PESTALOZ

Pestalozzi and Pestalozzianism.

LIFE,

EDUCATIONAL PRINCIPLES, AND METHODS,

OF

JOHN HENRY PESTALOZZI;

WITH

BIOGRAPHICAL SKETCHES

OF SEVERAL OF HIS

ASSISTANTS AND DISCIPLES.

Reprinted from the American Journal of Education.

EDITED BY HENRY BARNARD, LL.D.,
Chancellor of the University of Wisconsin.

IN TWO PARTS.

NEW YORK:
PUBLISHED BY F. C. BROWNELL
NO. 12 APPLETON'S BUILDING.
1859.

SECOND EDITION.

THE following Memoirs and Papers were originally prepared by the editor, or at his request, for "*The American Journal of Education*," as part of the History and Discussion of the great subject to which that periodical is devoted. They are collected in the present volume, as a Tribute to the Character and Services of one of the great Champions of Popular Enlightenment, and as a valuable contribution to the department of Educational Literature in the English language.

Pestalozzi and Pestalozzianism.

PART I.

MEMOIR OF PESTALOZZI, AND BIOGRAPHICAL SKETCHES OF SEVERAL OF HIS ASSISTANTS AND DISCIPLES.

PART II.

SELECTIONS FROM THE PUBLICATIONS OF PESTALOZZI.

CONTENTS.

PART I.

LIFE AND EDUCATIONAL SYSTEM OF PESTALOZZI.

PART II.

SELECTIONS FROM THE PUBLICATIONS OF PESTALOZZI.

PART I.

MEMOIR OF PESTALOZZI.

Assistants and Disciples of Pestalozzi.

PESTALOZZI'S EDUCATIONAL LABORS FOR THE POOR,

AND FOR

POPULAR SCHOOLS.

"It is to the charitable efforts of Pestalozzi"—remarks M. Demetz, the founder of the most complete and successful institution of reformatory education in the world, in a report on the Agricultural Reformatory Colonies of France,—"that we owe the establishment of agricultural colonies," that is, of institutions, organized on the basis, and in the spirit of the family, with agricultural employment as the principal means of industrial training, and with methods of instruction, moral, intellectual, and physical, so far as applied, good enough for children of any class of society, and yet capable of being followed by an intelligent mother in the home of the poor. Not that Pestalozzi's own plans and methods under his own application, were eminently successful—for they were not. His institution at Neuhof, was a disastrous failure, in its immediate results, both as a school, and as a pecuniary speculation. But the christian spirit in which this excellent man labored—the family organization into which he gathered, even the outcasts of society, living among such pupils as a father, as well as pastor and teacher, and denying himself the quiet seclusion and comforts of the home which the fortune of his noble minded wife had secured for him, that he might inspire the orphan, and the abandoned and even criminal child with filial attachments, cultivate habits of self-reliance and profitable industry, and thus enable them "to live in the world like men"—this spirit, system and aim, the dream and labor of his long and troubled life, imperfectly inaugurated at Neuhof, and never fully realized at Stanz, Burgdorf, and Yverden, but widely diffused by his writings, and the better success, under more favorable conditions, of his pupils and disciples in Switzerland and Germany, have led to the establishment of new educational institutions for rich and poor, of schools of practical agriculture, as well as of agricultural reformatories, and at the same time has regenerated the methods of popular education generally. To the connected and comprehensive survey of Pestalozzi's Life and Educational System by von Raumer, we add a notice of his labors at Neuhof by Dr. Blochmann, of Dresden, and by Dr. Diesterweg, of Berlin, from discourses pronounced on the occasion of the Centennial celebration of Pestalozzi's birth-day on the 12th of January, 1846.

PESTALOZZI'S POOR SCHOOL AT NEUHOF.

Pestalozzi having failed in a plantation of madder which he had commenced in connection with a mercantile house of Zurich, on an estate of about one hundred acres of land on which he commenced a house in the

Italian villa style, to which he gave the name of Neuhof, projected the plan of an educational establishment respecting which Dr. Blochmann,* an admiring pupil and avowed follower thus writes:

It was not in Pestalozzi's nature to sink under misfortune, so long as he could pursue the attainment of the object of his life. He had early learned and deeply fixed in his mind the maxim,

"Tu ne cede malis, sed contra fortior ito."

He advanced like a roused lion, with resolute courage, against all unfriendly influences. In spite of the severe distress into which the unforseen withdrawal of the Zurich house plunged him, he determined to go on, and to make his landed estate the centre of operations for his educational and agricultural plans. He resolved even upon more and higher designs. Henceforward he will live amongst beggar children, and share his bread in poverty amongst them; will live like a beggar himself, that he may learn to teach beggars to live like men.

He also proposed to render his establishment an institution for the poor. This undertaking attracted attention. It was considered a noble and benevolent enterprise; and his views and principles had so much influence, in spite of the mistrust of his practical ability, that he found assistance in Zurich, Bern and Basle, and was able without much difficulty to obtain the necessary funds for the institution, by the aid of a loan, for several years, without interest. His friends on all sides assisted him; more especially Iselin of Basle, whom he had met and known in the Helvetic Diet, and who introduced the beloved enterprise to public notice in his Ephemerides.

The Institution for the Poor at Neuhof was opened in 1775. Poor children flocked in from all directions, many of them gathered by Pestalozzi himself from their misery, and out of the streets. He had soon fifty children, whom he kept busy in summer with field labor, and in winter with spinning and other handicrafts, instructing them all the time, and developing and clearing up their mental faculties, especially by oral recitations and mental arithmetic.† Pestalozzi had early perceived

* HENRY PESTALOZZI. Touches at a Picture of his Life and Labors: from his own testimony, from observation, and communication. By Dr. Karl Justus Blochmann, Privy School Councilor and Professor: Leipsic. 1846.

† The idea of such a school for the poor, in which agricultural and industrial labor were to be combined with instruction, accompanied Pestalozzi, to whose mind it was so new and stimulating, all his life; and even remained like a sunbeam shining from behind the dark sad clouds of the past, his last love, his last active desire. What, however, he never completely accomplished, has been done by Emanuel von Fellenberg, who was assisted in the work, not only by his certain and practical skill and experience, but especially by his good fortune in discovering in Vehrli, such a man as is very seldom to be found, but absolutely necessary in the actual realization of such a school. Whoever, like myself—and there are thousands—has become thoroughly acquainted with Vehrli's school in Hofwyl, must be convinced that in institutions for the education of the poor so organized, conducted in such a spirit, with such love and self-sacrifice, there is to be found an inestimable blessing for the state and the people. Fellenberg has shown from his account books, that a poor boy, received at his ninth year, and remaining in the institution through his eighteenth, pays by his labor during the last half of his stay, for the excess of the expense of maintaining him over his earnings, during the first half. Lange, in his work on "The Country Educational Institutions for Poor Children," (*Landlicln Erziehungs Anstalten für Armenkinder,*) has made very thorough researches into this

that in the nature of every man are innate powers and means sufficient to assure him an adequate support; and that the hindrances arising from exterior circumstances, to the development of the natural endowments, are not in their nature insuperable.

The usual means of benevolence and mercy (as he was accustomed to name the orphan houses, institutions for supporting the poor, &c., of the period,) seemed to him to stimulate and encourage the evil, instead of helping it. The thousand public and private ways of spending alms, with which the times were crowded to nauseation, the beggar making and hypocrite training modes of assisting the poor, seemed to him only a palliative. The only means of affording real assistance he saw to lie in this; that the inborn natural powers of every man to provide for his own necessities, and sufficiently to perform the business, duties and obligations of his being, should be developed, encouraged, and set upon an independent footing. With this conviction the impulse increased within him to labor for this definite purpose; that it should become practicable for the poorest in the land to be assured of the development of their bodily, spiritual and moral powers both in relation to their own characters, and to their personal, domestic and social relations; and through this development to obtain the sure basis of a peaceful and sufficient means of existence. He had already taken the first step in this direction, by admitting into his house beggar children and others abandoned to neglect, that he might rescue them from their debasing condition, lead them back to manhood and a higher destiny, and thus prove to himself and those around him more and more clearly the truth of his opinion. His institution was to comprise the means for a sufficient instruction in field labor, in domestic work, and in associated industry. This was not, however, the ultimate purpose. That was, a training to manhood; and for it, these other departments were only preparatory.

First of all, he proposed to train his poor children to exertion and self-control, by forbearing and assiduous discipline, and by the ever powerful stimulus of love. He aimed to possess himself of their hearts, and from that starting point to bring them to the consciousness and the attainment of every thing noble and great in humanity. "I had from my youth" he says, "a high instinctive value of the influence of domestic training in the education of poor children, and likewise a decided preference for field labor, as the most comprehensive and unobjectionable external basis for this training, and also for another reason: as it is the condition of the manufacturing population which is increasing so rapidly amongst us, who, abandoned to the operations of a mercantile and speculating

---

subject, not only from other writings upon institutions for the poor after the model of Fellenberg's, but from his own repeated and extensive travels and personal observation. Our own teacher's association (*pädagogische verein*, at Dresden,) has proposed as a chief aim of its practical efforts, the realization of an institution for the education of poor and abandoned children, after Pestalozzi's model; for which purpose, it purchased some eight years since, a property in great part already in cultivation, and with a roomy mansion house, near the Löbtaner Schlage, which was dedicated on the 12th of January, 1845, by the name of the Pestalozzi Foundation, (Pestalozzi Stiftung.)

interest, wholly destitute of humanity, are in danger, in case of unforseen accident, of being able to find within themselves no means of escape from entire ruin.* Full of a love for my father-land, which hoped for it almost impossible things, and longed to lead it back to its native dignity and power, I sought with the greatest activity not only for the possible but for the certain means of averting the coming evil, and of awakening anew the remainder of the ancient home happiness, home industry, and home manners. These designs sank deep into my heart and often made me feel with sorrow what a high and indispensable human duty it is to labor for the poor and miserable, with all the means which our race possesses, in church, state or individuals, that he may attain to a consciousness of his own dignity through his feeling of the universal powers and endowments which he possesses, awakened within him; that he may not only learn to gabble over by rote the religious maxim that 'man is created in the image of God, and is bound to live and die as the child of God,' but may himself experience its truth by virtue of the divine power within him, so that he may be irresistibly and really elevated not only above the ploughing oxen, but above the man in purple and silk, who lives unworthily of his high destiny."

With such lofty and magnificent views, and with a heart at even a higher level of love, Pestalozzi labored at Neuhof from sunrise to sunset, amongst his beggar children. He lived steadily up to his principles, laboring in his vocation to the full extent of his powers; always knew what he was seeking, cared not for the morrow, but felt from moment to moment the needs of the present. Among his children were very many ungovernable ones of a better class, and still worse, many who had brought themselves from a better condition to beggary, and who were presumptuous and pretentious by reason of their former situation; to whom the energetic discipline which he applied, according to his design, was at first hateful. They considered their situation with him as more degrading than that in which they had been before. Neuhof was full every Sunday of the mothers and relatives of children who found their situation not what they had expected. All the impertinences which a miserable rabble of beggars could indulge in a house without visible protection or imposing exterior, were practiced, to encourage the children in their discontent; even so far that they were often tempted to run away by night just after they had been washed clean and clad in their Sunday clothes. However, these difficulties would little by little

* Upon the influence of manufacturing wealth amongst the Swiss at that time. Pestalozzi expresses himself thus in another place: "The paternal love of the upper and the filial love of the lower classes, in consequence of the increase of the manufacturing interest, is going more and more to ruin under the effects of ignoble wealth. The blinding height of arrogance derived from an eminent position obtained by money, the deceitful cornucopia of an unreliable life of mere pleasure, has drawn all within its destructive influence, even down to the commonest of the people, and carried them into the crooked path of a spiritless and powerless routine life. Truth, honor, sympathy, moderation, are daily vanishing. Pride, insolence, recklessness, contemptuousness, laxity, immorality, the eager pursuit of vain and ostentatious pleasure, the cherishing of boundless selfishness, have taken the place of the ancient simplicity, faith and honor.

have been overcome, had not Pestalozzi pushed his undertaking to an extent altogether beyond his means, and undertaken to modify it according to the original design, which supposed the possession of the utmost knowledge of manufacturing and of human nature; qualities in which he was lacking in the same measure in which he needed them urgently for managing his institution. Moreover, he hurried on to the higher branches of instruction, before supplying the solid foundation of acquaintance with the lower; an error recognized as the leading one of the teaching of the age, against which he had striven in his scheme of education with all his strength. For the sake of a fallacious prospect of greater profit, in higher branches of industry, he committed, in teaching his children to spin and weave, the very faults which he had so strongly abjured in all his expressed opinions upon education, and which he saw to be so dangerous to children of all classes. He would attempt to secure the finest spinning, before his children had acquired even a small amount of firmness and surety of hand in coarse work; and undertook to manufacture muslin before his weavers had attained skill in weaving common cotton stuff.

Through these and the like mistakes, through his ignorance of business, and his great lack of a sound practical faculty of learning it, it happened that Pestalozzi fell every year deeper in debts; and when these also from time to time had been paid by the self-sacrificing generosity of his noble wife, there came at last an end of this means of help, and in a few years the greater part of his substance and his expected inheritance was dissolved into smoke. The great confidence which he had enjoyed among his neighbors, changed when his undertaking failed so soon, into an utter and blind rejection of any shadow even of faith in his enterprise, or of belief in his possessing any capacity at all as a teacher. But such is the way of the world; it treated Pestalozzi, when poor, as it treats all who become poor by their own faults. Their money being gone, it withdraws also its confidence from them, in matters where they really are capable and efficient.

His enterprise failed, in a manner excessively painful, both to himself and his wife, in the year 1780, in the fifth year of its existence. His misfortune was complete; he was now poor. He felt most deeply the condition of his noble hearted wife, who in the excess of her devotion had mortgaged away for him nearly all her possessions. His situation was indeed shocking. In his over handsome country house, he was often destitute of bread, wood, and a few pennies, wherewith to defend himself from cold and hunger. Only the entire forbearance of his creditors and the kind help of his friends preserved him from despair and entire ruin.

Thus he lived a poor and destitute life in Neuhof for eighteen years, fighting with want and misery. He lived as a poor man amongst the poor; suffered what the common people suffered, and saw what they were. He studied the wants of the lower classes and the sources of their misery, in a manner which would have been impossible for one in better circumstances.

PESTALOZZI AND THE SCHOOLS OF GERMANY.

FROM THE GERMAN OF DR. DIESTERWEG.

Every one considers it a matter of course that all our children go to school until they grow up to be youths and maidens. The observance of this custom begins at the sixth year. But the parents have long before spoken of the school to the child; he looks eagerly forward to the day of entrance; and when it takes place, he is absorbed in his school and his teacher for the next six or eight years or more. We always think of children and schools or children and books together. To be a child and to learn, have become almost synonymous terms. To find children in school, or passing along the streets with the apparatus which they use there, makes no one wonder. It is only the reverse, which attracts attention. The school fills a very important part in the life of the young. In fact school life is almost the whole life of childhood and youth; we can hardly conceive of them without it. Without school, without education, what would parents do with their children? Without them, where would they secure the young the necessary preparation for actual life?

With our present organization of society, schools are indispensable institutions. Many others may perish in the course of time; many have already perished; but schools abide, and increase. Where they do not exist, we expect barbarity and ignorance; where they flourish, civilization and knowledge.

No apology is necessary for sending our children to school. At school they learn. There they acquire mental activity and knowledge; the manifold varieties of things; to gain the knowledge of things in heaven above and in the earth beneath, and under the earth; of stones, and plants, and animals, and men; of past, present, and future.

[The remainder of the discourse treats of three points:—

1. What were the schools before Pestalozzi?

2. What did they become by his means, and since; that is, what are they now?

3. What was Pestalozzi's life and labors?]

I. The Old Schools.

Our present system of common or public schools—that is schools which are open to all children under certain regulations—date from the discovery of printing in 1436, when books began to be furnished so cheaply that the poor could buy them. Especially after Martin Luther had translated the Bible into German, and the desire to possess and understand that invaluable book became universal, did there also become universal the desire to know how to read. Men sought to learn, not only for the sake of reading the Scriptures, but also to be able to read and sing the psalms, and to learn the catechism. For this purpose schools for children were established, which were essentially reading schools. Reading was the first and principal study; next came singing, and then memorizing texts, songs, and the catechism. At first the ministers taught; but afterward the duty was turned over to the inferior church officers, the choristers and sextons. Their duties as choristers and sextons were paramount, and as schoolmasters only secondary. The children paid a small monthly fee; no more being thought necessary, since the schoolmaster derived a salary from the church.

Nobody either made or knew how to make great pretensions to educational skill. If the teacher communicated to his scholars the acquirements above mentioned, and kept them in order, he gave satisfaction; and no one thought any thing about separate institutions for school children. There were no school books distinctively so called; the children learned their lessons in the Bible or the Psalter, and read either in the Old or the New Testament.

Each child read by himself; the simultaneous method was not known. One after another stepped up to the table where the master sat. He pointed out one letter at a time, and named it; the child named it after him; he drilled him in recognizing and remembering each. Then they took letter by letter of the words, and by getting acquainted with them in this way, the child gradually learned to read. This was a difficult method for him; a very difficult one. Years usually passed before any facility had been acquired; many did not learn in four years. It was imitative and purely mechanical labor on both sides. To understand what was read was seldom thought of. The syllables were pronounced with equal force, and the reading was without grace or expression.

Where it was possible, but unnaturally and mechanically, learning by heart was practiced. The children drawled out texts of Scripture, psalms, and the contents of the catechism from the beginning to end; short questions and long answers alike, all in the same monotonous manner. Anybody with delicate ears who heard the sound once, would remember it all his life long. There are people yet living, who were taught in that unintelligent way, who can corroborate these statements. Of the actual contents of the words whose sounds they had thus barely committed to memory by little and little, the children knew absolutely almost nothing. They learned superficially and understood superficially. Nothing really passed into their minds; at least nothing during their school years.

The instruction in singing was no better. The master sang to them the psalm-tunes over and over, until they could sing them, or rather screech them, after him.

Such was the condition of instruction in our schools during the sixteenth, seventeenth, and two-thirds of the eighteenth centuries; confined to one or two studies, and those taught in the most imperfect and mechanical way.

It was natural that youth endowed, when healthy, with an ever increasing capacity for pleasure in living, should feel the utmost reluctance at attending school. To be employed daily, for three or four hours, or more, in this mechanical toil, was no light task; and it therefore became necessary to force the children to sit still, and study their lessons. During all that time, especially in the seventeenth century, during the fearful thirty years' war, and subsequently, as the age was sunk in barbarism, the children of course entered the schools ignorant and untrained. "As the old ones sung, so twittered the young." Stern severity and cruel punishments were the order of the day; and by them the children were kept in order. Parents governed children too young to attend, by threats of the schoolmaster and the school; and when they went, it was with fear and trembling. The rod, the cane, the raw-hide, were necessary apparatus in each school. The punishments of the teacher exceeded those of a prison. Kneeling on peas, sitting in the shame-bench, standing in the pillory, wearing an ass-cap, standing before the school door in the open street with a label on the back or breast, and other similar devices, were the remedies which the rude men of the age devised. To name a single example of a boy whom all have heard of, of high gifts, and of reputable family,—Dr. Martin Luther reckoned up fifteen or sixteen times that he was whipped upon the back in one forenoon. The learning and the training corresponds; the one was strictly a mechanical process; the other, only bodily punishment. What wonder that from such schools there came forth a rude generation; that men and women looked back all their lives to the school as to a dungeon, and to the teacher as a taskmaster, and jailer; that the schoolmaster was of a small repute; that understrappers were selected for school duty and school discipline; that dark, cold kennels were used for school-rooms; that the schoolmaster's place especially in the country, was assigned him amongst the servants and the like.

This could not last; it has not, thank God! When and by what efforts of admirable men the change took place, I shall relate a little on. Let us now look at the present.

II. The Modern Schools.

What are our schools in this present fifth decade of the nineteenth century, and what are they from year to year growing to be? Upon this subject I can of course only give my readers a fresher and livelier impression of matters which they already understand. I begin with the exterior—not only every town, but every village of our father-land has at present its own school-houses. They are usually so noticeable for architecture, airiness and dimensions, as to be recognized at the first glance. The districts often compete amicably with each other in their appearance, and make great sacrifices for superiority.

In the school-house resides the teacher; a man who is often an object of the ridicule of the young, but who, if really a *teacher*, deserves and possesses the respect of the old. Many of course fail to obtain an adequate reward, especially for their highest aspirations, in their important calling; but their internal sources of satisfaction increase from day to day, in the power of lifting them above the depressing and wearing cares of their office. The conviction is daily gaining ground, that "what men do to the teacher, they are doing to their own children." The teacher is an educated man. He is trained in seminaries established and maintained for the purpose by the state. The time is past when teaching was practiced along with some handicraft; now undivided strength is devoted to it. How deeply teachers are themselves impressed with the importance, and engaged in the work, of steadily and continually improving themselves, is shown in the zeal with which they organize and maintain reading societies and associations for improvement.

Let us now consider the interior condition of the school, and observe its instruction:—

The children are kept quiet far otherwise than by blows. Each sits in his own place, busy at his lessons. Nowhere in the light, roomy and cleanly school rooms or halls is there any interruption, or any thing that could interrupt the attention of the young students. The walls are adorned with all manner of apparatus.

Far otherwise than by blows is the intercourse between teacher and children characterized. He greets them with a friendly word, and they him by rising up. He opens school with a prayer, and a hymn follows, sung well and sweetly. Now begins the business of instruction. All are earnest in it; every one has his work to do. There is no longer more than a slight trace of the plan of single instruction. All learn together every thing that is taught. Formerly the only thing taught to all was to read, and that by rote; for writing and arithmetic were required an extra payment; now, their work is regulated by a carefully considered plan of study, prepared by the teacher and superintending authorities of the school, which includes all subjects essential to the attainments of all; all the elements, that is of a general education.

At the head of all instruction is that concerning God's providence and man's destiny; in religion and virtue. To instruct the children in these great truths, to lay the secure foundation of fixed religious habits, is the highest aim of the teacher. Maxims, songs, &c., chosen with wise foresight, are ineradicably planted in his memory,and become a rich treasure to the scholar in after life. The singing as a part of the religious exercises. In solo, duet, or chorus, the scholars sing to the edification of all who take pleasure in well doing. They also learn secular songs, suitable in words and melody, and promotive of social good feeling.

The second chief subject of school instruction is reading. One who can not read easily, loses the principal means of acquiring knowledge during his future life. And how is it taught? The frightful old-fashioned drawl is done away with even to its last vestiges. Children now read, after two years' regular school attendance, not only fluently, but with just tone and accent, in such wise as to show that they understand and feel what they read. Is not that alone an immeasurable advance?

Formerly, the children studied each by himself, and where they barely learned to write by continual repetition of the letters and long practice, they now acquire facility in noting down and drawing up in the form of a composition, whatever they think or know. From the beginning, they are invariably trained to recite distinctly and correctly, speaking with proper tone, and as nearly as possible all together. This exercise has completely proved for the first time, how important it is that the teacher should understand and observe the rules of syntax and correct speaking. In this point, our present school instruction is an entirely new art. The old-fashioned teachers themselves could scarely read; now, the scholars learn it.

It is needless to detail all that remains; the entire revolution in teaching arithmetic, where, for unintelligent rule-work, has been substituted the means of developing the intellect, inasmuch that the scholars can not only reckon easily both mentally and in writing, but can also understand, judge, and form conclusions. It is needless to detail the instruction in the miscellaneous departments of geography, history, natural history, popular astronomy, physics, &c., which is intended for every man who pretends, even to the beginning of an education, and by means of which only is man enabled to comprehend the wonder of existence, and to grow up intelligently into an active life amongst its marvelous machinery.

No; it is needless to speak of those things and of many more; but it would be wrong not to devote a few words to the means by which the teacher of the present day maintains discipline; that is, seeks to train his scholars to obedience, good order, good conduct and deportment, and to all other good qualities. In truth, no one who should overlook our immense improvement in this department can be said to know the proposed aim of our good schools and skillful educators and teachers; or ever to understand our schools at all. The well-disposed scholar is received and managed by love. But if the teacher finds himself forced to punish an ungoverned, disobedient, or lazy scholar, he at one puts a period to the indulgence of his base or wicked practices. It pains him, but his sense of duty prevails over his pain, and he punishes him as a man acquainted with human nature and as a friend, first admonishing him with words. Fear is not the sceptre with which he governs; that would train not men, but slaves. It is only when admonition, stimulation, and example have failed, and when duty absolutely demands it, that he makes use of harsher means. It is above all his endeavor to treat his children like a conscientious father. Their success is his pride and happiness; in it he finds the blessing of his difficult calling. He daily beseeches God for it, and looks with a thankful heart to him, the giver of all good, upon whose blessing every thing depends, and without whom the watchman of the house watches in vain, if under the divine protection any thing has prospered under his hands.

Instead of a dark and dreary dungeon, the school has become an institution for training men. Where the children formerly only remained unwillingly, they now like best to go. Consider, now, what the consequences of this change of training must be on the hearts and lives of the children. How many millions of tears less must flow every year down childrens' cheeks! In Germany alone, more than five millions of children are attending school at the same time. Is the inspiration of such a number to future goodness a fantastic vision? Must not every department of school management assume great importance? It is with joy and pride that I say it; I myself am a teacher. Nowhere, in general, do children spend happier hours, than in school; at morning, and at noon, they can not wait for the time of departing for school; they willingly lose their breakfast, rather than to be late. How was it formerly? How often did fathers or mothers drag their screaming children to the school? And what awaited them there? God bless the men who have been and still are laboring, to the end that the pleasant season of youth, which will never return, the happy time of innocent childhood, may not be troubled with the dark barbaric sterness of pedantic school-tyrants; but that the school may be a place where the children may learn all that is good and praiseworthy, in milder and more earnest ways; a place in which earnest and thoughtful men, friends of children, and loving the teacher's profession, may feel and admit that they have passed the happiest hours of their lives. From schools so conducted, a blessing must go forth over the earth. Indeed, the ancients knew this. Thousands of years ago, it was high praise to say "He has built us a school;" and not less to say, "He has prepared praise for himself in the mouths of children."

The school has become an institution for training men and women; the old "school-masters" have become teachers. Pupils are now educated from the very foundations of their being, and by intelligible means. The scholar is not a machine, an automaton, a log; and accordingly the system of learning unintelligently by rote has come to be reckoned a slavish and degrading drudgery. The laws of human training and development are no longer arbitrarily announced, but are investigated, and when discovered, are faithfully followed. These laws lie within human nature itself. Beasts may be drilled at pleasure into external observances; but human beings must be educated and developed with reason and to reason, according to the laws impressed by God upon human nature. Of these laws, the schoolmaster handcraftsmen of former centuries knew nothing. Now, every thoughtful teacher adjusts his course of education and all his efforts whatever, as nearly as possible to nature. The consequences of this magnificent endeavor, in pedagogic science and art are plain before our eyes in our school-rooms. Instead of the former damp and gloomy prisons, we have light, healthy, clean and pleasant rooms; instead of dry and mechanical drilling in reading and other studies, effective and skillful education in the elements of all the knowledge and attainments required by man; instead of the ancient stick-government and bastinado system, a mild, earnest, paternal and reasonable method of discipline; loving instruction from well written books; teachers zealously discharging their duties; in short, we in Germany, by full consciousness that something better is always attainable, by laboring forward always to better methods, and by actual attainment, that the best educated nations on earth, the French and English, are behind us in respect to educational matters, we may justifiably take pride in knowing that men from all the civilized nations in the world, even from beyond the ocean, travel hither to observe the German common schools, to understand the German teachers, and to transplant into their own countries the benefits of which we are already possessed.

The young reader who has followed me thus far will naturally inquire, how all this happened; in what manner this better school system came into being. And among the names of those noble men to whose thoughts and deeds we owe so invaluable a creation, all historians will record with high honor that of Pestalozzi.

III. Influence of Pestalozzi's Life and Labors on the Schools of Europe.

[We omit much of the details of Pestalozzi's career as they will be found in Raumer's Life already refered to.—Barnard's Journal of Education, Vol. III, p. 401.]

As Pestalozzi grew up, he studied to become a minister, but finally decided to study law. In this profession he found no pleasure, although he completed his studies in it; his attention being involuntarily drawn aside to the unhappy condition of society around him. In the high places of his native city, prodigality, luxury, and contempt of the lower classes, were rife; while the poor in the other hand, regarded their superiors with hatred, but were prostrate in misery, want, ignorance, and immorality. The contemplation of these immeasurable evils of the age filled Pestalozzi's heart with grief and pain, and these feelings directed his thoughts to a search for some remedy. The result of a year's reflection upon the means of assisting his unfortunate fellow-men was, that it could only be done by training; by a better education of youth, especially of the children of the poor and the lower classes generally. Like a flash the idea came into his mind, "I will be a schoolmaster;" a teacher and educator of poor children. He consulted within himself upon this changed design; and seem to hear a voice replying, "you shall;" and again, "you can." So he answered, "I will." How well he fulfilled the promise! He now became the schoolmaster of a world.

Intention, Power, and Resolve; wherever these three operate together, there result not only promising words, but efficient actors.

He was filled with a sublime conception, which remained with him until after his eightieth year. His ideal was, the ennobling of mankind by education and culture. To this he devoted his whole life. He could pursue nothing else; he neglected every thing else; he thought of himself last of all. Ordinary men called him a fanatic, and cast nicknames at him and his enterprise.

He continued his special affection and love for the children of the poor. He was very early convinced that their education could not be successfully conducted within the close-shut, artificially organized public orphan-houses. He considered that they could only develop properly, in body and mind alike, in the country; that they ought at an early age to commence at some country occupation; especially at some useful and practical kind of labor; and that by that means their minds would develop in a simple and natural manner.

[Here follows a sketch of his labors at Neuhof.]

Every child who was capable of it was set at some out door work, and suitable labor was also provided in the house; during which last time he instructed them. He was surprised to see how little use they made of their faculties; how blind and deaf they seemed to the most striking phenomena, and how incorrectly they spoke. Accordingly he concluded even then that the development of the faculties, learning to see and hear aright, and speak correctly, were worth more than facility in reading and writing. The enterprise was too large for means, and too complicated for his practical ability.

[The experiment failed, but out of his painful experience and observation he wrote "Leonard and Gertrude," which was published by Decker of Berlin, in 1781.]

Amongst the nobles, princes, citizens, and philanthropists, both of Germany and Switzerland, there had been since 1770 a growing desire for social improvements. The conviction was all the time spreading, that there was a necessity for bestowing a better education upon the lower classes; of opposing the spread of superstition, and of diffusing more light and knowledge. In educational directions, Basedow and the Canon von Rochow had already distinguished themselves; and thousands had enlisted in aiding their enterprises. A book like Leonard and Gertrude, full of nature and truth, must necessarily be received with enthusiasm. The author, hitherto unappreciated even in his own neighborhood, immediately came into repute and honor. Encouraged by this success, he made in 1782 a tour through Germany, in search of model schools, studying the experience and operations of others, and gaining an acquaintance with the first men in Germany; Klopstock, Wieland, Goethe, Herder, Jacobi, &c. On his return he delighted the world with other useful writings. But still he did not succeed in finding any place where he could pursue undisturbed the object of his life.

Meanwhile—for we must hasten—the French Revolution broke out, and proceeded onward to the most horrible excesses. Switzerland was attacked, and in 1798 was invaded and overrun. The usual consequences of war, impoverishment, demoralization and barbarism did not fail to follow. Such news made the patriotic heart of Pestalozzi beat higher. At the information that troops of destitute children were wandering helplessly about, particularly in the vicinity of the Catholic town of Stanz, he proceeded thither, obtained from the authorities the gift of an empty house, and gathered into it eighty mendicant children. He says in relation to this occurrence, "The unfortunate and ruined condition of Stanz, and the relations into which I came with a great crowd of entirely destitute, partly wild, but powerful children of nature and of the mountains, gave me an excellent basis of operations, and though in the midst of manifold hindrances, an opportunity for a decisive experiment upon the scope and grade of the faculties which exist universally in children, as a base for education; and likewise to determine whether and to what extent the requisites are possible and practicable, which the necessities of the case demands, for the education of the common people." He became their father, educator and teacher. Day and night he was with them, the earliest in the morning, and the last at night; he ate, slept and played with them. In a single month, they had learned as much of the profit and pleasure of his instructions, that often in the evening when he requested them to go to bed, they begged that he would stay a little longer and teach them. Content and happiness, the blessing of God, rested upon the house. When in 1799 the village of Altdorf was burnt, Pestalozzi asked his children, "How is it? Can we receive about twenty of these houseless children amongst us? If we do we must divide our food with them." "Yes, yes," they all cried out, shouting for joy.

But this pleasure lasted not long. In that same year the French entered the neighborhood, took possession of the building for a hospital, and Father Pestalozzi was forced to disperse his children. His health was broken down with care, sorrow and over-exertion; and he was obliged once more to seek the means of support. He therefore went to Burgdorf, and established himself near the town as an assistant teacher without wages. His new modes of instruction displeased the country people. He did not let the children study the Heidelberg Catechism enough; and his instruction in thinking and speaking seemed to them entirely superfluous. But after eight months, the superintending authority, presenting themselves at the school, were much astonished at what he had accomplished. Unfortunately, his strength was exhausted in his oral labors; at the end of a year he had to resign his situation for the sake of his health.

During all his experiments thus far, his purpose of founding a self-supporting educational institution remained unaltered. He ceased operations at Burgdorf in 1801; was afterward established at München-Buchsee in Berne, near Hofwyl, where Fellenberg was laboring, and finally at Yverdun (Iferten,) where he entirely broke down in 1825. The last establishment was named the Pestalozzian Institute; and as such it became famous in all Europe, and even beyond the ocean, in America, &c. Neither before nor since has any similar institution ever attained to so great fame.

The work done in that institution became the foundation of the common schools of Germany; and changed the ancient mechanical schools into institutions for real human training.

The fundamental maxims upon which the instruction there proceeded, were as follows:

The basis of education is not to be constructed, but to be sought; it exists in the nature of man.

The nature of man contains an inborn and active instinct of development; is an organized nature; and man is an organized being.

True education will find that its chief hindrances are, passive obstructions in the way of development; its work is more negative than positive.

Its positive work consists in stimulation; the science of education is a theory of stimulation, or the right application of the best motives.

The development of man commences with natural perceptions through the senses; its highest attainment is, intellectually, the exercise of reason; practically, independence.

The means of independence and self-maintenance is, spontaneous activity.

Practical capacity depends much more upon the possession of intellectual and corporeal power, than upon the amount of knowledge. The chief aim of all education, (instruction included,) is therefore the development of these powers.

The religious character depends much less upon learning the Scriptures and the catechism, than upon the intercourse of the child with a God-fearing mother and an energetic father. Religious education, like all other, must begin with the birth of the child; and it is principally in the hands of the mother.

The chief departments for the development of power, are form, number and speech. The idea of elementary training is, the notion of laying, within the nature of the child, by means of domestic education, (the influence of father, mother, brothers and sisters,) the foundations of faith, love, of the powers of seeing, speaking and reflecting, and by the use of all the means of education, according to the laws and methods of development included within nature itself.

Such is the actual substance of Pestalozzi's principles of education. The consequences follow of themselves. They are these:

The family circle is the best place for education; the mother's book the best school-book.

All instruction must be based upon training the intuitive faculty. The first instruction is altogether instruction in seeing: the first instruction on any subject must be the same, in order to fruitful, active and real comprehension of it. The opposite of this is the empty and vain mode of mere verbal instruction. First the thing itself should be taught, and afterward, as far as possible, the form, the representation, and the name.

The first portion of instruction consists in naming things and causing the names to be repeated, in describing them and causing them to be described. After this, it should be the teacher's prime object to develop spontaneous activity, and for that purpose to use the fore-mentioned progressive and inventive method of teaching.

Nothing should be learnt by rote without being understood; the practice of learning by rote should be confined to mere matters of form. In the method of oral communication with the scholars is to be found an adequate measure for estimating the clearness and activity of the scholar's power of seeing, and his knowledge.

The chief inducements to the right and the good are not fear and punishment, but kindness and love.

These conclusions flow naturally from Pestalozzi's fundamental principles. If I were to give a brief statement of his method for intellectual training, I should call it "Education to spontaneous activity, by means of knowledge acquired by the perceptions."

This system has changed the whole condition of schools. It has not, it is true, yet penetrated all the schools, or all the teachers; but this is not the fault of the founder. To change a system established for centuries, is the work of centuries; not of a year, nor ten years. In the development of a nation, and in like manner of a school system, there are epochs, stationary periods, crises and reactions.

While the best men in Prussia, after 1808, were laboring to effect a a regeneration of their unfortunate country, King Frederic William the Third* summoned C. A. Zeller the pupil of Pestalozzi, to Königsberg, with the commission of awakening the intellectual faculties of the people, as the only dependence for the rescue of the country. The great Fichte had already drawn attention to Pestalozzi, in his lectures and publications at Berlin. Afterward, the eminent minister, Von Altenstein, sent some young men to Yverdun to be trained.† By these means, and by means of the numerous publications of Pestalozzi and his followers, with some

---

* Ramsauer writes as follows of the visit of Frederic William III. to Pestalozzi:

"When the king of Prussia came to Neufchatel in 1814, Pestalozzi was very ill. Nevertheless, he insisted that I should carry him to the king, that he might thank him for his zeal in the cause of common schools, and for having sent so many pupils to Yverdun. On the way he fainted several times, and I was obliged to take him from the vehicle and carry him into a house. I urged him to return, but he replied, 'No; say nothing about it. I must see the king, if I die after it: if by means of my visit to him, a single Prussian child obtains a better education, I shall be well repaid.'"

The benefits which this noble man wished for one child, have been secured already to millions.

† Extract from a letter which the Baron Von Altenstein wrote to Pestalozzi, dated 11th Sept., 1808, at Königsberg:

"The king's majesty, with a view to the efficient improvement of the national system of education, which always lies so near his heart, has lately entrusted me, as directing minister, with the oversight of the schools and educational system in the proper Prussian provinces of his dominions.

Being fully convinced of the great value of the system of instruction discovered, and so skillfully carried into practice by yourself, and expecting from it the most favorable influence upon the culture of the people, I am desirous of making its introduction into the elementary schools the basis of a thorough educational reform in those provinces. Among the measures which I contemplate for this purpose, one of the principal is, forthwith to send to you two suitable young men, that they may drink in the spirit of your entire system of education and instruction, at the purest source. I desire them not only to learn some one department of it, but to master all of them, in their various connections and deepest unity, under the guidance of yourself, the eminent founder of the system, and with your efficient assistance. I desire them by this intercourse with you, not only to acquire the spirit of your system, but to become trained into a complete fitness for the teacher's vocation; to acquire the same conviction of its holiness, and the same ardent impulses to pursue it, which have induced you to devote to it your whole life.

In order to the best mode of procedure, I desire in the meanwhile to hear from yourself what class of young men you consider fittest to learn your method; what age, natural disposition, and previous mental training would suit you best, in order that the individuals selected may meet your wishes in every respect."

In 1809, the minister of public instruction writes as follows to the teachers who had been sent to Yverdun: "The section of public instruction begs you to believe, and to assure Mr. Pestalozzi, that the cause is the interest of the government, *and of his majesty, the king, personally*, who are convinced that liberation from extraordinary calamities is fruitless, and only to be effected by a thorough improvement of the people's education."

help from the pressure of circumstances, the Prussian, or rather the Prussian-Pestalozzian school-system, was established. For he is entitled to at least half the fame of the German common schools. Whatever of excellence or eminence they have, they really owe to no one but him. Wherever his principles have been deviated from, there has followed a decline. Whatever of progress yet remains visible is a development of his principles. Whatever in our system is based on human nature, is taken from him. His experiments have secured their world-wide fame to the German schools. From France, England, Italy, Spain, Russia, Poland, Norway, Sweden, Holland, Denmark, America, whoever desires to study the best schools, resorts to Germany. Whatever fame they have, they owe to Pestalozzi. Wise people have made use of his creations for organizing improved institutions for training teachers. But the first impulse was given to the movement by the noble Swiss. As the waters flow from that land in every direction, in like manner have fruitful principles of instruction been diffused from it into every country where improvement can be detected.

The men and women by whom especially the method and spirit of Pestalozzi were diffused in Germany are; Frederick William III and his consort Louise;* state-councilors Nicolovius and Suvern; the philosopher Fichte, by his immortal addresses to the German nation; high school-councilor Zeller in Königsberg; the Prussian teachers trained at Yverdun; namely, Kawerau, Dreist, Henning, Braun, Steger Marsch, the two Bernhards, Hänel, Titze, Runge, Baltrusch, Patzig, Preuss, Kratz, and Rendschmidt; royal and school councilor Von Türk in Potsdam, seminary-director Gruner in Idstein; professor Ladomus in Carlsruhe; the prelate Denzel in Esslingen; seminary-director Stern in Carlsruhe; principal Plamann, in Berlin; seminary-director Harnisch in Breslau; Karoline Rudolphi in Heidelberg; Betty Gleim in Bremen and Elberfeld; Ramsauer, royal tutor in Oldenberg; professor Schacht in Mentz; seminary inspector Kruger in Bunzlau; seminary-director Hientzsch in Potsdam; principal Scholz in Breslau, Dr. Tillich in Dessau; director Blochmann in Dresden; principal Ackermann in Frankfort on the Mayne; principal de Laspé in Wiesbaden; seminary-inspector Wagner in Brühl; seminary-director Braun in Neuwied; seminary-preceptor Muhl in Trier; seminary-director Graffmann in Stettin; catechist Kröger in Hamburg; inspector Collmann in Cassel; and others. By means of these men the Pestalozzian common schools were set in operation throughout all Germany; and in Prussia, the Prussian-Pestalozzian system. As during Pestalozzi's life Yverdun was a place of pilgrimage for teachers, so afterward, from Europe, America and elsewhere, men came to observe the German and Prussian common schools. May this reputation never decrease; may it ever grow greater and greater! Much yet remains to be done.

* Queen Louise, who superintended the education of her own children, visited frequently the schools conducted on the plans and methods of Pestalozzi, spending hours in each visit, and aided in many ways those who labored to regenerate the popular schools of Prussia.

The foregoing sketch of Pestalozzi's labors, and of their influence on the popular schools of Germany, abridged from the Centennial Discourses of two of his avowed disciples, Dr. Blochmann, of Dresden, and Dr. Diesterweg, of Berlin, represent the extreme views entertained by the admirers of the great Swiss educator. There is a large number of educators and teachers, at the head of whom is Karl von Raumer, at one time a resident at Yverdun, for the purpose of studying the system and methods of the Pestalozzian Institution, who, while they acknowledge the value of Pestalozzi's services to the instruction and industrial training of the poor, and to the true theory of education, maintain that his principles and methods as developed and applied by himself, are in some respects unsound and incomplete.

The following summary and comparative view of his principles, is taken from an article by William C. Woodbridge, in the American Annals of Education, for January, 1837.

As the result of his investigations, Pestalozzi assumed as a fundamental principle, that education, in order to fit man for his destination, must proceed according to the laws of nature. To adopt the language of his followers—that it must not act as an arbitrary mediator between the child and nature, between man and God, pursuing its own artificial arrangements, instead of the indications of Providence—that it should assist the course of natural development, instead of doing it violence—that it should watch, and follow its progress, instead of attempting to mark out a path agreeably to a preconceived system.

I. In view of this principle, he did not choose, like Basedow, to cultivate the mind in a material way, merely by inculcating and engrafting every thing relating to external objects, and giving mechanical skill. He sought, on the contrary, to develope, and exercise, and strengthen the faculties of the child by a steady course of excitement to self-activity, with a limited degree of assistance to his efforts.

II. In opposition to the haste, and blind groping of many teachers without system, he endeavored to find the proper point for commencing, and to proceed in a slow and gradual, but uninterrupted course, from one point to another—always waiting until the first should have a certain degree of distinctness in the mind of the child, before entering upon the exhibition of the second. To pursue any other course would only give superficial knowledge, which would neither afford pleasure to the child, nor promote its real progress.

III. He opposed the undue cultivation of the memory and understanding, as hostile to true education. He placed the essence of education in the harmonious and uniform development of every faculty, so that the body should not be in advance of the mind, and that in the development of the mind, neither the physical powers, nor the affections, should be neglected; and that skill in action should be acquired at the same time with knowledge. When this point is secured, we may know that education has really begun, and that it is not merely superficial.

IV. He required close attention and constant reference to the peculiarities of every child, and of each sex, as well as to the characteristics of the people among whom he lived, in order that he might acquire the development and qualifications necessary for the situation to which the Creator destined him, when he gave him these active faculties, and be prepared to labor successfully for those among whom he was placed by his birth.

V. While Basedow introduced a multitude of subjects of instruction into the schools, without special regard to the development of the intellectual powers, Pestalozzi considered this plan as superficial. He limited the elementary subjects of instruction to Form, Number and Language, as the essential condition of definite and distinct knowledge; and believed that these elements should be taught with the utmost possible simplicity, comprehensiveness and mutual connection.

VI. Pestalozzi, as well as Basedow, desired that instruction should commence with the intuition or simple perception of external objects and their relations. He was not, however, satisfied with this alone, but wished that the *art of observing* should also be acquired. He thought the things perceived of less consequence than the cultivation of the perceptive powers, which should enable the child to observe completely,—to exhaust the subjects which should be brought before his mind.

VII. While the Philanthropinists attached great importance to special exercises of reflection, Pestalozzi would not make this a subject of separate study. He maintained that every subject of instruction should be properly treated, and thus become an exercise of thought; and believed, that lessons on Number, and Proportion and Size, would give the best occasion for it.

VIII. Pestalozzi, as well as Basedow, attached great importance to Arithmetic, particularly to Mental Arithmetic. He valued it, however, not merely in the limited view of its practical usefulness, but as an excellent means of strengthening the mind. He also introduced Geometry into the elementary schools, and the art connected with it, of modeling and drawing beautiful objects. He wished, in this way, to train the eye, the hand, and the touch, for that more advanced species of drawing which had not been thought of before. Proceeding from the simple and intuitive, to the more complicated and difficult forms, he arranged a series of exercises so gradual and complete, that the method of teaching this subject was soon brought to a good degree of perfection.

IX. The Philanthropinists introduced the instruction of language into the common schools, but limited it chiefly to the writing of letters and preparation of essays. But Pestalozzi was not satisfied with a lifeless repetition of the rules of grammar, nor yet with mere exercises for common life. He aimed at a development of the laws of language from within—an introduction into its internal nature and construction and peculiar spirit—which would not only cultivate the intellect, but also improve the affections. It is impossible to do justice to his method of instruction on this subject, in a brief sketch like the present—but those who have witnessed its progress and results, are fully aware of its practical character and value.

X. Like Basedow, Rochow and others, Pestalozzi introduced vocal music into the circle of school studies, on account of its powerful influence on the heart. But he was not satisfied that the children should learn to sing a few melodies by note or by ear. He wished them to know the rules of melody and rhythm, and dynamics—to pursue a regular course of instruction, descending to its very elements, and rendering the musical notes as familiar as the sounds of the letters. The extensive work of Nageli and Pfeiffer has contributed very much to give this branch of instruction a better form.

XI. He opposed the abuse which was made of the Socratic method in many of the Philanthropinic and other schools, by attempting to draw something out of children before they had received any knowledge. He recommends, on the contrary, in the early periods of instruction, the established method of dictation by the teacher and repetition by the scholar, with a proper regard to rhythm, and at a later period, especially in the mathematical and other subjects which involve reasoning, the modern method, in which the teacher merely gives out the problems in a proper order, and leaves them to be solved by the pupils, by the exertion of their own powers.

XII. Pestalozzi opposes strenuously the opinion that religious instruction should be addressed exclusively to the understanding; and shows that religion lies deep in the hearts of men, and that it should not be enstamped from without, but developed from within; that the basis of religious feeling is to be found in the childish disposition to love, to thankfulness, to veneration, obedience and confidence toward its parents; that these should be cultivated and strengthened and directed toward God; and that religion should be formally treated of at a later period in connection with the feelings thus excited. As he requires the mother to direct the first development of all the faculties of her child, he assigns to her especially the task of first cultivating the religious feelings.

XIII. Pestalozzi agreed with Basedow, that mutual affection ought to reign between the educator and the pupil, both in the house and in the school, in order to render education effectual and useful. He was, therefore, as little disposed as Basedow, to sustain school despotism; but he did not rely on artificial excitements, such as those addressed to emulation. He preferred that the children should find their best reward in the consciousness of increased intellectual vigor; and expected the teacher to render the instruction so attractive, that the delightful feeling of progress should be the strongest excitement to industry and to morality.

XIV. Pestalozzi attached as much importance to the cultivation of the bodily powers, and the exercise of the senses, as the Philanthropinists, and in his publications, pointed out a graduated course for this purpose. But as Gutsmuths, Vieth, Jahn, and Clias treated this subject very fully, nothing further was written concerning it by his immediate followers.

Such are the great principles which entitle Pestalozzi to the high praise of having given a more natural, a more comprehensive and deeper foundation for education and instruction, and of having called into being a method which is far superior to any that preceded it.

But with all the excellencies of the system of education adopted by Pestalozzi, truth requires us to state that it also involves serious defects.

1. In his zeal for the improvement of the mind itself, and for those modes of instruction which were calculated to develop and invigorate its faculties, Pestalozzi forgot too much the necessity of general positive knowledge, as the material for thought and for practical use in future life. The pupils of his establishment, instructed on his plan, were too often dismissed with intellectual powers which were vigorous and acute, but without the stores of knowledge important for immediate use—well qualified for mathematical and abstract reasoning, but not prepared to apply it to the business of common life.

2. He commenced with intuitive, mathematical studies too early, attached too much importance to them, and devoted a portion of time to them, which did not allow a reasonable attention to other studies, and which prevented the regular and harmonious cultivation of other powers.

3. The *method* of instruction was also defective in one important point. Simplification was carried too far, and continued too long. The mind became so accustomed to receive knowledge divided into its most simple elements and smallest portions, that it was not prepared to embrace complicated ideas, or to make those rapid strides in investigation and conclusion which is one of the most important results of a sound education, and which indicates the most valuable kind of mental vigor both for scientific purposes and for practical life.

4. He attached too little importance to testimony as one of the sources of our knowledge, and devoted too little attention to historical truth. He was accustomed to observe that history was but a 'tissue of lies;' and forgot that it was necessary to occupy the pupil with man, and with moral events, as well as with nature and matter, if we wish to cultivate properly his moral powers, and elevate him above the material world.

5. But above all, it is to be regretted, that in reference to religious education, he fell into an important error of his predecessors. His too exclusive attention to mathematical and scientific subjects, tended, like the system of Basedow, to give his pupils the habit of undervaluing historical evidence and of demanding rational demonstration for every truth, or of requiring the evidence of their senses, or something analogous to it, to which they were constantly called to appeal in their studies of Natural History.

It is precisely in this way, that many men of profound scientific attainments have been led to reject the evidence of revelation, and some, even, strange as it may seem, to deny the existence of Him, whose works and laws they study. In some of the early Pestalozzian schools, feelings of this nature were particularly cherished by the habit of asserting a falsehood in the lessons on Mathematics or Natural history, and calling upon the pupils to contradict it or disprove it if they did not admit its truth. No improvement of the intellectual powers, can, in our view, compensate for the injury to the moral sense and the diminished respect for truth, which will naturally result from such a course.

6. While Pestalozzi disapproved of the attempts of the Philanthropinists to draw forth from the minds of children, before they had stores of knowledge, he seemed to forget the application of his principle to moral subjects, or to imagine that this most elevated species of knowledge was innate. He attempted too much to draw from the minds of his pupils those great truths of religion and the

spiritual world which can only be acquired from revelation; and thus led them to imagine they were competent to judge on this subject without external aid. It is obvious that such a course would fall in most unhappily with the tendencies produced by other parts of the plan, and that we could not hope to educate in such a mode, a truly Christian community.

The personal character of Pestalozzi also influenced his views and methods of education on religious subjects. He was remarkably the creature of powerful impulses, which were usually of the most mild and benevolent kind; and he preserved a child-like character in this respect even to old age. It was probably this temperament, which led him to estimate at a low rate the importance of positive religious truth in the education of children, and to maintain that the mere habit of faith and love, if cultivated toward earthly friends and benefactors, would, of course, be transferred to our Heavenly Father, whenever his character should be exhibited to the mind of the child. The fundamental error of this view was established by the unhappy experience of his own institution. His own example afforded the most striking evidence that the noblest impulses, not directed by established principles, may lead to imprudence and ruin, and thus defeat their own ends. As an illustration of this, it may be mentioned that, on one of those occasions, frequently occurring, on which he was reduced to extremity for want of the means of supplying his large family, he borrowed four hundred dollars from a friend for the purpose. In going home, he met a peasant, wringing his hands in despair for the loss of his cow. Pestalozzi put the entire bag of money into his hands, and ran off to escape his thanks. These circumstances, combined with the want of tact in reference to the affairs of common life, materially impaired his powers of usefulness as a practical instructor of youth. The rapid progress of his ideas rarely allowed him to execute his own plans; and, in accordance with his own system, too much time was employed in the profound development of principles, to admit of much attention to their practical application.

But, as one of his admirers observed, it was his province to educate ideas and not children. He combated, with unshrinking boldness and untiring perseverance, through a long life, the prejudices and abuses of the age in reference to education, both by his example and by his numerous publications. He attacked with great vigor and no small degree of success, that favorite maxim of bigotry and tyranny, that obedience and devotion are the legitimate offspring of ignorance. He denounced that degrading system, which considers it enough to enable man to procure a subsistence for himself and his offspring—and in this manner, merely to place him on a level with the beast of the forest; and which deems every thing lost whose value can not be estimated in money. He urged upon the consciences of parents and rulers, with an energy approaching that of the ancient prophets, the solemn duties which Divine Providence had imposed upon them, in committing to their charge the present and future destinies of their fellow-beings. In this way, he produced an impulse, which pervaded the continent of Europe, and which, by means of his popular and theoretical works, reached the cottages of the poor and the palaces of the great. His institution at Yverdun was crowded with men of every nation; not merely those who were led by the same impulse which inspired him, but by the agents of kings and noblemen, and public institutions, who came to make themselves acquainted with his principles, in order to become his fellow-laborers in other countries."

INFLUENCE OF PESTALOZZI ON THE INFANT SCHOOL SYSTEM

OF

ENGLAND.

THROUGH the efforts of Dr. Mayo, Dr. Biber, and Mr. Greaves, (each of whom spent several months at Yverdun, and subsequently made publications on the subject,) and especially through the labors of the Infant School Society, a knowledge of Pestalozzi's educational principles and methods has been gradually infused into the popular schools of England. The following syllabus of "*Lessons on Education*," will show the extent to which Pestalozzi is now recognized as authority in the best infant schools of Great Britain.

EXTRACTS FROM SYLLABUS OF LESSONS ON EDUCATION, GIVEN TO STUDENTS IN TRAINING AT THE HOME AND COLONIAL SCHOOL SOCIETY.

I.—THE PRINCIPLES OF EDUCATION AS SET FORTH BY PESTALOZZI.

1. *On the Aim proposed by Pestalozzi in Education.*—This the first point to be considered—Mistakes with respect to—The true aim of education as it respects knowledge—intellectual and moral character—Social relations—Moral and religious duties—Principles on which based—The proper work of the Teacher reduced—Results.

2. *The Influence of a good Education.*—The little that has been done by education as hitherto pursued—Causes of this—Influence of a good education on thought, feeling, sentiment, opinion, &c.—Different senses in which the child may be said to be father of the man—Influence of education established from examples—Necessity of faith in this principle on the part of the Teacher—Incidental and systematic education, difference between—The Teacher to form a good intellectual and moral atmosphere round the child—Means of effecting this.

3. *Education, Organic.*—Organs and organized bodies considered to illustrate this—Difference between growth from within carried on by organic action or development, and increase from without effected by accretion—Application—Difference between ordinary elementary education and elementary education on the system of Pestalozzi—Deductions as to liberty, activity, and power—The application, especially as to liberty, in the school-room and play-ground.

4. *On Education being an entire Work.*—Pestalozzi's motto, "Education has to work on the head, the hand, and the heart"—Dugald Stewart on the same point—Pestalozzi introduced the principle into popular education—The perfection to be aimed at in education, moral,—Mistakes that have been made as to Pestalozzi's practice—Pestalozzi's estimate of the relative importance of the different elements of a child's nature, and method of dealing with each.

5. *Education should aim at the Gradual and Progressive Development of the Faculties.*—Examples of graduated and progressive instruction as—Proceeding from realities to signs, first natural, then artificial—From particular facts to general truths—From what is simple to what is complex—From the exercise of observation to the exercise of conception—From the conception of material things to abstract ideas, &c.—The first step—to find something analogous in the experience of the child to the subject presented, thus proceeding from the known to the unknown—The child to be firm on one step before proceeding to the next—The extent to which graduation should be carried—Extremes to be avoided—The graduations not to be too minute to prevent healthy exercise.

6. *Education should be Harmonious.*—The cultivation of all the faculties, not singly and apart, but simultaneously.

7. *The Character or Spirit of Education.*—"Not to teach religion alone but all things religiously"—Illustration drawn from the circulation of the blood in the body—Exemplification of this spirit in the instruction, general management, and discipline of the school—Results to be expected.

8. *Early Education chiefly by Intuition.*—What is meant by intuition—Examples—Value of what is learned from experience—Early education to lead to and prepare the mind for books—When commenced with books the mind often loaded with words conveying no definite meaning to children—The powers of the mind in consequence often cramped—Intuitive teaching one of the leading features of Pestalozzi's system—Connection between intuitive and logical knowledge—The assistance the former gives to

the latter—Difference between the instruction of infants and juveniles, the one mainly intuitive, the other principally logical.

9. *Difference between Education and Instruction.*—An idea put forth strongly by Pestalozzi—Origin and application of the words—Points of difference—Instruction communicated (though the subject may be clearly explained) does not produce the same good effect, as instruction employed as a means of mental discipline—The proper bearing of this distinction on the lessons of the Teacher.

10. *Education of a Mixed Character.*—What this means—Principle on which based—Examples—Education should be practical as well as preceptive—Illustrated by the Teacher as well as enforced upon the child—Applied individually as well as collectively—Direct instruction to be followed by study—Public education united with private and domestic—Children to be carried rapidly over some subjects to develop power and energy,—slowly over others to give habits of minute investigation—Subjects of instruction enumerated.

11. *Systems of Education.*—Application of the word system—Views generally taken of systems of education—Characteristics of the chief popular systems, especially those of Stow and Pestalozzi—The one teaching chiefly through words "picturing out," as it is called, the other by things and words in their appropriate place—The specious boast of selecting what is good from every system—The motto, "That is the best system which brings the powers of the mind under the best discipline," a test—The system of Pestalozzi founded on principles and adapted to the human mind, consequently a philosophical system, might be called the natural system—Different value of *principles* and *plans*—Illustration of this shown in the different kinds of value appertaining to wheat and bread—Advantage of principles in every thing—Many Teachers appreciate plans only—Principles the only true and safe guide.

12. *Summary of the leading Principles of Pestalozzi.*

1. Education ought to be essentially religious and moral.
2. Education ought to be essentially organic and complete, and not mechanical, superficial, and partial, it should penetrate and regulate the entire being.
3. Education ought to be free and natural instead of being cramped, confined, survile—The child should have sufficient liberty to manifest decidedly his individual character.
4. Education ought to be harmonious in all its parts—It should be so carried on that all the natural faculties, and all the acquired knowledge agree and harmonize.
5. Education should be based on intuition, on a clear and distinct perception of the subject to be learned.
6. Education should be gradual and progressive, united in all parts, like a chain, forming a continued series without gaps.
7. Education should be of a mixed character, uniting the private and the public; it should cultivate at the same time the social and domestic spirit.
8. Education should be synthetical—every thing taught should be first reduced into its elements by the Teacher.
9. Education should be practical, drawing its means of development from the actual circumstances of life.

II.—The Art of Teaching.

1.—INTRODUCTORY COURSE.

1. *Instructions as to the Mode of giving Familiar or Conversational Lessons*, and on the subjects chosen for such lessons in the Practicing Schools of the Institution.
2. *The Examination and Analysis of Lessons* selected from "*Model Lessons*," a work published by the Society.
3. *Drawing out Sketches of Lessons on various Subjects*, taking those before analyzed as examples.
4. *Different Methods of giving Lessons Compared*, with a view to point out which are bad and which good, also the methods suitable to different subjects.
5. *On the Art of Questioning.*—The importance of understanding this art—One of the plans of teaching much used by Pestalozzi—Different objects in view in questioning—Questions which only exercise memory—Advantages of questioning—Rules to be observed and mistakes avoided—Examples of different kinds of questions—Of a train of questions—Practice in the art of questioning.

2.—ON GALLERY INSTRUCTION.

1. *Introduction.*—The nature and importance of gallery instruction—Children brought under the direct influence of the Teacher—Facility thus afforded for securing order, attention, progress, moral training—Value in economizing labor—The principle of success to be found in the power of the sympathy of numbers—Extent to which Teachers should avail themselves of this sympathy—Its abuses—Duties connected with gallery instruction.

2. *Preparation of Lessons.*—Directions for making a good sketch—Advantages of a

full sketch—Importance of determining beforehand the chief points of the lesson, and the method of working them out.

3. *The Subject matter.*—Importance of attention to quantity and quality—Rules by which to be guided, and the principles upon which based—Advantage of clear and natural arrangement—The ideas to be thoroughly worked into the minds of the children—sufficient but not too much new matter to be presented properly, it being almost "as important how children learn as what they learn."

4. *The Summary.*—Definition of a summary—The qualities of a good summary—Its uses—Various ways of making a summary—Advantage of its being well committed to memory or written out by the children.

5. *Application of Moral and Religious Lessons.*—The nature of this application explained—The importance of *applying* moral and religious instruction—Of requiring the children to make the application themselves—What is meant by impression—Causes of failure in making religious instruction impressive.

6. *Order, Interest, and Attention.*—The importance of order—Causes of disorder—Various means of obtaining and regaining order—Difference between order and stiffness or restraint—Importance of exciting interest—Means of doing it—Difference between healthful activity of mind and excitement—Attention how to be obtained and kept up.

7. *The Exercise to be given to the Minds of Children.*—Importance of producing activity of the mind—Amount of mental exercise to be given—Means of giving it—Teachers tell too much—Ways of doing so, and causes.

8. *The Manner of the Teacher.*—Importance of manner, especially with young children—Different kinds of manner—How each affects children—The power of a decided manner—Its abuse—The effects of the voice in exciting different feelings—Tones of voice suited to different subjects.

9. *Attention to the whole Gallery.*—Temptations to attend to a few children only—Effects—Means of keeping up general attention—Difficulties where a gallery is unhappily composed of children of different degrees of attainment—How in part to be obviated.

10. *The Use to be made of Incidental Circumstances, especially in Moral Training.*—Enumeration of those which most commonly occur in a gallery, and also in the playground—The influence that the notice of incidental circumstances has on the children, as well in an intellectual as in a moral point of view—Cautions against the abuse of this practice.

11. *On the Language given to Children.*—Relation of language to ideas—Right time of supplying language—Necessity for clearness and simplicity—Fine words and technical terms to be avoided.

3.—ON CLASS INSTRUCTION.

Use of class lessons—Mechanical arrangements—Apparatus—Amount of class instruction to be given—Subjects.

4.—ON THE SUBJECTS OF INSTRUCTION, ETC., PROPER FOR AN INFANT SCHOOL.

1. *On the Principles that should Regulate.*—The choice of subjects should be suitable to the children's age—Elementary character of the subjects—Necessity of having a general design in each course of lessons, as well as a particular design in each lesson—The importance of the instruction being of a graduated character—Of its commencing at the right starting point—Subjects should be varied—The reason and principles upon which this is founded.

2. *The subject stated.*—Color—Object in view in lessons on color, and their suitableness to this object and to infant minds—The graduated course of these lessons, with reference to the work published by the Society, entitled, "*Graduated course of Instruction for Infant Schools and Nurseries*"—Methods to be adopted in giving lessons—Principles to be deduced.

3. The other subjects treated in a similar manner—Form—Size—Weight—Place—Number—Physical actions and employments—Sounds, including practice in singing—Common objects—Pictures of common objects—Drawing before children—Human body—Animals—Plants—Language—Reading, Spelling, Writing—Pieces of poetry—Moral instruction—Religious instruction.

5.—ON THE SUBJECTS OF INSTRUCTION, ETC., PROPER FOR A JUVENILE SCHOOL.

1. *Points in which a Juvenile School differs from an Infant School.*—As to its organization—Division of time—Classification of children—Home-work—Employment of Pupil-Teachers—Subjects of instruction calling the reasoning powers more into exercise—Method of giving such subjects a more continuous and systematic character—Mode of treating the children—Morally, throwing them more upon their own responsibility—Intellectually, making them more independent of their Teachers, and more accustomed to gain information and knowledge from books, teaching them early "to learn how to learn," *i. e.*, to be self-educators.

III.—The School-room, as to its Arrangement and Management.

1. *The School-room.*—Influence of the appearance of the school-room on the children's character—Its effect on visitors—Desks and their arrangement—Cleaning—Ventilation—Temperature—Order and decoration—Apparatus—What it is—Its right appreciation—Care to be taken of it.

2. *The Opening of a New School, &c.*—Preliminary steps to be taken—Difficulties—Spirit in which to commence—Plans to be adopted—Admission of children—Register and other books—Payments.

3. *The Organization of a School.*—What it means—Importance of good organization—Plans to be adopted—Treatment of new scholars—Points requiring attention, as time-tables, programmes, distribution of work, &c.

4. *Division or Classification of the Children.*—Importance of classification of the children of an Infant School—Too much neglected hitherto—The advantage seen in the Model Schools of the Institution—Arrangement in galleries and classes—Principle upon which this is made, of proficiency, not age or size—The difficulties of Infant Schools, when Teachers have no assistance.

5. *Regular and punctual Attendance, and the means of insuring it.*—Importance of the subject—Different causes of irregular attendance—Method of dealing with each—Means for securing attendance, supplying a good education, having well defined and positive rules—Quarterly pre-payment—Punctual attendance—How much depending on the Teacher's own habits—Closing the door at a fixed hour—Visiting the parents, &c.

6. *The Dinner hour and arrangements for it.*—The Teacher's presence necessary—Its inconvenience considered—The social and moral effects of superintending children at dinner.

7. *The Physical State of the Children.*—Teacher's duties with respect to health, cleanliness, and neatness—Duties of parents not to be too much interferred with—Means of cultivating cleanliness, neatness, &c.—The effects.

8. *The Play-ground.*—Physical education—Its importance—Provision to be made for its connection with a school—Advantages of the play-ground in reference to moral instruction and moral training—Its bearing on the health and comfort of the Teacher—Their objections answered—Tact required in the superintendence of the play-ground—Apparatus, games, &c.—Time to be allotted to exercise—Objections of parents met.

9. *Monitors, Pupil-Teachers, and Paid-Assistants.*—Monitors, these "*necessary evils*," as they have been called, fast disappearing—Still often found useful—Relative value of Monitors and Pupil-Teachers, and principle on which to be ascertained—The departments of labor for which each best fitted—Pestalozzi's method of preparing Monitors, and the work allotted them—Instruction of Pupil-Teachers, general and special—Their management—Special cases examined—Pupil-Teachers almost essential to a good school, and amply repay labors of first year or two—to be early trained to "self-education"—When so trained a great relief to the Teacher—Always to be had where practicable.

10. *Examinations*, for the satisfaction of the public—The parents—The Teacher—The design and special advantages of each—Manner of conducting them—Abuses—Addresses to parents a most desirable adjunct—Suitable topics for such addresses.

11. *Holidays*, their use and number—Never to be given at fairs, wakes, &c.—Not generally desired by children in a well-conducted school.

12. *Dealing with Parents.*—Position of the parent—Its relation to the Teacher—Conclusions—The double duty of a Teacher to the parent and the school—Course to be taken—Necessity of a conciliatory manner in dealing with parents who will not submit to rules—On punishing children at the request of parents.

13. *Visitors*, special and casual—Connection of the former with the school—Attention and courtesy due to them—How far the usual arrangement of a school may be changed for visitors—Their suggestions—Spirit in which to be taken—Use to be made of them.

14. *Inspectors.*—The peculiar character of their office—Inspection always to be obtained when practicable—Its value to a good Teacher—Their view of a school contrasted with that of the Teacher—Their relation as well to the Teacher as to the Patron—The Teacher's best friend—Inspection anticipated—Preparation to be made—Lessons to be given before Inspector, as at other times.

15. *Patrons and Committees.*—Relation to the school—Claims—The blessing of a good Patron—Difficulties with Patrons or Committees—The self-will and pride of a Teacher not to be mistaken for conscience, or the love of doing good—Principles and ends to be kept in view rather than plans—Not to thwart or oppose even when not convinced—to give way in minor matters if vital points are untouched—Circumstances which appear to justify giving up a school.

IV.—The Government of a School.

1. *The Nature and Object of this Government.*—All plans of government, if good, must be adapted to the uniform tendencies of human nature—Qualifications required in order to govern well—Importance of government in a school, as often giving to the

child first ideas of subordination—Essential also to the comfort of the Teacher—To the progress and happiness of the children—Disorder the master defect of many schools —Dislike to Teachers often caused by misgovernment.

2. *A knowledge of the Principles of Action in Childhood required in order to Govern well.*—The principles enumerated—Their importance—Scripture references on the influence of habits—Wisdom and beneficence of the Creator seen in the early formation and power of habits—Difficulty of ascertaining motives—Importance of knowing them—The use to be made of them in governing a school.

3. *Parental Government.*—Different kind of rule as to their spirit—The political—The military—The family—Characteristics of each—Reasonableness of requiring the parental spirit in Teachers—In what it consists—Effects of possessing the spirit—The parental spirit manifested by God—Seen in Christ—The parental spirit should govern our schools—Our debt to Pestalozzi for advocating it so powerfully—His fundamental principle in all moral development and training.

4. *Authority*—Meaning of the term—Abuses of authority—Modern mistakes—Importance of authority in the school-room—How to be used—Adaptation to the nature of the child—Mistakes as to governing by love alone—Rules to be adopted in establishing and maintaining authority.

5. *Kindness.*—Distinguished from other affections—Love essential to a Teacher—Shock often received by children when transferred from a mother to an unkind Teacher—Influence of Kindness—Principles on which based—Manner of carrying them out—Caution against extremes.

6. *Justice.*—Definition—Temptations to partiality—Children's appreciation of justice—Written rules often useful.

7. *Fear.*—Its abuses as a principle of government shown in the conduct of parents, teachers, and nurses—The use of fear in the moral economy of the child, and consequently its use by the Teacher—Cautions.

8. *Influence.*—What it is to govern with the will of a child—Means of obtaining inflence—its true value both in the Infant and Juvenile School.

9. *Appeal to Principle.*—Nature of principle, or sense of right and wrong—Relative position among motives of action—Advantages—The result, self-government, &c.—Perfection of a school as to government, when good conduct proceeds from principle.

10. *Prevention.*—Importance of this principle as applied to the government of a school—Children to have full occupation—To associate pleasure with learning—Teacher to call in aid the public opinion of the school—To obtain the co-operation of parents.

11. *Rewards.*—What they are—How they act—Injurious as being an artificial excitement—As giving wrong views both of justice and merit—As rousing a mercenary spirit—As exciting vanity and pride—Means to be used to make promised rewards unnecessary—Example of Hofwyl—From our Infant Schools—The highest motives to be cultivated—Animal motives to be properly directed—Different ways of rewarding merit—Value of a reward consists not in the actual value of what is bestowed, but in the association created—Reward occasional and not expected—When it is not an incentive to exertion, but a proof that merit is recognized, it gives the idea of justice.

12. *Punishments.*—Nature, design, and spirit—Difference between punishment, correction, and discipline—The true end of punishment—Mistakes of the passionate Teacher—Effects of these on the child—Punishment should arise out of the fault—God's dealings with us our example—Natural punishments enumerated—Children to be shown the connection between sin and punishment—An unvarying punishment impossible—Should differ according to character and disposition, and the nature of faults, &c.—Evils of severe punishments—Importance of discrimination—Public exposure as a punishment—Spirit that leads a teacher to expose her pupils for her own gratification—Effects of exposure on different dispositions, and on spectators—Corporal punishment—Former and present practice contrasted—Opinion of Dr. Arnold and Dr. Bryce—Pestalozzi's rules for using it—Its absence in a good school—Expulsion when to be resorted to—Circumstances to attend it.

13. *Emulation.*—Nature of the principle—Usual application—Meaning of the word-Natural emulation, distinguished from Scripture emulation—"Generous rivalry," and "rivalry a means of self-knowledge," false ideas—Natural emulation not to be stimulated—Difficulties of a Teacher not using emulation—Substitutes for it, as—Desire to overcome difficulties—To gain knowledge—To please a much-loved Teacher, &c.

MEMOIR OF PESTALOZZI.

By Karl von Raumer.

CONTENTS.

INTRODUCTION.

BIOGRAPHICAL SKETCH OF KARL VON RAUMER.

Out of the numerous memoirs, brief and extended, which have appeared in Switzerland and Germany, of the great Swiss educator, we select that by Prof. Karl von Raumer, in the second volume of his elaborate "*History of Pedagogy*."* It is at once condensed and sufficiently full and minute to give a correct, vivid picture of Pestalozzi's own diversified and troubled career as a man and an educator, and of his numerous contributions to the literature of education. Beyond any other of his biographers, Prof. Raumer has not only a rich and varied scholarship, but full and accurate knowledge of the past history of education and of schools, and a disposition to do justice to Pestalozzi's large-hearted as well as original contributions to this department of human progress.

Karl von Raumer, was born at Worlitz, in the duchy of Anhalt-Dessau, on the 9th of April, 1783. Until his fourteenth year, he was under private instruction at home; was then, with his brother, (Frederic, the present Minister of Public Instruction in Prussia,) placed at the Joachimsthal Gymnasium at Berlin; in 1801, went thence to the university of Göttingen to study law; in 1803, to Halle, to attend the lectures of Wolf and Steffens, and in 1805, to Freiberg, where he devoted himself to mineralogy and geology under Werner. After exploring the mountain chains in Germany and France, he went to Paris, in the autumn of 1808 to prosecute his geological studies, where a change in his plans of life occurred, which he thus describes in a chapter of his published lectures on education:

"At Paris my views and intentions in regard to the future occupation of my life underwent a great change, which was brought about by two different causes. For one thing, I had learnt by my own experience how little a single individual is able to accomplish for the science of mineralogy, even if he goes to work with the best will and the most toilsome industry; that it required, much more, the united, intelligent and persevering labors of many, in order to pass from a mere belief in the laws of mineralogy to an actual perception of their operation in mountain chains. I thus became convinced that we ought not to work for science as individuals, but that we should, after passing through our own apprenticeship, instruct others and train them for the pursuit of science. How much more useful is it, thought I, to produce *one* new workman than *one*

---

* *Geschichte der Pädagogik vom Wiederaufblühen klassischer studien bis aus unsere zeit* Stuttgart, 1847. 3 vols.

single new work, seeing that the former can execute many works, and even train other workmen. This conviction caused me to turn my attention to the question of education. But a second cause operated in a still higher degree to produce the same result. The sad time that had passed since 1806 had affected me with horror and dismay; it had made me wish to shun the society of my fellow-men, and had quite disposed me to give myself up to the most solitary researches among the mountains. This disposition was strengthened at Paris, in the midst of the haughty despisers of our German fatherland. But it was here, too, where hope first dawned within me, where a solitary light beamed toward me through the darkness of night. I read Pestalozzi, and what Fichte says, in his 'Addresses to the German Nation,' about Pestalozzi and education. The thought, that a new and better Germany must rise from the ruins of the old one, that youthful blossoms must spring from the mouldering soil, took strong hold of me. In this manner, there awoke within me a determination to visit Pestalozzi at Yverdun.

Fichte's Addresses had great influence on me. Surrounded by Frenchmen, the brave man pointed out to his Berlin hearers in what way they might cast off the French yoke, and renew and strengthen their nationality.

He promised deliverance especially through a national education of the Germans, which he indicated as the commencement of an entire reformation of the human race, by which the spirit should gain a complete ascendency over the flesh. To the question, to which of the existing institutions of the actual world he would annex the duty of carrying out the new education, Fichte answered, 'To the course of instruction which has been invented and brought forward by Henry Pestalozzi, and which is now being successfully carried out under his direction.'

He then gives an account of Pestalozzi, and compares him with Luther, especially in regard to his love for the poor and destitute. His immediate object, says Fichte, was to help these by means of education, but he had produced something higher than a scheme of popular education,—he had produced a plan of national education which should embrace all classes of society.

Further on he expresses himself in his peculiar manner on the subject of Pestalozzi's method, which he criticises. He takes exception to Pestalozzi's view of language, namely, 'as a means of raising mankind from dim perceptions to clear ideas,' and to the Book for Mothers. On the other hand, he strongly recommends the development of bodily skill and dexterity proposed by Pestalozzi, for this, among other reasons, that it would make the whole nation fit for military service, and thus remove the necessity for a standing army. Like Pestalozzi, he attaches a high value to the skill necessary for gaining a livelihood, as a condition of an honorable political existence.

He especially insists that it is the duty of the State to charge itself with education. He spoke in the year 1808, in the capital of Prussia, which had been deeply humiliated by the unhappy war of the preceding years, and in the most hopeless period of Germany's history.

'Would that the state,' he said to a Prussian audience, among whom were several high officers of state, 'would look its present peculiar condition steadily in the face, and acknowledge to itself what that condition really is; would that it could clearly perceive that there remains for it no other sphere in which it can act and resolve as an independent State, except the education of the rising generation; that, unless it is absolutely determined to do nothing, this is now all it can do; but that the merit of doing this would be conceded to it undiminished and unenvied. That we are no longer able to offer an active resistance, was before presupposed as obvious, and as acknowledged by every one. How then can we defend our continued existence, obtained by submission, against the reproach of cowardice and an unworthy love of life? In no other way than by resolving not to live for ourselves, and by acting up to this resolution; by raising up a worthy posterity, and by preserving our own existence solely in order that we may accomplish this object. If we had not this first object of life, what else were there for us to do? Our constitutions will be made for us, the alliances which we are to form, and the direction in which our military resources shall be applied, will be indicated to us, a statute-book will be lent to us, even the administration of justice will sometimes be taken out of our hands; we shall be relieved of all these cares for the next years to come. Education alone has not been thought of; if we are seeking for an occupation, let us seize this! We may expect that in this occupation we shall be left undisturbed. I hope, (perhaps I deceive myself, but as I have only this hope still to live for, I can not cease to hope,) that I convince some Germans, and that I shall bring them to see that it is education alone which can save us from all the evils by which we are oppressed. I count especially on this, as a favorable circumstance, that our need will have rendered us more disposed to attentive observation and serious reflection than we were in the day of our prosperity. Foreign lands have other consolations and other remedies; it is not to be expected that they would pay any attention, or give any credit to this idea, should it ever reach them; I will much rather hope that it will be a rich source of amusement to the readers of their journals, if they ever learn that any one promises himself so great things from education.'

It may easily be imagined how deep an impression such words made on me, as I read them in Paris, the imperial seat of tyranny, at a time when I was in a state of profound melancholy, caused by the ignominious slavery of my poor beloved country. There also I was absorbed in the perusal of Pestalozzi's work, 'How Gertrude teaches her children.' The passages of deep pathos in the book took powerful hold of my mind, the new and great ideas excited strong hopes in me; at that time I was carried away on the wings of those hopes over Pestalozzi's errors and failures, and I had not the experience which would have enabled me to detect these easily, and to examine them critically.

About the same time I read the 'Report to the Parents on the state of the Pestalozzian Institution;' it removed every doubt in my mind as to the possibility of seeing my boldest hopes realized. Hereupon, I immediately resolved to go to Yverdun, which appeared to me a green oasis, full of fresh and living springs, in the midst of the great desert of my native land, on which rested the curse of Napoleon."

At an age when most men, of his acknowledged ability and scholarship, are only thinking of securing a civil employment, which shall bring both riches and honor, Von Raumer hastened to Pestalozzi at Yverdun, where he devoted himself, for nearly two years, to a study of the principles and methods of elementary instruction, as illustrated by the great Swiss educator.

Returning from Switzerland, in May, 1810, Von Raumer accepted an appointment of regular professor at Halle, with a handsome salary; but, not finding the pleasure he anticipated in his professorial lectures, he soon after gave up the post, and proceeded to establish a private school at Nuremberg, where he strove to realize his own ideal of an educational institution. In this enterprise he was not so immediately successful as he hoped to be. In 1822 he married a daughter of Kappellmeister Reichardt, and, by the advice of his friends, he returned to academic life by accepting the appointment of professor of natural history, at Erlangen. In addition to his regular duties, he found time to prepare and deliver occasional lectures on the "History of Pedagogy from the revival of classical learning to our own time." These lectures were subsequently published in three parts—the first of which was issued in 1843. Of the origin and plan of the work the author thus speaks in the preface to the complete edition in 1846.

"This work has grown out of a series of lectures, upon the history of education, which I delivered, in 1822, at Halle, and several years later, from 1838 to 1842, at Erlangen.

The reader may inquire, how it was that my attention was directed to this subject? If he should, it will perhaps be sufficient to say in reply, that during the thirty-one years of my professorship, I have not merely interested myself in the *science* to which my time was devoted, but also in its corresponding *art*, and this the more, because much of the instruction which I gave was additional to my regular lectures, and imparted in the way of dialogue. This method stimulated my own thoughts too, to that degree, that I was induced as early as the year 1819 to publish many didactical essays, and subsequently, a manual for instruction in Natural History. But were I called upon for a more particular explanation, it would be necessary for me to relate the many experiences of my somewhat eventful life, both from my passive years of training and instruction, and from my active years of educating and instructing others. This, however, is a theme, to which I can not do justice within the brief compass of a preface; if hereafter an opportunity shall offer, I may treat it in another place.

And yet after all, the book itself must bear testimony to the fitness of the author for his task. Of what avail is it to me, to say that I have been taught by Meierotto, Buttman, Frederick Augustus, Wolf, Steffens, Werner, Pestalozzi, and other distinguished men? When I have said all this, have I done any more than to show that the author of this book has had the very best opportunity to learn what is just and true?

My book begins with the revival of classical learning. And Germany I have had preëminently in view. Why, by way of introduction, I have given a brief history of the growth of learning in Italy from Dante to the age of Leo X., the reader will ascertain from the book itself. He will be convinced, if not at the outset, yet as he reads further, that this introduction is absolutely necessary to a correct understanding of German didactics.

A history of didactics must present the various standards of mental culture, which a nation proposes to itself during its successive eras of intellectual development, and then the modes of instruction which are adopted in each era, in order to realize its peculiar standard in the rising generation. In distinguished men that standard of culture manifests itself to us in person, so to speak, and hence they exert a controlling influence upon didactics, though they may not themselves be teachers. 'A lofty example stirs up a spirit of emulation, and discloses deeper principles to guide the judgment.'

But their action upon the intellectual culture of their countrymen has a redoubled power, when at the same time they labor directly at the work of teaching, as both Luther and Melancthon did for years. This consideration has induced me to select my characters for this history among distinguished teachers, those who were held in the highest respect by their contemporaries, and whose example was a pattern for multitudes. Such an one was John Sturm at Strasburg, a rector, who with steady gaze pursued a definite educational aim, organizing his gymnasium with the utmost skill and discernment, and carrying out what he had conceived to be the true method, with the most scrupulous care. An accurate sketch of the educational efficiency of this pattern rector, based upon original authorities, in my opinion conveys far more insight and instruction than I could hope to afford, were I to entangle myself amid fragmentary sketches of numberless ordinary schools, framed upon Sturm's plan.

Thus much in explanation of the fact that this history has taken the form of a series of biographies. And in view of the surprising differences among the characters treated of, it can not appear singular, if my sketches should be widely different in their form.

There was one thought, which I will own occasioned me abundant perplexity during my labors. If I was about to describe a man, who, I had reason to suppose, was more or less unknown to most of my readers, I went about the task with a light heart, and depicted his life and labors in their full proportions, communicating every thing which could, by any possibility, render his image clearer and more lifelike to the reader. But how different the case, when the educational efficiency of Luther is to be set forth. 'My readers,' I say to myself, 'have long been acquainted with the man, and they will not thank me for the information that he was born at Eisleben, on the 10th of November, 1483; as if they had not known this from their youth up.' I am, therefore, compelled to omit all such particulars, and to confine myself exclusively to his educational efficiency. And yet this did not stand alone; but was for the most part united, with its entire influence, both to the church and the state. As with Luther, so also was it with Melancthon and others. Considerate readers will, hence, pardon me, I hope, when, in cases of this kind, they are not fully satisfied with my sketches.

In another respect, too, I ought perhaps to solicit pardon, though I am reluctant to do so. We demand of historians an objective portraiture, especially such as shall reveal none of the personal sympathies or antipathies of the writer. Now it is proper to insist upon that truth and justice which will recognize the good qualities of an enemy, and acknowledge the faults of a friend. But free from likes and dislikes I neither am, nor do I desire to be, but, according to the dictates of my conscience and the best of my knowledge, I will signify my abhorrence of evil and my delight in good, nor will I ever put bitter for sweet or sweet for bitter. It may be, too, that a strict objectivity requires the historian never to come forward himself upon the stage, and never to express his own opinion in respect to the facts which he is called upon to chronicle. Herein he is not allowed so much freedom of action as the dramatist, who, by means either of the prologue and epilogue, or of the chorus between each of the acts, comes forward and converses with the public upon the merits of his play. Such an objectivity, likewise, I can not boast myself of; for I record my own sentiments freely where I deem it necessary. And surely will not the objectivity of history gain more by an unrestricted personal interview with the historian, at proper intervals, than by compelling him to a perpetual masquerade behind the facts and the narrative? Certainly it will, for in that case the reader discovers the character of the writer in his opinions, and knows what he himself is to expect from the narration. He likewise observes with the more readiness, where the writer, though conscientiously aiming at truth and impartiality, nevertheless betrays symptoms of human infirmity and party zeal. From a church historian, for instance, who should express his puritanical views without reserve, no intelligent reader would expect an impartial estimate of the middle ages.

Another motive also urges me to a free expression of my opinions, and that is, in order thereby to allure my readers to that close familiarity with many important educational subjects which the bare recital of facts seldom creates. If, in this history, the ideal and the methods of such different teachers are depicted, these diverse views can not but have the effect, especially those practically engaged in training the young, to induce a comparison of their own aims and procedure therewith. Sentiments that harmonize with our own give us joy, and inspire us with the pleasant consciousness that our course is the right one; differing or opposing opinions lead us to scrutinize our own course, even as were it another's; and from such scrutiny there results either perseverance based upon deeper conviction, or a change of course. I am happy to acknowledge, that this practical aim has been my chief motive in undertaking the present work, and has been uppermost in my thoughts during its prosecution.

As far as possible, I have depended on contemporaneous sources, and in part from exceedingly rare works, and such, as, for aught that I know to the contrary, in the present age, have fallen into almost total oblivion. And, for this reason, I was the more influenced to render a service to the reader, by bringing widely to his view the men and the manners of earlier centuries, through the medium of contemporaneous and characteristic quotations."

We give on the next page the Table of Contents of the three volumes of Raumer's great work.

GESCHICHTE DER PÄDAGOGIK vom wiederaufblühen klassischer studien bis unsere zeit. [*History of Pedagogics, or of the Science and Art of Education, from the revival of classical studies down to our time.*] By Karl von Raumer. 3 vols. Stuttgard, 2d edition, 1847.

VOLUME I.

PREFACE.

1. Middle Ages.

2. Italy, from birth of Dante to death of Petrarca and Boccaccio. 1. Dante. 2. Boccaccio. 3. Petrarca. Review of the period.

3. Development of classical studies in Italy, from death of Petrarca and Boccaccio until Leo X. 1. John of Ravenna and Emanuel Chrysoloras. 2. The educators, Guarino and Vittorino de Feltre. 3. Collection of MSS. Cosmo de Medici. Nicholas V. First printing. 4. Platonic Academy. Greek philologists. 5. Italians. Philadelphus. Poggius. Laurentius. 6. Lorenzo de Medici. Ficinus. Argyropulus. Landinus. Politianus. Picus de Mirandola.

4. Leo X. and his time; its lights and shadows.

5. Retrospect of Italy. Transition to Germany.

6. *Germans and Dutch*, from Gerhardus Magnus to Luther, 1340–1483. 1. The Hieronymians. 2. John Wessel. 3. Rudolf Agricola. 4. Alexander Flegius. 5, 6. Rudolf von Lange and Herman von den Busch. 7. Erasmus. 8. School at Schlettstadt. Ludwig Dringenberg. Wimpheling. Crato. Lapidus. Platter. 9. John Reuchlin. 10. Retrospect.

Reformation. Jesuits. Realism.

From Luther to the death of Bacon, 1483–1626. 1. Luther. 2. Melancthon. 3. Valentin Friedland. Trotzendorf. 4. Michæl Neander. 5. John Sturm. 6. Wurtemberg. 7. Saxony. 8. Jesuits. 9. Universities. 10. Verbal Realism. 11. Francis Bacon. 12. Montaigne.

Appendix.—I. Thomas Platter. II. Melancthon's Latin grammar. III. John Sturm.

VOLUME II.

New ideas and methods of education. Struggle, mutual influence, and gradual connection and exchange between the old and the new.

From Bacon's death to that of Pestalozzi. 1. The Renovators. 2. Wolfgang Ratich. 3. The Thirty Years' War. 4. Comenius. 5. The Century after the Thirty Years' War. 6. Locke. 7. A. H. Franke. 8. Real Schools. 9. Reformatory Philologists. J. M. Gesner. J. A. Ernesti. 10. J. J. Rousseau. 11. Philanthropists. 12. Hamann. 13. Herder. 14. F. A. Wolf. 15. Pestalozzi.

Appendix.—I. Wolfgang Ratich and his literature. II. Pedagogical works of Comenius. III. Interior of the Philanthropinum. IV. Pestalozzi and his literature. V. Pestalozzi's Evening Hour of a Hermit. VI. Pestalozzi on Niederer and Schmid. VII. Strangers who remained some time at Pestalozzi's institution. VIII. Rousseau and Pestalozzi.

VOLUME III.

Early childhood. Schools for small children. School and home. Educational institutions. Tutors in families.

Instruction. 1. *Religion.* 2 *Latin.* Preface.

I. History of Latin in Christian times. Speaking Latin. Writing Latin.

II. Methods of reading Latin. 1. These methods changed within the last three centuries. 2. Adversaries of the old grammatical method. 3. New methods. A. Learning Latin like the mother tongue. B. Latin and real instruction in connection. Comenius. C. Combination of A and B. D. Ratich and similar teachers. a. Ratich. b. Locke. c. Hamilton. d. Jacotot. e. Ruthardt. f. Meierotto. g. Jacobs. Concluding remarks.

Aphorisms on the teaching of *history.*

Geography.

Natural history and philosophy. Preface. 1. Difficulties. 2. Objections against this instruction in gymnasia answered. 3. Grades of natural knowledge. 4. Beginnings. 5. Science and art. 6. Mathematical instruction and elementary instruction in the knowledge of nature. 7. Instruction in mineralogy. 8. Characteristics of scholars. 9. Instruction in botany. 10. Unavoidable inconsistency. 11. "Mysteriously clear," (*Goethe.*) 12. Law and liberty. Concluding remarks.

Geometry.

Arithmetic.

Physical training. 1. Hygiene. 2. Hardening the body to toil and want. 3. Gymnastics. 4. Cultivation of the senses. Concluding observations.

Appendix.—I. Ruthardt's new *Loci Memoriales.* II. Teachers of mineralogy. III. Use of counters in the elementary instruction in arithmetic. IV. Explanation of the common abbreviated counting with cyphers.

Since the foregoing sketch of Prof. Raumer's own educational life and labors was published, we have received a fourth and concluding volume of his "*History, &c.*," entitled "*The German Universities*," in which he introduces his own experience as a student and professor, to give personal interest to the narrative. We copy the Dedication and Preface, and give the Contents of the American edition, as translated originally for the "*American Journal of Education.*"

TO THE

STUDENTS OF THE PAST AND PRESENT,

WHO HAVE BEEN MY COMPANIONS FROM 1811 TO 1854,

I DEDICATE THIS BOOK,

IN TRUE AND HEARTFELT LOVE.

KARL VON RAUMER.

PREFACE.

The reader here receives the conclusion of my work.

It is a contribution to the history of the Universities. When I commenced it, I hoped confidently to be able to make it greater; but in proportion as I gained an insight into the difficulty of the enterprise of writing a complete history of the German Universities, my courage failed. Many of the difficulties which the historian of the German people has to overcome, are here also found in the way, and in much increased dimensions.

If all the German universities possessed the same features, if the characteristics of one of them—important modifications excepted—would stand for all, then the task of their historian would, apparently, be quite simple. But how different, and how radically different, are the universities from each other!

Even the multiplicity of the German nationalities, governments, and sects had much to do in distinguishing them. To compare, for instance, the universities of Göttingen and Jena, as they were at the beginning of the present century; what a contrast appears between them! And how much greater is the difference between these two Protestant universities and the Catholic one of Vienna!

Further than this, each single university undergoes such changes in the course of time, that it appears, as it were, different from itself. To instance the University of Heidelberg: Catholic in the beginning, it became Lutheran in 1556, Reformed in 1560, Lutheran in 1576, Reformed again in 1583; afterward came under the management of the Jesuits; and, at the destruction of their order, returned to Protestantism.

To these difficulties, in the way of the historian of all the German universities, is added this one: that the most important sources of information fail him; as we have, namely, but few competent histories of single universities—such, for example, as Klüpfel's valuable "*History of the University of Tubingen.*"

These considerations will sufficiently excuse me for publishing only contributions to a history of the German universities, which will sooner or later appear.

What I have added under the name of "Academical Treatises," is also a contribution to history; for the reason that these treatises will, of necessity, not be worthless for some future historian of the present condition of our universities.

In conclusion, I desire gratefully to acknowledge the goodness of Chief Librarian Hoeck, for books furnished me from the Göttingen library. Mr. Stenglein, librarian at Bamberg, also most willingly furnished me with books from it. The use of the Royal Library at Berlin was also afforded me, with distinguished friendliness and kindness; for which I would once more most heartily thank Privy Councilor and Chief Librarian Pertz, and Librarians Dr. Pinder and Dr. Friedlander.

ERLANGEN, 9*th April*, 1854. KARL VON RAUMER.

THE GERMAN UNIVERSITIES. Being the fourth volume of the *History of Education.* By KARL VON RAUMER. Re-published from the "*American Journal of Education,*" edited by HENRY BARNARD. LL.D. New York: F. C. BROWNELL, No. 346, Broadway. 250 pages. Price $1.50.

CONTENTS.

THE LIFE AND EDUCATIONAL SYSTEM OF PESTALOZZI.

BY CARL VON RAUMER,*

JOHN HENRY PESTALOZZI was born at Zurich on the 12th of January, 1746. His father was a medical practitioner; his mother, whose maiden name was Hotze, was a native of Wädenschwyl on the Lake of Zurich, and first cousin to the Austrian general Hotze, who fell at Schännis in 1799.

The father died prematurely, when Pestalozzi was only six years old; from this time forward, therefore, "every thing was wanting, in the influences around him, which a manly education of the faculties so urgently requires at that age." "I was brought up," he relates, "by the hand of the best of mothers like a spoilt darling, such that you will not easily find a greater. From one year to another I never left the domestic hearth; in short, all the essential means and inducements to the development of manly vigor, manly experience, manly ways of thinking, and manly exercises, were just as much wanting to me, as, from the peculiarity and weakness of my temperament, I especially needed them."

This peculiarity, according to Pestalozzi's own statement, was, that with the most sensitive feelings and the liveliest imagination, he was deficient in the power of sustained attention, in reflection, circumspection, and foresight.

His mother devoted herself wholly to the education of her three children, in which she was assisted by a faithful servant girl from the country, of the name of Babeli. Pestalozzi's father, on his deathbed, sent for this girl. "Babeli," said he, "for the sake of God and mercy, do not leave my wife; when I am dead, she will be forlorn, and my children will fall into strange and cruel hands." "I will not leave your wife when you die," replied Babeli; "I will remain with her till death, if she has need of me." Her words pacified the dying father; she kept her promise, and remained till her death with the

* In this article we follow literally, but with occasional abridgments, the translation of Prof. J. Tilleard, originally published in the Educational Expositor for 1853–4, and afterward collected in a volume of 80 pages, by Longman, Brown, Green and Longmans, London: 1855.

mother. "Her great fidelity," Pestalozzi says, "was the result of her strong, simple, and pious faith." As the mother was in very straitened circumstances, Babeli economized wherever she could; she even restrained the children when they wanted to go into the street, or to any place where they had no business to go, with the words, "why will you needlessly wear out your shoes and clothes? See how much your mother denies herself, in order to be able to give you an education; how for weeks and months together she never goes out any where, but saves every farthing for your schooling." Nevertheless, the mother was liberal in those expenses which respectability requires, nor did she let the children be without handsome Sunday clothes. These, however, they were allowed to wear but seldom, and they had to take them off again as soon as they came home.

"I saw the world," says Pestalozzi, "only within the narrow limits of my mother's parlor, and within the equally narrow limits of my school-room; to real human life I was almost as great a stranger, as if I did not live in the world in which I dwelt."

Pestalozzi's grandfather on the mother's side was minister at Höngg, a village three miles from Zurich. With him Pestalozzi spent several months every year, from the time when he was nine years old. The old man conscientiously cared for the souls of his flock, and thereby exercised a great influence upon the village school; his piety made a deep and lasting impression on his grandson.

Of his early school days, Pestalozzi relates the following:—

"In all boys' games, I was the most clumsy and helpless among all my school fellows, and nevertheless, in a certain way, I always wanted to excel the others. This caused some of them very frequently to pass their jokes upon me. One of them gave me the nickname 'Harry Whimsical of Foolstown.' Most of them, however, liked my good natured and obliging disposition; though they knew my general clumsiness and awkwardness, as well as my carelessness and thoughtlessness in everything that did not particularly interest me.

"Accordingly, although one of the best pupils, I nevertheless committed, with incomprehensible thoughtlessness, faults of which not even the worst of them was ever guilty. While I generally seized with quickness and accuracy upon the essential matter of the subjects of instruction, I was generally very indifferent and thoughtless as to the forms in which it was given. At the same time that I was far behind my fellow scholars in some parts of a subject, in other parts of the same subject I often surpassed them in an unusual degree. This is so true, that once, when one of my professors, who had a very good knowledge of Greek, but not the least eloquence of style, translated and published some orations of Demosthenes, I had the boldness, with the limited school rudiments which I then possessed, to translate one of these orations myself, and to give it in, at the examination, as a specimen of my progress in this branch of study. A portion of this translation was printed in the Linden Journal, in connection with an article entitled 'Agis.' Just in the same manner as I made incomparably more progress in certain parts of my subjects of instruction than in others, so generally it was of far more importance to me to be sensibly affected by, (I dare not say to understand thoroughly,) the branches of knowledge which I was to learn, than to exercise myself in the means of practicing them. At the same time, the *wish* to be acquainted with some branches of knowledge that took hold on my heart and my imagination, even though I neglected the means of acquiring them, was nevertheless enthusiastically alive within me; and unfortunately, the tone of public instruction in my native town at this period was in a high degree calculated to foster this visionary fancy of taking an active interest in, and believing one's self capable of, the practice of things in which one had by no means had sufficient exercise, and this fancy was very prevalent among the youth of my native town generally." What a foreshadowing is Pestalozzi's childhood of the whole of his subsequent career!

Among Pestalozzi's teachers, there were three who exercised an influence upon him in his youth,—Bodmer, Breitinger, and Steinbrüchel. Bodmer was Professor of History from 1725 to 1775; he is known by his literary controversies with Gottsched and Lessing, his edition of the Minniesingers, and his epic poem upon the Deluge. Breitinger, Professor of Greek and Hebrew from 1731 to 1776, edited the Septuagint. Steinbrüchel is described as a witty and learned man, but very much inclined to infidel "illumination." "Independence, freedom, beneficence, self-sacrifice, and patriotism, were the watchwords of our public education," says Pestalozzi. "But the means of attaining all this which was particularly commended to us —mental distinction—was left without solid and sufficient training of the practical ability which is its essential condition. We were taught, in a visionary manner, to seek for independence in an abstract acquaintance with truth, without being made to feel strongly what was essentially necessary to the security both of our inward and of our outward domestic and civil independence. The tone of the instruction which we received, led us, with much vivacity and many attractive representations, to be so short-sighted and inconsiderate as to set little value upon, and almost to despise, the external means of wealth, honor, and consideration. This was carried to such a length, that we imagined, while we were yet in the condition of boys, that, by a superficial school acquaintance with the great civil life of Greece and Rome, we could eminently prepare ourselves for the little civil life in one of the Swiss cantons."

Pestalozzi further relates, that the appearance of the writings of Rousseau was a great means of keeping alive the errors into which the noble flight of true and patriotic sentiment had led the more distinguished of the young Swiss. "They had run," he says, "into one-sided, rash, and confused notions, into which Voltaire's seductive infidelity, being opposed to the pure holiness of religion, and to its simplicity and innocence, had helped to lead them. Out of all this," he tells us, "a new tendency was produced, which was totally inconsistent with the real welfare of our native town, constituted as it was according to the old-fashioned style of the imperial free cities, which was neither calculated to preserve what was good in the old institutions, nor to introduce any that were substantially better."

At this time, Pestalozzi's contemporary, Lavater, founded a league which Pestalozzi joined, being then a lad of fifteen. The young men who formed this league, with Lavater at their head, brought a public charge of injustice against Grebel, the governor of the canton, impeached the character of Brunner, the mayor of Zurich, and declared war against unworthy ministers of religion.

"The moment Rousseau's *Emile* appeared," says Pestalozzi, "my visionary and highly speculative mind was enthusiastically seized by this visionary and highly speculative book. I compared the education which I enjoyed in the corner of my mother's parlor, and also in the school which I frequented, with what Rousseau demanded for the education of his Emilus. The home as well as the public education of the whole world, and of all ranks of society, appeared to me altogether as a crippled thing, which was to find a universal remedy for its present pitiful condition in Rousseau's lofty ideas.

"The ideal system of liberty, also, to which Rousseau imparted fresh animation, increased in me the visionary desire for a more extended sphere of activity, in which I might promote the welfare and happiness of the people. Juvenile ideas as to what it was necessary and possible to do in this respect in my native town, induced me to abandon the clerical profession, to which I had formerly leaned, and for which I had been destined, and caused the thought to spring up within me, that it might be possible, by the study of the law, to find a career that would be likely to procure for me, sooner or later, the opportunity and means of exercising an active influence on the civil condition of my native town, and even of my native land."

There was at this time a great controversy in the canton of Zurich, particularly between the town and the country. Pestalozzi had already as a boy, when living with his grandfather, the village pastor, won the affection of the people of the country, and might early have heard the complaint of the country clergy, *omne malum ex urbe*,—"all harm comes from the town." A fierce hatred toward the aristocracy who oppressed the country people was kindled in his young heart, and even in old age it was not altogether extinguished. This warmth of anger coëxisted in him with great warmth of love for the people; Göthe's saying—

> "Youth's wings should trim themselves for flight
> Ere youthful strength be gone,
> Thro' hate of wrong and love of right
> To bear him bravely on—"

characterizes not only the young Pestalozzi, but also the old man; it characterizes most of his writings.

He was seconded at this time by a friend of the name of Bluntschli, but a pulmonary complaint laid this young man upon his deathbed. He sent for Pestalozzi, and said to him, "I die, and when you are left to yourself, you must not plunge into any career which from your good natured and confiding disposition, might become dangerous to you. Seek for a quiet, tranquil career; and unless you have at your side a man who will faithfully assist you with a calm, dispassionate knowledge of men and things, by no means embark in any extensive undertaking whose failure would in any way be perilous to you." An opinion of Pestalozzi's character which was strikingly confirmed by almost every subsequent event of his life.

Soon after his friend's death, Pestalozzi himself became dangerously ill, probably in consequence of his overstrained exertion in the pursuit of his legal and historical studies. His physicians advised him to give up scientific pursuits for a time, and to recreate himself in the country. This advice, which was strengthened by Rousseau's anti-scientific diatribes, Pestalozzi followed too faithfully. He renounced the study of books, burnt his manuscripts, went to his maternal relation, Dr. Hotze at Richterswyl, and from thence to Kirchberg, in the canton of Bern, to Tschiffeli, a farmer of considerable reputation. From him Pestalozzi sought advice as to how he might best realize his plans for the country people. "I had come to him," says Pestalozzi, "a political visionary, though with many profound and correct attainments, views, and prospects in political matters; and I went away from him just as great an agricultural visionary, though with many enlarged and correct ideas and intentions in regard to agriculture. My stay with him only had this effect—that the gigantic views in relation to my exertions were awakened within me afresh by his agricultural plans, which, though difficult of execution, and in part impracticable, were bold and extensive; and that, at the same time, they caused me, in my thoughtlessness as to the means of carrying them out, to fall into a callousness, the consequences of which contributed in a decisive manner to the pecuniary embarrassment into which I was plunged in the very first years of my rural life."

Tschiffeli's plantations of madder were exciting great attention at that time, and induced Pestalozzi to make a similar experiment. He learnt that near the village of Birr there was a large tract of barren chalky heath-land to be sold, which was only used for a sheep-walk. He joined a rich mercantile firm in Zurich, and bought about 100 acres of this land, at the nominal price of ten florins. A builder erected for him, on the land he had purchased, a dwelling house in the Italian style; Pestalozzi himself calls this an injudicious and imprudent step. To the whole estate he gave the name of Neuhof.

Among the friends of Pestalozzi's youth, was Schulthess, (the son of a wealthy merchant in Zurich,) for whose beautiful sister, Anna Schulthess, Pestalozzi entertained an affection. A letter which he wrote to the beautiful maiden, gives us a profound insight into the workings of his heart, and even into his future life. In this letter he lays before her his hopes and resolutions, and also, with the utmost candor and with great self-knowledge, his faults. He thus writes :—

"My dear, my only Friend.

"Our whole future life, our whole happiness, our duties toward our country and our posterity, and the security of virtue, call upon us to follow the only correct guide in our actions—Truth. I will, with all candor, made known to you the serious reflection I have had in these solemn days upon the relation subsisting between us; I am happy that I know before-hand, that my friend will find more true love in the calm truth of this contemplation, which so intimately concerns our happiness, than in the ardor of pleasant, but often not too wise, outpourings of a feeling heart, which I now with difficulty restrain.

"Dear friend, first of all I must tell you that in future I shall but seldom dare to approach you. I have already come too frequently and too imprudently to your brother's house; I see that it becomes my duty to limit my visits to you; I have not the slightest ability to conceal my feelings. My sole art in this respect consists in fleeing from those who observe them; I should not be able to be in company with you for even half an evening, without its being possible for a moderately acute observer to perceive that I was in a disturbed state of mind. We know each other sufficiently, dear, to be able to rely upon mutual straightforward honesty and sincerity. I propose to you a correspondence in which we shall make our undisguised thoughts known to each other with all the freedom of oral conversation. Yes, I will open myself fully and freely to you; I will even now with the greatest candor, let you look as deep into my heart as I am myself able to penetrate; I will show you my views in the light of my present and future condition, as clearly as I see them myself.

"Dearest Schulthess, those of my faults which appear to me the most important in relation to the situation in which I may be placed in after-life, are improvidence, incautiousness, and a want of presence of mind to meet unexpected changes in my future prospects, whenever they may occur. I know not how far they may be diminished by my efforts to counteract them, by calm judgment and experience. At present, I have them still in such a degree, that I dare not conceal them from the maiden whom I love; they are faults, my dear, which deserve your fullest consideration. I have other faults, arising from my irritability and sensitiveness, which oftentimes will not submit to my judgment. I very frequently allow myself to run into excesses in praising and blaming, in my likings and dislikings; I cleave so strongly to many things which I possess, that the force with which I feel myself bound to them often exceeds the limits which reason assigns; whenever my country or my friend is unhappy, I am myself unhappy. Direct your whole attention to this weakness; there will be times when the cheerfulness and tranquillity of my soul will suffer under it. If even it does not hinder me in the discharge of my duties, yet I shall scarcely ever be great enough to fulfill them, in such adverse circumstances, with the cheerfulness and tranquillity of a wise man, who is ever true to himself. Of my great, and indeed very reprehensible negligence in all matters of etiquette, and generally in all matters which are not in themselves of importance, I need not speak; any one may see them at first sight of me. I also owe you the open confession, my dear, that I shall always consider my duties toward my beloved partner subordinate to my duties toward my country; and that, although I shall be the tenderest husband, nevertheless I hold it to be my duty to be inexorable to the tears of my wife, if she should ever attempt to restrain me by them from the direct performance of my duties as a citizen, whatever this might lead to. My wife shall be the confident of my heart, the partner of all my most secret counsels. A great and honest simplicity shall reign in my house. And one thing more. My life will not pass without important and very critical undertakings. I shall not forget the precepts of Menalk, and my first resolutions to devote myself wholly to my country; I shall never from fear of man, refrain from speaking, when I see that the good of my country calls upon me to speak: my whole heart is my country's; I will risk all to alleviate the need and misery of my fellow countrymen. What consequences may the undertakings to which I feel myself urged on, draw after them; how unequal to them am I; and how imperative is my duty to show you the possibility of the great dangers which they may bring upon me!

"My dear, my beloved friend, I have now spoken candidly of my character and my aspirations. Reflect upon every thing. If the traits which it was my duty to mention, diminish your respect for me, you will still esteem my sincerity, and you will not think less highly of me, that I did not take advantage of your want of acquaintance with my character, for the attainment of my inmost wishes. Decide now whether you can give your heart to a man with these faults and in such a condition, and be happy.

"My dear friend, I love you so truly from my heart, and with such fervor, that this step has cost me much; I fear to lose you, dear, when you see me as I am; I had often determined to be silent; at last I have conquered myself. My conscience called loudly to me, that I should be a seducer and not a lover, if I were to hide from my beloved a trait of my heart, or a circumstance, which might one day disgust her and render her unhappy; I now rejoice at what I have done. If the circumstances into which duty and country shall call me, set a limit to my efforts and my hopes, still I shall not have been base-minded, not vicious; I have not sought to please you in a mask,—I have not deceived you with chimerical hopes of a happiness that is not to be looked for; I have concealed from you no danger and no sorrow of the future; I have nothing to reproach myself with."

It was in the year 1767 that Pestalozzi removed to Neuhof. On the 24th of January, 1769, two years later, he married Anna Schulthess, being then only twenty-four years old. It was not long before troubles came upon the young married couple. The madder plantation did not prosper; an assistant whom Pestalozzi had engaged, caused himself to be hated by every body; the Zurich firm, which had advanced money to Pestalozzi, sent two competent judges to examine into the condition of the estate—both of them reported so unfavorably upon it, especially upon the buildings, that the firm preferred taking back their capital with loss, to trusting it any longer in Pestalozzi's hands. "The cause of the failure of my undertaking," says he, "lay essentially and exclusively in myself, and in my pronounced incapacity for every kind of undertaking which requires eminent practical ability."

Notwithstanding the great distress into which he fell, he resolved not only to go on with farming, but to combine with it a school for poor children. "I wished," says he, "to make my estate a centre for my educational and agricultural labors. In spite of all difficulties, I wanted, like a visionary, to reach the highest point in every respect, at the same time that I lacked the faculties, abilities, and skill, from which alone can proceed a proper attention to the first and humblest beginnings and preparatory steps to the great things which I sought after. So great, so unspeakably great, in consequence of the peculiarity of my mind, was the contrast between what I wished to do and what I did and was able to do, which arose from the disproportion between my good natured zeal, on the one side, and my mental impotency and unskillfulness in the affairs of life on the other."

By mental impotency, we must understand only a want of schooling or intellectual disciplining of the mind, for just at this time Pestalozzi's literary talent made itself known. He came forward with a plan for the establishment of the Poor School. His views and principles met with so much approbation in an economical point of veiw, in spite of the want of confidence, in his practical ability, that he received offers of assistance from Zurich, Bern, and Basel, and many poor children were sent to him.

Thus began the Neuhof Poor School in the year 1775; it had soon fifty pupils. In the summer, the children were to be chiefly employed in field-work,—in winter, with spinning and other handicrafts. During the time that they were engaged in the handicrafts, Pestalozzi gave them instruction; exercises in speaking were predominant.

But no long time elapsed before the establishment declined; to which result many things contributed. The children, who were to earn their support by their work, were, although beggar children, spoilt and full of demands. Their parents, who every Sunday besieged Neuhof, confirmed them in this, and also ran off with them as soon as they had got new clothes. None of the authorities protected Pestalozzi against this misconduct, from which the farming suffered a great deal. "But these difficulties," says Pestalozzi, "might gradually have been more or less overcome, if I had not sought to carry out my experiment on a scale that was quite disproportioned to my strength, and had not, with almost incredible thoughtlessness, wanted to convert it, in the very beginning, into an undertaking which presupposed a thorough knowledge of manufactures, men, and business, in which I was deficient in the same proportion as they were rendered necessary to me by the direction which I now gave my undertaking. I, who so much disapproved of the hurrying to the higher stages of instruction, before a thorough foundation had been laid in the elementary steps of the lower stages, and looked upon it as the fundamental error in the education of the day, and who also believed that I was myself endeavoring with all my might to counteract it in my plan of education, allowed myself to be carried away by illusions of the greater remunerativeness of the higher branches of industry, without knowing even remotely either them or the means of learning and introducing them, and to commit the very faults in teaching my school children spinning and weaving which, as I have just said, I so strongly reprobated and denounced in the whole of my views on education, and which I considered dangerous to the domestic happiness of all classes. I wanted to have the finest thread spun, before my children had gained any steadiness or sureness of hand in spinning even the coarser kinds, and, in like manner to, make muslin fabrics, before my weavers had acquired sufficient steadiness and readiness in the weaving of common cotton goods. Practiced and skillful manufacturers ruin themselves by such preposterous conduct,—how much more certain to be ruined by such conduct was I, who was so blind in the discernment of what was necessary to success, that I must distinctly say, that whoever took but a thread of mine into his hand was at once in a position to cause half of its value to vanish for me! Before I was aware of it, too, I was deeply involved in debt, and the greater part of my dear wife's property and expectations had in an instant, as it were, gone up in smoke. Our misfortune was decided. I was now poor. The extent and rapidity of my misfortune was owing to this among other causes—that, in this undertaking, as in the first, I readily, very readily, received an unquestioning confidence. My plan soon met with a degree of confidence which an attentive consideration of my former conduct would have shown that which I did not merit in the present undertaking. After all the experience they had had of my errors in this respect, people still did not think the extent of my incapacity for everything practical was so great as it really was. I even yet enjoyed for a while, to all appearance, an extensive confidence. But when my experiment went rapidly to wreck, as it necessarily did, this feeling changed, in my neighborhood, into just as inconsiderate a degree of the contrary, into a totally blind abandonment of even the last shadow of respect for my endeavors, and of belief in my fitness for the accomplishment of any part of them. It is the course of the world, and it happened to me as it happens to every one who thus becomes poor through his own fault. Such a man generally loses, together with his money, the belief and the confidence in what he really is and is able to do. The belief in the qualifications which I really had for attaining my objects was now lost, along with the belief in those which, erring in my self-deception, I gave myself credit for, but which I really had not."

Thus it happened, that in the year 1780, Pestalozzi was obliged to break up the establishment at Neuhof, after it had been five years in operation. His situation was frightful. Frequently in his only too elegant country house he wanted money, bread, fuel, in order to protect himself against hunger and cold. His faithful wife, who had pledged nearly the whole of her property for him, fell into a severe and tedious illness. "My friends," relates Pestalozzi, "now only loved me without hope; in the whole circuit of the surrounding district it was every where said that I was a lost man, that nothing more could be done for me."

The breaking up of the establishment at Neuhof was a fortunate thing for Pestalozzi—and for the world. He was no longer to fritter away his strength in efforts to which he was not equal. And, nevertheless, his severe mental and physical labor was not to have been in vain, but was to bear precious fruits. As the first of these fruits, there appeared in 1780 a paper of his, brief but full of meaning, in Iselin's Ephemerides, under the title, The Evening Hour of a Hermit. It contains a series of aphorisms, which nevertheless are cast in one mould, and stand among one another in the closest connection. Fruits of the past years of Pestalozzi's life, they are at the same time seeds of the following years, programme and key to his educational labors. "Iselin's Ephemerides," he writes in 1801, alluding to this Evening Hour, "bear witness, that the dream of my wishes is not more comprehensive now, than it was when at that time I sought to realize it.

It is scarcely possible to make a selection from these concise and thought-teeming aphorisms, the more so because they form, as I have said, a beautiful and ingenious whole, which suffers in the selection. Nevertheless, I will run the risk of selecting some of the principal thoughts.

The paper begins with melancholy seriousness. "Pastors and teachers of the nations, know you man; is it with you a matter of conscience to understand his nature and destiny?

"All mankind are in their nature alike, they have but *one* path to contentment. The natural faculties of each one are to be perfected into pure human wisdom. This general education of man must serve as the foundation to every education of a particular rank.

"The faculties grow by exercise.

"The intellectual powers of children must not be urged on to remote distances before they have acquired strength by exercise in things near them.

"The circle of knowledge commences close around a man, and from thence stretches out concentrically.

"Real knowledge must take precedence of word-teaching and mere talk.

"All human wisdom is based upon the strength of a good heart, obedient to truth. Knowledge and ambition must be subordinated to inward peace and calm enjoyment.

"As the education for the closest relations precedes the education for more remote ones, so must education in the duties of members of families precede education in the duties of citizens. But nearer than father or mother is God, 'the closest relation of mankind is their relation to Him.'

"Faith in God is 'the confiding, childlike feeling of mankind toward the paternal mind of the Supreme Being.' This faith is not the result and consequence of cultivated wisdom, but is purely an instinct of simplicity; a childlike and obedient mind is not the consequence of a finished education, but the early and first foundation of human culture. Out of the faith in God springs the hope of eternal life. 'Children of God are immortal.'

"Belief in God sanctifies and strengthens the tie between parents and children, between subjects and rulers; unbelief loosens all ties, annihilates all blessings.

"Sin is the source and consequence of unbelief, it is acting contrary to the inward witness of right and wrong, the loss of the childlike mind toward God.

"Freedom is based upon justice, justice upon love, therefore freedom also is based upon love.

"Justice in families, the purest, most productive of blessings, has love for its source.

"Pure childlike feeling is the true source of the freedom that is based upon justice, and pure paternal feeling is the source of all power of governing, that is noble enough to do justice and to love freedom. And the source of justice and of all worldly blessings, the source of the love and brotherly feeling of mankind toward one another, this is based upon the great thought of religion, that we are children of God, and that the belief in this truth is the sure ground of all worldly blessings. In this great thought of religion lies ever the spirit of all true state policy that seeks only the blessing of the people, for all inward power of morality, enlightenment and worldly wisdom, is based upon this ground of the belief of mankind in God; and ungodliness, misapprehension of the relation of mankind as children to the Supreme Being, is the source which dissolves all the power with which morals, enlightenment, and wisdom, are capable of blessing mankind. Therefore the loss of this childlike feeling of mankind toward God is the greatest misfortune of the world, as it renders impossible all paternal education on the part of God, and the restoration of this lost childlike feeling is the redemption of the lost children of God on earth.

"The Son of God, who with suffering and death has restored to mankind the universally lost feeling of filial love toward God, is the Redeemer of the world, He is the sacrificed Priest of the Lord, He is Mediator between God and sinful mankind. His doctrine is pure justice, educative national philosophy; it is the revelation of God the Father to the lost race of his children."

Much might be said upon these aphorisms; each is a text for a discourse; indeed, Pestalozzi's life is a paraphrase in facts of these texts. We must accuse human weakness, if the realization of his great anticipations henceforward also turns out but miserably, nay, only too often stands in the most glaring contradiction with them. The plan of an inventive builder, however, retains its value, if even the builder himself lack the skill to carry out the building according to the plan.

Rousseau's *Emile* appeared eighteen years before Pestalozzi's Evening Hour; in what relation does Rousseau stand to Pestalozzi? In particular points they frequently agree. Like Pestalozzi, Rousseau requires real knowledge and trained skill in the business of life, not an empty display of words, without an insight into the things themselves, and a ready power of acting. Like Pestalozzi, Rousseau also ridicules the plan of giving children a discursive knowledge about things remote, and leaving them in ignorance of the things in their immediate vicinity; he requires, like Pestalozzi, that they should first be at home in this vicinity.

In this manner many other things might be pointed out in which both men agree, arising principally from their common aversion to a baseless, dead talkativeness, without any real intelligence, activity of mind, or readiness of action. But when viewed more closely, how immensely different are the two men in all that is most essential.

Rousseau will not have God named before children; he is of opinion that long physical and metaphysical study is necessary to enable us to think of God. With Pestalozzi, God is the nearest, the most intimate being to man, the Alpha and Omega of his whole life. Rousseau's God is no paternal God of love, his Emile no child of God. The man who put his children into a foundling hospital, knew nothing of paternal and filial love; still less of rulers as the fathers of the nations, and of the childlike obedience of subjects; his ideal was a cold, heartless freedom, which was not based upon love, but was defensive, isolating, and altogether selfish.

While, therefore, according to Pestalozzi, the belief in God penetrates, strengthens, attunes, sanctifies all the relations of men; while the relations between ruler and subjects, between fathers and children, and the paternal love of God to his children, men, are every where reflected in his paper—with Rousseau there is never any mention of such bonds of love.

A year after the publication of the Evening Hour, namely, in 1781, appeared the first part of that work of Pestalozzi's which established his reputation, which exercised an extensive and wholesome influence at the time, and which will continue to exercise an influence in future. That work is "Leonard and Gertrude: A Book for the People." It was undertaken at a time, when, as he relates, "my old friends looked upon it as almost settled that I should end my days in a workhouse, or in a lunatic asylum." The form was suggested by Marmontel's *Contes moraux*; and he was stimulated to effort, by a few words of encouragement from the bookseller Füssli, of Zurich, or rather of the brother better known as *Fuseli*, the painter. After a few attempts at composition with which he was not satisfied, "the history of Leonard and Gertrude flowed from my pen, I know not how, and developed itself of its own accord, without my having the slightest plan in my head, and even without my thinking of one. In a few weeks, the book stood there, without my knowing exactly how I had done it. I felt its value, but only as a man in his sleep feels the value of some piece of good fortune of which he is just dreaming. "The book appeared, and excited quite a remarkable degree of interest in my own country and throughout the whole of Germany. Nearly all the journals spoke in its praise, and, what is perhaps still more, nearly all the almanacs became full of it; but the most unexpected thing to me was that, immediately after its appearance, the Agricultural Society of Bern awarded me their great gold medal, with a letter of thanks."

Pestalozzi himself has repeatedly spoken of the character and object of Leonard and Gertrude. In the preface to the first edition of the work, he says: "In that which I here relate, and which I have for the most part seen and heard myself in the course of an active life, I have even taken care not once to add my own opinion to what I saw and heard *the people themselves feeling, judging, believing, speaking, and attempting.* And now this will show itself:—If the results of my observation are true, and if I gave them as I received them, and as it is my aim to do, they will find acceptance with all those who themselves have daily before their eyes the things which I relate. If, however, they are incorrect, if they are the work of my imagination and the preaching of my own opinions, they will, like other Sunday sermons, vanish on the Monday." In the preface to the second edition, Pestalozzi gives as the object of the book, "To bring about a better popular education, based upon the true condition of the people and their natural relations." "It was," he says, "my first word to the heart of the poor and destitute in the land. It was my first word to the heart of those who stand in God's stead to the poor and destitute in the land. It was my first word to the mothers in the land, and to the heart which God gave them, to be to theirs what no one on earth can be in their stead."

"I desired nothing, and to-day, (1800,) I desire nothing else, as the object of my life, but the welfare of the people, whom I love, and whom I feel to be miserable as few feel them to be miserable, having with them borne their sufferings as few have borne them."

The remarks which I have cited characterize the soul of Leonard and Gertrude. In the severe years of suffering at Neuhof, Pestalozzi appeared to have wrought and suffered in vain. "To the accomplishment of my purpose," he says, "there stood opposed my entire want of trained practical skill, and a vast disproportion between the extent of my will and the limits of my ability."

He did not work in vain, however; what was denied him on the one side turned out to his advantage on the other. If he lacked all skill in carrying out his ideas, he possessed on the other hand, in the highest degree, the faculty of observing, comprehending, and portraying character. If he was not able to exhibit to the world his ideal realized, it was given to him to infuse the loving desires of his heart into the hearts of others, by means of his talent of poetical delineation. He might hope that men of practical ability would be among the readers of his book, and would be incited by it to realize what he only knew how to picture. He has found such readers. Leonard and Gertrude is in so many hands, that it is almost superfluous to give a selection from the work. Only this. The principal person in it is Gertrude, the wife of Leonard, a good-natured but rather weak man, whose stay and guardian she is. The manner in which she keeps house and instructs and trains her children, is Pestalozzi's ideal. Such house-keeping, such a manner of instructing and training, he desires for all people. Gertrude is consulted even in the management of the village school. Her house-keeping is the bright side of the circumstances depicted; in contrast with her is a terribly dark side, a peasant community in the deepest depravity. It is related of what Arner, the equally benevolent and intelligent lord of the village, does to check the depravity.

Pestalozzi wished to give the people the knowledge and skill needful for them chiefly by means of a good elementary instruction. If this instruction began at the right place, and proceeded properly, what an entirely different race would arise out of the children so instructed, a race made independent by intelligence and skill!

In vain, however, did Pestalozzi look around him for elementary teachers who could and would instruct after his manner and in his spirit. Seminaries, too, were wanting in which such teachers could be trained. Then the thought occurred to him who had grown up in his mother's parlor: "I will place the education of the people in the hands of the mothers; I will transplant it out of the school-room into the parlor." Gertrude was to be the model of mothers. But how are the mothers in the lower classes to be qualified for instructing?—We shall see how Pestalozzi's Compendiums are meant to be an answer to this question, to supply the place of knowledge and teaching talent. The mothers have only to keep strictly to these books in the instruction of their children; if they do this, the mother of the most limited capacity will instruct just as well as the most talented; compendiums and method are to equalize their minds: such was Pestalozzi's ideal, to which I shall afterward come back.

With extreme short-sightedness, the persons in immediate intercourse with Pestalozzi saw in this book of his dearly-bought experience nothing more than a proof that its author was born for novel-writing, and would in future be able to earn his bread by it.

Others understood better the value of the book. Karl von Bonstetten entreated Pestalozzi to come and live with him on his estate in Italian Switzerland; the Austrian Minister of Finance, Count Zinzendorf, wished to have him in his neighborhood. Subsequently, he became known, through Count Hohenwart, in Florence, to the Grand Duke Leopold of Tuscany, who was about to give him an appointment, when he was called by the death of Joseph II., to the imperial throne of Germany, and the appointment, was therefore not made.

If it be asked whether he would have been of any use in a post of importance, a word of Lavater's upon this subject may contain the answer. Pestalozzi tells us—"He once said to his wife, 'If I were a prince, I would consult Pestalozzi in every thing that concerns the people and the improvement of their condition; but I would never trust him with a farthing of money.' At another time, he said to myself, 'When I only once see a line of yours without a mistake, I will believe you capable of much, very much, that you would like to do and to be.'"

For seventeen years after the publication of Leonard and Gertrude, Pestalozzi continued to drag on his needy and depressed existence at Neuhof, where he spent altogether thirty years. Of his outward life during those seventeen years, we learn little else, besides the general fact just stated. It is worthy of mention, that in this period he entered the order of Illuminati, an order which was characterized by infidelity, exaggerated ideas of enlightenment, and destructive but not reconstructive principles, and that he even became eventually the head of the order in Switzerland. He soon discovered his mistake, however, and withdrew from it. "That which is undertaken by associations," he says, "usually falls into the hands of intriguers."

In this period he wrote several books.

In the year 1782, he published "Christopher and Alice." He himself relates the origin of this work. People had imbibed from Leonard and Gertrude the idea, that all the depravity among the common people proceeded from the subordinate functionaries in the villages. "In Christopher and Alice," says Pestalozzi, "I wished to make apparent to the educated public the connection of those causes of popular depravity which are to be found higher in the social scale, but which on this account are also more disguised and concealed, with the naked, undisguised, and unconcealed causes of it, as they are manifested in the villages in the persons of the unworthy functionaries. For this purpose, I made a peasant family read together Leonard and Gertrude, and say things about the story of that work, and the persons introduced in it, which I thought might not occur of themselves to everybody's mind."

So says Pestalozzi in the year 1826; but he spoke otherwise in the preface to the book when it first appeared, in 1782. "Reader!" he says, "this book which thou takest into thy hand is an attempt to produce a manual of instruction for the use of the universal school of humanity, the parlor. I wish it to be read in every cottage."

This wish was not accomplished, as we learn from the preface to the second edition, (1824,) which commences thus, "This book has not found its way at all into the hands of the people. In my native land, even in the canton of my native town, and in the very village in which I once lived, it has remained as strange and unknown, as if it had not been in existence."

In the same year, 1782, and the one following, Pestalozzi edited "A Swiss Journal," of which a number appeared every week. In this Journal, he communicated, among other things, memoirs of deceased friends. Thus he wrote the memoirs of Frölich, the pastor of Birr, who had died young. Pestalozzi says of him, "he dedicated himself to the work of the great divine calling, but eternal love dedicated him to the liberty of eternal life." The way in which he speaks of the excellent Iselin, who had died in 1782, is particularly affecting. "I should have perished in the depths into which I had fallen," he says, "if Iselin had not raised me up. Iselin made me feel that I had done something, even in the poor school."

The discourse "on Legislation and Infanticide" also appeared in 1782.

About 1783, Pestalozzi contemplated the establishment of a lunatic asylum and a reformatory institution, and wrote upon the subject; the manuscript, however, was lost.

In the years between 1780 and 1790, in the days of the approaching French revolution, and in the first symptoms of the dangers which its influence on Switzerland might entail," * he wrote "The Figures to my ABC-Book; they were not published, however, till 1795: a new edition, under the title of "Fables," came out in 1805. They relate principally to the condition of Switzerland at that time.

In the summer of 1792, he went to Germany, at the invitation of his sister in Leipzig, and became acquainted with Göthe, Herder, Wieland, Klopstock, and Jacobi; he also visited several normal schools.

In 1798 appeared Pestalozzi's "Researches into the Course of Nature in the Development of the Human Race." He says himself, speaking of this book, "I wrought at it for three long years with incredible toil, chiefly with the view of clearing up my own mind upon the tendency of my favorite notions, and of bringing my natural feelings into harmony with my ideas of civil rights and morality. But this work too is, to me, only another evidence of my inward helplessness, the mere play of my powers of research; my views were

*Pestalozzi's words in the preface to the "Figures."

altogether one-sided, while I was without a proportionate degree of control over myself in regard to them, and the work was left void of any adequate effort after practical excellence, which was so necessary for my purpose. The disproportion between my ability and my views only increased the more. The effect of my book upon those by whom I was surrounded was like the effect of all that I did; scarcely any one understood me, and I did not find in my vicinity two men who did not half give me to understand that they looked upon the entire book as so much balderdash."

Pestalozzi here assumes three states of man: an original, instinct-like, innocent, *animal* state of nature, out of which he passes into the social state, (this reminds us of Rosseau;) he works himself out of the social state and raises himself to the moral. The social man is in an unhappy middle condition between animal propensities and moral elevation.

The original animal state of nature can not be pointed to in any one individual man; the innocence of that state ceases with the first cry of the new-born child, and "animal depravity arises from whatever stands opposed to the normal condition of our animal existence." Against this depravity, man seeks for aid in the social state, but finds it not; it is only the moral will that can save him, "the force of which he opposes to the force of his nature. He *will* fear a God, in order that the animal instincts of his nature shall not degrade him in his inmost soul. He feels what he can do in this respect, and then he makes what he can do the law to himself of what he ought to do. Subjected to this law, *which he imposes upon himself*, he is distinguished from all other creatures with which we are acquainted."

Where and when, for example, did Pestalozzi's man of nature ever exist—an innocent *animal* man, endowed with instinct? * This character does not apply to Adam in Paradise, who was not an animal, but a lord of the animals, and still less does it apply to any child of Adam. In how simple and sublime a manner, on the

* Voltaire wrote the following characteristic letter to Rosseau about his discourse, prepared and offered for the prize proposed by the Academy of Dixon, on the origin of the inequality among men, and published in 1775:—"I have received your new book against the human race, and thank you for it. You will please men, to whom you speak the truth, but not make them better. No one could paint in stronger colors the horrors of human society, from which our ignorance and weakness promise themselves so many delights. Never has any one employed so much genius to make us into beasts; when one reads your book, one is seized with a desire to go down on all fours. Nevertheless, as I have left off this habit already more than sixty years, I feel, unfortunately, that it is impossible for me to take to it again, and I leave this natural mode of walking to others who are more worthy of it than you and I. Neither can I take ship, in order to visit the savages of Canada, firstly, because the maladies to which I am condemned, render a European physician necessary to me; then again, because there is at present war in that country, and the examples of our nations has made the savages almost as bad as we are ourselves. I am content to live as a peaceful savage in the lonely district adjoining your native land, &c."

contrary, do the Holy Scriptures comprehend and characterize the whole human race.

Thus we see Pestalozzi but little or not at all engaged in educational undertakings during the eighteen years from 1780 to 1798; his writings too, during this time are mainly of a philosophical and political character, and relate only indirectly to education. But the French revolution introduced a new epoch, for Pestalozzi, as well as for Switzerland.

The revolutionary armies of France pressed into the country, old forms were destroyed, the whole of Switzerland was consolidated into an "inseparable republic," at the head of which stood five directors, after the model of the French directional government of that time. Among these was Legrand, a man of a class that is always becoming more rare. I visited the amiable octogenarian in Steinthal, where formerly, with his friend Oberlin, he had labored for the welfare of the communes. When the conversation turned on the happiness or the education of the people, or on the education of youth generally, the old man became animated with youthful enthusiasm, and tears started to his eyes.

Legrand was a friend of Pestalozzi's; no wonder, seeing that the two men very nearly resembled each other in their way of thinking, as well as in their enthusiastic activity and their unbounded hopefulness. Pestalozzi joined the new republic, while, at the same time, he did all in his power to subdue the jacobinical element in it. He wrote a paper "On the Present Condition and Disposition of Mankind." In this paper, as also in the "Swiss People's Journal," which he edited at the instigation of the government, he pressed upon the attention of the people the necessity of a return to the integrity and piety of their ancestors; the instruction and education of youth, he represented, were the means for attaining this object.

Although, in pointing to an ennobling education of youth, and especially the youth of the people and the poor, as the securest guarantee of a lawfully ordered political condition, he only did that which he could not leave undone; still most people believed that he was speaking and writing thus industriously, merely with the view of procuring for himself an office under the new government, when an opportunity should arise. The government on whom he urged with far too much vehemence the importance of order, justice, and law, actually offered him an appointment, in the hope that he would then be quiet. But what was their astonishment, when, in reply to their inquiry as to what office he would be willing to accept, he said, "I WILL BE A SCHOOLMASTER." But few understood him, only those who, like himself, were earnestly desirous for the foundation of a truly equitable political condition.

Legrand entered into the idea; and Pestalozzi was already about to open an educational institution in the canton of Argovia, when one of the misfortunes of war intervened. On the 9th of September, 1798, Stanz in Unterwalden was burnt by the French, the entire canton was laid waste, and a multitude of fatherless and motherless children were wandering about destitute and without a shelter. Legrand now called upon Pestalozzi to go to Stanz and undertake the care of the destitute children.

Pestalozzi went; what he experienced he has himself told us.

The convent of the Ursulines there was given up to him; he took up his abode in it, accompanied only by a housekeeper, before it was even put into a fit condition for the reception of children. Gradually he gathered around him as many as eighty poor children, from four to ten years old, some of them orphans, horribly neglected, infected with the itch and scurvy, and covered with vermin. Among ten of them, scarcely one could say the alphabet. He describes the educational experiments which he made with such children, and speaks of these experiments as "a sort of feeler of the pulse of the science which he sought to improve, a venturesome effort." "A person with the use of his eyes," he adds, "would certainly not have ventured it; fortunately, I was blind."

For example, under the most difficult circumstances, he wanted to prove, by actual experiment, that those things in which domestic education possesses advantages must be imitated in public education.

He gave the children no set lessons on religion; being suspected by the Roman Catholic parents, as a Protestant, and at the same time as an adherent of the new government, he did not dare; but whenever the occurrence of daily life presented an opportunity, he would make them the groundwork of inculcating some religious or moral lesson. As he had formerly done at Neuhof, he sought to combine intellectual instruction with manual labor, the establishment for instruction with that for industrial occupations, and to fuse the two into each other. But it became clear to him, that the first stages of intellectual training must be separated from those of industrial training and precede the fusion of the two. It was here in Stanz also that Pestalozzi, for want of other assistants, set children to instruct children, a plan which Lancaster was similarly led to adopt in consequence of the inability of the teacher to instruct the large numbers of children who were placed under his charge.* Pestalozzi remarks,

* Lancaster's monitors, *i. e* children, set to teach and superintend other children. "At that time, (1798,)" says Pestalozzi, "nobody had begun to speak of mutual instruction."

without disapprobation, that a feeling of honor was by this means, awakened in the children; a remark which directly contradicts his opinion, that the performance of the duties of the monitor proceeded from a disposition similar to brotherly love.

Another plan, which is now imitated in countless elementary schools, was likewise tried by Pestalozzi at Stanz, namely, that of making a number of children pronounce the same sentences simultaneously, syllable for syllable.* "The confusion arising from a number of children repeating after me at once," he says, "led me to see the necessity of a measured pace in speaking, and this measured pace heightened the effect of the lesson."

Pestalozzi repeats, in his account of the Stanz institution, what he had brought forward in Leonard and Gertrude. "My aim," he says, "was to carry the simplification of the means of teaching so far, that all the common people might easily be brought to teach their children, and gradually to render the schools almost superfluous for the first elements of instruction. As the mother is the first to nourish her child physically, so also, by the appointment of God, she must be the first to give it spiritual nourishment; I reckon that very great evils have been engendered by sending children too early to school, and by all the artificial means of educating them away from home. The time will come, so soon as we shall have simplified instruction, when every mother will be able to teach, without the help of others, and thereby, at the same time, to go on herself always learning."

I refer the reader to Pestalozzi's own description of his singularly active labors in Stanz, where he was not only the teacher and trainer of eighty children, but, as he says, paymaster, manservant, and almost housemaid, at the same time. In addition to this, sickness broke out among the children, and the parents showed themselves shamelessly ungrateful.

Pestalozzi would have sunk under these efforts had he not been liberated on the 8th of June, 1799, by the French, who, being hard pressed by the Austrians, came to Stanz, and converted one wing of the convent into a military hospital. This induced him to let the children return to their friends, and he went himself up the Gurnigel mountains, to a medicinal spring. Only twenty-two children remained; these, says Mr. Heussler, "were attended to, taught, and trained, if not in Pestalozzi's spirit, still with care and with more order and cleanliness, under the guidance of the reverend Mr. Businger."

---

* The plan of simultaneous reading and speaking had been introduced into the Austrian schools at an earlier period.

"On the Gurnigel," says Pestalozzi, "I enjoyed days of recreation. I required them; it is a wonder that I am still alive. I shall not forget those days, as long as I live: they saved me, but I could not live without my work."

Pestalozzi was much blamed for giving up the Stanz institution, although necessity had compelled him to do so. "People said to my face," he says, "that it was a piece of folly, to believe that, because a man had written something sensible in his thirtieth year, he would therefore be capable of doing something sensible in his fiftieth year. I was said to be brooding over a beautiful dream."

Pestalozzi came down from the Gurnigel; at the advice of Chief Justice Schnell, he went to Burgdorf, the second town in the canton of Bern, where through the influence of well-wishers, Pestalozzi obtained leave to give instruction in the primary schools.* He had many enemies. The head master of the schools imagined that Pestalozzi wanted to supplant him in his appointment: the report spread that the Heidelberg catechism was in danger: "it was whispered," says Pestalozzi, "that I myself could not write, nor work accounts, nor even read properly. Popular reports are not always entirely destitute of truth," he adds; "it is true that I could not write, nor read, nor work accounts well.

As far as the regulations of the school would allow, Pestalozzi prosecuted here the experiments in elementary instruction which he had begun at Stanz. M. Glayre, a member of the executive council of the canton, to whom he endeavored to explain the tendency of these experiments, made the ominous remark, "You want to render education mechanical." "He hit the nail on the head," says Pestalozzi, "and supplied me with the very expression that indicated the object of my endeavors, and of the means which I employed for attaining it."

Pestalozzi had not been schoolmaster at Burgdorf, quite a year, when he had a pulmonary attack; in consequence of this he gave up the appointment, and a new epoch of his life commenced. M. Fischer, secretary to the Helvetian minister of public instruction, had entertained the idea of founding a normal school in the castle of Burgdorf, but had died before carrying it into execution. With this end in view, he had induced M. Krüsi to come to Burgdorf. Krüsi was a native of Gaiss, in the canton of Appenzell, was schoolmaster there at the early age of eighteen, and had migrated thence in the year 1799, taking with him 28 children. Pestalozzi now proposed

* In a school in which children from four to eight years old received instructions in reading and writing, under the general superintendence of a female teacher.

to Krüsi to join him in establishing an educational institution: Krüsi willingly agreed, and through him the coöperation of M. Tobler, who had been for the last five years tutor in a family in Basel, was obtained; through Tobler, that of M. Buss, of Tübingen. With these three assistants, Pestalozzi opened the institution in the winter of 1800.

It was in Burgdorf that Pestalozzi commenced a work which, with the "Evening Hour," and "Leonard and Gertrude," stands out conspicuously amongst his writings. It was commenced on the 1st of January, 1801.

It bears the queer title, "How Gertrude teaches her children: an attempt to give Directions to Mothers how to instruct their own Children." The reader must not be misled by the title; the book contains any thing but directions for mothers."

There are numerous contradictions throughout the book, as well as on the title page; and it is therefore a most difficult task to give a condensed view of it. Almost the only way to accomplish this will be to resolve it into its elements.

Nothing can be more touching than the passage in which the author speaks of the desire of his whole life to alleviate the condition of the suffering people—of his inability to satisfy this desire—of his many blunders—and of his despair of himself; and then humbly thanks God, who had preserved him, when he had cast himself away, and who graciously permitted him, even in old age, to look forward to a brighter future. It is impossible to read any thing more affecting.

The second element of this book is a fierce and fulminating battle against the sins and faults of his time. He advances to the assault at storm-pace, and clears every thing before him with the irresistible force of truth. He directs his attack principally against the hollow education of our time, particularly in the higher ranks of society. He calls the members of the aristocracy "miserable creatures of mere words, who by the artificialities of their mode of life are rendered incapable of feeling that they themselves stand on stilts, and that they must come down off their wretched wooden legs, in order to stand on God's earth with even the same amount of firmness as the people."

In another part of the book, Pestalozzi declaims warmly against all the education of the present age. "It sacrifices, (he says,) the substance of all instruction to the nonsense about particular isolated system of instruction, and by filling the mind with fragments of truth, it quenches the spirit of truth itself, and deprives mankind of the power of independence which is based thereon. I have found, what was very obvious, that this system of instruction, does not base the use of particular means either on elementary principles or elementary forms. The state of popular instruction rendered it inevitable that Europe should sink into error, or rather madness, and into this it really did sink. On the one hand, it raised itself into a gigantic height in particular arts; on the other, it lost for the whole of its people all the stability and support which are to be obtained by resting on the guidance of nature. On the one side, no quarter of the globe ever stood so high; but on the other, no quarter of the globe has ever sunk so low. With the golden head of its particular arts, it touches the clouds, like the image of the prophet; but popular instruction, which ought to be the basis and support of this golden head, is every where, on the contrary, the most wretched, fragile, good-for-nothing clay, like the feet of that gigantic image."

For this incongruity in our intellectual culture, he blames chiefly *the art of printing*, through which, he says, the eyes have become book-eyes—men have become book-men.

Throughout the work, he speaks against the senseless use of the tongue—against the habit of talking without any real purpose. "The babbling disposition of our time, (he says,) is so much bound up with the struggle of tens of thousands and hundreds of thousands for their daily bread, and with their slavish adherence to custom, that it will be long, very long, before this temporizing race shall gladly receive into their hearts truths so much opposed to their sensual depravity. Wherever the fundamental faculties of the human mind are allowed to lie dormant, and on those dormant faculties empty words are propt up, there you are making dreamers, whose visions are all the more visionary because the words that were propt up on their miserable yawning existence, were high-sounding, and full of pretensions. As a matter of course, such pupils will dream any and every thing before they will dream *that they are sleeping and dreaming;* but all those about them who are awake, perceive their presumption, and, (when it suits,) put them down as somnambulists.

"The meaningless declamation of this superficial knowledge produces men who fancy that they have reached the goal in all branches of study, just because their whole life is a belabored prating about that goal; but they never accomplish so much as to make an effort to reach it, because through their life it never had that alluring charm in their eyes which any object must possess to induce a man to make an effort to attain it. The present age abounds in men of this class, and is diseased by a kind of wisdom which carries us forward *pro formâ*, as cripples are borne along a race-course, to the goal of knowledge, when, at the same time, it could never enable us to advance toward this gaol by our own efforts, before our feet had been healed."

In other parts of the book he attacks governments as indifferent to the welfare of the people. "The lower classes of Europe, (he says,) are neglected and wretched: most of those who stand sufficiently near to be able to help them, have no time for thinking what may be for their welfare—they have always something to do quite different from this."

From this, the second and polemical element of the book, I pass to the third and positive one, namely, the kind of education by which Pestalozzi proposes to replace the false education of our time. This might in some measure be anticipated from the polemical passages which have been cited.

He thus enunciates the problem which he proposed to himself to solve: "In the empirical researches which I made in reference to my subject, I did not start from any positive system; I was not acquainted with any one; I simply put to myself the question, What would you do, if you wanted to give a single child all the theoretical knowledge and practical skill which he requires in order to be able to attend properly to the great concerns of life, and so attain to inward contentment?"

Theoretical knowledge and practical skill constitute, accordingly, the most important subjects of the work. They are treated with a special relation to the two questions,—What knowledge and skill do children require? and, How are these best imparted to them? The aim is to point out the proper object of education, and the way to attain that object.

Of practical skill, however, there is comparatively very little said, notwithstanding that Pestalozzi sets so high a value upon it. "Knowledge without skill, (he says,) is perhaps the most fatal gift which an evil genius has bestowed upon the present age." But Pestalozzi's ideas in relation to practical skill, and the method of attaining it, seem to have been still indistinct.

On the other hand, he is quite at home in the region of theoretical knowledge: to show the starting-point, the road, and the destination, in the journey through this region, is the main design of his work.

His polemic against senseless talking shows that he had sought and found the real root of the tree of which words are the spiritual blossoms.

The beginning of all knowledge, according to Pestalozzi, is *observation;* the last point to be attained, *a clear notion.* He says: "If I look back and ask myself what I really have done toward the improvement of the methods of elementary instruction, I find that, in recognizing observation as the absolute basis of all knowledge, I have established the first and most important principle of instruction, and that, setting aside all particular systems of instructions, I have endeavored to discover what ought to be the character of the instruction itself, and what are the fundamental laws according to which the education of the human race must be determined by nature." In another place, he requires it to be acknowledged, "that observation is the absolute basis of all knowledge, in other words, that all knowledge must proceed from observation and must admit of being retraced to that source."

But what does Pestalozzi understand by observation? "It is, (he says,) simply directing the senses to outward objects, and exciting consciousness of the impression produced on them by those objects." He refers, of course, principally to the sense of sight. But the ear is not to be neglected. "When sounds are produced so as to be heard by the child, and its consciousness of the impression which these sounds make on its mind through the sense of hearing is aroused, this, to the child, is just as much observation, as when objects are placed before its eyes, and consciousness is awakened by the impression which the objects make on the sense of sight. By the aid of his spelling book, therefore, the child's ear is to be familiarized with the series of elementary sounds which constitutes the foundation of a knowledge of language, just as it is to be made acquainted with visible objects by the aid of his Book for Mothers.

According to this, observation would mean every impression which the mind receives through the eye and the ear.

Does Pestalozzi exclude the remaining senses? No; for he frequently speaks of the impressions of the *five* senses, and he says that the understanding collects the impressions which the senses receive from external nature into a whole, or into a notion, and then develops this idea until it attains clearness. And elsewhere he says that the mechanical form of all instruction should be regulated by the eternal laws according to which the human mind rises from the perceptions of sense to clear notions.

Pestalozzi repeatedly dwells upon this process of intellectual development.

Above every thing, he will have attention given to the first step in the process, namely observation. Care is to be taken that the objects are seen separately by the children, not dimly at a distance, but close at hand and distinctly; then also that there shall be placed before the children, not abnormal, but characteristic specimens of any class of objects—such as will convey a correct idea of the thing and of its most important properties. Thus, for example, a lame, one-eyed, or six-fingered man, he says, would not be proper to convey the idea of the human form.

Out of the observation of an object, the first thing that arises, he says, is the necessity of naming it; from naming it, we pass on to determining its properties, that is to description; out of a clear description is finally developed the definition—the distinct idea of the object. The full maturity of this, the last fruit of all instruction, depends materially on the vigorous germination of the seed sown in the first instance—on the amount of wisdom exercised in guiding the children to habits of observation. Definitions not founded on observations, he says, produce a superficial and unprofitable kind of knowledge.

Just when we begin to think that we understand Pestalozzi's views, he again leads us into uncertainty as to the idea which he attaches to observation.

He says the idea had only lately struck him, "that all our knowledge arises out of number, form, and words." On this triple basis, he says, education must proceed; and—

"1. It must teach the children to look attentively at every object which they are made to perceive as unity, that is, as separated from those other objects with which it appears in connection.

2. It must make them acquainted with the form of every object, that is, its size and proportion.

3. It must teach them as early as possible the names and words applicable to all the objects with which they are acquainted."

Pestalozzi found it difficult, however, to answer the question, "Why are not all the other properties which the five senses enable us to perceive in objects, just as much elements of our knowledge, as number, form, and name?" His answer is, "All possible objects have necessarily number, form, and name; but the remaining properties which the senses enable us to perceive are not possessed by any object in common with all others, but this property is shared with one object, and that with another."

When Pestalozzi made form a category to embrace all and every thing, he only thought of the visible, as is evidenced by the further development of his instruction in form, which deals chiefly with the measuring of visible objects.

But there are innumerable observations which have nothing whatever to do with form and number; for example, tasting honey, smelling roses, &c.

The prominence which Pestalozzi gave to form and number caused him to undertake a new treatment of the subjects of geometry and arithmetic. Subsequently he divided geometry into instruction in form and instruction in spaces, for the reason that we perceive shape and size, (mathematical quality and quantity,) independently of each other; drawing he made a part of the instruction in form—writing a part of drawing.

But what became of Pestalozzi's principle, that observation is the foundation of all intelligence, when he thus gave an undue prominence to form and number, and neglected all other properties? Suppose that we put a glass cube into the hands of a child and he observes in respect to it nothing else, but that it has the cubic form, and, over and above this, that it is *one* cube,—so far this glass cube is in no way distinguished from a wooden one. But if I require to take notice of other properties, such as color, transparency, weight, &c., in order that I may form a correct idea of the glass cube, as a separate object, and so describe it that it shall be distinguished with certainty from every other cube,—then I must fix my attention, not only on form and number, but on all apparent properties, as elements in a complete observation.

Lastly, language itself has nothing to do with observation. Why should I not be able to form a perfectly correct notion of an object that has no name—for instance a newly-discovered plant? Language only gives us the expression for the impressions of the senses; in it is reflected the whole world of our perceptions. "It is," as Pestalozzi rightly observes, "the reflex of all the impressions which nature's entire domain has made on the human race." But what does he go on to say? "Therefore I make use of it, and endeavor, by the guidance of its uttered sounds, to reproduce in the child the self-same impressions which, in the human race, have occasioned and formed these sounds. Great is the gift of language. It gives to the child in one moment what nature required thousands of years to give man."

In that case, every child would be a rich heir of antiquity, without the trouble of acquisition; words would be current notes for the things which they designate. But both nature and history protest against payment in such currency, and give only to him that hath. Does not Pestalozzi himself repeatedly protest against this very thing? "The christian people of our quarter of the world, (he says,) have sunk into these depths, because in their lower school establishments the mind has been loaded with a burden of empty words, which has not only effaced the *impressions of nature*, but has even destroyed the inward susceptibility for such impressions."

Pestalozzi's further treatment of the instruction in language clearly proves that, contrary to his own principles, he really ascribed a magical power to words—that he put them more or less in the place of observation—and, (to speak with a figure,) that he made the reflected image of a thing equal to the thing itself.

As this error of Pestalozzi's is of the greatest consequence, I will examine it more closely. In the instruction in language, he begins with lessons on sounds; these are followed by lessons on words; and these again by lessons on language.

I. LESSONS ON SOUNDS.—"The spelling book, (says Pestalozzi,) must contain the entire range of sounds of which the language consists, and portions of it should be repeated daily in every family, not only by the child that is going through the exercises to learn how to spell, but also by mothers, within hearing of the child in the cradle, in order that these sounds may, by frequent repetition, be so deeply impressed upon the memory of the child, even while it is yet unable to pronounce a single one of them, that they shall never be forgotten. No one imagines to what a degree the attention of infants is aroused by the repetition of such simple sounds as ba, ba, ba, da, da, da, ma, ma, ma, la, la, la, &c., or what a charm such repetition has for them."

And so the child in the cradle is to have no rest from elementary teaching; the cradle songs sung to it are to consist of such delightful bawling and bleating as ba, ba, ba, &c., which might well scare away the child's guardian angels.

As soon as the child begins to talk, it is to "repeat some sequences of these sounds every day;" then follow exercises in spelling.

II. "LESSONS IN WORDS, or rather, LESSONS IN NAMES."—According to Pestalozzi, "all the most important objects in the world are brought under the notice of the child in the Book for Mothers."

"Lessons in names consist in giving the children lists of the names of the most important objects in all three kingdoms of nature, in history, in geography, and in the pursuits and relations of mankind. These lists of words are placed in the hands of the child, merely as exercises in learning to read, immediately after he has gone through his spelling book; and experience has shown me that it is possible to make the children so thoroughly acquainted with these lists of words, that they shall be able to repeat them from memory, merely in the time that is required to perfect them in reading: the gain of what at this age is so complete a knowledge of lists of names so various and comprehensive, is immeasurable, in facilitating the subsequent instruction of the children."

Here again it is not even remotely hinted that the children ought to know the things named; words, mere words, are put in the place of observation.

3. Lessons in Language.—The highest aim of language, according to Pestalozzi's idea, is to lead us from dim perceptions to clear notions, and that by the following process:—

1. "We acquire a general knowledge of an object, and name it as unity, as an object.

2. We gradually become conscious of its distinguishing qualities, and learn how to name them.

3. We receive through language the power of designating these qualities of the objects more precisely by means of verbs and adverbs."

The first step in this process is, as we have seen, the object of the Pestalozzian lessons in names; but, when viewed more closely, the lessons are found to consist, not in the naming of objects arising out of knowing them, but in the names for their own sake.

In reference to the second operation, when Pestalozzi writes on the black-board the word "eel," and adds the qualities, "slippery, worm-shaped, thick-skinned," the children by no means become conscious of the distinguishing qualities of an eel, and learn to name them, through observing an eel; they rather get adjectives to the noun "eel." Of the process by which these adjectives arise from the observation of the qualities which they express, there is again nothing said.

This neglect of observation is still more striking, when Pestalozzi, further on, classifies what is to be learned under the following heads:

1. Geography. 3. Physics. 5. Physiology.
2. History. 4. Natural History.

Each of these five heads he divides again into forty subdivisions, so that he makes two hundred subdivisions. He now proceeds to give lists of words in all these subjects in alphabetical order, which lists are to be impressed upon the childrens' memories, "till it is impossible they should be forgotten." Afterward, this alphabetical nomenclature is to be transformed into a "scientific" one. "I do not know, (says Pestalozzi,) whether it is necessary to illustrate the matter further by an example; it appears to me almost superfluous: nevertheless, I will do so, on account of the novelty of form. *E. G.* One of the subdivisions of Europe is Germany: the child is first of all made well acquainted with the division of Germany into ten circles, so that he shall not be able to forget it; then the names of the towns of Germany are placed before him, at first in mere alphabetical order for him to read, but each of these towns is previously marked with the number of the circle in which it lies. As soon as the child can read the names of the towns fluently, he is taught the connection of the numbers with the subdivisions of the main heads, and in a few hours he is able to determine the place of the entire number of German towns in these subdivisions. For example, suppose the names of the following places in Germany are set before him, marked by numbers:—

Aachan, (Aix-la-Chapelle,) 8.
Aalen, 3.
Abenberg, 4.
Aberthan, 11.
Acken, 10.
Adersbach, 11.
Agler, 1.
Ahrbergen, 10.
Aigremont, 8.
Ala, 1.
Allenbach, 5.
Allendorf, 5.
Allersperg, 2.
Alschaufen, 3.
Alsleben, 10.
Altbunzlau, 11.
Altena, 8.
Altenau, 10.
Altenberg, 9.
Altenburg, 9.
Altensalza, 10.
Altkirchen, 8.
Altona, 10.
Altorf, 1.
Altranstädt, 9.
Altwasser, 13.
Alkerdissen, 8.
Amberg, 2.
Ambras, 1.
Amöneburg, 6.
Andernach, 6.

He reads them all in the following manner:—

Aachen lies in the Westphalian circle;

Abenberg in the Franconian circle;

Acken in the Lower Saxony circle; and so on.

In this manner the child is evidently enabled, at first sight of the number or mark referring to the subdivisions of the main head, to determine the place of each word of the list in the scientific classification of the subject, and thus, as I before said, to change the alphabetical into a scientific nomenclature."

It is quite unnecessary to give a refutation of these views.*

Further on in the book, there follow some directions "how to explain more fully to the pupil the nature, qualities, and functions of all the objects with which the lessons in names have made him acquainted, and which have already been explained to him, to a certain extent, by placing their qualities side by side with their names." For this purpose, the mother is to read to the child certain sentences, and the child is to repeat them after her. Many of these sentences would be quite unintelligible to a child; for instance, "The creditor desires payment," "The right must be maintained." They are mere exercises in reading, not based in the slightest degree on observation.

We have seen that Pestalozzi fixed his attention chiefly on the principle that instruction must be based on observation, out of which the clear idea is at last developed. He says that we are dazzled by the charm of a language, "which we speak without having any real

* Observe, too, how Pestalozzi has taken the names of any obscure places that occurred to him at the moment, such as *Aberthan*, *Ala*, &c. Out of the 31 places whose names are given, five at most would deserve to be included in a school geography. Not a word is said about maps.

knowledge of the ideas conveyed by the words which we allow to run through our mouths." He combats "all scientific teaching which is analyzed, explained, and dictated by men who have not learnt to think and speak in harmony with the laws of nature," whose "definitions must be conjured into the soul like a *deus ex machinâ*, or must be blown into the ears as by stage-prompters;" the effect of which is that men "sink into a miserable mode of education, fit only for forming play-actors." He speaks with great warmth against "definitions not founded on observation." "A definition, (he says,) is the simplest expression of clear ideas, but for the child it contains truth only in so far as he has a clear and comprehensive view of the groundwork of observation on which these ideas are based; whenever he is left without the greatest clearness in the observation of a natural object which has been defined to him, he only learns to play with words like so many counters, deceives himself, and places a blind belief in sounds which will convey to him no idea, nor give rise to any other thought, except just this, that he has uttered certain sounds.*

Hinc illæ lacrymæ.

These excellent principles can not receive too much attention; but if Pestalozzi's own method of instruction be squared by them, it will be found to run quite counter to them. He begins, not with observations, but with words; with him, substantives stand in the place of the observation of objects, adjectives in the place of the observation of the properties of objects. His polemic against empty word-wisdom hits therefore his own method of instruction. Fichte says very truly in regard to Pestalozzi's idea: "In the field of objective knowledge, which relates to external objects, the acquaintance with the literal sign that represents the clearness and definiteness of the knowledge, adds nothing whatever for the student himself; it only heightens the value of the knowledge with reference, to its communication to others, which is a totally different matter. The clearness of such knowledge can result only from observation, and that which we can at pleasure reproduce in all its parts, just as it really is, in the imagination, is perfectly known, whether we have a word for it or not.

We are even of the opinion that this perfection of observation

* Pestalozzi also shows briefly and truly that none but those who have a thorough knowledge of a subject can possibly give a real explanation of it in words. "If I have not a clear perception of a thing," he says, "I can not say with certainty what its attributes are, much less what it is; I can not even describe it, much less define it. If then a third person puts into my mouth the words by means of which some other person, who had a clear conception of the thing, makes it intelligible to people of his own stamp, it is not on this account any clearer to me; but it is clear to the other person and not to me so long as the words of this person are not for me what they are for him: the definite expression of the full clearness of an idea."

should precede the acquaintance with the literal sign, and that the opposite way leads directly to that world of fog and shadows, and to that early use of the tongue, both of which are so justly hateful to Pestalozzi; nay even, that he who is only concerned to know the word at the earliest possible moment, and who deems his knowledge complete so soon as he knows it, lives precisely in that world of fog, and is only concerned for its extension."

We should have expected from Pestalozzi some directions, first, how to exercise the senses of children, and cultivate in them the power of rapidly arriving at clear conceptions of objects; second, how we should teach them to express in language the impressions of their senses—to translate their mute observations into words.

But Pestalozzi does give some hints, particularly as to the method in which instruction in natural history should be imparted. We must not allow the child to go into the woods and meadows, in order to become acquainted with trees and plants. "Trees and plants, (he says,) do not there stand in the order best adapted to make the character of each class apparent, and to prepare the mind by the first impressions of the objects for a general acquaintance with this department of science. It would make me too far away from my purpose, were I to refute this excessive pedantry of method, (with the best will in the world, I can find no better word for it,) against which every mind that has any degree of freshness, and is alive to the beauties of nature, will at once rise up in condemnation.

But, though nothing further is said, in the work before us, on the education of the senses, and the instruction in language connected therewith, Pestalozzi refers us to his "Book for Mothers," for more on these points. His principle, that the learning of a child must commence with what lies near to it, appears to have led him to the idea, that no natural object lay nearer to a child than its own body, and that therefore it should commence by observing that. The Book for Mothers describes the body, with all its limbs and parts of limbs, down to the minutest joints. Few persons, (I do not speak of surgeons,) are so well acquainted with the structure of the body as the child is to be made. Few people will understand, for instance, the following description: "The middle bones of the index finger are placed outside, on the middle joints of the index finger, between the back and middle members of the index finger," &c. The mother is to go through the book, word for word, with the child, making constant reference to the child's own body.

It was a great mistake on the part of Pestalozzi, to select the child's body as the first object on which it should exercise its faculties of sight and speech, and, generally, the so-called exercises in observation employed by Pestalozzi and his school, ought properly to be regarded as exercises in reading, in which the object is far more to make the children acquainted with words and sentences than to give them distinct and lasting impressions, and a real knowledge of the thing spoken of. He who yesterday saw a man, with whose image he was so strongly impressed that he can to-day depict it from his inward conception—he who to-day can correctly sing from memory a melody which he heard yesterday—he who yesterday smelt vinegar, and to-day feels the water gather in his mouth at the recollection of the smell—gives proof of his observation by the conception which he has formed, even though he does not translate that conception into words. The generality of the exercises of Pestalozzi and his followers never produced such an imagination of perceptions as this.

Toward the conclusion of the work, Pestalozzi asks himself: "How does the question of religion stand with relation to the principles which I have adopted as true in regard to the development of the human race in general?"

It is difficult to follow him in his answer to this question. Every thing that is lofty in man is founded, according to him, in the relationship which subsists between the infant and its mother. The feelings of gratitude, confidence and love in the child toward the mother gradually unfold themselves, and are, at a later period, transferred by the child, on the admonition of the mother, to God. This, with Pestalozzi, is the *only* way of training the child in religion. It presupposes a mother pure as an angel, and a child originally quite innocent. The mother is also, like a saint, to take the child under her wings, when it grows up and is enticed to evil by the world, which is not innocent, "as God first created it." According to this view, motherless orphans must remain entirely without religious training. There is scarcely a word about the father; just once he is mentioned, and then it is said that he is "tied to his workshop," and can not give up his time to the child.

In short, the mother is represented as the mediator between God and the child. But not once is it mentioned that she herself needs a mediator; not once in the whole book does the name of Christ occur. It is nowhere said that the mother is a christian mother, a member of the church, and that she teaches the child what she, as a member of the church, has learnt. Holy writ is ignored; the mother draws her theology out of her own heart. There pervades this work therefore a decided alienation from Christ. But we shall afterward see that it would be unjust to measure Pestalozzi's ideas on religious instruction by the untenable theory brought forward in the last chapters of this work.

Having thus considered the contents of this book, which was written and had its origin in Burgdorf, which contains fundamental educational principles of the highest value and importance, side by side with the most glaring educational blunders and absurdities, it will be of the greatest interest to hear how Pestalozzi performed his work as a teacher, and as the director of his institution, in Burgdorf. We shall obtain information on this point from a small but in many respects highly interesting and valuable pamphlet, entitled "A Short Sketch of my Educational Life, by John Ramsauer."* The writer, who was the son of a tradesman, and was born in 1790 at Herissu in the Swiss canton of Appenzell, migrated thence in 1800, along with forty-four other children from ten to fourteen years of age, at a time when several cantons, Appenzell among the rest, had been totally desolated in consequence of the French revolution; and he came thus to Schleumen, not far from Burgdorf. While at Schleumen, he attended the lower burgh school of Burgdorf, in which, as already stated, Pestalozzi taught. He gives the following account of Pestalozzi's teaching:—

"I got about as much regular schooling as the other scholars, namely, none at all; but his, (Pestalozzi's,) sacred zeal, his devoted love, which caused him to be entirely unmindful of himself, his serious and depressed state of mind, which struck even the children, made the deepest impression on me, and knit my childlike and grateful heart to his forever.

It is impossible to give a clear picture of this school as a whole; all that I can do is to sketch a few partial views.

Pestalozzi's intention was that all the instruction given in this school should start from form, number, and language, and should have a constant reference to these elements. There was no regular plan in existence, neither was there a time-table, for which reason Pestalozzi did not tie himself down to any particular hours, but generally went on with the same subject for two or three hours together. There were about sixty of us, boys and girls, of ages varying from eight to fifteen years; the school-hours were from 8 till 11 in the morning, and from 2 to 4 in the afternoon. The instruction which we received was entirely limited to drawing, ciphering, and exercises in language. We neither read nor wrote, and accordingly we had neither reading nor writing books; nor were we required to commit to memory any thing secular or sacred.

For the drawing, we had neither copies to draw from nor directions what to draw, but only crayons and boards; and we were told to draw "what we liked" during the time that Pestalozzi was reading aloud sentences about natural history, (as exercises in language.) But we did not know what to draw, and so it happened that some drew men and women, some houses, and others strings, knots, arabesques, or whatever else came into their heads. Pestalozzi never looked to see *what* we had drawn, or rather scribbled; but the clothes of all the scholars, especially the sleeves and elbows, gave unmistakable evidence that they had been making due use of their crayons.

For the ciphering, we had between every two scholars a small table

* When Pestalozzi himself speaks of his teaching, he is too apt to mix up what he intended with what he really effected.

pasted on mill-board, on which in quadrangular fields were marked dots, which we had to count, to add together, to subtract, to multiply, and divide by one another. It was out of these exercises that Krüsi and Buss constructed, first, the Unity Table, and afterward the Fraction Tables. But, as Pestalozzi only allowed the scholars to go over and to repeat the exercises in their turns, and never questioned them nor set them tasks, these exercises, which were otherwise very good, remained without any great utility. He had not sufficient patience to allow things to be gone over again, or to put questions; and in his enormous zeal for the instruction of the whole school, he seemed not to concern himself in the slightest degree for the individual scholar.

The best things we had with him were the exercises in language, at least those which he gave us on the paper-hangings of the school-room, and which were real exercises in observation. These hangings were very old and a good deal torn, and before these we had frequently to stand for two or three hours together, and say what we observed in respect to the form, number, position and color of the figures painted on them, and the holes torn in them, and to express what we observed in sentences gradually increasing in length. On such occasions, he would say: "Boys, what do you see?" (He never named the girls.)

Answer. A hole, (or rent,) in the wainscoat.

Pestalozzi. Very good. Now repeat after me:—

I see a hole in the wainscoat.
I see a long hole in the wainscoat.
Through the hole I see the wall.
Through the long narrow hole I see the wall.

Pestalozzi. Repeat after me:—

I see figures on the paper-hangings.
I see black figures on the paper-hangings.
I see round black figures on the paper-hangings.
I see a square yellow figure on the paper-hangings.
Besides the square yellow figure, I see a black round figure.
The square figure is joined to the round one by a thick black stroke.

And so on.

Of less utility were those exercises in language which he took from natural history, and in which we had to repeat after him, and at the same time to draw, as I have already mentioned. He would say:—

Amphibious animals.	Crawling amphibious animals.
	Creeping amphibious animals.
Monkeys.	Long-tailed monkeys.
	Short-tailed monkeys.

And so on.

We did not understand a word of this, for not a word was explained, and it was all spoken in such a sing-song tone, and so rapidly and indistinctly, that it would have been a wonder if any one had understood any thing of it, and had learnt any thing from it; besides, Pestalozzi cried out so dreadfully loud and so continuously, that he could not hear us repeat after him, the less so as he never waited for us when he had read out a sentence, but went on without intermission and read off a whole page at once. What he thus read out was drawn up on a half-sheet of large-sized mill-board, and our repetition consisted for the most part in saying the last word or syllable of each phrase, thus "monkeys—monkeys," or "keys—keys." There was never any questioning or recapitulation.

As Pestalozzi in his zeal, did not tie himself to any particular time, we generally went on till eleven o'clock with whatever he had commenced at eight, and by ten o'clock he was always tired and hoarse. We knew when it was eleven by the noise of other school children in the street, and then usually we all ran out without bidding good-bye.

Although Pestalozzi had at all times strictly prohibited his assistants from using any kind of corporal punishment, yet he by no means dispensed with it himself, but very often dealt out boxes on the ears right and left. But most of the scholars rendered his life very unhappy, so much so that I felt a real sympathy for him, and kept myself all the more quiet. This he soon observed, and many a time he took me for a walk at eleven o'clock, for in fine weather he went every day to the banks of the river Emme, and for recreation and amusement looked for different kinds of stones. I had to take part in this occupation

> myself, although it appeared to me a strange one, seeing that millions of stones lay there, and I did not know which to search for. He himself was acquainted with only a few kinds, but nevertheless he dragged along home from this place every day with his pocket and his pocket handkerchief full of stones, though after they were deposited at home, they were never looked at again. He retained this fancy throughout his life. It was not an easy thing to find a single entire pocket handkerchief in the whole of the institution at Burgdorf, for all of them had been torn with carrying stones.
>
> There is one thing which, though indeed unimportant, I must not forget to mention. The first time that I was taken in to Pestalozzi's school he cordially welcomed and kissed me, then he quickly assigned me a place, and the whole morning did not speak another word to me, but kept on reading out sentences without halting for a moment. As I did not understand a bit of what was going on, when I heard the word "monkey, monkey," come every time at the end of a sentence, and as Pestalozzi, who was very ugly, ran about the room as though he was wild, without a coat and without a neck-cloth, his long shirt-sleeves hanging down over his arms and hands, which swung negligently about, I was seized with real terror, and might soon have believed that he himself was a monkey. During the first few days too, I was all the more afraid of him, as he had, on my arrival, given me a kiss with his strong, prickly beard, the first kiss which I remembered having received in my life.

Ramsauer does not relate so much about the instruction given by the other teachers. Among the fruits of their instruction were two of the three elementary works which appeared in 1803, under Pestalozzi's name: (1.) "The ABC of Observation, or Lessons on the Relations of Size," (2.) "Lessons on the Relations of Number." (3.) The third elementary work alone was written by Pestalozzi himself; it is the one already mentioned, the "Book for Mothers, or Guide for Mothers in teaching their children to observe and speak."

The institution at Burgdorf attracted more and more notice; people came from a distance to visit it, induced particularly by Pestalozzi's work, "How Gertrude teaches her children." Decan Ith, who was sent by the Helvetian government in 1802, to examine the institution, made a very favorable report on it, in consequence of which the government recognized it as a public institution, and granted small salaries to the teachers out of the public funds.

But that government was dissolved by Napoleon the very next year, and the constitution of the cantons restored. The Bernese government now fixed on the castle of Burgdorf, as the seat of one of the chief magistrates of the canton; and Pestalozzi had to clear out of it, on the 22d of August, 1804.

In 1802, during Pestalozzi's stay at Burgdorf, Napoleon required the Swiss people to send a deputation to him at Paris. Two districts chose Pestalozzi as a deputy. Before his departure, he published a pamphlet, entitled "Views on the Objects to which the Legislature of Helvetia has to direct its attention." He put a memorandum on the wants of Switzerland into the hands of the First Consul, who paid as little attention to it as he did to Pestalozzi's educational efforts, declaring that he could not mix himself up with the teaching of the ABC.

The Bernese government gave up the monastery of Buchsee to Pestalozzi for his institution, and had the building properly arranged for him. Close by Buchsee lies the estate of Hofwyl, where Fellenberg resided, and to whom the teachers gave the principal direction of the institution, "not without my consent," says Pestalozzi, "but to my profound mortification."

Notwithstanding, Pestalozzi allows Fellenberg to have possessed in a high degree the talent of governing. In Fellenberg the intellect predominated, as in Pestalozzi the feelings; in the institution at Buchsee, therefore, "that love and warmth was missing which, inspiring all who came within its influence, rendered every one at Burgdorf so happy and cheerful: at Buchsee every thing was, in this respect, totally different. Still Buchsee had this advantage, that in it more order prevailed, and more was learned than at Burgdorf."

Pestalozzi perceived that his institution would not become independent of Fellenberg, so long as it should remain at Buchsee, and he gladly accepted, therefore, a highly advantageous proposal on the part of the inhabitants of Yverdun, that he should remove his institution to their town. He repaired thither, with some of his teachers and eight pupils; half a year later, the remaining teachers followed, having, as Pestalozzi remarks, soon found the government of Fellenberg far more distasteful than the want of government, under him, had ever been to them.

We now enter on a period when Pestalozzi and his institution acquired a European reputation, when Pestalozzian teachers had schools in Madrid, Naples, and St. Petersburg, when the emperor of Russia gave the venerable old man a personal proof of his favor and esteem, and when Fichte saw in Pestalozzi and his labors the commencement of a renovation of humanity.

But to write the history of this period is a task of unusual difficulty. On one side stand extravagant admirers of Pestalozzi, on the other bitter censurers; a closer examination shows us that both are right, and both wrong. A fearful dissension arises, in the institution itself, among the teachers; at the head of the two parties stand Niederer and Schmid, who abuse each other in a manner unheard of. With which party shall we side; or shall we side with neither, or with both?

If we ask to which party Pestalozzi inclined, or whether he held himself above the parties, and then go entirely according to his judgment, our embarrassment will only be increased. He pronounced a very different opinion on the same man at different times: at one time he saw in him a helping angel, before whom he humbled himself more than was seemly, and from whom he expected every benefit to his institution; at another time, he saw in him an almost fiendish being, who was only bent on ruining the institution.

If any fancy that they have a sure source of information in the account drawn up by Pestalozzi and Nieder, and published in 1807, namely, the "Report on the State of the Pestalozzian Institution, addressed to the Parents of the Pupils and to the Public;" they will be undeceived by some remarks which Pestalozzi himself added to that report at a later period, in the collected edition of his works, but still more so in, "The Fortunes of my Life." This work is altogether at variance with those which give a high degree of praise to the Pestalozzian Institution, in its former condition. From the year in which the dispute between Niederer and Schmid, broke out, (1810,) most of those who give any information on the subject range themselves on Niederer's side; while Pestalozzi himself, from the year 1815 till his death, holds unchangeably with Schmid.

I should despair of ever being able to thread my way in this labyrinth with any degree of certainty, were it not for the fact that I resided some time in the institution, namely, from October, 1809, till May, 1810, and there became more intimately acquainted with persons and circumstances than I could otherwise have been.

A friend, (Rudolph von Przystanowski,) accompanied me to Yverdun, where we arrived toward the end of October. It was in the evening of a cold rainy day that we alighted at the hotel called the Red House. The next morning we went to the old castle, built by Charles the Bold, which with its four great round towers incloses a courtyard. Here we met a multitude of boys; we were conducted to Pestalozzi. He was dressed in the most negligent manner: he had on an old grey overcoat, no waistcoat, a pair of breeches, and stockings hanging down over his slippers; his coarse bushy black hair uncombed and frightful. His brow was deeply furrowed, his dark brown eyes were now soft and mild, now full of fire. You hardly noticed that the old man, so full of geniality, was ugly; you read in his singular features long continued suffering and great hopes.

Soon after, we saw Niederer,* who gave me the impression of a young Roman Catholic priest; Krüsi,* who was somewhat corpulent, fair, blue-eyed, mild and benevolent; and Schmid,* who was, if possible, more cynical in his dress than Pestalozzi, with sharp features and eyes like those of a bird of prey.

At that time 137 pupils, of ages varying from six to seventeen

* A biographical sketch of Niederer, Krüsi, and Schmid, will be given at the close of the life of Pestalozzi.—Ed.

years, lived in the institution; 28 lodged in the town, but dined in the institution. There were in all, therefore, 165 pupils. Among them there were 78 Swiss; the rest were Germans, French, Russians, Italians, Spaniards, and Americans. Fifteen teachers resided in the institution, nine of whom were Swiss teachers, who had been educated there. Besides these, there were 32 persons who were studying the method: seven of them were natives of Switzerland. The interior of the building made a mournful impression on me; but the situation was extremely beautiful. An extensive meadow separates it from the southern end of the glorious lake of Neufchâtel, on the west side of which rises the Jura range of mountains, covered with vineyards. From the heights of the Jura, above the village of Granson, rendered famous by the defeat of Charles the Bold, you survey on the one side the entire chain of the Alps, from Mount Pilatus, near Lucerne, to Mount Blanc; on the other side you see far away into France.

A short time after my arrival, I went to live in the institution, where I took my meals, and slept along with the children. If I wanted to do any work for myself, I had to do it while standing at a writing desk in the midst of the tumult of one of the classes. None of the teachers had a sitting-room to himself. I was fully determined to devote all my energies thenceforth to the institution, and accordingly I had brought with me Freddy Reichardt, the brother of my future wife, a boy of eight years, and now placed him among the other scholars. My position was well suited to enable me to compare the reports on the institution with what I daily saw and experienced. The higher my expectations had been raised by that report, the deeper was my pain, as I was gradually undeceived; I even thought I saw the last hopes of my native land disappear.

It is scarcely necessary for me to particularize the respects in which I was undeceived; they may be learnt from Pestalozzi's notes to the latter copy of his report, but especially from his work, "The Fortunes of my Life." Nevertheless I will advert to one or two principal points.

I will particularly advert to what is said in the report about the spirit of the institution, which is represented as being similar to that which pervades a family.

"We may with a good conscience, declare publicly, that the children in our institution are happy and cheerful; that their innocence is preserved, their religious disposition cherished, their mind formed, ther knowledge increased, their hearts elevated. The arrangements which have been adopted for attaining these objects possess a quiet inward power. They are based principally on the benevolent and amiable character which distinguishes the teachers of our house, and which is supported by a vigorous activity. There reigns throughout the entire institution the spirit of a great domestic union, in which, according to the requirements of such a union, a pure paternal and fraternal feeling every where shines forth. The children feel themselves free, their activity finds even a powerful charm in their employments; the confidence reposed in them, and the affection shown toward them, elevate their sentiments." "The life in the house is, to a rare extent, a school for cultivating domestic affection and domestic unity." "All the teachers in common, acting as an organized whole, do for all the children what a careful mother does for the few children of her own family." The body of teachers "attains the most perfect unity of thought and action, and appears to the children as only one person."

"In general, it is to be remarked that we seek throughout to awaken and to foster the spirit of peace, of love, and of mutual brotherly fellowship. The disposition of the great body of our inmates is good. A spirit of strength, of repose, and of endeavor rests on the whole. There is much in our midst that is eminently good. Some pupils evince an angelic disposition, full of love and of a presentiment of higher thoughts and a higher existence. The bad ones do not feel themselves comfortable in the midst of our life and labor; on the other hand, every spark of good and noble feeling which still glimmers even in the bad ones encouraged and developed. The children are in general neither hardened by punishment, nor rendered vain and superficial by rewards. The mild forbearance of the most amiable household has the most undisturbed play in our midst. The children's feelings are not lightly wounded. The weak are not made to compare themselves with the strong, but with themselves. We never ask a pupil if he can do what another does. We only ask him if he can do a thing. But we always ask him if he can do it perfectly. As little of the struggle of competition takes place between one pupil and another, as between affectionate brothers and sisters who live with a loving mother in a happy condition."

"We live together united in brotherly love, free and cheerful, and are, in respect to that which we acknowledge as the one thing needful, one heart and one soul. We may also say that our pupils are one heart and one soul with us. They feel that we treat them in a fatherly manner; they feel that we serve them, and that we are glad to serve them; they feel that we do not merely instruct them; they feel that for their education we give life and motion to every thing in them that belongs to the character of man. They also hang with their whole hearts on our actions. They live in the constant consciousness of their own strength."

Must not even a sober reader of these passages be led to believe that a spirit of the most cordial love and concord reigned in a rare manner in the Pestalozzian institution. How much more did I believe so, who, deeply distressed by the calamities of those days, and inspired with hope by the eloquence of Fichte, perceived in Yverdun the commencement of a better time, and ardently longed to hasten its approach. Those who did not themselves live through those years of anguish, in which injustice increased and love waxed cold in the hearts of many, may perhaps smile at the enthusiasm of despair.

Pestalozzi himself says of the institution that, as early as the time when it was removed from Buchsee to Yverdun, it bare within itself "the seeds of its own internal decay, (these are his own words,) in the unequal and contradictory character of the abilities, opinions, inclinations, and claims of its members; although as yet this dissension had done any thing but declare itself general, unrestrained, and fierce." He says, that nevertheless many of the members were still desirous for peace, and that others were moderate in their views and feelings. "But the seeds of our decay had been sown, and though they were still invisible in many places, had taken deep root. Led aside by worldly temptations and apparent good fortune from the purity, simplicity, and innocence of our first endeavors, divided among ourselves in our inmost feelings, and from the first made incapable, by the heterogeneous nature of our peculiarities of ever becoming of one mind and one heart in spirit and in truth for the attainment of our objects, we stood there outwardly united, even deceiving ourselves with respect to the real truth of our inclination to this union, and unfortunately we advanced, each one in his own manner, with firm and at one time with rapid steps along a path which, without our being really conscious of it, separated us every day further from the possibility of our ever being united.

What Ramsauer says entirely agrees with this. In Burgdorf, he says, there reigned a kindly spirit. "This ceased when the family life was transformed in the institution into a constitutional state existence. Now the individual was more easily lost in the crowd: thus there arose a desire on his part to make himself felt and noticed. Egotism made its appearance every day in more offensive forms. Envy and jealousy rankled in the breasts of many." "Much indeed was said about 'a domestic life,' which ought to prevail in an educational establishment, just as a very great deal was said and written about an 'harmonious development of all the faculties of the pupil;' but both existed more in theory than in practice. It is true, that a good deal of common interest was evinced in the general working of the institution, but the details were allowed to go on or stand still very much as they might, and the tone of the whole house was more a tone of pushing and driving than one of domestic quietude."

In the report is this passage: "In respect to the execution of the design, we may say decidedly, that the institution has stood the fiery ordeal of eight severe years."

On this passage Pestalozzi remarks as follows in 1823: "What is here said in confirmation of this view is altogether a consequence of the great delusion under which we lay at that period, namely, that all those things in regard to which we had strong intentions and some clear ideas, were really as they ought to have been, and as we should have liked to make them. But the consequences of the partial truth which in this instance had hold of our minds were, from want of sufficient knowledge, ability, and skill for carrying it out, fixed in our midst, confused, and made the seed of countless weeds, by which the good seed that lay in the ground was on all sides crowded, and here and there choked. Neither did we perceive the weeds at that time; indeed, as we then lived, thought, acted, and dreamt, it was impossible that we should perceive them."

I am fully aware that by some these later observations of Pestalozzi have been attributed partly to the weakness of old age, partly to the influence of Schmid. To this I can not assent. As early as new year's day, 1808, at the same time as the report appeared, Pestalozzi said to his teachers:

"My work was founded in love; love vanished from our midst; it could not but vanish. We deceived ourselves as to the strength which this love demands; it could not but vanish. I am no longer in a position to provide any help for it. The poison which eats into the heart of our work is accumulating in our midst. Worldly honor will increase this poison. O God, grant that we may no longer be overcome by our delusion. I look upon the laurels which are strewn in our path as laurels set up over a skeleton. I see before my eyes the skeleton of my work, in so far as it is my work. I desire to place it before your eyes. I saw the skeleton which is in my house appear crowned with laurels before my eyes, and the laurels suddenly go up in flames. They can not bear the fire of affliction which must and will come upon my house; they will disappear; they must disappear. My work will stand. But the consequences of my faults will not pass away. I shall be vanquished by them. My deliverance is the grave. I go away, but you remain, Would that these words now stood before your eyes in flames of fire!—Friends, make yourselves better than I was, that God may finish his work through you, as he does not finish it through me. Make yourselves better than I was. Do not by your faults lay those same hindrances in your way that I have lain in mine. Do not let the appearance of success deceive you, as it deceived me. You are called to higher, to general sacrifice, or you too will fail to save my work. Enjoy the passing hour, enjoy the fullness of worldly honor, the measure of which has risen for us to its greatest height; but remember that it vanishes like the flower of the field, which blooms for a little while, but soon passes away."

What contradictions! Does then the same fountain send forth both sweet and bitter? Was the report actually intended to deceive the world?

Never; but Pestalozzi was not entirely free from an unfortunate spirit of worldly calculation, although his calculations in most cases turned out incorrect. Ever full of the idea of spreading happiness over many lands, in a short time, by means of his methods of instruction and education, he naturally considered it all-important that people should have a good opinion of his institution. By the bulk of the public, indeed, the institution was taken as substantial evidence for or against the excellence and practicability of his educational ideas: with it they stood or fell.

The concern which Pestalozzi felt about the reputation of his establishment became especially apparent when foreigners, particularly persons of distinction, visited Yverdun.

"As many hundred times in the course of the year," says Ramsauer, "as foreigners visited the Pestalozzian Institution, so many hundred times did Pestalozzi allow himself, in his enthusiasm, to be deceived by them. On the arrival of every fresh visitor, he would go to the teachers in whom he placed most confidence and say to them: 'This is an important personage, who wants to become acquainted with all we are doing. Take your best pupils and their analysis-books, (copy-books in which the lessons were written out,) and show him what we can do and what we wish to do.' Hundreds and hundreds of times there came to the institution, silly, curious, and often totally uneducated persons, who came because it was the 'the fashion.' On their account, we usually had to interrupt the class instruction and hold a kind of examination. In 1814, the aged Prince Esterhazy came. Pestalozzi ran all over the house, calling out: 'Ramsauer, Ramsauer, where are you? Come directly with your best pupils to the Red House, (the hotel at which the Prince had alighted.) He is a person of the highest importance and of infinite wealth; he has thousands of bond-slaves in Hungary and Austria. He is certain to build schools and set free his slaves, if he is made to take an interest in the matter.' I took about fifteen pupils to the hotel. Pestalozzi presented me to the Prince with these words: 'This is the teacher of these scholars, a young man who fifteen years ago migrated with other poor children from the canton of Appenzell and came to me. But he received an elementary education, according to his individual aptitudes, without let or hindrance. Now he is himself a teacher. Thus you see that there is as much ability in the poor as in the richest, frequently more; but in the former it is seldom developed, and even then, not methodically. It is for this reason that the improvement of the popular schools is so highly important. But he will show you every thing that we do better than I could. I will, therefore, leave him with you for the present.' I now examined the pupils, taught, explained, and bawled, in my zeal, till I was quite hoarse, believing that the Prince was thoroughly convinced about every thing. At the end of an hour, Pestalozzi returned. The Prince expressed his pleasure at what he had seen. He then took leave, and Pestalozzi, standing on the steps of the hotel, said: 'He is quite convinced, quite convinced, and will certainly establish schools on his Hungarian estates.' When we had descended the stairs, Pestalozzi said: 'Whatever ails my arm? It is so painful. Why, see, it is quite swollen, I can't bend it.' And in truth his wide sleeve was now too small for his arm. I looked at the key of the house-door of the *maison rouge* and said to Pestalozzi; 'Look here, you struck yourself against this key when we were going to the Prince an hour ago.' On closer observation it appeared that Pestalozzi had actually bent the key by hitting his elbow against it. In the first hour afterward he had not noticed the pain, for the excess of his zeal and his joy. So ardent and zealous was the good old man, already numbering seventy years, when he thought he had an opportunity of doing good. I could adduce many such instances. It was nothing rare in summer for strangers to come to the castle four or five times in the same day, and for us to have to interrupt the instruction on their account two, three or four times."

After this highly characteristic account, I ask the reader whether he will cast a stone at the amiable and enthusiastic old man? I certainly will not, though I could heartily have wished that, faithful in small things and mindful of the grain of mustard seed, he had planted his work in stillness, and that it had been slow and sound in its growth, even if it had been observed by only a few.

The source of the internal contradiction which runs through the life of Pestalozzi, was, as we saw from his own confessions, the fact that, in spite of his grand ideal, which comprehended the whole human race, he did not possess the ability and skill requisite for conducting even the smallest village school. His highly active imagination led him to consider and describe as actually existing in the institution whatever he hoped sooner or later to see realized. His hopeful spirit foresaw future development in what was already accomplished, and expected that others would benevolently do the same. This bold assumption has an effect on many, especially on the teachers of the institution. This appears to explain how, in the report on the institution, so much could be said *bonâ fide* which a sober spectator was forced to pronounce untrue.

But this self-delusion is never of long duration; the period of overstrung enthusiasm is followed by one of hopelessness and dejection. The heart of man is indeed an alternately proud and dejected thing! Such an ebb and flow of lofty enthusiasm and utter despair pervades the entire life of Pestalozzi. The address which he delivered to his teachers in 1808 appears almost as the *caput mortuum* of the report: the truth at last makes itself heard in tones of bitter remorse. Pestalozzi makes a more tranquil confession concerning the early times of Yverdun, at a later period of his life, in his autobiography. More than sixteen years had elapsed, and passion had cooled down. He states soberly what he had enthusiastically wished to accomplish in those earlier days; he acknowledges that he had deceived himself and he can now therefore relate the history of the institution clearly and truthfully. But the times less removed from him are still too present to his feelings, too near to his impassioned gaze, for him to be able to delineate them with the same historical clearness in that work.

The report speaks of the instruction imparted in the institution in a way which can not have failed to give offense to persons who were not enthusiastically prejudiced in favor of Pestalozzi. Listen to these remarks:—

"With regard to the subjects of the instruction generally, the following is what may be stated. The child learns to know and exercise himself, that is, his physical, intellectual, moral, and religious faculties. With this instruction to the child about himself, instruction about nature keeps pace. Commencing with the child in his domestic relations, the latter instruction gradually embraces human nature in all the above mentioned aspects. And in the same way, commencing with the circle of the child's observation, it gradually embraces the whole of external nature. From the first starting point, the child is led to an insight into the essential relations of mankind and society; from the second to an insight into the relations in which the human race stands to external nature, and external nature to the human race. Man and nature, and their mutual relation, constitute, therefore, the primary matter of the instruction; and from these subjects the knowledge of all separate branches of study is developed. It must here be remarked, however, that the aim of the instruction is not to make the pupils comprehend man and nature merely externally, that is, merely in so far as they present isolated imperical characteristics, capable of being arranged either in a logical sequence of separate units, or in any other order that may be convenient. The aim is rather to make the pupils observe things as a living and organic whole, harmoniously bound together by necessary and eternal laws, and developing itself from something simple and original, so that we may thus bring them to see how one thing is linked in another. The instruction, as a whole, does not proceed from any theory, but from the very life and substance of nature; and every theory appears only as the expression and representation of this observed life and substance."

I am relieved from the necessity of offering any criticism on this passage by a note which Pestalozzi added to it fifteen years later. "In this and several other passages," says the venerable old man, "I express, not so much my own peculiar views on education in their original simplicity, as certain immature philosophical views, with which, at that time, notwithstanding all our good intentions, most of the inmates of our house, myself among the rest, must needs perplex our heads, and which brought me personally to a standstill in my endeavors. These views caused the house and the institution, both of which attained at this period a seeming flourishing condition, to go rotten at the roots; and they are to be looked upon as the hidden source of all the misfortunes which have since come upon me."

It would take too long to follow the report in the accounts which it gives of the instruction in the separate branches of knowledge. In every thing Pestalozzi wants to be entirely novel, and just for this reason he falls into mistakes. Take, as a specimen, the following on the instruction in geography:—

"The instruction in this subject begins with the observation of the district in which we live, as a type of what the surface of the earth presents. It is then separated into elementary instruction, which includes physical, mathematical, and political geography, and (2,) the topographical part, in which each of the departments of the subject suggested by the observation of the surrounding district is prosecuted in a graduated course, and their reciprocal bearings brought out. By this foundation, the pupils are prepared for forming a clear and comprehensive view of the earth and man, and their mutual influence on each other, of the condition of states and peoples, of the progress of the human race in intellectual culture, and lastly of physical science in its broader outlines and more general relations. The children are made acquainted with the statistical portion of the subject, that is, the natural productions, the number of inhabitants, form of government, &c., by means of tabular views."

After this, need we wonder when we find Pestalozzi, in his memoirs, speaking of the earlier days of Yverdun in the following manner? "The desire of governing, in itself unnatural, was called forth among us at this period, on the one hand, by the reputation of our modes of instruction, which continued to increase after our return to Yverdun, and the intoxicating good fortune that streamed to nearly every fool who hung out the sign-board of an elementary method which, in reality, did not as yet exist; on the other, by the audacity of our behavior toward the whole world, and toward every thing that was done in education and was not cast in our mould. The thing is melancholy; but it is true. We poor weak birds presumed to take our little nestlings, ere they were fairly out of their shells, on flights which even the strongest birds do not attempt until their young ones have gained strength in many previous trials. We announced publicly things which we had neither the strength nor the means to accomplish. There are hundreds and hundreds of these vain boastings of which I do not like to speak."

No wonder that, in this state of things, there arose a determined opposition to the institution. In Switzerland especially, Pestalozzi says, the public journals began "to speak decidedly against our pretensions, asserting that what we did was by no means what we considered and represented ourselves to be doing. But, (he continues,) instead of penitently returning to modesty, we sturdily resisted this opposition. While participating in this temerity, which is now incomprehensible to me, I began to be sensible that we were treading in paths which might lead us astray, and that, in truth, many things in the midst of us were not as they should have been, and as we endeavored to make them appear in the eyes of the world."

Other members of the institution thought quite differently; full of self-confidence, they pressed for a formal examination; and in the month of May, 1809, an application to that effect was made to the Swiss Diet, then assembled at Freiburg. The request was granted, and Merian, member of the executive council of Basel; Trechsel, professor of mathematics, at Bern; and Père Girard, of Freiburg, were commissioned by Governor D'Affry to examine the institution.

In November, 1809, just after I had arrived in Yverdun, this commission of inquiry came down and remained five days. They were five sultry days for Pestalozzi and his teachers; it was felt that the commission, which confined itself strictly to actual results, would make no very enthusiastic report. Père Gerard wrote the report in French, Professor Trechsel translated it into German; on the 12th of May, 1810, it was presented to the Diet, then assembled at Solothurn. In the following year, the thanks of the country were accorded to Pestalozzi, by the Diet; and there the matter was allowed to rest.

I believe that the commission pronounced an impartial judgment; the conclusion of the report speaks for the whole. "The educational methods of the institution, (say the commissioners,) stand only in very imperfect connection with our establishments for public instruction. The institution has in no way aimed at coming into harmony with those public schools. Determined at any price to interest all the faculties of children, in order to guide their developmeut according to its own principles, it has taken counsel of its own views only, and betrays an irresistible desire to open for itself new paths, even at the cost of never treading in those which usage has now established. This was perhaps the right means for arriving at useful discoveries, but it was also a design which rendered harmony impossible. The institution pursues its own way; the public institutions pursue theirs; and there is no probability that both ways will very soon meet. It is a pity that the force of circumstances has always driven Mr. Pestalozzi beyond the career which his pure zeal and his fervent charity had marked out for him. A good intention, noble endeavors, indefatigable perseverance, should and will always meet with justice. Let us profit by the excellent ideas which lie at the foundation of the whole undertaking; let us follow its instructive examples; but let us also lament that an adverse fate must hang over a man, who, by the force of circumstances, is constantly hindered from doing what he would wish to do."

After the publication of the report, there arose a long and violent literary warfare, which did any thing but add to the credit of the institution.* With this war against external foes, was unfortunately associated an internal feud, which ended in the departure of Schmid and others of the teachers.

One of Pestalozzi's biographers states, that Schmid's pride and pretensions had grown to such an extent, that he had acted with the greatest harshness toward Pestalozzi, Niederer, and Krüsi. "This was caused," continues the biographer, "by some ideas which he had partially caught up from two scientific men who were then stopping with Pestalozzi, (one of them is now a man of note in Silesia.) Perhaps at that time these ideas were not very clearly defined in the minds of those men themselves."†

The biographer means me and my friend; I shall therefore not be misunderstood, if I relate briefly the matter to which he refers.

I had come to learn and to render service. On this account, I took up my quarters entirely in the old building of the institution, slept in one of the large dormitories, took my meals with the children, attended the lessons, morning and evening prayers, and the conferences of the teachers. I listened and observed attentively in silence; but I was far from thinking of commencing myself to teach. My opinion upon all the things that I saw and heard was formed very much with reference to the boy of eight years intrusted to my care, accordingly as they contributed to his comfort or otherwise. Several weeks had passed on in this way, when I was one evening with Pestalozzi and the rest of the teachers at the hotel of the Wild Man, where they used to meet I think once a fortnight. After supper, Pestalozzi called me into an adjoining room; we were quite alone. "My teachers are afraid of you," he said, "because you only listen and look on in silence; why do you not teach?" I answered that before teaching, I wished to learn—to learn in silence. After the

* The well-known K. L. von Haller noticed the report of the commission in terms of high praise, in the *Göttingen Literary Advertiser*, of the 13th of April, 1811, and at the same time accused the Pestalozzian Institution of inspiring its pupils with an aversion from religion, the constituted authorities, and the aristocracy. In reply to this, Niederer wrote "The Pestalozzian Institution to the Public." This pamphlet appeared in a new form in 1812, under the title, "Pestalozzi's Educational Undertaking in relation to the Civilization of the Present Time." Bremi, of Zurich, wrote in reply to the former pamphlet; Pestalozzi and Niederer wrote again in reply to Bremi. Niederer professes to have convicted Bremi of ninety-two lies, thirty-six falsifications, and twenty calumnies.

† Henning, in the Schulrath, (an educational periodical)

conversation had touched on one thing and another, he frankly told me things about several of his teachers which put me into a state of astonishment, and which stood in direct contradiction with what I had read in the report, but not with what I had myself already observed or expected. Pestalozzi followed up these disclosures with the proposal, that I and my friend, in company with Schmid, whom he highly praised, especially for his practical ability and his activity, should set to work to renovate the institution.

The proposal came upon me so unexpectedly, that I begged for time to think of it, and discussed the matter with my friend, who was just as much surprised as I was. We were both naturally brought by this means into a closer relation with Schmid, became in a short time acquainted with the *arcana imperii*, and honestly considered what obstacles stood in the way of the prosperity of the institution, and what could be done to remove them.

Foremost of these was the intermixture of German and French boys, which doubly pained me, as I had come from Paris. The parents thought otherwise: they perceived in this very intermixture a fortunate means of training their children in the easiest way to speak both languages: whereas the result was, that the children could speak neither. With such a medley of children, the institution was devoid of a predominant mother-tongue, and assumed the mongrel character of border-provinces. Pestalozzi read the prayers every morning and evening, first in German, then in French! At the lessons in the German language, intended for German children, I found French children who did not understand the most common German word. This, and much more that was to be said against this intermixture, was now discussed with Pestalozzi, and the proposal was made to him, to separate the institution into two departments, one for German, the other for French children. Only in this way, it was represented to him, could the education of each class of children be successfully conducted.

The proposal was not accepted, chiefly on account of external obstacles, which might however have been overcome. A passage in Pestalozzi's "Fortunes" shows that he afterward thoroughly agreed with us. In this passage he calls it an unnatural circumstance, that the institution was transplanted from Burgdorf to Yverdun, "from German to French soil." "When we first come here," he continues, "our pupils were nearly all Germans; but there was very soon added to them an almost equal number of French children. Most of the German children were now intrusted to us, not with any particular reference to any elementary or other education, but simply in order that they might learn to speak French in a German house, and this was the very thing that we were least able to teach them; so also most of the French parents intrusted their children to us, in order that they might learn German in our German house: and here we stood between these two claims, equally unable to satisfy either the one or the other. At the same time, the persons on either side, who committed their children to our care, saw with as little distinctness what they really wished of us, as we did the extent of our inability to satisfy their real wishes. But it had now become the fashion to send us children from all sides; and so, in respect to pecuniary resources and eulogistic prattle, things went on for a considerable time in their old glittering but deceptive path."

The second evil was this. Much as is said in the report about the life in the institution having quite the character of that in a family, and even excelling it in many respects, still nothing could be less domestic than this life was. Leaving out of consideration Pestalozzi's residence, there were indeed in the old castle class rooms, dining rooms, and bed rooms, but the parlor, so justly esteemed by Pestalozzi, was altogether wanting. Older boys who, as the expression is, had arrived at years of indiscretion, may have felt this want less; but so much the more was it felt by the youngest—by children of six to ten years. I felt deeply on this account for my little Freddy, who, until he came to the institution, had grown up under the care of a tender mother in a lovely family circle. His present uncomfortable and even desolate existence grieved me much, and troubled my conscience. For his sake, and at the same time, for the sake of the rest of the little boys, we begged Pestalozzi to rent a beautiful dwelling house in the vicinity of Yverdun, where the children might find a friendly compensation for the life of the family circle which they had lost. We offered to take up our abode with them.

This proposal also was declined. It may easily be supposed that in the consultation upon it, the weak side of the institution, the want of a parlor, and the impossibility even of supplying the place of the family life, was very fully discussed.*

Many of the conversations I had with Pestalozzi I shall never forget. One of them concerned the teachers of the institution, in particular the under-teachers. I saw that many of them labored with the greatest fidelity and conscientiousness, even sacrificing themselves

* We made a third proposal, because it appeared to us to be impossible that Pestalozzi's ideas could be realized in Yverdun under the then existing circumstances. We asked him to establish in the canton of Argovia the long promised poor school, and offered to engage in the work ourselves to the best of our ability. As he declined this proposal also, I thought it my duty, especially on account of the boy confided to me, to leave the institution.

for the good of the institution. I need only refer the reader to the autobiography of honest, manful Ramsauer, for evidence of this fact. But still there was something wanting in most of the teachers; this Pestalozzi himself could not help feeling. In his new year's address of 1811, he said to them: "Do not attach a higher value to the ability to teach well, than that which it really has in relation to education as a whole. You have, perhaps, too early in your lives had to bear burdens which may have diminished somewhat the lovely bloom of your youth; but to you as educators, that bloom is indispensable. You must seek to restore it. I am not ignorant of your ability, your worth; but just because I know them, I would wish to set upon them the crown of an amiable disposition, which will increase your worth and make even your ability a blessing."

In what then were the teachers deficient? Pestalozzi points out one thing: many who had grown up in the institution had too early borne burdens, and had been kept in uninterrupted exertion. "Those teachers who had been pupils of Pestalozzi," says Ramsauer, "were particularly hard worked, for he at all times required much more from them, than he did from the other teachers; he expected them to live entirely for the house,—to be day and night concerned for the welfare of the house and the pupils. They were to help to bear every burden, every unpleasantness, every domestic care, and to be responsible for every thing. Thus, for example, in their leisure hours, (that is when they had no lessons to give,) they were required at one time to work some hours every day in the garden, at another to chop wood for the fires, and, for some time, even to light them early in the morning, or transcribe, &c. There were some years in which no one of us were found in bed after three o'clock in the morning; and we had to work summer and winter, from three in the morning till six in the evening."* Nearly all the work consisted in the direct performance of school duties; the teachers had no time to think of their own improvement.

There was another thing. Most of the teachers of the institution might be regarded as so many separate and independent teachers, who had indeed received their first instruction there, but who had passed much too soon from learning to teaching, and wished to see how they could fight their way through. There was never any such thing as a real pedagogical lecture. Under such a course of training, it could not happen otherwise than that some of the teachers should strike into peculiar paths: of this Schmid gave an example. But it was an

* Ramsauer's time-table shows that, from two or three o'clock in the morning till nine in the evening, he was almost constantly occupied with official duties.

equally necessary consequence, that the usual characteristic of such teachers should make itself apparent: namely, a great want of self-knowledge and of a proper modest estimate of their own labors.

"Man only learns to know himself in man."

I must know what others have done in my department of science, in order that I may assign the proper place and rank to my own labors. It is incredible, how many of the mistaken views and practices of Pestalozzi and his teachers sprang from this source.

But there was a third thing that I brought against Pestalozzi: his view of the teachers, and their relation to the methods and the methodical compendiums. As already mentioned, the compendiums were to render all peculiar talent and skill in teaching as good as unnecessary. These methodical compendiums were like dressing machines, which did not, unfortunately, quite supply the place of the teachers, but still left the services of a man necessary; just as in the most perfect printing presses, a man must always be appointed, though indeed he scarcely requires the most ordinary degree of intelligence.

Pestalozzi's idea of a teacher was not much better than this; according to his views, such a one had nothing to do, but to take his scholars through the compendium, with pedantic accuracy, according to the directions how to use it, without adding thereto, or diminishing therefrom. He was never required to be more than just a step in advance of the scholars. Just as if a guide with a lantern were to be given to a man traveling in the night, and the guide had not only to light the traveler, but first to find out the way himself with the aid of the lantern. The real teacher must have the destination and the road to it so clear before his mind, that he shall be able to guide the scholars without a lantern—without a book of method. He must be able to say, *La méthode c'est moi.**

But can any one imagine a more miserable piece of slave-work than that of a teacher who is strictly tied to a Pestalozzian compendium? Is not all peculiar teaching power thereby fettered,—all disposition to sprightliness and decision in teaching and acting kept down,—all affectionate relation between teacher and scholar rendered impossible?†

At that time the institution appeared to me, in moments of sadness, as a great noisy education factory; many mistook the dull noise

* "Every teacher," says Herder, "must have his own method; he must have created it with intelligence for himself, otherwise he will not be successful."

† On leaving Yverdun in 1810 and going to Berlin, I attended an examination at Plamann's institution. How the free, independent, and untrammeled teaching of Friesen and Harnisch contrasted with the cold, methodical, and constrained teaching of many Pestalozzian teachers!

of the machines for an expression of youthful joyousness on the part of the pupils, while engaged in learning.

Pestalozzi's view of the task of the teachers was too intimately connected with his general views on education, and had been too much realized in the institution to allow me to entertain the idea of his changing it, although the good old man bitterly felt that my observation was not without foundation.

At a later period, when the brilliancy of the reputation of the institution was decreasing more and more, Pestalozzi saw his under-teachers in the year 1817, as he relates, "suddenly combine, like English factory work-people, desist by common consent from the performance of their duties, and declare in a body that they would give no more lessons, but would remain in a state of complete strike-idleness, until the salary of every one of them should be doubled."

Pestalozzi pressed me to teach mineralogy, and in doing so to make use of a small collection of minerals which the institution possessed. I replied that, if I did do so, I must entirely depart from the methods of instruction pursued in the institution. How so? asked Pestalozzi. According to that method, I replied, I should have to do nothing but to hold up before the boys one specimen of the collection after another, to give the name of each, for example, "that is chalk," and thereupon to make the class repeat in unison three times, "that is chalk." It was thought that in this way the observation of actual objects and instruction in language were provided for at the same time.

I endeavored to explain that such a mode of instruction made a mere show, giving the children words before they had formed an idea of the images of the minerals; that moreover this process of perception and conception was only disturbed by the talking of the teacher and the repetition of the scholars, and was therefore best done in silence. On Pestalozzi's opposing this view, I asked him why children are born speechless, and do not begin to learn to speak until they are about three years old; why we should in vain hold a light before a child eight days old, and say "light" three times, or even a hundred times, as the child would certainly not try to repeat the word; whether this was not an indication to us from a higher hand, that time is necessary for the external perception of the senses to become internally appropriated, so that the word shall only come forth as the matured fruit of the inward conception now fully formed. What I said about the silence of children struck Pestalozzi.

As far as my recollection extends, I have now related the most important matters that were discussed between Pestalozzi, Schmid, and myself. I should at the present day still uphold the views which I entertained at that time; but, taught by so much experience, I should perhaps be able to do so with greater "clearness" than I could then have done.

But here I will by no means represent myself as blameless, and accuse others. Although I believe that my opinions were right, I know that my conduct was wrong in several respects; but this the unhappy circumstances of the institution will perhaps in some measure excuse. I will only mention one thing. Unfortunately, Niederer and Schmid were already placed in complete opposition to each other by their different capabilities, labors, and aims; in spite of my best endeavors, I found it impossible to effect a mediation between them, there was nothing left me but to side with the one or the other. Pestalozzi himself allied me with Schmid, whose resolute and restless activity was a pledge to me that he would render powerful assistance in introducing reforms. I was thus brought almost involuntarily into opposition with Niederer. Even though I did not altogether agree with his views, I ought to have emphatically acknowledged his self-sacrificing enthusiasm. I felt myself drawn to Krüsi by his mild disposition, but he too was against Schmid.

My silent observation was distasteful to the younger teachers; can I blame them for it? While they were toiling with unheard of exertion from morning till night, and had been toiling in the same manner for years previously, I looked on at their toilsome life with a critical eye. I appeared to them as a strange, quizzing, inactive intruder, and it was inevitable that I should so appear to them. They did not know that I had come with so high an opinion of the institution, that I wished at first only to look on, only to learn, in order to be able afterward to teach and to assist wherever I could.

That high opinion I had imbibed chiefly from the report. The report led me to form an over-estimate of the excellence of the institution before I went to Yverdun, and this over-estimate led me when there to think too lightly of its labors. I ought to have acknowledged *then*, the honest, conscientious, toilsome industry of several of the teachers, for instance, Ramsauer, even though they did not always bring to light discoveries that were entirely new; misled by the report, I had hoped, it is true, to find there nothing else but new discoveries.

But, notwithstanding all these evils, I should certainly have remained longer at Yverdun, and should have wrought in patient and persevering hope, had I not held it to be my duty to take away the boy intrusted to my care. I quitted Yverdun with him in May, 1810.

Soon after my departure, the long restrained enmity there broke out into an open feud. Schmid left the institution, and wrote against it.

In the summer of 1811, Monsieur Jullien, Napoleon's companion in arms in Egypt, and Chevalier of the Legion of Honor, visited Yverdun. He remained in the institution six weeks; his observations were embodied in two works.*

During the war of 1814, the hospital department of the Austrian army required that the buildings of the institution should be given up for a hospital. Fortunately, the Emperor Alexander was then at Basel: Pestalozzi immediately went to him, and was received in the most friendly manner; in consequence of the interposition of the emperor, the hospital was not established at Yverdun at all, and in November of the same year Pestalozzi received the order of St. Vladimir, fourth class.

Schmid's departure from the institution caused a very sensible void, the existence of which was painfully felt. Letters which Pestalozzi wrote to Niederer at that time, bear witness to the evil plight in which the institution was placed. "O Niederer," he writes, "without strength and purity of purpose in those who surround us, all our endeavors after what is great and high are lost; the sublime and good can not easily unfold themselves where weakness and worthlessness peer forth from all corners—our greatest enemies are under our own roof, and eat from the same dish with us—it is better to be alone than to accept delusive aid from baseness."

In a second letter, Pestalozzi writes: "The internal weakness of our house has opened the mouth of the weakest among us, for them to give us monkey's advice and hold public conferences about us among themselves. The great evil of our house comes from boys who here play the part of men, but who at every other place would be schoolboys."

In this period falls also the visit of the Prussian Chancellor of State, von Beyme, who entered the institution "with a great predisposition in favor of Pestalozzi," and before he left it expressed himself to the effect, that if the institution held together for another year, he should look upon it as the greatest wonder, for that, in the instruction which he had seen given there, things were wanting which teachers in the lowest village schools would be ashamed to have neglected.

Niederer felt more than any one else the void created by the departure of Schmid. As early as the end of the year 1813, he wrote to Schmid in the most conciliatory manner, and writing on the 10th

* *Précis sur l'institut d'Yverdun en Suisse*, 1812; and *Esprit de la méthode d'éducation de M. Pestalozzi.*

of February, 1815, he says: "With Pestalozzi, I stake every thing I have upon bringing you back. Alone I can do nothing. You know wherein I am deficient, but with you and a few other distinguished and noble minded men, I do not doubt of the realization of an educational heaven on earth."

Pestalozzi adduces these passages as certain proofs of Schmid's ability, and the high value of his services to the institution: but they also testify to an honorable mind on the part of Niederer, who did not attempt to conceal his own practical incompetency, and who repressed a deep-seated antipathy to Schmid, in order to realize his educational ideal.

Schmid was then at the head of a school in Bregenz. At Niederer's pressing invitation, he returned to Yverdun in the Easter of 1815, and now commenced a comprehensive reform of the institution, especially in an economical point of view. There soon arose a silent but general antipathy to him.

On the 11th of the following December, Madame Pestalozzi died, aged nearly eighty years, having been the faithful and patient partner of her husband during forty-five years, through times of severe suffering. At her funeral, after a hymn had been sung, Pestalozzi, turning toward the coffin, said: "We were shunned and contemned by all, sickness and poverty bowed us down, and we ate dry bread with tears; what was it that, in those days of severe trial, gave you and me strength to persevere and not cast away our hope?" Thereupon he took up a Bible, which was lying near at hand, pressed it on the breast of the corpse, and said: "From this source you and I drew courage, and strength, and peace." Her grave is under two tall walnut trees in the garden of the castle.

On this sorrowful day, the antipathy of many of the teachers toward Schmid first broke out into open enmity, which was never again appeased, and which positively poisoned the last twelve years of the poor old man's life. From that time every blessing seemed to forsake the institution, and every new undertaking in which Pestalozzi engaged.

Most of the teachers were against Schmid. Blochmann, for many years director of a flourishing educational establishment at Dresden, drew up a formal complaint against him, which was signed by Krüsi, Ramsauer, Stern, Ackermann, and others, in all twelve teachers.

In the year 1816, these men left the institution, among them even Krüsi, so many years the fellow-laborer of Pestalozzi. "Father," he wrote to Pestalozzi, "my time of enjoying your presence is past. I must leave your institution, as it is now conducted, if I am not forever to lose my courage and strength to live for you and your work. For all that you were to me, and all that I was able to be to you, I thank God; for all my shortcomings, I pray God and yourself to forgive me.

At length, in 1817, Niederer also separated from the institution; Pestalozzi tried in vain the following year to reconcile him with Schmid. Both of them acknowledged Pestalozzi as their master, and yet the reconciliation was impossible. They were too much opposed to each other, not merely in natural endowments, but in their aim and object, in the educational idea which each endeavored to realize in the institution.

Niederer saw in Pestalozzi a man who had grasped with instinctive profundity the subject of human culture, but had given only a fragmentary view of it, and who could not control the ideas which, as it were, possessed him. Niederer felt himself called to control them philosophically—to build up out of those mighty educational fragments a complete systematic theory.

At first, Pestalozzi could not comprehend him, not understanding his philosophical language. At a later period, Pestalozzi saw in him the one man in the institution, who, standing on the pinnacle of German culture, was fitted to assign to the new method its proper place in the region of human culture generally. Only by such a man, he thought, could the educated world, especially Germany, be won over to his educational plans; by such a man must his Swiss idiom be translated into an intelligible *high* German. Nay, for some time he even thought that Niederer understood him better than he understood himself.

Niederer was deficient in the practical skill requisite for carrying out his educational theory, as he himself frequently acknowledged. His intention in the institution was more to observe the results of the practical talent at work there, and in this manner to learn what he could, but at the same time to see that all the teachers wrought together with one mind toward one and the same object—the realization of the educational theory.

No wonder that Pestalozzi, as he again and again affirmed, did not feel himself attracted by Niederer's peculiar character, even at times when the two men stood in a very friendly relation toward each other; and just as little need we wonder that the old man subsequently dissolved a connection, which had been formed by his will rather than his inclination.

But how entirely different was his relation to Schmid! "Inexplicaple feelings," he says, "drew me toward him from the moment of his appearance in our circle, as I have never felt myself drawn toward any other pupil." Pestalozzi writes characteristically: "I must trace from its origin the *strength* which alone appeared capable of holding us together in this unhappy state." This personified strength was no other than the shepherd boy Schmid, who had migrated from the Tyrolese mountains to Burgdorf. Pestalozzi says that he soon left his teachers behind him. "By his practical talent and incessant activity," continues Pestalozzi, "he soared above the influence of every other person in the house. I did not conceal that I looked upon the *strength* of this pupil, though still so young, as the main stay of my house." Pestalozzi characterizes Schmid in the same way in an address which he delivered in the year 1818. "I will not," he says, "make more of him than he is to me. I know him. He has a natural power which, in its artlessness, penetrates where much art has often before my own eyes failed to enter. Schmid threw a hard shell about the kernel of my vanishing labors, and saved me."

Niederer also acknowledged in the fullest measure, the ability and activity of Schmid. Like Pestalozzi, Niederer saw in him a most indefatigable teacher of mathematics and drawing, who, by his example, as well as by severe censure, could incite the remaining teachers to conscientious activity; he also saw in him a man who, being a pupil of Pestalozzi, was regarded as one of the fruits of the method, and who consequently impressed foreign visitors with a favorable idea of it. Thus it came that, in the year 1814, he hoped every thing from a reconciliation with Schmid. But how deceived he found himself, when Pestalozzi gave into Schmid's hands the sceptre over the entire institution.

Blochmann, too, in his complaint, acknowledges Schmid's "activity, perseverance, endurance, punctuality, administrative ability, his meritorious services in establishing greater order in the institution, his skill in teaching the elementary branches of mathematics—a rare talent." All these were qualities which neither Pestalozzi nor Niederer possessed, and which, therefore, marked out Schmid as an indispensable member of the staff of teachers. But, if Blochmann and the other teachers who signed the complaint acknowledged this, why did they press for Schmid's removal? Because, they answer, in that document, "the source of all that Schmid does is complete selfishness, ability without humility, without love, without self-denial, sounding brass, a tinkling cymbal, and Schmid himself is wise as the serpent, but not harmless as the dove."

In a letter, (19th March, 1818,) to Pestalozzi, Niederer reproaches him with having overrated the ability of Schmid, and ability generally.

"Ruin," he says, "entered your institution, when, dazzled and led away by individual instances of brilliant talents and results, you ceased to bestow any particular attention on that which by its nature can work only in silence, although it stands higher than talent, and alone can render the development of talent possible; when you began so to act as if you owed every thing to that with which you could make a display, and nothing to that which was not suited to this purpose. Under this fundamental error, I say more, under this fundamental injustice, the mathematical side of the method and the institution was made prominent, as if that singly and solely were the essence of the method and the salvation of humanity. Low and one-sided qualities were honored at expense of the higher ones. The qualities of good temper, fidelity, love, if they were not joined with those external qualities, were slighted and depreciated in the persons in whom they existed. In the kind of praise which you gave to the manual dexterity of utterly inexperienced youths in particular departments, you placed this dexterity above intelligence, knowledge and experience."

Let us now return to the history of the institution.

In the Easter of 1816, M. Jullien, already mentioned, came to Yverdun, bringing twenty-four pupils with him from France; but, annoyed, it is said, by Schmid, he quitted the institution the very next year.

As already stated, Niederer separated from the institution in 1817, from which time he conducted the girls' school only, in company with his wife. In the same year, a most ignominious and lamentable lawsuit, which lasted seven years, arose concerning the pecuniary affairs of this school, between Pestalozzi and Schmid, on one side, and Niederer, on the other. "It was in July, 1817," says Pestalozzi, "that a letter referring to that quarrel suddenly threw me into a state of inward rage, which was accompanied by an outbreak of real delirium, and placed me in danger of completely losing my reason, and sinking into utter insensibility." Schmid took the old man to Bület, on the Jura, whose cooling heights acted wholesomely on the endangered state of his nerves. There he poured out his sufferings in poems, in which his soul, now caught in the trammels of the most painful and ignoble relations, utters with wailing, its aspirations after heavenly freedom. Here is one of those poems:—

Fair bow, that smil'st amid the storm,
Thou tellest of the bliss of God!
With those soft beams of many hues,
O shine in this afflicted heart
Amid its wild and life-long storm!

Tell me of brighter morn to come,
O tell me of a better day,
Fair bow, that joinest earth to heav'n!

Through all the dark and stormy days,
The Lord hath been a rock to me,
My soul shall praise His holy name
Must I be call'd from this fair earth,
Ere thou appearest in my heart,
And bringest with thee heavenly joys
And that long wished for better day:
Must I drink out the bitter cup—
The cup of fierce contending strife
And enmity not reconciled—
Till I have drained the deepest dregs:
Must I from hence depart,
Ere peace, the peace I seek, is found?
I own my burthen of offense,
My many weaknesses I own,
And with affection and with tears,
All my offenders I forgive;
But death will bring me peace,
And after death's long night of rest,
A better day will dawn for me!
Thou herald of that better day,
How lovely then wilt thou appear
Above my still and lonesome grave:
Fair bow that shin'st like Hope through tears.

Like snow new fallen on the ground,
Like those bright flakes of winter-tide
Which, beaming lovely in the sun,
Sank into that new open'd grave,
Where lay the partner of my days:
Fair bow, that shin'st with heaven's light,
Thus lovely, in the hour of death,
Do thou appear once more to me.
Through all the dark and stormy days,
The Lord hath been a rock to me!
My soul shall praise his holy name!

An attempt, which Pestalozzi made in 1817, to enter into connection with Fellenberg, was unsuccessful. In 1818, Schmid made ar arrangement with Cotta, (the great Leipsig publisher,) for the publication of a complete edition of Pestalozzi's works; subscriptions to a considerable amount soon flowed in. The emperor of Russia subscribed 5,000 roubles; the king of Prussia, 400 dollars; the king of Bavaria, 700 guilders. Thereupon, Pestalozzi's hopes revived. In a remarkable address, already mentioned, which he delivered on his seventy-third birth-day, the 12th of January, 1818, he stated that he should appropriate to educational purposes, 50,000 French livres, which the subscription would yield.

In the same address, Pestalozzi speaks freely on the subject of his relations to Niederer and Schmid, and justifies himself for having separated from the former and joined with the latter. He hits off Niederer admirably when he says: "I am conscious of a high and fervent love for him. Only he should not require me to value in him what I do not understand; he should ascribe it to the weakness of my head, not to the hardness of my heart, if I fail to do so, and should not on that account pronounce me ungrateful. But what shall I say? Here lies the very ground of complaint against me, namely, that I am no longer capable of following the spirit of my endeavors, and that through my incapacity, I cripple and destroy the strength of those who are further advanced in that spirit than myself. It is an old complaint, that my spirit has left me; that I have outlived myself, and that the truth and the right of my labors have passed from mine into other hands. I know well, also, and I feel it deeply, that I do not possess, in the least degree, some qualifications which are essential to the furtherance of my views; on the other hand I know just as certainly, that all those qualifications which I formerly possessed, I still feel myself to possess in some vitality, and with an impulse to apply them to use."

Of this the address affords sufficient proofs; I will quote some passages.

"Man has a conscience. The voice of God speaks in every man, and leaves no one unconvinced as to what is good, and what bad; what is right and what wrong."

"Contemplate man in the entire range of his development. See, he grows, he is educated, he is trained. He grows by the strength of his own self; he grows by the strength of his very being. He is educated by accident, by the accidental that lies in his condition, in his circumstances, and in his relations. He is trained by art and by the will of man. The growth of man and his powers is God's doing. It proceeds according to eternal and divine laws. The education of man is accidental and dependent on the varying circumstances in which a man finds himself placed. The training of man is moral. Only by the accordance of the influences of education and training with the eternal laws of human growth is man really educated and trained; by contradiction between the means of his education and training and those eternal laws, man is mis-educated and mis-trained."

Pestalozzi gives a striking delineation of the contrast between the old time and the new.

"The time in which we live, is really a time of excessive artificial refinement, in contradistinction to a high and pure sense of innocence, love, and faith, and that powerful attachment to truth and right which springs from these virtues. Who among us, if he be not an alien that neither knows the present time and its spirit, nor has searched into the time of our fathers and its spirit, but must acknowledge that the time of our fathers was a better time, their spirit a better spirit; that their sincerity of purpose had its foundations laid immeasurably deeper, in the religion of the heart, in strong earnestness in domestic and civil life, and in the daily exercise of industry in the good works of a simple and satisfying professional life, than can possibly be the case in our paralysing refinement of the powers of body and soul. Our fathers were cheerful, reasonable, and benevolent, in all simplicity. Their circumstances were peculiarly fitted to lead them daily and hourly in all innocence, in faith, and in love, to be good-tempered, reflective, and industrious; but our artificial refinement has rendered us disgusted with our fathers' mode of life, and with the sources of their moral, domestic, and political elevation. We have almost entirely departed from their spirit and their mode of life. But it is for this reason that we have sunk so low in respect to the education of the people. We have the semblance of faith, love, and wisdom, but not the qualities themselves; and we live in a delusion, really without the virtues of our fathers, while they, though possessing those virtues, were by no means satisfied with themselves, as we are. The good and pious foundation which our fathers had in their mode of life itself for their views, feelings, opinions, and usages generally, and particularly in respect to the training of children and the relief of the poor, has sunk under our feet through the deception of our present artificial and frivolous mode of life. We are no longer what we were, and we have even lost the feeling that we ought to become again in spirit and in truth what we were. While we praise our fathers with our mouths, we are in heart far from them, and in our doings we stand at the very antipodes of them. We have substituted for their ability to do what was necessary, and their ignorance of what was useless, a large acquaintance with what is useless and an inability to do what is necessary. Instead of their healthy spirit, well exercised in mother-wit, we have forms, not so much of thinking as of verbal expressions about what has been thought, which suck the blood out of good sense, like a marten that fixes itself upon the neck of a poor dove. We no longer know our neighbors, our fellow citizens, or even our poor relations; but we make up for it by reading the newspapers and periodicals, by learning the genealogical register of the kings of the world, the anecdotes of courts, of the theatre, and of capital cities, and we raise ourselves to a daily change in our political and religious opinions, as in our clothes, running, on one side, from infidelity to *capucinade*, and from *capucinade* to infidelity, just as, on the other side, we run from sans-cullottism to tight-lacing and leading strings. Our fathers cultivated a general, simple, and powerful intellect; but few of them troubled themselves with researches into higher truths, which are difficult to fathom: we do very little indeed toward rendering ourselves capable of cultivating a general and profound spirit of thought and research: but we all learn to talk a great deal about sublime and almost unfathomable truths, and strive very zealously to get to read the results of the profoundest thinking in the popular descriptions of almanacs and daily pamphlets, and to put them into the mouth of people generally. Among our fathers, every honest man sought to do one thing well at least, namely, the work of his calling, and every man might with honor learn every trade; now our notables are mostly born to their callings. Numberless individuals are ashamed of the rank and profession of their fathers, and believe themselves to be called to pry into and carp at the professional knowledge of all ranks; and the habit of prating about all professions and discharging one's own imperfectly is becoming more general every day, among both the notable and unnotable men of our time. All spirit of political strength has fled from amongst us. In the present state of society we no longer ask what we really are, but what we possess and what we know, and how we may set out all our possessions and knowledge for show, put them up for sale, and barter them for the means of feasting ourselves, so that we may tickle our palates with the refined enjoyments of all the five divisions of the globe, whose appetites must by such conduct be almost inevitably engendered in us. And when we have in this way succeeded in rendering ourselves powerless and degraded in body and soul, in respect to the pure claims of the humanity of our nature, and of the eternal and divine essence which lies at its foundation,—then, in the state of debility and giddiness into which the fever has thrown us, we further seek to force up the appearance of a character whose truth and purity we entirely lack. In this state, we seek to cover over the outward appearances of our debility and desolation by a violent employment of the means of adjustment and concealment, which kill heart and spirit and humanity; and verily we have sunk to the employment of such means in many matters connected with the education of the people and the relief of the poor. Thus it is that we kill, in ourselves, the very essence of the powers of the soul, those human gifts divine; and then, when a shadow of the powers which we have killed flutters in us, we ornament the works of its fluttering with golden frames, and hang them up in splendid apartments, whose shining floors are unable to bear any of the good works of the ordinary life of man."

In another place, Pestalozzi says: "The gardener plants and waters, but God giveth the increase." It is not the educator that implants any faculty in man; it is not the educator that gives breath and life to any faculty: he only takes care that no external influence shall fetter and disturb the natural course of the development of man's individual faculties. "The moral, the spiritual, and the artistic capabilities of our nature must grow out of themselves, and by no means out of the results produced by art, which has been mixed up with their education. Faith must be called forth again by faith, and not by the knowledge of what is believed; thinking must be called forth again by thinking, and not by the knowledge of what is thought, or of the laws of thinking; love must be called forth again by loving, and not by the knowledge of what is loveable or of love itself; and art must be called forth again by ability, and not by endless talk about ability."

The reader can judge from the passages just cited whether any degree of youthful freshness still lingered in the mind and heart of the old man of seventy-three.

But his "unrivaled incapacity to govern," as he himself calls it, did not forsake him. He established a poor school in 1818 at Clindy, in the vicinity of Yverdun; a commencement was made with twelve boys. "They were to be brought up as poor boys," says Pestalozzi, "and receive that kind of instruction and training which is suitable for the poor." But after a short time, children were admitted to board in the establishment, at a fee of twelve louis d'or per annum; and in a few months the number of these pupils rose to thirty. It may be easily imagined that the presence of paying boarders would of itself destroy the character of the place as a school for the poor. But this result was occasioned in a still higher degree by some remarkably stupid experiments in teaching. An Englishman,* of the name of Greaves, visited Yverdun in 1819; he offered to teach these poor Swiss children English without remuneration, and his offer was accepted. On this step Pestalozzi himself remarks: "This created an impression, which, considering the original destination of these children, led us very far astray." To the instruction in English was added soon after instruction in French and Latin. Pestalozzi says, the poor children had made extraordinary progress in the elementary subjects. He adds, nevertheless, "I had no longer an establishment for the poor; but, on the contrary, two scientific ones, which I could not now allow to remain separated. Thus the so-called poor school at Clindy was amalgamated with the institution at Yverdun." According to Pestalozzi's account, the poor scholars were "models

* A second Englishman entered the establishment the same year, as the religious instructor of the English pupils who had been admitted. Later, "above half a dozen *poor* children" were even sent from England to the school!

worthy of imitation" to the pupils of the institution, especially in their acquirements. Many of them were employed as teachers. "The instruction which was given by the pupils of our poor school, (says he,) was preferred, on account of its solid and natural character to that of the most accomplished among the elder teachers of our house." (!) They threw their strength chiefly into arithmetic and geometry. Is it to be wondered at, that these poor children soon began to place themselves on a level with the children of the institution, and liked playing with them out of school hours better than chopping wood and carting manure;—that, instructed in three foreign languages, they did not like the idea of becoming masters of poor schools, and of having learnt Latin to no purpose?

Pestalozzi acknowledged, when it was too late, "that the establishment had taken such a direction that it was no longer to be looked upon as a poor school, but as a school for imparting the elements of a scientific education." The particular reason of the failure had been "that these children were led into acquirements, habits, pretensions, dreams, and appetites, which did not suit the character of their original destination, and even tended to unfit them for it."

Pestalozzi's unhappy disputes with Niederer and others went on uninterruptedly during this time. At last a reconciliation was brought about through the noble exertions of deputy governor Du Thou. On the 31st of December, 1823, Niederer wrote an apology to Schmid in the name of Krüsi and himself, in which, at the same time, it was said that any future dispute should be settled by an arbiter.

Unfortunately, newspapers and controversial writings of those years have made the public only too well acquainted with this dispute. Pestalozzi's worst enemies could not have conceived any thing that would have been more calculated to damp the public enthusiasm for him.

Who would like to undertake the task of placing before readers the details of these unfortunate occurrences, especially when it is considered that they almost exclusively concerned private interests? On February 1st, 1823, Pestalozzi wrote to Niederer a conciliatory letter, which shines forth in the midst of this lawsuit like a brilliant gem out of the mire. I give the following passage from this letter with pleasure:—

"DEAR MR. NIEDERER,*—Call to mind what we once hoped from each other and what we were to each other. I would again hope from you what I formerly hoped, and I would again be to you what I formerly was. But we must make the way to this possible for each other; we must help each other to clear the way to it, each from the point on which he stands. Let us do this. Above all,

* In November, 1824, the lawsuit which has been mentioned was terminated by arbitration.

let us, without circumlocution and without condition, forgive each other, and unite with a pure intention in true love, in true friendship, and in an undertaking which will be for our mutual happiness. Niederer, become again as far as you can my old Niederer—such as you were twenty years ago. Madame Niederer, be also to me again something of what you were then. I will readily be to both of you again, as far as I can, what I then was. How I long for the time when our hearts shall bring us to ourselves again, and when, in the path of real self-knowledge we shall attain to love, which is equally our duty as Christians, and the pressing need of our condition. Oh! Niederer, how I long for the time when strengthened and sanctified by this renewed love, we shall be able to go once more to the Holy Sacrament, when the festival comes round, without having to fear that the entire commune in which we live, scandalized by our conduct, will shudder at our coming to the Lord's table, and will cast upon us looks of indignation as well as pity. Oh! Niederer, the path of this renewed love is the only one which will lead to true honor, as it is also the only one which will lead to the restoration of a lost semblance of honor. Oh! Niederer, think not that the tricks and chicanery of law can ever bring us to the pinnacle of honor to which we can raise ourselves by the restoration of our love. My old friend, let us make clean the inside of the platter, before we trouble ourselves about the false glitter of the outside."

These lamentable lawsuits had naturally the worst influence on the hybrid institution. Pestalozzi felt this most painfully, and thought that his poor school would succeed, if he could only transfer it from unlucky Yverdun to Neuhof, in the canton of Argovia—the same Neuhof where, many years before, he had made his first important educational experiments. He had a new house built there for the purpose.

Each of the poor children who had been admitted into the school had bound himself to remain in it five years, from 1818 till 1823. The five years ran out. Pestalozzi confidently hoped that many of these children would follow him to Neuhof, and form the nucleus of the new establishment. But not one remained. As I have already remarked, they had imbibed grander ideas from the instruction which they had enjoyed, and they sought to make their fortune in other ways. "They considered it," says Pestalozzi, "beneath their dignity to be appointed teachers in a Pestalozzian poor school at Neuhof." When at last even a favorite pupil of his rejected all his offers, and went away clandestinely from Yverdun, the old man's heart was full. "The illusion, in my mind," he says, "as to the possibility of transplanting to Neuhof an establishment in Yverdun of which not an inch was in reality any longer mine, was now entirely dispelled. To resign myself to this conviction, required me to do no less than abandon all my hopes and aims in regard to this project, as for me completely unattainable. I did so at last, and on March 17th, 1824, I announced my total inability further to fulfill the expectations and hopes which I had excited, by my projected poor school, in the hearts of so many philanthropists and friends of education."

At length, in the year 1825, Pestalozzi also broke up the institution, after it had stood for a quarter of a century; and he returned, an old man of eighty years, and tired of life, to Neuhof, where, exactly half a century before, he had begun his first poor school. "Verily," he says, "it was as if I was putting an end to my life itself by this return, so much pain did it give me."

Pestalozzi had but one child, a son, who was born in 1770, and died at the early age of twenty-four, leaving a son himself.* This grandson of Pestalozzi was in possession of the estate of Neuhof; to him the old man went.

In these last years of his life, he wrote the "Song of the Dying Swan" and the "Fortunes of my Life." He looked back with deep pain on so many shipwrecked enterprises, and acknowledged that the blame was his, as the wreck had been brought on by his incompetency to manage the helm. He speaks, as we have seen, with equal candor of his fellow-workers.

These last writings of Pestalozzi have been regarded by many as the melancholy and languid outpourings of the heart of a dying old man. As far as concerns the old man's judgments on the institution, as it was at the time of my stay at Yverdun, I have already remarked that I consider them for the most part highly truthful, and as affording evidence that he was not deficient in manly clearness and penetration even in his old age.

In May of the year 1825, he was elected President of the Helvetian Society of Shinznach, of which he was the oldest member. The following year he delivered a lecture before the Education Society of Brugg, on, "The simplest means which art can employ to educate the child, from the cradle, to the sixth year, in the domestic circle." Thus the gentle influence of home education remained to the last the object of his love, as it had been fifty-six years before, when he wrote "Leonard and Gertrude."

On the 21st of July, 1826, Pestalozzi, in company with Schmid, visited the establishment of the excellent Zeller in Bruggen. The children received him with singing. An oak wreath was handed to him, but he did not accept it: "Not to me," he said, "but to Innocence belongs the wreath." The children sang to him the song by Goethe which he has introduced into "Leonard and Gertrude."

Thou art from highest skies,
Every storm and sorrow stilling;
Hearts that doubled anguish tries
Doubly with thy sweetness filling;
On the wave of passion driven,
Oh, how longs my soul for rest!
Peace of Heaven
Come, oh come within my breast.

Tears choked the voice of the old man.

* The widow, an excellent woman, subsequently married a Mr. Kuster, and remained attached to Pestalozzi with true affection.

From his youth, Pestalozzi had been weakly in constitution, and he had repeatedly suffered severe attacks of illness. In the year 1806, he was suddenly knocked down in the street by the pole of a carriage, and trampled under foot by the horses. "It is a great wonder," he said in an address on New Year's Day, 1808, "that I was saved from under the horses' feet. See, they tore the clothes from off my back, but did not touch my body."

In the year 1812, he suffered very severely for a long time from accidentally running a knitting needle into his ear.

But, notwithstanding slight ailments and dangerous accidents, his life was prolonged to a very advanced age.

At length he approached the end of his earthly existence. Some time before his death, he said: "I forgive my enemies; may they find peace now that I go to eternal rest. I should liked to have lived another month, to have completed my last labors; but I again thank God, who in His Providence calls me away from this earthly scene. And you, my children, remain in quiet attachment to one another, and seek for happiness in the domestic circle." Soon after, he breathed his last. He had lain ill only a few days. On the 15th of February, 1827, he had been removed from his country house to the town of Brugg, in order that he might be nearer to his physician; on the morning of the 17th he died, after violent paroxysms of fever; and on the 19th he was buried. His corpse was carried past the new poor school which he had begun to build, but could not complete, and was interred with a quiet and modest funeral service at the village of Birr. Few strangers attended his funeral, for the snow lay thick on the ground, and his interment took place sooner than might have been expected; the news of his death had scarcely been received in the canton of Argovia. Schoolmasters and children from the surrounding villages sang their thanks to the departed in artless strains over his grave.*

Pestalozzi rests from the labors of his toilsome life.

At the grave a Sabbath stillness sets in; we look back upon the past, but, at the same time, we look forward into the eternal life of the departed, and ask whether, in time, he seriously prepared himself for eternity—whether all the labors of his life were done in the Lord, and whether he died in the Lord.

Not as severe judges do we ask, but in all the humility of co-redeemed sinful fellow-men; we ask with the fond wish that he may be blessed eternally.

* Heussler.

In a letter written in the year 1793, Pestalozzi says, "Wavering between *feelings*, which drew me toward religion, and *opinions*, which led me away from it, I went the dead way of my time; I let the essential part of religion grow cold in my inmost heart, without really deciding against religion."

That is the judgment which he pronounced upon himself in his forty-eighth year; at the time of Robespierre, when the earthy political element reigned to such a degree in the minds of men, that no quiet abode remained for the religious element.

The "Evening Hour of a Hermit," written thirteen years earlier, when the world was more tranquil, and as yet not off its hinges, contains passages which are penetrated with true christian unction. To these belongs especially the concluding passage of the whole, already quoted, in which Pestalozzi speaks of Christ as "the Son of God, who with suffering and death has restored to mankind the universally lost feeling of filial love toward God—the Redeemer of the World —the sacrificed Priest of the Lord—the Mediator between God and sinful mankind;" and of his doctrine as "the revelation of God the Father to the lost race of his children."

But other passages of this paper, enticing as they sound, are at variance with essential doctrines of christianity. Thus the one in which Pestalozzi says, "Faith in God, thou art the pure sense of simplicity—the ear of innocence listening to the voice of nature, which proclaims that God is father."

Where is the ear of innocence to be found? The Scripture saith: "There is none righteous, no not one: There is none that understandeth, there is none that seeketh after God. They are all gone out of the way, they are together become unprofitable; there is none that doeth good, no, not one." (Romans iii., 10, 11, 12.)

Where is the ear of innocence? If it were to be found among men, then it might certainly hear a voice of nature, proclaiming that God is father. In that case, the heathen might also have prayed, "Our Father." But nowhere do we find the slightest evidence that the ancients loved their gods, not to say God, with filial love.

And, could man by nature love God, to what purpose were Christ the restorer of the lost filial love of mankind? But this very expression itself appears to me to be almost a euphemism for "The Lord hath laid on him the iniquity of us all." (Isaiah liii., 6.)

We saw, in considering the book, "How Gertrude teaches her Children," how deep an influence Pestalozzi's notion of the innocence of children exercised upon his educational theory; like Rousseau, he wanted to gather figs of thistles. Did he retain this notion to the end of his life? We shall answer this question in the negative.

In "Leonard and Gertrude," all the stress is laid upon active christianity, love is *occasionally* placed almost in opposition to faith: a dead, hypocritical faith not being always distinguished with sufficient exactitude from true faith, which is active in love. The clergyman in Leonard and Gertrude is an honest man, but strongly inclined to mere moralizing; his care of his flock is more that of a faithful personal friend, than of one acting in the spirit and strength of a church.

In the "Researches," christianity is styled a religion of morality—an effort to make the spirit subdue the flesh. If, according to the letter cited, Pestalozzi wavered between feelings, which drew him toward religion, and opinions, which led him away from it, both feeling and christianity give place, in the work just mentioned, to this belabored product of the intellect.

In the book, "How Gertrude teaches her children," the educational theory is, as we have seen, extremely weak on the religious side; it is more a rhetorical theory of intellectual developments estranged from Christ.

But in this book, also, Pestalozzi's feelings repeatedly glances through; there stand forth the aim and yearning desire of his toilsome life, the depth of a love which brought upon the poor helpless man countless sorrows and almost drove him to despair. From the depths of his necessity, he then cries to God, praying, hoping, offering up his thanks: "Friend," he writes to Gesner, "let me now for a moment forget my aim and my labors, and abandon myself entirely to the feeling of melancholy which comes over me, when I remember that I still live, though I am no longer myself. I have lost every thing, I have lost myself; nevertheless, thou, O Lord, hast preserved in me the desires of my life, and hast not shattered to pieces before my eyes the aim of my suffering, as thou hast shattered the aim of thousands of men, who corrupted themselves in their own ways. Thou hast preserved to me the work of my life, in the midst of my own ruin, and hast caused to arise upon me, in my hopeless declining age, an evening brightness, the sight of whose loveliness outweighs the sufferings of my life. Lord, I am not worthy of the mercy and faithfulness which thou hast shown toward me. Thou, thou alone, hast had mercy on the trampled worm; thou alone hast not broken the bruised reed; thou alone hast not quenched the smoking flax; and hast not, to the latest period of my life, turned away thy face from the offering, which from childhood I have desired to bring to the forsaken in the land, but have never been able to bring."

Before I consider the religious character of Pestalozzi's later works, I will first look at that of his institution. It is best delineated by Ramsauer. He entered the institution at Burgdorf in 1800, as a boy of ten years; he left it at the age of twenty-six, as head teacher, when he went from Yverdun to Würzburg. Thus he had, both as a learner and as a teacher, become acquainted with the religious tendency of the institution. When, in later years, the deep truth and solemn sanctity of christianity dawned upon his awakened conscience, which impelled him to self-knowledge, then first did he learn to form a just estimate of that religious tendency. He narrates as follows:—

"In Burgdorf, an active and entirely new mode of life opened to me; there reigned so much love and simplicity in the institution, the life was so genial—I could almost say patriarchal; not much was learned, it is true, but Pestalozzi was the father, and the teachers were the friends of the pupils; Pestalozzi's morning and evening prayers had such a fervor and simplicity, that they carried away every one who took part in them; he prayed fervently, read and explained Gellert's hymns impressively, exhorted each of the pupils individually to private prayer, and saw that some pupils said aloud in the bedrooms, every evening, the prayers which they had learned at home, while he explained, at the same time, that the mere repeating of prayers by rote was worthless, and that every one should rather pray from his own heart. Such exhortations became more and more rare at Yverdun, and the praying aloud ceased altogether, like so much else that had a genial character. We all felt that more must be learned than at Burgdorf; but we all fell, in consequence, into a restless pushing and driving, and the individual teachers into a scramble after distinction. Pestalozzi, indeed, remained the same noble-hearted old man, wholly forgetting himself, and living only for the welfare of others, and infusing his own spirit into the entire household; but, as it arose not so much from the religious arrangements and from Pestalozzi's principles, as from his personal character, that so genial a life had prevailed at Burgdorf, that spirit could not last long, it could not gain strength and elevate itself into a christian spirit. On the other hand, so long as the institution was small, Pestalozzi could, by his thoroughly amiable personal character, adjust at once every slight discordance; he stood in much closer relation with every individual member of the circle, and could thus observe every peculiarity of disposition, and influence it according to necessity. This ceased when the family life was transformed in the institution into a constitutional state existence. Now the individual was more easily lost in the crowd; thus there arose a desire, on the part of each, to make himself felt and noticed. Egotism made its appearance every day in more pointed forms. Envy and jealousy rankled in the breasts of many. The instruction, calculated only for the development of the mind, nourished feelings of selfishness and pride; and the counterpoise, which only the fear of God could have given, was not known. Instead of being told that only *that* teacher could labor with God's blessing who had attained to the knowledge and the belief of the highest truths, and had thus come to see that he was nothing of himself, but that he had to thank God for whatever he was enabled to be or to do, and that every christian, but especially the educator, had daily cause to pray to God for patience, love, and humility, and for wisdom in doing and avoiding; instead of this, we heard day after day that man could do every thing that he wished, that he could do every thing of himself, and that he alone could help himself. Had the otherwise so noble Pestalozzi made the Bible the foundation of all moral and religious education, I verily believe that the institution would still have been in existence, even as those institutions are still in existence and working with success which were founded by Franke, upward of one hundred years ago, with small means, but in full reliance on God. But, instead of making the pupils familiar with the Bible, Pestalozzi, and those of his assistants who gave the so-called religious instruction, or conducted the so-called morning and evening prayers, fell more and more in each succeeding year into a mere empty moralizing; and hence it may be understood how it could happen that I grew up in this institution, was confirmed there, and for sixteen years led a very active and morally good life, without acquiring even the slightest acquaintance with the word of God. I did, indeed, many a time hear the Bible named, and even heard

Pestalozzi complain that nobody read it, and say that in his youth things had been better in this respect; at the domestic worship on Sundays, and during my confirmation instruction, I also frequently heard individual texts read and arbitrarily explained; but neither I nor any other of the young men obtained any idea of the sacredness and connection of God's word. Just as Pestalozzi, by the force of his personal character, attached most of his assistants to himself for years, so that they forgot themselves as he forgot himself, when good was to be done, so also, and much more, might he have inspired them for the Gospel, and the blessing of God would then have rested on him and them, and the institution would have become a christian seminary. It would not have been necessary on this account to hang out a sign-board with the words "Christian Educational Institution," displayed upon it; on the contrary, the more quietly and modestly Pestalozzi and his assistants had conducted themselves, the more effectively would they have worked, and even the most noisy blusterer would soon have come to perceive how very little he could be and do of himself, and thus would have become capable of learning something from strangers. Perhaps some person or other may be disposed to reproach me with one-sidedness, injustice, or even ingratitude, toward Pestalozzi, and to oppose to my testimony the fact that at Yverdun Pestalozzi employed every Friday morning principally in representing Jesus to us as the great exemplar of love and self sacrifice; or I may be asked whether I have quite forgotten the zeal with which Niederer often gave the confirmation instruction. But, in reply to this, I can only refer to the facts which I have just detailed."

I could add but little to this statement of Ramsauer. When I was in the institution, the religious instruction was given by Niederer, but no stranger was allowed to be present at it. We may form a tolerably correct notion, however, of the manner in which he gave it, from what is said on the subject in the "Report to the Parents."*

"All the elder pupils, (says the report,) receive positive religious instruction twice a week. The guiding thread that is used for this purpose is the course of the religious development of the human race, as described in the Holy Scriptures, from the Mosaic records downward, and, based on this, the pure doctrines of Jesus Christ, as he announced them in his Gospel. We base the teaching of moral duties chiefly on Christ's sermon on the mount, and the teaching of doctrines chiefly on St. John's Gospel. The latter is read connectedly and explained from itself and from Christ's eternal fundamental view of God and of himself, as the visible image and representative of the god-head and the god-like, of the relation of mankind to God, and of the life in God. We seek, by the example of Christ, and by the manner in which he viewed and treated men and things and their relations, to awaken in the children an intuitive leaning toward the life and conduct, the belief and hope, which are founded in the unchangeable nature of religion, and to render these things habitual to them, and by the development of those graces through which the Father shone in Him, to raise them to such a mind and mode of life, that God may shine in them also. We do not combat religious error, but endeavor to impart only religious truth. We seek the ground of all dogmas and the source of all religious views in the nature of religion, in the nature of man, and in his propensities, powers, wants, and relations, in order that the child may learn to distinguish the truth in every garb and the substance in every form. The course pursued for the attainment of the last-named object, or the elementary religious instruction, preparatory to the positive doctrines of revelation, is based specially on the solution of the following questions: 1. What is the original religious capability in human nature, or what are the elements of all religious development and education, in so far as they exist in man himself, and proceed from him as something implanted in him by God? These elements are perceptions and feelings. 2. By what means and in what manner must these primitive religious perceptions and feelings necessarily be excited and brought to consciousness in him? Here it is especially the relation to father and mother, to nature, and to society, that is

* There is no doubt that this passage is from Niederer's pen.

regarded as a means of religious excitation and education. 3. By what means and in what manner does man originally and necessarily express the religious perceptions and feelings excited in him? And to what does all this lead man? We find here principally the expression of the religious disposition as a gesture; the expression of the religious notion as a word; the expression of the religious contemplation as an image. The first develops itself as ceremony, the second as instruction and doctrine, the last as symbol and image-worship. With the course of this development is connected the development of what utters itself unchangeably in human nature as veritable and eternal religion, every where operative, and of what, as sensual degeneracy, errors of the passions, and personal depravity, leads to superstition and infidelity, to idolatry and image-worship, to hypocritical self-delusion and deception of others, and lastly, to the contemptuous rejection of all that is divine and sacred. The pupil finds the key to the clear comprehension of this in the intuitive consciousness of the awaking and course of his own feelings, in the impressions which things make on his own mind, and in the religious arrangements by which he is surrounded. As matter of fact, the whole is exemplified in the history of the religious culture of mankind. The indication thereof, or the thread to which the explanation must be attached, in giving the instruction, exists in the language of every nation. The most important results to be accomplished by the instruction are: That the pupil shall lay hold of the true and the eternal in their origin; that he shall look upon the human race as essentially religious, and as an organic whole, developing itself according to necessary and divine laws; that, understanding also in its origin and in its consequences the fall from God and the god-like, he shall all the more earnestly and faithfully follow the way of return to God and to the life in Him, so that, being thus prepared, he may comprehend the worship of God in spirit and in truth, the significance of the eternal Gospel; so that he may attain to an inward godly existence, as he lives outwardly in an intelligent existence."

I have quoted the whole of this passage, because it shows how far the religious instruction was removed from all believing fervor and childlike simplicity, from christian simplicity, as we meet with it in Luther's small catechism. But this passage characterizes only the religious instruction in the institution, and by no means Pestalozzi's religious views and practice.

Still it is clear that at Yverdun he also had in view much less moral education than intellectual. He wished, by means of the latter, to lay before the world striking results of the method; but how shall he show passing strangers the results of moral education, a humble mind and a loving heart, or shall he even expose them rudely to public gaze by an examination? To which was added, that in the multitude of boys he despaired of being able to take each one individually to his heart as a father would do, who never loves his children only *en masse*.

I now return to Pestalozzi's writings, and come to those which he wrote in his old age.

In several of his addresses to the inmates of his house, there are passages which bear witness that even during the years which he passed at Yverdun, christianity still lived in his inmost soul; peaceful Sabbath and festival tones soar above the restless and noisy week-day work. So in his Christmas address of 1810.

"I have been told by old people, (he said,) and I have partly seen myself, that Christmas Eve used to be a night like no other. The day of the highest earthly joy was not its shadow. The anniversary of the deliverance of the country from slavery, the anniversary of freedom, was not to be compared to it. It was quite a heavenly night, a night of heavenly joy. In its still service dedicated to God, resounded the words: 'Glory to God in the highest, and on earth peace, good will toward men.' When the angels still assembled, as it were, over the heads of men, at this hour, and praised God that the Saviour of the world was born,—what a night was Christmas Eve! Who can describe its joy? Who can tell its bliss? The earth was, on that night, transformed into a heaven. On that night, God was celebrated on high, peace was on earth, and men showed a cheerful good will. Brothers, friends, children, could I but carry you back into the old christian world, and show you the celebration of this hour in the days of innocence and faith, when half the world still accounted it a small thing to die for the faith in Christ Jesus! Could I but show you the joy of Christmas Eve in the picture of those days! The heart full of the Holy Ghost, and the hand full of human gifts—thus stood the christian at this hour in the circle of his brethren. Thus stood the mother in the circle of her children. Thus stood the master in the circle of his workmen—the gentleman in the circle of his own people. Thus stood the commune before their pastor—thus went the rich man into the chamber of the poor. At this hour, enemy held out to enemy the hand of reconciliation. The sinner knelt down and wept over his transgressions, and rejoiced in the Saviour, who forgave him his sins. The hour of heavenly joy was the hour of heavenly sanctification. The earth was a heavenly earth, and the abode of mortal men emitted odors of immortal life. May the joys of this hour, may the joy at the birth of our Redeemer, so elevate us, that Jesus Christ may now appear to us as the visible divine love, as he sacrificed himself and gave himself up to death for us. May we rejoice in the hour in which he became man, because he brought into the world for us the great gift of his life, and laid it upon the altar of divine love. From this hour, he was the priest of the Lord, sacrificed for us. Friends, brothers, sisters, let us pray; O God, give us them again, those fair days of the world, in which the human race truly rejoiced in the birth of Jesus Christ, the Redeemer. Give us again the times in which the hearts of men were at this hour, full of the Holy Ghost, and their hands full of human gifts for their brethren. Father in heaven, thou wilt give us them again, if we but truly desire them."

In the address already mentioned, which Pestalozzi delivered in 1818, when he was seventy-two years old, occur passages which make a profound impression on the mind. He there declares that happiness is to be expected from christianity alone.

"The artificial spirit of our times, (he says,) has also annihilated the influence which the religious feeling of our fathers exercised upon this centre of human happiness. This religious spirit which caused the happiness of the quiet and circumscribed domestic relations, has sunk down amongst us into an insolent spirit of reasoning upon all that is sacred and divine; still we must also acknowledge that the prime source of the real poison of our artificiality, namely, the irreligious feeling of the present age, seems to be shaken in the very depths of its destructive powers; the blessed spirit of the true christian doctrine appears to strike deeper root again in the midst of the corruption of our race, and to preserve inward purity of life in thousands and thousands of men, and, indeed, with regard to popular education, it is from this quarter alone that we can derive the expectation, that we shall ever attain to measures really calculated to reach with sufficient efficacy the views, dispositions, appetites, and habits of our present mode of life, which we must look upon as the original source of our popular depravity and the misfortunes of our times."

The conclusion of the address is particularly important:—

Friends, brothers, become renovators of my house, restorers of its old spirit, and witnesses that the spirit of my youth, which is seen blossoming in 'Leonard and Gertrude,' and nearer maturity in 'How Gertrude teaches her children,' still lives in me. In that spirit, become joint founders of the present result of the old original, philanthropic and beneficent purpose of my institution. In that spirit, and in no other, I call you all, who are members of my institution, to a sacred union in and through love. Love one another, as Jesus Christ loved us. 'Love suffereth long, and is kind; love envieth not; love vaunteth not itself, is not puffed up, doth not behave itself unseemly, seeketh not its own, is not easily provoked, thinketh no evil; rejoiceth not in iniquity, but rejoiceth in the truth; beareth all things, believeth all things, hopeth all things, endureth all things.' Friends, brothers, bless them that curse you, do good to them that hate you. Heap coals of fire on the heads of your enemies. Let not the sun go down upon your wrath. If thou bring thy gift to the altar, first be reconciled to thy brother, and then come and offer thy gift. All unrelenting severity, even toward those who do us wrong, be far from our house. Let all human severity be lost in the gentleness of our faith. Let no one among you attempt to excuse his severity toward those who are in the wrong. Let no one say that Jesus Christ did not love those who did wrong. He did love them. He loved them with divine love. He died for them. He came not to call the righteous, but sinners, to repentance. He did not find sinners faithful, but made them faithful. He did not find them humble, but made them humble, by his own humility. Verily, verily, it was with the high and holy service of his humility that he conquered the pride of sinners, and chained them by faith to the heart of his divine love. Friends, brothers, if we do this, if we love one another, as Jesus Christ loved us, we shall overcome all the obstacles which stand in the way of our life's purpose, and be able to ground the welfare of our institution upon the everlasting rock, on which God himself has built the welfare of the human race, through Jesus Christ. Amen."

At the grave, I have asked after Pestalozzi's confession of faith; I have sought it in his writings, as well as in his life, and communicated to the reader what he himself confessed in 1793 about his christianity at that period of his life, when, perhaps, he had separated himself furthest from Christ, and lived only in a speculative and political element. "Wavering, (so went the confession,) between feelings which drew me toward religion, and opinions which led me away from it, I went the dead way of my time." This confession we have found confirmed in his writings, as in his life; but in his earliest, and again in his latest writings, religious feeling has been seen soaring above a sceptical intellect. And throughout his long life how high soars a love which would not despair under any suffering, any ingratitude; how high it soars above all doubts, in the pure air of heaven! Men are seduced into infidelity by superficial reflection, which, misapprehending and over-estimating the measure of insight possible to man, fails to judge aright where a clear self-knowledge believes with intelligent resignation. But Christ, who takes the strong for his spoil, reigns ever in the inmost heart of christians as *episcopus in partibus infidelium;* even in times, when their faith wavers, he remains faithful to them. This we see in Pestalozzi, both in his words and in his works.

Who shall dare cast a stone at him, who shall dare condemn him? To him shall much be forgiven, for he loved much. Aye, the whole of his toilsome life is pervaded by love—by a yearning desire to alleviate the condition of the poor suffering people. That love was the passion of his heart; it kindled in him a burning anger against all who stood in the way of the attainment of its object.

It is true, that the chief obstacle in his way was himself. With God, counsel and action go together; with men, they are only too often separated. Thus we have seen that Pestalozzi, with the clearest knowledge of men, was incapable of managing and governing them; with the most amiable ideals, he was blind when he had to show the way to those ideals. Nay, in endeavoring to realize his great conceptions, he frequently took the course most opposed to them.

No one was further than he was from a cleanly domestic existence; yet no one desired such an existence more earnestly, or understood its value better, than he did. The delineations of Gertrude's housekeeping prove that a poet can truthfully depict not only what he possesses in full degree, but what he longs for with his whole heart because he lacks it altogether.

He passed the greater part of his life in pressing want: thus he could scarcely fail to feel a true and spontaneous sympathy with the poor and abandoned.

If he was cynical in evil days from necessity; in better days, he was so on principle. Corresponding to the bodily cynicism, there was in the character of his mind, something which I would call, not spiritual poverty, but intellectual cynicism: an aversion to the aristocracy of education. And yet, as one of the contradictions of which his character is full, he felt himself called to lay new foundations under the lofty structure of this education, instead of the old pernicious ones. He wanted to support the upper story of the building, without troubling himself about that story itself. On one occasion, he even made it the subject of a boast, that he had not read a book for thirty years.

Hence it came, as I have already said, that he committed so many mistakes usual with self-taught men. He wants the historical basis; things which others had discovered long before appear to him to be quite new when thought of by himself or any one of his teachers. He also torments himself to invent things which had been invented and brought to perfection long before, and might have been used by him, if he had only known of them. For example, how useful an acquaintaince with the excellent Werner's treatment of the mineralogical characters of rocks would have been to him, especially in the definition of the ideas, observations, naming, description, &c. As a self-taught man, he every day collected heaps of stones in his walks. If he had been under the discipline of the Freiberg school, the observation of a single stone would have profited him more, than large heaps of stones, laboriously brought together, could do, in the absence of any such division.

Self-taught men, I say, want the discipline of the school. It is not simply that, in the province of the intellectual, they often find only after long wanderings what they might easily have attained by a direct and beaten path; they want also the ethical discipline, which restrains us from running according to caprice after intellectual enjoyments, and wholesomely compels us to deny ourselves and follow the path indicated to us by the teacher.

Many, it is true, fear that the oracular instinct of the self-taught might suffer from the school. But, if the school is of the right sort, this instinct, if genuine, will be strengthened by it; deep-felt, dreamy, and passive presentiments are transfigured into sound, waking, and active observation.

This self-taught character of Pestalozzi's mind showed itself in his treatment of several branches of instruction. What are his names of towns, which he takes in alphabetical order from the index of a geography book, without possessing any knowledge of the subject; what are the heaps of words transcribed from Scheller's Lexicon: what else are they but the trials of an undisciplined mind, to find out new ways of writing schoolbooks?

But when the self-taught man forsakes the old highways, he finds, in spite of much going astray, many short by-ways, the knowledge of which is welcome to the students of the subject, and induces them to make new experiments themselves. In this manner, Pestalozzi exercised an influence even upon his adversaries.

Generally, Pestalozzi's personal influence on the methods of teaching particular subjects was small; but, on the other hand, he compelled the scholastic world to revise the whole of their task, to reflect on the nature and destiny of man, as also on the proper way of leading him from his youth toward that destiny. And this was done, not in the superficial rationalistic manner of Basedow* and his school, but so profoundly, that even a man like Fichte anticipated very great things from it.

But it is to be lamented, that the actual attempts made by Pesta-

Basedow founded an educational institution called the "Philanthropin," at Dessua, in 1774. In this institution, the educational views of Rousseau, as expounded in his "Emile," were exclusively followed, and every effort made to realize them. Rousseau was at that time the pharos of many educationists in Germany and Switzerland, as he was the pharos of the men of the revolution in France. The Philanthropin excited a good deal of attention at the time. The name of the Philanthropin still survives, but it has almost become a term of reproach to signify any shallow educational enterprise. It appears, however, that, together with much that was whimsical and even foolish, the institution presented many honest and unselfish efforts on the part of faithful workers, and produced many wholesome fruits.—*See Raumer's account of the Philanthropin.*

lozzi and his fellow-laborers to set up new methods of teaching various subjects, have met with such especial approbation and imitation. An examination of Pestalozzi's profound principles, and an insight into the contradiction between these principles and his practice, would have conduced much more to the discovery of new methods, really answering to the principles. This is appplicable, for instance, to what I have said upon the exercises in observation, falsely so called. Most of the imitators of the great man have fallen in love with his dark side, the endeavor to mechanise education. When those purely external appliances and artifices which he employed for mechanising education shall have been so modified as to be no longer recognizable, or shall have been entirely laid aside and forgotten—then Pestalozzi's "Leonard and Gertrude," the "Evening Hour of a Hermit," and "How Gertrude teaches her Children," will still live on and exercise an influence, though even these works, like every thing else that is human, are not altogether free from spot or blemish. Profound thoughts, born of a holy love under severe pains, they are thoughts of eternal life, and, like love, shall never cease.

APPENDIX.

PESTALOZZI'S HUNDREDTH BIRTHDAY.

LET a graduate of any good public school imagine a system of schools permitting indeed, though after a most laborious and imperfect fashion, for the wealthy and noble, large acquirements; but, for all those likely to attend what answer to our common or public schools, teaching only reading, and that alone, or at most with church singing, and memorizing of texts and hymns; reading all day, by one pupil at a time, from the droning A, B, C, up to whatever rhetoric was highest in grade; in that even shrill yell which was the elocutionary rule fifty years ago, without any possible regard to the meaning of what was read, or indeed of what was committed to memory; no arithmetic, no geography, no grammar, no writing, even. Let him imagine this single study taught in dens almost like prisons; by men absolutely ferocious in manners and feelings: who whipped a single scholar—as Martin Luther's master did him—fifteen times in one forenoon; who feruled, caned, boxed, slapped, rapped, and punched, right and left; made children kneel on peas and sharp edges of wood; in short, ransacked their own dull brains for ingenious tortures, and a language twice as copious as English, besides Latin and Greek, for nicknames and reproaches, to inflict upon the youth of their charge; schools to which parents threatened to send contumacious children, as if to the "Black Man," or any other hideous, unknown torment; schools almost precisely as destitute of any kindly feeling, of any humanizing tendency, of any moral or religious influence, as any old-fashioned Newgate or Bridewell. Let our graduate imagine, if he can, all this. Then let him further imagine a state of society stiffened, by ages of social fixity, into immovable grades, and where "the lower classes" were to be permitted this, reckoned their appropriate education, but no more. Let him still further imagine great and far-reaching political, social, and intellectual disturbances, working in powerful conjunction, upsetting all manner of laws, systems, distinctions, and doctrines, preparing all minds to hope for, and to admit, better beliefs, and better opportunities, for themselves and for others. And, lastly, let him imagine a man possessed of the vastest capacity for labor, a mind fruitful of expedients and experiments to the very highest degree, and no less clear and firm in finding and adhering to fundamental generalizations, an absolutely unbounded and tireless benevolence, a love for humanity and a faith in his principles little less perfect and self-sustaining than that of an apostle; who steps forth just in that period of intense receptive mental activity, and in the place of that diabolical ancient school system, proceeds not only to propose, but to demonstrate, and in spite of sufferings, obstacles, and failures enough to have discouraged an army of martyrs, effectually to establish a system, which not only, in the words of its official investigators in 1802, was "that true elementary method which has long been desired, but hitherto vainly sought; which prepares the child for every situation, for all arts and sciences; which is appropriate to all classes and conditions, and is the first indispensable foundation for human cultivation; which not only was thus intellectually the absolute ideal of education, but whose very atmosphere was one of kindness and encouragement, whose perfection was to depend upon its identity with the affectionate discipline of a mother; which expressly included, and even preferred, the poor, the orphan, and the helpless; and which, last and best of all, was fundamentally inwrought with such hygienic, ethical, and religious principles that its legitimate result would be to make a strong, and wise, and just man, upright among his fellows, mutually respecting and respected, and a trusting worshiper of God."

Let our graduate imagine this, and he may comprehend what the Germans think of Pestalozzi. The reverence and gratitude which they, in common indeed with all Europe, though in somewhat higher degree, entertain toward him, were well exemplified in the festival observed in Germany, Switzerland, and Holland, on the 12th of January, 1846, the hundredth anniversary of his birthday, and in the consequent proceedings; of which a brief account follows.

The conception of this celebration originated with that veteran and most useful educator, Dr. Adolph Diesterweg, then director of a seminary at Berlin. A mistake of a year, founded on dates given by good authorities, occasioned a partial celebration on the 12th of January, 1845. This, however, was made a means of wider notification and effort for the following year, and we translate the most characteristic portion of the call, which was signed by forty-eight eminent teachers and educators, including Diesterweg himself.

"His (Pestalozzi's) life and labors testify that no object lay nearer his heart than to secure for neglected children an education simple, natural, pure in morals, re-enforced by the influence of home and school, and adequate to the needs of their future life. A concurrence of untoward circumstances prevented the permanent success of such an orphan asylum, or poor school, though proposed and often attempted by him. For this reason the idea has occurred to various of his admirers and friends, in various places, of establishing such institutions, and one first to be called 'Pestalozzi Foundation.' The undersigned, having the permission of the authorities, have associated for the establishment of such an institution, to be a monument of the gratitude of the whole German fatherland toward that noble man. This call is intended to inform the public of this design, and to request active co-operation, and contributions in money.

"The Pestalozzi Foundation is intended to afford to poor children and orphans an education suitable to their circumstances, and in accordance with Pestalozzi's views for this purpose.

"1. The institutions founded will be situated in the country, where only, as the undersigned believe, can the education of orphans succeed.

"2. The pupils will, from the beginning, besides intellectual, moral, and religious education, be trained to domestic, agricultural, or industrial knowledge and capacities.

"3. The managers and matrons to whom the family education of the pupils will be confided, are to labor in the spirit of '*Leonard and Gertrude*,' and '*How Gertrude Teaches her Children*,' and the supervisors and officers of instruction will endeavor not only to put in practice the principles of the '*Idea of Elementary Training*,' but to develop and propagate them.

"* * * We thus appeal with confidence to all who feel themselves bound to gratitude toward Heinrich Pestalozzi; to all who feel for the children of the poor and for orphans; to all who expect beneficial consequences to home and school education from the revival and development of the spirit of Pestalozzi, which the undersigned believe to be the true spirit of education; we appeal, in short, to all friends of the people and of the fatherland, for efficient aid to this undertaking--at once a monument of gratitude to a great man, and an attempt to supply an urgent want of the present age.

"BERLIN, *January* 12, 1845."

A second appeal was put forth, July 3d of the same year, by Diesterweg, "to the teachers of Germany," eloquently setting forth their professional obligations to Pestalozzi, calling upon them for corresponding efforts in aid of the enterprise, and proceeded to refer again, in very pointed terms, to the characteristically charitable and thoroughly practical aspirations of Pestalozzi for the education of neglected children, and to the similar character of the proposed institution.

"It was his chiefest wish to dry the tears from the cheeks of orphans, and to educate them; he longed to be the father, the friend, the teacher of the unfortunate and the neglected.

"Do you, therefore, teacher of the common school, friend of the people, prove your gratitude to Heinrich Pestalozzi, by doing your part for the Pestalozzi Foundation—no monument of bronze or of stone; for none but a living monument is worthy of him—which shall stand, within the territory of Germany, a proof of the thankfulness of posterity, an everlasting blessing to children, to the cause of education, and human development."

The institution spoken of in these documents was intended to be a single central one, to be endowed by the contributions of all donors, and to be a model and parent for others throughout Germany; the sum requisite being computed at 30,000 thalers, about $22,500.

But although sympathy with the general purpose thus brought into notice was universal and lively, difficulties, apparently chiefly sectarian, soon arose, in regard to the special feature of a first central institution; and these resulted in the holding of many local festivals instead of one great one, and the organization of many local Pestalozzi Foundations, or Pestalozzi Societies, instead of one general one. Such festivals were observed, and institutions or societies established, at Berlin, Dresden, Leipzig, Frankfort, Erfurt, Basle, and many other places. We proceed to give some account of some of them, with extracts from the more significant portions of the numerous addresses, and other documents connected with them.

Dr. Diesterweg delivered, at Berlin, a characteristic and interesting discourse. In describing the revolution caused by Pestalozzi in the estimation of different studies, he said:—

"After the Reformation, that is, after the establishment of German common schools, studies were divided into two classes: one including the Bible, catechism, and hymn-book, the other including the so-called trivial studies. The former were for heaven—that is, to prepare for eternal happiness; the latter for earth, and its ordinary employments. The consequence of this universally-received distinction was, that the religious teachers asserted a dignity far higher than that of the "trivial" teachers. This notion is theoretically denied by Pestalozzi—at least by immediate logical conclusion, though I do not think he discussed the subject specially—and by his school. We have learned to comprehend the moral influence of instruction in itself, aside from any peculiar character in the subject taught; and, still further, the direct influence of all true instruction upon the development of the pupil's character. This influence does not depend upon the thing taught, but in the manner of teaching. As in Hegel's system of philosophy, so it is in elementary instruction—and should be in all instruction—its strength is in its method. This principle will naturally not be understood by eloquent word-teachers and lecturers from chairs of instruction; and last of all by those dictating machines and note-readers, who, to the disgrace of pedagogy and the shame of the whole age, exist even at the present day. But we, Pestalozzi's scholars and followers, comprehend it, have mastered it, and can demonstrate its results in our schools. What would Adam Ries, that pattern of all blind guides, say, if he could come to life again after three hundred years, and taking up an arithmetic*—which has become capable of use, as an intelligently arranged elementary study, only since Pestalozzi's time—should find in it a chapter " On the *moral influence* of instruction in arithmetic?"

He sums up the changes brought about by Pestalozzi, thus:—

"Instead of brutal, staring stupidity, close and tense attention; for dull and blockish eyes, cheerful and pleased looks; for crooked backs, the natural erectness of the figure; for dumbness or silence, joyous pleasure in speaking, and promptitude that even takes the word out of another's mouth; for excessive verbosity in the teacher, and consequent stupidity in the scholar, a dialogic or, at least, a dialogic-conversational method; for government by the stick, a reasonable and therefore a serious and strict discipline; for mere external doctrines and external discipline, a mental training, in which every doctrine is a discipline also;

* Grube's Arithmetic.

instead of a government by force, and a consequent fear of the school and its pedant, love of school and respect for the teacher."

He proceeds to suggest how far-reaching was the influence of Pestalozzi's labors in mere school-rooms :—

"But is the spirit of Pestalozzi not entitled to some part of the credit of the elevation of the German people? Did this remarkable change spring up in a night, and from nothing? It is, rather, to be wondered at, that the Pestalozzian method should have brought about such vast results without foreseeing them. It would be unreasonable to claim that this alone accomplished the wonder; but it was certainly not one of the least of its causes. Lord Brougham said that the twenty-six letters of the present schoolmaster—those 'black hussars'—were mightier than the bayonet of the soldier. Consider what a child must become, who is taught as we have described, for six or eight years or more. Consider what a nation must become, all the youth of which have enjoyed the influence of such an education. What a project does this idea open in the future! The Jesuits of Freiburg had a glimpse of it, though no more, when they said that they wanted no schools which should educate 'Apostles of Radicalism;' an expression shameful, not to Pestalozzi, but to the utterer of it."

Further on, he forcibly portrays the need and the requisites of such an institution as the intended Pestalozzi Foundation.

"The help we would afford is radical, is the only help. We consider all institutions worthy of praise and of assistance, which contribute to the amelioration of human suffering, the advancement of morals and good training. Therefore we speak well of other institutions having the same general design with ours: institutions for the care of children; orphan houses; rescue institutions for neglected children; associations for changing prisons into institutions of reform, and for the care of dismissed criminals and prisoners. But none of these go to the root of the matter; they do not correspond with the precise want; they do not go deep enough. Many of them almost seem to be organized to make sport of the laws of human nature and reason. What, for instance, according to those laws, can a child be expected to become, who has grown up with ignorant parents, from whom it can learn nothing but vices; who has learned from them to lie and to steal, to wander about and be a vagabond? In general, we answer, only a man who will misuse his physical and mental powers; that is, a criminal, a wild beast, dangerous to the welfare of society. That society, for self-preservation, shuts up such men, like wild beasts, in a cage; or punishes, or kills him; although, nine times out of ten, he became such because he must; as probably any one of us would have done! Is this proceeding reasonable? Do we succeed when we try to reform an old rogue? Or do you suppose that children, if they only attend the infant school, are under school discipline, and are confirmed, can be otherwise left in charge of abandoned parents, and not be contaminated by the pestilent atmosphere around them? Experience teaches, and it can not be otherwise, that the influence of father and mother, whether good or bad, is infinitely greater than that of infant schools, or any schools. Those who have managed reform institutions understand this best. The reason of the ill-success of such is, that they first begin too late; for they take the children after they have shown ineradicable marks of debasement. It is easy to protect an uncontaminated child from vice; but to restore to a contaminated one its pristine health and purity, is infinitely difficult, if not impossible.

"Our intention therefore is, to receive into the Pestalozzi Foundation children who can not be expected to be educated in their own homes; and those will naturally be preferred, who are destitute of a father or mother, and are without means. The existing orphan houses do not fulfill their purposes; and their organization does not usually answer the requirements of the Pestalozzian principles. We would establish model institutions for the education of neglected children, which shall observe natural laws, in which the child shall receive a family education. An education together with hundreds is—it must be said—barrack instruction. A child who is to become an adult, with human feelings, must have enjoyed the thorough and kindly care of the feminine nature and of an affectionate father. All true education is individual. Where the letter of the law prevails, where each child is managed by general rules, where it is only a number or a figure, which it must be in a school of hundreds, there is no human education, in any higher sense. A girl even, brought up among hundreds, is, so to speak, even when a child, a public girl."

Adverting afterward to the financial economy of such institutions, he observes that Adam Smith remarks, that "The support of the poor and of criminals costs £8,000,000 a year in England and Wales. If £2,000,000 of this were invested in education and good bringing up, at least one-half of the whole amount would be saved."

He then adverts, with some feeling, but conciliatingly, to the unexpected breaking up of the original plan of one central society and institution, by means of denominational jealousies; and gives a brief summary of the finances, &c., of the undertaking, as follows:—

"Twelve thousand copies of our call were sent throughout all parts of Germany. The sympathy exhibited is altogether encouraging and delightful. Some hundreds over 2,000 thalers ($1,500) are already collected;* the beginning of the harvest. The ministries of the interior and of religion have recognized and approved the labors of the society; his excellency Postmaster-General Von Nagler has granted the franking privilege for sending copies of the call, and for remittances; the school councilors of the various governments, and those authorities themselves, have assisted earnestly in sending the call; and the school inspectors have assisted in collecting. Many of them also, as, for instance, at Potsdam and Frankfort-on-the-Oder, have sent us orders for the pamphlets published by us on account of the Foundation. Princes have kindly aided the purposes of the society by contributions, and

* January 12. In March, the sum reached about 7,000 thalers.

many private persons also have given, some in one amount, and some in subscriptions during five years. But what has encouraged us most, is the universal sympathy of the body of teachers; both of common schools, and upward, even to the universities. What has a poor common school teacher, or a seminary pupil, to give? But they *do* give. I have received with warm thankfulness their gifts, from one *silbergroschen* upward. They give with poor hands, but warm hearts.

"From five or six different places we have received offers of land for a location, sometimes for nothing; from the Mark of Brandenburg, Silesia, Saxony, &c.; we hear favorable accounts from Dessau and Saxe-Meiningen; in short, we have good hopes that the plan of the Pestalozzi Foundation will succeed. The festivals, held almost every where to-day, will assist us; and we count with certainty on the aid of our own fellow-citizens. The undertaking is spoken well of by every one. Even noble ladies are enthusiastic for the good cause. Three sisters, whom the Genius of Poetry overshadows, (I am proud of being their fellow countryman,) propose to publish their compositions together for for the benefit of the Foundation. Some gentlemen have already done the like. From almost every locality in Germany, from Tilsit to Basle, from Pesth to Bremen, I have received encouraging and sympathizing letters. In Pesth, a society of teachers is collecting for the German Pestalozzi Foundation; contributions have come in from the Saxons in Transylvania; in Amsterdam and Gröningen, committees have been formed for the same purpose; we are expecting money from across the ocean. In Königsberg, delegates of the magistracy and city authorities have joined with the committee of teachers, the more worthily to celebrate the day."

Several pastors, teachers, and officials in the Canton of Aargau put forth a call for a Pestalozzi festival at Brugg, in that canton. To this there soon afterward appeared a reply, signed by a number of Reformed clergymen of the same canton, which may illustrate the character of the difficulties to which Diesterweg alludes. This reply states, in substance, that the signers of it had, several years before, set on foot a subscription for a similar purpose, (it may be remarked that the call itself recited that the government of Aargau resolved, as early as 1833, to erect an institution for the education of neglected poor children, as a memorial of Pestalozzi; which, however, financial considerations rendered it necessary to postpone;) that the proposed plan of operations was unfortunate, inasmuch as

1. The estate of Neuhof, formerly Pestalozzi's, intended to be bought as a site for the Foundation, was unsuitable and ill-placed for such a purpose, too large, and too expensive.

2. Ostentatious commemorations of donors were promised, by votive tablets, &c.

3. The intended scheme of training the pupils of the Foundation into teachers for similar institutions is not practicable, because it can not be determined whether they are capable or inclined to that employment,

which requires rare and lofty qualifications; and because experience shows that such teachers are to be trained, not in such schools for them, but in a course of actual employment under proper conditions.

4. Experience shows that such institutions should not be commenced on a large and expensive scale, but by means of single individuals, properly trained, to supply the place, to the pupils, of fathers, and to begin quietly, with a small number.

5. The proposed institution is to receive both Reformed and Catholic children; a plan which experience shows to be unlikely to succeed. And, if the principal be decidedly either Catholic or Reformed, children of the other communion will not be intrusted to him; and if he is not decidedly of either, then those of neither will.

These reasons are clearly and strongly stated, and seem to have much force.

At the festival at Basle, Rector Heussler gave some odd details of Pestalozzi's early life; among others, "He was so careless and absent-minded at school, that his teacher once remarked, shrugging his shoulders, 'Heinrich will never come to any thing;' and it is well-known that, afterward, when he was at the summit of his fame, his assistant, Krüsi, confessed that he (Pestalozzi,) could not either write or compute decently; and that a moderately difficult problem in multiplication, or division, was an impossibility to him at the age of fifty, and when the most eminent Swiss teacher! As little promising, at the first view, was his exterior; and on this account he declared, very naïvely, to his bride, that he, her bridegroom, was outwardly a most dirty man, as all the world knew; and that he presumed that this was not the first time she had heard so."

Longer or shorter accounts are given in the *Allgemeine Schul-Zeitung*, and other periodicals, of many other celebrations. They usually consisted of a meeting, at which addresses were delivered, poems recited, hymns or songs sung; sometimes followed by a dinner, with toasts, short speeches, and convivial enjoyment. There was also a practical part of the ceremony, viz., either a collection for the central society, or the organization of a local one.

We subjoin, (from the *Allg. Sch.-Zeitung*,) parts of a quaint article, entitled "*Considerations on the character most suitable for a memorial to Pestalozzi*," and signed "Frankf. O.—P.—A.—Z.," which contains much humor and good sense.

"But by what means is it proposed to fulfill this obligation (to Pestalozzi?) Many persons are preparing a banquet of the usual character, at so many *silbergroschen* a head, including half a quart of wine. Provision is made, also, for toasts, solemn and not solemn, long and short; and, if the landlords do their duty, the consequent sickness will have been slept off by next morning. These good folks do not obstruct the progress of enlightenment, but they are not *par excellence* strict disciples of Pestalozzi. In other places, the teachers, especially, are to be assembled, inasmuch as they claim Pestalozzi as exclusively one of themselves, though he was also a theologian and jurist. These gentlemen take no particular measures for overloading their stomachs—for reasons best known to themselves. On the other hand, they are laboring upon poems and orations, and will, perhaps, produce some which will possess much unction. But in order that their lights may not put each other out, and that the *imperium in imperio* may not perish, they assemble parish-wise, renewing the idea of the Holy Roman Empire, which was neither holy, Roman, nor an empire, and in which there were so many principalities that the State was invisible. Naturally, where there is a festival to every ten schoolmasters, the 12th of January will be long enough for a speech and toast from every one. On this occasion the speakers will rather look away from the present, and consider the future. Very right: this was with Pestalozzi's custom. But Pestalozzi kicked down with his feet what he built with his hands; beware that you do not do so. Pestalozzi often used his heart instead of his head, and reckoned without his host; see that you do not imitate him in this. Pestalozzi understood children's hearts, but not men's; and did not avoid the appearance of evil, if only it did not appear so to him; beware of following in his footsteps in this. A great Foundation is to be erected, worthy of the German nation; all German heads are to be brought together under one German hat, for the sake of founding, somewhere—perhaps on the Blocksberg—a rescue institution for morally endangered children. These certainly need to be protected, and Pestalozzi drew attention to the fact fifty years ago, and sacrificed his health and his means in the cause. But will one such institution serve, however large—or ten, or twenty, or a hundred—for the forty millions of German population? There are already thirty such institutions in Wirtemberg; and there are still many children there in urgent need of education and aid. But what will this rescue institution do? Even if it does not remain without a roof, like the Teutoburger Hermann without a sword; even if the builders finish up windows, cellars, and stairs properly; the chief requisite of a model institution is wanting—the father of the family. Shall he be found in Diesterweg's seminary at Berlin, or among Harnisch's pupils at Weissenfels? Is pictism, or illuminism, to be taught in it? The question is important to Germany, and Pestalozzis and Oberlins are scarce. One Louise Schepler would be worth abundantly more than a council of ten seminary directors. This seems not to have been considered; the building, and always the building, of the institution, is urged. There is no lack of model institutions. Not to cite Wirtemberg, there is the Rauhe Haus, at Hamburg—is a better one wanted?

"Again; are neglected children to be sent fifty miles, or more, by mail-route, with a policeman, to the model institution? Or, are distant donors to have nothing but a distant view of it? Must they make a long journey merely to get a sight of it? 'But,' it is said, 'all this will do no harm, if the occasion shall succeed in causing a union of the German teachers.' A union—a significant word! Where did as many as three

Germans ever unite, unless it were over a bottle? And still more, three German schoolmasters, each quite right in his own school! Unite? With whom? Against whom? Does not 'unite' mean 'exclude?' For if the teachers are to unite, they will separate from the clergy. Are all the teachers in Germany to dissolve their present relations, and array themselves under a pedagogical general, as if to make an attack on the ministers?"

The writer then attacks the plan of selecting teachers' orphans, in particular, and concludes with a forcible suggestion of the necessity of individual sacrifice and effort, as the only true mode of reforming or protecting unfortunate children.

"Spend no more time in building and in choosing heating apparatus, but take vigorous hold of the work itself. Let each one take a child, and say, 'He shall be mine. I will win him to myself with love, so that he shall prefer to follow me rather than his thievish father and godless mother. He shall stop cursing, because he loves me; and stealing, because I will teach him better. He shall enjoy learning, because he shall find in the school a retreat from his parents. I will not be deterred by dirt or ignorance, if I can only save a soul, and spare the world one criminal. I would rather make my house a rescue house for him, than to send him to a Rauhe Haus, among the morally neglected.'

"If the admirers of Pestalozzi—and I do not mean teachers alone—would adopt this method on the 12th of January, 1846, and form an association, then the day would be and remain a blessing to Germany. God grant it!"

PUBLICATIONS BY AND RELATING TO PESTALOZZI.

I. Works by Pestalozzi.*

1. Pestalozzi's Works, (*Werke*,) Tübingen, 1819–26. Cotta. 15 vols. These include:—
   - a. *Leonard and Gertrude*, (*Lienhard und Gertrud*,) vols. 1—4.
   - b. *How Gertrude teaches her children*, (*Wie Gertrud ihr Kinder lehrt*,) vol. 5.
   - c. *To the innocence, earnestness, and nobility of my fatherland*, (*An die Unschuld, den Ernst und den Edelmuth meines Vaterlandes*,) vol. 6.
   - d. *My researches upon the course of nature in the development of the human race*, (*Meine Nachforschungen über den Gang der Natur in der Entwicklung des Menschengeschlechts*,) vol. 7.
   - e. *On legislation and child-murder*, (*Ueber Gesetzgebung und Kindermord*,) vols. 7 and 8.
   - f. *On the idea of elementary education. An address delivered at Lenzburg*, 1809, (*Ueber die Idee der Elementarbildung. Eine Rede, gehalten in Lenzburg*,) vol. 8.

     ("In great part the work of Niederer."—*Biber*. It first appeared in the "*Weekly for Human Development*," [*Wochenschrift für Menschenbildung*.])
   - g. *Pestalozzi's letter to a friend upon his residence at Stanz*, (*Pestalozzi's Brief an einen Freund über seinen Aufenthalt in Stanz*,) vol. 9.

     (This first appeared in the "*Weekly*.")
   - h. *Views on industry, education, and politics*, (*Ansichten über Industrie, Erziehung und Politik*,) vol. 9.
   - i. *Address to my household, delivered Jan.* 12, 1818, (*Rede an mein Haus, gehalten den* 12 *Jänner*, 1818,) vol. 9.
   - k. *Figures to my A B C-Book*, (*Figuren zu meinem A B C-Buch*,) vol. 10.
   - l. *Views and experiences relative to the idea of elementary education*, (*Ansichten und Erfahrungen, die Idee der Elementarbildung betreffend*,) vol. 11.

     (This had before appeared under the name of "H. Pestalozzi's views, experiences, and means to secure a mode of education adapted to human nature." Leipzig, 1807.)
   - m. *On the principles and plan of a periodical, announced in the year* 1807, (*Ueber die Grundsätze und den Plan einer im Jahre* 1807 *angekündigten Zeitschrift*,) vol. 11.
   - n. *Report to parents and the public* on the condition and organization of Pestalozzi's institution in the year 1807, (*Bericht an die Eltern und an das Publicum über den Zustand und die Einrichtungen der Pestalozzischen Anstalt im Jahre* 1807,) vol. 11.

     (This had already appeared in the "*Weekly for Human Development*," but in the collective edition it was materially enlarged.)
   - o. *A word on the condition of my pedagogical enterprises*, and on the organization of my institution during the year 1820, (*Ein Wort über den Zustand meiner pädagogischen Bestrebungen und über die Organisation meiner Anstalt im Jahr* 1820,) vol. 11.
   - p. *A few discourses in my house in the years* 1808, 1809, 1810, 1811, and 1812, (*Einige Reden an mein Haus in den Jahren* 1808, &c.,) vol. 11.
   - q. *Christoph and Else*, vol. 12.
   - r. *Swan-song*, (*Pestalozzi's Schwanengesang*,) vol. 13.
   - s. *Theory of Number and Form*, (*Zahl und Formlehre*,) vol. 14.

---

* This list is taken from Raumer's "*History of Pedagogy*," vol. ii, p. 489.

t. *Theory of Form and Dimension*, (*Form und Grossenlehre*,) vol. 15.

u. *Address at Langenthal*, Apr., 16, 1826, (*Rede, den 26sten April* 1826, *in Langenthal gehalten*,) vol. 15.

Some important objections have been made to this edition; primarily, that it is imperfect.

2. WORKS OF PESTALOZZI not included in the collected edition of 1819–26.

a. *Agis, or Spartan legislation*, (*Agis, über die Spartanische Gesetzgebung*.) (Pestalozzi's first work.)

b. *Evening hour of a Hermit*, (*Die Abendstunde eines Einsiedlers*.)

(This first appeared in Iselin's "*Ephemerides*" for 1780, and was reprinted in the "*Weekly for Human Development*," in 1807.)

c. *A Swiss Gazette*, (*Ein Schweizer-Blatt*,) in two volumes, 1782 and 1783.

(Not being acquainted with this, I do not know whether Pestalozzi was sole editor or not. About 1798 he published another "*Swiss Popular Gazette*," under authorization from government.)

d. *Pestalozzi's elementary works*, (*Pestalozzi's Elementarbucher*,) especially the "*Book for Mothers*," (*Buch der Mutter*,) Tübingen, 1803. The "*Intuitional Theory of the Relations of Size*," (*Anschauungslehre der Massverhältnisse*,) and the "*Intuitional Theory of the Relations of Numbers*," (*Anschauungslehre der Zahlenverhältnisse*,) by Krüsi, are quite as important for Pestalozzi's works as the theories of Number, Form, and Size, by Schmid, in vols. 14 and 15.

e. *Views on Subjects to which the Helvetian Legislature ought specially to direct its attention*, (*Ansichten über die Gegenstände auf welche die Gesetzgebung Helvetiens ihr Augenmerk vorzuglich zu richten hat*,) Bern, 1802.

f. *The Fate of my Life*, as Principal of my Educational Institutions at Burgdorf and Yverdun, by Pestalozzi, (*Meine Lebensschicksale als Vorsteher meiner Erziehungs-institute in Burgdorf und Iferten*,) Leipzig, 1826.

g. *The Instruction of the Sitting-Room*, (*Die Kinderlehre der Wohnstube*.)

(Published in "*Rossel's Monthly*.")

h. *Weekly for Human Development*, (*Wochenschrift für Menschenbildung*,) 4 vols., 1807—1811.

(In this, as was stated, are found Pestalozzi's Letter on his residence at Stanz, the Report on the Institution at Yverdun, and the Lenzburg address.)

i. *Pestalozzi's Educational Enterprise*, as related to the culture of the age, (*Pestalozzi's Erziehungs-Unternehmung im Verhältniss zur Zeit-cultur*,) (by Niederer,) 1812.

(In this is a letter from Pestalozzi to Niederer.)

k. *Declaration against Canon Bremi's three dozen Newspaper Questions*, (*Erklärung gegen Herrn Chorherr Bremi's drey Dutzend Bürklische Zeitungsfragen*,) Yverdun, 1812.

3. WORKS OF PESTALOZZI—in part not included in the above list, or in a new arrangement.

1. *Paternal Instruction, in moral explanation of words*. A legacy from Father Pestalozzi to his pupils. (*Vaterlehren in sittlichen Wortdeuteungen. Ein Vermächtniss von Vater Pestalozzi au seine Zöglinge*.) Revised and collected by Herman Krüsi. Trogen, 1829.

(The MS. of this work was presented by Pestalozzi to Krüsi, who edited it with addition and alteration.)

2. *Letters on Early Education*. Addressed to J. P. Greaves, Esq., with a memoir of Pestalozzi. London, 1829.

3. *Pestalozzi's Life and Views*, in verbatim extracts from the complete works of Pestalozzi. (*Pestalozzi's Leben und Ansichten, in wortgetreuen Auszuge seiner gesammten Schriften*.) Published with reference to the festival of his hundredth birthday. By Roget Christoffel. Zurich, 1847.

(An excellent selection, affording probably the best general view accessible of the whole subject, and made on a principle which renders it reliable for reference. We give the Table of Contents.)

CHRISTOFFEL, R., "Pestalozzi's, Life and Views," (*Leben und Ansichten, in wortgetreuen Auszuge seiner gesammten Schriften.*) Znrcih, 1847.

PART I.

PESTALOZZI'S BIOGRAPHY, IN EXTRACTS FROM HIS OWN WRITINGS.

PART II.

VIEWS OF NATURE AND MEN.

PART III.

VIEWS ON EDUCATION AND INSTRUCTION.

I. EDUCATION.

PART IV.

CONTRIBUTIONS TO A SYSTEM OF PUBLIC INSTRUCTION, AND WORDS TO THE FATHER-LAND.

II. Works Respecting Pestalozzi and His Educational System.

Bandlin, J. H., Pestalozzi; his times, his fate, and his labors. A work for friends of human culture and promoters of a better future. (*Pestalozzi, seine Zeit, seine Schicksale, und sein Wirken, &c.*) Schaffhausen: Brodtman. 1843.

Biber, Edward, Contribution to the Biography of Heinrich Pestalozzi, 1827. (*Beitrag Zur Biographie H. Pestalozzi.*) 1827.

(An important collection of documents for our knowledge of the last fourteen years of Pestalozzi's life; but as to opinions relative to Pestalozzi, a *non plus ultra* of impiety and injustice.)

Blochmann, K. J., Heinrich Pestalozzi.—Sketches from the pictures of his life and labors; from his own testimony, from inspection, and information. (*H. Pestalozzi. Züge aus dem Bilde seines Lebens und Wirkens nach Selbstzeugnissen, Anschauungen und Mittheilungen.*) Leipzig. 1846.

Burkhart. Was Pestalozzi an infidel? (*War Pestalozzi ein Unglaubiger?*) Leipzig: Hartknoch. 1841.

Diesterweg, A. H., Pestalozzi.—An Address at the festival on his hundredth birthday, January 12th, 1846, delivered at Berlin by A Diesterweg. (*H. Pestalozzi. Rede bei der Männer-Feier seines hundertjährigen Geburtstages am 12 Januar* 1846, *zu Berlin gehalten von Adolph Diesterweg.*) Berlin. 1846.

Same. Pestalozzi.—A word on him and his immortal services to children and their parents, at the first centennial festival of his birth. By A. D. Third edition. (*H. Pestalozzi. Ein Wort über ihn und seine unsterblichen Verdiente, fur die Kinder und deren Eltern, zu dem ersten Säcularfeste seiner Geburt. Von A. D. Dritte Auflage.*) Berlin. 1845.

Diesterweg, Ratisch, and Massmann. Festival of the hundredth birthday of H. Pestalozzi, Berlin, January 12, 1845. (*Die Feier des 100sten Geburtstages Heinrich Pestalozzi's, in Berlin am* 12 *Januar* 1845.) Berlin. 1845.

Essays for and against Pestalozzi's System of Instruction. 1806. (*Aufsätze für und gegen die Pestalozzische Unterrichtsmethode.*)

Ewald, J. Ludwig, Lectures on the theory and art of education, for fathers, mothers, and educators. (*Vorlesungen über die Erziehungskunst für Väter, Mütter, und Erzieher.*) 3 vols. Manheim. 1808.

Gruner, Anton, Letters from Burgdorf on Pestalozzi, his method and his institution. Second edition, enlarged. (*Briefe aus Burgdorf über Pestalozzi, seine Methode und Anstalt. Zweite Auflage.*) Frankfort-on-the-Maine. 1806.

Henning, (of Cöslin.) Information on Pestalozzi's peculiarities, life, and educational institutions. (*Mittheilungen über H. Pestalozzi's Eigenthumlichkeit, Leben, und Erziehungs-Anstalten.*)

(In Harnisch's "*School Councilor on the Oder*," (*Schulrath an der Oder*,) Part I. 1814.)

Herbart. Pestalozzi's idea of the rudiments of instruction. (*Pestalozzi's Idee eines A B C des Anschauungs, von Herbart.*) Gottingen. 1804.

Heussler. Pestalozzi's results in education, (*Pestalozzi's Leistungen im Erziehungsfache.*) Basle. 1836.

Itho, Johann, Official Report on the Pestalozzi Institution. (*Amtlicher Bericht über die Pestalozzische Anstalt.*)

Kroger, J. C., Information on Pestalozzi and his methods of education. (*Mittheilungen über Pestalozzi und seine Erziehungs-Methode.*) Hamburg. 1846.

Krusi. Recollections of my pedagogical life, before, during, and since my connection with Pestalozzi. (*Erinnerungen aus meinen pädagogischen Leben und Wirken, &c.*) Stuttgardt: Cast. 1840.

Monnich, W. B., J. H. Pestalozzi, painted by himself and by others. (*J. H. Pestalozzi, nach ihm selbst und Andern geschildert.*)

In the "*Cotemporaries*," (*Zeitgenossen.*) Leipzig. 1813.

Niederer. Pestalozzi's educational undertakings, in their relation to the culture of the age. (*Pestalozzi's Erztiehungs-Unternehmung im Verhältnisse zur Zeitcultür.*) 1812.

Pestalozzi-Foundation. The German Pestalozzi-Foundation. First financial report, by Diesterweg and Kalisch. (*Die Deutsche Pestalozzi-Stiftung. Erster Rechenschafts-bericht, erstattet von Diesterweg und Kalisch.*) Berlin. 1847.

PLAMANN, J. E., Some fundamental rules of the art of instruction, after Pestalozzi's method, applied to natural history, geography, and language. (*Einzige Grundregel der Unterrichts-kunst nach Pestalozzi's Methode, angewandt in der Naturgeschichte, Geographie, und Sprache.*) Halle. 1805.

RAMSAUER. Short sketches of my pedagogical life. (*Kurze Skizze meines pädagogischen Lebens.*) Oldenburg. 1838.

RAUMER, K. von, History of pedagogy. (*Geschichte der Pädagogik.*) Vol. 2, pp. 287, 412.

Remarks against Pestalozzi's system of instruction. By Steinmüller, pastor. 1803.

W. VON TURK. Letters from München-Buchsee upon Pestalozzi and his method of elementary training. (*Briefe aus München-Buchsee über Pestalozzi und seine Elementar-Bildungsmethod.*) Leipzig, 1806. 2 vols.

FRENCH WORKS ON PESTALOZZI.

JULLIEN, MARC ANTOINE, Spirit of the method followed and practiced by Pestalozzi in the educational institution at Yverdun. (*Esprit de la methode de Pestalozzi, suivie et pratiquée dans l' institut d' education d' Yverdun.*) 2 vols. Milan. 1812.

PESTALOZZI. Manuel des mères. Traduit del' Allemand. Geneva and Paris. 1821.

ENGLISH WORKS RELATIVE TO PESTALOZZI.

BIBER, E, Henry Pestalozzi, and his plan of education; being an account of his life and writings; with copious extracts from his works, and extensive details illustrative of the practical parts of his method. London. 1831.

BLACKWOOD'S MAGAZINE. Pestalozzi's system. Vol. 66, p. 93.

EDINBURGH REVIEW. Pestalozzi's system. Vol. 47, p. 119.

GREAVES, J. P., Letters and extracts from MS. writings. Ham Common. Surrey. 1843.

HINTS TO PARENTS on the cultivation of children, in the spirit of Pestalozzi's method. London. 1827. (Six parts.)

PESTALOZZI. Letters on early education. Addressed to J. P. Greaves, Esq. Translated from the German. With a memoir of Pestalozzi. London. 1827.

PESTALOZZI. Leonard and Gertrude. Translated from the German. 2 vols., 12mo. London. 1825.

AMERICAN WORKS ON PESTALOZZI.

ACADEMICIAN. This educational monthly, edited by A. and J. W. Pickett, N. Y., 1818–19, contains a brief article on Pestalozzi's system, p. 214, No. 14; and a series of seven articles on the same subject, in Nos. 16–23; the first on p. 245.

ALCOTT, A. B., Pestalozzi's principles and methods of instruction. (*Article in American Journal of Education, Vol. IV., No. 2, March and April,* 1829, *p.* 97.)

ALCOTT, A. B., Review of "*Maternal Instruction,* &c. In the spirit of Pestalozzi." "*American Journal of Education,*" Vol. IV., No. 1, January and February, 1829, p. 53.

DIAL. Memoir of J. P. Greaves. October 1842, and January 1843.

LIVING AGE. Pestalozzi's system. Vol. XXII., p. 461.

MATERNAL INSTRUCTION, OR HINTS TO PARENTS. In the spirit of Pestalozzi's method. Salem, Mass. 1825.

MUSEUM. Memoir. Vol. XIII., p. 278, and Vol. XIX., p. 493.

RIPLEY, GEORGE, Memoir of Pestalozzi, in "*Christian Examiner.*" Vol. XI., p. 347.

UNITED STATES LITERARY GAZETTE. Pestalozzi's system. Vol. I., pp. 344, 372.

ASSISTANTS AND DISCIPLES OF PESTALOZZI.

CONTENTS.

PREFACE.

Pestalozzi's power, as a doer of good, was based upon his untiring energy and his impregnable benevolence and faith in human nature. His intellectual endowments, in the endeavor to develop into a complete system the principles which he felt so strongly, failed him, and he continually became obscure and contradictory. His method of instruction was as spontaneously and unpremeditatedly the result of instinct, as the benevolence which inspired him; but he was unable to state its principles philosophically, or to develop his methodology logically.

Thus he was obliged to rely, to a degree unusual for the leader of a great reform, upon assistants, even for the statement of his views, and the details of his modes of operation; and, accordingly, an account of himself, and of his labors, must, in order to be complete, contain an apparently excessive proportion of narrative relating to them.

In finding such assistants, Pestalozzi was remarkably fortunate. Niederer, Schmid, Krüsi, Buss, Tobler, and many more of the numerous teachers at Burgdorf and Yverdun, were all men of remarkable capacity, either for some one department of investigation and instruction, or for good qualities of mind and heart, which endeared them to Pestalozzi, each other, and the pupils; often for both. And still more remarkable than such endowments is the eminent and persevering self-denial with which some of them—as Niederer—giving up positions of comfort and influence, already secured, entered the ill-managed and disorderly institution, and remained there, year after year, sometimes with small salaries and sometimes with none, and not even always finding abundance of ordinary food, through evil report and good report, until absolutely convinced that their usefulness in it was ended. Nor was this all. With the single exception of Schmid, Pestalozzi's teachers resigned to him whatever of fame and profit might have come from the manuals they compiled in their respective studies, and the books were published either as by Pestalozzi himself, or as the productions of the institution. Accounts of these assistants will be found in the following pages; some of them reasonably complete, but some, owing to the scarcity of accessible materials, somewhat scanty.

The present work also contains short biographies of some of the more prominent of those who were instrumental in propagating Pestalozzi's views and methods in Germany. The introduction of his system into Germany constitutes the most remarkable chapter in the history of modern education.

Of this chapter, a portion, complete within itself, and both interesting and important, consists of the introduction of Pestalozzianism into the kingdom of Prussia.

During the subjugation of Germany under Napoleon, the minds of the best and ablest of the Prussian statesmen and philosophers were most eagerly occupied in inventing means which, if not available for an immediate struggle for independence, should at once begin the work of raising the moral, mental, and physical character of the nation to a standard of elevated development, which might insure such a struggle in future, and its success.

Among the instrumentalities used for this purpose, which, together, amounted almost to an entire reorganization of the kingdom, the improvement in education, resulting from the introduction of the Pestalozzian system—and still more of the spirit of that system—occupied a prominent place. To the King and Queen, to the ministry of education, to Fichte, in short, to the most influential public men of that day, Pestalozzi's views seemed to promise the happiest results; and, with a rare liberality and decision, measures were at once taken to prove them experimentally and thoroughly.

These measures were two: the employment of an able Pestalozzian in founding or reforming institutions already existing, and the sending to Yverdun young men of promise, to draw their inspiration, as teachers, from the fountain-head of the new method.

Carl August Zeller was chosen to perform the former task, and was, in the year 1809, invited from Wirtemberg, where he had been laboring zealously among the teachers to introduce the new method, to Königsberg, in East Prussia, on terms honorable to the government and to himself. He was received with enthusiasm, and set himself earnestly to work, lecturing, instructing, reorganizing, with untiring zeal, industry, and efficiency. Notwithstanding a few errors of judgment, his labors gave a great and lasting impulse to education in that portion of Prussia; and one at least of the institutions he founded, at Karalene (*i. e.*, Livonian for "Queen,") in the government of Gumbinnen, is yet useful as an orphan-house and teachers' seminary.

The second measure taken by government was the sending of young men to be educated as teachers in the Pestalozzian principles. Those selected were mostly chosen from among the most promising of the theological students. Two, Marias Schmid and Dr. Harnisch,* were sent to Plamann's institution, at Berlin; the remaining ones, Henning, Dreist, Kawerau, Krätz, Rendschmidt, Preuss, Patzig, Braun, Steger, Marsch, Ksionzek, the brothers Bernhard, and four already teachers by profession, Hänel, Titze, Runge, and Baltrusch, were sent to Yverdun at various times during a series of years, their expenses being paid by government. Upon their return, they were employed in various institutions for the training of teachers, most of them with success. Thus a large body of

* Wilhelm Harnisch, the well-known educator, from whose "*Present Condition of the Prussian Common School System*," (Leipzig, 1844,) much of the information in this article is derived.

competent instructors in the new method was, in a comparatively short time, scattered among the Prussian schools; the spirit of the Pestalozzian method satisfied the needs of the age; and, with the powerful twofold aid of popular favor and the earnest influence of the whole power of the government, it speedily took possession of the entire common school system. Every where, the authorities co-operated zealously with the teachers under the new methods. Queen Louise, and under her influence the King, took so deep an interest in the reform, that they often visited the schools where it was introduced. The Queen, especially, often remained in them for hours; caused reports to be made to her on the progress of the schools generally; and was judicious and liberal in encouraging and rewarding instructors and educators.

While these measures effectually inaugurated the new system, a share of the credit of it is due to those teachers and school officers who, though not themselves trained under Pestalozzi, and not always accepting his methods of instruction, in every particular, yet entered fully into his spirit, and labored in union with his more immediate disciples, with a zeal and efficiency, perhaps, rather increased than decreased by the free development of the individualities of their various views. Indeed, one of the most valuable features of what may be called the Prussian-Pestalozzian system, was its deliberate and careful but free advance toward such improvements upon the system of Pestalozzi himself; a proceeding which has secured the highest excellence of the original system, has added to it much that is valuable, has insured that vivid and interested activity in the teachers which is the first requisite of successful instruction, and has prevented the decay and deadness into which servile followers of exclusive rules must necessarily fall.

The praises thus bestowed upon the Prussian common schools, as thus reformed, reflect no blame upon those teachers and conductors who neglected, or even opposed, the new methods. The principal among these were followers of Basedow and the Philanthropists; institutions of this class were the Schnepfenthal Institution, and the Hartung School, and the Real School, at Berlin; and among the men were Nolte, Zerrenner, and Dinter.*

The introduction of the Pestalozzian system into the schools of Prussia, may be said to have been in progress from 1812 to 1825; at the end of which time it had, substantially, possession of the whole common school system. Dr. Harnisch enumerates, as among the chief advantages resulting from it, 1. Patriotic feeling, causing more thorough study of the German language, home geography, &c.; 2. Giving a high value and place to vocal music, as a study; 3. The same of drawing, especially under the teachings of Peter Schmid; 4. Introduction of thorough musical instruction; 5. Introduction, or readoption of thorough system of bodily training.

* However strongly Dinter may have professed to hold on to the old ways, no avowed Pestalozzian ever labored more devotedly in the spirit, and with the aims and methods of Pestalozzi, as our readers will see in the memoir, p. 231.

From Prussia the principles and practice of the school of Pestalozzi were widely diffused in other countries, through travelers, often coming exclusively for the purpose of investigating the Prussian system, and sometimes sent by foreign governments for the purpose. Dr. Harnisch gives a long list of names of visitors to a single seminary only, mostly of persons eminent in education, among which are mentioned those of Hon. Horace Mann, and Profs. Stowe and Bache, from the United States.

The present occasion does not admit of any extended reference to the further spread of Pestalozzianism. We can only say that prominent among those who transferred the system into France, was Victor Cousin, whose able report is well known; and Chevalier Jullien, who, at an earlier date, drew up an extended report upon the school of Yverdun, and the educational principles and methods of Pestalozzi. The labors of Dr. Biber, Mr. Greaves, and at a later date of Dr. Mayo and Miss Mayo, and of Sir James Kay Shuttleworth, M. Tilleard, and Mr. Tait, have done much to spread the system in England. And among its advocates and propagators in America were William Russell, editor of the "*American Journal of Education;*" Warren Colburn, whose celebrated arithmetics are strictly Pestalozzian; A. Bronson Alcott; W. C. Woodbridge, the geographer and editor of the "*Annals;*" and Lowell Mason, the veteran and efficient instructor in vocal music.

It should be added, that the present work does not contain sketches of those who applied Pestalozzi's principles to reformatory schools proper, charitable schools, &c., for the reason that the accounts of those persons are contained in the editor's volume on REFORMATORY EDUCATION.*

* Papers on Prevention, Correctional, and Reformatory Institutions and Agencies for Juvenile Delinquency. New York, F. C. BROWNELL, 1859, 360 pages.

JOHANNES NIEDERER.

Johannes Niederer, whose reputation as a teacher is nearly connected with that of Pestalozzi, and stands high amongst those of his fellow-laborers, was born in 1778, in Appenzell. Having completed his studies, he was already settled as pastor when the fame of Pestalozzi's plans and labors reached him, and set his whole soul in motion. Unlike those who can not soon enough shake the dust of the school from their feet to seat themselves in the pulpit, Niederer resigned his pastorate in 1800, and hastened to connect himself with Pestalozzi. In the institution of the latter, he had special charge of the religious instruction. His manner in giving this, and in his whole labors as a teacher, is so well described by his efficient fellow-laborer, Krüsi, in his recent "*Recollections of my pedagogical life and work*," (*Erinnerungen aus meinem pädagogischen Leben und Wirken*,) p. 39, that we shall make an extract: Krüsi says, "To be present at the religious instruction of Niederer, and at his confirmations, was sure to have a good influence upon the heart. Good preparatory instruction in intellect and language was necessary, in order to appreciate it, it is true; but this was to be enjoyed in the institution. Although he soon passed over the history of creation, the gospel of John, and the sermon on the mount, yet the instruction he derived from these sources as to the faith, had a complete character, and afforded deep views of the essence of religion and of the scope of human duty. I several times attended the whole course; and how highly I valued the privilege may be inferred from the fact that I forthwith sent three of my children to attend, that they might learn from him the happiness of religion. Niederer filled an important part in Pestalozzi's institution and history. He earnestly devoted his time and strength to the subjects of religion, language, literature, and philosophy. He first studied Pestalozzi's works, in their various applications to pedagogy, politics, legislation, &c., not resting until he had ascertained the central point from which they all radiate; for to consider them only in their separate character, was insufficient for him as a thinker and investigator. But he did not limit his labors to writings and thinking only, nor even to the numerous studies successfully pursued in the institution, and the labors to be pursued in various directions, and amongst various materials, with reference to those studies; but embraced, in the scope of his inquiries, the nature, existence, powers, and weaknesses of man; his course of development, his future fate and destiny, in the individual, the nation, and the race.

Niederer possessed the fullest confidence of Pestalozzi, who consulted him on all occasions, and saved himself by his means from many mistakes. Niederer opposed himself to any views or efforts within the institution which threatened to break up or hamper its usefulness, and was variously active in contending against them.

In literature, Niederer has been less active than was to be wished from a man so rich in endowments and experience. Besides a series of small treatises, we have only one larger work: "*Pestalozzi's educational enterprise in its relations to cotemporary civilization,*" (*Pestalozzi's Erziehungsunternehmung im Verhältniss zur Zeitcultur,*) Stuttgart, 1812, 2 vols. The wish was often, and with good reason, expressed, that he would publish a scientific exposition of pedagogy on Pestalozzi's principles. A biography of the great teacher himself, from his pen, would have been gratefully received. Still more welcome, had it pleased him to write it, would have been an account of his method of religious instruction; especially now, when so many are endeavoring to fix that most important of all departments of instruction upon a half-ascertained psychological basis, and to entangle it with religious parties. He however died, in 1843, without having performed this work.

Niederer's wife, previously Rosette Kasthofer, of Berlin, where she was born, 3rd November, 1779, conducted for a long time the girls' school established by Pestalozzi at Yverdun, along with his boys' school. The institution was, however, transferred to Geneva, where it is now established. Madame Niederer has also established, in connection with it, a seminary for young women intending to become teachers; and in both she is yet laboring, with youthful freshness and enthusiasm. In 1828, was published a valuable work by her: "*Glances at the system of female education. For educated mothers and daughters,*" (*Blicke in das Wesen der weiblichen Erziehung. Für gebildete Mütter und Töchter.*) Berlin: Rücker. She has also published "*Dramatic Games for the Young,*" (*Dramatische Jugendspiele.*) Aarau, 1838, 2 vols.

We find the following estimate of Niederer, by Pestalozzi, expressed at different times.

"The mode in which Niederer looks at my work can not be separated from that in which I myself see it. His views are almost all the results of his reflections. I scarcely know what it is to reflect. My opinions and views are almost all the results of immediate intuition and of excited feelings. Moreover, I did not understand his language; but his Vindication taught me to understand it. I could not satisfy myself with reading that production. I found myself, in it, almost in every line, more clearly and distinctly stated, and more profoundly comprehended, than I had comprehended and expressed myself, on systems of education, on maternal instinct, on the nature and organization of schools, on my institution, in short, on all the principles and views which were in point at the time."—*Fortunes of My Life.*

"He has, at the same time, peculiarities which I often endure only with difficulty, since they are diametrically opposed to mine. But his friendship surpasses all the friendship that I have enjoyed or even dreamed of in my life. What more can a man do for a friend, than for his sake to give up a certain, quiet, and agreeable mode of living, and to put himself into a condition uncertain, unpleasant, oppressive, and in many respects dangerous? This Niederer has done. For my sake he gave up the pastorate where he was living, efficient, respected, and happy, joined himself to me and my poverty, threw himself into all my embarrassments, at a period when my work was not yet ripe in itself, and when I was almost wholly deprived of all external aid and co-operation in it. At that time he was the only man of any degree of literary cultivation who took a place at my side, and took part in all the perils to which my undertaking could and did expose him. And his friendship extended beyond me personally, and to the purpose of my life, in regard to which I so often saw myself deserted. He is drawn toward me personally as little as I toward him. I might say that, in this respect, we were not as near each other as is to be expected from men living so near; but his life is a friendship: his endurance and perseverance for my objects—even the contest which he continually keeps up with himself and with me, for the promotion of the purpose of my life—even his opposition to and arguments against me individually, when he finds himself in conflict with my designs—show the noble, remarkable, and pure character of his friendship. If he withstood me less, he would love me less."—*Declaration Against Canon Bremi's Questions*, p. 28.

"As early as at the begininng of our association in Burgdorf, there came amongst us a young clergyman, of thorough education, full of fire, power, and quiet though strong efficiency, and observed in silence the course of our labors. In this first stage of his design, he resembled nothing less than one seeking a predominant influence upon the general and practical course of our undertaking. On the contrary, his whole conduct indicated, at the beginning, very clearly, that he was investigating the psychological basis of the principles and essence of our idea of elementary training, more seriously, broadly, and

deeply than any one before him, by means of a free, individualized, and independent reflection upon them. By this course he very soon elaborated a system of his own, as to our idea of elementary training, which, it is true, was not made inwardly complete and outwardly applicable by any basis whatever of practical experience, but which inspired him with such a visionary enthusiasm for its infallibility and applicableness, that all at once he suddenly began to take an active and powerful part in the whole extent of our operations; so as gradually to acquire a universal and predominating influence over them, and to gain my own confidence to a high degree. His singular character inspired him with the definite design of opposing the weaknesses, faults, and defects of my establishment, by means of scientific expositions of the idea which lay at the base of our undertakings. He believed confidently that, by the magic touch of his lucid ideas, or frequently even by significant words, he could prevent the increase of that fatal influence whose greatness he deeply felt; and that, by verbal elucidations, he could control what he could not lead intellectually by the weight of his influence, nor practically manage, and could least of all carry forward by his creative energy by actual executive measures. Niederer's requirement of absolute acquiescence in his views, arose from ideas which he had not made clear and definite to himself in their whole extent and connection; for he was prone to lose himself in metaphysical expositions of his ideas, which he was neither fitted to do by possessing a solid substratum of intuitional knowledge, nor competent to express in any manner by simple, clear, and intelligible language, and thus to make properly comprehensible. Most of the objects he sought and urged were, to us, mere atmospheric phenomena, without any connection whatever with the basis of our actual life. He was, throughout, unfitted and almost incapable of giving the slightest practical demonstration of his high-sounding ideas. This he knew himself; and often required with earnestness that others should not only receive, as he did, what he had constructed in his ideal manner, but also that they should work them out in actual practice to his satisfaction, and that without requiring much co-operation from him."
—*Fortunes of My Life*, p. 29.

KARL CHRISTIAN WILHELM VON TÜRK

Karl Christian Wilhelm von Turk, was born at Meiningen, January 8, 1774. He was the youngest son of Chamber-president and High Marshal von Türk, who was of a noble Courland family, and in the service of the duke of Saxe-Meiningen. At his mother's death, when a boy of six years old, he was transferred to the family of his mother's brother, Grand Huntsman von Bibra, at Hildburghausen, where he was brought up with his cousins under a strict tutor. At seventeen and a quarter years old, without having attended any public school, he entered the University of Jena, where he found in his elder brother Ludwig, who had already been studying there a year and a half, a true friend and a pattern of industry and good conduct; and where he contracted a close friendship with several cotemporaries, amongst whom were T. von Hardenberg, known as a poet under the name of Novalis, and von Bassewitz, afterward Chief President and his own official superior.

After completing his legal studies, in 1793, he offered himself for an office under government in Meiningen, which had been promised him while his father was Chamber-president and his brother a government official, notwithstanding the strictness of the examination. What, however, his knowledge and capacity did not enable him to attain, he secured by means of a very ordinary social talent. During a visit in Hildburghausen, the Prince, then Duke Karl of Mecklenburg, father of Queen Louise of Prussia, found that he was a skillful ombre-player; and he took so strong a liking to him that afterward, upon receiving the principality by the unexpected death of his brother, he determined to fix him within his dominions. Accordingly, in the very next year, 1794, he appointed von Türk chancery auditor, and two years later, chamberlain and chancery councilor. In 1800, his official senior von Kamptz, afterward well known as Prussian minister, was appointed to a public station in Mecklenburg, and von Türk was appointed in his stead to take the oversight of the school system, with his judicial employments. The inquiries which his new place suggested to him drew his attention in such directions that he became gradually estranged from the occupations to which he had been earlier devoted.

In 1804, von Türk took a furlough for six months, visited various schools, and made the acquaintance especially, of Olivier, Tillich and Pöhlmann, then distinguished teachers of the day. In the same year, he remained during some months, at Pestalozzi's institution at München-Buchsee, and made himself acquainted with his views, and with J. Schmid's system for geometry and mathematics. He published the results of his stay with Pestalozzi, in his "*Letters from München-Buchsee*" (Leipzig, 1808); one of the most practical and useful accounts of Pestalozzi's method.

After his return to Mecklenburg, he could not resist his impulse to become a teacher. He gathered together a troop of boys, instructed them two hours daily and made teachers acquainted with Pestalozzi's method. During his educational journeys he had become acquainted with the prince of Oldenburg, and at the end of 1805, he was appointed to a lucrative office as Justice and Consistory Councilor in Oldenburg, with an annual salary of fourteen hundred thalers, (about $1050.)

In his new place he experienced the same impulse to exertion as a teacher and educator. Here also he gathered a troop of boys whom he instructed two hours a day; and he received into his house a number of young people, and gave them a complete education. These operations however did not meet the approval of the duke, who intimated a wish that he should devote himself wholly to the duties of his judicial station, and refused his request to be employed wholly in educational matters. This, together with the condition of Oldenburg (then threatened by the French,) which caused him much pecuniary difficulty, decided him to resign his place in Oldenburg and to give himself up entirely to the business of education.

In 1808, with some pupils, sons of a Bremen merchant, he went to Pestalozzi at Yverdun, and for some time instructed in that institution. His work, "Perception by the Senses," (*Die Sinnlichen Wahrnehmungen*,) is a fruit of his labors at that time in Pestalozzi's institution. But the situation of affairs there was unfavorable, and an increasing difference soon grew up between him and Pestalozzi. This decided von Türk to leave him and to establish an educational institution of his own at the castle of Vevay on the lake of Geneva. Here he lived amongst a small circle of children, but happily progressing in knowledge under his love and zeal. The financial results did not, however, answer his expectations, and he finally in 1814 transferred the care of the school to Latour de Peilz, at his castle not far from Vevay. Having offered his services to the Prussian monarchy, he was in 1815 appointed royal and school councilor at Frankfort on the Oder.

The course of instruction which he gave here in September of 1816 upon Pestalozzi's method, to nearly sixty clergymen and teachers, had upon many, who perhaps, then heard of Pestalozzi for the first time, an influence which did not remain fruitless. His efforts to improve the instruction in arithmetic, resulted in his publication of his "*Guide to Instruction in Arithmetic*," which is yet one of the best books of its class. Its fifth edition appeared in 1830. After Natorp's return to his native country in 1817, von Türk was appointed School Councilor in Potsdam, in which station he labored actively for sixteen years, but resigned it in 1833 to devote his whole time and powers to the benevolent institutions which he had founded.

These are (not including the Swimming Institution at Potsdam and the Association for the improvement of silk-raising,) the following:

1. The *Fund for School Teachers' Widows*, *a.* at Sorau, *b.* for the district of Frankfort, to which he has devoted the profits of his work on Arithmetic; and *c.* for the district of Potsdam.

In the district of Frankfort it has since been found better to establish, instead of one widow's society for the whole government, to establish a fund in each synod; an arrangement which has in most cases been entirely successful. In the case of the fund for the district of Potsdam, the plainest conclusions of experience were unfortunately so much overlooked, that after a few years the allowances, which are raised only from taxation, were materially reduced; the consequence of which has lately been many complaints.

2. The *Peace Society of Potsdam*, founded at the Reformation Festival in 1818; a society for the support of talented but poor young men, who are devoted to the arts or sciences. More than a hundred such have been supported by the society. Further information about this society, and its statutes, may be found in Guts-Muth's "New Library of Pedagogy."

3. The *Civil Orphan House*—a twin child, as von Türk calls it, in which about thirty orphan boys are supported. The original fund of this institution was raised from the sale of a collection of paintings belonging to von Türk. It received an express royal sanction in a cabinet order dated 21st February, 1825. Up to 1841, thirty-six young men had received their education in this establishment.

4. The *Fund for the Education and Support of Orphan Girls;* an institution which originated together with the Civil Orphan House, and which is managed in the same way. Up to 1841, twenty orphan girls had been supported by it.

5. The *Orphan House at Klein-Glienicke* near Potsdam, for the orphan children of artizans, elementary teachers and the lower grades of public officers.

It may not be uninteresting to describe the precise circumstances which led to the foundation of the Klein-Glienicke house. Von Türk heard that the Crown Prince was desirous of buying the hunting seat known as Klein-Glienicke, then occupied as a factory, in order to improve it into the counterpart of Prince Carl's adjacent beautiful estate in Glienicke. Von Türk accordingly quietly bought it, and offered it to the Crown Prince at the cost price, but received the answer that he would not be able to make use of the offer. Under these circumstances von Türk applied to his tried friend, Chief President von Bassewitz, and by his mediation gained permission to resign his hasty bargain at a small loss. He, however, made no use of the permission, but told his friend that he would retain the property, and found there another orphan house, to serve as a sort of supplement to the Civil Orphan House, which was intended for the sons of persons of rather higher rank. In fact he laid his plans before some of the higher authorities, but the means which he could show for the establishment of his intended institution were so small that permission was refused him. But promises of support gradually came in, and the heads of several departments, especially Postmaster-general von Nagler and the Ministers of Justice and of Finance declaring in its favor, on account of an arrangement to establish endowed places in it for orphans of their departments, the institution was finally set in operation. The plans for it were remodeled more than once, and more than one reckoning of the funds made; but at last, an association being formed which purchased the real estate from von Türk, and there were thus secured sufficient means to open the establishment for those at least for whom endowed places had been promised. Von Türk never lost his faith in ultimate success, though the funds still remained deficient. It happened that the disposition of some funds from a war-indemnity, not accepted by those entitled to them, were intrusted to the disposal of his chief, von Bassewitz, who, with the consent of the families of these proprietors, appropriated three thousand thalers (about $2,250,) from this source to the new Orphan House. Thus all difficulties were obviated. The association met, completed the purchase of Klein-Glienicke, leased it to von Türk, who was now able to proceed with the completion of his institution; and had the pleasure of seeing it flourish under his eyes.

In a letter of the present year, (1846,) relating to Klein-Glienicke, von Türk writes, "Here, the favorite idea of my teacher and master, Pestalozzi, is realized; education, combined with agriculture and gardening. My scholars now number about thirty. I have bout two hundred Magdeburg *morgen*, (the morgen is about fivethirteenths of an acre,) of tilled land, from sixteen to twenty *morgen* of garden and nurseries, twenty-four *morgen* of meadows, and a dairy which accommodates twenty cows and five horses, besides sufficient room for the silk-making, except that the latter is not comfortably accommodated in winter. I feel great interest in encouraging the establishment of similar institutions. What has been possible for me, without financial resources and in spite of the many prejudices with which I have had to contend, (for example, I have been a government official; and our burghers and laboring classes do not love the government officials; and I have had the little prefix 'von' before my name,) must be possible elsewhere under more favorable circumstances."

6. *Soup Distribution Institution for the Old, Sick, Feeble, and Poor, and Lying-in-Women.* By the day-book of the institution, 96.908 portions of soup were distributed in 1845. This was received by six hundred and fifty-one families, including four hundred and forty-one married persons, four hundred and thirty-eight widows and single persons, and thirteen hundred and forty children; in all two thousand two hundred and nineteen persons. The cost of one portion of soup was about 3⅛ pfennig, (about three-fifths of a cent.)

For some years von Türk had been complaining of the decay of his bodily strength and of his memory, when, in 1845, while he was in Berlin, a dangerous sickness seized him, from which he has never entirely recovered. He died July 31, 1846. His wife, two children and adopted daughter were by his side, and his last hours were peaceful and without pain. His memory will long endure.

On the 25th of the April before his departure from the world in which he had labored so nobly and benevolently, a letter, not without interest in this connection, from which a portion follows. To the request that he would communicate an autobiography for Hergang's Encyclopædia, he replies that he is unable. "My autobiography," he says, "lies ready written in my desk, but I propose to publish it for the benefit of the Teachers' orphans. I have established here an orphan house, especially intended for the orphans of teachers; but their numbers and necessities in the province of Brandenburg, for which the institution is founded, are so great, that I am obliged to refuse many applications; and thus I am contriving the means for assisting a larger number." "The motives which have impelled me to the establishment of the institutions which I have commenced, and the manner and means by which, without means of my own, and without the gift of eloquence, I have been able to accomplish these designs, will be related in my biography, that others, more richly endowed, may learn how to do the like." "I am in my seventy-third year, on the borders of the grave, in body much broken, but peaceful and happy in mind, and in all my efforts for the improvement and elevation of my fellow-citizens, having enjoyed a success far beyond my hopes." "At Easter I dismissed from the Civil Orphan House, a pupil, son of a country clergyman, who is now studying theology in Berlin. Several of my scholars are already laboring as preachers, judges, physicians, public officials, carpenters, architects, teachers and officers." How happy must we reckon thee, excellent man, who, while still living, hast experienced such intellectual and heartfelt pleasure! Thy works follow thee into eternity; their memory shall even give thee ever increasing pleasure, and many, happy through thy means, shall bring thee thanks.

Noble and venerable as von Türk was, he was yet attacked by the arrows of wicked calumny. On this point we shall only relate the following:

Bishop Eylert relates in his character of Frederic William III., (vol. 2,) that von Türk was suspected by that monarch of being an unprincipled demagogue. Von Türk was living amongst the common people, as his inborn and profound preference made it happiest for him to live, and laboring for their good by his writings and in his official station, according to his irresistible vocation; and some persons had concluded that to be doing this without apparent interested motives, and without remuneration for the necessary sacrifices of labor, means and time, was enough to stamp von Türk a dangerous demagogue. Bishop Eylert, who was a friend of von Türk, undertook to remove this impression from the king's mind. Having argued the case, the king said, "I am glad to have my former opinion corrected, and to be able to entertain a good opinion of one who has certainly been accused to me." At the next festival of the order, von Türk received the red order of nobility; the king immediately interested himself in the Civil Orphan House at Potsdam, and for the institution at Klein-Glienicke, where he endowed additional scholarships, made presents to the orphans, and continued to von Türk, at his resignation of his place as royal and school councilor, in order to devote himself wholly to his institutions, the whole amount of his salary as pension.

HERMANN KRÜSI.

Hermann Krusi was born March 12th, 1775, at Gais, in the canton of Appenzell. Of his parents he writes in his "Recollections," "they are entitled to the praise of having passed through life in quiet goodness and fear of God, and were careful to give their children a good education." After the good old fashion, they often read in the family Bible, and entered in its blank leaves the birth of each of their children, together with some pious prayer or saying. They also amused themselves, especially on Sundays, by singing from the then popular "Bachofen." Of learning they could of course give their poor children but very little, and what they afterward acquired in school was but little more. His earliest recollections was of a fire which laid the village of Gais in ashes; of which he thus speaks:—

It is natural that the first recollections of the mind should be of uncommon and striking events, such as make a profound impression upon one's whole being, and leave an indelible mark upon the character. This was the case with myself.

On the 7th of September, 1780, a violent south wind blew; bad weather for the weavers, but good for drying turf. "I will go to the turf-ground and turn and dry the turf," said my father; "there is nothing to do in the weaving-room." He took me with him that day for the first time to the turf-pits, which were a good four miles from the village. At half past eleven he heard the sound of a bell. "It can not be striking noon yet," he thought, looking at his work—"Ah God," he cried, "it is the alarm bell;" and we heard the cry of fire! fire! from all sides.

With this fragment, unfortunately, ends the account. The fact of the fire is well known. Notwithstanding his youth, our subject remembered many occurrences of that occasion; especially the next Sunday's service under the open sky. There was very general emotion, which, at the rather remarkable choice of the hymn, "As by the streams of Babylon we sat," &c., broke out into such loud lamentations that the singing could not proceed. These recollections may well have been terrible to the boy, although his father's house was spared by the flames. But a severer stroke came upon him, when his father, in the prime of his manhood, was suddenly snatched away by death from his numerous family. He had always supported his own household, and had taught them according to his ability; and it is difficult to tell what would have become of them, had not Krüsi, then in his fourteenth year, undertaken to perform his father's laborious duties of village errand-man and weaver; a service for which the consciousness that he was the trust and stay of an orphaned family gave him strength. Upon his solitary errands to St. Gall, and elsewhere, he used to recite to himself the instruction and counsel which his father had given.

Krüsi might have passed his whole life in his father's monotonous calling, had not a benign Providence given him an indication which had the most important consequences for his entire future. We shall permit Krüsi himself to tell the story, in the words of his own "Recollections," pp. 2–4, which give other and deeper views into his mind at that time:—

At the highest point of the pass, where the road turns away from toward Trogen, my life also took another direction. While earning my living as day laborer and errand-man, I was carrying, one cold day in 1793, to the establishment of Zellweger, with which I afterward came into very different relations, a great bundle of yarn from the mountain. As I stopped to rest, all dripping with sweat, at the very summit, a relative met me, who was then treasurer of the town, one Herr Gruber. After the usual greetings, the following conversation ensued, which I yet remember as the turning point of my life.

Gruber.—"It is warm."

Myself.—"Very warm."

Gruber.—"Now that schoolmaster Hörler is going away from Gais, you have a chance to earn your bread a little more easily. Have you no desire to offer yourself for his place!"

Myself.—"Wishing will not help me much. A schoolmaster must have knowledge; and I have none."

Gruber.—"What a schoolmaster among us needs to know, you at your age can very soon learn."

Myself.—"But how, and where? I see no possibility of it."

Gruber.—"If you wish it, the means will be easily found. Consider the matter and decide upon it."

He left me. I now had abundance of matter for reflection. But no ray of light came into my mind, although the natural sunlight surrounded my body with brightness and warmth. I scarcely felt my load as I proceeded along the ascents and steeps of the road. Whatever has fallen to my lot since that moment, I look upon as the fruit of this conversation.

Since my leaving the day school, where I had learned and practiced only reading, learning by rote, and mechanical copying, and while I was growing up to adult age, I had so far forgotten to write, that I no longer knew how to make all the capital letters; my friend Sonderegger therefore procured me a copy from a teacher in Altstätten, well known as a writing-master. This single copy I wrote over as often as a hundred times, for the sake of improving my handwriting. I had no other special preparation for the profession; but, notwithstanding, I ventured, when the notice was given from the pulpit, to offer myself as a candidate for the place, with but small hopes of obtaining it, but consoling myself with the thought that at least I should come off without shame.

The day of examination came. An elder fellow-candidate was first called before the committee. To read a chapter in the New Testament and to write a few lines, occupied him a full quarter of an hour. My turn now came. The genealogical register, from Adam to Abraham, from the first book of Chronicles, was given me to read. After this, chairman Schläpfer gave me an uncut quill, with the direction to write a few lines. "What shall I write?" I said. "Write the Lord's Prayer, or whatever you like," was the answer. As I had no knowledge of composition or spelling, it may be imagined how my writing looked. However, I was told to retire. After a short consultation, I was, to my wonder and pride, recalled into the room. Here chairman Schläpfer informed me that the whole committee were of opinion that both candidates knew little; that the other was best in reading, and I in writing.

The other, however, being over forty years old, and I only eighteen, they had come to the conclusion that I should learn what was necessary sooner than he, and as moreover my dwelling-house (the commune had then no school-house of their own) was better adapted for a school-house than his, I should receive the appointment. I was dismissed with friendly advice, and encouraging hopes of increased pay, if my exertions should be satisfactory.

Much attention was excited by the fact that my fellow-candidate, eight days afterward, took a situation as policeman, in which he received three *gulden* a week, while the schoolmaster, who was obliged to furnish his own school-room, had to satisfy himself with two and a half.

Krüsi, becoming schoolmaster at the age of scarcely eighteen, was destined to bear a responsibility almost greater than that which he had so lately laid down. This will easily be understood when it is known that, with his small knowledge of school matters, he had to manage and teach more than one hundred scholars, of various ages and both sexes, in the small school-room. In this situation many would have labored only for their money, as is unfortunately the case at this day even with better instructed teachers; but Krüsi's conduct in this respect may serve as a model. As soon as he had adopted this profession, it was his most earnest effort to live worthily of it, and to fit himself for it in the best possible way; a work in which pastor Schiess, his parish minister, materially assisted him, both with advice and help. Within a few years his school had the reputation of being the best in the canton; and he had the pleasure on Easter Monday of seeing his scholars take the six highest numbers in writing—a study on which the utmost value is placed. Krüsi had been laboring in his vocation now for six years, with zeal and faithfulness, when Providence destined him for another field of labor which he could not have foreseen, and which places the modest man in a situation to exert a wide influence upon the whole school system of our native land. The storm of the French Revolution broke out. In the year 1799, foreign armies swept across the plains of our fatherland, and encountered each other in murderous conflict; even the mountains and high alpine valleys did not escape from the bloody game. Poverty, hunger, and lack of occupation were especially severe in the eastern part of Switzerland; many parents could not maintain their children. Sympathy awoke in the hearts of the nobler men in the less severely pressed portions of the country; and from many sides there flowed in liberal gifts, often accompanied with the offer to receive and bring up needy children. Such an invitation came to pastor Steinmuller from his friend Fischer, in Burgdorf, who was then intrusted with the reorganization of the Swiss schools. The wish was at the same time expressed that he would also send a teacher of the requisite capacity and character for receiving a training as teacher and educator, and for undertaking the care of the children then in Burgdorf with certain benevolent families. Upon the communication of this invitation to Krüsi, he made no delay; an inner voice urged him not to let pass this opportunity for obtaining a further education. Twenty-six children of both sexes assembled for the expedition. Krüsi, as leader of the troop, was provided with twenty-four thalers for the journey, thirty leagues. Pastor Steinmuller, and bailiff Heim, of the district gave him a testimonial, which we may insert here as a noteworthy trait of the condition of the times:—

FREEDOM! EQUALITY! To all municipal authorities to whom these presents shall come. Citizen schoolmaster Hermann Krüsi is traveling hence from the canton Säntis to the canton Bern, with twenty-six poor children, whom he is taking to Burgdorf, where sympathizing benefactors will support and care for them for a time. It is my earnest and hopeful request to all municipalities, and especially to their citizen presidents, that they will kindly afford all needful help to the above named children and to their leader, sent forward by my means as above; that they will, as far as possible, kindly provide for them rest and refreshment at noon, and lodging at night, without pay. For such benevolent assistance, may the Lord bless you.

Thus asks and wishes
Gais, January 20, 1800. JOH. RUD. STEINMULLER, *Pastor.*

I join in the above request to all citizen presidents and citizen members of municipalities of all communes and districts, to which these needy children shall come, on their way hence to Burgdorf; and am fully convinced that all benevolent persons will, without further recommendation, assist the poor caravan to reach its destination as easily and successfully as possible.
The provincial under-bailiff of the circle of Teufen,

SAMUEL HEIM.

Of the journey itself we need only remark briefly that Krüsi, with his troop, was everywhere received in a friendly manner; and in many places they were entertained gratis, and even received gifts of money. His "Recollections" give an account of this. It deserves to be mentioned, as remarkable enough to remind us of the widow's cruse of oil, that, at Krüsi's arrival at Burgdorf, he was in possession not only of the twenty-four thalers with which he had set out, but of fifteen *gulden* besides; of which he retained the latter, but sent the former back to the authorities of Gais.

From Fischer, at Burgdorf, Krüsi received a most friendly welcome, and commenced his school. The former, however, soon after died, and Krüsi would have been left quite alone again, had not Providence pointed out to him a new path, by means of the appearance of a man whom he followed with entire confidence.

This was Pestalozzi, whose labors at his estate of Neuhof, and in Stanz, are among the noblest facts of history. It was when already of adult age that Pestalozzi, with warm enthusiasm and profound love, had conceived the idea of becoming an educator and teacher of the poorer classes, then deeply degraded both in intellect and morals; and giving to education in general a more natural direction. After Fischer's death, he therefore invited Krüsi to form a connection with himself, and with him to conduct the school which he had established in the castle of the place. This school, which Pestalozzi had at first commenced only with little children, was soon changed into an educational institution of a higher grade, which, by means of the entirely new direction of its operations, met with great success. Joy and pride must have filled Pestalozzi's breast, as he soon saw, one after another, young and talented men—Tobler from Wolfhalden, previously a tutor in Basle, Buss from Tübingen, Niederer from Lutzenberg, previously a pastor in Sennwald—full of enthusiasm, leaving each his sphere of labor and resorting to him as trustful disciples to a master who yet could reward them with no earthly treasure except a treasure of rich experience and of deep knowledge of the human heart.

The assemblage of these three Appenzellers will remain remarkable for all time. Each of them developed his own side of the Pestalozzian idea; and they were for a long time the ornament and strength of the institution; and, after subsequent successful labors in independent spheres of occupation, they all died within the same year. Krüsi's letters during this period to his early friend Kern, who is yet alive, and who lived in close personal relations with him for nearly forty years, are also of value to the student of human nature. What he wrote of Tobler, "he possesses my entire respect and love, for I recognize in him uncommon talent as a teacher, and goodness of heart," proved entirely true. Tobler had with enthusiasm taken up particularly the idea of Pestalozzi's "Lienhard and Gertrude;" that of replacing mothers in the position originally designed for them, of educators and instructors for early childhood. Seldom has any man labored with as benevolent and unostentatious a desire for the good of his fellow-men as he, although he was often rewarded by misunderstanding and ingratitude.

Niederer, also, besides immoveable integrity and warm feelings, possessed a far-seeing keenness of understanding, which had already appeared in his correspondence with Tobler, and which at a later period was displayed in the development of the method with so much power and breadth that even Pestalozzi himself had sometimes to yield to the clearness and thoroughness of his views.

It is astonishing to see with what uniformity these men, assembled from different directions, followed their new path. This was truly a power from on high. What else could have enabled the former errand-boy and village schoolmaster, Krüsi, to say in his letters to his friend, even before Tobler and Niederer came to Burgdorf,—

"In short, the enterprise advances. The seed of a better education, one more adapted to human nature, is already sown. It will bear fruit which as yet no man, not even its discoverer, the noble Pestalozzi himself, is expecting."

The self-denying spirit and lofty views with which Pestalozzi's assistants at this early period were imbued, is powerfully shown by the fact that Krüsi and Buss, being allowed a salary of about $125 a year each from the Helvetic government, appropriated the whole to the support of the institution, receiving from it only board and lodging.

We will here introduce Pestalozzi's own account of Krüsi's previous labors. It affords a valuable view of his character and gifts as a teacher, as well as hints of the general methods of teaching in those days, and of the power with which Pestalozzi's ideas, even in their then undigested and obscure condition, seized upon the minds of ignorant but earnest and unprejudiced men:—

Krüsi, the first of the three, whose acquaintance I made, had past his youth in a different kind of employment, whence he had acquired that variety of practical abilities, which, in the lower stations of life, so frequently gives the first impulse to a higher degree of development, and by which men, who have been in this school from their earliest childhood, are enabled to become more generally and extensively useful.

In his twelfth and thirteenth years, his father, who carried on a petty traffic, used to send him, with a small capital, amounting to about six or eight pounds sterling, for the purchase of different kinds of merchandise, to a distance of ten to twelve miles; to this employment he joined the trade of a sort of public messenger, carrying letters and executing various orders for the people of his village. When he grew older, he filled up his leisure days by weaving, or other daily labor. At the age of eighteen, he undertook the office of village schoolmaster at Gais,* his native place, without any kind of preparation. He says himself that he did not know the signs of punctuation, even by name; ulterior knowledge was out of the question, because he never had any other instruction than that of a common village school, which was entirely confined to reading, writing copies, and learning by rote the catechism, &c.; but he was fond of children, and he entertained the hope that, by means of this post, he should be enabled to gain for himself that knowledge and education, the want of which he had felt very oppressively, even in his expeditions as village messenger; for, being commissioned to buy a variety of articles, of artificial preparation, and of strange names which he had never heard in his life before, such as ammoniac, borax, and so on; and being at the same time placed in a responsible situation, in which he had to remember every, even the most trifling order, and to account for every farthing; he could not but be struck with the idea, what an advantage it would be, if every child could, by school instruction, be brought to that degree of ability in reading, writing, ciphering, in all sorts of mental exercises, and in the art of speaking itself, which he felt he ought to be possessed of, even for the discharge of his miserable post as village messenger.

Even so soon as the first week, the number of his scholars exceeded one hundred. But he was by no means competent to the task he had undertaken,

---

* A village, or, rather, a cluster of hamlets on the highest and most airy part of the canton Appenzell, celebrated as a place of resort for persons of consumptive habits, on account of its excellent milk, of which, however, the patients take only the whey.

for he knew not how to give proper employment to all these children, what to teach them, or by what means to keep them in order. All the notions he had hitherto acquired about keeping school were confined to the "setting" of spelling and reading lessons, to be "got by heart;" to the "saying" of the same lessons by turns, followed by the chastisement of the rod if the task was not properly got. From the experience of his own boyhood, however, he knew likewise that, with this mode of "keeping school," the greater part of the children are idling away most of the school-hours, and by idleness are led to a variety of follies and immoralities; that in this manner the time which is most available for education is allowed to pass by without any benefit to them, and that the few advantages which they may derive from their instruction are not even sufficient to counterbalance the ill effects which must necessarily result from such "school-keeping."

Pastor Schiess, the minister of the place, who was very actively combating the old routine, assisted him in his school, during the first eight weeks. From the very beginning they divided the scholars into three classes. With this division, and the use of some spelling and reading-books on an improved plan, which had recently been introduced in the school, they succeeded in making a number of children spell and read together, and thus keeping them generally occupied to a far greater extent than had been possible before.

The new reading-book, that had been introduced by the minister, contained religious truths in short paragraphs, and in biblical sentences; various facts of physical science, natural history, and geography, were concisely stated, and information was given on interesting points of the political constitution of the country. Krüsi observed his pastor, when he read it with the children, putting some questions at the end of each paragraph, in order to see whether they actually understood what they had read. Krüsi tried to do the same thing, and succeeded in making most of the scholars perfectly familiar with the contents of the reading-book. But this was only because, like good old Huebner,* he adapted his questions to the answers which were to be found, ready made, in the book, and because he neither demanded nor expected any other answer, except literally those which the book had put into the children's mouths, long before any question was devised to elicit them. The true reason of his success was, that there was a complete absence of all mental exercise in this his system of catechisation. It is, however, to be observed, that that mode of instruction which originally was termed catechisation, is, no more than Krüsi's system of questioning, an exercise of the mind; it is a mere analysis of words, relieving the child, as far as words are concerned, from the confusion of a whole sentence, the different parts of which are presented to the mind separately and distinctly; it can, therefore, only have merit when used as a preparatory step to the further exercise of clearing up the ideas represented by those words. This latter exercise, commonly termed Socratic instruction, has only of late been mixed up with the business of catechising, which was originally confined to religious subjects exclusively.

The children thus catechised by Krüsi were held up by the minister as examples to his elder catechumens. Afterward it was required of Krüsi, that he should, after the fashion of those times, combine this narrow analysis of words, called catechising, with the Socratic manner, which takes up the subject in a higher sense. But an uncultivated and superficial mind does not dive into those depths from which Socrates derived spirit and truth; and it was, therefore, quite natural that, in his new system of questioning, Krüsi should not succeed. He had no internal basis for his questions, nor had the children any for their answers. They had no language for things which they knew not, and no books which furnished them with a well-framed answer to every question, whether they understood it or not.

Krüsi, however, had not then that clear insight into the nature of those two methods which might have enabled him to apprehend their difference. He had not yet learned that mere catechising, especially if it runs upon abstract terms, leads to no more than the art of separating words and handling analytical forms; but that, in itself, it is nothing but a parrot-like repetition of sounds without understanding: nor was he aware that Socratic questions are not to be addressed

* "Good old Huebner" is the author of a Scripture history in German, to which are attached sets of "useful questions and answers," such as our readers may find in many a "good new" manual of our "enlightened and improved systems."

to children, such as his pupils at Gais, who were equally destitute of the internal fund, that is, of real knowledge,—and of the external means, that is, of language wherein to convey that knowledge. The failure of his attempt rendered him unjust to himself; he thought the fault lay entirely with himself, imagining that every good schoolmaster must be able, by his questions, to elicit from the children correct and precise answers on all manner of moral and religious subjects.

We have already noticed the circumstances which brought Krüsi to Burgdorf.

The more he labored with Fischer the higher seemed to him the mountain which lay in his way, and the less did he feel in himself of that power which he saw would be necessary to reach its summit. However, during the very first days after his arrival, Krüsi was present at some of the conversations I had with Fischer on the subject of popular education, when I expressed my decided disapprobation of the Socratic manner of our young candidates, adding, that it was not my wish to bring children to a premature judgment, on any subject, but that my endeavor was rather to check their judgment, until the children should have an opportunity of viewing the subject from all sides, and under a variety of circumstances, and until they should be perfectly familiar with the words expressive of its nature and its qualities. Krüsi was struck with these remarks; he felt it was there that his own deficiency lay; he found that he himself stood in need of that same elementary instruction which I designed for my children.

Fischer exerted himself with all his power to introduce Krüsi to different departments of science, that he might be able afterward to teach them. But Krüsi felt every day more that the way of books was not the one for him to make progress in, because on every subject he was destitute of that preliminary knowledge of things and their names, which, to a greater or lesser extent, books presuppose. On the other hand, he witnessed the effect which I produced upon my children, by leading them back to the first elements of human knowledge, and by dwelling on these elements with unwearied patience; and the result of his observation tended to confirm him in the notions he had formed concerning the causes of his own inability. Thus by degrees his whole view of instruction underwent a great change, and he began in his own mind to place it on a different foundation. He now perceived clearly the tendency of my experiments, which was to develop the internal power of the child rather than to produce those results which, nevertheless, were produced as the necessary consequences of my proceedings; and seeing the application of this principle to the development of different faculties by different branches of instruction, he came to the conviction that the effect of my method was to lay in the child a foundation of knowledge and further progress, such as it would be impossible to obtain by any other.

Fischer's death accelerated the union between Pestalozzi and Krüsi, which had been contemplated by the latter almost from the first moment of his acquaintance with his paternal friend. The following account of the view which he took of Pestalozzi's plan, after he had for some time enjoyed the advantage of practical co-operation with him, is, notwithstanding its great deficiencies, an interesting testimony in favor of the experiment, in the course of which these ideas urged themselves upon an evidently unprejudiced mind.

1. A well-arranged nomenclature, indelibly impressed upon the mind, is to serve as a general foundation, on the ground of which both teacher and children may, subsequently, develop clear and distinct ideas on every branch of knowledge, by a gradual but well-secured progress from the first elements.

2. Exercises concerning lines, angles, curves, &c., (such as I began to introduce at that time,) are calculated to give children such a distinctness and precision in the perception of objects, as will enable them to form a clear notion of whatever falls within the sphere of their observation.

3. The mode of beginning arithmetical instruction by means of real objects, or at least strokes and dots, representing the different numbers, gives great precision

and certainty in the elements, and secures the further progress of the child against error and confusion.

4. The sentences, descriptive of the acts of walking, standing, lying, sitting, &c., which I gave the children to learn, led Krüsi to perceive the connection between the beginnings of my instruction and the purpose at which I was aiming, viz., to produce a general clearness in the mind on all subjects. He soon felt, that if children are made to describe in this manner things which are so clear to them that experience can not render them any clearer, they must thereby be checked in the presumption of describing things of which they have no knowledge; and, at the same time, they must acquire the power of describing whatever they do know, to a degree which will enable them to give consistent, definite, concise, and comprehensive descriptions of whatever falls within reach of their observation.

5. A few words which I dropped on one occasion, on the tendency of my method to abate prejudice, struck him very forcibly. Speaking of the manifold exertions, and the tedious arguments, by which prejudices are generally combated, I observed that these means had about as much power to counteract them as the ringing of the bells had to disperse thunder-storms,* but that the only true safeguard against the influences of prejudice was a conviction of the truth, founded upon self-observation. For truth, so acquired, is in its very nature an impediment to the reception of prejudice and error in the mind; so much so, that if men thus taught are made acquainted with the existence of prevailing false notions by the never-ceasing cant of society, there is not in their minds any ground for that ignoble seed to rest on, or to grow up in, and the effect must therefore be very different from what it proves to be in the common-place men of our age, who have both truth and error thrust into their imagination, not by intuition and observation, but by the mere charm of words, as it were by a magic lantern.

When reflecting upon these remarks, he came to the conviction, that the silence with which, in my plan of instruction, errors and prejudice were passed over, was likely to prove more effectual in counteracting them than all the endless verbiage which he had hitherto seen employed for that purpose.

6. In consequence of our gathering plants during the summer, and of the conversations to which this gave rise, he was brought to the conviction that the whole round of knowledge, to the acquisition of which our senses are instrumental, depended on an attentive observation of nature, and on a careful collection and preservation of whatever she presents to our thirst of knowledge.

These were the views on the ground of which he conceived the possibility of establishing such a method of instruction as he felt was most needed; viz., one which would cause all the branches of knowledge to bear upon one another, with such coherence and consistency as would require, on the part of the master, nothing but a knowledge of the mode of applying it, and, with that knowledge, would enable him to obtain, not only for his children but even for himself, all that is considered to be the object of instruction. That is to say, he saw that, with this method, positive learning might be dispensed with, and that nothing was wanted but sound common sense, and practicable ability in teaching, in order not only to lead the minds of children to the acquirement of solid information, but likewise to bring parents and teachers to a satisfactory degree of independence and unfettered mental activity concerning those branches of knowledge, in which they would submit themselves to the course prescribed by the method.

During his six years' experience as village schoolmaster, a considerable number of children, of all ages, had passed through his hands; but with all the pains he took, he had never seen the faculties of the children developed to the degree to which they were carried by my plan; nor had he ever witnessed in them such an extent and solidity of knowledge, precision of thought, and independence of feeling.

He inquired into the causes of the difference between his school and mine.

He found, in the first instance, that, even at the earliest period of instruction, a certain feeling of energy was not so much produced,—for it exists in every mind not enervated by artificial treatment, as an evidence of innate power,—as kept alive in consequence of my beginning at the very easiest task, and exercising

* It is a superstitious practice, kept up to this day in many parts of Switzerland and Germany, to ring the church-bells at the approach of a thunder-storm, under the impression that the sacred toll will effectually remove the danger.

it to a point of practical perfection before I proceeded; which, again, was not done in an incoherent manner, but by a gradual and almost insensible addition to what the child had already acquired.

With this method, he used to say, you need not push on children, you have only to lead them. Formerly, whatever he wanted to teach, he was obliged to introduce by some such phrase as this: "Pray, do think, if you please!" "Can't you remember, now?"

It could not be otherwise. If, for instance, in arithmetic, he asked, "How many times seven are there in sixty-three?" the child had no palpable basis on which to rest his inquiry for the answer, and was, therefore, unable to solve the question, otherwise than by a wearisome process of recollection; but, according to my method, he has nine times seven objects before him, which he has learned to count as nine sevens; the answer to the above question is, therefore, with him, not a matter of memory; for although the question, perhaps, may be put to him for the first time, yet he knew long ago, by intuition and practice, that in sixty-three there are nine sevens; and the same is the case in all the other branches of my method.

To adduce another instance: he had in vain endeavored to accustom his children to write the initials of substantives with capital letters;* the rule by which they were to go was constantly forgotten. Now, on the contrary, the same children, having read through some pages of a vocabulary constructed on my plan, conceived of themselves the idea of continuing that vocabulary out of their own resources, and, by writing long lists of substantives, proved that they had a clear notion of the distinctive character of that sort of words. The remark which Krüsi made, that with this method children do not want to be pushed on, is so correct, that it may be considered as a proof of something imperfect in the mode of instruction, if the child still requires any kind of stimulus to thought; and the method can be considered as perfect only where every exercise proposed to the child is so immediately the result of what he has learned before, that it requires no other exertion on his part than the application of what he already knows.

Krüsi further observed that the detached words and pictures, which I used to lay before the children in teaching them to read, produced upon their minds a very different effect from that of the compound phrases commonly used in schools. He, therefore, now began to examine these phrases themselves somewhat more closely, and he found that it was utterly impossible for children to form any distinct notions of the different words of which they are composed; because they do not consist of simple elements before known to the children, and put together in an obvious connection, but that they are unintelligible combinations of objects mostly or entirely unknown. To employ children's minds in the unraveling of such phrases is contrary to nature; it exceeds their powers, and leads to delusion, inasmuch as it introduces them to trains of ideas which are perfectly foreign to them, as regards not only the nature of the objects to which they refer, but likewise the artificial language in which they are clothed, and of which the children have not even acquired the bare elements. Krüsi saw that I was no advocate for this hodge-podge of pedantry; but that I did with my children as nature does with savages, first bringing an image before their eyes, and then seeking a word to express the perception to which it gives rise. He saw that, from so simple an acquaintance with the object, no conclusions, no inferences followed; that there was no doctrine, no point of opinion inculcated, nothing that would prematurely excite them to decide between truth and error; it was a mere matter of intuition, a real basis for conclusions and inferences to be drawn hereafter; a guide to future discoveries, which, as well as their past experience, they might associate with the substantial knowledge thus acquired.

He entered more and more into the spirit of my method; he perceived that every thing depended on reducing the different branches of knowledge to their very simplest elements, and proceeding from them in an uninterrupted progress, by small and gradual additions. He became every day better fitted to second me in the experiments which I myself made on the ground of the above principles; and, with his assistance, I completed, in a short time, a spelling-book, and a course of arithmetic, upon my own plan.

* In the German language, every substantive, and every word used as a substantive is written at the beginning with a capital letter.

Krüsi himself considered the time he spent in Burgdorf the happiest and most fruitful of all his life. The conviction that they were laboring for a cause which was to exert an influence for good upon thousands of their fellow-men filled all the laborers there with enthusiasm, and made every effort and every new creation a delight which they would not have exchanged for all the treasures of earth.

The important year 1805, in which Napoleon decreed the reseparation of Switzerland, brought the institution at Burgdorf to an end; the castle reverted to the canton and was occupied by the high bailiff. Pestalozzi, after contemplating for some time the transfer of his institution to Münchenbuchsee, determined to continue it at Yverdun, on the lake of Neufchâtel. For this purpose he received permission to use the old castle there; and all his teachers joyfully gathered around him again. In Yverdun, the institution acquired a European reputation; from all directions there resorted to it not only pupils, (of whom it contained in its most prosperous condition above two hundred,) but also youths and men of riper age and experience, who sought to become acquainted with the discoveries of Pestalozzi, in order to fit themselves for learning and teaching in the great field of human education. An active and significant life grew up within the walls of the modest little institution, to which there gathered pilgrims both great and small from all parts of Europe. The seed there sown bore fruit a thousand-fold throughout all parts of Germany, and especially in Prussia, where the benevolent king highly valued the efforts and the method of Pestalozzi, and sent several young men of talents to make themselves acquainted with the latter.

Besides this undertaking, whose good influence was intended to reach boys, youths, and men of all classes and of all beliefs, Pestalozzi's scheme contemplated also the extension of the advantages of an improved education to girls, in order that they might be trained in their great vocation as mothers. To this end he connected with his institution, in 1806, a girls' institute, under the management of Krüsi and Hopf, the latter of whom was married. This institution succeeded. Pestalozzi's best teachers helped to instruct in it. Among those who patronized it, Krüsi always remembered with affection a wealthy landowner, (Stamm,) of Schleitheim, who sent to Yverdun not only four daughters, but a niece as a sort of guardian, two nephews, and a young man who he was assisting to train himself for the work of teaching. Truly we might almost say, in the words of Jesus, "I have not found such faith, no, not in Israel!" Of the operations of the institution Krüsi says: "It gives us heartfelt pleasure; but we had not foreseen the continually greater demands to be made upon our strength and time in order to comply with its requirements. We had, therefore, only the choice remaining to devote ourselves wholly to one institution or the other. Pestalozzi undertook the management of the new institution, with which I remained in friendly communication. The domestic management and moral instruction were all under the charge of several female teachers, until Rosette Kasthofer, afterward Niederer's wife, resolved to make it the object of her life to conduct the institution, in order to the accomplishment of Pestalozzi's views. To this purpose she yet remains true. Although the shortness of my experience will not allow me to claim the ability to educate skillful female teachers and good mothers of families, it will always give me pleasure to remember that the united efforts of my celebrated friend and myself called the institution into life."

Krüsi's wife also received her education in this institution; but after he had resigned the management of it. We, and all who knew him, must agree that the simplicity and goodness of his disposition peculiarly fitted him for teaching girls, although he first undertook it at the age of thirty.

Krüsi's recollections of this period were numerous; but we must confine ourselves to a very few of them. His acquaintance with Katherine Egger, afterward his wife, had already commenced in 1810–12. She subsequently removed to Mühlhausen, to assist her sister in her school there; and we shall derive part of our information from the correspondence between them.

In this correspondence he speaks most frequently of Father Pestalozzi, and of Niederer, who was always intellectually active, but at that time often depressed in spirits. The reverence and love with which all the friends and fellow-laborers there, to the ends of their lives, spoke of Father Pestalozzi, sufficiently refute the incorrect things now frequently heard on this subject.

Thus Krüsi says in one place:—

"Father Pestalozzi is always cheerful, and works with youthful energy. We often wonder at his enthusiasm, which will yield neither to labor nor to age. I seek to avoid unpleasant collisions between dissimilar views; and sincerely desire that my labor may always satisfy him."

And again, about Niederer.

"Niederer is working like a giant. A defence of the institution against wrong impressions and a true exposition of Pestalozzi's designs will soon appear in print. Few men are able to work like him."

Even from these few lines we obtain a deep view of the characters of these three fellow-workmen. Of Krüsi's own labors in the institution we shall let Pestalozzi himself speak, further on. A letter from Krüsi, January 15th, 1812, on occasion of Pestalozzi's birth-day, gives us a view of the feelings and relations of the pupils toward the father of the institution:

"The day," (writes Krüsi to his betrothed,) "was a glorious one, and rich in seeds and fruits for the growth and strengthening of the soul and the heart. I can give you only points of recollections of it: from these points you may complete the lines and the whole picture from your own fancy." He proceeds to give a circumstantial account of the festivities in the schoolroom of each class. The decorations in those of the third and fourth classes were especially ingenious. In the third were to be seen:

a. A transparency of Neuhof, the village of Birr, and the high land of Brunegg. (It was here that Pestalozzi first attempted to realize his benevolent plans for the education of poor factory children.)

b. Opposite to this Pestalozzi's bust, of wood, crowned with a wreath of laurels and immortals.

c. On each side of this, a transparency with an inscription: on the right, in German, "May God who gave thee to us, bless thy work and us long through thee!" on the left, in French, "Homage to our father! the pure joy of our hearts proclaims our happiness."

The room of the fourth class was arranged to represent a landscape, in which were to be seen:

a. Cultivated land and meadows.

b. A rock.

c. A spring rising at the foot of the rock, and a brook flowing from it and fertilizing the land.

d. Near this a poor dwelling; a hut roofed with straw.

e. Over its door the words, "May his age be peaceful."

f. In another place an altar.

g. Over it the words, in a transparency, "May poverty remember him!"

h. On one side of it, "May we live like him!"

i. Upon it, a poor's-box, with a letter from all the members of the class.

As soon as Father Pestalozzi entered the chamber, a little genius came forward from the hut to meet him, and handed him the poor's-box and the letter. He was so surprised and affected that he could scarcely read it. Its contents were as follows:

"Dear Herr Pestalozzi!

"It is very little, it is true, which we, both the present and former members of the class, save in the course of the year; which amount we now offer you as a feeble testimony of the depth of our love; but we are glad to be able to say that at least it comes from sincere hearts; and shall this please you, our end will have been gained. It may express to you our purpose hereafter doing still more for the poor, and like yourself, of finding our own happiness in that of others. May we use well the time of our stay here, and by our efforts evermore deserve your love. May you be happy among us! Full of gratitude to God, we embrace you affectionately, with the wish that you may live to see us fulfill this promise."

The money given amounted to fifty-two Swiss francs. Besides the displays of the children, the printers had a transparency with the words, "May the press send forth hereafter, no longer your life, but only the ripe and beautiful fruit of that life."

Krüsi also describes some festivities which Pestalozzi arranged for his pupils in order on his part to give them pleasure. From this production it is evident with what love and reverence he was regarded by the members of his household, and how they all endeavored to make his days pass in happiness and comfort.

In 1812 Pestalozzi contracted by carelessness a severe illness, during which he would have Krüsi almost incessantly with him as a nurse. The latter performed that office with his usual tenderness and self-sacrifice; bearing patiently with his weaknesses, and taking pleasure in every remarkable expression of his friend. Thus he writes from the side of the sick bed to his betrothed:

Our father is remarkable even in his sickness. He is wishing and longing to be well again, and to be able to apply himself to his labors once more with renewed strength; but yet he looks peacefully upon death, close before him. One day while his doctors were consulting about sending to Lausanne for a surgeon, he asked them cheerfully if he must set his house in order. When they were gone, he said to Elizabeth, his faithful housekeeper, (Krüsi's sister-in-law,) that he was willing to die; that the world cost him no regrets. To be able thus to look upon life and the eternity is a beautiful and soul-elevating thing. I am in hopes that God will spare him to us; but I can not tell you how much I am benefitted by seeing his peacefulness under such circumstances.

When the disease began to yield to the efforts of the physicians, Krüsi's joy expressed itself in the following language: "Had the inscrutable providence of God taken him from us, I would not resign for the whole world the recollections of having cared for him and of having been continually near him. He takes every occasion of expressing his pleasure at your return and of blessing. our union. May God make you happy with me. You know my faith in the wise saying, 'The father's blessing builds the childrens' house, &c.' He will build our house for us; not of wood or stone, but even if it be the most lowly hut, a dwelling of peace, love, truth, and pious labor."

Pestalozzi repaid this love with paternal tenderness. With such feelings he addressed to Krüsi's intended the following characteristic words: "Good day, Trineli! as long as things go well let us see each other and enjoy each others' society. When things no longer go well, and you see me no more, then do you and Krüsi continue to do right, and I shall take pleasure in you on the other side of the grave."

Still deeper in feeling are the words which Pestalozzi, in a Christmas address before all the members of the institution, addressed to Krüsi personally.*

To Niederer he says:—

Niederer, thou first of my sons, what shall I say to thee? what shall I wish thee? how shall I thank thee? thou piercest to the depths of truth, and with steady footsteps goest through its labyrinth. The love of high mysteries conducts thee. Courageously, with iron breast, thou throwest down the gauntlet to every one who, wandering in by-paths, strays from the ways of truth, regards appearances only, and would deceive his God. Friend, thou art my support; my house rests upon thy heart; and thine eye beams a light which is its health, though my weakness often fears it. Niederer! preside over my house like a protecting star. May peace dwell in thy soul, and may thine outward body be no impediment to thy spirit. Thus will a greater blessing arise to the help of my weakness from thy mind and thy heart.

Krüsi, be ever stronger in thy goodness. Among lovely children, thyself lovely and childlike, thou dost establish the spirit of the house in its goodness; in the spirit of holy love.

---

* Tobler had already left Yverdun.

At thy side and within thy loving influence, the child in our house no longer feels that he is without father or mother. Thou decidest the doubt whether a teacher can be in the place of a father and mother. Go and fill thy place still more efficiently and completely.

Krüsi, upon thee also I build great hopes. It is not enough to know the method of human education; the teacher must know the mild and easy steps with which the kind mother leads along that road. That way thou knowest and goest; and thou dost keep the child longer in that loving road of his first instruction than even his mother can. Complete thy knowledge; and tell us the beginnings of childish knowledge, with thine own inimitable union of childlikeness and definiteness. Thou didst bring Niederer hither as thy brother, and livest with him in oneness of mind and soul. May the bond of your old friendship ever knit itself more closely; you are the firstlings of my house; and the only ones that remain of them. I am not always of the same mind with you; but my soul depends upon you. I should no longer know my house, and should fear for its continuance, were your united strength to be removed from it. But you will not leave it, beloved, only remaining firstlings of my house.

We may see from the deep feeling and strong expressions of these words how much Pestalozzi valued Krüsi's quiet and modest labors, and how well Krüsi deserved that value. Scarcely one out of twenty teachers has the ability to enter fully into the nature and needs of children, to bear patiently with their weaknesses, to be pleased with the smallest step of progress, and to become fully accomplished in the profession. Upon the management of such young natures, Krüsi gives his opinion in a letter upon the significance of the smallest opinions. We give an extract from it, as useful and important to all teachers.

It requires much experience to develop the heavenly from the earthly. I can assure you of this, that the world is by no means the comedy that it seems; and what we call indifference is often far more definitely good or bad than men consider. The common appearances of life are only indifferent to us when we do not understand their connections, and set too little value upon their influence over us, for weal or woe. But the purer our soul is, the clearer is our perception of the value or worthlessness of every day and usual affairs; the more do we become able to perceive fine distinctions, and the freer do we become in our own choice and the more independent in our connections.

He whose perceptions of the infinite varieties of plants have not been cultivated sees nothing in the meadow but grass; and a whole mountain will contain for him scarcely a dozen blossoms which attract his attention. How different is the case with him who knows the wonders of their construction. He hears himself addressed from every side; the smallest thing has significance for him; he could employ a thousand eyes instead of his two. In their least parts, even to the very dust that clings to his fingers, he perceives mysteries which lead his mind to the loftiest views, and give his heart the liveliest pleasure. As it is here so it is everywhere. One mother will see only the coarsest physical wants of her child, and hears it only when it begins to cry. Another will penetrate entirely into its inner being; and as she is able to direct this, so she is entirely different in respect to its outward management. Nothing that concerns it is indifferent to her. Every thing is an expression of its being; and thus even the least thing acquires a high significance in her eyes.

The small and loveable children who were so often sent to the Pestalozzian institution—much to its credit—always attached themselves especially to Krüsi. From his views as above given, we may imagine with what wisdom he taught these little ones, and sought to awaken their minds and preserve their innocence. To the same purpose are the following notices in his diary, which it is true contain no very important facts, but which nevertheless, are the clear marks of a man inspired by the holiness of his calling:

"I often pray at evening when I go to bed, that the dear God will let me find something new in nature," said W. M.——, a boy of ten years old, who had found in one of his walks, a stone which he had not before known. This holy habit, (continues Krüsi,) of referring every thing immediately to the Almighty hand, is a sure sign of a pure soul; every expression of it was therefore of infinite value to me. I thanked God that by means of it I had been able to see further into the heart of this good child.

"It is hard for me to write a letter," said S——, when he was set to write to his parents, and found it difficult. Why? said I; adding, you are now a year older, and ought to be better able to do it. "Yes," said he, "but a year ago I could say every thing I knew; but now I know more than I can say." This answer astonished me. It came from deep within the being of the child. Every child, in his liking and capacity for writing letters, must pass through periods, which it is necessary for his parents or teachers to know, lest without knowing or wishing it, they should do the children some harm.

E——, nine years old, said yesterday, "One who is clever should not be told what 'clever' means. But one who is stupid will not understand it, and he may be told as much as you like."

Th. T——, six years old, sees God everywhere as an omnipresent man before him. God gives the birds their food; God has a thousand hands; God sits upon all the trees and flowers.

J. T——, on the contrary, has an entirely different view of God. To him he is a being far off, but who from afar sees, hears, and controls every thing. Are you also dear to God? I asked him. "I do not know," he answered; "but I know that you are dear to him. All good men are dear to him." I was so astonished to hear the child thus express his views of God, and of myself, and his childlike respect and dependence upon his teacher, that I dared question him no longer, lest I should not treat with sufficient tenderness and wisdom, this spark of the divine.

These extracts will sufficiently show that Krüsi considered the hearts of his pupils as holy things, which it was his business to keep in the right path. He was never ashamed, even in his old age, to learn from children; and the traits and efforts of earliest childhood often afforded him help in the construction of a natural system of instruction.

Every child that I have ever observed, writes Krüsi, in his "Efforts and Experiences," (*Bestrebungen und Erfahrungen*,) during all my life, has passed through certain remarkable questioning periods, which seem to originate from his inner being. After each had passed through the early time of lisping and stammering, into that of speaking, and had come to the questioning period, he repeated at every new phenomenon, the question, "What is that?" If for answer he received a name of the thing, it completely satisfied him; he wished to know no more. After a number of months, a second state made its appearance, in which the child followed its first question with a second: "What is there in it?" After some more months, there came of itself the third question: "Who made it?" and lastly, the fourth, "What do they do with it?" These questions had much interest for me, and I spent much reflection upon them. In the end it became clear to me, that the child had struck out the right method for developing its thinking faculties. In the first question, "What is that?" he was trying to get a consciousness of the thing lying before him. By the second, "What is there in it?" he was trying to perceive and understand its interior, and its general and special marks. The third, "Who made it?" pointed towards the origin and creation of the thing; and the fourth, "What do they do with it?" evidently points at the use, and design of the thing. Thus this series of questions seemed to me to include in itself the complete system of mental training. That this originated with the child is not only no objection to it, but is strong indication that the laws of thought are within the nature of the child in their simplest and most ennobling form.

That Krüsi was now writing his experiences with a view to others, and was continually occupying his mind with reflections upon all the appearances of nature and of life, the following words show:

Thus I have again gained a whole hour of instruction. I had four divisions in mental arithmetic. Each of them, as soon as it had found the clue, taught itself; all that I had to do was to oversee, and to assist. It is a pleasure to teach in that way, and a sweet consciousness rewards the labor. But still, arithmetic is not the chief subject which occupies my mind. For had I the opportunity, I could do something in the investigation of language. For if matters turn out as I am in hopes they may, I shall give some proof that I have not lived in vain. The study of language leads me on the one hand to nature and on the other to the Bible. To study the phenomena of the former, and to become familiar with the contents of the latter, are the two great objects which now demand from me much time, much industry, and a pure and natural observation of childish character.

The little work alluded to in the above lines, bears the title, "Biblical views upon the works and ways of God." (*Biblische Ansichten über die werke und wege Gottes;*) and in it the exposition of God's operations in nature, stated in Biblical language, was carried through upon a regular plan. Krüsi would perhaps have undertaken the work in a different manner at a later period; but the Bible was always to him a valued volume, in which he studied not only the divine teachings and similitudes of the New Testament, but also the lofty natural descriptions of Moses, Job, David, &c. The charge of deficiency in biblical religious feeling has often been brought against the Pestalozzians. For my part I can testify that even the first of them had studied the Bible through and through, and placed uncommon value upon it. Their child-like faith and love for everything good and true, fitted them especially for doing so; moreover, they were inspired by Pestalozzi's energetic Christianity. The fact that they always endeavored to bring a religious spirit into every study, and especially into that of language, by awakening a love of truth, and an active preparation for every thing good and beautiful, is a clear proof that a high and Christian ideal was always before their eyes.

Krüsi's heart was, so to speak, in love with the beauties of nature all his life. In his seventieth year, every flower, tree, sunrise and sunset, spoke to him as distinctly as the first time he saw them. He perceived in nature that plain impression of the divine energy which is often dim to adult men, and is most plainly seen by children. And he always returned to nature to learn from her. How she awakened his sensibilities will appear from the following extract which he wrote in his diary and afterward sent to his betrothed:

It is Sunday, and a divinely beautiful morning. More than an hour before the rising of the sun, the brightness of the morning light could be seen upon the summits of the great Alpine chain, from Mont. Blanc, to the Titlis in Unterwalden. Now the majestic sun himself in heavenly splendor, arises and lights up everything before me. Why does he begin his course so quietly that we must watch like a sparrow hawk, lest he escape our attention and stand there before us unawares? If the roll of the thunder were to accompany his rising, how exceedingly seldom would the dwellers in cities and villages keep themselves away from this divine spectacle, which no other earthly show even approaches? And yet none will be away when the roll of the drum announces the coming of an earthly prince. So I thought for a moment; but soon saw the silliness of my meditations. It is the very nature of light to distribute its blessings in silence. In the moral world it is the same. The nearer one approaches to the fountain of life, the more silent are his endeavors to spread around him light and blessings.

At the breaking of such a day it is as if a world were being created again. Light, air, water, land, plants, beasts, and men, appear to our eyes almost in the same order in which they were created.

How quickly is everything done which our Lord God creates! and how frightfully slow are we in understanding even the smallest of them! And besides all this quickness in creating, and slowness in comprehending, how infinite is the number of things which God places before our eyes! No wonder that our knowledge always remains mere patchwork, and that we have to postpone so many things to the other side of the grave, in the hope that there, free from the bonds of the earthly body, we shall progress with an ever increasing speed from knowledge to knowledge, and shall clearly understand how everything exists, in God, which was dim and perplexed to us here.

A strong and encouraging indication of our own inward worth appears in the expression, "The spirit explaineth all things, even the deep things of God." But it is a trouble to most men, that they cannot approach God by some other means than by the spirit; by their perceptions, or by their knowledge. He only can approach God by the spirit, to whom nature opens her mysteries; to whom her operations and her purposes are known. But how few are there who attain even to an A B C of knowledge of the world, from which, as from a living spring, they may gain a pure and worthy conception of their creator. How often must even he who has made the study of nature the business of his life, whose knowledge surpasses that of millions of his fellow beings, stand still before the most common physical, mental, or moral phenomenon, and exclaim: such mystery is too wonderful for me, and too high; I can not understand it.

Then hail to thee, human heart! Through thy feelings is it, that we can approach more nearly to God than through our intellectual powers.

The fundamental human relation is that of childhood. It is based entirely upon love. Without our own consent we enter into it. And this same condition is again the highest aim which man can propose to himself, as his best preparative for heaven. The mind loses nothing by this preëminence of the heart; on the contrary, it is this very preëminence in the growth of feeling, and in purity, which gives a higher character to the power and exercise of the mind.

The effort of men to know things here, as God knows them, to display the order of the heavens, the powers of the earth, and the relation of the mind, in the light of earthly truth, are a holy trait of humanity; but men in general can not find rest by these efforts. Everything elevating in the idea of the creator and ruler of the world must appear to them under the mild aspect of a father, if it is to be beneficial and elevating to them. Without this appearance, his omnipotence would be fearful to the weak mortal, his presence painful, his wisdom indifferent, and his justice a two edged sword, which hangs continually over his head and threatens to destroy him. Only by childlike faith in the fatherhood of God can our race feel itself cared for, elevated, supported and guided; or cultivate confidence, gratitude, love and hope, without a destructive conflict with opposing feelings.

The reëstablishment of this child-like condition and the revivification of the holiness which proceeds from it, are the things by which Christ has opened a way to God, and become the saviour of the world.

Through him is it that the pure in heart may see God. The simplest man has the powers necessary for this purpose. They are only the powers that the child exerts when he recognizes the love of his parents, in the care which they bestow upon him.

Truly, it is wonderful how both termini of the devclopment of our nature—the being a child, and the becoming a child of God, should be so nearly connected with each other.

A holy confidence in God is shown in the letters in which he speaks of his prospects for a certain support in the future. His betrothed, who like him had been left destitute by the storm of the revolution, had wandered away from Glarus, her native land, with a troop of poor children, and had been received and supported by some respectable and benevolent people in Zürich, had of course no property: and Krüsi's new place with Pestalozzi, had much more attraction for the friend and follower, than for one prudent in pecuniary matters. Although Krüsi's approaching marriage must have made a certain income more desirable to him, he still felt no solicitude about it, like a true believer in the words of Jesus, "Take ye no thought," &c., but expressed himself as follows:

God will provide. Whoever is conscious of strong love and honest aims in life, should act with freedom, and believe in the prophecy that all things will be for the best. Has not the being who guides all things, thus far watched wonderfully and benevolently over us and our connection? Many are troubled lest they shall not receive what is their own. Is it carelessness in me that I have no such feelings?

I thank God for the powers which he has given you and me for our duties; I feel much more solicitude that we may use these powers worthily of the benevolent God. At every rising of uneasiness I seem to hear God saying to me as Christ did to his disciples on the sea, "Oh ye of little faith!"

Krüsi at last managed to complete the indispensable arrangements for bringing his wife from Mühlhausen; and he was married at Lenzburg, in 1812. His wife entered with confidence upon her new sphere of life, with a man who was not only her lover, but her teacher and her paternal friend. He was not an inexperienced youth, but a man thirty-seven years old, in the prime of his strength, and with a ripeness of experience and thought, seldom found even at his years. His wife too, although considerably younger, had also seen the rougher side of life, and had also felt the inspiring influence of a right method of education.

After his marriage, Krüsi occupied a private house near the castle, where he had charge of the deaf and dumb children of his friend Näf, as long as his connection as teacher with the Pestalozzian institution continued. This now soon came to an end, and under circumstances so unpleasant that we should prefer to be silent upon them, were it not for removing from one of Pestalozzi's oldest teachers the charge of ingratitude, which many well informed readers have believed in consequence of this separation.

There has seldom been a man who has had so many friends and so few enemies, among so great a variety of men, as Krüsi; thanks to his mild and peace loving disposition. It was his principle always rather to withdraw himself, than to make the evil greater by obstinacy or violence in maintaining his views. This habit stood him in good stead in the quarrel which at this time threatened to destroy Pestalozzi's institution. But how was it possible, it may be asked, that men engaged in such a noble enterprise, could not go on in harmony with each other? It was the work of one man, a graduate of the Pestalozzian institution, endowed with uncommon mathematical talents, who sacrificed the peace of the institution to his unbounded ambition. This man, Schmid by name, had contrived, under the name of a guardian, to gain the entire control of the aged Pestalozzi, and little by little to alienate him from all his old friends. As early as 1808, Krüsi had concluded that he could not with honor remain longer in the institution, and had accordingly written an affecting letter of farewell to Pestalozzi, from which we make the following extracts:

Dear Herr Pestalozzi:

God knows that I have always sought with an honest heart, the accomplishment of your holy plans. Whenever I have thought it necessary to differ from you, it has been without any ulterior views, from love for you and for the good of humanity.

For eight years the undisturbed possession of your paternal love has made me the happiest of men. Your present expressions upon the sequel of this relation, pierce so much the more deeply, the less I feel that they are deserved. (Here follow some reasons for his withdrawal.)

If it shall be permitted to me to live for the darlings of your heart, the poor, and to prepare their children to receive the benefits which your efforts have secured for them, there will again awaken in your soul some faith in my gratitude, my love, and my earnest endeavor not to have lived by your side, in vain.

Still further, dearest Pestalozzi; if I have been to blame toward you, it was only by error. Forgive the child who with sorrow and grief tears himself away from his father and his friend.

Whether this letter was delivered to Pestalozzi, is not known. Krüsi did not leave at that time, although Tobler did, dissatisfied for various reasons, and sought another field of labor at Basle.

Schmid was at last, in 1810, removed from the institution, and for a few years the old good understanding prevailed there again. But when he returned and took charge of the financial department, (Pestalozzi, who was well known for a bad housekeeper, not being competent for it,) the quarrel came up again, directed this time chiefly against Niederer and his noble wife, but also against all the other faithful laborers in the institution. Thus, by a departure of many of the best teachers, especially the German ones, it lost many of its brightest ornaments; and in the year 1816, Krüsi also, with a bleeding heart, sent his resignation to Pestalozzi, whom even in his error he loved and respected; but for whom at that time another person spoke, in terms of the bitterest contempt, and most irritating coldness. There is, however, some trace of the old affection, in Pestalozzi's answer to Krüsi's letter:

With sorrow I see a connection dissolved, which I would willingly have continued unto my death, had it been possible. It was not, however, and I receive your explanation with the affection which I have always felt for you, praying God to better my pecuniary condition, so that I may be enabled before my death to show that I respect the relation in which I have so long stood to you. Greet your wife and embrace your child for me, and believe me ever your true friend,

Yverdun, 17th Feb., 1816. PESTALOZZI.

In the letter of Krüsi, just quoted, he expresses his earnest wish to labor for the education of the poor. The same is found in the following to his betrothed; "My inmost wish is to be able to labor in some way, according to the idea of our father, for the education of poor children. We both know what poverty is, and how sorely the children of the poor need help, that they may live worthy and satisfactory lives. It is for us to afford this help. I feel it my vocation, and feel that I have the ability, to do for the poor whatever God has rendered me capable of doing. You must help me. Female instinct must join with manly strength for the accomplishment of this object."

The wish thus expressed was never gratified. It was to be Krüsi's chief occupation to instruct the children of parents in good circumstances, until at a later period his situation in a seminary whose pupils were then, and have been since, mostly from the poorer classes, and who thus have influence both upon the poor and the rich, at least permitted it partial gratification.

After his separation from Pestalozzi, Krüsi set about the establishment of an institution of his own, which he did in fact afterward open, with very little other help than his confidence in God. He purchased a small house, pleasantly situated on the Orbe, by the assistance of a benevolent friend, who lent him a considerable sum, without security, and had the pleasure of seeing an increasing number of parents send their children to him. It was especially gratifying to his patriotism that his first pupils were from his native place of Gais, where they yet live as respectable citizens. In his institution he proceeded upon the Pestalozzian plans; and the happiness of his labors was only troubled by the knowledge that his paternal friend was continually more closely entangled in the snares of the intriguing Schmid, so that even Niederer was forced to leave the institution in 1817.

Although Krüsi was now happily established as father of a family, his first child was born in 1814, and teacher of a prosperous school, yet another destiny was before him, and as previously, without his own coöperation.

In his own little native territory, the public-spirited Hans Caspar Zellweger and others, had conceived the useful idea of seeing a cantonal school for the higher education of native youth, who were then able to command no other means of instruction in their own country than the ordinary village school. Herr Zuberbühler was appointed to the charge of the institution. He had been in the troop of poor children who went with Krüsi to Burgdorf; and was pecüliarly fitted for his place, by his acquirements and by the mildness of his character. But man proposes and God disposes. Zuberbühler was soon seized by an illness, which brought him to the edge of the grave, and which profoundly impressed him with the idea of his own helplessness and the danger from it to his institution. It being necessary to employ another teacher, he invited Krüsi, who was now well known in that neighborhood since his abode near it, and who had besides during the journey into Appenzell, in 1819, made himself acquainted with various influential men there. Soon after this journey he made another to Karlsruhe, Frankfort, Wiesbaden and Schnepfenthal, near Gotha, where he visited the excellent Gutsmuths, who has done so much for the art of gymnastics. It was in 1822 that the news of Zuberbühler's illness reached him, and of his own invitation to the place of director. The prospect of being useful to his fatherland was irresistible to him; and he was also influenced by the promises of an assured income and of entire freedom in modes of instruction. The reputation of his own institution was already great, as will be understood from Krüsi's own mention of the fact as a rare one, that even while he was at Yverdun, pupils were sent to him from three-quarters of the world; some by French merchants from Alexandria, in Egypt, and one from the capital of Persia, Teheran, 800 leagues distant. This may, however, be in some measure ascribed to the fame of the Pestalozzian institution. A very respectable lady from Memel had besides taken lodgings in Krüsi's house with her two daughters, in order to learn under his guidance how to instruct them; and the same thing happened afterwards with an English family at Gais. Krüsi, however, did not hesitate long, but accepted Zellweger's offer in a respectful letter. He himself went first alone to Trogen, and proceeded to his sick friend, Zuberbühler. He says, "When I entered the room Zuberbühler put his hands before his eyes and burst into tears. It relieved his heart to know that I had come to continue the work which he had so well begun." In fact, he grew better from that very day, and was soon completely well. In his native place of Gais, Krüsi attached himself, especially to his early friend Kern, who had traveled to Yverdun to see him. He also had the great pleasure of finding his old friend, the good-natured Tobler, at the head of an institution in St. Gall; where afterwards he often visited him. Having after a time removed thither his effects and his family, Krüsi with his two assistants, pastor Bänziger from Wolfhalden, and Egli from Hittnern, commenced operations in his new place, in the cantonal school at Trogen.

Want of space will oblige me to be brief in our account of Krüsi's stay at Trogen and Gais. Most readers are however better acquainted with this part of his life than with the earlier. This earlier period is especially valuable for teachers, as being that of the Pestalozzian discoveries, and of the enthusiasm which attended them. The later period is occupied more particularly with the further development of it. The institution at Trogen soon gained reputation. At first, most of the pupils were from Appenzell; but afterwards quite a number came from the canton and city of Zurich, and a less number from the cantons of Bündten, Thurgan, St. Gall and Basle, and several from Milan. There was an annual exhibition, which was always interesting, both as showing the progress of the pupils, and the spirit of the institution, and from the addresses made by the director, and Herren Kasper Zellweger, and Dean Frei; most of which have also appeared in print. The situation of the institution, in a somewhat retired place, had the advantage of withdrawing the pupils from material pleasures and the attractions of the world; in the stead of which were offered many enjoyments of a nobler kind in the pleasure of nature, and in the use of an excellent play-ground and garden. Although none of the studies, (which included the ancient and modern languages,) were carried so far as in many institutions of a higher grade, its results were very favorable, from the harmonious labors of the three teachers, and from the efficient character of the method by which Krüsi aimed always at increasing the capabilities of his scholars, and the industry of most of the pupils. There were, it is true, sad exceptions; and if the teachers did not succeed with any such pupils, there were often put under their charge a number of ill-taught or orphan children. Many were by Krüsi's friendly and earnest admonitions, caused to reflect, and brought into the path of virtue, no more to leave it. Krüsi, who always himself took charge of the instruction and management of such pupils, tried mild methods at first, as long as he had any hopes of succeeding with them; at lessons he was cheerful, pursuing every study with love and pleasantly encouraging every smile from his scholars which proceeded from honest animation. He became severe however upon the appearance of any falsehood, rudeness or immorality, and at such times every one feared the wrath of the angry and troubled father.

In 1832, one of the places of assistant teacher became vacant by the death of Herr pastor Bänziger, in whose stead he placed Herr

Siegfried of Zurich, an active and learned man. Meanwhile another change was at hand in Krüsi's lot. His earnest wish to devote himself to the training of teachers was to be gratified; although even in the cantonal school he had done something in this direction.

Since the year 1830 the cause of popular education had been gaining new life in many cantons of Switzerland. Funds were raised in many places for the establishment of new schools which were to be assisted by the State; the position of teacher began to be considered more respectable, and to be better paid; although neither a fair price nor this respect were paid in more than a few places. Clear-minded men however saw that in order to the improvement of popular education, the teacher must first be educated; that for this purpose teachers' seminaries must be established. The question of the choice of a director for the seminary at Zurich, being under consideration, Krüsi was mentioned by various persons, and particularly by the celebrated composer and firm admirer of Pestalozzi, Nägeli. Although this place, as the sequel showed, was not the right one for Krüsi, he still considered it his duty to think over the matter, and to communicate his views upon it, which he did in a letter to his friend Bodmer, at Zurich, from which we extract the following:

The higher education was always the field in which I hoped to labor, if it were the will of God, and to plant in it some good seed for the common schools of my native land. Thirty years ago, I hoped that I had found such a field, in the Swiss seminary, established in 1802, by the Helvetian government, under Pestalozzi as teacher. The act of mediation broke up the plan by disuniting the cantons, and the schools for the common people with them; but the investigation of the laws of education had always been since that a favorite pursuit with me. During a rich experience at Pestalozzi's side, and during researches up to this time uninterrupted, for the purpose of establishing a system of natural education, it has been my hope to be able to labor efficiently for the school system of my native land. The canton of Zurich is one which rather than any other I would glady see the first in Switzerland in furthering this most high and noble object. But I ought not to hide from you my fears, whether:

1. I can count upon being able to carry out Pestalozzi's system of elementary education, freely and without hindrance. In that I recognize the only means of awakening the intellectual life of the teacher, or of bringing the same into the school.

2. The strict necessity of coöperating labor would be regarded in the choice of a second teacher. They should each supplement the work of the other; and this can only happen when their efforts are put forth in the same spirit and for the same object.

3. There should be a model school, which I consider an indisputable necessity for the seminary. It is not as a place of probation for new scholars that I desire this, but as affording an example of the correct bodily, material, moral and religious training of the children.

4. Sufficient care should be taken in the selection of a place for the seminary, that the supervision of its morals should be as much facilitated as possible. The pupils of such a seminary are usually of an age most difficult to manage; and their own moral character subsequently has a strong influence upon that of their scholars.

When Krüsi at last entered upon his long desired field of labor, in 1833, being appointed director of the teachers' seminary, erected in that year, he felt the liveliest pleasure. The object of his life seemed to him now to stand in a clear light before him, and to open to him the prospect that his countrymen would reap the harvest, whose seed he had sown in the spring of youth, and watched over in the summer. Honor to our Grand Council, and to those who were the cause of the resolution, to spread such manifold blessings among our people and blooming youth. Honor to them, that they gave to poor but upright and study-loving youth, the means of training themselves for teachers in their own country, and of learning its necessities, that they might be able to labor for their relief. With gratitude to God, the wise disposer of his fate, Krüsi left the cantonal school, and proceeded to Gais; recalling with emotion the time forty years before, when as an ignorant youth he had there taken up the profession of teaching, himself afterward to become a teacher of teachers.

He considered the years of his labor in Gais, among the happiest of his life. To pass the evening of his days in his native country and his native town, to communicate the accumulated treasures of his teachings and experience to intelligent youth, to labor surrounded by his own family and with their aid, and to benefit so many pupils, all this was the utmost that he had ever dared wish for. This wish was however to be entirely realized. He conducted five courses, attended by sixty-four pupils, and with the assistance of his valued friend, pastor Weishaupt, of his own eldest son, and of Gähler, a graduate of the seminary itself. During the latter course death overtook him.

A boys' school, and a girls' school conducted by his second daughter, soon arose near the seminary, forming a complete whole, over which Krüsi's kind feeling and paternal supervision exercised a beneficial influence. Hardly ever did three institutions proceed in happier unity. Many pleasant reminiscences of this period present themselves; but the space is wanting for them. Krüsi's skill as educator and teacher were the same here as elsewhere. He used the same method, showed the same mild disposition, love of nature and enthusiasm for every thing beautiful and good. He occupied a position even higher in respect of insight and experience, in the completion of his system of education, as adapted to nature; and a more honorable one by reason of his old age and the gray hairs which began to ornament his temples. But despite of his age, whose weaknesses his always vigorous health permitted him to feel but little, he ever preserved the same freshness of spirit. His method of instruction did not grow effete, as is often the case with old teachers. He was always seeking to approach his subject from a new side; and felt the same animation as of old, at finding any new fruits from his method or his labors. His kind and friendly manners won all his pupils, whether boys and girls, or older youth. Nor is it strange that all the other members of the establishment also looked upon him as a father. An expression of their love and respect appeared on the occasion of his birthday, which they made a day of festival, with a simple ceremonial speeches and songs. Upon such occasions he was wont to recall the time of his abode with Pestalozzi; and his affectionate heart always impelled him to speak in beautifully grateful language of his never-to-be-forgotten father and friend, the originator of his own useful labors, and all his happiness. The crowning event of his happiness was the presentation on his sixty-ninth birthday, in 1843, the fiftieth year of his labors as a teacher, by all the teachers who had been instructed by him, of a beautiful silver pitcher, as an expression of their gratitnde. He looked hopefully upon so large a number of his pupils, and gave them his paternal blessing. Two of his birthday addresses have appeared in print.

Until April of that year, Krüsi continued to teach in the seminary and connected schools. After the completion of his fifth course, he had hoped to be able to completely work out his system of instruction, and more fully to write his biography; but this was not to be permitted him. He was able at leisure times to write and publish much matter; ·the last of these was a collection of his poems. These are valuable, not as artistic productions, but as true pictures of his pure and vivid feeling for every thing good and beautiful. The fact that he wrote many of his songs to the airs of his friend, pastor Weishaupt, shows that he valued high-toned musical instruction. This love of singing remained with him to the end of his life; and his face always grew animated if he saw men, youth and maidens, or young children, enjoying either alone or in pleasant companionship, that elevating pleasure.

At the annual parish festival of 1844, the old man now seventy, was present in Trogen, entering heartily into the exercises of the occasion, and particularly, the powerful chotal, "*Alles Leben stromt aus Dir*," which was sung by a thousand men's voices, and an eloquent discourse on common education, by Landarman Nagel. The fatigue, excitement, and exposure to the weather, which was damp and cold, were too much for his strength, and in the evening he was ill, and on the following day he was visited by a paralytic attack, from which he never recovered, but closed his earthly career on the 25th of July, 1844. His funeral was attended by a multitude of mourners from far and near, and his body was borne to its last resting place in the churchyard of Gais, by the pupils of the seminary.

XI. THE GENERAL MEANS OF EDUCATION.

WITH AN ACCOUNT OF A NEW INSTITUTION FOR BOYS.

BY HERMANN KRÜSI.

THE following "*Coup d'œil*" of the General Means of Education, with the Plan of the new Institution which Krüsi afterward organized and managed, was published at Yverdun, in 1818, and presents the ideas and methods of Pestalozzi, as held by one of his early assistants and avowed disciples.

The principal means for the education of man are three, viz., 1. Domestic Life. 2. Intellectual Education, or the Culture of the Mind. 3. Religious Training.

I. DOMESTIC LIFE.

The object of domestic life is the preservation of the body and the development of its powers. It may therefore be considered the basis of physical life.

The body is a seed, enveloping the germ of intellectual, moral and religious activity. Domestic life is the fertile soil in which this seed is deposited, and in which this germ is to expand and prosper.

There are three principal relations of domestic life; of parents to children, of children to parents, and of children to each other.

In domestic life, love is the center of all the sentiments and actions. It is manifested in the parents by unremitting care and unbounded self-sacrifice; in the children, in return, by perfect confidence and obedience; and among brothers and sisters, by endeavors to promote each other's happiness. Every event, almost every moment, of domestic life, stimulates the entire being, body, mind and soul, into activity. Beyond the domestic circle, and the further we move from it, the more remarkable does the particular tendency and the isolated action of each faculty become.

A seminary should exemplify domestic life in all its purity. The teachers should regard the pupils as their children; the children should regard the teachers as parents, and each other as brothers and sisters. The purest love should inspire all these relations; and the result should be cares, sacrifices, confidence, obedience, and reciprocal endeavors to aid in attaining the objects desired.

Such a domestic life prepares the child for mental improvement and religious development and habits. Without it, religion will gain no access to the heart, and intellectual cultivation will only be a means for satisfying the selfish demands of the animal nature. But with it, the child is prepared for the successful exercise of the same good qualities and the maintenance of the like relations in a wider sphere as a man, a citizen, and a Christian.

II. INTELLECTUAL EDUCATION.

The aim of this should be, on one hand, to develop the faculties, and on the other to develop executive power. The faculties must all be developed together; an end only to be attained by the exercises of the active and productive faculties. In order to real development, the mind must act of itself; and moreover, the active and productive faculties can not be exercised without at the same time exercising those which are passive and receptive, (namely, those of comprehension and retention,) and preparing them for future service with increased advantage.

That alone can be considered the elementary means of developing the mental faculties, which is essentially the product of the human mind; which the mind of each individual can, and does in fact, to a certain degree produce, independent of all instruction; that which spontaneously exhibits itself in each department, and is, as it were the germ of attainment in it. These essential productions of the human mind are three; *number*, *form*, and *language.*

The ultimate element of number is unity; of form, a line; of language, ideas, which are interior, and sound, which is exterior. Each of these three means may be employed in two different directions; to develop, on one hand, the power of discerning truth, and on the other, that of discerning beauty.

The faculties of the individual can not be developed without his acquiring, at the same time, a certain amount of knowledge, and a certain bodily skill in the execution of what the mind has conceived; and it is an important truth that an enlightened mind will succeed much better than an unenlightened one in the acquirement of knowledge as well as of every kind of executive ability.

Exercises intended to develop the faculties, like those intended to communicate knowledge, should succeed one another in a logical (natural or necessary) order; so that each shall contain the germ of that which is to follow, should lead to it, and prepare for it.

The development of the principal faculties, and the acquirement of a certain amount of information, are necessary to qualify every individual for his duties as a man, a citizen, and a Christian. This degree of development, and this amount of information, constitute the province of *elementary education*, properly so called, which would be the same for all. But beyond these limits, the character and extent of studies should vary, on one hand, according to the indications of nature, which destines individuals by different capacities for different callings; and on the other hand, according to his situation in life.

In the acquisition of knowledge, an elementary path should be followed, introductory and preparatory to a scientific method of study. This is suited to the child, because it leads from a series of particular facts, it leads upward to the discovery of general truths. The scientific method is suitable only to mature and enlarged minds, proceeding from general principles, displaying them in their whole extent, and thus arriving at particular truths.

We shall now point out the proper means of development, and the principal objects to be attained by them; afterward considering the different ages of childhood, and the successive steps in development and order of studies.

*First means of development. Number.**

SECTION 1. Exercises in number, with reference to truth.

A. Mental calculation; to give intuitive knowledge of numbers, and their relations: including

a. exercises on units.

b. " simple fractions.

c. " compound fractions or complex fractions.

In each of these three series there are different degrees, namely,

First, (Preparatory,) Numeration, or learning to count.

Second, Composition of Numbers; e. g., all numbers are composed of units. All even numbers are composed of twos; all triple ones of threes, &c. Also, decomposition of numbers, e. g.; all numbers may be decomposed into units; all even numbers into twos; all triple ones into threes, &c. Also, transformations of numbers. That is, the mode of composing new numbers from the threes, twos or units, coming from the decomposition of an old one.

Third, Determinations of simple relations and proportions.

B. Calculations by symbols. (Figures, letters, &c.) The object of this is to give an intuitive knowledge of rules, under which all operations on numbers may be performed, and also the ability to express numbers and operations by signs. Including,

a. A knowledge of the decimal numerical system.

* We state the means of development in the following order; *number*, *form*, *language;* because the development of number is simplest and has fewest applications, those of form are more varied, and language includes number, form, and all human knowledge. When we consider the child at different ages, we shall, on the contrary, begin with language, because by that, begins the development of his understanding.

b. The four simple rules, addition, subtraction, multiplication and division.
c. The rule of three, throughout.
d. Evolution and involution.
e. Algebra.

C. Applications both of mental and written calculation, to the discovery of relations between numbers and the attainment of skill in the common calculations. This application is to four principal objects, viz.,

a. Extent, according to natural and arbitrary measures.
b. Time and duration.
c. Weight.
d. Conventional values.

SEC. 2. Exercises on number, with reference to beauty, viz., Measure in music; the other musical element being sound.

*Second means of development. **Form.***

SEC. 1. Exercises in form, with reference to truth. (Geometry.)

A. Construction of figures from given conditions.

a. With lines determined by points.
b. With planes determined by lines and points.

B. Valuation of lines and surfaces, either by absolute measures, that is, by comparison of dimensions, or by arbitrary standards.

a. The measure of one dimension (length,) represented by a line.

b. The measure of two dimensions (length and breadth,) represented by surface. (Planimetry.)

c. The measure of three dimensions (length, breadth and thickness,) represented by solids. (Stereometry.) The higher development, of the same exercises leads to trigonometry and conic sections.

Together with the application of these exercises to surveying, drafting, &c.

SEC. 2. Exercises in form, with reference to beauty. (Drawing.)

A. Linear drawing, to form the eye and the hand, and to practice invention, under rules and in forms agreeable to the sight.

B. Perspective.

a. As a result of observation.
b. As the result of geometrical and optical laws.

C. Knowledge and imitation of light and shade.

D. Progressive exercises in drawing from nature.

Third means of development. Language.

SEC. 1. The interior view of language, *i. e.*, language considered chiefly with reference to the sense of the words. (Exercises to teach children to make observations and to express them with ease and correctness.)

A. Maternal and domestic language includes what relates to infancy; what a child can comprehend.

a. Exercises in naming objects. Review whatever the child has learned in actual life, and ascertain if he knows and can name the objects of which he must speak.

b. Exercises on the qualities of objects. A quality is explained to the child, and he is to search for objects possessing it. Both here and in every subsequent exercise, the child must be required to give each example in a complete, correct and strictly true proposition. Each example should contain something of positive interest.

c. Exercises on actions and their relations. An action is explained to the child, and he is to inquire and discover who does it, what is its object; its when, where, wherewith, how, why. In this practice of observing every action with reference to the agent, object, time, place, manner, principles and intention, we not only obtain what this exercise is primarily intended to promote, the development of the faculty of language, and thereby of general intelligence—but also the development in the child of a disposition to explain to himself all he does, and all others do; which is likely to have the happiest effect upon his judgment and conduct.

B. Social language; a development of maternal language.

a. Exercises on families of words. A radical word is chosen, and all its derivatives sought for with the child. He is made to distinguish with care the different meanings, proper or figurative, of each derivative, with a reference to the meaning of the radical word. He must give each word, and each meaning of it, in a phrase complying with these conditions, and those above laid down for propositions.

b. Exercises on synonyms.

c. Exercises in definitions.

SEC. 2. The exterior of language; *i. e.*, language with reference to the form of speech.

A. Exterior of language, with reference to truth.

First. Verbal language.

a. Composition of words.

1. With given sounds.

2. With given syllables. A final syllable, or an initial and final syllable, is given the child, and he is to find words formed with them; thus acquiring a knowledge of the roots of words.

3. With simple words. This and the last exercise are preparatory to exercises on the families of words.

b. Composition of phrases.

1. Knowledge of the constituent parts of phrases, (parts of speech.)

2. Inflection of those parts of speech susceptible of it.

3. Construction of phrases with given parts of speech.

c. Composition of periods.

1. Knowledge of the members of a period.

2. Combination of them.

d. Rules for the construction of language.

Second. Written language.

Besides the discourse of the living voice, which is the original and natural mode of representing our ideas, and which discovers them to the ear, there is an artificial method which displays them to the eye by means of signs called *letters.*

The desire of enjoying the ideas of others thus communicated, and of being able, in like manner, to communicate our own, leads to the study of written language, including the following exercises:

a. Combination of the pronunciation of sounds with the knowledge of the signs by which they are indicated to the eye. (Reading.)

b. Tracing these signs. (Writing.)

c. Expression of sounds by them. (Orthography.)

d. Knowledge and use of signs which indicate the relations of the members of the phrase or period composed. (Punctuation.)

B. The exterior of language with reference to beauty. (Modulation, accent, prosody, versification.)

C. Sound, the external element of language, developed in an independent manner with reference to beauty; constituting one of the elements of music.

REMARKS. The study of the construction of a language constitutes grammar; whose laws being correspondent to the laws of thought, grammar leads directly to logic, in which are united the studies of the interior and exterior of language.

By exercises in logic, and in the formation of language, the pupil is prepared to compose on given subjects, and to study the rules of composition, (Rhetoric.)

The same exercises will nourish and develop the talent for poetry or eloquence, where it has been given by nature.

Language, as a production of the human mind, and the expression of physical, intellectual, and moral life, should be universally the same in principle, since human nature is everywhere essentially the same. But as the development of human faculties, the circumstances of life, social and domestic relations, variously differ, this difference must have caused corresponding differences in this production of the mind; that is, different languages. Men associated in a social body have formed for themselves a certain tongue, which has become their national language. In order to intercourse between different nations, they must learn each other's language; hence the study of foreign tongues. This study enables us in a certain sense to hold intellectual and moral intercourse even with nations no longer existing; *i. e.*, by the study of the dead languages.

Those whose mother tongue is derivative, must, in order to understand it perfectly, study the primitive language from which it originated.

SEC. 3. Application of language to the acquirement of knowledge.

Man is the center of all knowledge.

A. Physical man. Knowledge of the body; not anatomical, but of the parts of the animated body..

First degree. Knowledge of the parts of the body.

a. Names of the parts.

b. Number of parts of each kind.

c. Their situation and connection.

d. Properties of each.

e. Functions of each.

f. The proper care of each.

Second degree. Knowledge of the senses.

a. Distinctions and names of the senses.

b. Their organs.

c. Functions of these organs.

d. Objects of these functions.

e. Means of the activity of each organ.

f. Consequences of the action of the senses, sensations, disposition, inclinations.

REMARKS. The child acquainted with the physical man, knows the highest link of external nature; the most perfect of organized beings.

Man belongs to the animal kingdom by his body and by his animal affections. He employs animals for different purposes. The knowledge of physical man conducts therefore to that of the *animal kingdom.*

Plants are also organized beings, but of an inferior organization.

Man obtains from plants the greater part of his food, his clothing and his remedies. They feed the animals he employs. They adorn his abode. Their fate in some respect resembles his, like him they grow, they expand, they produce, decline and die. The knowledge of the physical man conducts therefore to that of the vegetable kingdom.

The mineral kingdom forms the ground of our abode and of that of all organized bodies, and all return to it when they die. It supplies us with salt, many remedies, and the greater part of materials for our habitations. The knowledge of the physical man conducts then to that of the *mineral kingdom.*

Fire, air, water and earth compose all terrestrial bodies, wherefore to the observer, without instruments, they appear as elements. The preservation and the destruction of all bodies depend upon them. The constant property of fire is to consume, of air to volatilize, of water to liquify, of earth to mineralize. It is by their equilibrium that bodies are preserved; so soon as one of the four overpowers the rest, the body subject to its preponderating action must perish. Thus the study of the three kingdoms of nature leads to that of substances commonly called *elements* and this is a preparation and an introduction to the study of *physic* and *chemistry.*

Physical man, animals, minerals, and elements belong to the terrestrial globe, the knowledge of which constitutes *geography.* The study of the earth, regarded as a planet, leads to *astronomy.*

Man as a *physical* being, stands in relation with beings above him, on a level with him and beneath him. Above him are the elements considered at large and the laws of physical nature. On his level are his fellow creatures, and beneath him the individuals of the three kingdoms of nature, and the elements taken in detail.

B. Intellectual man.

a. Inferior faculties which animals possess in common with man. Faculties of perception and observation.

b. Intermediate faculties. The faculties of comparison, judgment, and inference.

c. Superior faculties. The faculty of seeing abstractly, the essence of each object, and the invariable laws of its nature. The faculty of believing divine revelation, which unites the most elevated powers of the soul and heart.

Faculties formed in each of the preceding degrees, are :—

The faculty of devoting the thoughts to one object, excluding every other· (*attention.*)

The faculty of creating any image: (*imagination.*)

The faculty of receiving and preserving every effort of the understanding. (*memory.*)

The faculty of discovering beauty: (*taste.*)

The study of the intellectual faculties leads to the study of intellectual productions.

a. For satisfying intellectual wants, that is to say, the essential means for the expansion of the mind: (*Language, number, form.*) These three productions of the human mind have been already represented as essential means for intellectual cultivation.

b. For satisfying corporal wants or to aid the bodily organs to serve the mind. General knowledge of arts and trades, of the materials they employ, of their mode of action: (*technology.*)

C. Moral man.

The germ of morality is in the sentiments of love, confidence, gratitude. Fruit of these sentiments: (*obedience.*)

Faculties whose action springs from intelligence and sentiment: *will, liberty.* The governing and representative faculty of the will, is with the child the will of his parents; among men grown, the will of God: (*conscience.*)

Man as a *moral, intellectual* and *physical* being is in affinity with his superiors, his equals, and his inferiors. Our relation with superior beings commences at our birth: those then above us are our father and mother. Those with whom we begin to be in connection when we enter into civil society are persons in authority. The highest points to which we can ascend in our relation to beings above us is as *children of God.* The fundamental relation of all those with beings on a level with us, is that of brothers and sisters in the interior of our family. These relations exist in full extent, and perfection, when we regard all mankind as brethren, and as forming with us a single family. The fundamental relations of all those with beings beneath us are those of a father and mother toward their children. These relations exist in all their perfection and true dignity when we are *the representatives of the Deity*, with those committed to our care. The knowledge of the relationships of which we have just spoken, existing in domestic life, in civil society, and in religion, the same conducts to that of our rights and duties as men, as citizens and as Christians.

By exercising a child in the study of himself and of the men around him, his faculties, the productions of his intellectual activity, the principles and the consequences of his actions, his relative situation to all beyond himself, the rights and duties resulting from this situation, he is prepared to study the same objects in a wider sphere, namely, in the human race, where appears in full, all that the individual offers in miniature; and this study is the main object of history. The study of history includes three successive degrees.

1st Degree. From the time a child begins to study human nature and as a confirmation of the truths this study will discover to him, he will be shown particular and well chosen facts, taken from the history of individuals or nations, facts, the circumstances of which compose a whole, and form in his imagination, as it were, a picture after nature. When the child shall have arrived at a certain degree of development, he will be made to bring home all these isolated events to the men, or to the people, as well as to the time and place, to which they belong. In this degree the study of history serves principally to feed the *imagination*, and the *memory.*

2d Degree. When the young man shall be more advanced in the knowledge of human nature, he may ascend to the origin of the actual state of the nations that surround him, beginning with the people of his own country. We may conduct him to the epoch which has been the germ of this actual state, and seek with him the successive degrees by which the nation has progressed, as well as the principles and consequences of each particular event. He will thus learn to know the current order of history, of the principal nations in existence. He will then pass on to the history of those now no more. In this degree, the study of history serves principally as food to the judgment, inasmuch as it connects actions, causes, and their consequences.

3d Degree. Only when the young man shall have become more matured, acquired a deep knowledge of human nature, and the consequences of the development of the individual, is it, that he can with advantage collect the particular facts, and the series of events which he has learned to know, in order to form one entire whole, and to study in mass, the consequences of the development of the human species and of each historical personage, which is the essential end of history, and the highest point to which it can lead. In this degree the study of history serves as food *to the mind in its most noble state of action.*

Auxiliary means for the development of the faculties and the acquisition of knowledge. The study of what men have produced, as true, beautiful and good.

1st. Progressive lessons according to the degree of development the child has attained and the branches of study to which he applies.

2d. Exercises for the memory. To learn by heart beautiful pieces of poetry, eloquence or music.

3d. Exercise of judgment and of taste: an examination of the productions of art, to trace therein the principles of truth and beauty.

4th. Imitation and reproduction: declamation of pieces of eloquence, or of poetry; execution of musical composition; copying drawings and paintings.

General means for rendering the body of man able to serve his soul and to execute its conceptions. (*Gymnastics.*)

In domestic life the child's body is the object of most tender care. As the child expands, he constantly exercises the organs of his senses and of all his members. Care on the part of the parents and exercises on that of the child are the double means of his preservation and his first development. Bodily exercise for a child comes in the form of plays destined to amuse and divert him. At first they vary at almost every instant. Gradually they become more steady, and more serious.

The art of education extends and perfects what life itself begins and prepares. Thus what in its birth was but play and amusement becomes the object of a complete development, of which the very organization of our body points out the aim and the laws.

Gymnastics present three different degrees.

a. Children's plays; free exercises produced by unconscious strength and activity, and determined by the impulse of the mind and the accidental circumstances of life.

b. Progressive and regulated exercises of the limbs. *Gymnastics* properly so called.

c. Exercises preparatory to occupations in active life, and to the employment the pupil is to embrace: *Gymnastics of Industry.*

By the gymnastic exercises, directed toward the essential object of developing the physical faculties in harmony with the intellectual and moral, and by care to preserve the strength and purity of the organs, the body may attain its true destination, namely to serve the mind by executing its conceptions.

Different ages of pupils.

These ages are fixed from a general view of children. In different individuals nature accelerates or retards the progress of development, so that some enter earlier, some later into each period. There are also individuals who develop more rapidly in some directions than in others. ***We must therefore take care that the backward faculties are not neglected, which would destroy in the individual, the harmony of human nature.***

A. First age; until five years old.

During this first age, the child is exclusively the object of maternal and paternal care. He only receives instruction occasionally; each moment, each circumstance may furnish a means to fix his attention upon the objects which surround him, and to teach him to observe them, to express his observations and to act upon them as far as his age will allow. The development which the child may acquire in this first period is of the greatest future importance. Every teacher will find a wide difference between the child whose parents have trained him with tenderness and judgment and him who has been in the first stage abandoned to himself, or what is worse, ill-directed or ill-associated.

B. Second age; from five to ten years.

It is at this period only that a regular course of instruction should begin. At first this should be but a recapitulation of all the child has learned by the habits of life, with the simple difference that the objects of the exercises should no longer be determined by accident, but fixed in one plan, adapted to the intellectual wants of the child. Domestic life thus furnishes, during the first period, the germs which a course of instruction ought to develop, and in a great measure decides its success.

The following exercises properly belong to this age.

1. Maternal and domestic language.

2. Exterior of language: composition of words, reading, writing, spelling.

We must always take care that the knowledge of the interior of language keeps a little before the exterior.

3. Elementary exercises in singing.

4. Mental arithmetic with units.

5. Construction of figures according to given conditions, and linear drawing.

6. Application of language and the acquisition of knowledge; knowledge of the human body.

There are other exercises which may be begun at this period, but which do not properly belong to it; for which reason we put off the mention of them to the following period.

C. Third age; from ten to fifteen.

1. Interior of language: social language.

2. Exterior of language: composition of phrases and of periods, orthography, punctuation.

3. Continuation of singing exercises.

4. Mental arithmetic with simple and with compound fractions.

Written arithmetic to the rule of three, in its full extent, inclusively.

5. *Geometry* properly so called: relation of forms, as far as, and including *stereometry.*

Drawing: perspective, shades, drawing from nature.

6. Application of language to the acquisition of knowledge.

a. Continuation of the study of the physical man: senses, sensations, inclinations, passions.

b. Intellectual man.

c. Moral man.

d. Knowledge of such natural objects in the three kingdoms as by a complete system of positive features, may serve as a representative of a series of other objects of like character.

e. Knowledge of the elements as far as it can be acquired by observation, without the aid of physical and chemical apparatus.

f. Geography.

g. Technology and notices of the principal inventions.

h. History, 1st degree.

7. Application of arithmetic to bulk: to duration, to weight, and to the conventional value of objects.

D. Fourth age; from fifteen to eighteen or twenty.

Language. Continuation of language. Rules for the construction of language. *Logic.*

Compositions on given subjects. *Rhetoric.* Continuation of singing exercises. Arithmetic, mental and written; evolution of powers; extraction of roots. Algebra, geometry, trigonometry and conic sections.

Drawing. Continuation of perspective, shades, and drawing from nature.

Application of language to the acquirement of knowledge.

Continuation of the study of the intellectual and moral man.

Relations of the physical, intellectual and moral man to other beings.

Continuation of the study of the three kingdoms of nature.

Elementary course of physic and chemistry.

Geography, mathematics and history.

History, 2d degree.

Application of arithmetic and geometry united, to agriculture, drafting, etc.

Observations on the study of foreign languages.

In each stage of development it is important that the mother tongue should always keep a little before all foreign languages, that the child should learn nothing in these he does not already know in that, so as to leave no deficiency in the mother tongue. If any study were pursued by the child in a foreign language only, such language would in this department take the lead; the child would find it difficult to express himself in his own tongue on subjects learned by means of a strange one. On the contrary, the study of all foreign languages should serve to make the mother tongue better known.

In a seminary where different pupils speak different languages, these must go hand in hand, and every branch of instruction must be cultivated in them both.

Hence results this advantage, that the pupil learns by *intuition* the meaning of the words of the language which is foreign to him, that is to say he every instant sees this meaning, and does not learn it solely from translation and memory. This mode of employing two languages singularly facilitates the communication of ideas in them both. It also gives the advantage of comparing them, and thereby teaches their actual relations and difference both as to ground and form. A knowledge of the genius, the peculiarities and the shades of meaning of each are the fruits of this comparison.

Dead languages are more foreign to the mind of a child, and more difficult for him. The study of them should be based upon a sufficient development of the living languages, and above all of the native language; without which they remain dead in the mind, without real fruit. This study should not therefore begin before the third period; and should not occupy all the pupils, but only those destined to walk in the paths of science. Those otherwise to be disposed of, may employ their time and their endeavors to much greater advantage.

III. RELIGION. THE SOUL AND THE FINAL END OF ALL EDUCATION.

Third means for the cultivation of man.

As the body is vivified by the soul, so domestic, social and intellectual life are animated and ennobled by religion. Without it the activity of man in each of these three spheres, has only a terrestrial object and falls short of its true dignity and destiny.

Thus the relations of father and mother are ennobled and sanctified when the father and the mother consider themselves, in respect to their children, as the representatives of God, the common father of all.

The state of the child is ennobled and sanctified, when we not only feel ourselves children of mortal parents, but at the same time children of God, destined to rise to perfection even as our heavenly father is perfect.

The state of brothers and sisters is also ennobled and sanctified when we recognise all mankind as brothers and sisters and members of one same family.

The endeavors we make to develop our intellectual faculties and to gain a knowledge of truth, are sanctified when we acknowledge God as the fountain of all wisdom and the eternal source of all virtue and goodness. All earthly life is sanctified when made a preparation for one heavenly and immortal.

The specific means which education may adopt to promote in the child a religious life are:

1. Pious exercises, the principal of which is prayer.

2. Religious conversations, in which we take advantage of the circumstances and events of life to raise the soul of the child from what is earthly and fugitive, to what is heavenly and everlasting.

3. The study of sacred history and important passages of Holy Writ, chosen with care, according to the degree of development the child may have attained, and which, committed to memory, are germs which religious instruction and the events of life will hereafter develop.

4. Religious instruction properly so called; or the regular explanation of the doctrine of our Saviour. This instruction should only take place in the 4th period of development; and the chief aim of every preceding period should be to prepare for it. It should close the child's career and become his support in the hour of trial, his guide to direct his steps to the highest point of perfection of which his nature is susceptible.

All education should proceed from man and lead to God. Man should endeavor to live in God and for God, and to devote to ***HIM*** all his terrestrial and intellectual existence. To this, domestic and social life, exterior nature, and all the circumstances through which he passes here below, should conduct him. But it is only through the influence of God, that all these can produce this effect; the sublime truths of the gospel can alone lead us into that way which leads to that heavenly life which is our true destination.

PROSPECTUS OF AN ESTABLISHMENT FOR THE EDUCATION OF BOYS.

From the earliest age at which they can receive regular instruction, to that in which they should enter into a scientific pursuit, a profession, or business.

This establishment was commenced three years ago. While I was yet with Mr. Pestalozzi, working with him in his undertaking and teaching in his institution, two pupils were unexpectedly committed to my particular care and direction. These were shortly followed by a third, their relation. From that time a combination of circumstances independent of my will induced me to leave the institution I had assisted to form and direct during sixteen years. I should above all things have preferred, after this separation, to have labored to form teachers for the people, taking poor children equal to the office. Seeing the accomplishment of this desire beyond my reach, I applied myself to measures more within my ability, and such as appeared appointed by Providence. I extended my sphere of activity, receiving such new pupils as were intrusted to my care unsought by me.

This train of circumstances on the one hand, and on the other my desire to remain attached to Messrs. Niederer and Naef, (during many years my friends and companions in labor,) and with them to devote my life to education, induced me again to choose Yverdun for the place of my intended labor, and for the gradual growth of my rising institution.

Our union enables us to find means and men competent in every respect to insure the prosperity of our three institutions, (that of Mr. Naef for the deaf and dumb, that of Mr. Niederer for youth of either sex, and mine.) Mr. Nabholz, whose sentiments and purposes resemble our own, will enter my institution as assistant. Mr. Steiner, a pupil of Pestalozzi, will teach mathematics, in which his talents and success afford the brightest hopes. Keeping up friendly intercourse with Mr. Brousson, principal of the College of Yverdun and with other respectable men, I receive from them, in the different branches of instruction, assistance of importance to me, and on the continuance of which I can depend. In my former situation the frequent changes which occurred among my companions in labor often pained me on account of its influence on the success of that undertaking to which I devoted my life.

To avoid a like inconvenience, which must inevitably produce every kind of discord, and expose an institution subject to it, to great dangers, we shall choose our assistants and fellow-laborers with the greatest circumspection.

The views which serve as the foundation of my enterprise are the same with those I have helped to develop under the paternal direction of Pestalozzi. All that I have found in many years' observation, both by my own experience and that with my pupils, to be true and conducive to the entire culture of man, I shall strive by unremitting efforts to develop more and more in myself and to apply in a natural manner for the advantage of my pupils.*

My first object is, to establish in my institution a true domestic life; that all the pupils may be considered as members of one family, and that thus all those sentiments and all those virtues which are necessary to a happy existence, and which render the connections of life pure and sweet, may be developed.

Without this foundation, I believe that the blessing of God is wanting on every means of education whatever.

The extent of knowledge and executive ability which the pupils will acquire is in part the same for all, and in part influenced by individual dispositions and destinations. It is the same for all inasmuch as it embraces the development of the faculties and powers most essential to human nature. Thus far, the method has acquired an invariable basis, inasmuch as it has established language, number and form, as productions of the human mind and as the universal means by which the mind should be developed.

The acquisition of knowledge and executive skill as a result of this development are secured either by means of exercises in language, number and form, or connect themselves with these in a very simple manner. Thus, with the study of numbers is connected mercantile and scientific calculation. The study of form and size leads to the art of drawing and writing. The exercises in the mother tongue as a means of developing the mind of the child, conduct to the study of foreign languages and to the knowledge of objects, which the tongue serves to seize and to define. Music as a combined production of two elements is allied to language by tone, and to number by measure.

In the circle of human knowledge, man as a compound being is the center of a double world: of an exterior and physical world to which the three kingdoms of nature

* I have endeavored in the Coup d'œil which precedes this announcement, to state the means of education such as I conceive them to be. This exposition will be the model and the basis of my work. It is evident that these views and these means can not all be developed by a single man or a single institution. It is a task in which all the friends of education must coöperate.

belong, and also the earth which contains them and all exterior nature ; and of an interior world, intellectual and moral, which, proceeding from the faculties and the powers of our nature, contains all the whole sphere of the connections of man, and of his duties toward himself, toward his fellow creatures, and toward God. The child should be as familiar with this interior world as with the exterior and physical world.

Intellectual cultivation should be accompanied by cultivation of the heart. The physical powers should also be developed, in order that the body may be able to perform what the mind has conceived and the will has resolved. Bodily exercise in this respect possesses an essential and incontestible value. The mind and the heart stand in need of the body in all the actions of life. The operations of the soul are hampered in proportion as the body is neglected, or unequal to execute its orders.

In regard to the admission and residence of pupils in my school, I desire parents who propose to intrust their children to my care, to fully weigh the following considerations.

The two most decisive epochs in education are that of early infancy under the mother's care, and that where the youth enters into manhood. If these two periods are successfully passed, it may be considered that the education has succeeded. If either has been neglected or ill-directed, the man feels it during his whole life. The age of boyhood being the intermediate period between early infancy and youth, is of unmistakable importance, as the development *of the first period, and the germ of the third;* but in no case does this age *influence either decisively, by repairing previous defects or neglects, or by insuring what shall follow.* In the first age the child belongs by preference to its mother, to be taken care of by her; in the second age it belongs by preference to its father, to be directed by him. As a young man, a new existence opens to him, he ceases to be the child of his parents; and becomes their friend. The son, at maturity, becomes the tender, intimate and faithful friend of his parents, as he was, in his minority, their amiable, docile, and faithful child.

With regard to exterior life, the child must sooner or later become an orphan, and when this misfortune befalls him in his minority, society provides that a guardian shall supply the place of parents until he comes of age. *For the interior life, no one can supply this place for him.* Nothing but intellectual and moral strength in the child himself, and strengthened by that wisdom and that love which proceed from God, can bring us near to HIM and supply the place of the wisdom and the love of our father and mother. When the young man has attained this point, it is only as a friend that he remains the child of his parents. If he is not brought up in these noble dispositions, an unhappy consequence follows; the bonds of nature are broken on his coming of age, because these bonds were only of force with respect to physical life; and *the child, who, in this first friendship—in this friendship whose objects are nearest to him—has not supported the trial of fidelity, will never bear the test for any being upon earth.*

Therefore it is that this period in education is so important, so decisive, and so exacting more than any other. On the one hand it requires the purity and tender affection of domestic life, and on the other side, solid and wholesome food for the mind.

In this exigency a means presents itself which ought to be the keystone in the education of the child, the resting place for the passage from minority to majority, the foundation of a new life; a means raised above every other, namely, *Religion*—the revelation of all that is divine in man manifested by Jesus Christ. The young man, who in body, as a mortal, ceases to be a child, should *become a new child in soul,* and as an immortal being. After entering this new state, he ought in general to cease to be the pupil of men, to raise himself above their direction, and to become the pupil of himself, that is to say, *of that wisdom and that love which comes to us from God and raises us to him.*

So long as a man has not attained this point, his education is incomplete. The aim of education is to enable him to reach it.

To strive incessantly toward this object, is the task of the institution here announced.

YVERDUN, Pestalozzi's birthday, 1818.

JOHANNES BUSS.

JOHANNES BUSS, an assistant teacher of Pestalozzi, especially in teaching drawing, was born at Tubingen, in Wurtemburg, in 1776. His father held a subordinate place about the theological school, and thus secured for the son better opportunities of early instruction than are usually enjoyed by persons in his condition. In the grammar school he acquired, before he was twelve years old, considerable knowledge in Greek and Hebrew, logic and rhetoric. His father applied for his gratuitous reception in an institution recently established by the reigning Duke Charles, at Stuttgardt, but this was refused; and about the same time an edict was promulgated, prohibiting children of the middle and lower class from embracing a literary career. The youth, although disappointed, did not despair, but applied himself to the study of drawing. This he was obliged to give up from the want of means, and at the age of sixteen he was apprenticed to a bookbinder—an art by which he hoped yet to get the means for a literary career.

We continue the narrative, in Buss's own language, down to his connection with Pestalozzi.

Having served my apprenticeship, I began to travel; but growing melancholy and sickly, I was obliged to return home; and here I made a new attempt to get rid of my trade, hoping that the little knowledge of music I had retained would enable me to earn my bread in Switzerland.

With this hope I went to Basel; but my circumstances, and the events of my past life, had given me a degree of shyness, which foiled me in all my attempts at money-getting. I had not the courage to tell the people all that a man must say to obtain from them what I wanted. A friend of mine, who met me by accident at that moment of embarrassment, reconciled me for a short time to the bookbinding business; I entered once more into a workshop; but the very first day I sat down in it, I began again to indulge myself in my dreams, thinking it still possible that a better chance might turn up for me in time, although I was quite aware that I had lost too much of my skill in music and drawing to rely upon those two attainments for an independent subsistence. I consequently changed my place, in order to gain time for practice in both, and I was lucky enough to get two spare hours a day, and to form acquaintances, which assisted me in my progress.

Among others I was introduced to Tobler, who soon perceived the gloom by which I was oppressed; and having ascertained the cause, was desirous of assisting me in gaining a more favorable position. When, therefore, Krüsi informed him that Pestalozzi stood in need of a drawing and music-master for the full organization of his new method, his thoughts immediately turned toward me.

I was, as I have before stated, fully aware of my deficiencies; and the hope that I should meet with an opportunity of improving myself, had no small share in my determination to go to Burgdorf, in spite of the warnings which I received from several quarters against forming any connection with Pestalozzi, who, they told me, was half mad, and knew not himself what he was about. In proof of this assertion they related various stories; as, for instance, that he once came to Basel, having his shoes tied with straw, because he had given his silver buckles to a beggar on the road. I had read "*Leonard and Gertrude*," and had, therefore, little doubt about the buckles; but that he was mad, that I questioned. In short, I was determined to try. I went to Burgdorf. I can not describe the feelings I had at our first interview. He came down from an upper room with Ziemssen, who was just then on a visit with him, his stockings hanging down about his heels, and his coat covered with dust. His whole appearance was so miserable that I was inclined to pity him, and yet there was in his expression something so great, that I viewed him with astonishment and veneration. This, then, was Pestalozzi? His benevolence, the cordial reception he gave to me, a perfect stranger, his unpretending simplicity, and the dilapidated condition in which he stood before me; the whole man, taken together, impressed me most powerfully. I was his in one instant. No man had ever so sought my heart; but none, likewise, has ever so fully won my confidence.

The following morning I entered his school: and, at first, I confess I saw in it nothing but apparent disorder, and an uncomfortable bustle. But I had heard Ziemssen express himself, the day before, with great warmth concerning Pestalozzi's plan; my attention was excited, and, conquering in myself the first impression, I endeavored to watch the thing more closely. It was not long before I discovered some of the advantages of the new method. At first I thought the children were detained too long at one point; but I was soon reconciled to this, when I saw the perfection which they attained in their first exercises, and the advantages which it insured to them in their further progress. I now perceived, for the first time, the disadvantages under which I myself had labored, in consequence of the incoherent and desultory manner in which I had been taught in my boyhood; and I began to think that, if I had been kept to the first elements with similar perseverance, I should have been able afterward to help myself, and thus to escape all the sufferings and melancholy which I had endured.

This notion of mine perfectly agrees with Pestalozzi's principle, that by his method men are to be enabled to help themselves, since there is no one, as he says, in God's wide world, that is willing or able to help them. I shuddered when I read this passage for the first time in "*Leonard and Gertrude*." But, alas, the experience of my life has taught me that, unless a man be able to help himself, there is actually no one, in God's wide world, able or willing to help him. I now saw quite clearly that my inability to pursue the plan of my younger years in an independent manner, arose from the superficiality with which I had been taught, and which had prevented me from attaining that degree of intrinsic power of which I stood in need. I had learned an art, but I was ignorant of the basis on which it rested; and now that I was called on to apply it, in a manner consistent with its nature, I found myself utterly at a loss to know what that nature was. With all the attention and zeal I brought to the subject, I could not understand the peculiar view which Pestalozzi took of drawing, and I could not at all make out his meaning, when he told me that lines, angles, and curves were the basis of drawing. By way of explanation, he added, that in this, as in all other matters, the human mind must be led from indistinct intuitions to clear ideas. But I had no idea, whatever, how this was to be done by drawing. He said it must be done by dividing the square and the curve, by distinguishing their simple elements, and comparing them with each other. I now tried to find out what these simple elements were, but I knew not how to get at simple elements; and, in endeavoring to reach them, I drew an endless variety of figures, which, it is true, might be called simple, in a certain sense, but which were utterly unfit, nevertheless, to illustrate the elementary laws which Pestalozzi was in search of. Unfortunately he was himself no proficient either in writing or drawing; though, in a manner to me inconceivable, he had carried his children pretty far in both these attainments. In short, months passed away before I understood what was to be done with the elementary lines which he put down for me. At last I began to suspect that I ought to know less than I did know; or that, at least, I must throw my knowledge, as it were, overboard, in order to descend to those simple elements by which I saw him produce such powerful, and, to me, unattainable effects. My difficulties were immense. But the constant observation of the progress which his children made in dwelling perseveringly on his "elements," brought my mind, at last, to maturity on that point; I did violence to myself, and, abandoning my preconceived notions of the subject, I endeavored to view all things in the light of those same elements; till, at last, having reached the point of simplicity, I found it easy, in the course of a few days, to draw up my sketch of an alphabet of forms.

Whatever my eyes glanced upon from that moment, I saw between lines which determined its outline. Hitherto I had never separated the outline from the object, in my imagination; now I perceived the outline invariably as distinct from the object, as a measurable form, the slightest deviation from which I could easily ascertain. But I now fell into another extreme. Before I had seen nothing but objects; now I saw nothing but lines; and I imagined that children must be exercised on these lines exclusively, in every branch of drawing, before real objects were to be placed before them for imitation, or even for comparison. But Pestalozzi viewed his drawing-lessons in connection with the whole of his method, and with nature, who will not allow any branch of art to remain isolated in the human mind. His intention was, from the first beginning, to lay before the child two distinct series of figures, of which one should be contained in his book for the earliest infancy, and the other should furnish practical illustrations for a course of lessons on abstract forms. The first were intended to form, as it were, a supplement to nature, in giving children an intuitive knowledge of things and their names. The second was calculated to combine the practical application of art with the theoretical knowledge of its laws, by connecting the perception of abstract forms with an intuitive examination of the objects that fitted into those forms. In this manner, he meant to bring nature and art to bear upon each other; so that, as soon as the children were able to draw a line, or a figure, real objects should be presented to them, so exactly corresponding as to render their imitation a mere repetition of the same exercise which they had before performed in the abstract.

I was afraid lest, by giving the child real objects, his perception of the outline should be disturbed; but Pestalozzi did not wish to cultivate any power against nature, and he said, concerning this subject: "Nature gives no lines, but only objects to the child; the lines must be given to the child, that he may view the objects correctly; but to take the objects from him, in order to make him see lines only, would be exceedingly wrong."

But there was another difficulty in which I had entangled myself. Pestalozzi told me that children must learn to read those outlines like so many words, by denominating the different parts, the lines, angles, and curves, with different letters, so that their combinations may be as easily expressed in language, and put down in writing, as any other word by the composition of its letters. In this manner an alphabet of forms was to be established and a technical language created, by means of which the nicest distinctions of the different forms might be clearly brought before the mind, and appropriately expressed in words calculated to illustrate them by the difference of the formation.

Pestalozzi persevered until I understood him. I saw that I gave him a great deal of trouble, and I was sorry for it. It was, however, unavoidable; and but for his patience we should never have made an alphabet of forms.

At last I succeeded. I began by the letter A. I showed him what I had done; he approved of it, and now one thing followed from the other without any difficulty. In fact, the figures being once completed, the whole was done; but I was unable to see all that I had done; I had neither the power of expressing myself clearly on the subject, nor the capability of understanding the expression of others.

To remedy the defect under which I labored is, however, one of the most essential objects of Pestalozzi's method, which connects language throughout with the knowledge gained from nature by the assistance of art, and supplies the pupil at every stage of instruction with appropriate expressions for what he has learned.

It was an observation which we all of us made upon ourselves, that we were unable to give a distinct and accurate account, even of those things of which we had a clear and comprehensive idea. Pestalozzi himself, when explaining his views on education, had great difficulties in finding always the precise term which would convey his meaning.

It was this want of precise language, in fact, which caused me to remain so long in the dark concerning the nature of my task, and prevented me from perceiving what Pestalozzi's views were on that subject.

After I had overcome all these difficulties, my progress was rapid, and I felt every day more the advantages of his method. I saw how much may be done by precision and clearness of language on the subject of instruction, whether it be one of nature or of art, to assist the mind in forming a correct notion of forms and their proportions, and in distinguishing them clearly from each other; and I could not, therefore, but be aware of the paramount importance of enlightened and careful instruction in the signs which language supplies for the designation of things, their properties, relations, and distinctions. Experience confirmed the conjecture which I had formed, that children taught upon this method would make more accurate distinctions, than even men accustomed, from early life, to measuring and drawing; and the progress which many of our children made was beyond comparison, greater than that which is commonly obtained in schools.

It is very true, I saw the whole of Pestalozzi's method only through the medium, as it were, of my peculiar branch of instruction, and judged of its value by the effects which it produced in particular application to my art. But my anxiety to enter fully into the spirit of it, led me, in spite of that limitation, by degrees to investigate the bearing which it had upon other branches; and, at last, assisted by the practical illustrations which drawing afforded me, I succeeded in comprehending Pestalozzi's views on language and arithmetic. I saw that, as it was possible to proceed from lines to angles, from angles to figures, and from figures to real objects, in the art of drawing, so it must likewise be possible, in language, to proceed by degrees from sounds to words, and from words to sentences, and thereby lead the child to equal clearness on that subject. As regards arithmetic, I was laboring under the same error as before, with reference to the intuition of objects. As I looked at these without reference to their outline, so did I view numbers without a clear notion of the real value or contents of each. Now, on the contrary, I acquired a distinct and intuitive idea of the extent of each number, and I perceived, at the same time, the progress which the children made in this branch of instruction. At length, it seemed to me a point of essential importance, that the knowledge and practice of the elements of every art should be founded upon number, form, and language. This led me to understand the difficulties with which I had so long been struggling in my own department. I saw how I had stuck fast from want of clearness of language, and how I was impeded by a confused idea of number. It seemed very obvious that the child can not imagine, with any degree of precision, the division of any figure into its component parts, unless he have a clear idea of the number of those parts; that, for instance, if he is in the dark as to the extent of the number four, he must be equally in the dark on the division of any figure into four parts.

I felt my own mind daily clearing up; I saw that what I had attained had in itself a power, as it were, to carry me further and further; and applying this experience to the child, I came to the conviction, that the effect of Pestalozzi's method is, to render every individual intellectually independent, by awakening and strengthening in him the power of advancing by himself in every branch of knowledge. It seemed like a great wheel, which, if once set going, would continue to turn round of itself. Nor did it appear so to me only. Hundreds came, and saw, and said: "It can not fail." Poor ignorant men and women said: "Why, that's what I can do myself at home with my child!" And they were right. The whole of the method is mere play for any one who has laid hold of the first elements, and has followed its progress sufficiently to be secured against the danger of straying into those circuitous paths which lead man away from the foundation of nature, on which alone all his knowledge and art can securely rest, and from which he can not depart without entangling himself in endless and inextricable difficulties. Nature herself demands nothing of us but what is easy, provided we seek it in the right way, and under her guidance.

One word more, and I have done. My acquaintance with Pestalozzi's method has in a great measure restored to me the cheerfulness and energy of my younger days, and has rekindled in my bosom those hopes of improvement for myself and my species, which I had for a long time esteemed as vain dreams, and cast away, in opposition to the voice of my own heart.

JOSEPH SCHMID.

JOSEPH SCHMID, one of the best known of Pestalozzi's assistants, was a native of Tyrol, and, when he entered the institution as a scholar, was a Catholic, and excessively ignorant. He possessed great native talent for mathematics, and this, together with his habits of industry, order, and thoroughness, raised him in time to the rank of the most influential of Pestalozzi's teachers. Although his talents as a mathematician, and still more his great business capacity, rendered him quite indispensable as a member of the institution, yet his conduct, and his demeanor in his intercourse with his fellow-instructors, became so unsatisfactory to them, that in 1810 he was dismissed from the institution. He soon after established himself as teacher of a school at Bregenz, and vindicated himself by publishing a work entitled "*My Experience and Ideas on Education, Institutions, and Schools.*"

But the absence of his financial guidance brought the institution to such a point of confusion, that, notwithstanding the deep ill-feeling against him on the part of the teachers, he was recalled five years afterward, in 1815. From this time onward, he was in opposition to all the remaining teachers, except Pestalozzi himself, who unflinchingly stood his friend to the day of his death. But the dislike of the other teachers against him, although unable to eject him from the institution, resulted, with other causes, in its ruin. Twelve of the teachers, including Blochmann, Krüsi, Stern, Ramsauer, Ackermann, &c., left at one time; having drawn up and signed a document attributing their departure to the faults and misconduct of Schmid. Others were appointed in their places, but the day of the institution was over, and it gradually sank into entire decay.

Schmid now conceived the idea of an edition of the complete works of Pestalozzi, and himself made the arrangements with the publisher, Cotta, and applied for subscriptions in all quarters, with so much vigor and success that the net profits of the undertaking to Pestalozzi were 50,000 francs. He also appears to have assisted in revising and rewriting portions of the works; which, however, do not contain a number of important compositions by Pestalozzi, while some of Schmid's own, embodying them, are published among them.

Schmid's personal appearance was somewhat striking. He was

muscular and strong, of dark complexion, and keen black eyes, with a harsh voice, and a sharp look. Of his life, subsequent to the year 1817, we have no precise information. We give below Pestalozzi's own estimate of Schmid, as published in 1825:—

"I must trace from its source the powers which seemed the only ones capable of holding us together in these sad circumstances. While we were at Burgdorf, in the beginning of the evil consequences of our unnatural union there, there came to us, from the mountains of Tyrol, a lad showing not a single trace of the exaggerated refinement of our time, but endowed with inward gifts whose depth and subsequent use were anticipated by none—not even by myself. But some unexplained feeling drew me toward him on the first instant of his appearance in our midst, as I had never been drawn to any other pupil. His characteristics were, from the first, quiet, efficient activity, circumscribed within himself; great religious fervency, after the Catholic persuasion, and of a simple but powerful kind; and eager efforts after every attainment in learning or wisdom which he judged necessary. In the exercises in elementary means of education, mental and practical, he soon surpassed all his teachers, and soon even became the instructor of those who a little before had looked upon him as the most uncultivated child they had ever seen in our institution. This son of nature—who even at this day owes nothing to the culture of the time, and, in all that he has accomplished, is as ignorant of the usual outward forms of every intellectual science as he was the day he came from the mountains into our midst, with his *Ave Maria* in his mouth and his beads in his pocket, but with a powerful intellect, a peaceful heart, and courage ready for every struggle—soon excited, by his whole conduct amongst us, extraordinary expectations; and, on my part, that close friendship which I felt for him almost as strongly in the first hour of our meeting.

Schmid passed the years of his youth in these quiet but active labors; and, recognized at his first appearance as an extraordinary child of nature, his mind, developed in the power of thinking and managing by many experiences of practical life, could not fail soon to recognize the unnaturalness and weakness of our organization, and of all our doings and efforts. As soon as the influence of his preponderating powers had insured him a recognized right to do it, he did not delay to declare himself, with Tyrolian open-heartedness, against the presumption of the one-sided and narrow views of the tablet-phantasts, and of the equally narrow and one-sided as well as superficial praises of our methods of intellectual instruction; and, most of all, against the continually-increasing inefficiency, love of mere amusement, disorder, insubordination, and neglect of positive duties therewith connected. He required, without any exception, of each and all of the members of our association, from morning to evening, the thorough performance of all the duties properly pertaining to the members of a well-ordered household. He was equally clear and distinct in rejecting every boast of the elevation and importance of our principles and efforts, which was not proved amongst us by actual facts, as idle babble; and was accustomed to ask, when any thing of this kind was said, 'How is this put into practice? What use is made of it?' And, if the answer did not please him, he would hear no more of the subject. This conduct, however, very soon and very generally gave very great offense."—*Fortunes of My Life*, pp. 22 to 24, 34, 35.

JOHN GEORGE TOBLER.

John George Tobler, an educator of the Pestalozzian school, was born at Trogen, in the canton of Appenzell-Ausserrhoden, in Switzerland, October 17, 1769. He lost his mother in his third year, and his father in his tenth. His education was very inadequate, as was usual in those times. His disposition inclined him to become a preacher. Want of means, however, prevented him until his twenty-third year, when with a very insufficient preparation he entered the University of Basle. With all the other qualifications for becoming a valuable preacher and catechist, his memory for words failed him in respect to the acquisition of foreign languages. This defect decided him entirely to give up entering for the examination as candidate. He was to find a greater sphere of usefulness in another career. He exchanged his theological studies for the practical employment of a tutor and teacher.

In 1799, he placed himself at the head of a school for the female children of emigrants at Basle. An invitation from Pestalozzi brought him to Burgdorf in May, 1800. He there became the friend of Buss and Krüsi, and married, and after a short disagreement with Pestalozzi, labored with him for seven years at Munchen Buchsee and Yverdun. Circumstances brought him to Mühlhausen, where, besides other exertions, he founded his labor-school, which quickly increased so as to contain from four to six hundred scholars, but which came to an end in 1811, in the midst of a prosperous career. Tobler returned to Basle, and set about collecting his pedagogical views and experiences, and preparing for the press a geography upon Pestalozzi's principles.

His pecuniary needs, however, obliging him to seek another situation, he obtained a place as teacher in a private institution in Glarus. On New Year's day of 1817, together with his fellow-teachers, he was dismissed, by reason of the famine. He immediately turned to his profession of tutor, and held a situation for three entire years, in an eminent family of the neighborhood. The children being afterward sent to a newly erected cantonal school, he went to Arbon on the Lake of Constance, with the design of erecting there, instead of a school, a superior orphan-house; but the place was too small. A year afterward he went to St. Gall. Here, the real star of his peda gogical career shone out upon him. That place deserves gratitude for having afforded him ten years together, of free and unimpeded room for the display of his talents as teacher and educator. One of the noblest fruits of this time, was the education of a son to follow his father's honorable example. In 1831, this son was able to graduate from school, and in 1836, he left St. Gall, and accompanied Niederer to Yverdun, and then to Geneva, at both of which places he was at the head of institutions of his own; and was also of very great service to Niederer's school for girls. At present he fills the place of director of a cantonal school at Trogen.

Tobler passed his latter years at Basle, in part with his second son, the principal of a boys' school at Nyon; where he died in his seventy-fourth year, after a short sickness, Aug. 10, 1843. The last months of his life were rendered happy by an elevated self-consciousness, by the pleasant prospect of ending his days at his native place, as he desired, and by incessant and active occupation in setting in order his writings and his domestic affairs. His inner life was as happy and elevated above earthly things as the evening sun, amidst the eternal blue of heaven.

After this short sketch of Tobler's life, varied and struggling as it was, although not fateful, we may devote a few words to his intellectual peculiarities, his rank as a teacher, and his services to humanity and human culture.

His moral and religious nature was his predominating trait; the key-tone of his mind. His father, who filled the place of both father and mother to his sensitive nature, inspired these sentiments into him while yet a child. The maxim "Seek first the kingdom of God (or what was with him its equivalent, the sphere of attainments according to Christ) and its righteousness, and all other things shall be added unto you," was his rule of life; and in his teaching and his example, afforded him constant assistance in answering such questions as arose during his labors for moral improvement.

As soon as he could write, he commenced the practice of taking down sermons and catechizings; and thus acquired great facility in his German style, and a mastery of analytic methods which afterward stood him in good stead by enabling him to deliver extemporaneous sermons and addresses to children, and to compose excellent sketches of sermons. His popular and instructive style occasioned various congregations, after hearing him, to desire him for a pastor. His morning and evening prayers with pupils and children were exceedingly simple, pathetic, clear, and impressive. In moments of higher excitement, the very spirit of the Apostle John's epistles spoke through him. His religious instruction and other Sabbath exercises exerted a profound influence upon the neglected children of the manufacturing school at Mühlhausen.

While a student at Basle, Tobler exercised a predominating influence over numbers of his fellow students, in inciting them to industry, and inspiring them with the idea of the honorableness of their future calling. He was one of the founders there of a society for intellectual improvement; an enterprise which later events rendered prophetical. A very remarkable difference was to be observed between the after lives of those who were his friends, and others.

While he was teacher and director of the female school at Basle, he followed in general the doctrines of Basedow, Campe, and Salzmann. His method of teaching was substantially that which has since been named the Socratic. By strictly adhering to this method he endeavored to call into life and to develop the minds and hearts of his scholars, not however in the ancient Greek spirit, but in that of Christ; and thus he proceeded until the man appeared upon the stage, who gave an entirely new meaning to the word Education, who completely apprehended the entire subjects of education and instruction, who established them as an independent art and science, and made an epoch in their history. To Pestalozzi Tobler adhered, and was afterward his steady disciple.

Tobler fully comprehended Pestalozzi's idea and method, in their general collective significance for humanity and education. Their individual principle separately was more difficult of comprehension to him. He understood it to be Spontaneous Activity. This, however, he considered only as a *receiving* and *working* faculty, to be developed by perception and drilling (*i. e.* Receptivity and Spontaneity; Nature and Capacity; Faculties;) and in this opinion he was quite correct, as well as in regard to the relation of these faculties to the three subjects of instruction, nature, man, and God. But Pestalozzi had determined a third sub-division of this Spontaneous Activity, before unrecognized, and had distinguished within it the elements pertaining to the intellect and to the feelings, viz., that of the *productive* spontaneous activity of the moral and intellectual powers, (the talents?) In this consists the peculiarity and importance of Pestalozzi's discoveries in method, and of the discoveries and the revolution thus originated. It is by operating according to this distinction that the progress of the development and general training of human nature is assured, and the real intellectual and moral emancipation of the schools substantially established.

During the first period of Pestalozzi's institution, Tobler took part with all in everything as a beloved teacher and pupil. In a general activity of this kind consisted what might be called Pestalozzi's jubilee. Then, all the teachers were pupils, and all the pupils teachers; so far as they brought forward independent matter of their own, and furnished results of their own inner activity. After a time, however, the necessity of the separation and ordering of different departments of instruction and drilling, rendered it necessary for Tobler to select some special department of labor; and he selected the real branches; and among them, that of elementary geography. He established the principles of this study by reference to the actual surface of earth, and to the pupil's own sphere of vision, with a success which entitles him to the name of the father of the new method in geography. Ritter, who knew his labors, and proceeded onward from their termination, passed beyond the sphere of education, by a giant stride forward in his science.

Tobler's personal relations with Pestalozzi were neither fortunate nor enduring. Pestalozzi had not the faculty of determining the proper place for each of his assistants, and of laying out for each of them his appointed work. He was neither an organizer nor administrator; and he regarded Tobler's wishes in this respect as mere assumption and weakness. Tobler could not bring out the real value of his views, without their complete display in actual operation. Whoever could at once put a matter into a distinctly practical form could in Pestalozzi's eyes do everything; and whoever fell at all short of this, nothing. Tobler, therefore, wholly absorbed in the business of elementarizing, did nothing to please or satisfy Pestalozzi. The elementarizing of instruction, and of the so-called "real branches," required too much at once; namely, the investigation and harmonious arrangement of the elements and laws of two spheres, viz., that of children's powers, and that of the proposed subject-matter of them. Pestalozzi required from Tobler, simple, rapid and immediate results from this investigation, even when the indispensable materials for them were wanting. Both Tobler and Pestalozzi, moreover, were in the habit of very plain speaking; and as husband and father, Tobler could not devote his entire life to Pestalozzi.

This false position of Tobler's gradually became that of the teachers and pupils of the institution. And Pestalozzi's disposition an opinions passed more and more under the influence of a single o of the assistant teachers (Schmid.)

At München Buchsee, Tobler was a promoter of the separation b tween Pestalozzi and von Fellenberg. Coöperation with the latt was possible only on condition of complete submission to his authority;

a claim which von Fellenberg made on the gronnd of his social position. But the views of the two men were too radically different; of the world, of men, and of pedagogy. It is true that pedagogically, von Fellenberg proceeded on Pestalozzi's principles; but it was upon those principles as he entertained them when he wrote Leonard and Gertrude; when he considered the common school as a valuable instrumentality for the training by society of its needed members; *i. e.*, for education to agriculture, manufacturing, and trades. This view was in harmony with the caste-spirit of society; "The individual was not considered as a moral person, and society subordinated to him as to a superior being, but he was placed quite below it." Pestalozzi had, while at Stanz and Burgdorf, risen very far above this view. He had turned about, let go his consideration of mere purposes, and had laid hold upon the principle of personal exterior independence not merely as a negative, but as a positive fact. This starting point von Fellenberg did not recognize; and Tobler, therefore, could not agree with him. The true reason why no union between von Fellenberg and Pestalozzi and the Pestalozzians never took place is, therefore, not to be sought amongst any accidental circumstances, but in their radical opposition of views.

In Mühlhausen, and afterward in Glarus, Tobler established new schools. His want of adaptedness to the demands of the times upon the teacher and educator here came sharply out. He experienced, by the severe lesson of falling into poverty and want, the truth, that no one, even if possessed of a lofty new truth, strong by nature, and really deserving of confidence and support, can unpunished oppose himself to the tendencies of the age. Every new truth has its martyrs; and a pedagogical truth as well as others.

His real excellence, and his maturest, he showed at St. Gall, while director and center of his school there, as educator and instructor of his pupils, as guide to his assistants, and as unwearied and unsatisfied investigator after new applications of the Pestalozzian method to language, geography and Natural History. He invented a useful alphabetical and reading machine, arranged a simplified mode of map-drawing, and a good though unfinished course of instruction in Natural History. Having continual reference to the common schools, he paid much attention to the subject of obtaining cheap materials for instruction, and took great interest in the training of teachers, for which also he accomplished considerable good.

An idea which never left him after his connection with Pestalozzi, was the training of mothers as teachers; and the establishment of the belief of the destiny and fitness of the female sex for this high calling. Even in his latter years he was still enthusiastic upon this subject, and Niederer's female school at Geneva, owes to him much that is valuable.

The following account of Tobler's educational experiments and failures, is given in his own words, in Pestalozzi's "*Eliza and Christopher.*"

"After having been, for six years, practically engaged in education, I found the result of my labors by no means answering my expectations. The energy of the children, their internal powers, did not increase according to the measure of my exertions, nor even in proportion to the extent of positive information which they had acquired: nor did the knowledge which I imparted to them appear to me to have a sufficiently strong hold upon their minds, or to be so well connected in its various parts, as I felt it ought to be.

I made use of the best juvenile works that were to be had at that time. But these books contained words, of which the greater part were unintelligible to children, and ideas far beyond the sphere of their own experience; and consequently formed, altogether, so strong a contrast with the mode of thinking, feeling, and speaking, natural to their age, that it took endless time and trouble to explain all that they could not understand. But this process of explaining was in itself a tedious job, and, after all, it did no more toward advancing their true internal development, than is done toward dispelling darkness by introducing a few detached rays of light in a dark room, or in the obscurity of a dense, impenetrable mist. The reason of this was, that these books descended to the profoundest depths of human knowledge, or ascended above the clouds, nay, and to the uppermost heavens of eternal glory, before an opportunity was offered to the children of resting their feet on the solid ground of mother earth; on which, nevertheless, it is absolutely necessary that men should be allowed to stand, if they are to learn walking before flying; and for the latter, moreover, if it is to be flying indeed, their wings must have time to grow.

An obscure foreboding of those truths in my mind, induced me, at an early period, to try to entertain my younger pupils with matters of immediate perception, and to clear up the ideas of the elder ones by Socratic conversations. The result of the former plan was, that the little ones acquired a variety of knowledge not generally to be met with at that age. I endeavored to combine this mode of instruction with the methods I found in the most approved works; but whichever of those books I took in hand, they were all written in such a manner as to presuppose the very thing which the children were in a great measure to acquire by them, viz., the knowledge of language. The consequence was, that my Socratic conversations with the elder pupils led to no better result than all other explanations of words by words, to which no real knowledge corresponds in the children's minds, and of which they have, consequently, no clear notion, as regards either each of them taken separately, or the connection in which they are placed together. This was the case with my pupils, and, therefore, the explanation which they seemed to understand to-day, would a few days after be completely vanished from their minds, in a manner to me incomprehensible; and the more pains I took to make everything plain to them, the less did they evince energy or desire to rescue things from that obscurity and confusion in which they naturally appear.

With such experience daily before me, I felt myself invincibly impeded in my progress to the end which I had proposed to myself. I began to converse on the subject with as many schoolmasters, and others engaged or interested in education, as were accessible to me, in whatever direction: but I found, that although their libraries were well furnished with works on education, of which our age has been so productive, yet they saw themselves placed in the same difficulty with myself, and were no more successful with their pupils than I was with mine. Seeing this, I felt with what an increased weight these difficulties must oppress the masters of public schools, unless, indeed, they were rendered too callous for such a feeling by a professional spirit. I had a strong, but, unfortunately, not a clear impression of the defects of education in all its departments, and I exerted myself to the utmost to find a remedy. I made a determination to collect, partly from my own experience, and partly from works on the subject, all the means, methods, and contrivances, by which it seemed to me possible that the difficulties under which I labored, might be removed at every stage of instruction. But I soon found that my life would not suffice for that purpose. Meanwhile I had already completed whole volumes of scraps and extracts, when Fischer, in several of his letters, drew my attention to the method of Pestalozzi. I soon began to suspect that he was about to reach the end I was aiming at, without my circuitous means; and that most of my difficulties arose out of the very nature of the plan which I followed, and which was far too scientific and systematic. I then began to see, that in the same manner the artificial methods, invented in our age, were the very sources of all the defects of modern education. On the contrary, I saw Pestalozzi equally free from my peculiar difficulties, and from the general failings, and I accounted for this by the fact, that he rejected all our ingenious contrivances, all our well-framed systems. Some of the means employed by him, that for instance of making children draw on slates, seemed to me so simple, that my only puzzle was, how I could have gone on so long without hitting upon them. I was struck with the idea that all his discoveries, seemed to be of the kind which might be termed "obvious," they were none of them far-fetched. But what most attached me to his method, was his principle of re-educating mothers for that for which they are originally destined by nature, for this principle I had long cherished and kept in view, in the course of my experiments.

I was confirmed in these views by Krüsi, who, at his visit in Basle, gave, in the girls' school, practical specimens of Pestalozzi's mode of teaching spelling, reading, and arithmetic. Pastor Faesch, and Mr. De Brunn, who had in part organized the instruction and management of that institution, according to the loose hints which had as yet reached us on the Pestalozzian method, perceived immediately what a powerful impression was produced upon the children by their spelling and reading together in a stated measure of time. Krüsi had also brought with him some school materials for the instruction in writing and arithmetic, and some leaves of a vocabulary, which Pestalozzi intended to draw up as a first reading-book for children; which enabled us to see the bearing which Pestalozzi's method had upon the development of the different faculties of human nature. All this contributed to mature in me, very rapidly, the determination to join Pestalozzi, according to his wish.

I went to Burgdorf, and the first impression of the experiment, in the state in which it then was, fully answered my expectations. I was astonished to see what a striking degree of energy the children generally evinced, and how simple, and yet manifold, were the means of development by which that energy was elicited. Pestalozzi took no notice whatever of all the existing systems and methods; the ideas which he presented to the minds of his pupils were all extremely simple; his means of instruction were distinctly subdivided, each part being calculated for a precise period in the progress of development; whatever was complicated and confused, he rejected; by a few words he conveyed much, and with little apparent exertion produced a powerful effect; he kept always close to the point then under consideration; some of his branches of instruction seemed like a new creation, raised from the elements of art and nature: all this I saw, and my attention was excited to the highest degree.

There were some parts of his experiment, it is true, which seemed to me rather unnatural; of this description was, for instance, the repetition of difficult and complicated sentences, which could not, at first, but make a very confused impression upon his pupils. But I saw, on the other hand, what a power he had of leading children into clear ideas; yet I mentioned my doubts to him. His answer was, that nature herself presented all sorts of perceptions to our senses in confusion and obscurity, and that she brings them to clearness afterward. To this argument I had nothing to reply,* especially as I saw that he attached no value to the details

* The obvious reply was, that the perceptions which nature presents, however confused, or otherwise obscure, they may be, are realities, and therefore contain in themselves the very elements of clearness, and at the same time, a strong inducement to search for those elements. But confused impressions made upon us by words, are not realities, but mere shadows; they have in themselves the elements of confusion, and they offer neither an inducement, nor the means, for clearing them up. The former call out the mind, the latter cramp it. The very power which Pestalozzi possessed over his pupils, what was it owing to, according to the statements both of himself and his friends, but to his making a rule of supplying the child with a clear and distinct notion of the reality, before he gave him the sign or shadow, the name?

cf his experiment, but tried many of them with a view to throw them aside again, as soon as they should have answered their temporary purpose. With many of them he had no other object than to increase the internal power of the children, and to obtain for himself further information concerning the fundamental principles on which all his proceedings rested. I resolved, therefore, not to mind the apparent inadequacy of some of his means, so much the more as I had come to the conviction, that the further pursuit of the experiment necessarily involved the improvement of the details of the method. This was perfectly evident already in arithmetic, in drawing, and in the rudiments of language.

I perceived, likewise, that by the connection which his different means of instruction had with each other, every one of them, individually, was instrumental in promoting the success of all the others, and, especially, in developing and strengthening the faculties generally. Long before he began to lay down his principles in stated terms, I saw, in the daily observation of their practical effect, the approaching maturity of the whole undertaking, and, as an infallible consequence of it, the gradual attainment of the object he had in view. In trying the details of his method, he never leaves any single exercise until he has so far investigated and simplified it, that it seems physically impossible to advance any further. Seeing the indefatigable zeal with which he did this, I was more and more confirmed in a sentiment, of which I had before had some indistinct notion, that all the attempts at fostering the development of human nature, by means of a complicated and artificial language, must necessarily end in a failure; but that, on the contrary, a method intended to assist nature in the course of human development, must be characterised by the utmost simplicity in all the means of instruction, and more especially in language, which should be a faithful expression of the simplicity of both the child's own mind, and the objects and ideas which are employed for its cultivation. I now began to understand, by degrees, what he meant by introducing a variety of distinctions in the instruction of language; by aiming, in his arithmetical instruction, at nothing else but producing in the child's mind a clear and indelible conviction that all arithmetic was nothing else but an abridgment of the simple process of enumeration, and the numbers themselves nothing but an abridgment of the wearisome repetition, one, and one, and one, and one; and, lastly, by declaring an early development of the faculty of drawing lines, angles, curves, and figures, to be the groundwork of art, and even of the capacity, which so few men possess, of taking a distinct view of visible objects.

I could not but feel every day more confirmed in the notions which I had formed of the manifold advantages of his method, by being a constant witness of the effects produced by general development of the mental faculties in the arts of measuring, calculating, writing, and drawing. I grew more and more convinced that it was possible to accomplish what I have before stated to have been the leading object of my own pursuits at a previous period, viz., to re-educate mothers for the fulfillment of that sacred task assigned to them by nature, the result of which would be, that even the first instruction imparted in schools, would have previous maternal tuition for a foundation to rest on. I saw a practical method discovered, which, admitting of universal application, would enable parents, who have the welfare of their offspring at heart, to become themselves the teachers of their little ones. From that moment, popular improvement ceased to be dependent on the circuitous plan of training teachers in expensive seminaries, and with the aid of extensive libraries.

In short, the result of the first impression produced upon my mind by the whole of Pestalozzi's experiment, and of the observations I have since been able to make on the details of his method, has been, to re-establish in my heart that faith which I held so dear at the onset of my career, but which I had almost lost under the pressure of systems sanctioned by the fashion of the day, faith in the practicability of popular improvement."

In the progress of his narrative he declares himself. that it was one of the characteristic features of his method of teaching language, that he reduced it to the utmost simplicity, "by excluding from it every combination of words which presupposes a knowledge of language." He was not, however, at all times, equally clear on this point, although it lies at the very foundation of all his improvements in elementary instruction.

JOHANN RAMSAUER.

JOHANN RAMSAUER was born in May, 1790, in Herisau, in the Swiss canton of Appenzell, where his father carried on a small manufactory, and a trade in the machines and tools used in spinning and weaving-factories. In his fourth year he lost his father, whose business was continued by his mother. He was the youngest of her seven remaining children; and was occupied in the labors of the establishment, and in accompanying his older brothers and sisters to market. At home he learned to work, and to be orderly, industrious, and obedient. At eight he was sent to a wretched school, where, in two years, he learned, with great difficulty, to write and read ill. During this period of his life he learned much more from the good examples set him at home than from the incompetent schoolmaster. In the "*Brief Sketch of My Pedagogical Life*," furnished originally for Diesterweg's "*Pedagogical Germany*," we are told:—

"When the French Revolution, during the years 1796 to 1799, caused stagnation of trade, general loss of employment, and even famine and all sorts of misery throughout Switzerland, especially the eastern part, there gradually wandered away, out of the cantons of Uri, Schwytz, Unterwalden, Zug, Glarus, and Appenzell, five thousand three hundred boys and girls of from seven to fourteen; partly to Basle and Neuenburg, but chiefly to the great cantons of Zurich and Bern, where they were received humanely, and in most cases treated even with parental kindness and fidelity. Although I did not belong to such a troop of utterly destitute children, my mother yielded to my often-repeated request to be also allowed to emigrate; and thus, in February, 1800, I left my home and wandered off with forty-four boys of from ten to fourteen years old." He entered, while a boy, a school at Burgdorf, which Krüsi was teaching; and soon after that of Pestalozzi. "In the public school, where Pestalozzi taught six hours daily, I learned, school-fashion, no more than the rest. But his holy zeal, his deep and entirely self-forgetting love, and his earnest manner, impressive even to the children, made the deepest impression upon me, and knit my childish, grateful heart to his forever." He continued for several years at Burgdorf, as scholar, table-waiter, and under-under-teacher. Ramsauer became a favorite scholar of Pestalozzi, and accompanied him, often acting as his private secretary, during his stay at Burgdorf, München-Buchsee, and Yverdun. At the latter place he acquired a knowledge of mechanics, with the view of assisting in a school planned by Pestalozzi for the education of the poor. He left Yverdun in April, 1816, to become a teacher in a school newly established at Würzburg; departing from Pestalozzi with great reluctance, but feeling that the influence and character of Schmid rendered him of little further use there, and in part induced by the privilege of free attendance upon lectures at the University of Würzburg.

Here Ramsauer lived happily, making short journeys from time to time, giving private instruction, acquiring new knowledge from the university lectures, of a kind which afforded a useful complement to his previous practical studies, and growing so rapidly in reputation that, in October, 1816, of four invitations to other situations as teacher, two were from Stuttgardt, one inviting him to become instructor of the princes Alexander and Peter of Oldenburg, and another to become head of an important school for the elementary instruction of children of the educated classes. Both these invitations he accepted, and went to Stuttgardt in March, 1817.

While here, he undertook a third employment as teacher in a new real school; his own institute being discontinued, and the male pupils entering the real school, while the female ones, whom he continued to teach, attended the *Katharinenstift*, a female school established by the Queen of Wirtemburg, and opened with an address by the queen herself.

The young princes of Oldenburg leaving Stuttgardt in 1820, for the court of their grandfather, the Duke of Oldenburg, Ramsauer attended them thither, to continue their education in mathematics, drawing, and gymnastics. Some months afterward he opened a school for girls of the educated classes, which he was still conducting with success in 1838.

In 1826 he was appointed teacher of the duchesses Amalia and Frederica of Oldenburg, whom he instructed for ten years. Afterward he established in Oldenburg a school for the daughters of persons of the educated classes. Here he published his "*Instruction in Form, Size, and Substance;* being the elements of Geometry methodized. With fifteen lithographic plates. 1826." He had before published his work on "*Drawing,*" in two volumes, thirty-one lithographic plates.

Ramsauer sums up his pedagogical experience as follows:—

1. I learned, in my father's house, up to my tenth year, to pray and to obey.
2. In Schleumen, to run, climb, and jump.
3. With Pestalozzi, from my eleventh to my twenty-sixth year, to work, to think, and to observe.

4. During my various journeys, to be independent, and to help myself.

5. In Würzburg and Stuttgardt, to be more modest, and to some extent a knowledge of the world and of family life.

6. In Oldenburg, the word of God; to endure good and evil with equanimity, well-knowing whence and why they come; and in many ways the knowledge that we live upon a beautiful and wonderful earth, but that to care and strive for things connected with it, is a troubled life; that it is well worth while to pay regard to the spirit of the age; and that it is possible to live very happily here below, and, at the same time, to prepare one's self well for the better future life.

We give some further extracts from the "*Sketches*," which may be interesting to readers connected with the work of education.

I have already said that the finer social graces must either be inborn or developed by culture. Even of the simple politeness of a boy's manners this is true. I have found this always to be the case. Those to whom this gift is natural are usually of rather weak or superficial intellects; but, as the saying is, they get well through the world—that is, easily attain eminence in society. This opinion has led me to another and a more important one, namely, that in practical life it is of little moment whether one has "a good head," (*ein guter kopf.*) It is of much greater importance, however, what is one's character for truthfulness and perseverance; and much more, that he keep his faith. Through this last, if it be of the right kind, comes the blessing. As to the point of practical efficiency, every one of even moderate experience in the world will agree with me that those men who have filled important places in the world, are indebted to their truthfulness, perseverance, and uprightness much more than to their "good head," or their "genius." This is especially true of those of the burgher class. Even in the elementary school, this truthfulness and perseverance can be cultivated, proved, and established; but it is home education which must do most of it.

It has often troubled me to hear of a "smart boy" (*guten kopfe,*) in a family or school, and to see those undervalued who lacked such a qualification. Such conduct discourages those reckoned inferior, (who subsequently very probably may excel them,) and only makes those possessed of this apparent talent conceited and heartless. Faith and good feeling forbid such doing; unless we are born merely for the span of present existence! Young teachers, just commencing, are especially prone to fix upon such smart boys; but commonly deceive themselves, by setting a high value upon a mere partial quickness of apprehension. There are even teachers, whether from the fear of men or from some other discreditable weakness, who praise every thing they see in their scholars; or who, after they have complained to their colleagues about scholars all the year, will, at the end of the term, make out for them certificates of unqualified excellence.

I have known not only hundreds but thousands of proofs that, however unpleasant a strict teacher my be to a bad scholar, such a scholar will, in the end, feel toward him more respect, and gratitude, and love; provided only that the strictness was just—that is, without respect of persons, partiality, or passionateness. Even the most spoiled of children will endure ten times more from such a teacher than from another, provided only that the parents acquiesce in it.

There are also teachers who lay great stress upon learning quickly; forgetting that the most superficial scholars are often the quickest. Such will find, by experiments enough, that these forget just as quickly; while things acquired with more pains remain longer in the memory, and are better understood. The principal thing is thoroughness; it is this only which truly educates—which tells upon character. Merely to know more or less is of little significance; whoever imagines that he knows very much, does, in fact, know pitifully little. This thoroughness should be a characteristic even of the lowest elementary school; and is a constituent of what I have already referred to as perseverance. A condition preparatory to this thoroughness is, that the scholar be constrained (without any apparent force, however,) into thinking and laboring independently. Thus I have often said to an indolent or compliant scholar, who imitated others rather too easily, "Your own eating must make you fat; that you know very well. Just so, your own thinking must make you wise; and your own practice must make you dexterous."

A condition of thoroughness is repetition; constant repetition. This means is, to many teachers, too wearisome, or too slow: the latter, to those who instruct mechanically only; the former, to those who have never perceived and learned for themselves, but only out of books. But a teacher whose heart is really in his work will be drilling often and earnestly, and always in new ways; so that both the scholar and he himself will always be getting at a new and interesting side of the subject. But a teacher who labors in two or three departments of study with vivacity and pleasure, and gives really thorough instruction—such as really educates—will naturally have neither time nor wish to expend several hours daily in a club or in other mere amusements. His greatest happiness will be in his calling; and in daily progress in whatever is truly useful for time and eternity. Such a teacher will live as much as possible amongst his own children, if he has them; and the more he does so, the better will he comprehend other children, and, therefore, the better will he manage them.

Among my own children, as well as among those of others, I have repeatedly experienced that there is a school understanding, a conversation understanding, and a life or practical understanding; all three very clearly distinct, especially the first and the third. If the teacher only understands the first of these, he only half-understands even that; and is in great danger of exacting too much or too little from his scholars. In like manner, parents are liable to do the teacher injustice, if they judge of their children only by their words and actions at home. Girls especially, who in school hardly dare open their mouths, often appear astonishingly quick and intelligent outside; so that those will be much deceived who overlook the multitude of cases in which children imitate the words and actions of adults, and pass off their sayings for their own coin. The school understanding is the most suitable for scholars; as their passions are less liable to come into play in connection with it, and all matters which are regularly arranged and under rules assist its onward progress. From this difference it often follows that the same scholar who is industrious, efficient, and intelligent in school, and seems there to be far forward for his age, is wholly a child when outside of it, childish and simple (as he should be,) and apparently quite backward in understanding, and this especially where he needs to govern himself and to exhibit character.

Such experiences of a hundred others will lead every observing teacher—I do not state this as any thing new, but merely as something of psychological importance, and therefore not susceptible of too frequent repetition—to require from his scholars neither too much nor too little, and to hope from them neither too much nor too little. And I believe that the frequent enforcement of such experiences would materially ease the difficult calling of the teacher, especially at its commencement, and would save beginners our trouble at Pestalozzi's Institute; that is, from spending all the first years of their work in proving and experimenting, without the advantage of being able to learn of their predecessors.

JOHN ERNST PLAMANN.

John Ernst Plamann, an earnest and influential teacher and apostle of the Pestalozzian system, in Prussia, was born on the 22d of June, 1771, at Repzin, of poor but respectable parents of the burgher class, and received his elementary education at the Royal Real School in Berlin, from which he was removed to the Joachimsthal Gymnasium, then under the charge of the celebrated Meierotto. In 1796 he resorted to Halle to study theology, and at the same time acquire the principles of pedagogy under Niemeyer. After spending a few years as a private tutor in the family of his brother-in-law, and passing his examination for a license to teach, he returned to Berlin, to continue his classical studies, and, at the same time, to give instruction in the Messow Institute and other industrial schools, preparatory to founding one of the same class for himself.

At this time the fame of Pestalozzi had spread into Germany, and Plamann resolved to see for himself the great schoolmaster who was so extravagantly praised and beloved. Having read "*How Gertrude teaches her Children*," he could not rest; but, borrowing some money to pay his expenses, he set out in May, 1803, for Switzerland; having announced his intention to Pestalozzi in a letter, from which the following is an extract:

> Thanks is a powerless word to express the enthusiasm which your letters upon instruction have kindled in me. But you will not despise my utterance; indeed you will not hear it, amid the loud praises which nations are giving you. Of that your heart assures me, noble man, who have so acutely and truly displayed the inmost laws of the development of the human soul, and with a wise and strong hand laid out the path and the art of training it. You have so radiated upon me the light of truth, and so inspired my breast, that I also feel the sacred call to labor in my fatherland to the same end, according to my powers. The saying of our great teacher, "Many are called, but few chosen," shall not discourage me if I can enjoy your instructions and wise direction. With that I can escape from the old, lifeless, beaten track, which I have been obliged to follow in my labor as a teacher, and will be able to do something in the necessary work of teaching the neglected to elevate themselves. O, if you will give me power; if you will make me an example of your methods; if you will instruct me thoroughly in your system; then I hope, with confidence and success, to sow the seed which your benevolence shall have entrusted to me, &c.

Pestalozzi was then at Burgdorf. There soon sprung up between him and Plamann a friendship based upon mutual appreciation; for Plamann, with his thorough knowledge of the labor of former schools in pedagogy, his scientific attainments, his philosophical intellect and psychological insight, was a valuable supplementary person to the Swiss reformer, who had only his own experience of the results of his always original mental action. The latter candidly explained to him what he was seeking, both by means of written and oral communication, until he understood him and his system thoroughly. Plamann writes:

> Pestalozzi received me like a father. No man ever looked so quickly and deeply into my soul as he. At once he comprehended my whole being, and pressed me to his breast with the warmth of a brother. At his side I learned to feel how many were my faults as a man. I was modest, and told him of my discovery with tearful eyes. "You are a child of nature," he answered; "an adept in the rules of science and art, which I am not; and which, nevertheless, a man must be in this world." Thus he used to encourage me to have more confidence in myself. A poem which I gave him moved him to tears. He smothered me with kisses, and said, "No one has understood me so well."

Plamann remained several months in Burgdorf, laboring zealously at the new method; and became so dear to Pestalozzi, that he could not endure to have him depart, and even offered him money sufficient to enable him to bring his betrothed to Switzerland. But he was impatient to introduce the new method into his fatherland. Immediately after his return to Berlin, Plamann proceeded to put his newly-gotten knowledge into practice in the institution where he was teaching, and to apply the method also to other subjects. He maintained a regular correspondence with Pestalozzi and his assistants, especially with Niederer. The Swiss took the utmost interest in his labors, kept him acquainted with their researches, and awaited with solicitude the result of his undertakings.

In 1805 Plamann published his work, "*Some Principles of the art of Instruction according to Pestalozzi's Method, applied to Natural History, Geography, and Language.*" (*Einzige Grundregel der Unterrichtskunst nach Pestalozzi's Methode, angewandt in der Naturgeschichte, Geographie und Sprache.*) In this publication, he showed upon what a deep psychological basis Pestalozzi's system rested, and how it is necessarily derived from the laws of human thought. While, however, they commence with the same principles, follow them out with like results, and in like manner connect them with others, their related ones, Plamann differs from Pestalozzi on the view laid down in the "*Book for Mothers,*" that education should begin with instruction on the human body, on the ground that the similarity of it with the bodies of animals does not much concern the child, and that instruction by a teacher should not be given so early. He thought it more proper for the mother to teach the child about such objects as are within the sphere of the child's knowledge; — the house, furniture, clothes, &c. He then proceeds to apply the method to the three departments of natural history, to geography, and to the German language. He promised in the second part to continue the course of instructions on language and geography, as well as on technology and history; but this has never been published.

On account of his high standing with Pestalozzi, his zeal in studying the method, and in extending it by his writings, he became a centre for the operations of those who were following the new views in Prussia, and were endeavoring to spread them there. All applied to him for directions, school-books, plans for schools, and information as to the spread and results of the new method; and he was also in communication with persons in foreign countries.

Soon after his return to Prussia from Switzerland, Plamann undertook himself to found an institution for the practice of Pestalozzi's methods. For this he obtained the royal permission, Nov. 29, 1803, and opened the institution at Michaelmas, 1805, with his friend Schmidt; obtaining also, soon after, an assistant from Switzerland, Breissig by name. His undertaking drew much attention, and proved quite successful. In the following year he published two instructive works:

"*Course of Instruction for a Pestalozzian School for Boys.*" (*Anordnung des Unterrichts für ein Pestalozzische Knaben Schule.*)

"*Elementary Methods of Instruction in Language and Science.*" (*Elementarformen, Sprach-u. wissenschaftlichen Unterrichtskunst.*)

At Easter, 1812, Plamann gave up his school, and visited once more his beloved Pestalozzi, to make himself acquainted with the progress of the method, and to observe what was going on in the schools of Switzerland. Upon his return he at once commenced again to "Pestalozzianize," as he expressed himself, and bought a house in Berlin, in which to erect an institution. In the same year he commenced a publication, which he finished in 1815, entitled, "*Contributions to Pedagogical Criticism; in Defence of the Pestalozzian Method.*" (*Beitrage zur Pädagogischen Kritik; zur Vertheidigung der Pestalozzischen Methode.*)

A full description of his new Pestalozzian institution will be found in the "*Biography of Plamann, by Doctor Franz Bredow.*" Plamann adhered closely to the Pestalozzian principles throughout; proceeding strictly according to the forms of the Swiss at first, but using more and more independent methods as he went on. His school was resorted to by young men from all quarters, who were ambitious to understand and disseminate the improved methods of teaching, and he was never more popular than when he gave up his school from the pressure of bodily infirmities, against which he had long struggled. He died on the 3d of September, 1834.

HANS GEORG NÄGELI.

Hans Georg Nageli, by whose compositions and teaching the Pestalozzian method of instruction was applied to the study of music, was born, May 17, 1773, at Wetzekon, a village in the canton of Zurich, of which his father was pastor. After receiving his rudimentary education at home, he went to Zurich in 1786, to continue his studies; but homesickness soon drew him back to his father's home, where he devoted himself carefully to the study of music, and in 1790 he again resorted to Zurich, when in a few years we find him in a music store and musical circulating library of his own, and at the same time giving lessons in singing. He became a composer and publisher of music, and in 1800 he established a periodical principally, devoted to his favorite art. His song, "Life let us cherish," accompaniments of harp and harpsichord, published in 1794, passed the parlor, and the fireside, and the social gathering of rich and poor, all over Europe; and the same popularity has marked other productions of his.

Nägeli was one of the earliest founders, even if he did not originate, the Swiss musical league or union, which set the example of great musical festivals, attended by concourses of people, practically engaged in or lovers of the art. He went out frequently to give instruction to musical societies in the different cantons, to lecture on the subject to conventions of teachers, and, in 1810, published, in connection with M. T. Pfeiffer, "*The Theory of Instruction in Singing, on Pestalozzian Principles*," (*Die Gesangbildungslehre nach Pestalozzischen Grundsätzen*,) by which a new epoch in this department of education was introduced. The treatise was the best realization of the method of Pestalozzi, and soon made singing a regular study in the popular schools of Europe, particularly those of Switzerland and Germany. By the efforts of William C. Woodbridge and Lowell Mason, the method of Nägeli was introduced into the United States; and, in consequence, the study of music became much more philosophical and general, and is fast passing into the course of instruction in our common schools.

Nägeli died at Zurich, on the 26th of December, 1836, from a cold he contracted in discharge of his duties as a member of the council of education.

WILHELM HARNISCH

WILHELM HARNISCH was born, August 28th, 1787, at Wilsnach, in the Prussian government of Potsdam—the only son of a prosperous master-tailor, who intended him for the study of theology, and accordingly placed him at the gymnasium in Salzwedel in 1800, and caused him to study from 1806 to 1808 at Halle and Frankfort-on-the-Oder. Here he already began to devote himself particularly to the study of pedagogy, and very soon commenced the practice of it, taking a situation as private tutor in a distinguished family in Mecklenburg, where a well-selected library was at his command, and Rousseau's "*Emile*" was the favorite study of the accomplished mistress of the family. In 1810 he had the good fortune to be summoned to Berlin, in order to be made acquainted with the Pestalozzian system in Plamann's institution, at the expense of the State. Here, in the society of Fichte, Schleiermacher, Köpfe, Zeune, Jahn, Klöden, and other eminent literati, statesmen, and educators, he completed his higher scientific education, and also took an active part in the first establishment of the fencing school, and the gymnastic and swimming institutions. In 1812 he took the degree of Doctor of Philosophy, married the daughter of a landed proprietor in Russian Lithuania, and became favorably known by his first work, "*The German Common Schools.*" Being appointed teacher in the new Teachers' Seminary at Breslau, established upon Pestalozzi's principles, he introduced, with excellent results, a system of instruction in reading and writing, which he also made known in various publications. While [illegible] he also wholly originated or took part in various academical [illegible]rs; established a Society of Teachers, took partial charge of the [illegible]ucation of Princess Charlotte, afterward Empress of Russia, and l[illegible]ed in friendly intercourse with Professors Schneider, Wachler, Steffens, Passow, Kaysler, &c. In 1822 he was appointed director of the Teachers' Seminary at Weissenfels, to which he gave a reputation second to no other in Germany, and which is well known in this country, through the Reports of Stowe, Bache, and Mann.

In 1834 he received from the King of Prussia the red order of nobility, fourth class; has received honorary gifts from the Emperor and Empress of Russia, and other royal personages; besides pecuniary means for various pedagogical journeys. In 1837 he was complimented by his colleagues and scholars with the celebration of a jubilee on occasion of the twenty-fifth anniversary of his labors as a teacher. He has rendered distinguished services toward the perfection of the common school system of Prussia, by his manifold practical and literary labors.

The principal of his numerous writings are the following:—

THE GERMAN COMMON SCHOOLS (*Die Deutscher Volksschulen,*) Berlin, 1812.

COMPLETE INSTRUCTION IN GERMAN (*Vollständiger Unterricht in der Deutschen Sprache,*) Breslau, 1814.

COMPLETE EXPOSITION OF THE BELL–LANCASTERIAN SYSTEM (*Ausführliche Darstellung des Bell-Lancasterschen Schulwesens,*) Breslau, 1819.

LIFE OF THE TUTOR FELIX KASKORBI (a pedagogical romance,) (*Das Leben des Hauslehrers Felix Kaskorbi, ein pädagogischer Roman,*) Breslau, 1820.

HAND-BOOK FOR THE GERMAN SCHOOL SYSTEM (*Handbuch für das Deutsche Volksschulwesen,*) Breslau, 1820.

THE EDUCATION AND SCHOOL COUNCILOR (*Die Erziehungs-und Schulrath.*) 24 parts. Breslau, 1815 to 1820.

THE COMMON SCHOOL TEACHER, (five years,) (*Die Volksschullehrer,*) (5 *jahrgänge,*) Halle, 1824 to 1828.

THE GERMAN BURGHER SCHOOLS (*Die Deutsche Bürgerschule,*) Halle, 1830.

THE WEISSENFELS SEMINARY (*Das Weissenfelser Seminar,*) Berlin, 1838. (Containing an autobiograph sketch.)

KARL AUGUST ZELLER.

Karl August Zeller, High School Councillor and Royal Councillor of the Kingdom of Prussia, was born August 15th, 1774, in Ludwigsburg, Wirtemberg. He was educated in a theological seminary, and in 1798 received an appointment as teacher and assistant preacher in the evangelical congregation at Brunn. In 1803, he proceeded to Pestalozzi's establishment at Burgdorf, for the purpose of making himself acquainted with his new system of instruction. An offer, which he accepted, to accompany a young man of the Von Palm family upon his travels, gave him occasion, while at Tubingen in the winter of 1804, to establish a charity school for the purpose of trying Pestalozzi's plans, and afterwards, at the request of some of his scholars at Brunn, a Sunday-school. Both are described in a work dedicated to that friend of education, the late Pauline, Princess of Detmold, who gave him the appointment of Councillor, and retained a decided interest in his prosperity until her death.

Zeller became pastor at St. Gall, and teacher in the gymnasium there, in 1805. In 1806, he became acquainted, in Zurich, with the Senator Rusterholz, who had a scheme for educating all the teachers of the cantons in normal schools, which he was prevented from carrying out by sickness. Becoming much interested for the sick man and his designs, he agreed to remain in Zurich and endeavor to assist him; to which coöperation the authorities of the cantons agreed.

The first course of instruction was opened in 1806, with thirty pupils, by a commission of school councillors, under the presidency of Superintendent Gessner. The lectures, here devoted to the principles of correct school discipline, gave Zeller an opportunity of composing his "*School for Teachers.*" After the decisive experiment of this course, seven thousand florins were appropriated to defray the expense of a Normal School, Pestalozzi's arithmetic was introduced, and a plan of teaching drawn up by Zeller was printed and introduced into the parochial schools of the canton. A second and a third part to this treatise soon followed. Being appointed Director of the Normal Institute, he trained, in 1807, among others, a Catholic clergyman, sent to him by the government of Lucerne, and who was followed by three canons from the same canton, who had been studying at Kreutzlingen in the

Thurgan, under the patronage of Von Wessenberg. Meanwhile, a favorable report was made by a commission of clergymen upon the result of the first three courses of the normal school; and, whereupon, Zeller published a work on the subject, in the form of letters addressed to the Princess Pauline. Three courses of lectures now followed, one of which was delivered before the Swiss Diet, and the attention of the Confederation was thus drawn to the subject of them.

The year 1808 found Zeller with Pestalozzi, teaching and learning, and enjoying himself amongst the children. In returning, he passed through Hofwyl, where a young Bernese gave him fifty *carolines*, with the request that he would undertake a school for teachers among his country people in that neighborhood. Upon the invitation of the consistory, who added thirty carolines, forty teachers assembled, and remained under his instruction ten months. A French teacher, under an assumed name, also attended this course, and afterwards pursued his vocation in his own country. By reason of the open recognition by the Bernese government of his efforts, in spite of malicious opposition, and having a little before received a call from Zofingen, Zeller had meditated spending the remainder of his life as a Swiss burgher; but the visit of the King of Wirtemberg to Hofwyl gave another direction to his life.

The king had attended five of his lectures, and was so much pleased with what he saw and heard, that he declared that he could not permit Zeller to remain in that place. In fact, he shortly after received the appointment of school-inspector at Heilbronn, and, two months later, an appointment at Königsberg from the Prussian minister of state, Von Schrötter, whom War-councillor Schiffner had made acquainted with the "*Letters to the Princess Pauline.*" Not yet actually employed in Heilbronn, Zeller requested permission to accept the latter; but an order to the teachers of the vicinity to assemble there, and to himself as the proper schoolmaster to instruct them, was the answer. Forty-two teachers assembled, including one minister, and remained, at their own expense, six weeks. The assembly was characterized by the same pleasant activity, good nature and success, which had appeared in Switzerland.

In April, 1809, with the office of Councillor in the government of East Prussia, he was authorized to organize the Orphan House at Königsberg as a model school, in which young clergymen and teachers might be instructed, with courses of lectures on the administration and instruction of schools, and traverse all the provinces of the kingdom for similar purposes. On condition that he should deliver one more course of lectures to clergymen of all three confessions, the King of Wirtemberg at length allowed him to accept the appointment. Fifty-two eminent clergymen and six teachers assembled, and remained under his instruction during four weeks. A commission from the High Consistory of the kingdom and from the Council of Catholic Clergy held an examination upon the result, and Zeller, accompanied by one of Pestalozzi's pupils, now for the first time proceeded to the Baltic.

The new organization of the orphan home at Königsberg in a short time excited so much interest, that a considerable number of official persons were desirous of some report upon Zeller's methods and organization. Further; the noble and intellectual men who were laboring with Scharnhorst to reëstablish the warlike fame of Prussia, learned hence to consider the relation between a correct school discipline and military discipline. October 7, the king, queen and ministry, made a personal inspection of the school, and the dignity of High School Councillor, conferred upon the director, showed their gratification with the visit. In May, 1810, the institution had so grown that the first course of lectures was attended by a hundred and four deans, superintendents and pastors, and the second by seventy clergymen and teachers.

In 1811, he organized a second institution at Braunsberg for the province of Ermeland, and a third at Karalene, for Lithuania. He would gladly have remained in the latter pleasant place, but his official duties would not permit. He was intending to go to Stettin also, but the approach of Napoleon's expedition to Russia prevented. An "extraordinary compensation" was now decreed him, in consequence of this disappointment, and as a testimony of the satisfaction of the king and the ministry with the results of his exertions in East and West Prussia and Lithuania. This was the gift of the domain of Munsterwalde, near Marienwerder, on the condition that he should continue to perform the functions of his appointment. He accordingly published a manual for the Prussian army-schools, and a work upon his experiments in organizing the school of correction at Graudenz, containing a statement of the methods upon which all his labors hitherto had been conducted.

For several years Zeller resided at Kreutznach, Wetzlar and Bonn, busily engaged in writing and in the support of his numerous family. His only son devoted himself to the study of theology at Bonn, and at the same place, his wife, the mother of his seven children, died. He became desirous of revisiting his native country; and, having been raised by the King of Prussia to the third class of the "red order of nobility," he removed to Stuttgart in 1834. His last labors were devoted to his own country; the institution at

Lichtenstein owes to him its foundation and progress, a building worth eleven hundred florins, and continued care and advocacy. The requirements of his situation obliged him to remove to Stuttgart again in the autumn of 1837.

His very busy and varied life came to an end in the beginning of the year 1847, while he was absent from home on a short journey; a life that knew no rest, and whose quiet pulses often seemed like restless wandering; a life which, without despising an open recognition of its deserts, yet often forgot itself in true sacrifices for the sake of doing good; that willingly bestowed its strength wherever any beneficial purpose was to be served, and especially if any alleviations in the condition of the children of the poor common people were in prospect. His mission was, not to maintain and carry on an enterprise already commenced, with long-suffering and victorious patience and constancy, but rather to erect edifices upon waste and desert ground for others to furnish. Especially valuable for young theologians are the many stirring thoughts contained in his "Thomas, or John and Paul?" published in 1833. The desire and labor of his life was to improve the common schools. The study of singing in that class of Prussian schools began with him. He was energetic, not only in introducing new discoveries in pedagogical science, but also in independently sifting and ingeniously improving its principles already accepted.

Zeller's best known educational works, as given in Hergang's "*Manual of Pedagogical Literature,*" are:

The Schoolmaster School; or, instructions in school education on the plan of the institutions for saving children (Kinder-Rettungsanstalt). Leipzig, 1839.

Elementary Schools; their personal, local and administrative organization. Königsberg, 1815.

The Evangel of Jesus Christ; or his character as such; not developed chronologically, but in its various elements and relations; as exhibited in a harmony of the four gospels. Stuttgart, 1839.

Methods of Learning, for use of common schools on the mutual system.

Elementary Geometry for Common Schools. Three parts. Stuttgart, 1839.

Elementary Singing-Book for Common Schools. Three parts. Stuttgart, 1839.

BERNHARD GOTTLIEB DENZEL.

BERNHARD GOTTLIEB DENZEL, an influential promoter of Pestalozzianism in the Kingdom of Wirtemberg and the Duchy of Nassau, was born at Stuttgardt, on the 29th of December, 1773. His father was a merchant and associate-judge, and secured for his son the best education which the gymnasia and university of the kingdom could give. After studying theology at Tübingen, under the profound Dr. Storr, he commenced his pedagogical career as private tutor in Frankfort-on-the-Maine. After two years' experience in that capacity, he served five years as curate and preacher in Pleidelsheim, where he exhibited an enthusiastic interest in the schools, and took the lead in introducing the new Pestalozzian system into Wirtemberg. His decided and influential labors in this work involved him, for a time, in bitter controversy with many old-fashioned schoolmasters, and municipalties; but he was sustained by the higher authorities. He made himself perfectly familiar with the publications of Pestalozzi, and visited both Burgdorf and Yverdun, to observe the practical operations of the system. Deeply in earnest himself, with a thorough practical knowledge of existing wants, and desirable remedies, with a conciliatory manner, and the confidence of all religious men, Denzel made more rapid progress than is usual with school reformers; but, as has been already remarked, he did not entirely escape the opposition of parties whose craft was interfered with.

In 1811, Denzel was appointed director of the Seminary for Teachers in Esslingen, and of the public schools in that circle. Under his oversight, the seminary and the schools made great progress, and were resorted to by teachers and educators as good working-models of the new system of instruction. In 1817, having obtained leave of absence for this purpose, he assisted in reorganizing the school system of the Duchy of Nassau, and establishing the Teachers' Seminary at Idstein, and received, for his service, the appointment of Ducal high school councilor, and the title and rank of prelate.

After performing good service to the cause of popular education throughout Germany, not only through the improvements introduced into the schools of Nassau and Wirtemberg, but by his writings on the science and art of teaching, he died, in the autumn of 1838, universally respected and beloved.

As a teacher, Director Denzel was distinguished by great quickness and clearness of understanding and expression, and by mildness, firmness, and justness in discipline. One who was for nineteen years associated with him in the Seminary at Esslingen says:—"Universally learned and completely master of every subject of instruction in the schools with which he was connected as teacher or inspector, his rare knowledge of the best method of communicating what he knew, enabled him to carry forward the best as well as the weakest minds in his classes, with great satisfaction to all, and at the same time to inspire a love of study, and impart to others the secret of his own success as a teacher." His principal pedagogical works are "*Experiences and Opinions on the Professional Training of Common School Teachers;*" "*The Common School—a course of lectures on Methodology at Idstein, in* 1816;" "*Introduction to the Science and Art of Education and Instruction of Masters of Primary Schools.*" The last named is a great work, and holds a high place in the pedagogical literature of Germany.

FRIEDRICH ADOLF WILHELM DIESTERWEG.

Friedrich Adolf Wilhelm Diesterweg, an eminent educator, and efficient promoter of the general principles of Pestalozzi, was born in the then Rhine provinces of Prussia, at Seigen, in Nassau, October 29th, 1790. His first education was received at the Latin school of his native place. Thence he went to the university of Herborn, intending to devote himself to the study of theology; but his academic course was finished at Tubingen. At first a private tutor in Manheim, he was afterward second teacher in the secondary school at Worms; and in 1811 entered the model school at Frankfort-on-the-Mayne, where his holy zeal accomplished much good. Having become known as a scientifically-trained and well-practiced educator, he was chosen second rector of the Latin school at Elberfeld. From this place he was called, in 1820, to be director of the teachers' seminary at Meurs. In this place he labored with intelligence, energy, and singleness of purpose, during a series of years, for the cause of elementary instruction, which, under the French domination, had been entirely neglected on the Rhine. He was, moreover, very useful as a writer—discussing more particularly mathematics and the German language. In 1827, he commenced publishing (by Schwerz, in Schwelin,) the "*Rhenish Gazette of Education and Instruction*" (*Rheinische Blätter fur Erziebung und Unterricht,*) with especial reference to the common schools. The first volume contained much valuable matter, much condensed; and the succeeding volumes (to 1859,) have not fallen beneath it in excellence. Through this periodical, the educationists of the Rhine provinces were afforded a good opportunity for discussing pedagogical subjects; upon which much interest was then beginning to appear.

In 1833, Diesterweg was appointed director of the royal seminary for city teachers, at Berlin. Here he labored for eighteen years; his eyes fixed fast and unvarying upon his object—exposing all sorts of pedagogical faults and weaknesses, seeking in every way to raise the position of teachers, and pursuing his work without any fear of men. The meetings of the Pedagogical Society of Berlin were set on foot by him. In 1849, his connection with the seminary was terminated by the government, in consequence of his popular sympathies in

1848. During this period, Diesterweg published "*Autobiographies of Distinguished Educators*," "*Education of the Lower Classes*," "*Degeneracy of our Universities*," "*Education for Patriotism, &c.*," "*Controversial Inquiries on Educational Subjects.*" In these writings, Diesterweg appears as a man of progress; as one who seeks to reconcile the existing discrepancy between actual life and learning; between living practice and dead scholastic knowledge; between civilization and learning. The works contain true and striking thoughts. In his zeal for good objects, the author sometimes overpassed the bounds of moderation, and assailed the objects of his opposition with too much severity.

His "*Pedagogical Travels through the Danish Territories*," (*Pädagogische Reise Nachden Dänischen Staaten*,) 1836, involved him in an active controversy with several Danish literati, and especially with Zerrenner, of Magdeburg. Diesterweg's objections to the monitorial system of instruction, which prevails in the schools of Denmark, are:—That it modifies, decreases, or destroys the teacher's influence upon his scholars; that it is disadvantageous to their outward and inward intercourse; reduces to a minimum the precious period of close intercourse between the ripe man and the future men; and sinks the school, in by far the majority of cases, into a mere mindless mechanism, by which the children, it is true, acquire facility in reading and writing, and in a manner outwardly vivid and active, but in reality altogether unintelligent; but become intellectually active not at all. That Diesterweg is in the right in this matter, is daily more extensively believed.

In 1846, Dr. Diesterweg took an early and influential part in the celebration by German teachers of the centennial birthday of Pestalozzi, and in founding an institution for orphans, as a living and appropriate monument to the great regenerator of modern popular education.

His "*Year Book*," or "*Almanac*," (*Jahrbach*,) which commenced in 1851, is a valuable contribution to the current discussion of educational topics, and to the history of the literature and biography of education.

Diesterweg's "*Guide for German Teachers*," (*Wegweiser für Deutscher Schrer*,) of which a third enlarged and improved edition appeared in 1854, in two large volumes, is one of the best existing manuals for teachers, of both elementary and high schools, and has been made a text-book in several teachers' seminaries. We give the contents of this valuable "*Guide*."

DIESTERWEG, F. A. W., "Guide for German Teachers," *Wegweiser für Deutscher Schrer.* 2 vols. pp. 675 and 700.

CONTENTS. VOL. I.

PART I.

GENERAL VIEWS.

PART II.

SPECIAL DEPARTMENTS.

VOL. II.

GUSTAV FRIEDRICH DINTER,

GUSTAV FRIEDRICH DINTER, whose life was a beautiful illustration of his noble declaration in a letter to Baron Von Altenstein—" I promised God that I would look upon every Prussian peasant child as a being who could complain of me before God, if I did not provide for him the best education, as a man and a Christian, which it was possible for me to provide "—was born, Feb. 29, 1760, at Borna, in Saxony, where his father was a lawyer, with the title of Chamber-Commissary. Dinter describes him in his autobiography as a cheerful and lively man, whose most prominent trait was always to look upon the bright side of things, and to oppose all moroseness. In accordance with this character was the bringing up which he gave his five sons; and particularly he would not endure any timidity in them, for which Dinter was always grateful to him. He also obliged them to strict obedience. His mother was a woman of strict religious character, careful foresight, and some vanity, which made her particular about appearances. His father employed a private tutor for him; but this instructor knew little or nothing of pedagogy or didactics, and his teaching looked to nothing except the good appearance of his scholar at examinations. This was very well for the memory; but his head and heart would have received little benefit, had it not been for the assistance of his intelligent mother. For example, Dinter had, when twelve years old, to read, translate, and commit to memory, Hutter's " *Compendium Theologiæ*," and then recite it; and to learn the texts quoted from the New Testament, in the original Greek.

April 27, 1773, he was examined for the national school at Grimma, where he found valuable teachers in Rector Krebs, Conrector Mücke, and Cantor Reichard. Mücke cultivated carefully the religious feelings which the boy's mother had implanted within him; and Reichard was not only his teacher, but his loving friend. While yet at school, his excellent mother died; whose loss he mourned even when grown up. In April, 1779, Dinter left the school at Grimma, and passed the interval of time, before entering the university at Leipzig, partly with his brother, and partly with his godfather, Superintendent Rickfels. In Leipzig, he almost overburdened himself with hearing lectures, during his first two years: attending, especially, Dathe, Ernesti, Morus, and Platner. For want of a competent guide, he fell into wrong directions in many studies, as is often the case. His sentiments, at a later day, upon the studies of the university, were thus expressed :—"It is not necessary that the scholar should learn, in special lessons, all that he is to know. Let him only have the ability, and take pleasure in his studies, and let the sources of assistance be pointed out to him, and he will accomplish more for himself than all the lessons and lectures will do for him."

Even in his student years, the study of men was a favorite pursuit with him. He had a great love for the theater; and says, regarding it :—"For young theologians, the drama is very useful. It furnishes them declamatory knowledge. Not that they are to theatricalize in the pulpit; but at the play they may acquire a feeling for modulations of voice, for strength and feebleness of accent, and an animated style of delivery. Young theologians, attend the theater industriously, if it is convenient. You will get much more good there than at the card-table. But the plays may be judiciously selected." He laments much over his incapacity for music. "I unwillingly find myself deprived of a pleasure which would have added to the enjoyments of my life, and would have rendered cheerful my troubled days, which, thank God, have been few."

After leaving Leipzig, he passed his examination for the ministry, receiving a first-class certificate, and became the private tutor in the family of Chamberlain von Pöllnitz. The years of his candidateship Dinter passed in studying clergy, schoolmasters, and people; a pursuit which has often cheered, taught, animated, and warned him. The common people liked him, and had confidence in him, listening to his preaching with pleasure, and he spoke kindly to every child whom he met. Thus Dinter entered upon the duties of the pastorate, not ill prepared by his experience as a private tutor; and he considers this intermediate training as far from useless. In such a place, the young man weans himself from his student-habits, and learns to accommodate himself to the ways of the people amongst whom he is probably to live; studies the pastors and the gentry; and collects a thousand experiences which will be of the greatest use to him, and which can not be learned out of books. He must, however, be careful not to be warped by the influences of the great house, to become accustomed to indulgences which his future scanty income will not allow him, nor to a style so lofty that his farmers will not understand it. To this end he must devote his leisure to the pastors, the schoolmasters, and the people. Dinter became a pastor in 1787, at Kitscher, a village in the government of Borna, with three hundred inhabitants; to the entire satisfaction of his wishes. He was now a village pastor, as he had so often desired to be. The village belonged to lieutenant-colonel Baron von Niebeker, a very benevolent man, who sympathized with all in misfortune; and Dinter came into most friendly relations with him. As a preacher, his pastoral influence accomplished much, and so did his truly and eminently practical character. In preaching, this thought was continually before him; the handicraftsman and the farmer have, usually, but this one day to devote to the cultivation of head and heart, and the country pastor should shape his efforts accordingly. While a tutor, he had adopted, as his models in preaching, Christ's sermon on the mount, and Paul's discourse at Athens; not merely in the sense of becoming an extemporaneous speaker, but in the spirit of his discourse. He never preached without careful preparation. He usually began to consider on the Sunday, his next Sunday's subject; and he reflected upon it from time to time, during his walks, for example; and on Friday he first wrote down the connected substance of the discourse, in one whole, as it were at one gush. During the ten years of his first pastorate, he thought out almost all his sermons word by word, and learned them so. He never read a sermon. At a later period, when the increase of his occupations disenabled him from using the time necessary for this purpose, he often had to content himself with determining the divisions of his subject; which made him sometimes preach too long. He relates that he learned to preach popularly from his maid-servant, who had a strong common-sense understanding, without much knowledge; and he often read large portions of his discourse to her, on Friday evenings, to see whether it were clear to her mind. In his first pastorate, he confined his choice of subjects mostly to the evangelists; but afterward, especially after his acquaintance with Reinhard, he alternated from them to the epistles, and other scriptures.

During this period, his labors as school-overseer were also very useful; instruction having been his favorite pursuit since his fourteenth year. School conferences were then neither established in Saxony, nor usual. Of his own three school-teachers, each was too old for improvement. Dinter accordingly spent, at first, only two half-days per week in the school. He himself took charge of religious instruction and arithmetic; leaving to the teachers only the repetition of the lessons in the former, and the necessary drilling in the latter. His farmers' children became a credit and a pleasure to him; they learned to take notes of his sermons, to understand their contents, and to take pleasure in them. The confirmation he made the great festival of the year. As to his other relations with his congregation, he did not live in a haughty seclusion from them, but followed them, like a father, into their own habitations. He entered no house where the family was in bad repute, but visited all others without distinction of rich or poor. Thus he gradually acquired an intimate knowledge of their every-day life, and was enabled to say many things to them which would not have been suitable for the pulpit. He gained an influence upon their modes of disciplining their children, and corrected many defects in it. Thus also he came to be considered an intimate family friend of all, and was frequently called upon to act as umpire in family quarrels; so that he was enabled to bring peace into many families. He was no less assiduous toward the sick, whom he visited without being summoned; making it his rule to visit any whose illness was serious, daily if near at hand, and thrice a week if more distant; but, for obvious reasons, he was not able to continue this practice. Thus, by words and deeds, he accomplished much good. But Providence had marked out for him another and wider sphere of action, which estranged him, for a time, from the duties of the ministry. Instruction, as we have remarked, being his favorite pursuit, he had established in Kitscher a sort of seminary, for the training of young people as teachers. This institution soon gained a reputation, and was the occasion of an invitation from first court-chaplain Reinhard, to become director of the teachers' seminary at Friedrichstadt, near Dresden. Dinter accepted, although the duties of the place were greater and the salary less than at Kitscher, from mere love for education; although there was mutual grief at his parting with his congregation. About this time, some sorrows came upon him: the death of a brother, and of his excellent father, who left the world with as much calmness as he had shown in enjoying it. He refused to admit his confessor, saying, "One who has not learned to die in seventy-five years, can not learn it from him now."

Reinhard, with satisfaction, introduced Dinter into his new place of labor, Oct. 21, 1797. The latter remained true to his principle, "Not the multiplicity of knowledge makes the skillful teacher, but the clearness and thoroughness of it, and skill in communicating it." As to his intercourse with the pupils of the seminary, his rule was this: "The seminarist is no longer a boy; he is a youth, who will in a few years be a teacher. It is by a distinct set of means, therefore, that he must be taught. These are Freedom, Work, Love, and Religion." In the first of these particulars he may have been sometimes too late; but he can not be charged with neglect. He expended much labor and time in Bible lessons; professing that religious knowledge should be gained, not from the catechism, but from the original sources.

In arithmetic, his rule was, "Where the scholar can help himself, the teacher must not help him;" for fear of making lazy scholars. In reading, he did not use Olivier's method, then in high repute, but a simplification of that of Stephan. He somewhat erred, at first, in his practice of Pestalozzian principles, adhering too exclusively to mere forms; but he soon perceived the mistake, and proceeded in the genuine spirit of that distinguished teacher, without his diffuseness. He believed that "Pestalozzi was king of the lower classes, and Socrates of the higher." Under Dinter's direction, the seminary became very prosperous.

But Dinter was not to remain always in this sphere of labor. Providence had destined him for another and a higher, although by a road which at first seemed retrograde. He fell very sick with a violent jaundice, which endangered his life; and, at his recovery, feeling still unable to perform the duties of his office without an assistant, whom the salary would not permit him to employ, he accepted again, in 1807, a situation as country clergyman at Görnitz, a village with a hundred and twenty inhabitants, also in the government of Borna. He was received at Görnitz with pleasure, as the son of the former justiciary of Lobstädt, whose jurisdiction had included Görnitz; and here again he established an educational institution—a sort of progymnasium, in which he appointed one of his former seminary pupils, assistant.

Besides these manifold labors, Dinter's productions as a writer gained a large circle of readers. His works made him well known abroad; and thus the humble village pastor unexpectedly received an invitation to Königsberg, in Prussia, to the place of school and consistorial counselor, which he accepted, in his fifty-seventh year. His official duty there was a singular union of the most different employments. He was obliged to consult with superintendents, to examine candidates for the ministry and for schools, to read Sophocles and Euripides with gymnasium graduates, to adjust a general literary course with the royal assessors, as member of the commission for military examinations, to determine whether one person and another was entitled to claim for one year's service, and to be ready to explain to the teachers of the lowest schools whether and why the alphabetical or the sound-method was preferable. His thoroughly practical mind, however, enabled him to fulfill these many duties with efficiency and usefulness. His chief object was the improvement of the common school system; which he found not in the best condition in East Prussia. His first effort was to accomplish as much as possible through the medium of the ignorant and inefficient teachers already employed. He made distinctions between country schools, city schools, seminaries, gymnasia, &c., and adapted his management to the peculiar needs of each. In the country schools he found much to blame; but was careful not to find fault with the teachers in the presence of their scholars, or of the municipal authorities. His only exceptions to this rule were two; where the teacher attempted to deceive him, and where the school was in so bad a condition that to retain the teacher would be an injury to the next generation. He was able to judge of the spirit of a school by a single recitation; and was accustomed to judge, from the prayer and the singing, whether the teacher possessed, and was able to communicate, æsthetical training, or not. Prayer in school he valued highly; and attached much importance to tone and accent in reading, as an indication of cultivated understanding and feeling. Intuitions for higher and lower classes were suitably kept distinct; and special attention was paid to orphan homes and teachers' seminaries. He also improved and extended the instruction of the deaf and dumb.

He declined a call to Kiel as regular professor; and, in consideration of this, received from the Prussian government an extraordinary professorship of theology, with a salary of two hundred thalers (about $150,) and the assurance that in a future *emeritus* appointment, not the years, but the quality, of his labor, should be considered. The German Society, and the society for maintaining poor scholars at gymnasia, elected him member. As an academical teacher, Dinter lectured upon the pastoral charge and upon homiletics, as well as upon popular dogmatics and catechetics; in which his own practical experience as pastor and seminary director assisted him materially. He also conducted disputations and exercises in exegesis. He selected such subjects as required careful preparation on his own part; e. g., the Revelation of St. John, some subject connected with the Hebrew language, æsthetics, &c. His plan was, however, not to train slaves to his opinions, but independent thinkers; and, in his private courses with students, his object was the same.

Dinter's influence as a writer was great; although his first appearance in that capacity was rather late.

We add a few words upon the private life of this remarkable man. His life, as a whole, may be called cheerful and happy; in sixty-nine years he was seriously ill only five times. He lived very simply and regularly. He was never married,* but adopted a son, and educated

* While yet a student, he became acquainted with a fatherless child, Friederike Pack, daughter of the late pastor of Raschan, of whom he says, in his autobiography, "My heart was entirely hers on the first day I saw her. It was not her beauty, but her unaffected goodness and unconscious innocence, which bound me to her." Dinter, however, never had the happiness of calling her his own. She died early; and even to his old age he mourned her loss.

his brothers. He suffered a severe misfortune by a fire in Görnitz, which, in his absence, burnt the parsonage, destroying not only his worldly property, but his intellectual treasures—his library and many valuable manuscripts. He had only sixty thalers left in money. A second was being plundered by the Cossacks a few days before the battle of Leipzig. His age, however, was entirely cheerful and happy. He wrote, "I can wish you no better wish than that God may grant you such an old age as mine has hitherto been. I am healthy, can work eighty-three hours a week, and am commonly as fresh at ten at night as I was in the morning. I often write on Sundays, even in the short winter days, thirteen hours, without spectacles and without fatigue. My superiors, in both consistory and civil government, comply with all my reasonable wishes. My pupils still love the old man who sometimes forgets the difference in their ages. Good teachers see me coming with pleasure; and lazy ones fear me, as an appointer of substitutes, and get the 'inspection-fever.' Without being actually rich, I have enough, and have always something for others; and I look fearlessly upon death, having hopes for the future." So strong an old man might have looked forward to an age of eighty or ninety years; but Providence had determined otherwise.

During a tour of inspection, in the spring of 1831, in which he exerted himself as much as usual, he caught a fatal cold, under the result of which he sank, May 29, 1831. His unexpected death was much lamented throughout Germany; for he was yet capable of much more usefulness, and was rather a citizen of all Germany than of any one nation in it. Even his adversaries were obliged to confess that in him was lost one of the most active, learned, and skillful educators and teachers of the world; who labored unweariedly for the realization of his great ideas, and worked as long as his day lasted. His memory will be revered as long as education and instruction shall be recognized as the first blessings of the human race.

PART II.

SELECTIONS

From the Publications of Pestalozzi.

CONTENTS.

PART II.

SELECTIONS FROM THE PUBLICATIONS OF PESTALOZZI.

PREFACE.

The choice of selections from the works of Pestalozzi is rendered difficult by the character of the mind that produced them. Taken as a whole, they display remarkable powers of observation, considerable insight into the operations of the mind and feelings, great appreciation of character, and a graphic and forcible style. But to select from their whole extent portions which shall give a connected view of his principles, is almost impossible, from the fact that his mind was strongly intuitional in tendency and habit, and rapid and impulsive in action, and that his powers of reflection, combination, and logical expression were not correspondingly great. Thus he often said too much or too little; was contradictory or inconsistent; and has nowhere, even where expressly undertaking to do it, as in "*How Gertrude Teaches Her Children*," given an adequate presentation of his principles or practice.

"*Leonard and Gertrude*" is presented as the book which, more than any other one work, was the foundation of Pestalozzi's fame, and as in itself to the present generation a new and interesting picture of life in the German Swiss villages of the last half of the last century. It has also additional value as containing many of the author's views on educational and social questions, although diffused throughout the work.

A brief extract from "*Christopher and Alice*" is given, sufficient to exhibit the mode of treatment of the subject. The work was comparatively a failure, and has moreover little interest to readers in this country and this age, being closely and exclusively local in aim.

"*The Evening Hour of a Hermit*" is termed by Karl von Raumer "the key of Pestalozzi's educational views." And Pestalozzi himself observed, in his old age, that even at the early date of its composition, he had already arrived at the fundamental principles which controlled the labors and expositions of all his subsequent life.

The various addresses from which extracts are next given are interesting as affording a view of one mode of communication between Pestalozzi and his associates. They are doubtless freer and more spontaneous expressions of his peculiar modes of thought and feeling than his more formal expositions.

"*How Gertrude Teaches Her Children*" was intended by Pestalozzi to give a logical and connected view of his methods of instruction, in some detail. The extracts presented embody the most important portion of the work, and exhibit also some of his characteristic defects in arrangement and exposition.

The extracts from the "*Paternal Instructions*" are valuable as a specimen of a mode of combining instruction in language with sound lessons in morals; upon a principle which Pestalozzi carried very far in theory, and to a great extent in practice; namely, that of teaching through one and the same vehicle, if possible, in the departments both of intellect and morals.

The London translation of "*Leonard and Gertrude,*" with corrections, has been followed in that work, except in the extracts added from the subsequently written part of the book. The liberty has been taken of extracting from Dr. Biber's valuable biography of Pestalozzi, his translation from "*Christopher and Alice,*" and from the "*Paternal Instructions.*" The "*Evening Hour of a Hermit,*" the extracts from the second part of "*Leonard and Gertrude,*" and from "*How Gertrude Teaches Her Children,*" and the several addresses of Pestalozzi, were translated by FREDERICK B. PERKINS, Esq., of Hartford, Librarian of the Connecticut Historical Society; and are from Cotta's edition of Pestalozzi's works, Von Raumer's "*History of Education,*" or Christoffel's "*Life and Views.*"

LEONARD AND GERTRUDE.

PREFACE

TO THE FIRST EDITION.

Reader—In the following pages I have attempted, through the medium of a tale, to communicate some important truths to the people, in the way most likely to make an impression upon their understandings and their feelings.

It has also been my endeavor, to ground both the tale and the instructions derived from it, upon the most careful imitation of nature, and upon the simple description of what is every where to be found.

In what is here related, (the greatest part of which I have, in the course of an active life, myself observed,) I have been careful never to set down my own opinions, instead of what I have seen and heard the people themselves feel, judge, say, and attempt.

If my observations be just, and if I have been successful in my endeavor to give them with the simplicity of truth, they will be well received by all those, before whose eyes the things which I relate are continually passing. If they be false, if they be the creatures of my imagination, the trifles of my own brain, they will, like other Sunday discourses, be forgotten on the Monday.

I will say no more, except to add two passages which appear calculated to illustrate my opinions as to the means to be adopted for a wise instruction of the people.

The first is from a work of our immortal Luther; every line of whose pen breathes humanity, insight into the character of the people, and a desire to instruct them. He says:—

"The holy scriptures are so graciously adapted to our wants, that they do not tell us merely of the great deeds of holy men, but also relate their common discourse, and disclose to us the inmost motives and principles of their hearts."

The second is from the writings of a Jewish Rabbi, and, according to a Latin translation, is as follows:—

"There were amongst the heathen nations, who dwelt round about the inheritance of Abraham, men full of wisdom, whose equals were not to be found far or near. These said: 'Let us go to the kings and to their great men, and teach them how to make the people happy upon the earth.'

"And the wise men went out, and learned the language of the houses of the kings and of their great men, and spoke to the kings and to their great men, in their own language.

"And the kings and the great men praised the wise men, and gave them gold, and silk, and frankincense; *but treated the people as before.* And the wise men were blinded by the gold, and the silk, and the frankincense, and no longer saw that the kings and the great men behaved ill and foolishly to all the people who lived upon the earth.

"But a man of our nation reproved the wise men of the heathens, and was kind to the beggar upon the highway; and took the children of the thief, of the sinner, and of the exile, into his house; and saluted the tax-gatherers, and the soldiers, and the Samaritans, as if they had been brethren of his own tribe.

"And his deeds, and his poverty, and the long-suffering of his love toward all men won him the hearts of the people, so that they trusted him as a father. And when the man of Israel saw that all the people trusted him as a father, he taught the people wherein their true happiness lay; and the people heard his voice, and the princes heard the voice of the people."

Such is the story of the Rabbi, to which I will not add a single observation.

And now must these pages go forth, from my peaceful home, into a world where the winds arise and the tempests blow, and where no peace is. May they be preserved from the storms of evil.

I take no part in the disputes of men about opinions, but I think all will agree, that whatever makes us pious, good, true, and brotherly, whatever cherishes the love of God and of our neighbor, and whatever brings happiness and peace into our houses, should be implanted in the hearts of all, for our common good.

THE AUTHOR.

FEBRUARY 25*th*, 1781.

PREFACE

TO THE SECOND EDITION.

This book, which was written more than twenty years ago, I now again present to my readers, without alteration, as it first came from my pen. It was an attempt to describe the condition of the people, according to what I had learned from my own immediate observation; and, by giving this description, to point out the means of really benefiting them. It has interested many, procured me many friends, and excited in many mothers the wish to be to their children what Gertrude was to hers. But to the age in general, my observations were not, and could not, be palatable. The ruling maxims of the latter half of the past century, were almost altogether deficient in the simplicity of strength, and in the strength of simplicity. They aimed at a high stretch of knowledge; but man, as a whole, remained ignorant, arrogant, and enslaved. Trusting in the extent of his knowledge, he, as it were, lost himself. It was a misfortune to the race of men, during this century, that, by this extension of their knowledge, they were prevented from seeing that they lived without real strength or stability; and, by this self-deception, they lost all feeling for the truth and greatness of the simple relations of nature and society. In these circumstances, it was natural that my book should fail in its chief object; which was, *by pointing out the real situation of the people, and their natural and durable connections with each other, to lay a foundation for their progressive improvement.* As a representation of the nature of domestic education, my book produced no effect; but made an impression chiefly as a tale. True to the object of my life, I persevered in endeavoring to lead the attention of my country to the aim of the book, whilst I, at the same time, labored to place myself in a situation which might enable me to offer to mothers and teachers, the means by which they might bring up their children according to its spirit.

All I have hitherto effected, is but, as it were, a continuation of the book itself, which I now again present to my readers. May it be received as kindly as before! It was my first address to the poor and desolate of the land. It was my first address to those who stand in the place of God to them. It was my first address to mothers, and to the hearts which God has given them, to induce them to be to their children what no one else can be to them. May it be to the poor a greater blessing than it has yet been! May it make upon those who stand in the place of God to them, the impression which it must make, before it can become a blessing to the poor and desolate! May many mothers, through its influence, become to their children what none can be in their stead! Let people say what they will, nature, and God its eternal Creator, have left nothing wanting. It is blasphemy to maintain that mothers have no desire to devote themselves to their children. Let people say what they will, I am full of trust in this desire, and full of hope for the consequences which the excitement of it will produce. The greatest corruption which can arise from the errors of man, does not entirely destroy human nature. Its strength is inextinguishable! Go into the poorest hut, and see there what a mother's heart, almost without means or help, can do for her children. It is equally false to say that mothers have no time to attend to the first formation of the minds and feelings of their children. Most of them, particularly those who live at home, have their children with them a great part of the day; and why can not they, whilst they are at work, as well behave to them, and talk to them, in a way which will instruct and improve them, as in one which will do neither? A mother's instruction requires no art. It is nothing but to excite the child to an active observation of the things which surround it. It is nothing but a regular exercise of the senses, of the warm feelings of the heart, of the powers of speech, and of the natural activity of the body. All that is necessary is to second the feelings of mothers, and their already prepared, and, as I may say, instinctively simple and upright understandings, and to place in their power the necessary means, so prepared as they may best use them.

Good mothers! let it not be unjustly said, any longer, that you have not understanding and strength for what, in your circumstances, is your highest and holiest duty. If you once go so far as to weep in the stillness of your chambers, because the good Gertrude did more for her children than you have hitherto done for yours, I am sure you will then try whether it be not possible to do what she did; and it is when you are arrived at this point, that I wish to offer you my elementary books.

My heart here bids me be silent; but one word more! Whoever wishes to do his duty to God, to posterity, to public right, and public order, and to the security of family happiness, must, in one way or other, accord with the spirit of my book, and seek the same object. This is my comfort. When these truths are ripened, as ripen they must, they will bear fruit; when they are become fitted for the poor and desolate, they will be enjoyed by them. Many good men and women, who have hitherto been unable, notwithstanding the best inclinations, to give a good piece of advice to a neighbor, will become the fathers and mothers of the poor and desolate. It is to this strength and greatness that I seek to elevate the minds and hearts of the nobles, and of the people, of my native country. After my death, may men of matured powers proceed in this great object of my life; and, before I close my eyes, may I enjoy the happiness of seeing both my object and the means which I employ to attain it, no longer misunderstood.

Alas! this misunderstanding prevents the happiness of thousands, who, but for it, would every where find wise and powerful assistance.

PESTALOZZI.

BURGDORF, *November*, 1803.

CONTENTS.

LEONARD AND GERTRUDE.

CHAPTER I.—A KIND-HEARTED MAN, WHO YET MAKES HIS WIFE AND CHILDREN VERY UNHAPPY.

THERE lived in Bonnal, a mason. He was called Leonard, and his wife, Gertrude. He had seven children and some property, but he had this fault; that he often let himself be tempted to the tavern. When he was once seated there, he behaved like a madman;—and there are in our village, cunning, good-for-nothing rogues, whose sole employment and business it is, to take in honest and simple people, and seize every opportunity of getting hold of their money. These were acquainted with poor Leonard, and often led him on from drinking to gaming, and thus cheated him of the produce of his labor. Whenever this had happened over-night, Leonard repented in the morning, and it went to his heart when he saw Gertrude and his children wanting bread, so that he trembled, wept, and cast down his eyes to conceal his tears.

Gertrude was the best wife in the village; but she and her blooming children were in danger of being robbed of their father, and driven from their home, and of sinking into the greatest misery, because Leonard could not let wine alone.

Gertrude saw the approaching danger, and felt it most keenly. When she fetched grass from the meadow, when she took hay from the loft, when she set away the milk in her clean pans, whatever she was doing, she was tormented by the thought that her meadow, her haystack, and her little hut, might soon be taken away from her; and when her children were standing around her, or sitting in her lap, her anguish was still greater, and the tears streamed down her cheeks.

Hitherto, however, she had been able to conceal this silent weeping from her children; but on Wednesday, before last Easter, when she had waited long and her husband did not come home, her grief overcame her, and the children observed her tears. "Oh mother," exclaimed they all with one voice, "you are weeping," and pressed themselves closer to her. Sorrow and anxiety were on every countenance—anxious sobs, heavy, downcast looks, and silent tears, surrounded the mother, and even the baby in her arms, betrayed a feeling of pain hitherto unknown—his first expression of care and sorrow, his staring eyes which, for the first time, were fixed upon her without a smile—all this quite broke her heart. Her anguish burst out in a loud cry, and all the children and the baby wept with their mother, and there was a dreadful sound of lamentation just as Leonard opened the door.

Gertrude lay with her face on the bed; heard not the opening of the door, and saw not the entrance of the father; neither did the children perceive him. They saw only their weeping mother, and hung on her arm and round her neck, and by her clothes. Thus did Leonard find them.

God in heaven sees the tears of the wretched, and puts a limit to their grief. Gertrude found in her tears the mercy of God. The mercy of God brought

Leonard to witness this scene, which pierced through his soul, so that his limbs trembled. The paleness of death was upon his countenance, and he could scarcely articulate, with a hasty and broken voice: "Lord Jesus! what is this?" Then the mother saw him for the first time, the children looked up, and their loud exclamations of grief were hushed. "O mother! here is our father," said the children all at once, and even the baby sobbed no longer.

As a torrent, or a raging flame, did their wild anguish subside into quiet, thoughtful anxiety. Gertrude loved Leonard, and in her deepest distress his presence was always a comfort. Leonard's horror also was now less overwhelming than at first.

"Tell me, Gertrude," said he, "what is this dreadful trouble in which I find thee?"

"O my dear," answered Gertrude, "heavy cares press upon my heart, and when thou art away sorrow preys more keenly upon me."

"Gertrude," said Leonard, "I know why thou weepest, wretch that I am!"

Then Gertrude sent away the children, and Leonard hid his face on her neck, and could not speak.

Gertrude too was silent for a few moments, and leaned sorrowfully against her husband, who wept and sobbed on her neck.

At last she collected all her strength, and took courage to urge him not to bring any further trouble and misery upon his children.

Gertrude was pious, and trusted in God; and before she spoke, she prayed silently for her husband and for her children; and her heart was evidently comforted as she said, "Leonard! trust in the mercy of God, and take courage to do nothing but what is right."

"O Gertrude, Gertrude!" exclaimed Leonard, and wept, and his tears fell in torrents.

"O my love! take courage and trust in thy Father in heaven, and all will be better with thee. It goes to my heart to make thee weep. My love, I would gladly keep every trouble from thee. Thou knowest that, by thy side, I could be content with bread and water, and the still midnight is often to me an hour of cheerful labor, for thee and my children. But, if I concealed my anxiety from thee, lest I be separated from thee and these dear little ones, I should be no mother to my children, nor true to thee. Our children are yet full of gratitude and love toward us,—but, my Leonard, if we do not continue to act as parents, their love and tenderness, to which I trust so much, must needs decrease, and think too what thou wilt feel, when thy Nicholas has no longer a home of his own, and must go out to service. He who now talks with so much delight of freedom and his own little flock. Leonard! if he, and all these dear children, should become poor through our fault, should cease to thank us in their hearts, and begin to weep for us their parents—Leonard! couldst thou bear to see thy Nicholas, thy Jonas, thy Liseli, and thy little Anneli, driven out of doors to seek their bread at another's table? Oh! it would kill me to see it." So spoke Gertrude, and the tears fell down her cheeks.

And Leonard was not less affected. "What shall I do, miserable creature that I am? What can I do? I am yet more wretched than thou knowest of—O Gertrude! Gertrude!" Then he was again silent, wrung his hands and wept in extreme misery.

"Oh, my dear husband, do not mistrust God's mercy! Whatever it be, speak! that we may consult together, and comfort each other."

CHAPTER II.—A WOMAN WHO FORMS A RESOLUTION, ACTS UP TO IT, AND FINDS A LORD OF THE MANOR, WHO HAS THE HEART OF A FATHER TOWARD HIS DEPENDENTS.

"OH Gertrude, Gertrude! it breaks my heart to tell thee my distress and add to thy anxieties; and yet I must do it. I owe Hummel, the bailiff, thirty florins; and he is a hound to those who are in debt to him, and not a man. I wish I had never seen his face! If I do not go to his house, he threatens me with law; and if I do go, the wages of my labor are in his claws. This, Gertrude, this is the source of our misfortunes."

"My dear husband," replied Gertrude, "canst thou not go to Arner, the father of the country? Thou knowest how all the widows and orphans praise him. I think he would give thee counsel and protection against this man."

"O Gertrude," said Leonard, "I can not, I dare not. What could I say against the bailiff? He would bring up a thousand different things against me! He is bold and cunning, and has a hundred ways and means of crying down a poor man before a magistrate, so that he may not be heard."

Gertrude. Dear husband, I never yet spoke to a magistrate, but if necessity and want carried me to him, I am sure I could speak the truth to any man. O do not be afraid; think of me, and of thy children, and go.

"Gertrude," said Leonard, "I can not, I dare not. I am not free from fault. The bailiff will coolly take the whole village to witness that I am a drunkard. O Gertrude, I am not blameless. What can I say? Nobody will stand up against him and say that he enticed me to it all. O Gertrude, if I could, if I durst, how gladly would I go; but if ventured, and did not succeed, think how he would revenge himself."

Gertrude. But even if thou art silent he will nevertheless bring thee to ruin, without a chance of escape. Leonard, think of thy children, and go. This anxiety of heart must have an end. Go,—or I will go myself.

Leonard. Gertrude, I dare not. If thou darest, for God's sake, go directly to Arner, and tell him all.

"I will go," said Gertrude; and she did not sleep one hour that night; but she prayed during that sleepless night, and was more and more resolved to go to Arner, the lord of the manor.

Early in the morning she took her baby, which bloomed like a rose, and went six miles, to the hall.

Arner was sitting under his lime-trees, before the door of his house, as Gertrude approached; he saw her, he saw the baby in her arms, and upon her countenance sorrow and suffering, and the traces of tears. "What do you want my good woman? Who are you?" said he, so kindly that she took courage to speak.

"I am Gertrude," said she, "the wife of Leonard, the mason of Bonnal."

"You are an excellent woman," said Arner. "I have observed your children more than all the rest in the village; they are more modest and better behaved than any of the others; and they appear better fed. And yet I hear you are very poor. Tell me what you wish for."

"O gracious sir, my husband has, for some time past, owed Urias Hummel, the bailiff, thirty florins; and he is a hard man. He entices him to gaming, and all kinds of waste; and because he is afraid of him, he dare not keep away from his tavern, though it costs him, almost every day, his wages and his children's bread. Honored sir! he has seven young children, and without help and counsel against the bailiff it is impossible that we should escape beggary. I know that you have compassion upon the widow and the orphan, and therefore I have made bold to come to you, and tell you our misfortunes. I have brought with me all my children's savings, to leave them with you, if I might venture to beg you to make some agreement for us, so that the bailiff, till he is paid, may not oppress and injure us any more."

Arner had long had suspicions of the bailiff. He perceived, therefore, immediately, the truth of this complaint, and the wisdom of what she asked. He took a cup of tea which stood before him, and said—"You are tired, Gertrude; drink this tea, and give your pretty child some of this milk."

Gertrude stood blushing; and this paternal kindness went to her heart, so that she could not restrain her tears. And Arner encouraged her to tell him what the bailiff and his companions had done, and the wants and cares of many years. He listened attentively, and than asked her, "How have you been able, Gertrude, through all this distress to keep your children's money?"

Then Gertrude answered:—"It was difficult indeed, gracious sir, to do so; but I always looked upon the money as not my own, as if some dying man had given it me on his death-bed to keep for his children. I considered it almost in this light; and if ever, in the time of our greatest need, I was obliged to buy the children bread with it, I never rested till I had made it up again for them by night labor."

"Was that always possible, Gertrude?" said Arner.

"O gracious sir, if we have once set our hearts upon any thing, we can do more than we could imagine possible, and God always helps us in our greatest need, if we are really doing our best to get what is absolutely necessary. O gracious sir, he helps us more than you in your magnificence can know or imagine."

Arner was deeply affected by the innocence and goodness of this poor woman; he made still further inquiries; and said, "Gertrude, where is this money?"

Then Gertrude laid down seven neat parcels upon Arner's table; and to every parcel was fastened a ticket, saying whose it was, and when Gertrude had taken any thing away from it, and how she had replaced it.

Arner read the tickets over attentively. Gertrude saw it, and blushed: "I ought to have taken away these tickets, gracious sir."

Arner smiled, and read on; but Gertrude stood there abashed, and her heart throbbed on account of these tickets; for she was modest, and troubled at the least appearance of vanity.

Arner saw her uneasiness because she had not taken off the tickets, and felt the simple dignity of innocence, as she stood ashamed that her goodness and prudence were noticed; and he resolved to befriend her more than she asked or hoped for; for he felt her worth, and that no woman was like her among a thousand. He added something to each of the parcels, and said "Take back your children's money, Gertrude, and I will lay down thirty florins for the bailiff, till he is paid. Go home, now, Gertrude; to-morrow I shall be in the village, and I will settle matters between you and Hummel."

Gertrude could not speak for joy; scarcely could she stammer out a broken, sobbing—"Heaven reward you, gracious sir!" and then she went with her baby, and with the comfort she had obtained, to her husband. As she went, she prayed and thanked God all the way, and wept tears of gratitude and hope, till she came to her cottage.

Leonard saw her coming, and saw the joy of her heart in her countenance.

"Art thou here again so soon?" said he, going to meet her. "Thou hast been successful with Arner."

"How dost thou know that already?" said Gertrude.

"I see it in thy face, thou excellent creature, thou canst not conceal it."

"That can I not," said Gertrude, "and I would not, if I could, keep the good news a moment from thee, Leonard." Then she related to him Arner's kindness; how he had believed her words, and how he had promised to help them. And she gave the children Arner's present, and kissed them all, more fondly and cheerfully than she had done for a long time past; and said to them: "Pray every day for Arner, my children, as you pray for your father and me. Arner cares for the welfare of all the country; he cares for your welfare; and if you are good and well-behaved, and industrious, you will be dear to him, as you are dear to me and to your father."

From that time forward the mason's children, every morning and evening, when they prayed for their father and mother, prayed also for Arner, the father of the country.

Gertrude and Leonard made fresh resolutions to look after the management of the house, and to bring up their children in every good way; and this day was a festival to them. Leonard's courage was renewed, and in the evening Gertrude prepared for him a supper that he was fond of; and they rejoiced together over the coming morning, the assistance of Arner, and the mercy of their God.

Arner, too, longed for the next morning, that he might do a deed, such as he did by thousands, to make his existence useful.

Chapter III.—A brute appears.

And when his bailiff came to him, that evening, to receive his orders, he said to him, "I am coming myself to Bonnal, to-morrow. I am determined to have the building of the church begun at last." The bailiff replied: "Gracious sir, is your grace's master-builder at liberty now? "No," answered Arner, "but there is a mason in the village, of the name of Leonard, whom I shall be glad to employ in this affair. Why have you never recommended him to me before as a workman?"

The bailiff made a low bow, and said: "I durst not have employed the poor mason in any of your magnificence's buildings."

Arner. "Is he a trusty man, bailiff, upon whom I can depend?"

Bailiff. "Yes—your grace may depend upon him; he is a very honest fellow."

"They say he has an excellent wife; is she not a talker?" said Arner emphatically.

"No, indeed," replied the bailiff, "she is a hard-working, quiet woman."

"Very well," said Arner, "be at the church-yard to-morrow morning, at nine o'clock. I will meet you there myself."

The bailiff went away, well pleased with this conversation; for he thought within himself, this is a fresh cow for my stall; and he already turned over in his mind the tricks by which he should get from the mason, the money he might gain by this building of the church. He went straight home, and then to the mason's cottage.

It was already dark, as he knocked impatiently at the door.

Leonard and Gertrude were sitting by the table. The remains of the supper were still before them. Leonard knew the voice of the envious bailiff, started, and pushed the food into a corner.

Gertrude encouraged him not to be afraid, and to trust in Arner; but he turned pale as he opened the door for the bailiff.

The latter smelt out the concealed supper as quick as a hungry hound, but he behaved civilly, and said, though with a smile; "You are well off, good people; it is easy to do without the tavern at this rate. Is it not, Leonard?"

The poor man cast down his eyes and was silent; but Gertrude was bolder, and said: "What are the bailiff's commands? It is seldom that he comes further than to the window of such a poor house as this."

Hummel concealed his anger, laughed, and said: "It is very true that I should not have expected to find such good cooking here; or perhaps I might have invited myself."

This vexed Gertrude. "Bailiff," said she, "you smell our supper, and grudge it us. When a poor man is enjoying a supper he likes, and which perhaps he does not get three times in a year, you should be ashamed to come in and spoil it."

"I had no such wicked intention," said the bailiff, still laughing. But soon afterward, he added more seriously, "You are too insolent, Gertrude; it does not become poor people. You should remember that we may have something to do with each other yet. But I will not begin upon this at present. I am always kindly disposed toward your husband; and whenever I can, I serve him. Of this I can give proof."

Gertrude. "Bailiff, my husband is enticed away, every day, to drink and game in your tavern, and then must I and my children, at home, suffer every possible misery. This is the service we have to thank you for."

Hummel. "You do me wrong, Gertrude. It is true that your husband is somewhat inclined to drinking. I have often told him so. But in my tavern, I can not refuse any man what he asks for, to eat and drink. Every body does the same."

Ger. "Yes; but every body does not threaten a poor unfortunate man with law, if he does not double his reckoning every year."

Here the bailiff could restrain himself no longer; he turned in a rage to Leonard: "Are you such a pitiful fellow, Leonard, as to tell these tales of me? Must I have it thrown into my very beard, what you ragamuffins are going to bring upon the credit and good name of an old man like me? Did I not reckon with you a short time ago, before the overseer? It is well that all the tickets are in my hands. Will you deny my claims, Leonard?"

"That is not the question," said Leonard. "Gertrude only wants me to make no fresh debts."

The bailiff considered a little, lowered his tone, and said: "There is nothing so much amiss in that. But you are the master—she does not wish to tie you up in leading-strings?"

Ger. "Far from it, bailiff. I only wish to get him out of the leading-strings in which he is now fast—and that is your book, bailiff, and those beautiful tickets."

Hum. "He has only to pay me, and then he will be out of the leading-strings, as you call them, in a twinkling."

Ger. "He will well be able to do that, if he makes no fresh debts."

Hum. "You are proud, Gertrude—we shall see. Confess the truth, Gertrude! you would rather sit junketing with him alone at home, than let him enjoy a glass of wine with me."

Ger. "You are a mean fellow, bailiff; but your speeches do me no harm."

Hummel could not continue this conversation any longer. He felt that something must have happened to make this woman so bold. Therefore he durst not indulge his anger, and took his leave.

"Have you any further commands?" said Gertrude.

"None if this is to be the way;" answered Hummel.

"What way?" replied Gertrude, smiling, and looking steadily in his face.

This put the bailiff still more out of countenance, so that he knew not how to behave.

He went out, muttering to himself down the steps; what can be the meaning of all this?

Leonard was not easy about the business, and the bailiff was still less so.

CHAPTER IV.—HE IS WITH HIS OWN SET, AND IT IS THERE THAT ROGUES SHOW THEMSELVES.

IT was now near midnight, and as soon as he got home, he sent for two of Leonard's neighbours, to come to him directly.

They were in bed when he sent, but got up again, without delay, and went to him through the dark night.

And he inquired about every thing which Leonard and Gertrude had done for some days past. But as they could tell him nothing which threw any light upon the subject, he turned his rage against them.

"You hounds, if one wants any thing from you, you are never ready with it. I don't know why I should always be your fool. Whenever you trespass in the woods, or steal fodder,—I am to take no notice of it.—When you turn cattle into the squire's pastures and destroy the hedges—I must not say a word"—

"You, Buller! more than a third part of thy reckoning was false, and I was silent about it. Dost thou think that bit of mouldy hay was enough to content me? but the year is not yet passed over. And you, Kruel! Thy half meadow belongs to thy brother's children. You old thief! what good hast thou done to me, that I should not give thee up to the hangman, whose property thou art?"

These speeches frightened the neighbors.

"What can we do? What must we do, Mr. Bailiff? By night or by day, we are always ready to do what you ask us."

"You dogs! You can do nothing—you know nothing—I am half mad with rage. I must know what the mason's people have been about this week—what is hidden in that poke." Thus he went on.

In the mean time Kruel recollected himself.

"Hold, bailiff, I have just thought of something. Gertrude went over the fields this morning; and this evening, her Liseli was praising the squire at the well. She must surely have been to the hall. The evening before, there was a great lamentation in the cottage; nobody knew why. To-day they are all cheerful again."

The bailiff was now convinced that Gertrude had been to the hall. Anger and alarm raged still more fiercely in his soul.

He uttered horrible curses, abused Arner violently for listening to every beggarly wretch; and swore to have revenge upon Leonard and Gertrude. "But you must say nothing about it, neighbors. I will treat these people civilly, till all is ripe. Look carefully after what they do, and bring me word—I will be your man when you want help."

Then he took Buller aside, and said, "Dost thou know any thing of the stolen flower-pots? Thou wert seen, yesterday, going over the borders with a laden ass. What wert thou carrying off?

Buller started. "I—I—had—" "Come, come," said the bailiff "be faithful to me, and I will help thee at a pinch."

Then the neighbors went away, but it was already near dawn.

And Hummel threw himself on his bed for about an hour—started, thought of vengeance, gnashed his teeth in uneasy slumber, and kicked with his feet—till the clear day called him from his bed.

He resolved to see Leonard once more, to master himself, and to tell him that Arner had appointed him to build the church. He summoned all his powers of deceiving, and went to him.

Gertrude and Leonard had slept more peacefully this night than they had done for a long time past; and at the dawn of morning they prayed for a blessing upon the day. They hoped also for prompt help from Father Arner. This hope spread tranquillity of soul, and unwonted delightful serenity around them.

Thus did Hummel find them. He saw how it was, and Satan entered into his heart, so that he was more than ever inflated with rage; but he commanded himself, wished them civilly good morning, and said:

"Leonard, we parted in anger with each other last night; but this must not last. I have some good news for thee. I am come from our gracious master; he has been speaking of building the church, and inquired about thee. I said thou wert equal to the work, and I think he will give it thee. This is the way neighbors can serve one another—we must not be so easily vexed."

Leonard. "He has agreed with his master-builder to build the church. You told the whole village so, long ago."

Hummel. "I thought it was so; but it proves a mistake. The master-builder has only made an estimate of it, and thou mayest easily believe he has not forgotten his own profit. If thou undertakest it according to this reckoning, thou mayst gather up gold like leaves. Leonard, see now how well I mean by thee."

The mason was overcome by the hope of having the work, and thanked him cordially. But Gertrude saw that the bailiff was white with smothered rage, and that bitter wrath was concealed under his smiles; and she could not yet rejoice. The bailiff retired, and as he went, he added, "Within an hour Arner will be here." And Leonard's daughter Lise, who was standing by her father, said to the bailiff,

"We have known that ever since yesterday."

Hummel started at these words, but pretended not to hear them.

And Gertrude, who saw that the bailiff was lying in wait for the money, which might be gained by the building of the church, was very uneasy about it.

CHAPTER V.—HE FINDS HIS MASTER.

IN the mean time Arner came to the churchyard, and many people collected together from the village to see the good squire.

"Are you so idle, or is this a holiday, that you have so much time to be gossiping here? said the bailiff to some who stood too near him; for he always took care

that nobody should hear the orders he received. But Arner observed it and said aloud: "Bailiff, I like my children to remain in the churchyard, and to hear, themselves, how I will arrange about the building. Why do you drive them away?"

Hummel bowed down to the ground, and called aloud to the neighbors: "Come back again! his grace will allow it."

Arner. "Have you seen the estimate for the building of the church?"

Bailiff. "Yes, gracious sir."

Arner. "Do you think Leonard can make the building good and durable, at this price?"

"Yes, gracious sir," answered the bailiff; and he added in a lower tone, "I think, as he lives on the spot, he might perhaps undertake it for something less."

But Arner said aloud, "As much as I would have given to my master-builder, so much will I give him. Call him here, and take care that he has as much from the wood and from the magazine as the master-builder would have had."

A few moments before Arner sent to call him, Leonard had gone to the upper village, and Gertrude resolved to go back herself to the churchyard with the messenger, and tell Arner her anxieties.

When the bailiff saw Gertrude coming back with the messenger instead of Leonard, he turned pale.

Arner observed it, and said, "What is the matter, bailiff?"

Bailiff. "Nothing, gracious sir! nothing at all; only I did not sleep well last night."

"One may tell that by your looks," said Arner, looking steadily into his inflamed eyes. Then he turned to Gertrude, spoke to her kindly, and said, "Is your husband not with you? You must tell him to come to me. I will intrust the building of this church to him."

Gertrude stood for a few moments silent, and durst not say a word before so many people.

Arner. "Why do you not speak, Gertrude? I will give your husband the work, upon the same terms on which my master-builder would have had it. This ought to please you, Gertrude."

Gertrude had now recovered herself, and said, "Gracious sir, the church is so near the tavern."

All the people began to smile; and as most of them wished to conceal this from the bailiff, they turned away from him toward Arner.

The bailiff, who clearly saw that Arner had perceived it all, got up in a passion, went toward Gertrude, and said, "What have you to say against my tavern?"

Arner quickly interrupted him and said, "Is this your affair, bailiff, that you interfere about it?" Then he turned again to Gertrude, and said, "What do you mean? Why is the church too near the tavern?"

Ger. "Gracious sir, my husband is easily enticed away by wine; and if he works every day so near the tavern, I am afraid he will not be able to resist."

Arner. "But can not he avoid the tavern, if it is so dangerous to him?"

Ger. "Gracious sir, when people are working hard, and get heated, it makes them very thirsty; and if he has always before his eyes people drinking together, and trying to entice him by every kind of joviality, and jesting, and buying wine, and laying wagers, oh! how will he be able to resist? and if he once gets ever so little into debt again, he is fast. Gracious sir, if you only knew how one single evening, in such houses, can bring poor people into slavery and snares, out of which it is scarcely possible to escape again!"

Arner. "I do know it, Gertrude! and I am angry about what you told me yesterday; and therefore, before your eyes, and before the eyes of all these people, I will show that I will not have the poor oppressed and ill-used. Then he turned to the bailiff, and said, with a solemn voice, and a look which thrilled through his bones and marrow: "Bailiff! is it true, that poor people are oppressed, and misled, and cheated in your house?"

Confused, and pale as death, the bailiff answered: "Gracious sir, such a thing never happened to me before in my life,—and so long as I live, and am bailiff"——; he wiped the perspiration from his face—coughed—cleared his throat, and began again. "It is dreadful"——.

Arner. "You are disturbed, bailiff! The question is a simple one. Is it true, that you oppress the poor, and lay snares for them in your tavern, so as to make their homes unhappy?"

Bailiff. "No, certainly not, gracious sir! This is the reward one gets for serving such beggarly folks. I might have foreseen it. One always gets such thanks instead of payment."

Arner. "Trouble not yourself about payment now. The question is, whether this woman lies."

Bailiff. "Yes, certainly, gracious sir! I will prove it a thousand fold."

Arner. "Once is enough, bailiff! but take care. You said yesterday, that Gertrude was a good, quiet, hard-working woman, and no talker."

"I don't know—I—I—thought—you have—I thought—her so——," said the gasping bailiff.

Arner. "You are so troubled, bailiff, that there is no speaking to you now. It will be better for me to find it out from these neighbors here; and immediately he turned to two old men who stood by quietly, and with interest, observing what passed, and said to them, 'Is it true, good neighbors? are the people led away to evil, and oppressed in the tavern?' The two men looked at each other, and durst not speak."

But Arner encouraged them kindly. "Do not be afraid! Tell me the plain truth!"

"It is but too true, gracious sir; but how can we poor people venture to complain against the bailiff?" said the elder of the two at last, but in so low a voice, that only Arner could hear it.

"It is enough, old man," said Arner; and then turned to the bailiff.

"I can not, at present, inquire fully into this complaint; but certainly I will have my poor people secure against all oppression; and I have long thought that no bailiff should keep tavern. But I will defer this till Monday. Gertrude, tell your husband to come to me; and be easy, on his account, about the tavern."

Then Arner transacted some other business; and when he had done, he went into the forest hard by; and it was late when he arrived at home. The bailiff, too, who was obliged to follow him into the forest, did not get back to the village till it was night.

When he came to his house, and saw no light in the room, and heard no voices, he foreboded some misfortune; for usually the house was full every evening, and all the windows were lighted up by the candles which stood upon the tables; and the shouts of those who were drinking, always sounded through the still night, so that you might have heard them at the bottom of the street, though it is a long one, and the bailiff's house stands at the top.

The bailiff was very much startled by this unusual silence. He opened his door impatiently, and said, "What is this? what is this? Why is nobody here?"

His wife was sobbing in a corner. "Oh husband! Art thou come back? Oh what a misfortune has befallen us! There is a jubilee of thy enemies in the village, and no man dares come and drink a single glass of wine with us. They all say thou hast been taken through the forest to Arnburg."

As an imprisoned wild boar foams in the trap, opens his jaws, rolls about his eyes, and roars with anger; so did Hummel rage. He stamped, and was full of fury, plotted revenge against Arner, and cursed him for his goodness. Then he spoke to himself:

"Is this the way to have justice done in the country? He will take away my license from me, and be the only person to hang up a sign in the manor. In the memory of man, the bailiffs have all been landlords. All affairs have gone through our hands. But this man thrusts himself into every thing, like a village schoolmaster. Therefore every knave is become insolent to the constables, and says he can speak to Arner himself. Thus the law loses all its credit, and we sit still under it and are silent, pitiful creatures as we are, whilst he thus wrongs and alters the rights of the land."

Thus did the old rogue misrepresent to himself the good and wise actions of his excellent master, raged and plotted revenge, till he fell asleep.

CHAPTER VI.—CONVERSATION AMONGST COUNTRY PEOPLE.

In the morning he rose early, and sang and whistled at his window, that people might think he was perfectly easy about what had happened yesterday. But Fritz, his neighbor, called to him across the street: "Hast thou customers so early, that thou art so merry?" and he smiled to himself as he said it.

"They will be coming soon, Fritz! Hopsasa and Heisasa! Plums are not figs," said the bailiff; and he held a glass of brandy out of the window, and said: "Wilt thou pledge me, Fritz?"

"It is too soon for me," answered Fritz, "I will wait till there is more company."

"Thou wert always a wag," said the bailiff, "but, depend upon it, yesterday's business will not turn out so ill. No bird flies so high that it never comes down again."

"I know not," answered Fritz. "The bird I am thinking of, has had a long flight of it; but perhaps we are not speaking of the same bird, Mr. Bailiff? They are calling me to breakfast!" and with this, Fritz shut down his window.

"Short leave-taking," murmured the bailiff to himself, and shook his head until his hair and his cheeks shook. "I shall have the devil to pay, to get this cursed business of yesterday out of these people's heads." Having said this to himself, he poured out some brandy, drank it off, and said again: "Courage! time brings counsel! This is Saturday. These simpletons will be going to be shaved. I will away to the barber's, and give them each a glass of wine. The fellows always believe me ten times before they would half believe the pastor once." So said the bailiff to himself; and then added to his wife: "Fill my box with tobacco: not with my own, but with that strong sort—it suits such fellows. And if the barber's boy comes for wine, give him that brimstoned three times over, and put into each can a glass of brandy."

He went out; but whilst he was in the street, and not far from home, he recollected himself, turned back, and said to his wife, "There may be knaves drinking with me. I must be upon my guard. Get me some yellow-colored water; and when I send for the La Côte, bring it thyself." He then went out again.

But before he arrived at the barber's, and under the lime-trees near the school he met Nickel Spitz and Jogli Rubel.

"Whither away, in thy Sunday clothes, Mr. Bailiff?" asked Nickel Spitz.

Bailiff. "I am going to get shaved."

Nickel. "It's odd thou hast time for it, on a Saturday morning."

Bailiff. "That's true. It is not so the year through."

Nick. "No! It is not long since thou camest always on a Sunday, between morning prayers, to the barber."

Bailiff. "Yes, a time or two."

Nick. "A time or two! The two last, I think. Since the pastor had thy dog driven out of the church, thou hast never been within his premises."

Bailiff. "Thou art a fool, Nickel, to talk so. We must forgive and forget; the driving the dog away, has long been out of my head."

Nick. "I would not trust to that, if I were the pastor."

Bailiff. "Thou art a simpleton, Nickel; why should he not? But come into the room, there will be some drinking ere long."

Nick. "Thou wouldst look sharp after the barber, if he had any drinking going on in his house."

Bailiff. "I am not half so jealous as that comes to. They are for taking away my license; but Nickel, we are not come to that yet. At all events, we shall have six weeks and three days, before that time arrives."

Nick. "So I suppose. But it is no good thing for thee, that the young squire does not follow his grandfather's creed."

Bailiff. "Truly, he does not believe quite as his grandfather did."

Nick. "I suspect they differ about every article of the twelve."

Bailiff. "It may be so. But the old man's belief was the best, to my fancy."

Nick. "No doubt! The first article of his creed was: I believe in thee, my bailiff."

Bailiff. "Thou art facetious, Nickel! but what was the next?"

Nick. "I don't know exactly. I think it was: I believe in no man but thee, my bailiff, not a single word."

Bailiff. "Thou shouldst have been a pastor, Nickel: thou couldst not only have explained the catechism, but put a new one in its place."

Nick. "They would not let me do that. If they did, I should make it so clear and plain, that the children would understand it without the pastor, and then he would naturally be of no use."

Bailiff. "We will keep to the old, Nickel. It is the same about the catechism as about every thing else to my mind. We shall not better ourselves by changing."

Nick. "That is a maxim which is sometimes true, and sometimes not. It seems to suit thee now with the new squire."

Bailiff. "It will suit others too, if we wait patiently, and for my own part, I am not so much afraid of the new squire. Every man finds his master."

Nick. "Very true: but there was an end of the old times for thee, last summer."

Bailiff. "At all events, Nickel, I have had my share of them. Let others try now."

Nick. "True, thou hast had thy share, and a very good one it was; but, how could it miss? The secretary, the attorney, and the late pastor's assistant, all owed thee money."

Bailiff. "People said so, but it was not true."

Nick. "Thou mayst say so now; but thou hadst an action brought against two of them, because the money did not come back."

Bailiff. "Thou fool, thou knowest every thing."

Nick. "I know a great deal more than that. I know thy tricks with Rudi's father, and how I caught thee by the dog-kennel, under the heap of straw, lying on thy face, close to Rudi's window; his attorney was with him. Till two o'clock in the morning, didst thou listen to what they were saying in the room. I was watchman that night, and had wine gratis at thy house, for a week after, for my silence."

Bailiff. "Thou heretic: there is not a word of truth in what thou sayest. It would be pretty work for thee, if thou wert made to prove it."

Nick. "I was not talking about proving it, but thou knowest whether it be true or not."

Bailiff. "Thou hadst better take back thy words."

Nick. "The devil put it into thy head to listen under the straw, in the night. Thou couldst hear every word, and then easily twist thy evidence with the attorney."

Bailiff. "How thou talkest!"

Nick. "How I talk? If the attorney had not wrested thy evidence before the court, Rudi would have had his meadow now, and Wast and Kaibacker needed not have taken their fine oaths."

Bailiff. "Truly, thou understandest the business, as well as the schoolmaster does Hebrew."

Nick. "Whether I understand it or not, I learned it from thee. More than twenty times thou hast laughed with me, at thy obedient servant, Mr. attorney."

Bailiff. "Yes, so I have; but he did not do what thou sayest. It is true, he was a cunning devil. God forgive him. It will be ten years, next Michaelmas, since he was laid in his grave."

Nick. "Since he was sent to hell, thou shouldst say."

Bailiff. "That is not right. We should not speak ill of the dead."

Nick. "Very true; or else I could tell how he cheated Roppi's children."

Bailiff. "He might have confessed himself to thee, on his death-bed, thou knowest it all so well."

Nick. "I know it, at any rate."

Bailiff. "The best part of it is, that I gained the action: if thou hadst known that I had lost it, it would have troubled me."

Nick. "Nay, I know that thou didst gain it, but I also know how."

Bailiff. "Perhaps; perhaps not."

Nick. "God keep all poor folks from law."

Bailiff. "Thou art right there. Only gentle-folks and people well off in the world, should go to law. That would certainly be a good thing; but so would many other things, Nickel. Well, well, we must be content with things as they are."

Nick. "Bailiff, that wise saying of thine puts me in mind of a fable I heard from a pilgrim. He came out of Alsace, and told it before a whole room full of people. A hermit had described the world in a book of fables, and he could repeat it almost from beginning to end. We asked him to tell us some of these fables, and he related that which thou remindest me of."

Bailiff. "Well, what was it, prater?"

Nick. "By good luck, I think I remember it. 'A sheep was complaining and lamenting that the wolf, the dog, the fox, and the butcher, tormented her terribly. A fox, that was standing near the fold, heard the complaint, and said to the sheep: we must always be content with the wise regulations of the world. If there were any change it would be for the worse.

That may be true, when the fold is shut, answered the sheep; but if it were open, I, for one, should not agree with you.

It is right enough that there should be wolves, foxes, and wild beasts; but it is also right, that the fold should be carefully looked after, and that poor weak animals should have watchful shepherds and dogs, to protect them from wild beasts.'

'Heaven preserve us,' added the pilgrim; 'there are everywhere plenty of wild beasts, and but few good shepherds.'

'Great God, thou knowest wherefore it is so, and we must submit silently.' His comrades added: 'yes, we must submit silently; and holy virgin, pray for us now, and in the hour of our death.'

We were all affected when the pilgrim spoke so feelingly, and we could not go on chattering our nonsense as usual."

Bailiff. "It's fine talking about such silly fancies of the sheep; according to which, wolves, foxes, and other wild beasts must die of hunger."

Nick. "It would be no great harm if they did."

Bailiff. "Art thou sure of that?"

Nick. "Nay, I spoke foolishly; they need not die of hunger: they might always find carrion and wild creatures, and these belong to them, and not tame animals, which must be brought up, and kept with labor and cost."

Bailiff. "Thou wouldst not then have them altogether die of hunger. That is a great deal for such a friend of tame animals to allow; but I am starved, come into the room."

Nick. "I can not, I must go on."

Bailiff. "Good-bye then, neighbors;" and he went away. Rubel and Nickel looked at each other for a moment, and Rubel said, "Thou hast salted his meat for him."

Nick. "I wish it had been peppered too, and so that it might have burnt his tongue till to-morrow."

Rubel. "A week ago, thou durst not thus have spoken to him."

Nick. "And a week ago he would not have answered as he did."

Rubel. "That is true. He is grown as tame as my dog, the first day it had its muzzle on."

Nick. "When the cup is full it will run over. That has been true of many a man, and it will be true of the bailiff."

Rubel. "Heaven keep us from officers! I would not be a bailiff, with his two courts."

Nick. "But if anybody offered thee half of one, and the office of bailiff, what wouldst thou do?"

Rubel. "Thou fool!"

Nick. "Thou wise man! what wouldst thou do? come, confess; thou wouldst quickly consent, wrap the cloak of two colors around thee, and be bailiff."

Rubel. "Dost thou think so?"

Nick. "Yes, I do think so."

Rubel. "We are losing time chattering here. Good-bye, Nickel."

Nick. "Good-bye, Rubel."

CHAPTER VII.—THE BAILIFF BEGINS SOME BAILIFF'S BUSINESS.

As soon as the bailiff entered the barber's room, he saluted him, and his wife, and the company, before he seated himself, or made any bustle. Formerly, he used to make a great spitting and coughing first, and took no notice of anybody, till he had seated himself.

The country people answered, smilingly, and put their hats on again, much sooner than they usually did, when the bailiff spoke to them. He began the conversation by saying, "Always good pay, Mr. Barber, and so much custom; I wonder how you manage to get through it, with one pair of hands."

The barber was a quiet man, and not in the habit of replying to such speeches; but the bailiff had been teasing him with these jests for several months past, and every Sunday morning in sermon-time; and as it happened, he took it into his head to answer him for once, and said:

"Mr. Bailiff, you need not wonder how people manage to work hard, with one pair of hands, and get little; but it is, indeed, a wonder how some people manage to sit with their hands before them, doing nothing at all, and yet get a great deal."

Bailiff. "True enough, barber; but thou shouldst try. The thing is, to keep the hands still, in the right way: then, money showers down like rain."

The barber made another attempt, and said: "Nay, bailiff, the way is, to wrap one's self up in a two-colored cloak, and say these three words: *It is so*, on my oath, *It is so.* If the time be well chosen, one may then put two fingers up, three down—*abracadabra!* and behold a bag full of gold."

This put the bailiff into a passion, and he answered, "Thou art a conjuror, barber! but there is no wonder in that. People of thy trade always understand witchcraft and conjuring."

This was too sharp for the good barber, and he repented having meddled with the bailiff; so he held his peace, and let the others talk, and began quietly lathering a man who was sitting before him. The bailiff continued, maliciously: "The barber is quite a fine gentleman, he will not answer one again. He wears smart stockings, town-made shoes, and ruffles on a Sunday. He has hands as smooth as a squire's, and his legs are like a town-clerk's."

The country people liked the barber, had heard this before, and did not laugh at the bailiff's wit.

Only young Galli, who was being shaved, could not help smiling at the idea of the town-clerk's legs; for he was just come from the office, where the jest had begun; but when his face moved, the barber's razor cut his upper lip.

This vexed the people; they shook their heads, and old Uli took his pipe out of his mouth, and said:

"Bailiff, it is not right to disturb the barber in this way."

And when the others saw that old Uli was not afraid, and said this boldly, they murmured still more loudly, and said: "Galli is bleeding, nobody can be shaved at this rate."

"I am sorry for what has happened," said the bailiff, "but I will set all to rights again."

"Boy! fetch three flasks of good wine, which heals wounds without needing to be warmed."

The moment the bailiff spoke of wine, the first murmur subsided.

Some did not believe that he was in earnest; but Lenk, who was sitting in a corner, solved the riddle, saying: "The bailiff's wine was tapped yesterday, in the church-yard."

The bailiff, taking his tobacco-box out of his pocket, laid it on the table, and Christian, the ballad-singer, asked him for a pipe-full. He gave it him; then more followed his example, and the room was soon full of the smoke of this strong tobacco, but the bailiff smoked a better kind himself.

Meantime the barber and the other neighbors kept quiet, and made light of it.

This disturbed Master Urias. He went up and down the room, with his finger on his nose, as he always did, when he could not get rid of his vexation.

"It is devilish cold in this room; I can never smoke when it is so cold," said he. So he went out of the room, gave the maid a kreuzer to make a larger fire, and it was soon warm enough.

CHAPTER VIII.—WHEN THE WHEELS ARE GREASED THE WAGON GOES.

Now came the brimstoned wine. "Glasses, glasses here, Mr. Barber," said the bailiff. And the wife and the boy soon brought plenty.

All the neighbors drew near the wine flasks, and the bailiff poured out for them.

Now were old Uli, and all the rest, content again; and young Galli's wound was not worth mentioning. "If the simpleton had only sat still, the barber would not have cut him."

By degrees they all grew talkative, and loud sounds of merriment arose.

All praised the bailiff; and the mason, Leonard, was at one table abused for a lout, and at the other for a beggar.

One told how he got drunk every day, and now played the saint; another said, "He knew well why pretty Gertrude went, instead of the mason, to the squire at the hall:" and another, "That he dreamed, last night, that the bailiff would soon serve the mason according to his deserts."

As an unclean bird buries its beak in the ditch, and feeds upon rotten garbage, so did Hummel satiate his wicked heart on the conversation of the neighbors. Yet it was with great caution and watchfulness that he mingled in the wild uproar of the chattering drunkards.

"Neighbor Richter," said he, giving him a glass, "you were yourself at the last reckoning, and are a qualified man. You know that the mason owed me thirty florins. It is now half a year since, and he has not paid me any part of it. I have never once asked him for the money, nor given him a hard word, and yet it is likely enough that I shall lose every farthing of it."

"That is clear enough," swore the farmers, "thou wilt never see another farthing of thy money;" and they poured out more wine.

But the bailiff took out of his pocket book the mason's promissory note, laid it on the table, and said, "There you may see whether it be true, or not."

The countrymen looked over the writing, as if they could read it, and said, "He is a rogue, that mason."

And Christian, the ballad-singer, who, till now, had been quietly swallowing down the wine, wiped his mouth with his coat sleeve, got up, raised his glass, and shouted out,

Long life to the bailiff, and away with all firebrands;" so saying, he drank off the glass, held it to be filled, drank again, and sang:

" He who digs another's grave,
Into it, himself may slip;
Who ne'er lifts a hand to save,
Should be careful not to trip.

"Be he lifted e'er so high,
And cunning as the deuce withal,
He who will still in ambush lie,
Is sure, at last, himself to fall—
Himself to fall.
Juhe, mason! juhe!"

CHAPTER IX.—ON THE RIGHTS OF THE COUNTRY.

"NOT so riotous, Christian," said the bailiff; "that is of no use. I should be very sorry if any ill luck happened to the mason. I forgive him freely. He did it from poverty. Still it is hard that the country must lose its rights."

The neighbors opened their ears when he spoke of the country's rights.

Some put down their glasses, when they heard of the country's rights, and listened.

"I am an old man, neighbors, and it can not signify much to me. I have no children, and it is almost over with me. But you have sons, neighbors; to you, your rights are of great consequence."

"Ay! our rights!" called out the men. "You are our bailiff. Do not let us lose a hair of our rights."

Bailiff. "Yes, neighbors. The landlord's license is a parish concern, and a valuable one. We must defend ourselves."

Some few of the men shook their heads, and whispered to each other, "He never looked after the parish before—he wants to draw us into the mud where he is sticking,"

But the majority shouted louder and louder, stormed, and cursed, and swore that to-morrow there must be a parish meeting.

The wiser amongst them were silent, and only said, quietly, to each other, "We shall see what they do when the wine is out of their heads."

Meantime the bailiff kept prudently drinking of the colored water, and began again to rouse up the people about their rights.

"You all know," said he, "how our forefather, Ruppli, two hundred years ago, had to fight with the cruel ancestors of this squire. This old Ruppli, (my grandfather has told me of it a thousand times,) had a favorite saying, 'When the squires welcome beggars at the hall, God help the country people.' They do it only to make mischief amongst them, and then to be masters themselves. Neighbors, we are thus always to be the fools in the game."

Countrymen. "Nothing is clearer. We are thus always to be the fools in the game."

Bailiff. "When your lawyers can be of no more use, you are as ill off as soldiers, who have their retreat cut off. The new squire is as sharp and cunning as the devil. No man can see through him; and certainly he gives no one a good word for nothing. If you knew but half as much as I do, there would be no need for me to say another word to you. But you are not quite blockheads; you will take heed, and be on your guard."

Abi, to whom the bailiff was speaking, and to whom he made a sign, answered,

"Do you think, bailiff, that we do not perceive his drift? He wants to take the landlord's license into his own hands."

Bailiff. "You see through it, do you?"

Countrymen. "Ay, by G——! but we will not allow it. Our children shall have a free tavern, as we have had."

Abi. "He may choose to make us pay a ducat for a measure of wine; and we should be false to our own children."

Bailiff. "That is going too far, Abi. He can never make you pay a ducat for a measure of wine."

Abi. "I don't know. The smith and the cartwright are raising their prices shamefully; and even wood is dearer than it has been these fifty years. What say you, bailiff? As the twig is bent, so grows the tree. How can you tell how high a measure of wine may get, when nobody can sell it but the squire? It is devilish dear already, on account of the duty."

Bailiff. "So it is. There is always some new plague and difficulty, and that makes every thing dearer."

"Yes, yes, if we will submit to it!" said the men, shouting and roaring, and threatening. Their conversation became, at last, the wild uproar of a set of drunkards, which I can describe no further.

CHAPTER X.—THE BARBER'S DOG DRINKS UP WATER AT AN UNLUCKY MOMENT, AND PLAYS THE BAILIFF A SAD TRICK.

MOST of them were, by this time, pretty well intoxicated, particularly Christian the ballad-singer, who sat next the bailiff; and, in one of his drunken huzzas, knocked over the jug of water.

The bailiff, alarmed, wiped the colored water off the table as quickly as he could, that nobody might detect the cheat. But the barber's dog, under the table, was thirsty, and lapped the water from the ground; and, unluckily, one of the neighbors, who was looking sorrowfully after the good wine under the table, observed that Hector licked it up.

"Wonder and marks, bailiff" said he, "how long have dogs drank wine?"

"You fool, long enough!" answered the bailiff, and made signs to him with his hands and head, and pushed him, with his foot, under the table, to be silent. He kicked the dog, at the same time, to drive him away. But Hector did not understand him, for he belonged to the barber. He barked, snarled, and lapped up the colored water a little further off. The bailiff turned pale at this; for many of the others now began to look under the table, and lay their heads together, and point to the dog. The barber's wife took up the fragments of the broken pitcher, and smelt at them, and perceiving that it was only water, shook her head, and said, aloud, "This is not right."

The men murmured all round; "There's something hidden under this;" and the barber told the bailiff, to his face, "Bailiff, your fine wine is nothing but colored water."

"Is it not, indeed?" exclaimed the men.

"What the devil is the meaning of this, bailiff? Why do you drink water?"

The bailiff, confused, answered, "I am not very well; I am obliged to spare myself."

But the men did not believe the answer; and right and left they murmured more and more; "There is something wrong in this."

And now some began to complain that the wine had got into their heads, which such a small quantity should not have done.

The two wisest amongst them got up, paid the barber, and said, "good-bye, neighbors," and went toward the door.

"So soon, gentlemen! Why do you leave the company so soon?" said the bailiff.

"We have something else to do," answered the men, and went out.

The barber accompanied them out of the room, and said, "I wish the bailiff had gone instead of you. He has had no good intention, either with the wine or the water."

"So we think, or we would have staid," answered the men.

Barber. "And I can not endure this drunken rioting."

Men. There is no reason why thou shouldst; and it may bring thee into difficulties. "If I were in thy place, I would put an end to it," said the elder of the two.

"I dare not do that," replied the barber.

"Things are not as they were, and thou art master in thy own house," said the men.

"I will follow your advice," said the barber, and went back into the room.

"What is the matter with these gentlemen, that they are gone off so suddenly?" said the bailiff.

And the barber answered, "I am of their mind. Such rioting is unseemly, and does not suit my house."

Bailiff. "So, so! and is this your answer?"

Barber. "Yes, indeed, it is, Mr. Bailiff. I like a quiet house."

This dispute did not please the honorable company.

"We will be quieter," said one of them.

"We will behave well," said another.

"Come, come, let us all be friends," said a third.

"Bailiff, another flask!" said Christian.

"Ha, neighbors! I have a room of my own. We will leave the barber in peace," said the bailiff.

"I shall be very glad of it," answered the barber.

"But the parish business is forgotten, and the landlord's rights, neighbors!" said old Abi, who was thirsty yet.

"Follow me, all who are true men," said the bailiff, threateningly,—muttering "donner and wetter," and looking fiercely round the room. He said good-bye to nobody, and clapped the door after him so furiously, that the room shook.

"This is shameful!" said the barber.

"Yes; it is shameful," said many of the men.

"It is not right," said young Meyer. "I, for one, will not enter the bailiff's house."

"Nor I," added Laupi.

"The devil, nor I!" said Reynold. "I remember yesterday morning. I stood next to him and Arner, and saw how it was."

The neighbors looked at each other, to see what they should do; but most of them sat down again, and staid where they were.

Only Abi and Christian, and a couple of blockheads more, took up the bailiff's empty cans, and went after him.

The bailiff was looking out of his window, down the street, which led to the barber's house, and as nobody followed at first, he was vexed at himself.

"What a lame ox I am! It is almost noon, and I have done nothing yet.

The wine is drunk and now they laugh at me. I have blabbed to them like a child, and let myself down, as if I had been one of them. Now, if I had really meant well by these fellows; if I had really desired to serve the parish; or, if I had only kept up the appearance of it a little better, I should have succeeded. Such a parish as this will dance after any cunning piper, who can only persuade them he means well by them. But times have been only too good for me. In the old squire's time, I led the parish about like a he-goat. Ever since I have been bailiff, it has been my pastime and delight to abuse them, tease them, and master them; and even now I mean to do so more than ever. But then, I must and will keep them at a distance. Shaking hands and lowering one's self; asking advice, and acting like everybody's brother-in-law, does not do, where people are so well known. Such a man as I am, must quietly act for himself; only employ such people as he knows, and let the parish alone. A herdsman does not ask advice of his oxen, and yet I have been fool enough to do so to-day."

Now came the men with the empty cans.

"Are you alone? Would not the dogs come with you?"

"No, not a man," answered Abi.

Bailiff. "That is going a good way."

Christian. "I think so too."

Bailiff. "I should like to know what they are talking and consulting together. Christian, go and seek the other cans."

Christian. "There are none left there."

Bailiff. "Blockhead! It's all one for that. If thou findest none, get thyself shaved or bled, and wait to listen to what they say. If thou bringest me any news, I will drink with thee till morning. And thou, Loli, go to the mason's old comrade, Joseph, but take care that no one observes thee, tell him to come to me at noon."

"Give me another glass first, I am thirsty," said Loli, "and then I'll run like a greyhound, and be back again in a twinkling."

"Very well," said the bailiff, and gave him one.

These two went off, and the bailiff's wife set some wine before the others.

Chapter XI.—Well-laid plots of a rogue.

The bailiff himself went, in some perplexity, into the next room, and considered how he should manage matters when Joseph came.

"He is faithless, that I may depend upon, and cunning as the devil. He has drunk away several crowns of his master's money; but my demand is a great one. He will be afraid, and not trust me. It is almost noon. I will offer him as much as ten crowns. If he will do as I bid him, within three weeks all the plaster will fall off the building. I shall not grudge ten crowns," said the bailiff; and as he was speaking thus to himself, Loli arrived, with Joseph behind him. They did not come together, that they might excite less suspicion.

"Good day, Joseph! I suppose thy master does not know that thou art here."

Joseph answered, "He is still at the hall, but he will come back at noon. If I am at work again by one o'clock, he will never miss me."

"Very well. I have something to say to thee, Joseph. We must be alone," said the bailiff; and, taking him into the inner room, he shut the door and bolted it. There were bacon, vegetables, wine, and bread, upon the table. The bailiff placed two chairs by the table, and said to Joseph, "Thou wilt miss thy dinner; sit down and eat it with me."

"With all my heart," answered Joseph—sat down, and said, "Mr. Bailiff, what is it you want? I am at your service."

The bailiff answered, "To thy good health, Joseph!" drank, and then continued the conversation. "Try these vegetables: they are good. Why dost thou not help thyself? Thou hast hard times enough with thy master."

Joseph. "True; but it will be better when he has work at the hall."

Bailiff. "Thou art a fool, Joseph! Thou mayest easily imagine how long that will last. I wish him joy of it; but he is not the man for such a thing. He has never had the management of any thing of the sort; but he will trust all to thee, Joseph."

Joseph. "May be so."

Bailiff. "I foresaw that, and therefore wished to speak to thee. Thou canst do me a great favor."

Joseph. "I am all attention, Mr. Bailiff. Here's luck to my master," (*drinking.*)

"It shall not be for nothing, mason," said the bailiff, and helped him again to the vegetables. "I should be very glad if the foundation of the church, which is to be of hewn stone, were got from the quarry at Schwendi."

Joseph. "Potz blitz, Mr. Bailiff! It can never be! The stone is bad, and good for nothing, as a foundation—"

Bailiff. "O the stone is not so bad: I have often seen it used. It is good, I say, Joseph; and it would be a great pleasure to me if this quarry were to be opened again."

Joseph. "It can not be done, Mr. Bailiff."

Bailiff. "I will be grateful for the service, Joseph."

Joseph. "The wall will be down in six years if it be built of this stone."

Bailiff. "I can't hear that. That is a foolish story."

Joseph. "By G——, it is true! There are two dung-heaps next the wall, and the stables drain past it. The stone would rot away like a fir plank."

Bailiff. "After all, what is it to thee, whether the wall be good or not, in ten years? Dost thou fear that the squire can not make a new one? Do what I say, and thou mayst expect a good handsome present."

Joseph. "That is all very well. But what if the squire should find out that the stone is not good."

Bailiff. "How should he find it out? There is no fear of that."

Joseph. "He knows more about things than any body would believe. But you know him better than I."

Bailiff. "He will understand nothing about this."

Joseph. "I almost think so myself; for the stone looks very well on the outside, and is very good for some purposes."

Bailiff. "Give me thy hand upon it, that thy master shall use the stone out of this quarry. If thou wilt, thou shalt have five crowns for thyself."

Joseph. "It's a good sum, if I had only hold of it."

Bailiff. "I am in earnest, by G——! I will give thee five crowns, if thou wilt do it!"

Joseph. "Well, there you have my word, Mr. Bailiff; and he stretched out his hand and pledged it him. It shall be done, Mr. Bailiff. Why should I trouble myself about the squire?"

Bailiff. "One word more, Joseph. I have a bag full of stuff, from an apothecary's shop, which a gentleman gave me. They say, that when it is mixed with the lime, the mortar sticks to a wall like iron. But these gentlemen are such queer folks, that one can not trust them about any thing. I would rather not try it first on a building of my own."

Joseph. "I can manage that for you. I will try it on a corner of a neighbor's house."

Bailiff. "It is of no use to try it in such a small way. Whether it succeeds or fails, one is at no certainty. There is no knowing how it might do on a larger scale. I should like it to be tried on the church, Joseph! can not it be done?"

Joseph. "Is it necessary to put much of it into the lime?"

Bailiff. "I think about two pounds to a barrel."

Joseph. "Then it will be easy enough."

Bailiff. "Wilt thou do it for me?"

Joseph. "Yes, that I will."

Bailiff. "And if it should fail, say nothing about it?"

Joseph. "It can not fail, so as to signify; and, of course, one should say nothing about it!"

Bailiff. "Thou wilt find the stuff at my house, whenever thou art ready for it; and a glass of wine with it."

Joseph. "I will not fail, Mr. Bailiff. But I must go now. It has struck one. Here's my thanks to you," said he, taking up his glass.

Bailiff. "Thou hast nothing to thank me for yet. Keep thy word, and thou shalt have the five crowns."

"I will do my part, Mr. Bailiff," said Joseph, getting up and putting by his chair. "My best thanks to you"—and he drank off his parting glass.

Bailiff. "Well, if thou must go, good-bye, Joseph; and remember our agreement."

Joseph went away, and, as he was going, said to himself, "This is a strange fancy of his about the stone; and still stranger about the stuff in the lime. It's a fine way to try a thing, to begin upon a church. But, at all events, I'll get hold of the money; and I can do as I like afterward."

"This has turned out very well," said the bailiff to himself. "Better than I expected, and for half the money. I should have promised him ten crowns, as easily as five, if he had understood how to make his bargain. I am well pleased that the thing is set a going. No, no! one should never despair. O that the wall were but already above the ground! Well, patience! on Monday they will begin to prepare the stone. Poor mason! Thy wife has cooked up a pretty mess for thee."

CHAPTER XII.—DOMESTIC HAPPINESS.

THE mason Leonard, who had gone up to the hall early in the morning, was now come back to his wife.

She had been very busy in getting her Saturday's work done, against her husband's return. She had combed the children, made them tidy, mended their clothes, cleaned up the little room, and, whilst she was at work, had taught them a song. "You must sing it for your dear father," said she; and the children gladly learned any thing which would please their father, when he came home. Whilst they were working, and without any trouble or loss of time, without book, they sang it after her till they knew it.

When their father came home, the mother welcomed him; and then she and the children sang:

Heav'nly Guest, who hast the power, Sorrow, pain, and care con-
trolling; O'er the suff' rer's saddest hour, To throw a ra - diant
beam con - sol - ing; Weary now of care and ri - ot,
cease - less chang-es with - out rest, Heaven - ly

> **Heavenly guest! who hast the pow'r—**
> **Sorrow, pain, and care controlling,**
> **O'er the suff'rer's saddest hour,**
> **To throw a radiant beam consoling:**
>
> **Weary now of care and riot,**
> **Ceaseless changes, without rest;**
> **Heavenly quiet!**
> **Come and reign within my breast.**

The tears came into Leonard's eyes, as the children and their mother sang so happily together, to welcome him. "God bless you, my darlings! God bless thee, my love!" said he to them, with great emotion.

"My dear husband," answered Gertrude, "it is heaven upon earth to seek for peace, do what is right, and wish for little."

Leon. "If I have ever enjoyed an hour of that happiness which peace of mind brings, I owe it to thee. Till my last moment I will thank thee for saving me; and these children will be grateful to thee for it, after thy death. O, my dear children! always do what is right, and follow your mother, and you will prosper."

Ger. "How cheery thou art to-day, Leonard!"

Leon. "I have gone on well with Arner."

Ger. "Ah! God be thanked for it, my dear husband."

Leon. "He is a man who has not his equal. How childish it was in me to be afraid of going to him."

Ger. "And how wise we have been at last, love. But come, tell me how it all was." And as she sat down by him, and took out the stocking she was knitting, he said to her:—

Chapter XIII.—A proof that Gertrude was dear to her husband.

Leonard. "If thou sittest down in such state, as thou dost to thy Bible on a Sunday evening, I must prepare to tell thee a great deal."

Gertrude. "Every thing! thou must tell me every thing, love!"

Leon. "Yes, if thou hadst time for it; but, Gertrude, dear, it is Saturday, when thou art always so busy."

Ger. (*Smiling.*) "Look about thee!"

Leon. "Ah! is every thing done already?"

Lise. "She has been very busy, father; and Enne and I have helped her to clean up. Is not that right?"

"It is, indeed, right," answered the father.

"But now begin to tell me," said Gertrude.

Leon. "Arner asked me my father's name, and the street where I lived, and the number of my house."

Ger. "O, thou art not telling it right, Leonard; I know he did not begin so."

Leon. "And why not, darling? What wouldst thou have?"

Ger. "First, thou wouldst make thy bow to him, and he would take notice of thee. How did he do that?"

Leon. "Thou little conjuror; thou art right. I did not begin at the beginning."

Ger. "I told thee so, Leonard."

Leon. "Well, then, as soon as he saw me, he asked whether I was still afraid of him. I made a bow, as well as I could, and said 'Forgive me, gracious sir.' He smiled, and ordered a jug of wine to be set before me."

Ger. "Come now, this is quite a different beginning. Well, wert thou ready enough to drink the wine? no doubt!"

Leon. "No, wife, I was as shamefaced as a young bride, and would not touch it. But he did not let it pass so. 'I know you can tell what good wine is,' said he, 'help yourself.' I poured out a little, drank his health, and tasted it—but he looked at me so steadily, that the glass shook in my hand."

Ger. "What it is to have a tender conscience, Leonard! It had got into thy fingers. But thou wouldst recover thyself, I suppose."

Leon. "Yes, very soon. He was very kind, and said, 'It is very natural that a man who works hard should like a glass of wine. It does him good too. But it is a misfortune when, instead of taking one glass to refresh himself, he lets wine make a fool of him, and thinks no more of his wife and children, nor of his old age. This is a great misfortune, Leonard.'

Wife! I felt it strike through my heart as he said this; but I took courage, and answered, 'That by unlucky circumstances I had got so entangled, that I did not know how in the world to help myself; and that I had not, in all that time, drunk one glass with a merry heart.'"

Ger. "And didst thou really get through all that?"

Leon. "If he had not been so very kind, I could not have managed it."

Ger. "And what did he say next?"

Leon. "'That it was a misfortune that poor folks, when they were in trouble, generally got hold of people they should avoid as the plague.' I could not help sighing; and I think he observed it, for he went on, very kindly: 'If one could only teach good people this, before they learn it by sad experience!—a poor man is half saved, if he can only keep out of the claws of these blood-suckers.' Soon afterward he went on again: 'It goes to my heart, when I think how often the poor will go on suffering the greatest misery, and have not the sense and courage to tell their situation to those who would gladly help them, if they only knew how things were. It is really unpardonable to think how you have let yourself be ensnared, day after day, by the bailiff, and brought your wife and children into such trouble and danger, without once coming to me, to ask for help and counsel. Only consider, mason, what would have been the end of all this, if your wife had had no more sense and courage than you.'"

Ger. "And did he say all this before he asked after the number of thy house?"

Leon. "Thou hearest how it was."

Ger. "Thou didst not mean to tell me all this in a hurry, didst thou?"

Leon. "Why, indeed, I think it would have been more prudent not. Thou wilt grow too proud for me; because thou hast had so much courage."

Ger. "Thinkest thou so, my good master? Yes, indeed, I will plume myself upon this as long as I live; and as long as it does us any good. But what said Arner besides?"

Leon. "He began to examine me about the building. It was well I had not forgotten every thing. I had to reckon it all up by measurement, and set down every item for carrying lime, and sand, and stone."

Ger. "Didst thou make no mistake at all in the reckoning?"

Leon. "No; not this time, love."

Ger. "God be thanked for it."

Leon. "Yes, indeed, God be thanked."

Ger. "Is every thing ready now?"

Leon. "Yes; all will very soon be ready. Guess now much he has given me in hand, said he, (shaking the money in a bag.) It is long since I heard the sound of so much silver." Gertrude sighed.

Leon. "Do not sigh now, my dear wife, we will be prudent and saving; and we shall certainly never come into the same distress again."

Ger. "God in heaven has helped us."

Leon. "Yes; and many more in the village besides us. Only think; Arner has chosen out ten fathers of families, who were poor and in want, as day-laborers at this building; and he gives each of them twenty-five kreutzers a day. Thou shouldst have seen, Gertrude, how carefully he chose them all out."

Ger. "O, tell me how it all was?"

Leon. "Yes; if I could remember I would."

Ger. "Try what thou canst do, Leonard."

Leon. "Well then: he inquired after all the fathers of families who were poor; how many children they had; how old they were; and what property or help they had. Then he asked which were the worst off, and had the most young children; and said to me, twice over, 'If you know of any body else, who is in trouble, as you were, tell me.' I thought of Hubel Rudi, and he has now work for a year certain."

Ger. "Thou didst very right not to let him suffer for having taken thy potatoes."

Leon. "I can never bear malice against any poor man, Gertrude; and they are terribly ill off. I met Rudi, near the potato hole two days ago, and pretended not to see him. It went to my heart, he looked such a picture of want and misery; and, thank God, we have always yet had something to eat."

Ger. "Thou art quite right, my dear husband! but still it can not be a help to any body to steal; and the poor who do so, are only doubly wretched."

Leon. "True; but when people are very hungry, and see food before them, and know how much of it must go to waste in the hole, and that even the cattle have enough to eat;—O Gertrude! it is hard work to let it lie there and not touch it."

Ger. "It is very hard! but the poor man must learn to do it, or he will be wretched indeed."

Leon. "Oh, who could punish him for it? who could ask it of him again?"

Ger. "God!—He who requires this from the poor man, gives him strength to do it, and leads him on, through trouble, and want, and the many sufferings of his situation, to that self-denial which is required from him. Believe me,

Leonard, God helps the poor man in secret, and gives him strength and understanding to bear, and to suffer, and to endure, what appears almost incredible. And, when it is once gone through, with an approving conscience, Leonard, then it brings happiness, indeed; greater than any one can know, who has had no occasion to practice self-denial."

Leon. "I know it, Gertrude. I know it by what thou hast done. I am not blind. I have often seen how, in the greatest need, thou couldst still trust in God and be content. But few are like thee in trouble, and there are many who, like me, are very weak creatures, when want and distress are heavy upon them; and therefore I always think, that more should be done, to provide all the poor with work and food. I think too, that they would then all be better than they now are, in the distraction of their poverty, and of their many troubles."

Ger. "O my love! that is not the state of the case. If nothing were wanting but work and gain, to make the poor happy, they would be easily helped. But it is not so. Both rich and poor must have their hearts well regulated before they can be happy. And more arrive at this end, by means of trouble and care, than through rest and joy. If it were not so, God would willingly let us all have joys in abundance. But since men can only know how to bear prosperity, and rest, and joy, when their hearts have been trained to much self-denial, and are become steadfast, firm, patient, and wise, it is clearly necessary that there should be much sorrow and distress in the world; for without it, few men can bring their hearts into due regulation, and to inward peace; and, if these be wanting, a man may have work or no work, he may have abundance or not, it is all one. The rich old Meyer has all he wants, and spends every day in the tavern: but for all that, he is no happier than a poor man who has nothing, works hard all day, and can only now and then have a glass of wine in a corner." Leonard sighed. Gertrude was silent for a short time. Then she continued: "Hast thou seen whether the men are at work? I should tell thee, that Joseph has again slipped away to the tavern."

Leon. "That looks ill! I am sure the bailiff must have sent for him. He goes on very strangely. Before I came home, I went to them at their work, when he was just come back from the tavern; and what he said made me uneasy. It is not his own thought then."

Ger. "What was it?"

Leon. "He said the stone out of the quarry at Schwendi was excellent for the church wall; and when I told him the great flint stones, which lay near in heaps, were much better, he said, 'I should always be a fool, and not know my own business. The wall would be much better and handsomer of Schwendi stone.' I thought, at the time, he said it with a good intention. But he began so suddenly about the stone, that it seemed very strange; and if he has been with the bailiff,—there is certainly something more in it. The Schwendi stone is soft and sandy, and not fit for such work. If it should be a snare laid for me!"—

Ger. "Joseph is not a man to depend upon, be careful about him."

Leon. "They will not take me in, this time. The squire will have no sandstone in the wall."

Ger. "Why not?"

Leon. "He says that sandstone where there are dung heaps and stable drainage will decay, and be eaten up with saltpetre."

Ger. "Is that true?"

Leon. "Yes. When I was from home once, I worked at a building, where they were obliged to take away a very good foundation of this kind of stone."

Ger. "To think of his understanding it so well!"

Leon. "I was surprised myself; but he understands a great many things. He asked me where the best sand was. I said, near the lower mill. 'That is very far to fetch it, and up the hill too,' answered he: 'We must be careful of men and cattle. Do you not know of any nearer?' I said, there certainly was very good sand in a meadow near the church; but it was private property, and we should have to pay for the hole; and could go no way but through the meadow, where we must make a road. 'There is no harm in that,' said he. 'It is better than fetching sand from the mill.' I must tell thee one thing more: As he was speaking of the sand, a servant came from the squire of Oberhofen, and I thought then, that I ought to say I would not detain him, but come another time. He laughed, and said: 'No, mason, I like to finish what I am about; and when I have done, I see what any body else wants from me. But it is like you, to be taking leave. It is a part of your old ways, which you must give up—to be so ready at every opportunity to leave your business and work.'

"I looked like a fool, wife; and heartily wished I had kept my tongue quiet, and not said a word about coming another time.'"

"It was partly thy own fault, indeed!" said Gertrude; and at that moment somebody called out at the door: "Holla! is nobody at home?"

Chapter XIV.—Mean selfishness.

The mason opened the door, and Margaret, the sexton's daughter-in-law, and the bailiff's niece, came into the room. As soon as she had very slightly saluted the mason and his wife, she said to him: "You will not be for mending our old oven, now, I suppose, Leonard!"

Leonard. "Why not, neighbor? Does it want any thing done to it?"

Margaret. "Not just now. I only ask in time, that I may know what to trust to."

Leon. "You are very careful Margaret; but there was no great need to be afraid."

Marg. "Ay! but times change, and people with them."

Leon. "Very true. But one may always find plenty of people to mend an oven."

Marg. "That is some comfort, at all events."

Gertrude, who had been silent all this time, took up the cleaver to cut some hard rye-bread for supper.

"That is but black bread," said Margaret; "but you will soon have better, as your husband is become builder to the squire."

"You talk foolishly, Margaret. I shall be thankful if I have enough of bread like this, all my life;" said Gertrude.

Marg. "But white bread is better; and you will find it so. You will now be a bailiff's wife, and your husband, Mr. Bailiff; but it will be a bad thing for us."

Leon. "What do you mean by your sneers? I like people to speak out; if they have any thing on their minds, and dare say it."

Marg. "Ay, mason! and I dare say it, if it comes to that. My husband is the sexton's son, and since the church was first built, it was never heard of before, but that his people had the preference, when there was any thing to be done at it!"

Leon. "Well! what more?"

Marg. "Why, now, at this very moment, the bailiff has a list in his house, in which more than a dozen blockheads, out of the village, are marked out to work at the building of the church, and there is not a word said of the sexton's people."

Leon. "But, neighbor! what have I to do with it? Did I write out the list?"

Marg. "No, you did not write it out, but I suppose you dictated it."

Leon. "It would be a fine thing for me, indeed, to dictate his own list to the squire."

Marg. "O! we all know that you go every day to the hall; and you have certainly been there again to-day; and if you had only told him how it was before, things would have gone on in the old way.

Leon. "You are mistaken, Margaret, if you think so. Arner is not the man to let things go on in the old way, if he can mend them by a new one."

Marg. "We see how it is!"

Leon. "And he means to help the poor and needy, by giving them work."

Marg. "Yes! he means to help all the blockheads and beggarly rabble."

Leon. "All poor folks are not rabble, Margaret; and it is not right to talk so. No one knows what may happen to himself before he dies."

Marg. "No; and therefore every body should look after his own bread; and it is no wonder we are troubled to be so forgotton."

Leon. "Ah, Margaret! it is a very different thing. You have good property, and live with your father, who has the best situation in the village; and you have no need to work for your bread like us poor folks."

Marg. "You may say what you will: every one is vexed when he thinks a thing belongs to him, and another dog comes and snatches it out of his mouth."

Leon. "Don't talk of dogs, Margaret, when you are speaking of men, or you may find one that will bite you. But if you think the situation belongs to you, you are young and strong, and a rare talker; you can manage your own affair, and take it to the place where you may be helped to your right."

Marg. "Many thanks, Mr. Mason, for your fine piece of advice."

Leon. "I can give you none better."

Marg. "One may find an opportunity to remember the service. Farewell, Leonard."

Leon. "Farewell, Margaret. It is all I can do for you."

Margaret went away, and Leonard to his men."

CHAPTER XV.—THE WISE GOOSE LAYS AN EGG; OR, A BLUNDER WHICH COSTS A GLASS OF WINE.

LEONARD had no sooner left the hall, than Arner sent the list of day-laborers which he had written out, by Flink, his huntsman, to the bailiff, with orders to give them all notice.

The huntsman brought the list to the bailiff before noon; but formerly, all the writings which came from the hall, were directed "To the honorable and discreet, my trusty and well-beloved Bailiff Hummel in Bonnal," and on this, there was only, "To the Bailiff Hummel in Bonnal."

"What is that damned Spritzer, the secretary, about, that he does not give me my right title?" said the bailiff to Flink, as he took the letter.

But the huntsman answered: "Take care, bailiff, what you say. The squire directed the letter himself."

Bailiff. "That's not true. I know the writing of that powdered beggar the secretary!"

Flink shook his head, and said: "You are a bold man. I saw the squire write it, with my own eyes, and I stood by him in the room whilst he did it."

Bailiff. "Then I have made a damned blunder, Flink! The words escaped me. Forget them, and come into the house, and drink a glass of wine with me."

"Take care the next time, bailiff! I don't like to make mischief, and will pass it over for once," said Flink, going with the bailiff into the house. He set his short gun in a corner, drank one glass, and then went away.

The bailiff opened the paper, read it, and said: "These are all mere blockheads and beggars, from first to last. Donner! what a business this is! Not one of my own people, except Michael. I am not even to recommend a day-laborer to him! And here I am to give them all notice to-day. It will be hard work for me—but I will do it. It is not evening all day long. Truly, I will tell them of it, and advise them all to go on Monday to the hall, to return thanks to the squire. He does not know one of these fellows. It must be the mason who has recommended them to him. When they arrive at the hall, on Monday, all in tatters, some without shoes, others without hats, and stand before the squire, I shall wonder if he does not say something I can turn to use." Thus he laid his plans, dressed himself, and took up the list to see how they lay near each other, that he might not go roundabout.

Hubel Rudi was not the next to him; but ever since he had gained the meadow from his father by a lawsuit, he kept, as much as he could, away from his house, on account of certain uneasy thoughts which occurred to him, when he saw these poor people. "I will go first to these folks," said he, and went up to their window.

CHAPTER XVI.—THE DEATH-BED.

HUBEL RUDI was sitting with his four children. It was only three months since his wife's death, and now his mother lay dying upon a bed of straw, and said to Rudi: "I wish thou wouldst collect some leaves this afternoon, to put into my coverlid; I am very cold."

Rudi. "Oh, mother! as soon as ever the fire in the oven is put out, I will go."

Mother. "Hast thou any wood left, Rudi? I think not, for thou canst not leave me and the children, to go into the forest—alas, Rudi, I am a burthen to thee!"

Rudi. "My dear mother, do not say that thou art a burthen to me! Oh, if I could only give thee what thou hast need of! Thou art hungry and thirsty, and makest no complaint. It goes to my heart, mother!"

Mother. "Do not make thyself unhappy, Rudi. Thanks be to God, my pain is not severe—he will soon relieve it, and my blessing will repay thee what thou hast done for me."

Rudi. "O mother, my poverty was never such a trouble to me as now, when I can give thee nothing, and do nothing for thee. Alas! thou sufferest from sickness and misery, and sharest my wants."

Mother. "When we draw near our end, we want little on earth, and what we do want, our heavenly Father supplies. I thank him, Rudi; for he strengthens me in my approaching hour."

Rudi. (Weeping.) "Dost thou think then, mother, that thou wilt not recover?"

Mother. "Never, Rudi! it is most certain."

Rudi. "Gracious heaven!"

Mother. "Take comfort, Rudi! I go into a better life."

Rudi. (Sobbing.) Alas, alas!"

Mother. "Do not grieve, Rudi! Thou hast been the joy of my youth, and the comfort of my old age. And now I thank God that thy hand will soon close my eyes! Then shall I go to God, and I will pray for thee, and all will be well with thee for ever. Think of me, Rudi. All the sufferings and all the troubles of this life, if they are well borne, end in good, All I have undergone comforts me, and is as great a blessing to me, as any of the pleasures and joys of life. I thank God for the gladsome days of my childhood; but when the fruit of life ripens for harvest, and when the tree drops its leaves before its winter sleep,—then are the sorrows of life hallowed, and its joys but as a dream. Think of me, Rudi!—all thy sufferings will end in good."

Rudi. "Oh, mother! dear mother!"

Mother. "Yet, one thing more, Rudi."

Rudi. "What, mother?"

Mother. "Ever since yesterday it has lain like a stone on my heart. I must tell thee of it, Rudi."

Rudi. "What is it, dear mother?"

Mother. "Yesterday I saw our little Rudeli creep behind my bed, and eat roasted potatoes out of his bag. He gave some to his sisters, and they also ate these potatoes, which must have been stolen. Rudi, they could not be ours!—or the boy would have thrown them upon the table, and called his sisters loudly; and he would have brought me some of them, as he had done a thousand times before. Oh, how it used to gladden my heart, when he flew towards me with something in his hand, and said, so fondly to me: "Eat, eat, grandmother?" Rudi, if this darling child should become a thief! O, this thought has been a sad weight upon me since yesterday. Where is he? bring him to me—I will speak to him."

Rudi ran quickly, sought the boy and brought him to his mother's bed-side.

The mother, with great difficulty, raised herself up, for the last time, turned toward the boy, took both his hands in hers, and bent forward her weak, dying head.

The little fellow wept aloud. "Grandmother! what is it you wish? you are not dying yet! O, do not die yet, grandmother."

She answered in broken words: "Yes, Rudeli, I must certainly die very soon."

"O my God! do not die, grandmother," said the boy.

The sick woman lost her breath, and was obliged to lie down again.

The boy and his father burst into tears—but she soon recovered herself, and said:

"I am better again, now that I lie down."

And Rudeli said: "And you will not then die now, grandmother?"

Mother. "Say not so, my darling! I die willingly; and shall then go to a kind father! If thou couldst know, Rudeli, how happy I am, that I shall soon go to Him, thou wouldst not be so sorrowful."

Rudeli. "I will die with you, grandmother, if you must die!"

Mother. "No, Rudeli, thou must not die with me. If it be the will of God, thou must live a long time yet, and grow up to be a good man; and when thy father is old and weak, thou must be his help and comfort. Tell me, Rudeli, wilt thou follow after him, and be a good man, and do what is right? Promise me thou wilt, my love!"

Rudeli. "Yes, grandmother, I will do what is right, and follow after him."

Mother. "Rudeli, our Father in heaven, to whom I am going, sees and hears all that we do, and what we promise. Tell me, Rudeli, dost thou know this, and dost thou believe it?"

Rudeli. "Yes, grandmother! I know it, and I believe it."

Mother. "But why didst thou then eat stolen potatoes, yesterday, behind my bed?"

Rudeli. "Forgive me this once, grandmother; I will never do so again. Forgive me! I will certainly never do so again, grandmother."

Mother. "Didst thou steal them?"

Rudeli. (Sobbing.) "Yes, grandmother, I did!"

Mother. "From whom didst thou steal them?"

Rudeli. "From the ma—ma—son."

Mother. "Thou must go to him Rudeli, and beg him to forgive thee."

Rudeli. "O, grandmother, for God's sake! I dare not."

Mother. "Thou must Rudeli! that thou mayst not do so another time. Thou must go, without another word! and for heaven's sake, my dear child, if thou art ever so hungry, never take any thing again. God will not forsake any of us. He provides for all. O, Rudeli, if thou art ever so hungry, if thou hast no food, and knowest of none, yet trust in God, and do not steal any more."

Rudeli. "Grandmother, I will never steal again. If I am hungry, I will never steal again."

Mother. "Then may the God, in whom I trust, bless thee, and keep thee, my darling!" She pressed him to her heart, wept, and said: "Thou must now go to the mason, and beg his pardon; and, Rudi, do thou also go with him, and tell the mason, that I too beg his pardon; and that I am very sorry I can not give him back the potatoes. Tell him I will pray for the blessing of God upon what he has left, I am so grieved! They have so much need of all they have—and if his wife did not work so hard, day and night, they could not possibly maintain their own large family. Rudi, thou wilt willingly work a couple of days for him, to make it up."

Rudi. "I will, indeed, dear mother, with all my heart."

As he spoke, the bailiff tapped at the window."

Chapter XVII.—The Sick Woman's Behavior.

And the sick woman knew him by his cough, and said: "O Rudi! here is the bailiff!—I am afraid the bread and butter thou art preparing for me are not paid for."

Rudi. "For heaven's sake, do not distress thyself, mother. It is of no consequence. I will work for him; and, at harvest time, reap for him, as much as he likes."

"Alas! he will not wait," said the mother; and Rudi went out of the room to the bailiff.

The sick woman sighed to herself, and said: "Since this affair of ours, God forgive him, the poor blinded creature, I never see him without a pang. And to think that, at my last hour, he must come and talk under my window. It is the will of God that I should forgive him, entirely and immediately, and overcome my last resentment, and pray for his soul—and I will do so."

"O God, thou hast overruled the whole affair. Forgive him, Father in heaven, forgive him." She heard the bailiff talking loudly, and started. "Alas! he is angry! O my poor Rudi! it is owing to me that thou art in his power!" Again she heard his voice, and fainted away.

Rudeli sprang out of the room to his father, and called him: "Father, come, come! I think my grandmother is dead."

And Rudi exclaimed: "Gracious heaven! Bailiff, I must go into the room."

"Much need of that," said the bailiff. "It will be a great loss, truly, if the old witch should be gone at last."

Rudi heard not what he said, but rushed into the room.

The sick woman soon recovered herself, and as she opened her eyes, she said: "Is he angry, Rudi? I am sure he will not wait."

Rudi. "No, indeed, mother! It is some very good news. But art thou quite recovered?"

"Yes!" said the mother, and looked at him very earnestly and mournfully,—"What good news can this man bring? what dost thou say? Dost thou wish to comfort me, and to suffer alone? He has threatened thee."

Rudi. "I do assure thee it is not so, mother. He has told me that I am to be a day-laborer, at the building of the church, and the squire pays every man twenty-five kreutzers a day, wages."

Mother. "Lord God! Can this be true?"

Rudi. "Yes, mother, it is indeed! And there is work for more than a whole year."

Mother. "Now I shall die more easy, Rudi. Great God, thou art merciful! O, be so to the end! And, Rudi, be thou sure, that the greater our want, the nearer is his help."

She was silent for a while, and then said again, "I believe it is all over with me! my breath grows shorter every moment—we must part, Rudi—I will take leave of thee."

Rudi trembled, shuddered, took off his cap, and knelt down by his mother's bed, folded his hands, raised his eyes to heaven, and tears and sobs choked his speech.

Then said his mother: "Take courage, Rudi! I trust in an eternal life, where we shall meet again. Death is a moment which passes away—I do not fear it—I know that my Redeemer liveth, and that he shall stand at the latter day upon the earth: and though, after my skin, worms destroy this body, yet in my flesh shall I see God: whom I shall see for myself, and mine eyes shall behold, and not another."

Rudi had now recovered himself, and said: "Give me thy blessing, mother! If it be the will of God, may I soon follow thee to eternal life."

Then said his mother: "Hear me, heavenly Father, and grant thy blessing upon my child! Upon this, the only child whom thou hast given me, and who is so dear to me! Rudi, may my God and Saviour be with thee, and as he showed mercy unto Isaac and Jacob, for their father Abraham's sake, so may he show mercy unto thee, abundantly, for the sake of my blessing; that thy heart may rejoice and be glad, and praise his name."

"Hear me now, Rudi! and do as I say. Teach thy children regularity and industry, that they may never come to want, nor grow disorderly and idle. Teach them to hope and trust in Almighty God, and to be kind to each other in joy and in sorrow. So will it be well with them, even in poverty.

"Forgive the bailiff; and, when I am dead and buried, go to him, and tell him that I die in charity with him, and if God hears my prayer, he will yet do well and come to the knowledge of himself, before he must depart hence."

After a pause, the mother said again: "Rudi, give me my two bibles, my prayer-books, and a paper, which is lying under my handkerchief, in a little box."

And Rudi rose from his knees and brought them all to his mother.

Then she said: "Now bring all the children to me." He brought them from the table, where they were sitting weeping, and they all knelt down by her bed-side.

Then she said to them: "Weep not so, my children! your heavenly Father will support and bless you—you are very dear to me, and I grieve to leave you so poor, and without a mother. But hope in God, and trust in him, whatever may befall you; so will you always find in him, more than a father's help, or a mother's kindness. Remember me, my darlings! I have nothing to leave you, but I have loved you tenderly, and I know that you love me also. My bibles and my prayer-books are almost all I have left, but do not think them trifles, my children!—They have comforted and cheered me, a thousand times, in my troubles. Let the word of God be also your comfort and your joy; and love one another; and help and advise one another, as long as you live; and be honest, true, kind, and obliging, to all men—so will you pass well through life.

"And thou, Rudi, keep the great bible for Betheli, and the smaller one for Rudeli; and the two prayer-books for the little ones, for a remembrance of me.

"I have nothing for thee, Rudi! but thou needest no remembrance of me—thou wilt not forget me."

Then she called Rudeli again to her: "Give me thy hand, my dear child! Be sure thou never stealest again."

"No indeed, grandmother, believe me! I will never take any thing from any body again," said Rudeli, with burning tears.

"And I do believe thee, and will pray to God for thee," said the mother. "See, my love, I give thy father a paper which the pastor, with whom I lived servant, gave me. When thou art older read it, and think of me, and be good and true."

It was a certificate from the late pastor of Eichstatten, that Catharine, the sick woman, had served him ten years, and helped him, indeed, to bring up his children, after the death of his wife; that all had been intrusted to Catharine; and that she had looked after every thing most carefully. The pastor thanked her in it, and said that she had been as a mother to his children, and he should never forget the assistance she had been to him in his difficulties. She had also earned a considerable sum of money in his service, which she gave to her deceased husband to buy the meadow, which the bailiff had afterward taken from him by a law suit.

After she had given Rudi this paper, she said: "There are two good shifts there. Do not put either of them on me when I am buried—the one I have on, is good enough. And when I am dead, let my gown and my two aprons be cut up for the children."

Soon afterward, she added: "Look carefully after Betheli, Rudi! She is such a delicate child; and always let the children be kept clean, and well washed and combed; and every year let them have spring herbs to sweeten their blood; they do them so much good. And if thou canst manage it, keep a goat for them, during the summer—Betheli can take care of it now. It grieves me to think that thou wilt be so solitary, but keep up thy courage, and do what thou canst. This work at the church will be a great help to thee—I thank God for it."

The mother was now silent, and the children and their father remained for a time upon their knees, praying. Then they stood up, and Rudi said to his mother: "Mother, I will now go and get the leaves for thy coverlid."

She answered: "There is no hurry for that, Rudi! The room is warmer now, thank God! and thou must go to the mason's with the child."

And Rudi beckoned Betheli out of the room, and said: "Watch thy grandmother carefully, and if any thing happens to her, send Anneli after me. I shall be at the mason's."

CHAPTER XVIII. A POOR BOY ASKS PARDON FOR HAVING STOLEN POTATOES, AND THE SICK WOMAN DIES.

AND he took the little one by the hand, and went with him.

Gertrude was alone in the house when they arrived, and soon saw that both the boy and his father had tears in their eyes. "What dost thou want, neighbor Rudi? Why art thou weeping? Why is the little fellow weeping?" said she, kindly taking his hand.

"Alas, Gertrude? I am in trouble," answered Rudi. "I am come to thee, because Rudeli has taken potatoes out of your heap. Yesterday his grandmother found it out, and he has confessed it—forgive us, Gertrude.

"His grandmother is on her death-bed—she has just taken leave of us. And I am so wretched, I scarcely know what I am saying—Gertrude! she begs thy forgiveness too—I am sorry I can not pay thee back now; but I will willingly work a couple of days for thee, to make it up. Forgive us!—The boy did it from hunger."

Gertrude. "Say not another word about it, Rudi: and thou, dear little fellow! come and promise me never to take any thing from any body again." She kissed him, and said: "Thou hast an excellent grandmother! only grow up as pious and as good as she is."

Rudeli. "Forgive me, Gertrude! I will never steal again."

Ger. "No, my child, never do so again. Thou dost not yet know how miserable and unhappy all thieves become. Do so no more: and if thou art hungry, come to me instead, and tell me. If I can, I will give thee something to eat."

Rudi. "I thank God, I have now got work at the building of the church, and I hope hunger will never lead him to do any thing of the kind again."

Ger. "My husband and I were very glad to hear that the squire had fixed upon thee as one."

Rudi. "And I am so glad that my mother has lived to have this comfort! Tell thy husband, I will work under him honestly and truly, and be there early and late; and I shall be very glad to allow any wages, to pay for the potatoes."

Ger. "Say nothing of that, Rudi. I am sure my husband will never take it. God be praised, we are now much better off, on account of this building. Rudi, I will go with thee to thy mother, as she is so very ill."

She filled Rudeli's pocket with apples, and said to him once more: "Remember, my dear child, never to take any thing from any body again;" and she then went with Rudi to his mother.

And as he was collecting some leaves under a nut-tree, to fill his mother's coverlid, Gertrude helped him—and then went with him to her.

Gertrude spoke kindly to the sick woman, took her hand, and wept.

"Dost thou weep, Gertrude?" said the grandmother. "It is we who should weep. Hast thou forgiven us?"

Ger. "O, do not talk of forgiveness, Catharine! Your distress goes to my heart, and still more thy goodness and carefulness. Thy carefulness and honesty will certainly bring down the blessing of God upon thy children, Catharine."

Catharine. "Hast thou forgiven us, Gertrude?"

Ger. "Say no more about that, Catharine. I only wish I could do any thing to give thee ease, in thy sickness."

Cath. "Thou art very good, Gertrude, and I thank thee; but God will soon help me. Rudeli, hast thou asked her pardon? Has she forgiven thee?"

Rudeli. "Yes, grandmother: see how good she is." He showed her his pocket full of apples.

"How very sleepy I am," said the grandmother. "Hast thou asked her forgiveness properly?"

Rud. "Yes, grandmother, with my whole heart."

Cath. "A slumber creeps over me, and my eyes grow dim. I am going, Gertrude!" said she softly, and in broken words. "There is one thing more, I wish to ask thee; but I don't know whether I dare. This unfortunate child has stolen from thee—may I ask thee, Gertrude, when—I am dead—these poor—desolate children—they—are so desolate"—she stretched out her hand—(her eyes were already closed,) "may I—hope—follow her—Rud"—she expired, unable to finish.

Rudi thought she had only dropped asleep, and said to the children: "Do not speak a word, she is asleep. O, if she should yet recover!"

But Gertrude thought it was death, and told Rudi so.

How he and all the little ones wrung their hands in anguish, I can not describe. Reader! let me be silent and weep—for it goes to my heart to think how man, in the dust of earth, ripens to immortality; and how, in the pomp and vanity of the world, he decays without coming to maturity. Weigh then, O man, weigh the value of life, on the bed of death; and thou who despisest the poor, pitiest and dost not know him—tell me whether he can have lived unhappy, who can thus die!—But I refrain. I wish not to teach you, O men! I only wish you to open your eyes, and see for yourselves, what really is happiness or misery, a blessing or a curse in this world.

Gertrude comforted poor Rudi, and told him the last wish of his excellent mother, which, in his trouble, he had not heard.

Rudi took her by the hand, confidingly—"What a sad affliction it is to lose my dear mother! How good she was! I am sure, Gertrude, thou will remember her wish."

Ger. "I must have a heart of stone if I could forget it. I will do what I can for thy children."

Rudi. "God will repay thee what thou dost for us."

Gertrude turned toward the window, wiped the tears from her face, raised her eyes to heaven, and sighed deeply. Then she took up Rudeli and his sisters, one after the other, kissed them with warm tears, prepared the corpse for the grave, and did not go home till she had done every thing which was necessary.

CHAPTER XIX.—GOOD SPIRITS COMFORT, CHEER, AND SUPPORT A MAN, BUT ANXIETY IS A CONTINUAL TORMENT.

THE bailiff, after he had been to Rudi, proceeded to the other day-laborers. And first he went to Jogli Bar. He found him splitting wood, and singing and whistling over his chopping-log; but when he saw the bailiff, he looked up in astonishment: "If you are come for money, bailiff, I have none."

Bailiff. "Thou art singing and whistling like a bird in a granary. How canst thou be without money?"

Bar. "If crying would bring bread, I should not be whistling. But, in good earnest, what do you want!"

Bailiff. "Nothing; but to tell thee, that thou art to be a helper at the building of the church, and to have twenty-five kreutzers a day."

Bar. "Can that be true?"

Bailiff. "It is, indeed. Thou must go up to the hall on Monday."

Bar. "If it is really true, I am very thankful for it, Mr. Bailiff. You see now that I might well be singing and whistling to-day."

The bailiff went away, laughing; and said to himself: "I never know what it is to be as merry as this beggar."

Bar went into the house, to his wife. "Keep up a good heart, wife. I am to be day-laborer at the building of the church!"

Wife. "It will be long enough before thou hast such a piece of luck. Thou hast always a bag full of hope, but not of bread."

Bar. "There shall be no want of bread, when once I get my daily wages."

Wife. "But there may be want of wages."

Bar. "No, child, no! Arner pays his laborers well. No fear of that."

Wife. "Art thou joking, or can it be true about the building?"

Bar. "The bailiff has just been here to tell me to go on Monday to the hall, with the other laborers who are to work at the church; so it can not well miss."

Wife. "Heaven be praised, if it prove so: if I may hope to have one comfortable hour!"

Bar. "Thou shalt have many a one. I am as light-hearted as a child about it. Thou wilt no longer scold me, when I come home laughing and merry. I will bring thee every kreutzer, as fast as I get it. I should have no pleasure in life, if I did not hope that the time would yet come, when thou shouldst think, with joy, that thou hast a good husband. If thy little property was soon lost in my hands, forgive me. God willing, I will yet make it up to thee."

Wife. "I am glad to see thee merry; but I am always afraid it is from thoughtlessness."

Bar. "What have I neglected? or what have I done that was wrong?"

Wife. "Nay, I do not accuse thee of that; but thou art never troubled when we have no bread."

Bar. "Would my being troubled bring us bread?"

Wife. "Do what I will, I can not help it:—it always makes me low."

Bar. "Take courage, and cheer up, wife. It makes things easier."

Wife. "Thou hast never a coat to go up to the hall in on Monday."

Bar. "Oh, then I will go in half of one. Thou always findest something to fret about," said he; and went off to his log, and split wood until dark.

From him, the bailiff went to Laupi, who was not at home; so he left the message with Hugli, his neighbor, and went on to Hans Leemann.

CHAPTER XX.—FOOLISH GOSSIPING LEADS TO IDLENESS.

HE was standing at his door, staring around him, saw the bailiff at a distance, and said to himself: "Now we shall have some news." "What brings you this way, Mr. Bailiff?"

Bailiff. "I am in search of thee, Leemann."

Leemann. "It is doing me a great honor, Mr. Bailiff—but tell me, how is the mason's wife going on? Is she as pert as she was yesterday in the church-yard? What a witch she was, bailiff!"

Bailiff. "Thou must not say so now. Thou art to be helper to her husband."

Leemann. "Is there no other news, that you come to me with such a tale?"

Bailiff. "Nay, it is true enough, and I am come, by the squire's orders, to tell thee of it."

Leemann. "How did I come to this honor, Mr. Bailiff?"

Bailiff. "I think it must have been in thy sleep."

Leemann. "I will awake, however, if this be true. What time must one go to the work?"

Bailiff. "I suppose in a morning."

Leemann. "And in an afternoon too, I fancy. How many of us are there, Mr. Bailiff?"

Bailiff. "Ten."

Leemann. "I wonder who they are! Tell me."

The bailiff told him all the names in order. Between every one Leemann guessed twenty others—not such a one? nor such a one?—"I am losing time," said the bailiff at last, and went on.

CHAPTER XXI.—INGRATITUDE AND ENVY.

FROM him, the bailiff went to Jogli Lenk. He was lying on the stove-bench, smoking his pipe. His wife was spinning, and five half naked children were sprawling around.

The bailiff told his message in few words.

Lenk took the pipe out of his mouth, and answered: "It's a wonder that any good thing comes to me! I have always been far enough out of the way of such luck, till now."

Bailiff. "And many others with thee, Lenk."

Lenk. "Is my brother amongst the day-laborers?"

Bailiff. "No."

Lenk. "Who are the others?"

The bailiff told him their names.

Lenk. "But my brother is a far better workman than Rudi, or Bar, or Marx. I say nothing of Kriecher. On my life, there is not another amongst the ten, except myself, who is half so good a workman. Bailiff, can not you manage to get him in?"

"I don't know" said the bailiff; and cutting short the discourse, he went away.

Lenk's wife, who was at her wheel, said nothing till the bailiff was out of hearing; but the conversation troubled her; and as soon as the bailiff was gone she said to her husband: "Thou art thankless both to God and man. When

God sends thee help in thy great distress, thou dost nothing but abuse thy neighbors, whom he has also helped."

Lenk. "I shall have to work for the money, and not get it for nothing."

Wife. "Till now, thou hadst no work to get any by."

Lenk. "But then I had no labor."

Wife. "And thy children no bread."

"What had I more than you?" said the lazy lubber. His wife was silent, and wept bitter tears.

CHAPTER XXII.—REMORSE FOR PERJURY CAN NOT BE ALLAYED BY CRAFTY ARTS.

FROM Lenk the bailiff went to Kriecher, and as he was going, came unexpectedly upon Hans Wust.

If he had seen him in time, he would have slipped out of the way; for, since Rudi's affair, the bailiff and Wust never met without feelings of self-reproach; but the bailiff met him unawares, at the corner of the side street, near the lower well.

"Art thou there, Wust?" said the bailiff.

"Yes, bailiff," answered Wust.

Bailiff. "Why dost thou never come near me? Hast thou forgotten the money I lent thee?"

Wust. "I have no money at present, and when I look back, I am afraid I have paid too dearly for your money already."

Bailiff. "Thou didst not talk in this way, Wust, when I gave it thee. It is serving a man ungraciously."

Wust. "Serving a man is one thing—but, serving a man so that one can never have another comfortable hour on God's earth, is another."

Bailiff. "Talk not so, Wust! Thou didst not swear any thing but what was true."

Wust. "So you always say. But I can not but feel in my heart that I swore falsely."

Bailiff. "That is not true, Wust! On my soul, it is not true. Thou didst but swear to what was read to thee, and it was very carefully worded. I read it to thee more than a hundred times, and it appeared to thee in the same light as it did to me, and thou saidst always 'Yes; I can swear to that!' Was it not so, Wust? And why art thou now fretting about it? But it is only on account of thy debt. Thou wouldst have me wait longer."

Wust. "No, bailiff; you are mistaken. If I had the money, I would pay it down this moment, that I might never see your face again; for my heart smites me whenever I look at you."

"Thou art a fool!" said the bailiff; but his own heart smote him also.

Wust. "I saw it as you do, for a long time; for it did not come to me at first, that the squire spoke as if he saw it in quite a different light."

Bailiff. "Thou hast nothing to do with what the squire said about it. Thou didst but swear to the paper that was read to thee."

Wust. "Yes; but he passed judgment according to what he had understood from it."

Bailiff. "If the squire was a fool, let him look after it. What is that to thee? He had the paper in his hand; and if it did not seem clear to him, he should have had it written differently."

Wust. "I know you can always out-talk me; but that does not comfort my conscience. And at church, on a sacrament day, I am in such a horrible state, that I could sink into the earth! O bailiff, would that I had never owed you any thing! Would that I had never known you, or that I had died the day before I was forsworn!"

Bailiff. "For God's sake, Wust, do not fret in this way. It is folly. Think of all the circumstances. We went about it very carefully. In thy presence I asked the pastor's assistant, point-blank: Will Wust have sworn to any thing but what is in the paper, supposing he does not understand it right? Dost thou not remember his answer?"

Wust. "Yes; but still——"

Bailiff. "Nay, he said these very words;—Wust will not have sworn to a hair more than is in the paper. Were not these his words?"

Wust. "Yes; but then is it so, because he said it?"

Bailiff. "Is it so? What, art thou not satisfied?"

Wust. "No, bailiff? I will speak out for once. The late pastor's assistant owed you money, as well as myself; and you know what a fellow he was, and how disorderly. It is little comfort to me what such a reckless creature said."

Bailiff. "His way of life was nothing to thee. He understood the right doctrine, and that thou knowest."

Wust. "Nay, I know it not. But I know he was good for nothing."

Bailiff. "But what did that signify to thee?"

Wust. "Why, for my part, if I know a man has been very wicked and bad in one point, I dare not trust to his goodness in any other. Therefore I am afraid that this worthless man deceived me, and then what is to become of me?"

Bailiff. "Let these thoughts go, Wust! Thou hast sworn to nothing but what was true."

Wust. "I did so, for a long time; but it's over now. I can not cheat myself any longer. Poor Rudi! Wherever I go or stand, I see him before me. Poor Rudi! how his misery, and hunger, and want, must rise up to God against me! O, and his children, they are such sickly, starved, ricketty things; and as yellow as gipsies. They were fine, stout, healthy children; and my
the meadow from them,"

Bailiff. "I had a right to it. It was as I told thee. And now, Rı
work at the building of the church, and may come round again."

Wust. "What good can that do me? If I had not sworn, it would be all the same to me, whether Rudi were rich or a beggar."

Bailiff. "Do not let it disturb thee so! I had a right to it."

Wust. "Not disturb me? If I had broken into his house and stolen all his goods, it would trouble me less. O bailiff, bailiff! that I should have acted thus! It is now near Easter again. I wish I were buried a thousand feet deep in the earth!"

Bailiff. "For heaven's sake, Wust, do not go on in this way in the open street, before all the people. If any body should hear thee! It is thine own stupidity that plagues thee. All that thou hast sworn to was true."

Wust. "Stupidity here, stupidity there! If I had not sworn, Rudi would still have had his meadow."

Bailiff. "But thou didst not say it was not his, or that it was mine. What in the devil's name is it to thee who has the meadow?"

Wust. "It is nothing to me who has the meadow, but it is that I have sworn falsely."

Bailiff. "I tell thee it is not true that thou hast sworn falsely. That which thou didst swear to, was true."

Wust. "But it was a deceit! I did not tell the squire how I understood the writing; and he understood it differently. Say what you will, I know, I feel it in myself, that I was a Judas, and a betrayer; and that my oath was a false one, words or no words."

Bailiff. "I am sorry for thee, Wust, that thou art so stupid; but thou art ill; thou lookest like one risen from the grave; and when a man is not well he sees things so differently. Compose thyself, Wust. Come home with me, and let us drink a glass of wine together."

Wust. "I can not, bailiff. Nothing upon earth can cheer me now."

Bailiff. "Comfort thyself, Wust. Drive it out of thy head, and forget it till thou art well again. Thou wilt then perceive that I was in the right, and I will tear thy note in pieces. Perhaps it will be a relief to thee."

Wust. "No bailiff! keep the note. If I must eat my own flesh for hunger, I will pay you that debt. I will not have the price of blood upon my soul. If you have betrayed me, if the pastor's assistant has deceived me, perhaps God will forgive me. I did not mean it to turn out so."

Bailiff. "Here is thy note, Wust. See, I destroy it before thy eyes; and I take it on my own responsibility that I was in the right; and now be comforted."

Wust. "Take what you will upon yourself, bailiff, I will pay you my debt. The day after to-morrow I will sell my Sunday coat, and pay you."

Bailiff. "Think better of it. Thou deceivest thyself, upon my life. But I must go away now."

Wust. "It is a mercy that you are going. If you were to stay much longer, I should go mad before your eyes."

Bailiff. "Quiet thyself, for heaven's sake, Wust." They then separated.

But the bailiff, when he was alone, could not help saying to himself, with a sigh: "I am sorry he met me just now. I have had enough before to-day, without this." He soon, however, hardened himself again, and said: "I am sorry for the poor wretch; he is so troubled! but he is in the wrong. It is nothing to him how the judge understood it. The devil might take the oaths, if the exact meaning of them were to be looked after so sharply. I know that other people, and those who should understand the thing best, take oaths after their own way of interpreting them, and are undisturbed, where a poor wretch, who thinks like Wust, would say he saw as clear as day that it was a deceit. But I wish these thoughts were out of my head, they make me uncomfortable! I will go back and drink a glass of wine." He did so, and then went to Felix Kriecher.

Chapter XXIII.—A Hypocrite, and a Suffering Woman.

Felix Kriecher was a man who always had the air of enduring the greatest afflictions with the patience of a martyr. To the barber, the bailiff, and every stranger, he bowed as low as to the pastor; and he went to all the weekly prayers at church, and to all the Sunday evening singing. Sometimes he got, by this means, a glass of wine; and occasionally, when he was very late, and managed well, had an invitation to supper. He took great pains to be in favor with all the pietists of the village, but could not quite succeed; for he was very careful not to offend the other party on their account, and this does not suit fanatics. They will not let their disciples be well with both sides; and thus, notwithstanding his appearance of humility, and all the hypocritical arts he practiced and even his spiritual pride, which generally suits fanatics, he was not admitted into their set.

With all these exterior and acknowledged qualities, he had some others; and though these were only for secret use in his domestic life, I must now speak of them.

To his wife and children he was a devil. In the most extreme poverty he still insisted upon having something dainty to eat; and if he did not get it, all went wrong—the children were not properly combed and washed; and if he could find nothing else to blame, and one of his little children of four years old stared at him, he would beat it, to teach it proper respect to him.

"Thou art a fool!" said his wife to him one day when this had occurred. But, though she was quite right, and had told him nothing but the simple truth, he kicked her for it; and as she was running away from him, she fell by the door, and made two deep wounds in her head. This frightened the man; for he thought, wisely enough, that a broken head might tell tales.

And as all hypocrites, when they are alarmed, crouch, and fawn, and humble themselves, so did Kriecher to his wife. He coaxed her; and begged and entreated, for God's sake, not that she would forgive him, but that she would promise to tell nobody of it. She did so, and patiently endured the pain of a very bad wound, and told the barber and the other neighbors that she had fallen; but many of them did not believe her. Poor woman! she might have known beforehand that no hypocrite was ever grateful, or kept his word, and should not have trusted him. But what do I say? Alas! she knew all this; but she thought of her children, and knew that God only could change his heart, and that it was of no use to be talking about it. She is an excellent woman, and it is grievous to think how unhappy he makes her, and what she suffers daily by his means. She was silent, but prayed to God; and thanked him for the afflictions with which he tried her.

O eternity!—when thou revealest the ways of God, and the blessedness of those to whom he teaches steadfastness, courage, and patience, by suffering, want, and sorrow—O eternity! how wilt thou exalt those tried ones who have been so lowly here.

Kriecher had forgotten the wounds, almost before they were healed, and went on as usual. He tormented and harassed his wife, without cause or excuse, every day, and embittered her life. A quarter of an hour before the bailiff came, the cat had overturned the lamp, and wasted a drop or two of oil. "Thou stupid creature, thou shouldst have taken better care," said he to his wife, with his accustomed fury; "thou mayst now sit in the dark, and light the fire with cow-dung, thou horned beast!" His wife said not a word, but the tears streamed down her cheeks, and the children cried in the corners with their mother.

At this moment the bailiff knocked. "Hush! for heaven's sake, be quiet! What is to be done? The bailiff is at the door," said Kriecher, and, hastily wiping off the children's tears with his handkerchief, he threatened to cut them in pieces, if he heard another whimper; then opened the door to the bailiff, bowed, and said: "What are your commands, Mr. Bailiff?" The bailiff told him his errrand, briefly.

But Kriecher, who was listening at the door, and heard no more crying, answered: "Come into the room, Mr. Bailiff, and I will tell my dear wife what a piece of good fortune has befallen us." The bailiff went into the room, and

Kriecher said to his wife: "The bailiff has just brought me the good news that I am to be one of the day-laborers at the building of the church; and a great favor it is, for which I can not be sufficiently thankful."

The wife answered, "Thank God!" and a sigh escaped from her.

Bailiff. "Is something the matter with thy wife?"

"She is not very well to-day, Mr. Bailiff," said Kriecher, throwing an angry, threatening look toward his wife.

Bailiff. "I must be going on. I wish her better."

Wife. "Good-bye, Mr. Bailiff."

Kriecher. "May I beg you, Mr. Bailiff, to be so good as to thank the squire, in my name, for this favor."

Bailiff. "Thou canst thank him thyself."

Kriech. "You are right, Mr. Bailiff. It was a great liberty in me to ask you to do it. I will go to-morrow to the hall. It is my duty to do so."

Bailiff. "All the others are going on Monday morning, and I think thou hadst better go with them."

Kriech. "Of course, yes, certainly, Mr. Bailiff. I did not know they were going."

Bailiff. "Good-bye, Kriecher."

Kriech. "I am greatly indebted to you, Mr. Bailiff.

Bailiff. "Thou hast nothing to thank me for." And he went away, saying to himself, "I am much mistaken, if this fellow is not one of the devil's own. Perhaps he is the kind of man to suit me with the mason—but who dare trust a hypocrite? I would rather have Shaben Michel. He is a downright rogue."

CHAPTER XXIV.—AN HONEST, JOYFUL, THANKFUL HEART.

FROM Kriecher the bailiff went to young Abi, who jumped for joy when he heard the good news; and sprang up like a young heifer when it is turned out in spring. "I will go and tell my wife, that she may rejoice with me. No! I will wait till to-morrow. To-morrow it will be eight years since we were married. It was St. Joseph's day. I remember it, as if it were yesterday. We have had many a hard hour since; but many a happy one, too. God be thanked for all. To-morrow, as soon as she wakes, I will tell her. I wish the time were come! I can see just how she will laugh and cry over it; and how she will press her children and me to her heart for joy. O that to-morrow were come! I will kill the cock, and boil it in the broth, without her knowing any thing about it. She would enjoy it then, though she would be sorry to have it killed. No, no! it will be no sin to kill it for such a joyful occasion. I will venture it. I will stay at home all day and make merry with her and the children. No, I will go with her to church and to the sacrament. We will rejoice and be glad; and thank God for all his goodness."

Thus did young Abi talk to himself, in the joy of his heart, at the good news the bailiff had brought him. He could scarcely, in his eagerness, wait till the morrow came, when he did as he had said he would.

CHAPTER XXV.—HOW ROGUES TALK TO EACH OTHER.

FROM Abi the bailiff went to Shaben Michel, who saw him at a distance, beckoned him into a corner, behind the house, and said: "What the deuce art thou about now?"

Bailiff. "A merry-making."

Michel. "Truly, thou art a likely fellow to be sent out to invite guests to weddings, dances, and merry-makings."

Bailiff. "Well, it is nothing dismal, at all events."

Mich. "What then!"

Bailiff. "Thou art got into new company."

Mich. "Who are they, and what is it for?"

Bailiff. "Hubel Rudi, Jenk, Leemann, Kriecher, and Marx Reuti."

Mich. "Nonsense! What have I to do with these fellows?"

Bailiff. "To build up and adorn the house of the Lord in Bonnal, and the walls round about it."

Mich. "In sober earnest?"

Bailiff. "Yes, by G——!"

Mich. "But who has chosen out the blind and lame for this work?"

Bailiff. "The well and nobly born, my wise and potent master, the squire!"

Mich. "Is he mad?"

Bailiff. "How should I know?"

Mich. "This looks like it."

Bailiff. "Perhaps it would not be the worst thing that could happen. Light wood is easily turned. But I must away. Come to me to-night, I want to speak to thee."

Mich. "I will not fail. Who art thou for next?"

Bailiff. "Marx Reuti."

Mich. "He is a proper fellow for work! a man must be out of his mind to choose him. I do n't believe he takes a mattock or spade into his hand the year through; and he is half lame on one side."

Bailiff. "What does that signify? Only do thou come to me to-night."

The bailiff then went on to Marx Reuti.

CHAPTER XXVI.—PRIDE, IN POVERTY AND DISTRESS, LEADS TO THE MOST UNNATURAL AND HORRIBLE DEEDS.

THIS man had formerly been well off, and carried on business for himself; but he was now without occupation, and lived almost entirely upon the charity of the pastor and some of his relations, who were able to help him.

In all his distress, he always kept up his pride, and concealed, as much as he could, the want and hunger of his family, except from those who gave him assistance.

When he saw the bailiff, he started—I can not say he turned pale, for he was always as white as a ghost. He took up the rags which lay about, and thrust them under the coverlid of the bed, and ordered the half-naked children to hide themselves directly in the next room. "Lord Jesus!" said the children, "it snows and rains in. Only listen what a storm it is! There is no window in the room."

"Get along, you godless brats! how you distract me. Do you think there is no need for you to learn to mortify the flesh?"

"We can not bear it, father!" said the children.

"He will not stay long, you heretics!" said the father; and pushing them in, he fastened the door, and then invited the bailiff into the house.

When he had delivered his message, Marx thanked him, and said: "Am I to be an overlooker over these men?"

"What art thou thinking of, Marx?" answered the bailiff. "No! thou art to be a day-laborer with the rest."

Marx. "So, Mr. Bailiff!"

Bailiff. "It is at thy own choice, if thou dost not like the work."

Marx. "In truth, I am not accustomed to any thing of the kind; but, if the squire and the pastor wish it, I can not decline, and will undertake it."

Bailiff. "It will rejoice them greatly; and I think the squire will almost send me again to thank thee."

Marx. "Nay, I do n't mean exactly that; but, in a common way, I can not serve every body as a day-laborer.

Bailiff. "Then thou hast enough to eat, I suppose."

Marx. "Thank God! I have as yet."

Bailiff. "But I know well enough where thy children are."

Marx. "They are dining with my wife's sister."

Bailiff. "I thought I heard children crying in the next room."

Marx. "There is not one of them in the house."

The bailiff heard the cry again, opened the door, without ceremony, saw the almost naked children shivering and sobbing with the wind, rain, and snow, which came in through the window, so that they could hardly speak, and said: "Is this the place where thy children dine, Marx? Thou art a hound, and a hypocrite, and thy damned pride often makes thee act in this way."

Marx. "For heaven's sake, do not tell any body; do not betray me, Bailiff! I should be the most miserable man in the world if it were known."

Bailiff. "Art thou out of thy senses? Even now thou dost not tell them to come out of such a dog-kennel. Dost thou not see that they are yellow and blue with cold? I would not use my poodle in such a way."

Marx. "Come out, then, children—but, bailiff, for mercy's sake, tell nobody."

Bailiff. "And all this time, forsooth, thou playest the saint before the pastor."

Marx. "I beseech you tell nobody."

Bailiff. "Thou art worse than a brute. Thou a saint! Thou art an infidel. Dost thou hear? thou art an infidel, for no true man would act in such a way. And why must thou go and tell tales to the priest about the battle which took place last week. It must have been thou who told him; for at twelve o'clock, when it happened, thou wert going home, past my house, from one of thy holy banquets."

Marx. "No, on my life! Do not believe it. I assure you it was not so."

Bailiff. "Darest thou say so?"

Marx. "God knows it was not so, bailiff! May I never stir from this spot if it was!"

Bailiff. "Marx! darest thou maintain what thou sayest before me to the pastor's face? I know more about it than thou thinkest."

Marx stammered: "I know—I could—I did not begin"—

"Such a brute, and such a liar as thou art, I never saw in my life! We understand each other now," said the bailiff; and he went that moment to the pastor's cook, who laughed till she was half dead at the pious Israelite, Marx Reuti, and faithfully promised to bring it to the pastor's ears.

And the bailiff rejoiced in his heart that, probably, the pastor would give the wicked heretic his weekly bread no longer; but he was mistaken, for the pastor had, before this, given him the bread, not on account of his virtues, but of his hunger.

CHAPTER XXVII.—ACTIVITY AND INDUSTRY, WITHOUT A KIND AND GRATEFUL HEART.

FROM Marx the bailiff went to the last of the number. This was Kienast, a sickly man. He was not yet fifty years old, but poverty and anxiety had worn him out, and this day, in particular, he was in terrible distress.

His eldest daughter had, the day before, hired herself out to service in the town, and had showed her father the earnest-money that morning, which made the poor man very uneasy.

His wife was with child, and near her time; and Susan was the only one of the children who could be any help to them, and now she was to go to service in a fortnight.

The father begged her, with tears in his eyes, to return the money, and stay with him, till after her mother's confinement.

"I will not," answered the daughter. "Where shall I find another service, if I give up this?"

Father. "After thy mother is brought to bed, I will go myself into the town, and help thee to find another. Only stay till then."

Daughter. "It will be half a year before I can hire myself again; and the service I have got is a good one. Who knows how you will help me? and, in short, I will not wait for another attempt."

Father. "But thou knowest, Susan, that I have done all I could for thee. Think of thy childhood, and do not leave me in my necessity."

Daughter. "Do you wish then, father, to stand in the way of my happiness?"

Father. "Alas! it is not for thy happiness, that thou shouldst leave thy poor parents in such circumstances. Do not go, Susan, I beg of thee. My wife has a very handsome apron, it is the last she has left, and she values it very much; it was a keepsake; but she shall give it thee, after her confinement, if thou wilt only stay."

Daughter. "I will not stay, either for your gifts or your good words. I can earn such as that, and better. It is time for me to be doing something for myself. If I were to stay ten years with you, I should not get a bed and a chest."

Father. "Thou wilt not get these in one half-year. After this once, I will not seek to detain thee. Stay only these few weeks."

"No, I will not, father!" answered the daughter; and she turned away, and ran into a neighbor's house.

The father stood there, bent down by anxiety and care, and said to himself: "What shall I do in this misfortune? How shall I deliver such a Job's message to my poor wife? I have been very much to blame for not doing my duty better by this child. I always passed over every thing, because she worked so well. My wife said to me a hundred times: 'She is so pert and rude to her parents; and if she has to teach her sisters, or do any thing for them, she does it so hastily and saucily, and so entirely without kindness and affection, that they can none of them ever learn any thing from her!' But she works so well, we must excuse something, and perhaps it is the fault of the others, was always my answer; and now I have my reward. I should have remembered that if the heart be hard, whatever other good qualities any one may have, they are all in vain. One can not depend upon them. I wish my wife did but know."

As the man was speaking thus to himself, the bailiff came close up, without his being aware.

"What darest thou not tell thy wife?" said he.

Kienast looked up, saw the bailiff, and said: "Is that you, bailiff? What dare I not tell my wife? Susan has hired herself out to service in the town, and we have such need of her at home! But I had almost forgotten to ask what you wanted with me."

Bailiff. "If this be the case with Susan, perhaps my news will be a comfort to thee."

Kienast. "That would, be help indeed."

Bailiff. "Thou art to have work at the building of the church, and twenty-five kreutzers a day, wages."

Kienast. "Lord God in heaven! May I hope for such a help as this?"

Bailiff. "Yes, Kienast. It is, indeed, as I tell thee."

Kienast. "Then God be praised for it." He turned faint, and his limbs shook. "I must sit down. This joy, in my troubles, has overcome me."

He sat down on a log of wood, and leaned against the wall of the house, to keep himself from falling.

The bailiff said: "Thou canst bear but little!"

And Kienast answered: "I have not broken my fast to-day."

"And so late!" said the bailiff; and he went on his way.

The poor wife, from the house, had seen the bailiff join her husband, and groaned aloud.

"This is some fresh misfortune! My husband has been like one beside himself all day, and knows not what he is doing; and just now I saw Susan, in the next house, lift up her hands in a passion; and here is the bailiff—what can have happened? There is not a more unfortunate woman under the sun! So near forty, and a child every year, and care and want and pain all the time!" Thus did the poor woman grieve in the house.

The husband, in the mean time, had recovered himself, and came to her with such a cheerful, happy face as she had not seen for many a month.

"Thou lookest merry! Dost thou think to keep it from me that the bailiff has been here?" said the woman.

And he answered. "He is come, as it were, from heaven to comfort us."

"Is it possible?" said the woman.

Kienast. "Sit down, wife! I must tell thee the good news." Then he told her what Susan had done, and what trouble he had been in; and how, now, he was helped out of all his distress.

Then he ate the food, which in his trouble he had left standing there at noon; and he and his wife shed tears of thankfulness to God, who had thus helped them in their distress. And they let Susan go, that very day, into service, as she wished.

Chapter XXVIII.—A Saturday Evening in the House of a Bailiff, who is a Landlord.

Now came the bailiff home from his journey, tired and thirsty. It was late; for Kienast lived up the hill, two or three miles from the village.

In the mean time he had had it given out, by his friends, that he was not at all alarmed by what had happened yesterday; and had not been so merry and jovial as he was to-day, for a year.

This made some take courage, toward evening, to creep quietly to the tavern.

When it began to be dark, still more came; and at night, by seven o'clock, the tables were almost as full as usual.

Thus it happens, when a fowler, in autumn, shoots a bird in a cherry-tree, all the others, which were pecking at the cherries, fly fearfully and hastily away from the tree, chirping the note of alarm. But, after a while, one, a solitary one at first, perches upon the tree—and, if it no longer sees the fowler, it whistles, not the sound of danger, but the bold, loud note of joy at finding food. At the call of the daring adventurer, the others flock timidly back again, and all feed upon the cherries, as if the fowler had never fired.

So it was here; and thus was the room once more filled with neighbors, who yesterday, and even this morning, would not have ventured to come.

In all mischievous, and even wicked deeds, people are always merry and bold, when they are in a crowd, and when those who give the tone to it are daring and impudent; and, as such leaders are not wanting in taverns, it can not be denied that such places tempt the common people to all wickedness, and are much more likely to lead them on to rash and thoughtless deeds, than poor simple schools are to bring them up to a quiet and domestic life.

The neighbors in the tavern were now the bailiff's friends again; for they sat over his ale. One began to say, that the bailiff was a manly fellow, and that, by G——, nobody had ever yet mastered him. Another, that Arner was a child, and the bailiff had managed his grandfather. Another, that it was not right; and, by heaven, he could not answer it to his conscience, thus to cheat the parish of the landlord's right, which had belonged to it ever since the days of Noah and Abraham. Another swore, that he had not got possession, by thunder! and that there should be a struggle for it yet, in spite of all the devils, and a parish meeting held to-morrow.

Then again, one said, there is no need of that, for the bailiff had always overcome all his enemies; and would not turn over a new leaf, either with his honor the squire, or with the beggarly mason.

Thus did the men go on, talking and drinking.

The bailiff's wife laughed to herself, set one pitcher after another upon the table, and marked all carefully down with chalk upon a board in the next room.

Now came the bailiff home; and he rejoiced in his heart to find the tables surrounded by the old set.

"This is hearty in you, my good fellows, not to forsake me," said he to them.

"We are not tired of thee yet," answered the countrymen; and drank his health, with loud shouts and huzzas.

"There is a great noise, neighbors! We must keep out of trouble; and this is Saturday night," said the bailiff. "Put the shutters to, wife; and put out the lights toward the street. We had better go into the back room. Is it warm, wife?"

Wife. "Yes, I made a fire there on purpose."

Bailiff. "Very well; carry all off the table into the back room."

His wife and the neighbors carried the glasses, pitchers, bread, cheese, knives, plates, cards, and dice, into the back room; from which, if they had been murdering one another, nothing could have been heard in the street.

"There now, we are safe from rogues and eavesdroppers, and from the holy servants of the black man.* But I am as thirsty as a hound: give me some wine."

* Certain church officers, who reported disturbances to the pastor, disrespectfully called "the black man" by the godless bailiff.

His wife brought some.

And Christian said: "Is that of the kind the barber's dog laps up?"

Bailiff. "Yes, indeed, I 'm likely to be such a fool again!"

Chris. "But what devil's scheme had you in your head?"

Bailiff. "By G—, none! It was mere folly. I had eaten nothing, and did not like to drink."

Chris. "Whistle that to a dog; perhaps it may believe you: not I."

Bailiff. "Why not?"

Chris. "Why not? Because the wine we were drinking smelt of sulphur like the plague."

Bailiff. "Who says so?"

Chris. "I, Mr. Urias! I said nothing of it at the time; but when I carried home the empty jug, it reeked in my nose so that it almost knocked me down. All things considered, you have certainly had some scheme in your head to-day."

Bailiff. "I know no more than the child in the cradle what wine my wife sent. Thou art a fool with thy fancies."

Chris. "Ay, but you know, well enough, what a fine sermon you made on the rights of the land. I suppose you said all that with as little meaning as a man has when he takes a pinch of snuff."

Bailiff. "Hold thy foolish tongue, Christian. The best thing I could do, would be to have thee well beaten for upsetting my jug. But I must know now how they went on at the barber's after I left them."

Chris. "And your promise, bailiff."

Bailiff. "What promise?"

Chris. "That I should have wine till morning for nothing, if I got to know it."

Bailiff. "But if thou knowest nothing, wouldst thou still be drinking?"

Chris. "If I know nothing! Send for the wine, and you shall hear."

The bailiff had it brought, sat down by him; then Christian told him all he knew, and more besides. Sometimes he contradicted himself so barefacedly, that the bailiff perceived it, and called out: "You dog, do 'nt lie so that a man can take hold of it with his hands!"

"No, by G——," answered Christian, "as true as I am a sinner, every hair and point of it is true."

"Come, come," said the bailiff, who by this time had had enough, "Shaben Michel is here, and I must speak to him;" and he then went to the other table where Michel was sitting, slapped him on the shoulder, and said:

Chapter XXIX.—Continuation of the Conversation of Rogues with Each Other.

"Art thou also amongst the sinners? I thought, since thou wert called to the church building, thou hadst become a saint; like our butcher, because he once had to ring a week for the sexton."

Michel. "No, bailiff! My calls are not so sudden; but, when I once begin, I will go through with it."

Bailiff. "I should like to be thy father confessor, Michel."

Mich. "Nay, I can not consent to that."

Bailiff. "Why not?"

Mich. "Because thou wouldst double my score with thy holy chalk."

Bailiff. "Would not that suit thee?"

Mich. "No, bailiff! I must have a father confessor who will forgive and look over sins, and not one who will chalk them down against me!"

Bailiff. "Well, I can forgive and overlook sins, as well as another."

Mich. "What! sins in thy books?"

Bailiff. "Truly, I am often obliged to do so; and it is better people should think I do it willingly."

Mich. "Is that possible, Mr. Bailiff?"

"We shall see," said the bailiff, making a sign to him.

They went together to the little table, near the fire.

And the bailiff said: "It is well thou art come; and lucky for thee."

Mich. "I have great need of luck."

Bailiff. "So I suppose; but if thou art willing, thou canst not fail to make money by this new place."

Mich. "And how must I manage it?"

Bailiff. "Thou must get into favor with the mason, and seem very hungry and poor."

Mich. "I can do that without lying."

Bailiff. "Thou must also often give thy supper to thy children, that people may think thy heart is as soft as melted butter; and thy children must run after thee bare-footed and bare-legged."

Mich. "There is no difficulty in that either."

Bailiff. "And when thou art the favorite of all the ten, then comes the true work."

Mich. "What is that to be?"

Bailiff. "To do all that thou canst to make quarrels and misunderstandings about the building; to throw things into confusion, and to make mischief between the laborers and their masters and the squire."

Mich. "There will be more difficulty in that part of the business."

Bailiff. "But it is a part by which thou mayst get money."

Mich. "Ay, if it were not for the hope of that, a cunning man might give such a direction, but only a fool would follow it."

Bailiff. "It is a matter of course, that thou wilt get money by it."

Mich. "Two crowns in hand, Mr. Bailiff. I must have so much paid down, or I will have nothing to do with it."

Bailiff. "Thou art more unconscionable every day, Michel. I show thee how thou mayst get wages for nothing, and thou wouldst have me also pay thee for taking my good advice."

Mich. "What is all that to the purpose? Thou wilt have me play the rogue in thy service, and so I will, and be true and hearty in it; but payment in hand, that is two crowns, and not a kreutzer less, I must have, or thou mayst do it thyself."

Bailiff. "Thou dog! thou knowest well enough how to get thy own way. There are thy two crowns for thee."

Mich. "Now it is all right, master! thou hast nothing to do but to give thy orders."

Bailiff. "I think thou mayst easily by night break down some of the scaffolding, and knock out a couple of the windows; and of course thou wilt make away with ropes and tools, and such light things as are lying around."

Mich. "Naturally."

Bailiff. "And it would be no very difficult affair to carry some of the timber over the hill to the river, and send it back again toward Holland."

Mich. "No, no! I can manage that. I will hang a great white shirt upon a pole, in the middle of the churchyard, that if the watchman, or any of the old women in the neighborhood hear a noise, they may fancy it is a ghost, and keep away from me."

Bailiff. "Thou art a rascally heretic. What a scheme!"

Mich. "I will do so, however; it may serve to keep me from the pillory."

Bailiff. "Well, but there is another thing. If thou canst find any drawings, or calculations, or plans of the squire's, lying about, thou must quietly put them out of the way, where nobody would think of looking for them, and at night mend thy fire with them."

Mich. "Very well, Mr. Bailiff."

Bailiff. "And thou must contrive so as to make thy honorable comrades inclined to be merry, and work idly, and particularly when the squire or any body from the hall comes down, and then thou canst wink, as much as to say: You see how it is."

Mich. "Well, I will do what I can. I see plainly enough what thou art after."

Bailiff. "But, of all things, the most important is, that thou and I should be enemies."

Mich. "Very true."

Bailiff. "We will begin directly. There may be tell-tales here, who will talk of how we held counsel secretly together."

Mich. "Thou art right."

Bailiff. "Drink another glass or two, and I will pretend as if I would reckon with thee, and thou wouldst not agree. I will make a noise about it, thou must abuse me, and we will thrust thee out of the house."

Mich. "Well thought of." He drank what was in the pitcher, and then said to the bailiff, "Come, begin."

The bailiff muttered something about reckoning, and then said aloud: "I never received the florin."

Mich. "Recollect yourself, bailiff!"

Bailiff. "By heaven, I know nothing of it! Wife! didst thou receive a florin last week from Michel?"

Wife. "Heaven bless us! not a kreutzer."

Bailiff. "It is very strange. Give me the book!" She brought it, and the bailiff read: "Here it is—Monday—nothing from thee. Tuesday—nothing. Wednesday—Didst thou say it was on Wednesday?"

Mich. "Yes!"

Bailiff. "Here is Wednesday—look! there is nothing from thee—and on Thursday, Friday, and Saturday—not a syllable of the florin."

Mich. "The devil! I tell you I paid it."

Bailiff. "Softly, softly, good neighbor—I write down every thing."

Mich. "What the deuce is your writing to me, bailiff? I paid the florin."

Bailiff. "It is not true, Michel."

Mich. "Here's a rogue, to say I have not paid him!"

Bailiff. "What dost thou say, thou unhanged rascal?"

Some of the countrymen got up:—"He has given the bailiff the lie, we heard him."

Mich. "No, I did not. But I paid the florin."

Men. "What dost thou say, thou knave, that thou didst not give him the lie? We all heard it."

Bailiff. "Turn the dog out of the room."

Michel took up a knife, and called out: "Let any one who touches me look to it."

Bailiff. "Take the knife away from him."

They took the knife from him, turned him out of the room, and sat down again.

Bailiff. "It's well he is gone. He was only a spy of the mason's."

Countrymen. "By G——, so he was. We are well rid of him."

Chapter XXX.—Continuation of the Conversation of Rogues with Each Other, in a Different Style.

Bring us some more wine. Bailiff! we will drink on the strength of the harvest, and let you have one sheaf out of every ten for a measure of wine.

Bailiff. "You will not pay me soon, then."

Countrymen. "No; but you will have heavier weight for that."

The bailiff sat down with them, and drank to their hearts' content, on the strength of the future tithe.

Now their mouths were opened, and there arose from all the tables a wild uproar of oaths and curses, of dissolute, idle talk, of abuse and insolence. They told stories of licentiousness and theft, of blows and insults, of debts they had cunningly escaped paying, of lawsuits they had won by clever tricks, of wickedness and riots, which for the most part were false; but, alas! too much was true. How they had stolen from the old squire's woods, and fields, and tithes—and how their wives whined over their children—how one took up a prayer-book, and another hid the jug of wine in the chaff and straw. Also of their boys and girls,—how one helped his father to cheat his mother, and another took part with the mother against the father—and how they had all done as much or more when they were lads. Then they got to talking about old Uli, who had been caught in such fool's talk, and cruelly brought to the gallows; but how he had prayed at last and made a holy end of it. And how, when he had confessed, (though, as every body knew, but half,) still the hard-hearted pastor had not saved his life.

They were in the midst of this history of the pastor's cruelty, when the bailiff's wife beckoned him to come out. "Wait till we have finished the story of the hanged man," was his answer.

But she whispered in his ear: "Joseph is come."

He replied: "Hide him somewhere, and I will come soon."

Joseph had crept into the kitchen; but there were so many people in the house, that the bailiff's wife was afraid of his being seen. She put out the light, and said to him: "Joseph! take off thy shoes, and come after me into the lower room. My husband will be with thee directly."

Joseph took his shoes in his hand, and followed her on tip-toe into the lower room.

He had not waited long, before the bailiff came to him, and said: "What dost thou want so late, Joseph?"

Joseph. "Not much! I only want to tell you I have ordered all about the stone."

Bailiff. "I am glad of it, Joseph."

Joseph. "The master was talking to-day of the wall, and said that the flint stone, hard by, was very good—but I told him he was a fool, and did not know his own business; and that the wall would look much handsomer, and more polished, of Schwendi stone. He answered not a word; and I went on to say that, if he did not use Schwendi stone, it would be a loss to him."

Bailiff. "Did he resolve upon it?"

Joseph. "Yes, he did, immediately. We are to begin with it on Monday."

Bailiff. "The day-laborers are all going to the hall on Monday."

Joseph. "They will be back by noon, and busy with the stuff in the lime. It is as good as mixed."

Bailiff. "That is all right and well; if it were only begun—thy money is ready for thee, Joseph."

Joseph. "I am in great want of it just now, bailiff."

Bailiff. "Come on Monday, when you have begun with the quarry. It is put aside for thee."

Joseph. "Do you suppose I shall not keep my word?"

Bailiff. "Nay, I can trust thee, Joseph."

Joseph. "Then give me three crowns of it, now. I should like to get my new boots, at the shoemaker's, for to-morrow; it is my birth-day, and I dare not ask the master for any money."

Bailiff. "I can not well give it thee now; come on Monday evening."

Joseph. "I see how you trust me. It's one thing to promise, and another to perform. I thought I could depend upon the money, bailiff."

Bailiff. "On my soul thou shalt have it."

Joseph. "Ay, I see how it is."

Bailiff. "It will be time enough, on Monday."

Joseph. "Bailiff! you show me, plainly enough, that you do not trust me: and I will make bold to tell you, that I fear, if the quarry is once opened, you will not keep your word with me."

Bailiff. "This is too bad, Joseph! I shall most certainly keep my word with thee."

Joseph. "I do not believe it. If you will not give it me now; it is all over."

Bailiff. "Canst thou not manage with two crowns?"

Joseph. "No! I must have three; but then you may depend upon having every thing done."

Bailiff. "Well, I will give thee them: but thou must keep thy word."

Joseph. "If I do not, I give you leave to call me the greatest rogue and thief upon the earth."

The bailiff now called his wife and said: "Give Joseph three crowns."

His wife took him aside and said: "Do not let him have them."

Bailiff. "Do as I bid thee, without a word."

Wife. "Be not so foolish! Thou art in liquor and wilt repent to-morrow."

Bailiff. "Answer me not a word. Three crowns this moment! Dost thou hear what I say?"

His wife sighed, reached the money, and threw it to the bailiff. He gave it to Joseph, and said: "Thou wilt not, surely, deceive me."

"Heaven forbid! what dost thou take me for, bailiff?" answered Joseph. And he went away, counted over his three crowns, and said to himself: "Now I have my reward in my own hands, and it is safer there than in the bailiff's chest. He is an old rogue, and I will not be his fool. The master may now take flint or blue stone for me."

The bailiff's wife cried for vexation, over the kitchen fire, and did not go again into the room, till past midnight.

The bailiff too, as soon as Joseph was gone, had a foreboding that he had overreached himself, but he soon forgot it again, amongst his companions. The riot of the drinkers lasted till after midnight.

At last the bailiff's wife came out of the kitchen, into the room, and said: "It is time to break up now; it is past midnight, and Easter Sunday."

"Easter Sunday!" said the fellows, stretched themselves, yawned, and got up, one after the other.

They tottered and stumbled along, catching hold of the tables and walls, and went with difficulty home again.

"Go, one at once, and make no noise," said the wife, "or the pastor and his people will get hold of you, and make you pay the fine."

"Nay, we had better keep our money for drinking," answered the men. And the wife added: "If you see the watchman, tell him there is a glass of wine and a piece of bread for him here."

They had scarcely got out of the house when the watchman appeared before the alehouse windows, and called out:

"All good people hear my warning,
'Tis one o'clock, and a cloudy morning."

The bailiff's wife understood his call, and brought him the wine, and bade him not to tell the pastor how late they had been up.

And now she helped her sleepy, drunken husband off with his shoes and stockings.

And she grumbled about Joseph's crowns. and her husband's foolishness. But he slept and snored, and took notice of nothing. And at last they both fell asleep, on the holy evening before Easter.

And now, thank God, I have no more to relate about them, for some time.

I return to Leonard and Gertrude.

What a world is this! A garden lies near a dog-kennel, and in the same field an offensive dunghill and sweet nourishing grass. Yes, it is indeed a wonderful world! The beautiful pasture itself, without the manure which we throw upon it, could not produce such delicious herbage.

Chapter XXXI.—The Evening Before a Sabbath in the House of a Good Mother.

Gertrude was now alone with her children. The events of the week and the approach of the Sabbath filled her heart.

Thoughtfully and silently she prepared the supper, and took out of the chest her husband's, her children's, and her own Sunday clothes, that nothing might distract her attention in the morning. And when she had arranged every thing, she sat down at the table with her children.

It was her custom every Saturday, when the time for evening prayer came, to impress upon their hearts the recollection of their various failings, and of all the events of the week which might be of consequence to them.

And this day she was particularly alive to the goodness of God toward them throughout the week, and wished to fix it as deeply as possible upon their young hearts, that they might never forget it.

The children sat around her, folded their little hands for prayer, and their mother thus addressed them:—

"I have something very good to tell you, my children! Your dear father has got some very good work this week, by which he will be able to earn much more than usual; and we may venture to hope that we shall in future have our daily bread with less care and anxiety.

"Thank your heavenly father, my children, for his mercy to us, and do not forget the former times, when I had to be sparing of every mouthful of bread. It was often a great trouble to me, not to be able to give you enough, but God Almighty knew that he would help us in his own good time, and that it was better for you, my darlings, to be brought up in poverty, in patience, and in the habit of overcoming your desires, than in abundance. It is very difficult for people, who have all they wish for, not to become thoughtless and forgetful of God, and unmindful of what is for their real good. Remember then, my children, as long as you live, the want and care you have undergone; and when you are yourselves better off, think of those who suffer as you have suffered. Never forget what it is to feel hunger and want, that you may be tender-hearted to the poor, and willingly give them all you have to spare. Do you think you shall be willing to give it to them, my children?" "O yes, mother, that we shall!" said all the children.

Chapter XXXII.—The Happiness of the Hour of Prayer.

Mother. "Nicholas, who dost thou think suffers most from hunger?"

Nicholas. "Rudeli, mother! you were at his father's yesterday. He must be almost dying of hunger, for he eats grass off the ground."

Mother. "Shouldst thou like sometimes to give him thy afternoon's bread?"

Nich. "O yes, mother! may I give it him to-morrow?"

Mother. "Yes, thou mayst."

Nich. "I am glad of it."

Mother. "And thou, Lise! to whom wilt thou sometimes give thy piece?"

Lise. "I can not tell, just now, whom I shall like best to give it to."

Mother. "Dost thou not recollect any poor child who is very hungry?"

Lise. "O yes, mother."

Mother. "Then why canst thou not tell to whom thou wilt give it? thou art always so overwise, Lise."

Lise. "I know now, mother."

Mother. "Who is it?"

Lise. "Marx Reuti's daughter, Betheli. I saw her picking up rotten potatoes, from the bailiff's dunghill, to-day."

Nich. "Yes, mother, and I saw her too; and felt in all my pockets, but I had not a mouthful of bread left. If I had only kept it a quarter of an hour longer!"

The mother then asked the other children the same questions, and they were all glad in their hearts to think that they should give their bread to the poor children to-morrow.

The mother let them enjoy this pleasure a while longer. Then she said to them: "That is enough, children! think how good the squire has been to make you each a present."

"O yes, our pretty money! Will you show it us, now, mother?"

"By and by, after prayer," said the mother; and the children jumped about for joy."

CHAPTER XXXIII.—THE SERIOUSNESS OF THE HOUR OF PRAYER.

"YOU are noisy, my children," said the mother. "When any thing good happens to you, think of God, who gives us all things. If you do so, you will never be wild and riotous in your joy. I am very glad to rejoice with you, my darlings, but when people are wild and riotous in their joy, they lose the serenity and peace of their hearts; and, without a quiet, tranquil heart, there is no true happiness. Therefore must we keep God ever in view. This is the use of the hour for morning and evening prayer, that you may never forget him. For whoever is praying to God, or thinking of him, can neither be extravagant in joy, nor without comfort in sorrow. But then, my children, he must always endeavor, particularly when he is praying, to keep himself quiet and untroubled. Consider, whenever you thank your father for any thing sincerely, you are not noisy and riotous. You fall softly, and with few words, on his neck; and when you feel it really in your hearts, the tears come into your eyes. It is the same toward God. If his loving kindness really rejoices you, and your hearts are truly thankful, you will not make a great noise and talking about it—but the tears will come into your eyes, when you think how merciful he is toward you. Thus all that fills your hearts with gratitude to God and kindness to men, is a continual prayer; and whoever prays as he ought, will do what is right, and will be dear to God and man, as long as he lives."

Nicholas. "And, mother, you said, yesterday, that we should be dear to the gracious squire, if we did what was right."

Mother. "Yes, my children, he is a good and religious gentleman. May God reward him, for all he has done for us. I wish thou mayst become dear to him, Nicholas!"

Nich. "I will obey him, because he is so good, as I obey you and my father."

Mother. "That is right, Nicholas! always think so, and thou wilt certainly become dear to him."

Nich. "If I durst but speak a word to him!"

Mother. "What wouldst thou say to him?"

Nich. "I would thank him for the pretty money."

Anneli. "Durst you thank him?"

Nich. "Why not?"

Anneli. "I durst not."

Lise. "Nor I!"

Mother. "Why durst you not, children?"

Lise. "I should laugh."

Mother. "Why wouldst thou laugh, Lise, and so show him, plainly, that thou wert but a silly child? If thou hadst not many foolish fancies in thy head, thou wouldst never think of doing such a thing."

Anneli. "I should not laugh; but I should be sadly frightened."

Mother. "He would take thee by the hand, Anneli, and smile upon thee, as thy father does when he is very kind to thee, and then thou wouldst not be frightened any longer."

Anneli. "No, not then."

Jonas. "Nor I, then."

Chapter xxxiv.—A mother's instruction.

Mother. "But, my dear children, how have you gone on, as to behavior, this week?"

The children looked at each other, without speaking.

Mother. "Anneli, hast thou done what was right this week?"

Anneli. "No, mother, you know I did not do right about little brother."

Mother. "Anneli, some misfortune might have happened to him. There have been children suffocated with being left in that way. And how wouldst thou like, thyself, to be shut up in a room, and left to hunger, and thirst, and cry alone? Besides, little children, when they are left long without any body to help them, get into a passion, and scream so dreadfully, that it may do them a mischief as long as they live. Anneli! God knows, I could not have a moment's peace out of the house, if I had reason to be afraid that thou wouldst not take proper care of the child."

Anneli. "Indeed, mother, I will not go away from him any more."

Mother. "I do trust thou wilt never put me into such a fright again. And Nicholas, how hast thou gone on this last week?"

Nicholas. "I do n't know of any thing wrong."

Mother. "Hast thou forgotten knocking over thy little sister on Monday?"

Nich. "I did not do it on purpose, mother."

Mother. "If thou hadst done it on purpose, it would have been bad indeed. Art thou not ashamed of talking so?"

Nich. "I am sorry I did it, mother; and will not do so again."

Mother. "When thou art grown up, if thou takest no more heed of what is near thee and about thee, thou will have to learn it to thy cost. Even amongst boys, those who are so heedless are always getting into scrapes and disputes; and I am afraid, my dear Nicholas, that thy carelessness will bring thee into great trouble and difficulties."

Nich. "I will take pains to be more thoughtful, mother."

Mother. "Do so, my dear boy, or, believe me, thou wilt often be very unhappy."

Nich. "My dear mother, I know it, and am sure of it, and I will certainly take heed."

Mother. "And thou, Lise, how hast thou gone on?"

Lise. "I know of nothing at all this week, mother."

Mother. "Art thou sure?"

Lise. "I can not now think of any thing, mother; or I am sure I would willingly tell you of it."

Mother. "Thou hast always, even when thou knowest nothing, as many words to utter as if thou hadst a great deal to say."

Lise. "What have I been saying now, mother?"

Mother. "Nothing at all, and yet many words. It is in this way, as we have told thee a thousand times, that thou art foolish. Thou dost not think about any thing thou hast to say, and yet must always be talking. What need was there for thee to tell the bailiff, yesterday, that we knew that Arner was coming soon?"

Lise. "I am sorry I did so, mother."

Mother. "We have so often told thee not to talk of what does not concern thee, particularly before strangers, and yet thou dost so still. Suppose thy father had been afraid of telling him that he knew it before, and thy prating had brought him into trouble."

Lise. "I should have been very sorry, but neither of you had said a word that it was to be a secret."

Mother. "Well, I will tell thy father, when he comes home, that whenever we are talking to each other in the room, we must add, after every sentence: 'Lise may tell this to the neighbors, or at the well—but not this—nor this—but again she may—and then thou wilt know what thou mayst chatter about.'"

Lise. "Forgive me, mother, I did not mean it so."

Mother. "We have told thee repeatedly, that thou must not talk about what does not concern thee; but it is useless. We can not cure thee of this failing, but by treating it seriously; and the first time that I find thee again chattering so thoughtlessly, I will punish thee with the rod."

The tears came into Lise's eyes when her mother talked of the rod. The mother saw them, and said to her: "Lise, the greatest misfortunes often happen from thoughtless chattering, and thou must be cured of this fault."

In this manner she spoke to them all, even to the little one; "Thou must not call out so impatiently for thy supper any more, or I shall make thee wait longer the next time; or, perhaps, give it to one of the others."

When this was all over, the children said their usual evening prayer, and afterward the Saturday prayer, which Gertrude had taught them, and which was as follows:—

CHAPTER XXXV.—A SATURDAY EVENING PRAYER.

"HEAVENLY Father! thou art ever kind to the children of men, and thou art kind also to us. Thou suppliest our daily wants. All comes from thee. Our bread, and all that we receive from our parents, thou hast first bestowed upon them, and they willingly give it to us. They rejoice in all which thou enablest them to do for us, and bid us be thankful unto thee for it. They tell us that if they had not learned to know and love thee, they should not so love us; and that if they were unmindful of thee, they should do much less for us. They bid us be thankful to the Saviour of men, that they have learned to know and love thee; and they teach us that those who do not know and love him, and follow all the holy laws which he has given to men, can neither so well love thee, nor bring up their children so piously and carefully as those who believe in the Saviour. Our parents teach us many things of Jesus, the Messiah; what great things he did for the children of men; how he passed his life in suffering and distress, and at last died upon the cross, that he might make men happy in time and eternity; how God raised him again from the dead; and how he now sits at the right hand of the throne of God his Father, in the glory of heaven, and still loves all the children of men, and seeks to make them blessed and happy. It goes to our hearts when we hear of our blessed Saviour. O, may we learn so to live as to obtain favor in his sight, and at last be received unto him in heaven.

"Almighty Father! we poor children, who here pray together, are brothers and sisters; therefore may we always love one another, and never hurt each other, but be kind and good to each other whenever we have the opportunity. May we carefully watch over the little ones, that our dear parents may follow their work and earn their bread, without anxiety. It is all we can do, to help them for the trouble and care they have had on our account. Reward them, O, heavenly Father, for all they have done for us; and may we be obedient to them in all which they require from us, that they may love us to the end of their lives, and be rewarded for all the faithful kindness they have shown us.

"O, Almighty God! may we, on the approaching Sabbath, be truly mindful of all thy goodness, and of the love of Christ Jesus; and also of all that our dear parents and friends do for us, that we may be thankful and obedient to God and man, and walk before thee in love all the days of our lives."

Here Nicholas paused, and Gertrude added, with reference to the events of the week: "We thank thee, Heavenly Father, that thou hast this week relieved our dear parents from their anxious care for our nourishment and support, and given unto our father a good and profitable employment. We thank thee that our chief magistrate is, with a truly parental heart, our protector and our help in all misfortunes and distress. We thank thee for the goodness of the lord of the manor. If it be thy will, may we grow up to serve and please him, who is to us as a father."

Then Lize repeated after her: "Forgive me, O, my God, my besetting fault, and teach me to bridle my tongue; to be silent when I ought not to speak, and carefully and thoughtfully to answer the questions I am asked."

And Nicholas: "Guard me in future, O, Heavenly Father, from my hastiness; and teach me to give heed to what I am doing, and to those who are near me."

And Anneli: "I repent, O my God, that I so thoughtlessly left my little brother, and alarmed my dear mother. May I do so no more."

Then the mother said, further:

"Lord! hear us!

"Father, forgive us!

"Christ have mercy upon us!

Then Nicholas repeated the Lord's prayer.

And Enne added: "May God bless our dear father, and mother, and brothers, and sisters, and our kind benefactor, and all good men."

And Lise: "In the name of the Father, and of the Son, and of the Holy Ghost."

Mother. "May God be with you, and keep you! May he lift up the light of his countenance upon you, and be merciful to you for ever!"

The children and their mother remained for a time in that stillness, which must always succeed a prayer from the heart.

Chapter XXXVI.—Pure Devotion and Lifting up of the Soul to God.

Lise broke this silence: "Now will you show us our presents," said she to her mother.

"Yes, I will," replied the mother. "But Lize, thou art always the first to speak."

Nicholas jumped from his seat, rushed past his little sister, to be nearer the light, that he might see the money, and, in so doing, pushed the child so that it cried out.

Then said the mother: "Nicholas, this is not right. It is not a quarter of an hour since thou gavest thy promise to be more careful, and now thou art doing the same thing again."

Nicholas. "O, mother, I am very sorry. I will never do so again."

Mother. "So thou saidst just now before God, and yet thou dost it again. Thou art not in real earnest."

Nich. "O, indeed, mother, I am in earnest. Forgive me! I am, indeed, in earnest, and very sorry."

Mother. "And so am I, Nicholas; but thou wilt forget again if I do not punish thee. Thou must go without supper to bed. As she spoke, she led the boy away from the other children into his room. His sisters stood all sorrowfully around. They were troubled, because Nicholas might not eat with them."

"Why will you not let me teach you by kindness alone, my children," said the mother.

"O, let him be with us this once," said the children.

"No, my loves, he must be cured of his carelessness," said the mother.

"Then do not let us see the presents till to-morrow, when he can look at them with us," said Anneli.

Mother. "That is right, Anneli. Yes, he may see them with you then."

Then she gave the children their supper, and went with them into their room, where Nicholas was still weeping.

"Take care, another time, my dearest boy," said his mother to him.

Nicholas. "Only forgive me, my dear, dear mother. Only forgive me and kiss me, and I will willingly go without supper.

Then Gertrude kissed her son, and a warm tear fell upon his cheek, as she said to him: "O, Nicholas, Nicholas, be careful!" Nicholas threw his arms around his mother's neck and said: "My dear mother, forgive me."

Gertrude then blessed her children, and went again into her room.

She was now quite alone. A little lamp burnt faintly in the room, her heart was devoutly still; and the stillness was a prayer which, without words, moved her inmost spirit. A feeling of the presence of God, and of his goodness; a feeling of hope of an eternal life, and of the inward happiness of the man who puts his trust and confidence in his Almighty Father; all this filled her soul with deep emotion, so that she sunk upon her knees, and a flood of tears rolled down her cheeks.

Blessed are the tears of the child, when, touched by a father's goodness, he looks sobbing back upon the past, dries his eyes, and seeks to recover himself, before he can stammer out the thankfulness of his heart. Blessed were the tears of Nicholas, which he wept at this moment, because he had displeased his good mother, who was so dear to him.

Blessed are the tears of all who weep from a pure child-like heart.

The Lord of heaven looks down upon the sobbing forth of their gratitude, and upon the tears of their eyes, when they spring from affection.

He saw the tears of Gertrude, and heard the sobbing of her heart; and the offering of her thanks was an acceptable sacrifice to him; Gertrude wept long before the Lord her God, and her eyes were still moist when her husband came home.

"Why dost thou weep, Gertrude? thy eyes are red and full of tears! Why dost thou weep to-day, Gertrude?"

Gertrude answered: "My dear husband, these are not tears of sorrow:—be not afraid. I wished to thank God for this week, and my heart was so full that I fell upon my knees; I could not speak for weeping, and yet it seemed to me as if I had never so thanked God before."

"O, my love," answered Leonard, "I wish I could so quickly lift up my soul, and pour forth my heart in tears. It is now my firm resolution to do what is right, and to be just and thankful toward God and man; but I shall never be able to fall upon my knees thus and shed tears."

Gertrude. "If thou art only earnestly resolved to do what is right, all the rest is of little consequence. One has a weak voice and another a strong one, but that signifies little. It is only the use to which they are applied, which is of importance. My dear husband, tears are nothing, and bended knees are nothing; but the resolution to do justly, and be thankful toward God and man is every thing. That one man is more easily affected and another less so, is of no more consequence than that one worm crawls through the earth more easily than another. If thou art only in earnest, my love, thou art sure to find him who is the father of all men."

Leonard, with tears in his eyes, let his head fall upon her neck, and she leaned her face over his, with melancholy tenderness.

They remained thus for a while, still and deeply affected, and were silent.

At last Gertrude said: "Wilt thou not eat to-night?"

"I can not," answered he, "my heart is too full. I can not eat any thing at present." "Nor can I, my love," said she; "but I'll tell thee what we will do. I will take the food to poor Rudi. His mother died to-day."

CHAPTER XXXVII.—KINDNESS TOWARD A POOR MAN.

Leonard. "Is she then at last freed from her misery?"

Gertrude. "Yes, God be praised! But thou shouldst have seen her die, my dear husband. Only think! she found out on the day of her death that Rudeli had stolen potatoes from us. She sent the boy and his father to me, to ask forgiveness. She desired them earnestly to beg us, in her name, to forgive her, because she could not pay back the potatoes; and poor Rudi promised so heartily to make it up by working for thee. Think, my dear husband, how all this affected me. I went to the dying woman, but I can not tell thee, it is impossible to describe, with what a melancholy dying tone she asked me whether I had forgiven them; and when she saw that my heart was touched, how she recommended her children to me; how she delayed it to the last moment, and then, when she found she was going, how she at last ventured, and with what humility and love toward her children, she did it; and how in the midst of it she expired. O, it is not to be told or described."

Leon. "I will go with thee to them."

Ger. "Yes, come, let us go."

So saying, she took up the broth, and they went.

When they arrived, Rudi was sitting on the bed by the corpse. He wept and sighed, and his little boy called out from the other room, and asked him for bread—or even raw roots—or any thing at all.

"Alas! I have nothing whatever. For God's sake, be quiet till morning. I have nothing," said the father.

And the little fellow cried out: "But I am so hungry, father, I can not go to sleep! O, I am so hungry, father!"

Leonard and Gertrude heard this, opened the door, set down the food before the hungry child and said to him, "Eat quickly, before it is cold."

"O, God!" exclaimed Rudi, "What is this? Rudeli, these are the people from whom thou hast stolen potatoes; and, alas, I myself have eaten of them!"

Ger. "Say no more about that, Rudi."

Rudi. "I dare not look you in the face, it goes so to my heart to think what we did."

Leon. "Eat something, Rudi."

Rudeli. "Eat, eat; let us eat, father."

Rudi. "Say the grace then."

Rudeli.

> **"May God feed,**
> **And God speed**
> **All the poor**
> **On the earth's floor,**
> **In body and soul, Amen!"**

Thus prayed the boy, took up the spoon, trembled, wept, and ate.

"May God reward you for it a thousand fold," said the father; and he ate also, and tears fell down his cheeks.

But they did not eat it all, but set aside a plate full for the children who were asleep. Then Rudeli gave thanks.

> **"When we have fed,**
> **Let's thank the Lord,**
> **Who all our bread**
> **Doth still afford.**
> **To him be praise, honor, and thanksgiving,**
> **Now and forever, Amen."**

LEONARD AND GERTRUDE.

CHAPTER XXXVIII.—THE PURE AND PEACEFUL GREATNESS OF A BENEVOLENT HEART.

As Rudi was about to thank them again, he sighed involuntarily.

"Dost thou want something, Rudi? If it is any thing we can do for thee, tell us," said Leonard to him.

"No, I want nothing more, I thank you," answered Rudi.

But he evidently repressed a deep sigh, which struggled to escape from his heart. Leonard and Gertrude looked at him with sorrowful sympathy, and said: "But thou sighest, and we see that thy heart is troubled about something."

"Tell them, tell them, father," said the boy, "they are so kind."

"Do tell us, if we can help thee," said Leonard and Gertrude.

"Dare I venture?" answered the poor man. "I have neither shoes nor stockings, and to-morrow I must follow my mother to her grave, and the day after go to the hall."

Leonard. "To think that thou shouldst fret thyself thus about it! Why didst thou not tell me directly? I can and will willingly give thee them."

Rudi. "And wilt thou believe, after what has happened, that I will return them safe and with thanks?"

Leon. "Say nothing of that, Rudi. I would trust thee for more than that; but thy misery and want have made thee too fearful."

Gertrude. "Yes, Rudi, trust in God and man, and thou wilt be easier in thy heart, and better able to help thyself in all situations."

Rudi. "Yes, Gertrude, I ought to have more trust in my father in heaven; and I can never sufficiently thank you."

Leon. "Say nothing of that, Rudi."

Ger. "I should like to see thy mother again."

They went with a feeble lamp to her bedside; and Gertrude, Leonard, Rudi, and the little one, all with tears in their eyes, looked at her awhile, in the deepest silence; then they covered her up again, and kindly took leave of each other, almost without words.

As they went home, Leonard said to Gertrude: "What a dreadful state of wretchedness this is! Not to be able to go any longer to church, nor to ask for work, nor return thanks for it, because a man has neither clothes, nor shoes, nor stockings."

Ger. "If he were suffering it from any fault of his own, it would almost drive him to despair."

Leon. "Yes, Gertrude, he would despair, he certainly would despair, Gertrude. If I were to hear my children cry out in that way for bread, and had none, and it was my own fault, Gertrude, I should despair; and I was on the road to this wretchedness."

Ger. "We have indeed been saved out of great danger."

As they thus spoke, they passed near the tavern, and the unmeaning riot of drinking and talking reached their ears. Leonard's heart beat at a distance, but, as he drew near, he shuddered with painful horror. Gertrude looked at him tenderly and sorrowfully, and Leonard, ashamed, answered the mournful look of his Gertrude and said: "O what a blessed evening have I spent with thee! and if I had been here instead!"

Gertrude's sadness now increased to tears, and she raised her eyes to heaven. He saw it. Tears stood also in his eyes, and the same sadness was upon his countenance. He, too, raised his eyes to heaven, and both gazed for a time upon the beautiful sky. They looked with admiration upon the silvery brightness of the moon; and a rapturous inward satisfaction assured them that the pure and innocent feelings of their hearts were acceptable in the sight of God.

After this short delay, they went into their cottage.

Gertrude immediately sought out shoes and stockings for Rudi, and Leonard took them to him that evening.

When he came back, they said a preparation prayer for the sacrament of the next day, and fell asleep with devout thankfulness.

In the morning they arose early, and rejoiced in the Lord; read the history of the Saviour's sufferings, and of the institution of the holy supper; and praised God in the early hours, before the Sabbath sun arose.

Then they awoke their children, waited for them to say their morning prayer, and then went to church.

A quarter of an hour before service-time, the bailiff also arose. He could not find the key of his clothes-chest; uttered dreadful curses; kicked the chest open with his foot; dressed himself; went to church; placed himself in the first seat in the choir; held his hat before his mouth; and looked into every corner of the church, whilst he repeated his prayer under his hat.

Soon afterward the pastor entered. Then the people sang two verses of the hymn for Passion week: "O man, repent thy heavy sins," and so on.

Then the pastor went into the pulpit; and this day he preached and instructed his people as follows:—

Chapter XXXIX.—A Sermon.

"My children!

"He who fears the Lord, and walks piously and uprightly before him, walks in light.

"But he who in all his doings is forgetful of his God, walks in darkness.

"Therefore be ye not deceived, one only is good, and he is your Father.

"Wherefore do you run astray, and grope about in darkness? No one is your Father but God.

"Beware of men, lest ye learn from them what will be displeasing in the sight of your Father in heaven.

"Happy is the man who has God for his Father.

"Happy is the man who fears wickedness and hates deceitfulness: for they who commit wickedness shall not prosper, and the deceitful man is taken in his own snare.

"The man shall not prosper, who oppresses and injures his neighbor.

"The man shall not prosper, against whom the cry of the poor man rises toward God.

"Woe to the wretch who in the winter feeds the poor, and in the harvest takes from him double.

"Woe to the godless man who causes the poor to drink wine in the summer, and in the autumn requires from him double.

"Woe to him, when he takes away from the poor man his straw and his fodder, so that he can not till his ground.

"Woe to him, by the hardness of whose heart the children of the poor want bread.

"Woe to the godless man, who lends money to the poor that they may become his servants, be at his command, work without wages, and yet pay rent.

"Woe to him, when they give false testimony for him before the judge, and swear false oaths that his cause is just.

"Woe to him, when he assembles sinners in his house, and watches with them to betray the just man, that he may become as one of them, and forget his God, his wife, and his children, and waste, with them, the wages of his labor, upon which his wife and children depend.

"And woe to the miserable man, who suffers himself to be led astray by the ungodly, and, in his thoughtlessness, squanders the money which is wanted at home.

"Woe to him, when the sighs of his wife arise to God, because she has no food for her infant.

"Woe to him, when his child starves, that he may drink.

"Woe to him, when she weeps over the wants of her children, and her own excessive labor.

"Woe to him, who wastes the apprentice-fee of his sons; when his old age comes, they will say unto him, 'Thou didst not behave as a father to us, thou didst not teach us to earn bread, how can we now help thee?'

"Woe to those, who go about telling lies, and make the crooked straight, and the straight crooked: for they shall come to shame.

"Woe to you, when ye have bought the land of the widow, and the house of the orphan, at an unfair price. Woe to you, for this is your Lord; father of the widow and of the orphan, and they are dear to him; and ye are a hatred and an abomination in his sight, because ye are cruel and hard to the poor.

"Woe to you, whose houses are full of what does not belong to you.

"Though you riot in wine which came from the poor man's vines:

"Though you laugh, when starved and miserable men shake their corn into your sacks with sighs:

"Though you sneer and jest when the oppressed man writhes like a worm before you, and entreats you, in God's name, to lend him a tenth part of what you have cheated him of; though you harden yourselves against all this, yet have you never an hour's peace in your hearts.

"No! there lives not the man upon God's earth, who oppresses the poor and is happy.

"Though he be raised out of all danger, out of all fear of iniquity or punishment, on this earth; though he be a ruler in the land, and imprison with his hand, and accuse with his tongue, miserable men who are better than himself:

"Though he sit aloft, and judge them to life or death, and sentence them to the sword, or the wheel:

"He is more miserable than they!

"He who oppresses the poor man from pride, and lays snares for the unfortunate, and swears away widows' houses; he is worse than the thief and the murderer, whose reward is death.

"Therefore, has the man who does these things no peaceful hour, throughout his life.

"He wanders on the face of the earth laden with the curse of a brother's murder, which leaves no rest for his heart.

"He wanders around, and seeks, and tries continually to conceal from himself the horror of his inward thoughts.

"With eating and drinking, with insolence and malice, with hatred and strife, with lies and deceit, with buffoonery and licentiousness, with slander and abuse, with quarreling and backbiting, he seeks to get through the time which is a burthen to him.

"But he will not always be able to suppress the voice of his conscience; he will not always be able to escape the fear of the Lord; it will fall upon him like an armed man, and you will see him tremble and be dismayed, like a prisoner whom death threatens.

"But happy is the man who has no part in such doings.

"Happy is the man who is not answerable for the poverty of his neighbor.

"Happy is the man who has nothing in his possession which he has forced from the poor.

"Happy are you, when your mouth is pure from harsh words, and your eyes from harsh looks.

"Happy are you, when the poor man blesses you, and when the widow and the orphan weep tears of gratitude to God for you.

"Happy is the man who walks in love before his God, and before his people.

"Happy are you who are pious; come and rejoice at the table of the God of love.

"The Lord your God is your Father.

"The signs of love from his hands will refresh your spirits, and the blessedness of your souls will increase, because your love toward God your Father, and toward your brethren of mankind, will increase and strengthen.

"But ye who walk without love, and in your deeds consider not that God is your Father, and that your neighbors are the children of your God, and that the poor man is your brother; ye ungodly, what do ye here? ye, who to-morrow will injure and oppress the poor as ye did yesterday, what do ye here? Will ye eat of the bread of the Lord, and drink of his cup, and say that ye are one in body, and mind, and soul, with your brethren?

"Leave this house, and avoid the meal of love.

"And ye poor and oppressed ones of my people, believe and trust in the Lord, and the fruit of your affliction and suffering will become a blessing to you.

"Believe and trust in the Lord your God, and fear not the ungodly; but keep yourselves from them. Rather suffer, rather endure any want, rather bear any injury, than seek help from their hard-heartedness. For the words of the hard man are lies, and his help is a decoy by which he seeks to entrap the poor man and destroy him. Therefore flee from the ungodly man when he salutes you with smiles, when he gives you his hand, and takes yours with friendliness. When he offers you his assistance, then flee from him; for the ungodly man insnares the poor. Avoid him, and join not yourselves with him; but fear him not:—though you see him standing fast and great, like a lofty oak, fear him not!

"Go, my children, into the forest, to the place where the lofty oaks stand, and see how the little trees, which withered under their shade, now being removed from them, flourish and bloom. The sun shines again upon the young plants, the dew of heaven falls upon them in its strength, and the great spreading roots of the oaks, which sucked up all the nourishment from the ground, now decay, and nourish the young trees which withered in the shade.

"Therefore hope in the Lord, for his help never fails those who hope in him.

"The day of the Lord will come to the ungodly man; and on that day, when he shall see the oppressed and the poor man, he will cry out and say: 'O, that I had been as one of these!'

"Therefore trust in the Lord, ye who are troubled and oppressed, and rejoice that ye know the Lord, who has appointed the supper of love.

"For through love ye bear the sufferings of this earth, even as a treasure from the Lord; and your burthens only increase your strength and your blessedness.

"Therefore rejoice that ye know the God of love; for without love ye would sink and become as the ungodly, who torment and betray you.

"Praise the God of love, that he has appointed this sacrament, and has called you, amongst his millions, to partake in his holy mysteries.

"Praise ye the Lord!

"The revelation of love is the salvation of the world.

"Love is the band which binds the earth together.

"Love is the band which unites God and man.

"Without love, man is without God; and without God and love, what is man?

"Dare ye say? can ye utter or think what man is without God, and without love?

"I dare not; I can not express it—man, without God and without love, is no longer a man, but a brute.

"Therefore rejoice that ye know the God of love, who has called the world from brutishness to love, from darkness to light, and from death to eternal life. Rejoice that ye know Jesus Christ, and through faith in him are called to be children of God, and to eternal life.

"And yet once more I say unto you, rejoice that ye know the Lord; and pray for all those who do not know him; that they may come to the knowledge of the truth and of your joy.

"My children, come to the holy supper of your Lord. Amen."

When the pastor had said this, and instructed his congregation for nearly an hour, he prayed with them, and then the whole congregation partook of the Lord's supper.

The bailiff, Hummel, assisted in distributing the Lord's supper; and when all the people had given thanks unto the Lord, they sang a hymn, and the pastor blessed his people, and every one returned to his own house.

CHAPTER XL.—A PROOF THAT THE SERMON WAS GOOD; *Item*, ON KNOWLEDGE AND ERROR, AND WHAT IS CALLED OPPRESSING THE POOR.

THE bailiff, Hummel, was furious at the discourse which the pastor had delivered about the ungodly man; and on the Lord's day, which the whole parish kept holy, he raged, and swore, and abused the pastor, and said many violent things against him.

As soon as he got home from the sacrament, he sent for his dissolute companions to come to him directly. They soon arrived, and joined the bailiff in saying many shameful and abusive things of the pastor and his Christian discourse.

The bailiff began first: "I can not endure his damned taunts and attacks."

"It is not right, it is a sin, and particularly on the Sabbath day, it is a sin to do so," said old Abi.

Bailiff. "The rascal knows very well that I can not endure it, and he only goes on so much the more. It will be a fine thing for him, if he can bring the people, by his preaching and his abuse, to hate and despise what he does not understand, and has nothing to do with."

Abi. "Ay, indeed! our blessed Saviour, and the evangelists, and the apostles in the New Testament, never attacked any body."

Christian. "Thou canst not say that. They did attack people, and still more than the pastor does."

Abi. "It is not true, Christian."

Chris. "Thou art a fool, Abi. Ye blind guides, ye serpents,—ye generation of vipers, and a thousand such. Thou knowest a great deal about the Bible, Abi."

Countryman, "Yes, Abi! they certainly did attack people."

Chris. "They did. But as for affairs of law, which they did not understand, and reckonings which had been settled before the judges according to law, they did not meddle with them, and those who do are very different kind of people."

Count. "Yes, that they are."

Chris. "They must be very different, or people would not be so bold. Only think what they did. There was one Annas—yes, Annas was his name—and his wife after him, only for telling one lie, they fell down and died."

Count. "Die they indeed? For only one lie?"

Chris. "Yes, as true as I am alive, and standing here."

Abi. "It's a fine thing, too, to know one's Bible."

Chris. "I have to thank my father, who is dead and buried for it. For the rest he was, God forgive him, no great things. He ran through all my mother's property to the last farthing,—but I could have got over that, if he had not leagued himself so much with Uli, who was hanged. Such a thing as that injures children and children's children. But he could read his Bible as well as any pastor, and made us all learn too. He would not excuse one of us."

Abi. "I have often wondered how he could be so good-for-nothing, when he knew so much."

Count. "It is very strange."

Jost. (A stranger, who happened to be in the tavern.) "I can not help laughing, neighbors, at your wonder about it. If much knowledge could make people good, your attorneys, and brokers, and bailiffs, and magistrates, with respect be it spoken, would be always the best."

Count. "Ay, and so they would, neighbor."

Jost. "Depend upon it, there is a wide difference between knowing and doing. He who is for carrying on his business by knowledge alone, had need take care lest he forget how to act."

Count. "Yes, so it is. A man soon forgets what he does not practice."

Jost. "Of course. When a man is in habits of idleness, he is good for nothing. And so it is with those who, from idleness and weariness, get to chattering and talking. They become good for nothing. Only attend, and you will find that the greatest part of those fellows who have stories out of the Bible, or the newspapers, and new and old pamphlets, constantly in their hands and mouths, are little better than mere idlers. If one wants to talk with them about housekeeping, bringing up children, profit, or business, when they should give one advice how to set about this thing or that, which is of real use, they stand there like blockheads, and know nothing, and can tell nothing. Only where people meet, for idleness, in taverns, and at dances, and gossipings on Sundays and holidays; there they show off. They tell of quack cures, and foolish stories and tales, in which there is not a word of truth; and yet a whole room full of honest folks will sit listening for hours to such a prating fellow, who tells them one lie after another."

Abi. "By my soul, it is as he says! and, Christian, he has drawn thy father to the life. Just so we went on with him. He was as stupid as an ox about every thing relating to wood and fields, cattle, fodder, ploughing, and such like; and knew no more about his own business than a sheep. But in the tavern, and at parish meetings, and in the churchyard, after service, he spoke like a wise man from the East. Sometimes of Doctor Faustus, sometimes of our Saviour, sometimes of the Witch of Endor, or of the one of Hirzau, and sometimes of bull-fights at Maestricht, or of horse-races at London. Stupidly as he did it, and evident as it was that he was telling them lies, people went on willingly listening to him, till he was near being hanged, which did at last hurt his credit as a story-teller."

Jost. "It was high time."

"Yes, we were fools long enough; and gave him many a glass of wine for pure lies."

Jost. "To my mind it would have been better for him if you had never given him any."

Abi. "Indeed, I believe if we had never given him any, he would not have come so near the gallows. He would have been obliged to work."

Jost. "So you see your good will toward him did him an injury."

Count. "Yes, that it did."

Jost. "It is a wicked and ruinous thing to drag the Bible into such idle telling and hearing of profane stories."

Leupi. "My father once beat me soundly for forgetting, over one of these stories, (I think it was out of the Bible,) to fetch the cow from the pasture."

Jost. "He was in the right. To do what is in the Bible is our business, and to tell us about it is the pastor's. The Bible is a command, a law; what would the governor say to thee, if he had sent a command down to the village that we were to cart something to the castle, and thou, instead of going into the wood to get thy load, wert to seat thyself in the tavern, take up the order in thy hand, read it aloud, and, whilst thou wert sitting over thy glass, explain to thy neighbors what he meant and wished for?"

Abi. "What would he say to me? He would abuse me, and laugh at me, and throw me into prison for taking him for a fool."

Jost "And just so much do the people deserve, who read the Bible from mere idleness, and that they may be able to tell stories out of it at the tavern."

Chris. "Yes, but yet we must read in it, to know how to keep in the right way."

Jost. "Of course. But those who are always stopping at every resting-place, and standing still to talk at every well, and finger-post, and cross, which is put down to show the way, are not those who will get on the fastest?"

Abi. "But how is this neighbor? They say one can not pay too dear for knowledge; but it seems to me one may easily pay too dear for knowledge of many things."

Jost. "Yes, indeed! We always pay too dear for every thing which keeps us away from active duties and business of importance. We should seek to gain information that we may know how to act, and if people try to know many things, merely for the sake of talking about them, they will certainly avail them nothing.

"It is, with respect to knowledge and performance, as it is in a trade. A shoemaker, for instance, must work, that is the first thing; he must also be able to judge of leather and know how to buy it; this is the means by which he can carry on his trade to advantage; and so it is in every thing else. Execution and practice are the chief things for all men; knowledge and understanding are the means by which they can carry on their business to advantage.

"But for this purpose the knowledge of every man should relate to what he has to do and perform, or in other words to his chief business."

Abi. "Now I begin to see how it is. When a man has his head full of various and foreign affairs, he does not give his mind to his own business, and to what is of the most importance to him."

Jost. "Just so. The thoughts and understanding of every man should be intent upon the things which are of the greatest consequence to him. I have no meadows to be cultivated by irrigation, therefore it is nothing to me how people manage to overflow them; and, till I have a wood of my own, I shall take no pains to know how it may be best taken care of. But my reservoirs for manure are often in my thoughts, because they make my poor meadows rich. Every thing would prosper, if every body were properly attentive to his own affair. People get plenty of knowledge, soon enough, if they only learn to know things well; but they never learn to know them well, if they do not begin by knowing, and looking after what belongs to them. Knowledge rises by degrees from the lowest thing to the highest, and we shall make great progress in our lives, if we begin thus; but from idle talking, and stories, and foolish dreams of things in the clouds, or in the moon, people learn only to become good for nothing."

Abi. "They begin to learn that, even at school."

During the whole of this conversation, the bailiff stood by the fire, stared into it, warmed himself, scarcely listened to any thing, and joined seldom, and without any connection, in what they were saying. He forgot the wine in his abstraction, and therefore it was that the conversation between Abi and the stranger had lasted so long. Perhaps, too, he was not willing to express his vexation till the stranger had finished his glass and left them.

Then at last he began all at once, as if, during his long silence, he had been learning it off by heart.

"The pastor is always talking about oppressing the poor. If what he calls oppressing the poor were done by nobody, the devil take me if there would be any poor in the world. But when I look around me, from the prince to the nightwatchman, from the first council in the land to the lowest parish meeting, every one seeks his own profit, and presses against whatever comes in his way. The late pastor sold wine, as I do, and took hay, and corn, and oats, in payment for it, as much as I do. Throughout the world every one oppresses his inferiors, and I am obliged to submit to oppression in my turn. Whoever has any thing, or wishes to have any thing, must oppress, or he will lose what is his own, and become a beggar. If the pastor knew the poor as well as I do, he would not trouble himself so much about them; but it is not for the sake of the poor. All he wants is to find fault, and lead the people to judge one another wrongfully. The poor are a good-for-nothing set: if I wanted ten rogues I could soon find eleven amongst the poor. I wish people would bring me my income regularly home every quarter-day, I would soon learn to receive it piously and devoutly. But in my business, in a tavern and in poor cottages, where every farthing must be forced out, and one is plagued at every turn, it is a very different thing. I would lay a wager that any landlord, who would act considerately and compassionately toward day-laborers and poor people, would soon lose all he had. They are rogues every one."

Thus spoke the bailiff, and perverted the voice of his conscience, which made him uneasy, and told him that the pastor was right, and that he was the man who oppressed all the poor of the village, even until the blood started under their nails.

But, however he reasoned to himself, he was not at rest. Anxiety and care visibly tormented him. He paced uneasily up and down the room.

At last he said: "I am so angry about the pastor's sermon, that I know not what to do, and I am not well. Are you cold, neighbors? I have been as cold as ice, ever since I came home."

"No," answered the neighbors, "it is not cold; but every body saw at church that thou wert not well, thou wert so deadly pale."

Bailiff. "Did every body see it at church? I was indeed strangely ill!—I am very feverish—and so faint—I must drink something. We will go into the back room, during service-time."

CHAPTER XLI.—A CHURCHWARDEN INFORMS THE PASTOR OF IMPROPER CONDUCT.

BUT a churchwarden, who lived in the same street with the bailiff, and had seen Abi, Christian, and the other fellows go into the tavern, between the services, was angry in his heart, and thought at that moment of the oath he had taken to look after all improper and profane conduct, and to inform the pastor of it. And the churchwarden set a man, he could depend upon, to watch the fellows, and see whether they went out of the tavern again before service.

It was now nearly time for the bell to ring, and, as nobody came out, he went to the pastor, and told him what he had seen, and that he had set Samuel Treu to watch them.

The pastor was troubled by this intelligence, sighed to himself, and said little.

The churchwarden thought he was studying his sermon, and spoke less than usual over his glass of wine.

At last, as the pastor was preparing to go into the church, Samuel came, and the churchwarden said to him:

"Thou canst tell the honorable Herr Pastor, thyself, all about it."

Then Samuel said: "May heaven bless you, honorable Herr Pastor, sir."

The pastor thanked him, and said: "Are these people not gone home yet?"

Samuel. "No, sir! I have kept in sight of the tavern ever since the elder told me to watch, and nobody has left the house, except the bailiff's wife, who is gone to church."

Pastor. "And thou art quite certain that they are all still in the tavern?"

Sam. "Yes, sir, I am sure of it."

Churchwarden. "Your reverence sees that I was not mistaken, and that it was my duty to let you know of it."

Pastor. "It is a great pity that such things should take up any one's time and thoughts on a Sabbath day."

Churchwarden. "We have only done what was our duty, please your reverence."

Pastor. "I know it, and I thank you for your watchfulness. But, neighbors, take care that, for the sake of a trifling duty, you do not forget one of more difficulty and importance. To watch over ourselves, and over our own hearts, is our first and most important duty. Therefore it is always unfortunate when such evil deeds distract a man's thoughts."

After a while, he added: "No! such shameful disorder must no longer be endured—forbearance only increases it."

And he then went with the men into the church.

Chapter XLII.—An Addition to the Morning's Discourse.

As he was reading the account of our Saviour's sufferings, he came to these words:—

"And when Judas had taken the sop, Satan entered into his heart."

And he discoursed to his people upon the whole history of the traitor; and his feelings were so strongly excited, that he struck the cushion, vehemently, with his hand, which he had not done for years before.

And he said that all those who, as soon as they went out from the Lord's supper, ran off to drinking and gaming, were not a jot better than Judas, and would come to the same end.

And the congregation began to wonder, and consider, what could be the meaning of this great indignation of the pastor.

People began to lay their heads together; and a murmur went round that the bailiff had his house full of his associates.

And all the people began to turn their eyes toward his empty seat, and toward his wife.

She observed it—trembled—cast down her eyes—durst not look any body in the face; and, as soon as the singing began, made her way out of the church.

When she did that, the excitement grew still greater, and some pointed at her with their fingers; some women even stood up on the furthest benches on the women's side to see her, and there was so much disturbance that the singing went wrong.

Chapter XLIII.—The Countrymen in the Tavern are Disturbed.

She ran home as fast as she could; and, when she entered the room, she threw the prayer-book, in a rage, amongst the glasses and jugs, and burst into a violent fit of crying.

The bailiff, and the neighbors, inquired what was the matter

Wife. "I'll soon let you know that. It's a shame for you to be drinking here on the Sabbath day."

Bailiff. "Is that all? Then there is not much amiss."

Men. "And it is the first time it ever made you cry."

Bailiff. "I thought, to be sure, thou hadst lost thy purse, at the least."

Wife. "Don't be talking thy nonsense now. If thou hadst been at church, thou wouldst not be so ready with it."

Bailiff. "What is the matter then? Do n't make such a blubbering, but tell us."

Wife. "The pastor must have got to know that these fellows of thine were drinking here during service-time."

Bailiff. "That would be a cursed business, indeed."

Wife. "He knows it, to a certainty."

Bailiff. "What Satan could tell him of it just now?"

Wife. "What Satan, thou simpleton? They come here smoking their pipes along the street, instead of by the back way; and so pass close by the elder's house. It is impossible to tell thee in what a way the pastor has been talking, and all the people have been pointing at me with their fingers."

Bailiff. "This is a damned trick that some Satan has been playing me."

Wife. "Why must you come just to-day, you drunken hounds?—you knew well enough that it was not right."

Men. "It is not our fault. He sent for us."

Wife. "Did he?"

Men. "Ay, that he did."

Bailiff. "I was in such a strange way, I could not bear to be alone."

Wife. "Well, it is no matter how it was. But, neighbors, go, as quickly as you can, through the back door, home; and take care that the people, as they come out of the church, may find every one of you at his own door—and so you may put a cloak over the thing. They have not yet quite finished the hymn, but go directly. It is high time."

Bailiff. "Yes; away with you. It is well advised."

The men went, and the bailiff's wife told him that the pastor had preached about Judas, how the devil had entered into his heart, how he had hanged himself;—and how those who went from the Lord's supper to drink and game would come to a like end."

"He was so earnest," said the woman, "that he struck the cushion with his fist, and I turned quite sick and faint."

The bailiff was so much terrified by this account that it struck him dumb, and he could not utter a word; and heavy groans escaped from the proud man, who had not been heard to utter such for years.

His wife asked him, repeatedly, why he groaned in such a manner?

He answered her not a word; but more than once he muttered to himself: "What is to be the end of this? what will become of me?"

He paced up and down the room in this way for a long time, and at last said to his wife: "Get me a cooling powder from the barber's; my blood is in a fever, and oppresses me. I will be bled to-morrow, if the medicine does not remove it."

His wife fetched him the powder; he took it, and, after a while, became easier.

CHAPTER XLIV.—DESCRIPTION OF A WICKED MAN'S FEELINGS DURING THE SACRAMENT.

THEN he told his wife how in the morning he had gone with right feelings to church, and in the beginning of the service had prayed to God to forgive his sins; but that the pastor's discourse had driven him mad, he had not had one good thought since, and dreadful and horrible things had occurred to him during the sacrament. "From the beginning to the end," said he to his wife, "I could not utter a single prayer. My heart was like a stone; and when the pastor gave me the bread, he looked at me in a way I can not describe. No, it is impossible to give an idea of it; but I shall never forget it. When a judge condemns a poor sinner to the wheel, or the flames, and breaks his rod of office over him, he does not look at him in such a way. I can never forget how he looked at me. A cold sweat ran down my face; and my hands trembled as I took the bread from him.

"And when I had eaten it, a furious, horrible rage against the pastor took possession of me, so that I gnashed with my teeth, and durst not look round me.

"Wife! one dreadful idea after another came into my mind, and terrified me like a thunderbolt; but I could not get rid of them.

"I shuddered at the altar, so that I could not hold the cup fast; and then came Joseph, with his torn boots, and threw down his rogue's eyes when he saw me. And my three crowns!—O, how I shuddered at the thought of my three crowns.

"Then came Gertrude, who raised her eyes to heaven, and then fixed them on the cup, as if she had not seen me, as if I had not been there. She hates me, and curses me, and wishes to ruin me; and yet she could behave as if she did not see me, as if I had not been there.

"Then came the mason, and looked so sorrowfully at me, as if he would have said, from the bottom of his heart: 'Forgive me, bailiff.' He, who would bring me to the gallows, if he could.

"Then came Shaben Michel, as pale and frightened as myself, and trembling as much. Think, wife, what a state all this put me into.

"I was afraid Hans Wust would be coming too; I could not have stood that—the cup would certainly have fallen out of my hand, and I should have dropped upon the ground. As it was, I could scarcely keep upon my feet; and, when I got back to my seat, all my limbs shook, so that when they were singing I could not hold the book.

"And all the time I kept thinking—'Arner, Arner is at the bottom of all this!' and anger, fury, and revenge raged in my heart the whole time. A thing I had never thought of in my life came into my head during the sacrament. I dare scarcely tell thee what it was. I am frightened when I only think of it. It came into my head to throw his great landmark, on the hill, down the precipice. Nobody knows of the landmark but myself."

Chapter XLV.—The Bailiff's Wife Tells Her Husband Some Weighty Truths, But Many Years Too Late.

The bailiff's speech alarmed his wife, but she knew not what to say, and was silent whilst he spoke.

Neither of them said any thing more for some time. At last the wife began, and said to him: "I am very uneasy on account of what thou hast been saying. Thou must give up these companions of thine. This business can not end well, and we are growing old."

Bailiff. "Thou art right enough there. But it is not so easy to do it."

Wife. "Easy or not, it must be done. Thou must get rid of them."

Bailiff. "Thou knowest well enough how I am tied to them, and what they know about me."

Wife. "Thou knowest still more about them. They are a parcel of rogues, and dare not peach. Thou must get rid of them."

The bailiff groaned, and his wife continued:—

"They sit eating and drinking here constantly, and pay thee nothing; and when thou art intoxicated they can persuade thee to any thing. Only think how Joseph tricked thee last night. I wanted to advise thee for thy good, and pretty treatment I got for my pains. And, moreover, since yesterday two crowns more have walked out of thy waistcoat pocket, without being so much as set down. How long can this last? If thou wilt only reckon up how much thou hast spent over thy misdeeds, thou wilt find that thou hast lost by them every way. And yet thou goest on still with these people; and many a time and oft it is for the sake of nothing in the world but thy godless pride. Sometimes thou wilt have one of these hounds to say something for thee, and then another must hold his tongue for thee; and so they come and eat and drink at thy cost, and, for their gratitude, they are ready at the first turn to ruin and betray thee.

"Formerly, indeed, when they feared thee like a drawn sword, thou couldst keep these fellows in order; but now thou art their master no longer, and depend upon it, thou art a lost man in thy old age, if thou dost not look sharply after them. We are in as slippery a situation as can well be. The moment thou turnest thy back, the lads begin laughing and talking, and will not do a stroke of work, nor any thing but drink." So said the wife.

The bailiff answered her not a word, but sat staring at her, without speaking, whilst she spoke. At last he got up, and went into the garden, and from the garden into his meadow, and then into the stables. Trouble and anxiety followed him every where; but he stood still for a while in the stables, and reasoned thus with himself:—

CHAPTER XLVI.—SOLILOQUY OF A MAN WHOSE THOUGHTS UNHAPPILY LEAD HIM TOO FAR.

"WHAT my wife says is but too true; but what can I do? I can not help it; it is impossible for me to escape out of this net." So said the bailiff, and again cursed Arner, as if he had been the cause of his getting into all these difficulties; and then abused the pastor for driving him mad at church. Then he recurred again to the landmark, and said: "I will not touch the cursed stone; but if any one did remove it the squire would lose the third part of his wood. It is clear enough, that the eighth and ninth government landmark would cut through his property in a straight line. But heaven forbid that I should remove a landmark!"

Then he began again: "Suppose after all it should be no true landmark. It lies there, as if it had been since the flood, and has neither a letter nor a figure upon it."

Then he went again into the house, took down his account book—added it up—wrote in it—blotted it—separated his papers, and laid them back again—forgot what he had read—looked up again what he had written—then put the book into the chest—walked up and down the room, and kept thinking and talking to himself of "a landmark without a letter or a figure upon it. There is not such another to be found any where! What an idea is come into my head! Some ancestor of the family may have made an inroad into the government wood, and suppose this stone were of his placing! By G——, it must be so! It is the most unaccountable bend in the whole government boundary. For six miles it goes in a straight line till it comes here, and the stone has no mark upon it, and there is no trench of separation.

"If the wood really belongs to the government, I should be doing nothing wrong. It would be only my duty to the government. But if I should be mistaken! No, I will not touch the stone. I should have to dig it up and to roll it, on some dark night, to the distance of a stone's throw over the level part to the precipice; and it is a great weight. It will not fall down like a stream of water. By day every stroke of the mattock would be heard, it is so near the highway; and at night—I dare not venture. I should start at every sound. If a badger came by, or a deer sprang up, I could not go on with the work. And who knows whether really a goblin might not catch me while I was doing it? It is not safe around the landmark in the night; I had better let it alone!"

After a while he began again: "To think that there are so many folks who don't believe either in hell or in spirits! The old attorney did not believe a word of them, nor did the pastor's assistant. By heaven, it is impossible that he could believe in any thing. And the attorney has told me plainly, a hundred times, that, when I was once dead, it would be all the same with me as with my dog or horse. This was his belief, and he was afraid of nothing, and did what he would. Suppose he were to prove right! If I could believe it, if I could hope it, if I could be assured in my heart that it was so, the first time Arner went out to hunt, I would hide myself behind a tree and shoot him dead. I would burn the pastor's house—but it is to no purpose talking. I can not believe it; I dare not hope it. It is not true; and they are fools, mistaken fools, who think so! There must be a God! There certainly must be a God! Landmark! Landmark! I will not remove thee!"

So saying the man trembled, but could not drive the thought out of his head. He shuddered with horror! He sought to escape from himself; walked up the street, joined the first neighbor he met with, and talked to him about the weather, the wind, and the snails which had injured the rye harvest for some years past.

After some time he returned home with a couple of thirsty fellows, to whom he gave something to drink, that they might stay with him. Then he took another cooling powder, and so got over the Sunday.

Chapter XLVII.—Domestic Happiness on the Sabbath Day.

And now I leave the house of wickedness for a time. It has sickened my heart to dwell upon its horrors. Now I leave them for a time, and my spirit is lightened and I breathe freely again. I approach once more the cottage where human virtue dwells.

In the morning, after Leonard and his wife were gone to church, the children sat quietly and thoughtfully together in the house, said their prayers, sang and said over what they had learned in the week; for they always had to repeat it to Gertrude every Sunday evening.

Lise, the eldest, had the care of her little brother during service time. She had to take him up, dress him, and give him his porridge; and this was always Lise's greatest Sunday treat; for, when she was looking after and feeding the child, she fancied herself a woman. You should have seen how she played the part of mother, imitated her, fondled the baby in her arms, and nodded and smiled to it; and how the little one smiled again, held out its hands, and kicked with its little feet; and how it caught hold of Lise's cap, or her hair, or her nose, and pointed to the smart Sunday handkerchief on her neck, and called out, ha! ha! and then how Nicholas and Anneli answered it, ha! ha! whilst the little one turned its head round, to see where the voice came from, spied out Nicholas and laughed at him; and then how Nicholas sprang up to kiss and fondle his little brother; and how Lise then would have the preference, and insisted upon it that the little darling was laughing at her; and how carefully she looked after it, anticipated all its wants, played with it, and tossed it up toward the ceiling, and then carefully let it down again almost to touch the ground; how the baby laughed and crowed with delight, whilst she held it up to the looking-glass, that it might push its little hands and face against it; and how at last it caught a sight of its mother in the street, and crowed and clapped its hands, and almost sprang out of Lise's arms.

Such were the delights of Leonard's children on a Sunday or a feast day; and such delights of good children are acceptable in the sight of their God. He looks down with complacency upon the innocence of children, when they are enjoying existence; and, if they continue good and obedient, he will bless them, that it may be well with them to the end of their lives.

Gertrude was satisfied with her children, for they had done every thing as they had been told.

It is the greatest happiness of good children to know that they have given satisfaction to their father and mother.

Gertrude's children had this happiness. They climbed their parents' knees, jumped first into the arms of one, and then of the other, and clasped their little arms round their necks.

This was the luxury in which Leonard and Gertrude indulged on the Lord's day. Ever since she became a mother, it had been Gertrude's Sunday delight to rejoice over her children, and over their tender affection for their father and mother.

Leonard sighed this day, when he thought how often he had deprived himself of such pleasures.

Domestic happiness is the sweetest enjoyment of man upon earth; and the rejoicing of parents over their children is the holiest of human joys. It purifies and hallows the heart, and raises it toward the heavenly Father of all. Therefore the Lord blesses the tears of delight which flow from such feelings, and richly repays every act of parental watchfulness and kindness.

But the ungodly man, who cares not for his children, and to whom they are a trouble and a burthen—the ungodly man, who flies from them on the week day, and conceals himself from them on the Sabbath; who escapes from their innocent enjoyment, and finds no pleasure in them till they are corrupted by the world, and become like himself—this man throws away from him the best blessing of life. He will not in his old age rejoice in his children, nor derive any comfort from them.

On the Sabbath days Leonard and Gertrude, in the joy of their hearts spoke to their children of the goodness of their God, and of the compassion of their Saviour.

The children listened silently and attentively, and the hour of noon passed swiftly and happily away.

Then the bells began to ring, and Leonard and Gertrude went again to church.

On their way they passed by the bailiff's house, and Leonard said to Gertrude: "The bailiff looked shockingly this morning. I never in my life saw him look so before. The sweat dropped from his forehead as he assisted at the sacrament. Didst thou not notice it, Gertrude? I perceived that he trembled when he gave me the cup."

"I did not notice it," said Gertrude.

Leonard. "I was quite disturbed to see the man in such a state. If I durst, I would have asked him to forgive me; and if I could in any way show him that I wish him no ill, I would do it gladly."

Gertrude. "May God reward thee for thy kind heart, Leonard. It will be right to do so, whenever thou hast an opportunity. But Rudi's poor children, and many others, cry out for vengeance against this man, and he will not be able to escape."

Leon. "I am quite grieved to see him so very unhappy. I have perceived, for a long time past, amidst all the noisy merriment of his house, that some anxiety preyed upon him constantly."

Ger. "My dear husband, whoever departs from a quiet, holy life can never be really happy."

Leon. "If I ever in my life saw any thing clearly, it was this: that however the bailiff's followers, whom he had about him in the house, might help him in the way of assistance, or advice, or cheating, or violence, they never procured for him a single hour of contentment and ease."

As they were thus conversing, they arrived at church, and were there very much moved by the great earnestness with which the pastor discoursed upon the character of the traitor.

Chapter XLVIII.—Some Observations upon Sin.

Gertrude, amongst the rest, had heard what was said, in the women's seats, about the bailiff's house being again full of his people, and after church she told Leonard of it. He answered: "I can scarcely believe it, during church time, and on a Sunday."

Gertrude. "It is indeed very sad. But the entanglements of an ungodly life lead to all, even the most fearful wickedness. I shall never forget the description our late pastor gave us of sin, the last time we received the sacrament from him. He compared it to a lake, which from continual rains overflowed its banks. The swelling of the lake, said he, is imperceptible, but it increases every day and hour, and rises higher and higher, and the danger is as great as if it overflowed violently with a sudden storm.

"Therefore the experienced and prudent examine, in the beginning, all the dams and embankments, to see whether they are in a fit condition to resist the force of the waters. But the inexperienced and imprudent pay no attention to the rising of the lake, till the dams are burst, and the fields and pastures laid waste, and till the alarm bell warns all in the country to save themselves from the devastation. It is thus, said he, with sin and the ruin which it occasions.

"I am not yet old, but I have already observed, a hundred times, that the good pastor was right, and that every one who persists in the habitual commission of any one sin, hardens his heart, so that he no longer perceives the increase of its wickedness, till destruction and horror awaken him out of his sleep."

Chapter XLIX.—The Character and Education of Children.

Conversing in this manner, they returned to their own cottage.

The children ran down the steps to meet their father and mother, and called out: "O, come, pray come mother! we want to repeat what we learned last week, that we may be ready directly."

Gertrude. "Why are you in such haste, my loves? What need is there for it?"

Children. "O, when we have repeated, mother, you know what we may do then with our afternoon bread. You know, mother, what you promised yesterday."

Mother. "I shall be very glad to hear whether you can say what you have learned."

Chil. "But then we may do it afterward, mother! may we not?"

Mother. "Yes, if you are perfect."

The children were in great delight, and immediately repeated what they had learned, very perfectly.

Then the mother gave them their pieces of bread and two bowls of milk, from which she had not taken the cream, because it was Sunday.

She then took the baby in her arms, and rejoiced in her heart to hear the children laying their plans, and telling each other how they would give their bread. Not one of them ate a mouthful of it, not one of them dipped a morsel into the milk, but each rejoiced over his piece, showed it to the others, and maintained that it was the largest share.

The milk was soon finished, but the bread was all lying by the mother. Nicholas crept up to her, took her hand, and said: "You will give me a piece of bread for myself too, mother?"

Mother. "Thou hast got it already, Nicholas."

Nicholas. "Yes; but that is what I must give to Rudeli."

Mother. "I did not bid thee give it to him; thou mayst eat it thyself, if thou wilt."

Nich. "No, I will not eat it; but will you not give me another piece for myself, mother?"

Mother. "No, certainly not."

Nich. "Why not, mother?"

Mother. "That thou mayst not fancy that people should begin to think of the poor, only when they are satisfied, and have eaten as much as they can."

Nich. "Is that the reason, mother?"

Mother. "Wilt thou now give him the whole?"

Nich. "O, yes, to be sure I will, mother. I know he is terribly hungry, and we shall eat again at six o'clock."

Mother. "And, Nicholas, I think Rudeli will get nothing then."

Nich. "No, indeed, mother; he will have no supper."

Mother. "The want of those poor children is great indeed, and one must be very hard and cruel not to spare, whatever one can, from one's own food, to relieve them in their distress."

Tears came into the eyes of Nicholas. The mother then turned to the other children: "Lise, dost thou mean to give away all thy piece?"

Lise. "Yes, certainly, mother."

Mother. "And thou too, Enne?"

Enne. "Yes, mother."

Mother. "And thou too, Jonas?"

Jonas. "I think so, mother."

Mother. "I am glad of it, my children. But how will you set about it? Every thing should be done in the right way, and people who mean very well, often manage very ill. Tell me, Nicholas, how wilt thou give thy bread?"

Nich. "I will run, as fast as I can, and call him, Rudeli, I mean; but I will not put it into my pocket, that I may give it him sooner. Let me go now, mother."

Mother. "Stop a moment, Nicholas. And how wilt thou manage, Lise?"

Lise. "I will not do like Nicholas. I will beckon Betheli into a corner; I will hide the bread under my apron, and I will give it her, so that nobody may see it, not even her father."

Mother. "And what wilt thou do, Enne?"

Enne. "I do n't know where I shall meet with Heireli: I will give it as I find best at the time."

Mother. "And thou, Jonas! Thou hast some trick in thy head, little rogue. How wilt thou do?"

Jonas. "I will stick my bread into his mouth as you do, mother, when you are playing with me. I shall say to him: Open your mouth and shut your eyes, and then I shall put it between his teeth. I am sure he will laugh then, mother."

Mother. "Very well, my children. But I must tell you one thing. You must give the children the bread quietly, and so as not to be observed; lest people should think you fancy you are doing a very fine thing."

Nich. "Potz tausend, mother! then I had better put the bread into my pocket, after all."

Mother. "I think so, Nicholas."

Lise. "I thought of that before, mother; and that was the reason why I said I should not do like him."

Mother. "Thou art always the cleverest, Lise. I ought not to have forgotten to praise thee for it, and thou dost well to remind me of it."

Lise blushed and was silent, and the mother said to the children: "You may go now, but remember what I have said to you." The children went.

Nicholas ran and leaped, as fast as he could, down to Rudi's house, but Rudeli was not in the street. Nicholas shouted, and whistled, and called, but in vain; he did not come out, even to the window. Then said Nicholas to himself: "What must I do now? Must I go into the house to him? But I must give it him alone. I will go and tell him to come out into the street."

Rudeli was sitting with his father and sisters by the open coffin of his dear grandmother, who was to be buried in two hours; and the father and his children were talking, with tears in their eyes, of the kindness and love which she had always shown them. They wept over her last trouble about the potatoes, and promised again, as they looked at her, that, however hungry they might be, they would never steal from any body.

At this moment Nicholas opened the door, saw the dead body, was frightened, and ran out of the house again.

Rudi, who thought he might have some message to him from Leonard, went after the boy, and asked what he wanted. "Nothing, nothing," answered Nicholas, "only I wanted to speak to Rudeli, but he is at his prayers."

Rudi. "You may come in, if you want him."

Nich. "Let him come here to me for a moment."

Rudi. "It is so cold, and he does not like to leave his grandmother. Come into the house to him."

Nich. "I can not go in, Rudi. Let him come to me for a moment."

"Well then, he shall," answered Rudi, and went back into the house.

Nicholas followed him to the door, and called: "Rudeli, come here just for one moment."

Rudeli. "I can not come into the street, Nicholas! I would rather stay with my grandmother. They will soon take her away from us."

Nich. "It is but for a moment."

Rudi. "Go and see what he wants."

Rudeli went out, and Nicholas took him by the arm, and saying: "Come here, I have something to say to you," led him into a corner, thrust the bread quickly into his pocket, and ran away.

Rudeli thanked him, and called after him: "Thank your father and your mother too."

Nicholas turned round, made a sign to him, with his hand, to be quiet, said: "Do n't tell any body," and went off again like an arrow.

CHAPTER L.—CONCEIT AND BAD HABITS INTERFERE WITH OUR HAPPINESS, EVEN WHEN WE ARE DOING A KIND ACTION.

LISE, in the meantime, walked deliberately to the higher village, to Betheli, Marx Reuti's daughter. She was standing at the window.

Lise beckoned to her, and Betheli crept out of the house. But her father, who observed it, followed her, and hid himself behind the door.

The children thought not of him, and chattered away to their hearts' content.

Lise. "Betheli, I have brought you some bread."

Betheli. (Shivering, and stretching out her hand.) "You are very kind, Lise; and I am very hungry. But why do you bring me bread to-day?"

Lise. "Because I like you, Betheli. We have now bread enough. My father is to build the church."

Beth. "And so is mine, too."

Lise. "Yes; but your father is only a day-laborer."

Beth. "It is all the same thing, if it brings us bread."

Lise. "Have you been very ill off?"

Beth. "O! I do hope we shall do better now."

Lise. "What have you had for dinner?"

Beth. "I dare not tell you."

Lise. "Why not?"

Beth. "If my father were to find it out, he would—"

Lise. "I shall never tell him."

Betheli took a piece of a raw turnip out of her pocket, and said: "See here."

Lise. "Goodness! nothing better than that?"

Beth. "We have had nothing better this two days."

Lise. "And you must not tell any body; nor ask any body for any thing—"

Beth. "If he only knew I had told you, it would be a pretty business for me."

Lise. "Well, eat the bread before you go in again."

Beth. "Yes, that I will, or I shall not get it."

She began to eat, and at that moment Marx opened the door, and said: "What art thou eating, my child?"

His child gulped and swallowed down the unchewed mouthful, and said: "Nothing, nothing, father."

Marx. "Nothing was it? but stop a moment! Lise, I do n't like people to give my children bread, behind my back, for telling them such godless lies about what is eaten and drunk in the house. Thou godless Betheli! dost thou not know that we had a chicken for dinner to-day?"

Lise now walked off as fast, as she had come deliberately.

But Marx took Betheli by the arm, and dragged her into the house, and Lise heard her crying bitterly, even when she was a great way off.

Enne met Heireli in the door-way of his own house, and said: "Would you like a piece of bread?"

Heireli. "Yes, if you have any for me." Enne gave it him; he thanked her, and she went away again.

Jonas crept about Shaben Michel's house, till Robert saw him, and came out. "What are you after, Jonas?" said Robert.

Jonas. "I want to have some play."

Robert. "Well, I will play with you, Jonas."

Jonas. "Will you do what I tell you, Robert? and then we shall have some sport."

Robt. "What do you want me to do?"

Jonas. "You must shut your eyes, and open your mouth."

Robt. "Ay, but perhaps you will put something dirty into my mouth."

Jonas. "No, I promise you, faithfully, I will not, Robert."

Robt. "Well—but look to it if you cheat me, Jonas!" (He opened his mouth, and half shut his eyes.)

Jonas. "You must shut your eyes quite close, or it will not do."

Robt. "Yes! but if you should prove a rogue, Jonas;" said Robert, shutting his eyes quite close.

Jonas popped the bread into his mouth directly, and ran off.

Robert took the bread out of his mouth, and said: "This is good sport, indeed," and sat down to eat it.

CHAPTER LI.—NO MAN CAN TELL WHAT HAPPY CONSEQUENCES MAY RESULT FROM EVEN THE MOST TRIFLING GOOD ACTION.

SHABEN MICHEL saw the sport of the children from the window, and knew Jonas, Leonard's son, and it struck him to the heart.

"What a Satan I am!" said he to himself. "I have sold myself to the bailiff, to betray the man who provides me with work and food, and now I must see that even this little fellow has the heart of an angel. I will not do any thing to injure these people. Since yesterday, the bailiff has been an abomination to me. I can not forget his look when he gave me the cup!" So said the man, and he remained at home the rest of the evening, thinking over his past conduct.

Leonard's children were now all returned, and told their father and mother how they had gone on, and were very merry—all except Lise, who tried, nevertheless, to look like the rest, and said a great deal about Betheli's delight when she received the bread.

"I am sure something has happened to thee," said Gertrude.

"O, no, nothing has happened; and she was very glad, indeed, to have it," answered Lise.

Her mother inquired no further, but prayed with her children, gave them their suppers, and put them to bed.

Afterward Leonard and Gertrude read for an hour in the Bible, and talked about what they had read, and passed a very happy Sunday evening together.

CHAPTER LII.—EARLY IN THE MORNING IS TOO LATE FOR WHAT OUGHT TO BE DONE THE EVENING BEFORE.

VERY early in the morning, as soon as the mason awoke, he heard some one calling to him, in the front of the house, and got up immediately, and opened the door.

It was Flink, the huntsman, from the hall. He wished the mason good morning, and said: "Mason, I should have told thee, last night, to set the men to work this morning without delay, at breaking stone."

Mason. "From what I hear, the bailiff has told all the workmen to go to the hall this morning. But it is early yet, they can scarcely be set out, and I will tell them."

He called to Lenk, who lived next door, but got no answer.

After some time, Keller, who lodged in the same house, came out, and said: 'Lenk went half an hour ago to the hall, with the rest of the men. The bailiff told them last night, after supper, that they must, without fail, be at the hall betimes, as he had to be at home again by noon."

The huntsman was very uneasy at the intelligence, and said: "This is a cursed business!" "But what must be done?" said the mason.

Flink. "Is there any chance of overtaking them?"

Mason. "From Marti's hill thou mayst see them a mile and a half off; and, if the wind be fair, thou mayst call them back so far."

Flink made no delay, but ran quickly up the hill, called, whistled, and shouted with all his might, but in vain. They did not hear him, but went their way, and were soon out of sight.

The bailiff, who was not so far off, heard him call from the hill, and looked out. The huntsman's gun glittered in the sun, so that the bailiff recognized him, and wondered what the man wanted, and went back to meet him.

Flink told him that he had had a terrible headache the day before, and had delayed going, to tell the mason to set the men to work to break stone the first thing this morning.

CHAPTER LIII.—THE MORE CULPABLE A MAN IS HIMSELF, THE MORE VIOLENTLY DOES HE ABUSE ANOTHER WHO HAS DONE WRONG.

"THOU cursed knave! what a trick thou hast played now!" said the bailiff.

Flink. "Perhaps it will not turn out so ill. How the deuce could I tell that the fellows would all run off to the hall before daybreak! Was it by your orders?"

Bailiff. "Yes, it was, thou dog; and I suppose I shall now have to answer for thy fault."

Flink. "I wish I may come clear off myself."

Bailiff. "It is a cursed—"

Flink. "That was the very word I used myself, when I heard they were gone."

Bailiff. "I want no nonsense now, knave."

Flink. "Nor I neither; but what is to be done?"

Bailiff. "You fool, think."

Flink. "It is half an hour too late for my brains to discover any."

Bailiff. "Stop—one must never despair! A thought strikes me. Maintain boldly that thou gavest the order last night to the mason's wife, or to one of his children. They will not out-talk thee, if thou art resolute."

Flink. "I will not try that plan. It may miss."

Bailiff. "Nay, it could not miss, if thou wert steady. But, upon second thoughts, I have hit upon another which is better."

Flink. "What 's that?"

Bailiff. "Thou must run back to the mason, and lament and grieve over it; and tell him, it may be a great loss to thee to have neglected the order; but that he may get thee out of trouble by speaking one word for thee, and telling the squire that he received his note on the Sunday; and, by mistake, as it was the Sabbath, had not opened it till to-day.

"This will not hurt him in the least, and will get thee out of the scrape, if thou canst persuade him to do it."

Flink. "You are right there, and I think it will do."

Bailiff. "It can not miss."

Flink. "I must go now. I have other letters to take, but I will return some time this morning to the mason. Good-by, Bailiff."

When the bailiff was left alone, he said: "I will go now and give this account at the hall. If it does not agree, I will say it is what the huntsman told me."

CHAPTER LIV.—USELESS LABOR FOR POOR PEOPLE.

IN the meantime, the day-laborers arrived at the hall, sat down on the benches near the door, and waited till they were summoned, or till the bailiff, who had promised to follow them, should arrive.

When the squire's footman saw the men at the door, he went down to them, and said: "What are you here for, neighbors? My master thinks you are at work at the building."

The men answered: "The bailiff told us to come here to thank the squire for giving us the work."

"That was not necessary," answered Claus. "He will not keep you long for that; but I will tell him you are here."

The footman told his master, and the squire ordered the men to come in, and asked them, kindly, what they wanted.

When they had told him, and, awkwardly and with difficulty, stammered out something of thanks, the squire said: "Who told you to come here on this account?"

"The bailiff," replied the men, and again attempted to give him thanks.

"This has happened against my wish," said Arner. "But go away now, and be diligent and faithful, and I shall be glad if the work is of use to any of you. And tell your master that you must begin to break the stone to-day."

Then the men went home again.

CHAPTER LV.—A HYPOCRITE MAKES FRIENDS WITH A ROGUE.

AND as they returned, one of the men said to the others: "This young squire is a very kind-hearted man."

"And so would the old one have been too, if he had not been imposed upon, in a thousand ways," said the old men with one voice.

"My father has told me, a hundred times, that he was very well inclined in his youth, and would have continued so, if he had not been so infatuated by the bailiff," said Abi.

"And then it was all over with the squire's kindness. It dropped only into the bailiff's chest, and he led him about, as he chose, like a great Polar bear," said Leemann.

"What a shameful trick he has played us now, to send us all this way without orders, and then leave us to get out of the scrape ourselves," said Lenk.

"That is always his way," said Kienast.

"And a villainous way it is," answered Lenk.

"Yes, but the bailiff is a worthy man! People like us can not always judge of the reasons for such things," answered Kriecher, in a raised tone; for he saw the bailiff creeping along the hollow, and very near them.

"The devil! thou mayest praise him if thou wilt, but I will praise the squire for the future," said Lenk, almost as loudly; for he did not see the bailiff below.

The latter now, as he was speaking, came up out of the hollow, wished them good morning, and then said to Lenk: "And why art thou praising the squire at this rate?"

Lenk answered, in some confusion: "Because we were talking together about his being so good-natured and kind to us."

"But that was not all," answered the bailiff.

"I know of nothing more," said Lenk.

"It is not right for a man to take back his words in that way, Lenk," said Kriecher, and continued: "He was not alone in what he said, Mr. Bailiff. Some of the others were murmuring that you had left them in such a way, and I was saying that such as we could not judge of your reasons; and upon this, Lenk said: 'I might praise the bailiff if I would, but that he would praise the squire for the future.'"

"Aye, indeed! and so thou wert comparing the squire with me," said the bailiff, sneeringly.

"But he did not mean it, as it is now represented," said some of the men, shaking their heads, and murmuring against Kriecher.

"There is no need of any explanation and no harm done. It is an old proverb, Whose bread I eat, his praise I sing," said the bailiff, and shaking Kriecher by the hand, he said no more upon the subject, but asked the men whether Arner had been angry.

"No;" answered the men, "not at all. He only said, we must go home again, and without fail begin the work to-day."

"Tell the mason so, and that the mistake is of no consequence—my respects to him," said the bailiff, and proceeded on his way; as did the men.

Some time before this, the huntsman had been to the mason, and begged and entreated him to say that he had received the note on the Sunday.

The mason was willing to oblige the bailiff and the huntsman, and mentioned it to his wife.

"I am afraid of every thing which is not straight-forward," said she, "and I dare say the bailiff has already made his own excuse. If the squire asks thee, I think thou must tell him the truth; but perhaps he will not inquire any thing more about it; and then thou canst leave it as it is, that nobody may be brought into trouble." Leonard accordingly told the huntsman that he would do this.

In the mean time the men returned from the hall.

"You are soon back again," said the mason.

"We might have spared our labor altogether;" replied they.

Leonard. "Was he angry about the mistake?"

Men. "No, not at all! He was very friendly and kind, and told us to go back and begin the work to-day.

Flink. "You see it will be of no consequence to you. It is a very different thing for me and the bailiff."

"O, but the bailiff's message; we had nearly forgotton it," said Hubel Rudi; "he sent his respects to thee, and the mistake was of no consequence."

Leon. "Had he been with the squire, when you met him?"

Men. "No; we met him on his way."

Leon. "Then he knew no more than what you told him, and what I now know myself?"

Men. "No! to be sure he did not."

Flink. "You will keep your promise, mason?"

Leon. "Yes, but exactly as I told you."

The mason then ordered the men to be at their work early, prepared some tools, and, after he had got his dinner, went with the men, for the first time, to the work.

"May God Almighty grant his blessing upon it," said Gertrude, as he went out.

Chapter LVI.—It is decided that the bailiff must no longer be a landlord.

When the bailiff came to the hall, Arner kept him waiting some time. At last he came out of the avenue and asked him, with some displeasure: "What is the meaning of this? Why did you send all these people to the hall to-day, without orders?"

"I thought it was my duty to advise them to thank your honor for your goodness," answered the bailiff.

Arner replied, "Your duty is to do what is useful to me and to my people, and what I order you, but not to send poor folks all this way for nothing, to teach them to make fine speeches, which are of no use, and which I do not seek for. But the reason why I sent for you, was to tell you, that I will no longer have the situation of bailiff and landlord filled by the same person."

The bailiff turned pale, trembled, and knew not what to reply; for he was quite unprepared for such a sudden resolution.

Arner continued, "I will leave you to choose which of the two you prefer; but in a fortnight I must know your determination."

The bailiff had somewhat recovered himself again, and stammered out some thanks for the time allowed him to think of it. Arner replied, "I should be sorry to be hasty with any body, and I do not wish to oppress you, old man. But the two offices are incompatible with each other."

This kindness of Arner encouraged the bailiff. He answered, "Till now all the bailiffs in your employ have kept tavern, and it is a common practice throughout the country."

But Arner answered him shortly, and said: "You have heard my decision." He then took out his almanac, and said again, "This is the 20th of March, and in a fortnight it will be the 3d of April; therefore, upon the 3d of April, I expect your answer. Till then, I have no more to say." Arner then marked down the day in his almanac, and went into the house.

Chapter LVII.—His conduct upon the occasion.

Anxious and troubled at heart, the bailiff also departed. This blow had so much overcome him, that he took no notice of any of the people he met on his way down the steps, and through the avenue; and he scarcely knew where he was, till he came to the old nut-tree. There he stopped, and said to himself, "I must take breath. How my heart beats! I don't know whether I stand on my head or my feet. Without making a single complaint, without making any inquiry, merely because it is his pleasure, I am either to give up being bailiff, or landlord. This is beyond all bounds. Can he compel me to it? I think not. He can not take away my bailiff's coat, without bringing some charge against me; and the landlord's license is paid for. But if he should try, if he should seek for open accusation, he may find as much as he will. Of all the damned fellows I have served, there is not one who would be true to me. What must I do, now! A fortnight is something, however; I have often done a great deal in that time. If I can only keep up my spirits! The mason is at the bottom of all this. If I can only ruin him, it will be every thing. I can manage all the rest. But how very faint and weak I am!" So saying, he took a brandy bottle out of his pocket, sat down in the shade of the tree, applied to his constant remedy, and swallowed down one draught after another. A thief or a murderer, who is pursued by a warrant, is not more refreshed by his first draught of water in a free land, than the bailiff's rancorous heart was encouraged by his brandy bottle. He felt himself better again immediately, and, with his strength, his wicked daring also revived. "This has refreshed me greatly," said he to himself. And he got up again, with the air of a bold man who bears himself loftily. "A little while ago," said he, "I thought they would eat me up for their supper, but now I feel once more as if I could crush the mason, and the fine young squire himself, with my little finger. It is well I did not leave the bottle behind me. I am a sad poor creature without it."

Thus reasoned the bailiff with himself. His fears had now entirely given place to anger, pride, and his brandy bottle.

He walked along once more, as insolently and as full of malice as usual.

He nodded to the people in the fields, who saluted him, with almost his wonted bailiff's pride. He carried his knotted stick in a commanding manner, as if he were of more importance in the country than ten Arners. He pursed up his mouth, and opened his eyes, as wide and round as a plough-wheel, as they say in this country. Thus did the blockhead behave at a time when he had so little cause for it.

Chapter LVIII.—His Companion.

By his side walked his great Turk; a dog who, at a word from the bailiff, showed his great white teeth and snarled at every body, but faithfully followed his master through life and death. This great Turk was as much the terror of all the poor folks around, as his master was of all his oppressed dependents and debtors. This powerful Turk walked majestically by the side of the bailiff—but I dare not utter what is at my tongue's end, only it is certain that the bailiff, who was in a furious rage, had something in the expression of his face which reminded one very much of the dog.

Chapter LIX.—Explanation of a Difficulty.

Perhaps some simple inquirer may wonder how the bailiff, after yesterday's trouble, and his fright this morning, could still bear himself so haughtily. An experienced man will see the reason at once. Pride never torments a man more, than when he is under a cloud. As long as all is prosperous, and nobody can doubt a man's greatness, he seldom thinks it necessary to look so very big. But when on all sides people begin to rejoice over his failures, it is no longer the same thing—then the blood gets heated, foams, and runs over like hot butter in a kettle, and this was exactly the bailiff's case. Moreover, it was very natural, and the most simple may understand it, that after he had recruited himself under the nut-tree, he should be able to conduct himself as haughtily as I have described. Besides this, he had slept better than usual the night before, on account of having taken his two powders, and drunk little, and his head, this morning, was quite cleared from the uneasiness and anxiety of the preceding day.

Chapter LX.—A Digression.

It would, indeed, have been better for the bailiff if he had broken his brandy bottle to atoms, under the nut-tree, and gone back to his master to explain to him his situation, and to tell him that he was not rich, and had need both of his office of bailiff, and of his tavern, on account of his debts, and entreat him to show compassion and mercy toward him. I am sure Arner would not have driven away the old man, if he had acted thus.

But such is always the ill fate of the ungodly. Their crimes deprive them of their reason, and they become, as it were, blind in their greatest difficulties, and act like madmen in their distress; whilst, on the contrary, good and honest men, who have pure and upright hearts, keep their senses much better in their misfortunes, and therefore generally know better how to help themselves, and how to act in all the chances of life.

They bear their misfortunes with humility, ask forgiveness for their faults, and in their necessity look up to that Power who always lends assistance in need to those who seek his help with pure hearts.

The peace of God, which passeth all understanding, is a protection and star to them, through life, and they always so pass through the world, as, in the end, to thank God from their hearts.

But the wickedness of the ungodly man leads him from one depth to another. He never uses his understanding in the straight paths of simplicity, to seek for repose, justice, and peace. He uses it only in the crooked way of wickedness, to create distress, and to bring about disturbance. Therefore he is always unhappy, and in his necessity becomes insolent.

He denies his faults, he is proud in his distress. He seeks to help and save himself either by hypocrisy and servility, or by force and cunning.

He trusts to his own misled and disordered understanding. He turns away from the hand of his father, which is stretched out toward him, and when his voice says: "Humble thyself! it is a father's hand which chastens and will help thee," he despises the voice of his deliverer, and says: "With my own hand, and with my own head, will I save myself." Therefore the end of the ungodly man is always utter misery and woe.

Chapter LXI.—An Old Man Lays Open His Heart.

I have been young, and now am old, and I have many times, and often, observed the ways of the pious, and of the ungodly. I have seen the boys of the village grow up with me. I have seen them become men, and bring up children and grand-children—and now have I accompanied all those of my own age, except seven, to the grave. O God! thou knowest the hour, when I too must follow my brethren! My strength decays, but my eyes are fixed upon the Lord! Our life is like a flower of the field, which in the morning springs up, and in the evening withers away. O Lord, our God! thou art merciful and gracious toward those who put their trust in thee—therefore does my soul hope in thee; but the way of the sinner leads to destruction. Children of my village, O listen to instruction. Hear what is the life of the ungodly, that you may become holy. I have seen children who were insolent to their parents, and heeded not their affection. All of them came to a bad end. I knew the father of the wretched Uli. I lived under the same roof with him; and saw, with my own eyes, how the godless son tormented and insulted his poor father. And as long as I live, I shall never forget how the old man wept over him, an hour before his death. I saw the wicked boy laugh at his funeral! Can God suffer such a wretch to live? thought I.

What followed? He married a woman who had a large property, and he was then one of the richest men of the village, and went about, in his pride and in his wickedness, as if there were none in heaven, or upon earth, above him.

A year passed over, and then I saw the proud Uli sorrow and lament at his wife's funeral. He was obliged to give back her property, to the last farthing, to her relations. He was suddenly become as poor as a beggar, and in his poverty he stole, and you know what was his end. Children, thus have I always seen that the end of the ungodly man is misery and woe.

But I have also seen the manifold blessings and comforts in the quiet cottages of the pious. They enjoy whatever they have; they are content if they have little, and sober if they have much.

Industry is in their hands, and peace in their hearts—such is their lot in life. They enjoy their own with gladness, and covet not what is their neighbors.

Pride never torments them, envy does not embitter their lives. Therefore they are always more cheerful and contented, and generally more healthy, than the ungodly. They go through the necessary evils of life more safely and peacefully; for their heads, and their hearts, are not turned to wickedness, but are with their work, and the beloved inmates of their own cottages. Therefore they enjoy life. Their heavenly Father looks down upon their cares and anxieties, and assists them.

Dear children of my native village! I have seen many pious men and women upon their death-beds, and I have never heard any—not a single one, amongst them all—complain, in that hour, of the poverty and hardships of life. All, without exception, thanked God for the thousand proofs of his paternal goodness, which they had enjoyed through life.

O my children! be then pious, and remain single-hearted and innocent. I have seen the consequences of sly and cunning habits.

Hummel and his associates were much more crafty than the rest. They knew a thousand tricks, of which the others never dreamed. This made them proud, and they thought that sincere men were only to be their fools. For a time they devoured the bread of the widow and of the orphan—they raged and were furious against all who would not bow down the knee to them. But their end is approaching. The Lord in heaven heard the sighs of the widow and of the orphan, and saw the tears of the mother, which she shed with her children, on account of the wicked men who led away and oppressed the husband and the father; and the Lord in heaven helped the oppressed ones and the orphans, when they had given up all hope of recovering their rights.

Chapter LXII.—The Horrors of an Uneasy Conscience.

On Saturday evening, when Hans Wust left the bailiff and went home, the pangs of perjury tormented him still more, so that he threw himself upon the ground and groaned in anguish.

Thus was he distracted the whole night, and on the following sabbath he tore his hair, struck his breast with his hands, violently, could neither eat nor drink, and called out: "O, O, this meadow of Rudi's! O, O, his meadow, his meadow! It tortures my very soul! O, O, Satan has got possession of me! O, woe is me! Woe to my miserable soul!"

Thus he wandered about, tormented and distracted by the thoughts of his perjury, and groaned in the bitter agony of his spirit.

Worn out with such dreadful sufferings, he at length, on Sunday evening, fell asleep for a time.

In the morning he was a little easier, and came to the resolution no longer to keep his sufferings to himself, but to tell all to the pastor.

He took his Sunday coat, and whatever else he could find, and fastened all together in a bundle, that he might borrow upon them the money he owed the bailiff.

He then took up the bundle, trembled, went to the pastor's house, stood still, was very near running away again, stood still once more, threw the bundle in at the door-way, and gestured like one out of his mind.

Chapter LXIII.—Kindness and Sympathy Save a Wretched Man from Becoming Utterly Distracted.

The pastor saw him in this situation, went to him, and said: "What is the matter, Wust? What dost thou want? Come into the house, if thou hast any thing to say to me."

Then Wust followed the pastor into his room.

And the pastor was as kind and friendly as possible to Wust; for he saw his confusion and distress, and had, the day before, heard a report that he was almost in despair on account of his perjury.

When Wust saw how kind and friendly the pastor was toward him, he recovered himself a little, by degrees, and said:—

"Honorable Herr Pastor! I believe I have sworn a false oath, and am almost in despair about it. I can not bear it any longer. I will willingly submit to all the punishment I have deserved, if I may only again hope in the mercy and goodness of God."

Chapter LXIV.—A Pastor's Treatment of a Case of Conscience.

The pastor answered: "If thou art truly grieved at heart, on account of thy fault, distrust not God's mercy."

Wust. "O sir, may I, may I ever, in this my crime, hope for God's mercy, that he will forgive me my sins?"

Pastor. "If God has brought a man to a true repentance of his sins, so that he earnestly longs and sighs after pardon, he has already pointed out to him the way to forgiveness, and to the obtaining of all spiritual mercies. Depend upon this, Wust! and if thy repentance be really from thy heart, doubt not that it will be acceptable in the sight of God."

Wust. "But can I know that it is acceptable to him?"

Pastor. "Thou mayest easily know, by faithfully examining thyself, whether it be really sincere, and from the bottom of thy heart; and if it be, it will certainly be acceptable to God. This is all I can say. But, Wust! if any one has encroached upon his neighbor's land, and repents of it, he goes, without his neighbor's knowledge or request, and, quietly and of his own accord, restores the land, and gives back rather more than less than what he had taken from him. In this case, we can not but be convinced that his repentance is sincere.

"But if he does not restore it, or only part of it, to him—if he gives it back unfairly—if he is only anxious not to be brought before a magistrate—if it is all for his own sake and not for the sake, of his neighbor whom he has injured —then are his repentance and his restoration only a cloak with which the foolish man cheats himself. Wust! if thou, in thy heart, seekest for nothing, but to amend and rectify all the mischief which thy wickedness has caused, and all the trouble which it has occasioned, and to obtain the forgiveness of God and man; if thou wishest for nothing else, and wilt willingly do and suffer any thing, to make all possible amends for thy fault; then is thy repentance certainly sincere, and there is no doubt that it will be acceptable to God."

Wust. "O, sir! I will most willingly do and suffer any thing whatever, upon God's earth, if this weight may only be removed from my heart. It is such a dreadful torment! Wherever I go, whatever I do, I tremble under this sin."

Pastor. "Fear not! Set about the business with sincerity and truth, and thou wilt certainly become easier."

Wust. "If I might only hope for that!"

Pastor. "Be not afraid! Trust in God! He is the God of the sinner who flies unto him. Only do all thou canst, with sincerity and uprightness. The greatest misfortune which has happened, in consequence of thy oath, is the situation of poor Rudi, who, owing to it, has fallen into grievous distress; but I hope the squire, when thou tellest him the whole affair, will himself take care that the man is comforted in his necessity."

Wust. "It is, indeed, poor Rudi, who is a continual weight upon my heart. Does your reverence think the squire will be able to help him to his meadow again?"

Pastor. "I don't know that. The bailiff will certainly do all in his power to throw suspicion upon thy present testimony. But, on the other hand, the squire will do his best, to help the unfortunate man to get his own again."

Wust. "O, if he can only accomplish that!"

Pastor. "I wish he may, with all my heart! and I hope he will—but, whatever may happen to Rudi, it is necessary that, for thine own sake and for thy peace of mind, thou shouldst tell the whole truth to the squire."

Wust. "I will willingly do that, your reverence."

Pastor. "It is the right way, and I am glad that thou dost it so willingly. It will bring back rest and peace to thy heart. But, at the same time, this acknowledgment will bring blame, and trouble, and imprisonment, and grievous distress upon thee."

Wust. "O, sir! all that is nothing in comparison of the horrors of despair, and the fear of never again obtaining the forgiving mercy of God."

Pastor. "Thou seest the thing so properly and sensibly, that I am glad at heart on thy account. Pray unto God, who has given thee so many good thoughts, and so much strength for good and right resolutions, that he will grant thee still further favor. Thou art now in an excellent way, and wilt, with God's assistance, bear with patience and humility whatever may await thee—and, whatever happens to thee, open thy heart to me. I will certainly never forsake thee."

Wust. "O, sir! how kind, how tender you are to such a wicked sinner!"

Pastor. "God himself is all love and forbearance in his dealings with us poor mortals, and I should indeed be a faithless servant to him, if I were cruel, and unfeeling, and severe to one of my own erring brethren, whatever might be his situation."

In this paternal manner did the pastor talk to Wust, who burst into tears, and for some time could not speak.

The pastor also remained silent.

Wust, at last, began again and said: "Please your reverence, I have one thing more to say."

Pastor. "What is it?"

Wust. "Since this affair, I have owed the bailiff eight florins. He said, the day before yesterday, that he would tear the note; but I will not receive any thing from him. I will pay it back to him."

Pastor. "Thou art right. Thou must certainly do that, and before thou speakest to Arner upon the subject."

Wust. "I have brought a bundle with me. It is my Sunday coat and some other things, which together are well worth eight florins. I must borrow this money, and I thought you would not be angry, if I were to beg you to lend it me, upon this pledge."

Pastor. "I never take security from any body, and I am obliged often to refuse such requests, sorry as I may be to do so; but in thy case I will not refuse."

Immediately he gave him the money, and said: "Take it directly to the bailiff, and carry thy bundle home with thee."

CHAPTER LXV.—THERE IS OFTEN A DELICACY IN THE POOREST PEOPLE, EVEN WHEN THEY ARE RECEIVING FAVORS FOR WHICH THEY HAVE ASKED.

WUST trembled when he received the money from the pastor, and said: "But I will certainly not take the bundle home, your reverence."

"Well then, I must send it after thee, if thou wilt not take it thyself," said the pastor, smiling.

Wust. "For heaven's sake, sir, keep the bundle; that you may be sure of your money."

Pastor. "I shall be sure of it any way, Wust! Don't trouble thyself about that, but think only of the much more important things thou hast to do. I will write to the squire to-day, and thou canst take the letter to him to-morrow."

Wust. I thank your reverence. But, for heaven's sake, keep the bundle. I dare not take the money else. I dare not, indeed!"

Pastor. "Say no more about it; but go directly to the bailiff, with the money, and come to me again to-morrow, at nine o'clock."

Then Wust went, relieved and comforted in his mind, from the pastor to the bailiff's house; and, as he was not at home, he gave the money to his wife. She said to him: "Where did you get so much money at once, Wust?" Downcast and briefly, Wust answered: "I have managed as well as I could. God be praised that you have it."

The bailiff's wife replied: "We never troubled you for it."

Wust. "I know that well enough, but it was no better for me on that account."

Bailiff's Wife. "You speak strangely, Wust! What is the matter with you? All seems not right with you."

Wust. "You will soon know more: but count the money, I must go."

The bailiff's wife counted the money, and said it was right.

Wust. "Well then, give it to your husband properly. Good-by."

Wife. "If it must be so, good-by, Wust."

CHAPTER LXVI.—A FORESTER WHO DOES NOT BELIEVE IN GHOSTS.

THE bailiff, in his way from the hall, called at the tavern at Hirzau, and sat there drinking and talking to the countrymen. He told them of the lawsuits he had gained, of his influence over the late squire; how he, and he alone, had kept the people in order under him; and how all was now confusion.

Then he gave his dog as much dinner as a hard-working man would eat, except the wine; and laughed at a poor fellow who sighed, as he saw the good meat and drink set before the dog. "Thou wouldst be glad enough to take it away from him," said he to the poor man; patted the dog, and talked, and drank, and boasted to the countrymen till evening.

Then came the old forester from the hall, and, as he went by, he called for a glass of wine; and the bailiff, who was never willingly alone for a moment, said to him: "We will go home together."

"If you are coming now," said the forester; "I must follow a track."

"This moment," answered the bailiff; asked first for his dog's reckoning and then for his own, paid both, gave the waiter his fee, and they went out together.

When they were alone on the road, the bailiff asked the forester if it were safe to go through the woods at night, on account of spirits.

Forester. "Why do you ask?"

Bailiff. "Only because I wonder how it is."

Forester. "You are an old fool then. To think of having been bailiff thirty years, and asking such a nonsensical question. You should be ashamed of yourself."

Bailiff. "No, by G—! About ghosts I never know what to think, whether to believe in them or not. And yet I never saw any."

Forester. "Come, as you ask so honestly, I will help you out of your wonder—but you will give me a bottle of wine for my information?"

Bailiff. "I will gladly give you two, if you can explain it."

Forester. "I have now been a forester forty years, and was brought up in the woods, by my father, ever since I was a boy of four years old. He was always talking to the countrymen, in taverns and at drinking bouts, about ghosts and horrible sights he saw in the woods—but he was only playing the fool with them. He went on very differently with me—I was to be a forester, and therefore must neither believe nor fear any such stuff. Therefore he took me by night, when there was neither moon nor stars, when it was very stormy, and on festivals and holy nights, into the woods. If he saw a fire, or an appearance of any kind, or heard a noise, I was obliged to run toward it with him, over shrubs, and stumps, and holes, and ditches, and to follow him over all cross roads, after the noise: and it was always gypsies, thieves, or beggars—and then he called out, with his terrible voice: 'Away rogues!' and though there were twenty or thirty of them, they always made off; and often left pots, and pans, and meat behind them, so that it was laughable to behold. Often indeed the noise was nothing but wild animals, which sometimes make a strange sound;

and decayed old trunks of trees will give out a light, and have an appearance which often frightens people, who dare not go up to them; and these are all the ghosts I ever in my life saw in the wood. But it always is, and will be, a part of my business to make my neighbors believe that it is well filled with spirits and devils: for, look ye, one grows old, and it is a comfort, on a dark night, not to have to turn out after the rascals."

CHAPTER LXVII.—A MAN WHO DESIRES TO REMOVE A LANDMARK, AND WOULD WILLINGLY DISBELIEVE IN THE EXISTENCE OF SPIRITS, BUT DARES NOT.

As the man was thus speaking, they came to the by-path, through which the forester went into the wood, and the bailiff, who was now left alone, reasoned thus with himself:—

"He has been a forester now for forty years, and has never seen a ghost, and does not believe in them, and I am a fool and believe in them, and dare not pass a quarter of an hour in the wood, to dig up a stone.

"The squire takes away my license from me, like a thief and a rogue, and that dog of a stone upon the hill is no true landmark: I will never believe it is; and, suppose it be, has he a better right to it than I have to my tavern?

"To take a man's property from him by violence in this way! Who but the devil could put such a thing into his head? And since he does not spare my house, I have no reason to spare his damned flint-stone. But I dare not touch it! By night I dare not go to the place, and by day I can not manage it, on account of the high-road." Thus he talked to himself, and came to Meyer's hill, which is near the village.

He saw the mason at work upon the great flint stones which lay around, for it was not yet six o'clock, and he was vexed in his soul to see it.

"Every thing I plan and contrive, fails me! They all play the rogue with me. Must I now go quietly past this damned Joseph, and not say a word to him? No, I can not do it! I can not go by him, without a word. I would rather wait here, till they go home."

He sat down, and soon afterward got up again: "I can not bear to sit here, looking at them. I will go to the other side of the hill. O, thou damned Joseph!" He went a few steps back, behind the hill, and sat down again.

CHAPTER LXVIII.—THE SETTING SUN AND A POOR LOST WRETCH.

THE sun was now setting, and its last beams fell upon the side of the hill, where he sat. The field around him, and all below the hill, were already in deep shade. The sun set in majesty and beauty, serenely and without a cloud; God's sun; and the bailiff, looking back, as the last rays fell upon him, said to himself, "It is going down;" and he fixed his eyes upon it, till it was lost behind the hill.

Now all was in shade, and night came on rapidly. Alas! shade, night, and darkness surround his heart! No sun shines there! Do what he would, the bailiff could not escape this thought. He shuddered and gnashed his teeth—instead of falling down in prayer to the Lord of heaven, who calls forth the sun again in his glory—instead of hoping in the Lord, who saves us out of the dust and out of darkness, he gnashed with his teeth! The village clock at that moment struck six, and the mason went home from his work. The bailiff followed him.

CHAPTER LXIX.—HOW A MAN SHOULD CONDUCT HIMSELF WHO WOULD PROSPER IN THE MANAGEMENT OF OTHERS.

THE mason had, during this first afternoon of their being together, gained the good-will of most of the laborers. He worked the whole time as hard as they did—himself lifted the heaviest stones, and stood in the mire, or in the water, where it was necessary, as much or more than any of them. As they were quite inexperienced in such labor, he showed them, kindly and patiently, the best way of doing every thing to advantage, and betrayed no impatience even toward the most awkward. He called no one an ox, or a fool; though he had provocation enough, a hundred times over. This patience and constant attention of the master, and his zeal in working himself, caused all to succeed extremely well.

CHAPTER LXX.—A MAN WHO IS A ROGUE AND THIEF BEHAVES HONORABLY, AND THE MASON'S WIFE SHOWS HER GOOD SENSE.

MICHEL, as being one of the stoutest and best workmen, was by the master's side the whole afternoon, and saw with what kindness and goodness he behaved even to the most stupid; and Michel, though a thief and a rogue, became fond of Leonard, on account of his fair and upright conduct, and resolved not to be the cause of any injury to this good and honest man.

But Kriecher and the pious Marx Reuti were not so well pleased, that he made no distinction amongst the people, but behaved well, even to the rogue Michel. Lenk, too, shook his head often, and said to himself: "He is but a simpleton! If he had taken people who could work, like me and my brother, he would not have had half so much trouble." But the greater number, whom he had kindly and patiently instructed in the work, thanked him from the bottom of their hearts, and some of them prayed for him to that God, who rewards and blesses the patience and kindness, which a man shows toward his weaker brethren.

Michel could no longer keep to himself the wicked engagement into which he had entered with the bailiff, on Saturday evening, and said to the master, as they returned: "I have something to tell you, and will go home with you."

"Well! come then," said Leonard.

So he went with the master into his cottage, and told him how the bailiff, on Saturday evening, had bribed him to treachery, and how he had received two crowns in hand for it. Leonard started, and Gertrude was horror-struck, at this account.

"It is dreadful!" said Leonard.

"Dreadful, indeed!" said Gertrude.

"But don't let it distress thee, Gertrude, I beg of thee."

"Be not at all disturbed about it, master," said Michel, "I will not lift a hand against you, depend upon that!"

Leonard. "I thank you, Michel! but I did not deserve this from the bailiff."

Michel. "He is a devil incarnate. Hell has no match for him, when he is furious and seeks for revenge."

Leon. "It makes one shudder to think of it."

Gertrude. "I am quite bewildered!"

Mich. "Don't be like children about it; all things have an end."

Ger. and *Leon.* "Yes; thanks be to God."

Mich. "You may have it just your own way. If you like, I will let the bailiff go on thinking I am still true to him, and to-morrow, or the next day, take some tools from the building and carry them to his house. Then do you go quickly to Arner, and get a search warrant to examine all houses, and begin with the bailiff's, and go directly into the further room, where you will be sure to find them; but mind, you must rush in, the very moment you have shown the warrant, or it will be all in vain. They will have warning and get the things out of your sight, through the window, or under the bed-clothes—and, if you are civil, and do not search for them, you will be in a fine situation. But, indeed, I almost think it would be better for you to send somebody else; you are not fit for such a job."

Leon. "No, Michel; this kind of work certainly will not suit me."

Mich. "It is all one. I will find somebody to manage it cleverly for you."

Ger. "Michel! I think we should thank God, that we have escaped from the danger which threatened us, and not be laying a snare for the bailiff, from revenge."

Mich. "He deserves what he will get. Never trouble your head about that."

Ger. "It is not our business to judge what he deserves, or does not deserve; but it is our business to practice no revenge, and it is the only right conduct for us to pursue in this case."

Mich. "I must confess that you are in the right, Gertrude. It is a great blessing to be able so to govern one's self. But you are right. He will meet with his reward, and it is best to keep entirely away from him, and have nothing to do with him. And so I will directly break with him, and take him back his two crowns. But just now, I have but a crown and a half!" He took it out of his pocket, counted it, and then said: "I don't know whether to take him the other half by itself, or wait for my week's wages on Saturday, when I can give it him altogether."

Leon. "It will be no inconvenience to me to advance you the half-crown now."

Mich. "Well, if you can do so, I shall be very glad to have done with the man to-day. I will take it to him, this very hour, as soon as I get it."

"Master! since yesterday's sacrament, it has been heavy at my heart, that I had promised him to do such wicked things; and, in the evening, came your Jonas, to give his afternoon bread to my child, and that made me repent still more of behaving so ill to you. I never knew you properly before, Leonard, and I have never had much to do with you; but to-day I saw you wishing to help every body kindly and patiently, and I thought I could never die in peace, if I were to reward such an honest, good man with treachery. (The tears came into his eyes.) See, now, whether I am in earnest or not."

Leon. "Then never do an injury to any man again."

Mich. "With God's help, I will follow your example."

Ger. "You will certainly be a happier man if you do."

Leon. "Do you wish to go to the bailiff this evening?"

Mich. "Yes, if I can."

The mason gave him the half-crown and said: "Do not put him into a passion."

Ger. "And don't tell him that we know any thing about it."

Mich. "I will be as short as I can; but I will go this moment, and then it will be done with. Good-by, Gertrude! I thank you, Leonard! Good night."

Leon. "Good-by, Michel." He went away.

Chapter LXXI.—The Catastrophe Draws Near.

When the bailiff arrived at home, he found only his wife in the house; and therefore was able, at last, to give vent to all the rage and anger which had been rising in him throughout the day.

At the hall, at Hirzau, and in the fields, it was a different thing. A man like him is not willing to lay open his heart to others.

It will be said: a bailiff who should do so would, indeed, be as simple as a shepherd's lad; and Hummel was never accused of this. He could, for days together, smother his rage, envy, hatred, and vexation, and keep laughing, and talking, and drinking; but when he came home, and, by good or ill-luck, found the house empty, then the rage which he had before concealed, burst forth fearfully.

His wife was crying in a corner, and said: "For heaven's sake, do not go on in this way. This violence of thine will only drive Arner still further. He will not rest till thou art quiet."

"He will not rest, do what I will! He will never rest, till he has ruined me. He is a rogue, a thief, and a dog. The most cursed of all the cursed," said the man.

Wife "Do not talk in such a shocking way. Thou wilt go out of thy mind."

Bailiff. "Have I not cause? Dost thou not know that he will take my license or my bailiff's coat from me in a fortnight?"

Wife. "I know it; but, for heaven's sake, do not go on at this rate. The whole village knows it already. The secretary told the attorney, who has published it every where. I did not know it till tea-time this evening. All the people were laughing and talking on both sides of the street about it; and Margaret, who was at tea with me, took me aside, and told me the bad news. And, besides this, Hans Wust has brought back the eight florins. How comes he by eight florins? Arner must be at the bottom of it. Alas! a storm threatens us on every side!" So said the wife.

The bailiff started, as if he had felt a thunder-bolt, at the words "Hans Wust has brought back the eight florins!" He stood still for a time, staring at his wife, with open mouth—and then said: "Where is the money?—where are these eight florins?"

His wife set the money on the table, in a broken ale-glass. The bailiff fixed his eyes for some time upon it, without counting it, and then said: "It is not from the hall! The squire never pays any body in this coin."

Wife. "I am very glad it is not from the hall."

Bailiff. "There is something more in this. Thou shouldst not have taken it from him."

Wife. "Why not?"

Bailiff. "I could have got to know from whom he had it."

Wife. "I did think of that; but he would not wait; and I do not think thou couldst have got any thing out of him. He was as short and close as possible."

Bailiff. "All comes upon me at once. I know not what I am doing!—give me something to drink!" She set it before him, and he paced up and down the room in a frenzy—drank and talked to himself. "I will ruin the mason! That is the first thing to be done—if it cost me a hundred crowns. Michel must ruin him, and then I will go after the landmark." Thus he spoke; and, at that moment, Michel knocked at the door. The bailiff started in a fright, said: "Who can be here so late at night?" and went to look through the window.

"Open the door, bailiff," called out Michel.

Chapter LXXII.—His last hope forsakes the bailiff.

"He comes just at the right moment," said the bailiff, as he opened the door. "Welcome, Michel! What good news dost thou bring?"

Michel. "Not much. I only want to tell you—"

Bailiff. "Don't talk outside the door, man. I shall not go to bed for some time. Come into the room."

Mich. "I must go home again. I only want to tell you, that I have changed my mind about Saturday's business."

Bailiff. "Ay, by G—! that would be complete! No! thou must not change thy mind. If it is not enough, I will give thee more—but come into the room. We are sure to agree about it."

Mich. "At no price, bailiff. There are your two crowns."

Bailiff. "I will not receive them from thee, Michel! Don't play the fool with me. It can not hurt thee; and, if the two crowns are too little, come into my room."

Mich. "I will not listen to another word about it, bailiff. There is your money."

Bailiff. "By G—, I will not receive it from thee, in this way. I have sworn it, so come into the room."

Mich. "Well, I can do that. There; now I am in the room, and here is your money," said he, laying it upon the table; "and now good-by, bailiff!" and therewith he turned about, and away he went.

Chapter LXXIII.—He sets about removing the landmark.

The bailiff stood for a while, stock-still and speechless, rolled about his eyes, foamed with fury, trembled, stamped, and then called out: "Wife, give me the brandy. It must be done. I will go!"

Wife. "Whither wilt thou go, this dark night?

Bailiff. "I am going—I am going to dig up the stone—give me the bottle."

Wife. "For God's sake, do not attempt it."

Bailiff. "It must be done!—I tell thee I will go."

Wife. "It is as dark as pitch, and near midnight; and this week before Easter, the devil has most power."

Bailiff. "If he has got the horse, let him e'en take the bridle too. Give me the bottle. I will go."

He took a pickaxe, a shovel, and a mattock, upon his shoulder, and went, in the darkness of the night, up the hill, to take away his master's landmark.

Drunkenness, and revenge, and rage, emboldened him; but when he saw a piece of shining wood, or heard a hare rustling along, he trembled, stopped for a moment, and then went raging on, till at last he came to the landmark—set to work directly, and hacked and shoveled away, with all his might.

Chapter LXXIV.—Night greatly deceives drunkards and rogues, especially when they are in trouble.

Suddenly a noise startled him, and, looking up, he saw a black man coming toward him. A light shone about the man in the dark night, and fire burned upon his head. "This is the devil incarnate!" said the bailiff. And he ran away, screaming horribly, and leaving behind him mattock, pickaxe, and shovel, with his hat and the empty brandy bottle,

It was Christopher, the poulterer of Arnheim, who had been buying eggs at Oberhofen, Lunkofen, Hirzau, and other places, and was now on his way homeward. He had covered his basket with the skin of a black goat, and had hung a lantern from it, that he might find his way in the dark. This egg-carrier knew the voice of the bailiff, as he was running away; and, as he suspected that he was about some evil deed, he grew angry, and said to himself: "I will give the cursed knave his due for once. He thinks I am the devil."

Then quickly setting down his basket, he took up the mattock, pickax, and shovel, and his own iron-bound walking-stick, fastened them all together, dragged them behind him over the stony road, so that they rattled fearfully, and ran after the bailiff, crying out, with a hollow, dismal voice: "Oh!—Ah—Uh!—Hummel! Oh!—Ah!—Uh!—thou art mine—sto—op!—Hummel!"

The poor bailiff ran as fast as he could, and cried out pitifully, as he ran: "Murder! help! watchman! the devil is catching me!"

And the poulterer kept shouting after him: "Oh!—Ah!—Uh! bai—liff—sto—op—bailiff! thou art—mine!—bailiff."

Chapter LXXV.—The village is in an uproar.

The watchman in the village heard the running and shouting upon the hill, and could distinguish every word; but he was afraid, and knocked at some neighbors' windows.

"Get up, neighbors!" said he, "and hear what is going on upon the hill. It sounds as if the devil had got hold of the bailiff. Hark! how he shouts murder! and help! And yet, God knows, he is at home with his wife. It is not two hours since I saw him through the window."

When about ten of them were assembled, they declared they would go altogether, with torches, and well armed, toward the noise; but that they would carry with them, in their pockets, new bread, a testament, and psalter, that the devil might not prevail against them.

The men accordingly went, but stopped first at the bailiff's house, to see whether he were at home.

The bailiff's wife was waiting in deadly fear, wondering how he might be going on upon the hill, and when she heard the uproar in the night, and that men with torches were knocking at the door, she was dreadfully frightened, and called out: "Lord Jesus! what do you want?"

"Tell your husband to come to us," said the men.

"He is not at home; but do tell me what is the matter? Why are you here?" said the woman.

The men answered: "It is a bad business if he is not at home. Hark! how he is crying murder! help! as if the devil were taking him."

The wife now ran out with the men, as if she had been beside herself.

The watchman asked her, by the way: "What the devil is your husband doing now upon the hill? He was at home two hours ago."

She answered him not a word, but screamed terribly.

And the bailiff's dog growled, at its chain's length.

When the poulterer saw the people coming to help the bailiff, and heard his dog bark so fearfully, he turned round, and went, as quickly and quietly as he could, up the hill again to his basket, packed up his booty, and pursued his way.

Kunz, however, who, with the bailiff's wife, was a few steps before the rest, saw that it could not be the devil; and taking the roaring bailiff rather roughly by the arm, said to him: "What is the matter? why dost thou go on in this way?"

"Oh—Oh—let me alone—O—devil! let me alone!" said the bailiff, who in his terror could neither see nor hear.

"Thou fool, I am Kunz, thy neighbor; and this is thy wife," said the man.

The others first looked very carefully, to see whether the devil were any where about; and those who had torches, held them up and down, to examine carefully above and below, and on every side; and each man put his hand into his pocket to feel for the new bread, the testament, and psalter.

But as they still saw nothing, they began to take courage by degrees, and some grew bold enough to say to the bailiff: "Has the devil scratched thee with his claws, or trodden thee under his feet, that thou art bleeding in this manner?"

The others exclaimed: "This is no time for joking! we all heard the horrible voice."

But Kunz said: "I suspect that a poacher or a woodman has tricked the bailiff and all of us. As I came near him, the noise ceased, and a man ran up the hill as fast as he could. I have repented ever since, that I did not run after him; and we were fools for not bringing the bailiff's dog with us."

"Thou art a fool thyself, Kunz! That was certainly no man's voice. It ran through bone and marrow, and a wagon load of iron does not rattle over the streets as it rattled."

"I will not contradict you, neighbors! I shuddered as I heard it. But yet I shall never be persuaded that I did not hear somebody run up the hill."

"Dost thou think that the devil can not run so that one may hear him?" said the men.

The bailiff heard not a word of what they were saying; and, when he got home, he asked the men to stay with him that night, and they willingly remained in the tavern.

Chapter LXXVI.—The Pastor Comes to the Tavern.

In the mean time, the nightly uproar had roused the whole village. Even in the parsonage-house, they were all awake; for they anticipated some evil tidings.

When the pastor inquired what was the cause of the noise, he heard fearful accounts of the horrible adventure.

And the pastor thought he could, perhaps, turn the bailiff's fright (foolish as its cause might be,) to a good use.

He therefore went that night to the tavern.

Quick as lightning, vanished the wine jug as he entered.

The men stood up and said: "Welcome, honorable Herr Pastor!"

The pastor thanked them, and said to the neighbors: "It is a credit to you to be so ready and active when a misfortune happens. But will you now leave me alone with the bailiff, for a short time?"

"It is our duty to do as your reverence pleases. We wish you good-night."

Pastor. "The same to you, neighbors! but I must also beg that you will be careful what you relate about this business. It is very disagreeable to have made a great noise about a thing which afterward proves nothing at all, or something very different from what was expected. So far, nobody knows any thing about what has happened; and you know, neighbors, night is very deceitful."

"It is so, your reverence!" said the men, as they left the room; "and a great fool he always is, and will believe nothing!" added they, when they were outside of the door.

CHAPTER LXXVII.—CARE OF SOULS.

THE pastor began at once: "Bailiff! I have heard that something has happened to thee, and I am come to help and comfort thee, as far as I am able. Tell me honestly what has really happened."

Bailiff. "I am a poor unfortunate wretch, and Satan tried to get hold of me."

Pastor. "How so, bailiff? where did this happen?"

Bailiff. "Upon the hill, above."

Pastor. "Didst thou really see any body? Did any body touch thee?"

Bailiff. "I saw him as he ran after me. He was a great black man, and had fire upon his head. He ran after me to the bottom of the hill."

Pastor. "Why does thy head bleed?"

Bailiff. "I fell down as I was running."

Pastor. "Then nobody laid hold of thee?"

Bailiff. "No! but I saw him with my own eyes."

Pastor. "Well, bailiff, we will say no more about that. I can not understand how it really was. But be it what it may, it makes little difference. For, bailiff, there is an eternity when, without any doubt, the ungodly will fall into his hands; and the thoughts of this eternity, and of the danger of falling into his hands after thy death, must make thee anxious and uneasy in thy old age, and during thy life."

Bailiff. "O, sir! I know not what to do for anxiety and uneasiness. For heaven's sake, what can I do, what must I do, to get out of his hands? Am I not already entirely in his power?"

Pastor. "Bailiff! do not plague thyself with idle and foolish talking. Thou hast sense and understanding, and therefore art in thine own power. Do what is right, and what thy conscience tells thee is thy duty to God and man, and thou wilt soon see that the devil has no power over thee."

Bailiff. "O, sir! what must I do to obtain God's mercy?"

Pastor. "Thou must sincerely repent of thy faults, amend thy ways, and give back thy unrighteous possessions."

Bailiff. "People say I am rich, your reverence! but heaven knows I am not so."

Pastor. "That makes no difference. Thou keepest possession of Rudi's meadow unjustly, and Wust and Keibacher have sworn falsely. I know it, and I will not rest till Rudi has got his own again."

Bailiff. "O, sir! for heaven's sake, have compassion upon me."

Pastor. "The best compassion any one can show thee, is this: to persuade thee to do thy duty to God and man."

Bailiff. "I will do whatever you wish, sir."

Pastor. "Wilt thou give Rudi his meadow again?"

Bailiff. "Yes, I will, your reverence!"

Pastor. "Dost thou also acknowledge that thou possessest it unlawfully?"

Bailiff. "I can not deny it—but it will bring me to beggary if I lose it."

Pastor. "Bailiff! it is better to beg, than to keep unjust possession of poor people's property."

The bailiff groaned.

Pastor. "But what wert thou doing upon the hill?"

Bailiff. "For heaven's sake, sir, do not ask me that? I can not, I dare not tell you. Have mercy upon me, or I am a lost man."

Pastor. "I will not urge thee to confess more than thou desirest. If thou dost it willingly, I will advise thee like a father; but if thou wilt not, then it is thy own fault if I can not give thee the advice which is perhaps most needful to thee. But though I do not seek to inquire after what thou art not willing to tell me, yet I can not see what thou canst gain by concealing any thing from me."

Bailiff. "But will you never repeat what I say to you, without my consent, whatever it may be?"

Pastor. "I certainly will not."

Bailiff. "Then, in plain truth, I will tell you. I wanted to remove one of the squire's landmarks."

Pastor. "Gracious heaven! and why wouldst thou injure the excellent squire?"

Bailiff. "Because he wants to take away from me either my tavern or my office of bailiff."

Pastor. "Thou art indeed an unhappy creature, bailiff! And he was so far from intending any unkindness toward thee, that he would have given thee an equivalent, if thou hadst freely given up thy office of bailiff."

Bailiff. "Can that be true, your reverence?"

Pastor. "Yes, bailiff, I can assure thee of it with certainty; for I had it from his own lips. He was out hunting on Saturday afternoon, and I met him on the road from Reutihof, where I had been to see the old woman, and there he told me expressly that young Meyer, whom he wished to have for bailiff, should give thee a hundred florins yearly, that thou mightest have no reason to complain."

Bailiff. "O, if I had only known this before, your reverence, I should never have come to this misfortune."

Pastor. "It is our duty to trust in God, even when we can not see how his fatherly mercy will show itself; and we should hope well from a good master on earth, even when we can not see how he means to manifest his kindness toward us. If we do this, we shall always remain true and faithful to him, and, in all our mischances, find his heart open to compassion and paternal kindness toward us."

Bailiff. "O, what an unfortunate man I am! If I had only known half of this before!"

Pastor. "We can not alter what is past! But what wilt thou do now, bailiff?"

Bailiff. "I know not what in the world to do! To confess it, would endanger my life. What does your reverence think?"

Pastor. "I repeat what I told thee just now. I do not wish to force thee to any confession; what I say is merely in the way of advice; but it is my opinion, that the straight way never turned out ill to any body. Arner is merciful, and thou art guilty. Do as thou wilt, but I would leave it to his compassion. I see clearly that it is a very difficult step to take, but it will also be very difficult to hide thy fault from him, if thou seekest true peace and satisfaction for thy heart."

The bailiff groaned, but did not speak.

The pastor proceeded: "Do as thou wilt, bailiff! I do not wish to urge thee; but the more I consider it, the more it appears to me that it will be the wisest plan to leave it to Arner's compassion: for I must confess to thee, I do not see what else thou canst do. The squire will inquire why thou wert off the road so late at night."

Bailiff. "Mercy on me! what a thought is just come into my head. I have left a pickaxe, shovel, and mattock, and I know not what besides, by the landmark, which is half dug up already. This may discover it all. I am in a dreadful fright about the pickaxe and mattock!"

Pastor. "If thou art in such a fright, bailiff, about a poor pickaxe and mattock, which may be easily removed before daybreak, think what hundreds of such chances and accidents will occur, if thou concealest it, to poison all the remainder of thy life with uneasiness and constant bitter anxiety. Thou wilt find no rest for thy heart, bailiff, if thou dost not confess."

Bailiff. "And there is no chance of my obtaining mercy from God, without it?"

Pastor. "Bailiff! if thou thyself thinkest and fearest this, and yet art silent against the voice of thy conscience and thine own conviction, how is it possible that this conduct can be pleasing to God, or restore thee to his favor?"

Bailiff. "And is there no other remedy?"

Pastor. "God's mercy will assist thee, if thou dost what thy conscience bids thee."

Bailiff. "I will confess it."

The moment he said this, the pastor prayed thus, in his presence.

"All praise, and thanksgiving, and adoration, be unto thee Almighty Father! Thou didst stretch forth thy hand toward him, and the work of thy love appeared to him anger and wrath! But it has touched his heart, so that he no longer hardens himself against the voice of truth, as formerly. O, thou, who art all mercy, and compassion, and loving-kindness, graciously accept the sacrifice of his confession, and remove not thy hand from him. Fulfill the work of thy compassion, and let him again become one of thy favored children! O, heavenly Father, the life of man upon earth is erring and sinful, but thou art merciful to thy frail children, and forgivest their excesses and sins when they amend.

"All praise and adoration be unto thee, Father Almighty! Thou hast stretched forth thy hand toward him, that he might turn unto thee. Thou wilt fulfill the work of thy compassion; and he will find thee, and praise thy name, and acknowledge thy mercies amongst his brethren."

The bailiff was now thoroughly moved. Tears fell from his eyes.

"O, sir, I will confess it, and do whatever is right. I will seek rest for my soul, and God's mercy."

The pastor remained some time longer with him, comforting him, and then went home. It was striking five as he arrived at his own house, and he immediately wrote to Arner. His letter yesterday and that to-day were as follows:—

Chapter LXXVIII.—Two letters from the Pastor to Arner.

FIRST LETTER.

"High and nobly born, gracious sir!

"The bearer of this, Hans Wust, has this day revealed a circumstance to me, which is of such a nature, that I could not do otherwise than advise him to confess it to you, as to his judge. He maintains, on his conscience, that the oath which he and Keibacher took ten years ago, about the affair between Rudi and the bailiff, was a false one. It is a distressing story, and there are some remarkable circumstances belonging to it, relating to the conduct of the late secretary, and of the unhappy assistant of my deceased predecessor, which this confession will bring to light, and thereby I fear give rise to much scandal. But I thank God that the poorest of all my many poor people, the long oppressed and suffering Rudi, with his unhappy family, may, by means of this confession, again obtain possession of what belongs to them. The daily increasing wickedness of the bailiff, and his daring conduct, which he now no longer restrains even on sacred days, convince me that the time of his humiliation is approaching. For the poor unhappy Wust, I earnestly and humbly entreat your compassion, and all the favor which the duty of justice can permit your benevolent heart to show him.

"My wife desires her best respects to your lady, and my children their grateful remembrances to your daughters. They send a thousand thanks for the bulbs, with which they have enriched our little garden. They will be most zealously watched over, for my children have quite a passion for flowers.

"Permit me, high and nobly born, gracious sir, with the sincerest respect and esteem, to subscribe myself

"Your high and nobly born grace's
"Most obedient servant,
"Joachim Ernst."

"*Bonnal*, 20*th March*, 1780."

SECOND LETTER.

"High and nobly born, gracious sir!

"Since yesterday evening, when I informed you (in a letter now lying sealed beside me,) of some circumstances relating to Hans Wust, an all-seeing Providence has strengthened my hopes and wishes for Rudi, and my anticipations respecting the bailiff, in a manner which I can not yet either comprehend or explain. Last night there was a general uproar in the village, so violent that I apprehended some misfortune, and, upon inquiring, was told that the devil wanted to seize the bailiff. He screamed pitifully, on the hill, for assistance, and all the people heard the horrible rattling noise of the pursuing devil. I could not help laughing heartily at this intelligence; but many more people came in, who confirmed the fearful story, and at last told me that the bailiff was now returned home again, with the men who had gone to help him; but that he had been so dreadfully dragged about and injured by his terrible enemy, that it was not likely he would recover.

"This was a business quite out of my line—but what was to be done? We must make the best of the world as it is, since we can not alter it. I thought that whatever this affair might be, the bailiff was probably in a state to be worked upon, and that I ought not to lose the opportunity; so I went immediately to his house. I found him in a pitiful condition. He was firmly persuaded that the devil had really been in pursuit of him. I made a few inquiries, in hopes of getting a clue to the business, but could make nothing out. The only thing certain is, that nobody has touched him, and that the wound on his head, which is but trifling, was caused by a fall. Moreover, as soon as the people approached, the devil ceased his rattling and roaring—but it is time to come to the most important part of the story.

"The bailiff was humbled, and confessed to me two shocking deeds, which he freely permitted me to communicate to your grace. First, that what Hans Wust had told me yesterday was true—namely, that he had deceived your late grandfather about Rudi, and obtained possession of the meadow unjustly. Secondly, that this night he intended to remove one of your grace's landmarks, and was busy at the work when the fearful accident happened to him.

"I humbly entreat your compassion and forbearance toward this unhappy man also, who appears, God be praised for it, to be brought to repentance and submission. As the circumstances are changed since yesterday, I will not send Hans Wust with his letter, but Wilhelm Abi shall deliver them both. I wait your further commands about them, and remain

"With true regard,

"Your high and nobly born grace's

"Most obedient servant,

"*Bonnal*, 21*st March*, 1780." "JOACHIM ERNST."

CHAPTER LXXIX.—THE POULTERER'S INFORMATION.

WILHELM ABI set out for Arnburg with the letters, but Christopher, the poulterer, was at the hall before him, and told the squire the whole of what had happened, from beginning to end.

The squire, as he sat in his arm-chair, laughed until he had to hold his sides, at the account of the bailiff's fright, and of the fearful Oh!—Ah!—Uh! of the poulterer.

His wife Theresa, who was in the next room, heard the bursts of laughter and the poulterer's exclamations, and called out: "Charles, what is the matter? Come and tell me what it is all about!"

Then the squire said to the poulterer: "My wife wants to hear how you perform the devil: come in."

And he took the poulterer into his wife's room.

The man there repeated his tale—how he had driven the bailiff down into the field—how the neighbors had come out by dozens, with spits, and cudgels, and torches, to the poor bailiff's help—and how he had then crept up the hill again.

The squire and his lady were much diverted, and the squire gave the poulterer some glasses of good wine, and bade him tell nobody a single word of the affair.

In the mean time Wilhelm Abi arrived, with the pastor's letters.

Arner read them, and was the most touched by Hans Wust's story.

The negligence of his grandfather, and the misery of Rudi, deeply grieved him; but the pastor's judicious conduct rejoiced his heart. He gave the letters to Theresa, and said: "My pastor in Bonnal is a most excellent man. Nobody could have acted more kindly and prudently."

Theresa read the letters, and said: "This is a sad business about Wust! You must help Rudi to recover his property without delay; and, if the bailiff refuses to give up the meadow, throw him into prison. He is a wretch who must not be spared."

"I will have him hanged, to a certainty!" answered Arner.

"O, no! you will not put any body to death!" replied Theresa.

"Do you think not, Theresa?" said Arner laughing.

"Yes, Charles! I am sure of it!" said Theresa, affectionately kissing him.

"You would not kiss me any more, I suspect, if I were to do so, Theresa," said Arner.

"No, indeed!" said Theresa, smiling.

Arner then went into his own room, and answered the pastor's letters.

CHAPTER LXXX.—THE SQUIRE'S ANSWER TO THE PASTOR.

"DEAR AND REVEREND SIR,

"An hour before I received your letters, I had heard the story from the very devil who chased the bailiff down the hill; and who was no other than your old acquaintance, Christopher, the poulterer. I will give you an account of the whole affair, which was very laughable, to-day; for I am coming to the village, where I will hold a parish-meeting about the landmark. I mean at the same time to have a comedy with the people, about their belief in ghosts; and you, my dear sir, must be present at this play. I think you have not been at many, or you would not be so shy, and perhaps not so truly good and contented a man.

"I beg your acceptance of some of my best wine, with my heartfelt thanks for the upright and excellent assistance you have given me, in making amends for my grandfather's failings.

"We will this afternoon drink some of it to his memory. Believe me, he was a good man at heart, though rogues too often abused his kindness and confidence. I thank you, my dear sir, for the pains and care you have taken about Hubel Rudi. I will certainly assist him. This very day he must be in charity with my dear grandfather, and I trust he will never again lament over the recollection of him. I am grieved at heart, that he has suffered so much, and I will do my best, in any way I can, to comfort him for his past distress, by future ease and happiness. We are certainly bound to make good the failings of our parents wherever it is in our power. O, my dear sir, it is a sad mistake, to say that a judge is never answerable, nor obliged to make reparation. How little is he acquainted with mankind, who does not see that all judges are bound, at the risk of their property, continually to rouse and exert all their powers, not only to be honorable, but to be careful and watchful. But I am going from the purpose.

"My wife and children desire me to give their kind regards to your family, and send your daughters another box of flower-roots. Farewell, my dear sir! and do not trouble yourself to get all the rooms into such order, and to provide so many good things, as if I were coming from pure hunger. If you do, I will not visit you any more, dear as you are to me.

"Once more accept my best thanks, and believe me ever

"Your faithful and affectionate friend,

"CHARLES ARNER VON ARNHEIM."

"*Arnburg*, 21*st March*, 1780."

"P. S. My wife has just told me that she wishes to be present at the comedy of the poulterer, so we shall pour down upon you, with all the children, in the family coach."

Chapter LXXXI.—A good cow-man.

When Arner had dismissed Wilhelm, he went into his cow-house, and, from amongst his fifty cows, he chose out one for Hubel Rudi, and said to his cow-man: "Feed this cow well, and tell the boy to drive it to Bonnal, and put it up in the pastor's cow-house, till I come."

The cow-man replied: "Sir! I must obey your orders; but there is not one amongst the fifty, I would not rather part with. She is such a fine, young, handsome cow; and just at her best time for milking."

"It is to your credit, cow-man, to be so sorry to lose the good cow; but I am glad I chose it, I was looking for the best. She is going to belong to a poor man, cow-man, so don't grieve over her. She will be a treasure to him."

Cow-man. "O, sir, it is a sad pity to send her. She will fall off so in a poor man's hands, grow so thin, and lose her looks. O, sir, if I find he starves her, I shall be running off to Bonnal every day, with all my pockets full of bread and salt for her."

Squire. "Thou art a good fellow; but the man has an excellent meadow of his own, and plenty of food for her."

Cow-man. "Well, if she must go, I do hope she will be well treated."

Squire. "Depend upon it, she will want for nothing, cow-man."

The man fed the cow, and sighed to himself, because his master had chosen the best of all his set, to give away. He gave his favorite Spot his own bread and salt from breakfast, and then said to the boy: "Put on thy Sunday coat and a clean shirt, brush thy shoes, and make thyself neat; thou must drive Spot to Bonnal."

And the boy did as the cow-man bade him, and drove away the cow.

Arner stood still for a while, earnestly considering what he should decide about the bailiff.

As a father, when he restrains his wild untoward boys, seeks only the welfare of his children—as a father grieves at the punishment he is obliged to inflict, and would gladly exchange it for forgiveness and approbation—as he shows his sorrow in punishing, and touches his children's hearts still more by his tender regret than by the chastisement—so, thought Arner, must I punish, if I would perform my duty as judge, in the spirit of a father to my dependants.

With these feelings he formed his decisions about the bailiff.

In the mean time his wife and her maidens had hastened dinner, that it might be over sooner than usual.

Chapter LXXXII.—A coachman who loves his master's son.

And little Charles, who had already been more than a dozen times to the coachman, to desire him to make haste and get the coach ready, ran again to the stables and called out: "We have done dinner, Francis! Put to, and drive round to the door, directly."

"You are mistaken, young master; I heard the dinner-bell ring just now."

Charles. "How dare you say I am mistaken? I will not bear that, old moustache!"

Francis. "Hold, my boy! I will teach you to call me moustache! I will plait the horses' tails and manes, and put on the ribands and the rosettes, and that will take me an hour—and, if you say another word, I will tell your papa that Herod is ill—See how he shakes his head! And then he will leave the black horses in the stable and take the little carriage, and you can not go with him."

Charles. "No, no, Francis! Stop—don't begin to plait their manes. I love you, Francis! and will not call you moustache any more."

Francis. "You must give me a kiss then, Charles, in my beard; or I will take the ribands and plait them."

Charles. "No, don't do so, pray."

Francis. "Why did you call me moustache? You must kiss me, or I will not drive the black horses."

Charles. "Well, then, if I must! But you will get the coach ready very soon then."

Francis put down the curry-comb, lifted up the boy, who kissed him; said: "There's a good little fellow!"—put the horses to the coach, and drove quickly round to the hall-door.

Arner was sitting with his wife and children, and Charles begged his papa to let him ride upon the coach-box with Francis. "It is so hot and crowded inside."

"With all my heart," said Arner; and called out to Francis: "Take good care of him."

Chapter LXXXIII.—The Squire with His Workmen.

And Francis drove his spirited horses fast, and was soon on the plain near Bonnal, where the men were breaking stones.

Then Arner got out of the coach, to look at their work, and he found all the men in their right places.

They had got on with their work very well for the time.

And Arner praised the regularity and good appearance of the work, in a manner which convinced the dullest amongst them, that the slightest irregularity or neglect would not have escaped him.

Leonard was very glad of this, for he thought within himself, now they will all see that it is impossible for me to allow any carelessness or neglect.

Arner asked the master which was Hubel Rudi; and, at the moment Leonard pointed him out, poor Rudi, who was pale and evidently very weak, was raising a very heavy stone with his iron crow. Arner called out immediately: "Do not overwork yourselves, my good fellows; and take care not to do yourselves an injury." Then he ordered the master to give them each a glass of wine, and went toward Bonnal.

Chapter LXXXIV.—A Squire and a Pastor, Who Have Equally Kind Hearts.

He soon saw the good pastor coming to meet him, and the squire ran quickly toward him, and called out: "You should not have troubled yourself to come out such weather as this? It is not right, with your delicate health;" and he then went into the house with him.

There he told him the whole history of the poulterer, and then said: "I have some business to transact, but will be quick about it, that we may enjoy a couple of hours quietly together."

He sent immediately for young Meyer, and said to the pastor: "The first step shall be to seal up all the bailiff's accounts and books of reckoning; for I am resolved to know who are concerned with him, and he shall settle with them all, in my presence."

Pastor. "By doing this, you will get to know a great deal about the people of the village."

Squire. "And, as I hope, find out the way to put an end to a great deal of domestic unhappiness; if I can by this means make it clear and evident to every man how irrevocably people ruin themselves when they get ever so little into debt to such grasping men as the bailiff. In my opinion, my good friend, the laws do too little against this ruinous practice."

Pastor. "No law can do so much to counteract it, as the paternal kindness of the lord of a manor."

CHAPTER LXXXV.—THE SQUIRE'S FEELINGS TOWARD HIS GUILTY BAILIFF.

As they were speaking, young Meyer arrived, and Arner said to him: "Meyer, I mean to dismiss my bailiff; but, notwithstanding his offenses, some circumstances lead me to wish him to receive, for life, a part of the emolument of his office. You are well off in the world, Meyer! and I think, if I were to make you bailiff, you would willingly allow the old man a hundred florins yearly, out of your salary."

Meyer. "If your honor thinks me equal to the situation, I shall wish in this, as to every other respect, to do according to your pleasure."

Arner. "Well then, Meyer, come to me to Arnburg to-morrow, and I will arrange this business. For the present, I will only tell you that you must take my secretary and Abi, who is a qualified man, with you, and seal up all Hummel's writings and accounts. You must carefully see after it, that not one of his papers or accounts be secreted."

Immediately young Meyer and the squire's secretary took Abi with them, and sealed up the bailiff's papers. His wife went with a wet sponge toward the chalked board; but Meyer saw her, and hindered her from touching it, and had a copy of it taken immediately.

And Meyer, the secretary, and Abi, wondered to see on the board: "On Saturday, 18th, to Joseph, Leonard's man, three crowns." "What was this for?" said they to the bailiff and his wife; but they gave them no answer.

And when the men arrived at the parsonage-house, with the copy of the board, the squire also wondered at the three crowns, and asked the men if they knew the meaning of it.

"We inquired, but nobody would give us an answer," replied the men.

"I will soon find it out," said the squire. "When Flink and the gaoler come, tell them to bring the bailiff and Hans Wust here."

CHAPTER LXXXVI.—THE PASTOR AGAIN SHOWS HIS KINDNESS OF HEART.

THE good pastor had no sooner heard this, than he slipped out of the room, went to the tavern, and said to the bailiff: "For God's sake what is the meaning of these three crowns to Joseph? It will be a double misfortune to thee, if thou dost not tell me. The squire is angry about it."

Then the bailiff sorrowfully confessed to the pastor, the whole affair about Joseph and the money.

And the pastor went immediately back to Arner, and told him all, and how penitently the bailiff had owned it to him; and he again entreated the squire to be merciful toward this unhappy man.

"Be not uneasy, my good friend! You may depend upon finding me humane and compassionate toward him," said Arner.

He then had Joseph taken from his work, and brought before him, with Wust and the bailiff.

The bailiff trembled like an aspen leaf. Wust appeared very sorrowful, but composed and patient.

But Joseph was in a rage, and said to the bailiff: "Thou old wretch, this is all thy fault."

Arner had the prisoners brought, one after the other, into the inner room of the parsonage-house, and there he examined them, in the presence of Meyer, Abi, and the attorney. And when the secretary had written down their depositions, word for word, and read them over to the prisoners, and these had again repeated and confirmed them, he had them all brought to the place where the parish-meetings are held, under the lime-trees, and ordered the bell to be rung, to assemble all the people.

CHAPTER LXXXVII.—ON A CHEERFUL DISPOSITION, AND ON GHOSTS.

BUT before this, the squire went for a few moments into the other room, to the pastor, and said: "I will take a draught of something to refresh me, my good friend. For I mean to be merry with the people. It is the best way to convince them of any thing."

"Nothing is more certain," said the pastor.

And the squire made him pledge him, and said: "I wish all clergymen would learn thus to go amongst the people in a straight-forward, unceremonious manner. When people see a man good-humored, and with an open, unrestrained manner, they are half won already."

"Alas, sir!" said the pastor, "this cheerfulness, and open, unrestrained manner, are exactly what we are least allowed to practice."

Squire. "It is a misfortune, belonging to your situation, reverend sir."

Pastor. "You are quite right. None should go amongst the people with a more unrestrained, cheerful, open manner, than the ministers of religion. They should be the friends of the people, and known to be such. They should be influenced by a regard to them in their speech, and in their silence. They should carefully consider their words, and yet dispense them freely, benevolently, and to the purpose, like their Master. But, alas! they form themselves in other schools, and we must have patience, squire. In all situations of life, there are many impediments to the practice of what is simple and natural."

Squire. "It is true. In all ranks people wander continually further and further from the path they should follow. Much time, which ought to be employed upon important duties, is wasted upon ceremonies and nonsense: and there are few men who, under the burthen of forms of etiquette and pedantry, preserve due attention to their duties, and to the really important objects of their lives, as you have done, my dear friend. But, by your side, it is my delight and joy to feel it my happy destination to act the part of a father, and I will endeavor to fulfill it with a pure heart, and, like you, with as little of the ceremony and nonsense of the world as possible."

Pastor. "You make me ashamed, my dear sir."

Squire. "I feel what I say! but the bell will soon ring. I am impatient for the comedy at the parish-meeting. I do expect, this time, to cure them of some of their superstitions."

Pastor. "May God grant you success! This superstition of theirs, interferes sadly with the good one seeks to do them."

Squire. "I find, from my own experience, that it often makes them very stupid, timid, and irresolute."

Pastor. "It warps a man's understanding, and has a bad effect upon all he does, and says, and thinks. And, what is still worse, it injures his heart, and hardens it with pride and uncharitableness."

Squire. "Very true. There is a wide distinction between the pure simplicity of nature, and the blind stupidity of superstition."

Pastor. "Yes. The uncorrupted simplicity of nature is alive to every impression of truth and virtue: it is like a blank tablet. But the stupidity of superstition is like melted ore, incapable of receiving any impression, except from fire and flame. And now that you have introduced the subject of this distinction, which is of so much importance to me, in my avocation, will you permit me to say a few more words about it?"

Squire. "Pray do. The subject is very interesting to me."

Pastor. "Man, in the uncorrupted simplicity of his nature, knows little; but what he does know, is well arranged. His attention is firmly and steadily directed toward what is useful and comprehensible to him. He does not seek to know what he can neither comprehend nor turn to use. But the stupidity of superstition has no clear arrangement in its knowledge. It boasts of knowing what it neither knows nor comprehends; it persuades itself that the disorder of its ideas is heavenly illumination, and that the fleeting splendor of its airy bubbles is divine light and wisdom.

"The simple innocence of nature, makes use of all the senses, judges nothing inconsiderately, examines every thing quietly and attentively, endures opposition, earnestly seeks and desires what is necessary, not what is mere matter of speculation, and conducts itself peacefully, gently, kindly, and benevolently. But superstition believes in contradiction to its own senses, and to the senses of mankind; never rests but in the triumph of its own obscurity, and rages rudely, wildly, and unfeelingly, wherever it exists.

"Man, in a state of simplicity, is guided by his uncorrupted heart, upon which he can always depend; and by his senses, which he uses peacefully.

"But the superstitious man is guided by his opinions, to which he sacrifices his feelings, his senses, and often his God, his country, his neighbor, and himself."

Squire. "Every page of history confirms the truth of your statement; and a very small share of experience and knowledge of the world, is sufficient to convince any man that hardness of heart and superstition are inseparable companions, and always followed by pernicious and grievous consequences."

Pastor. "From this essential difference between the simplicity of the honest, unprejudiced man, and the stupidity of the superstitious man, it appears that the best method of opposing superstition, is: 'In educating the poor, to ground their knowledge of the truth upon the pure feelings of innocence and love; and to turn their attention chiefly to the surrounding objects which interest them in their individual situations.'"

Squire. "I understand you, my good friend! and I think, with you, that by this means superstition and prejudice would lose their sting, their hurtfulness, and their accordance with the passions and desires of wicked hearts, and with the groundless terrors and weak fancies of a busy, speculative knowledge.

"And thus all that would remain of prejudice and superstition would be but empty words, and shades of things without inward poison, and these would die away of themselves."

Pastor. "It appears to me in the same light. The education of the poor should be founded upon clear ideas, surrounding objects, and the cautious development of the impulses of human nature; because these are, undoubtedly, the foundation of true human wisdom.

"To fix the attention strongly upon speculative opinions and distant objects, and feebly upon our duties, our actions, and the objects which surround us, is to create disorder in the soul of man. It leads to ignorance about our most important affairs, and to a foolish predilection for information and knowledge, which do not concern us.

"Roughness and hardness of heart are the natural consequences of all pride and presumption; and the source of the inward poison of superstition and prejudice is clearly derived from this: that in the education of the people, their attention is not steadily turned to the circumstances and objects around them, which have a strong and near relation to their individual situation, and would lead their hearts to pure and tender feelings of humanity upon all occasions.

"If people sought thus to instruct them, as earnestly and zealously as they do to teach them particular opinions, superstition would be torn up by the roots, and deprived of all its power; but I feel daily, more and more, how little we are advanced in this good work."

Squire. "In the world all is comparatively true, or not true. There have been rude times—times when a man who did not believe in ghosts was esteemed a heretic; times when a man was obliged, on pain of forfeiting his rights and his situation of judge, to order old women to the rack, to make them confess their dealings with the devil."

Pastor. "God be praised, those times are gone by; but much of the old leaven still remains."

Squire. "Yet, be of good cheer, my friend! One stone after another falls away from the temple of superstition; and it would be well if people were only as zealous to build up the temple of God, as they are to overthrow that of superstition!"

Pastor. "There again we are wanting: and this checks and destroys my rejoicing in the attacks made upon superstition; because I see that those who are so active against it, trouble themselves very little about upholding religion, the sanctuary of God, in its strength."

Squire "It is too true. But in all revolutions people will always begin by rejecting good and bad together. They were in the right to purify the Lord's temple; but they will soon perceive that, in their zeal, they have injured the walls, and then they will return and repair them again."

Pastor. "I trust it will be so! and, indeed, I see myself that people begin to feel that destructive irreligion strikes at the root of human happiness."

Squire. "We must now go; and I will make one attempt this very day to attack superstition, and overthrow the belief in ghosts which exists in Bonnal."

Pastor. "May you be successful! I have as yet been able to do very little against it by my arguments and preaching."

Squire. "I will not attempt it by words. My poulterer must spare me that trouble, with his basket and lantern, his pickaxe and mattock."

Pastor. "I really believe it will succeed admirably. It is certain that, when people know well how to turn such accidents to advantage, they may do more by means of them in a moment, than they can in half a century by all the arts of eloquence."

CHAPTER LXXXVIII.—ON GHOSTS, IN A DIFFERENT TONE.

In the mean time the country people were all assembled at the place of meeting. Yesterday's adventure, and the report of the prisoners, brought them together in crowds. The alarming appearance of the devil had greatly agitated them, and they had already, early that morning, taken council together what was to be done under the circumstances, and had come to a resolution that the pastor ought no longer to be allowed to teach and preach so incredulously, and to laugh at all stories of ghosts. They determined to request Hartknopf, the church-warden, to make a proposal to this effect at the meeting; but young Meyer was against this, and said: "I can not agree that the old miser, who starves his own children, and is constantly hunting about for all sorts of refuse, should speak for us. It will be an eternal shame for us to appoint such a hypocrite."

The men answered: "We know well enough that he is a hypocrite and a miser, and we know that the way in which he and his maid-servant live together is scandalous. It is true, also, that we have not such a liar amongst us, nor one who encroaches so much upon his neighbor's land, or clears his field so carefully at harvest-time; but then, there is not one of us who can talk to a minister, or discuss spiritual matters, as he can. If you can tell us of any one, who will do it only half so well, we will be content." But Meyer knew of nobody.

So the men made their request to the church-warden, in these words: "Hartknopf, you are the man amongst us who best knows how to answer a clergyman; and when the squire holds the meeting to-day, we wish you to make a complaint against the pastor, on account of his unbelief, and to ask for the appointment of a day of prayer, on account of the fearful appearance of Satan."

They did not talk to him publicly about this, but the cleverest amongst them explained the business to him; for the pastor had many friends amongst the poorer part of them. Some of the richer country people disliked him the more on this account, particularly since he had maintained, in one of his morning discourses, that it was not right in them to oppose the division of a waste common, which the squire had proposed for the advantage of the poor.

The church-warden Hartknopf, accepted the appointment, and said: "You have given me rather late notice of this, but I will study the proposition;" and he went away to his own house, and thought over what he had to say, from morning until evening, when the bell rang for the meeting. When those who were in the plot were all assembled together, they wondered why he did not join them, and could not imagine what kept him away. Then Nickel Spitz said: "He is only waiting till you go in form to fetch him."

"What is to be done?" said the men. "We must e'en do as the simpleton wishes, or he will not come."

So they sent three of their officers to fetch him; and these soon returned with him.

The churchwarden saluted the people, with as much dignity as if he had been a pastor; and, with great importance and gravity, assured all those who had entered into the agreement, that he had now studied the proposition.

In the mean time, Arner had told the poulterer that, when he made a signal, by taking a large white handkerchief out of his pocket, he must come forth, and do all that they had agreed upon together.

Then he went with the pastor and the secretary to the meeting.

All the people stood up, and welcomed the worthy squire and the reverend pastor.

Arner thanked them with paternal kindness, and then told the men to sit down upon benches, that all might be done in proper order.

Theresa and the pastor's wife, and the children and servants, from the hall and the parsonage-house, stood in the churchyard, from whence they could see what passed at the meeting.

Arner now ordered the prisoners to be brought forth, one after the other, and their depositions to be read in their presence.

And when they had confirmed them before the meeting, he told the bailiff to kneel down and hear his sentence, and addressed him as follows:—

Chapter LXXXIX.—A Judgment.

"Unhappy man!

"It grieves me to the heart, to pronounce against thee, in thy old age, the doom which must follow evil deeds like thine. Thou hast deserved death; not because Hubel Rudi's meadow or my landmark are worth a man's life, but because perjury and daring robbery bring innumerable dangers and evils upon a country.

"The perjured man and the robber becomes a murderer, when circumstances tempt him to it; and is already a murderer in many senses, through the consequences of the error, suspicion, distress, and misery, which he occasions.

"Therefore, thou hast deserved death.

"I will, however, spare thy life, in consideration of thy old age, and because a part of thy crimes were committed against myself, individually.

"This is thy punishment:—

"Thou shalt this day, in the presence of appointed persons and of all who wish to accompany thee, be carried to the landmark, and there, in chains, replace every thing as it was before.

"Thence thou shalt be taken to the village prison, when the pastor will examine thee, for the space of fourteen days, about thy past life, that the causes of thy great recklessness and hardness of heart may be clearly and evidently discerned: and I will myself use my utmost endeavors to discover the circumstances which have led thee to these crimes, and which may lead others of my dependants into similar misfortunes.

"After this fortnight is expired, the pastor will, on the Sunday following, openly, before the whole community, relate the history of thy past life, of the disorders of thy house, thy hardness of heart, thy contempt of oaths and duties, and thy way of keeping accounts against the poor and rich—and the whole must be confirmed by thy own confession.

"I will myself be present; and, with the assistance of the pastor, will endeavor to preserve my dependents from such dangers in future, and to provide them with assistance and counsel against all such sources and causes of domestic misery.

"And with this I would willingly discharge thee, were my people sufficiently peaceable and well brought up to follow after the truth and what pertains to their temporal and eternal welfare, for their own sake, and not from the fear of severe, painful, and loathsome punishment; but, with so many rude, uncontrolled, and boisterous people, as are still amongst us, it is necessary for me to add:—

"That the executioner must conduct thee to-morrow under the gallows at Bonnal, and there bind thy right hand to a stake, and mark the first three fingers with an indelible black stain.

"But it is my express desire, that no man imbitter this thy hour of suffering, by jest or laughter, or any mark of redicule; but that, on the contrary, all the people look on, without noise or speech, and with their heads uncovered."

The squire then condemned Hans Wust to eight days' punishment in prison. And Joseph, as being a stranger, he immediately expelled from his territories, and forbade him to labor or to appear upon his land any more, on pain of being sent to the house of correction.

In the mean time the pastor's god-father, Hans Renold, had secretly told him what the country people had settled with the church-warden, and that they would certainly and without doubt attack him on account of his unbelief.

The pastor thanked Renold, and told him, laughingly, not to be uneasy; the thing would not end ill.

"This is excellent," said the squire, to whom the pastor told this, "that they should themselves begin the game:" and, whilst he was speaking, the church-warden got up and said:—

Chapter XC.—The Proposal of Hartknopf, the Church-Warden.

"Honored sir!

"May I be permitted, in the name of your faithful people of Bonnal, to state to you an affair of conscience?"

Arner answered: "I am ready to hear. Who are you? What have you to say?"

The church-warden replied: "I am Jacob Christopher Frederick Hartknopf, church-warden and elder of Bonnal, and fifty-six years of age. And the principal people of the village, being themselves inexperienced and unaccustomed to speak upon spiritual subjects, have chosen and requested me to lay a statement before you."

Arner. "Now then, Mr. Church-warden Hartknopf, to the point."

Then the church-warden began again:—

"Honored sir!

"We have received from our forefathers a belief that the devil and his spirits often appear to men; and, since it is now become very evident that this our old belief in spirits is true, as indeed we never for a moment doubted it to be, we are compelled to take the liberty of informing your honor, that our reverend pastor (may God forgive him,) is not of this belief. We well know that your honor is of the same opinion with the pastor on this subject. But since, in sacred things, we must obey God rather than man, we hope your honor will forgive our freedom, when we entreat that the reverend pastor may, in future, teach our children our old belief, about the appearance of the devil, and that he may say nothing to them against ghosts, in which we believe, and will continue to believe. It is also our wish, that some Sunday, at no great distance, may be fixed upon for a day of fasting, and prayer, and humiliation; that we may all, upon an appointed day, penitently implore forgiveness, in dust and ashes, for the increasing sin of want of belief in spirits."

The squire and the pastor, though they were scarcely able to restrain their laughter till he had finished, yet heard him with all possible patience.

But the country people rejoiced in their hearts over this discourse, and resolved to accompany this able orator home, by hundreds, though they had sent only three to fetch him.

They now rose up on all sides, and said: "Honored sir! we all agree in what the church-warden has declared."

But the poor, and all those who loved the pastor, were very sorry and grieved about it, and said here and there to each other: "If he had only the luck to believe like other people—he is such an excellent man!" But these durst not speak out, so that his enemies triumphed.

Chapter XCI.—The Squire's Reply.

The squire took off his hat, looked earnestly around him, and said:—

"Neighbors! you had no need of an orator for such nonsense as this. The whole affair, and the appearance of the devil, is all a mistake; and your pastor is one of the wisest of ministers. You ought to be ashamed of insulting him through such a poor blockhead as your church-warden. If you had a proper regard for his learning and judgment, you would be wiser, lay aside your belief in old women's tales, and not seek to restrain intelligent people to foolish opinions, which are entirely without foundation."

Here the country people all exclaimed: "But it was only last night that the devil appeared to the bailiff, and sought to lay hold of him."

Squire. "You are mistaken, neighbors; and before supper-time you will be ashamed of your credulity. But I hope you are not all equally hardened in your folly. Meyer! are you also of the opinion, that it is past all doubt that it was the devil who frightened the bailiff so terribly upon the hill?"

Young Meyer answered: "What do I know about the matter, your honor?"

The church-warden and many of the men were angry at Meyer for answering thus.

And the church-warden muttered over the bench to him: "How canst thou talk so against thy knowledge and conscience, Meyer?" But many of the men exclaimed: "We all heard the horrible voice of the pursuing devil."

Squire. "I know very well that you heard a shout, and a roaring, and a rattling. But how can you tell that all this was the devil? Might it not be a man, or several men, who, unluckily for the bailiff, who seems to have been there at an improper time, wished to frighten him? The wood is scarcely ever without somebody in it, and the high road is near, so that it may as easily have been men as the devil."

Countrymen. "Twenty or thirty men could not have made such a noise; and, if your honor had been there and heard it, you would never have thought of its being men."

Squire. "Night is deceitful, neighbors! and, when people are once frightened, they see and hear double."

Countrymen. "It is of no use to talk of being mistaken. It is impossible."

Squire. "But I tell you it is altogether certain that you were mistaken."

Countrymen. "No, please your honor, it is entirely certain that we were not mistaken."

Squire. "I have a great notion I could convince you that you were mistaken."

Countrymen. "We should like to see that, your honor."

Squire. "Many things would be more difficult."

Countrymen. "Your honor is joking."

Squire. "No, I am not joking. If you think I can not do it, I will try. And if you will agree to divide the common, I will perform my promise, and convince you that all the roaring and rattling was made by one man."

Countrymen. "That is impossible."

Squire. "Will you venture it?"

Countrymen. "Yes, sir, we will! We durst venture two commons upon it, that you will not be able to prove this."

Here there arose a murmur amongst the countrymen. Some of them said: "People should take care what they promise." Others replied: "He can no more prove this, than that the devil will go to heaven!" Others again said: "We have nothing to fear; he must give it up. We will venture; he can never prove it."

Countrymen (aloud.) "Yes, squire; if you will keep your word; speak on. We are content that if you can prove what you say, that one man made the noise we heard yesterday, we will divide the common. That is to say, if you can prove it entirely to our satisfaction; not otherwise."

The squire took out a large white handkerchief, gave the poulterer the signal, and said to the men: "I must have a quarter of an hour for preparation."

The people smiled all around, and said: "Till to-morrow, squire, if you will."

The squire said not a word in answer to their rudeness; but those who were in the churchyard, and could see the poulterer approaching the place of meeting, laughed heartily.

The men anticipated some mischance when they heard the bursts of laughter, and saw the stranger, with his dark basket and lantern, drawing near.

"What fool is this, who walks with a lighted lantern in broad daylight?" said they.

Arner answered: "It is my poulterer from Arnheim!" and called out to him: "Christopher, what is your business here?"

"I have a tale to tell, please your honor."

"With all my heart," answered Arner.

Then the poulterer set down his basket, and said:—

Chapter XCII.—Speech of the Poulterer to the Meeting.

"Honored sir, reverend pastor, and you neighbors, here are the pickaxe, the mattock, the spade, the brandy-bottle, the tobacco-pipe, and the cocked hat of your bailiff, which, in his fright, he left by the landmark last night, when I drove him away from his work on the hill."

Countrymen. "And are we to believe that it was you who made all the noise? That can never be. The proof is not sufficient; we beg for another."

Squire. "Wait a little longer. He has a lantern by his side. Perhaps it may enlighten you a little." And then he added, loudly and very seriously: "Be silent, if you please, till he has finished what he has to say."

The men obeyed.

Then the poulterer continued: "You are not so civil as people usually are in this country. Why don't you let me finish? Remember the poulterer of Arnheim. If you do not hear every word I have to say, the next newspaper will be full of you; for there is not a syllable of truth in the devil's having appeared to the bailiff. It was I who frightened him! I, the poulterer, just as I now stand before you, with this basket, and this new black goat-skin, which I had put over my basket, because it rained yesterday, and I had hung the lantern before the basket, as you saw it when I came here. I filled it full of oil at Hirzau, that it might burn well; for it was very dark, and the road, as you well know, is bad near Hirzau. At eleven o'clock I was in the tavern at Hirzau. I can bring the landlord, and at least ten men more, who were there, to prove this. As I came over the top of the hill, it struck twelve at Bonnal; and then I heard the bailiff, not half a stone's throw from the high-road, swearing and working away; and, as I knew him immediately by his voice and his swearing, I began to wonder what he was doing there at that hour of night. I half suspected that he was searching for hidden treasures, and that he might share them with me if I hit the right time. I followed the noise. But the bailiff, it seems, had yesterday, contrary to his usual custom, drunk rather more than was necessary; for, the moment he beheld me, he took me—a poor sinful man—for the devil in a bodily form! and when I saw that he was about removing a landmark in our master's wood, I thought to myself: come, he deserves to be frightened. I will make him think hell is gaping for him! So I bound the mattock, pickaxe, spade, and my walking-stick, all together, dragged them down the hill, over the stones, after me, and shouted out, with all my might: Oh!—Ah!—Uh!—bai—liff!—thou art mine! Hum—me!! And I was not more than a stone's throw from you, when you crept out softly and cautiously with your torches, to the bailiff's assistance. But as I had no wish to frighten innocent folks with making a noise so near them, I gave over, and went up the hill again, with my booty, to my basket, and then took the nearest way home. It was a quarter past two when our watchman met me, and asked why I was carrying workmen's tools upon my egg-basket.

"I forget what I answered, but certainly nothing to the purpose; for I did not wish to say any thing of it, till I had told the squire my story; which I did at six o'clock this morning.

"And now, neighbors, how do you think I could come by this story and these tools so early, if what I tell you is not true?"

Some of the countrymen scratched their heads, others laughed.

The poulterer continued: "If such a thing should happen to you again, neighbors, let me just, in a friendly way, advise the watchman, the authorities, and all the honorable commonalty of Bonnal, to let loose the greatest dog in the village, and he will soon discover the devil."

The poulterer here ceased, and there was a general murmur on every side.

CHAPTER XCIII.—THE POOR ARE GAINERS BY THE COMEDY.

Some countrymen. "It is as he says, by G—! all the circumstances agree."

Other countrymen. "What a set of fools we were."

Kunz. "I wanted to run after the rogue."

Some of the leaders. "If we had only not staked the common upon it."

The rich countrymen. "This is a cursed business."

The poor. "Heaven be praised for it."

Theresa. "The master-stroke of all, is getting the common divided."

Pastor's wife. "The whole is a master-stroke."

The church-warden. "It is enough to make the very stones weep blood! Our belief is lost for ever. Elias! Elias! Fire from heaven."

The children (from the churchyard.) "Thou art mine!—Oh!—Ah!—Uh!—bailiff!"

The pastor. "I never saw the people so much moved."

The bailiff. "Am I in a dream, or awake? All was a mistake, and I must go under the gallows. And yet I feel no anger; no desire of vengeance rages within me."

Thus in a general murmur did every man speak according to his own feelings.

After a while Arner stood up, smiled, and said: "How are you now inclined about the fast-day, on account of the fearful appearance of the devil upon the hill?"

Do what is right! Love God!
And fear God, but neither man nor devil.

This is the old and true belief; and your stories of apparitions and spirits are idle follies, which ruin your heads and hearts.

"Now at last the division of your common is agreed upon, and you will find, in a few years, how useful and beneficial it will be to your children and grandchildren, and how much reason I had to wish for it so earnestly. I have ordered some drink to be brought to you. Drink it to my health, and to the health of your numerous poor, who, in the division of the common, will receive no more than the rest; but to whom it will be a treasure, because they have nothing besides. There is not one of you who knows how much his children may stand in need of it."

Then Arner left the meeting, and told Hubel Rudi to follow him, in a quarter of an hour, to the parsonage-house.

And the squire and the pastor went to their wives in the churchyard, and afterward, with them, to the parsonage-house.

The pastor praised Arner for the wisdom and humanity with which he had treated his flock, and said to him: "I shall never again urge you to show forbearance and compassion toward any body, for your own benevolent heart has exceeded all I could have asked or advised."

Chapter XCIV.—The Squire Thanks the Pastor.

The squire replied: "Say no more, my dear friend, I beseech you. I go straight to the point, and am as yet young and without experience. But, with God's assistance, I hope to learn how to manage things better. I am truly rejoiced that you approve of my decisions. But you must not imagine that I am not aware that your exertions have been much greater than mine, and that your care and kindness had prepared every thing, so that little remained for me, but to pronounce the sentence."

Pastor. "My dear sir, you go too far!"

Squire. "No, my friend. It is the simple truth, and I should be indeed unthankful and unjust, if I did not acknowledge it. You have labored with great care and intelligence to throw light upon my dear grandfather's inconsiderate decisions, and to put an end to their consequences. That good and upright man will rejoice, in heaven, over what you have done, and that the evil has at last been remedied; and he certainly would not forgive me, if I were to leave your goodness unrewarded. Here are the deeds of a small piece of land in your village, which I hope you will accept as a testimony of my gratitude."

Thus saying, he gave him a sealed deed of gift, which was expressed with the greatest warmth of gratitude.

Theresa stood by Arner's side, and presented the pastor with the most beautiful nosegay ever seen in a parsonage-house.

"This is in remembrance of the best of grandfathers, reverend sir," said she.

And in the morning the pastor's wife discovered, for the first time, that it was bound together by a string of pearls.

The good pastor was much overcome: tears filled his eyes, and he could not speak.

"Say not a word about it," added the squire.

"Your heart is worthy of a kingdom!" said the pastor at last.

"Do not make me blush, my dear sir," answered the squire. "Be my friend; and, hand in hand, let us strive to make our people as happy as we can. I hope to see more of you in future, and you will come more to me, will you not? My carriage is always at your service. Send for it, without ceremony, whenever you like to come to me."

Chapter XCV.—The Squire Asks Forgiveness from a Poor Man, Whom His Grandfather Had Injured.

In the mean time Hubel Rudi arrived, and the squire held out his hand to the poor man, and said: "Rudi! my grandfather did you injustice, and deprived you of your meadow by his decision. It was a misfortune. He was deceived. You must forgive him, and not bear malice against him."

Rudi answered: "Alas! your honor! I knew very well that it was not his fault."

"Did you never hate him for it?" said the squire.

Rudi. "In my poverty, and particularly at first, I was indeed often very much troubled that I had not the meadow any longer; but I never felt hatred toward his honor."

Squire. "Is this really true, Rudi?"

Rudi. "It is, indeed, your honor! God knows that it is, and that I never could feel angry with him. I knew in my heart that it was not his fault. What could he do, when the bailiff found false witnesses, who swore an oath against me? The good old squire, whenever he saw me afterward, gave me money, and on all holidays sent me meat, and bread, and wine. May God reward him for it. It often cheered me in my poverty."

Rudi had tears in his eyes, and continued: "Alas! your honor! if he had only talked with us, by ourselves, as you do, many, very many things would never have happened; but the bloodsuckers were always by his side, whenever we saw him, and that spoiled all."

Squire. "You must forget this now, Rudi. The meadow is again yours. I have effaced the bailiff's name from the deed, and I wish you joy of it with all my heart, Rudi!"

Rudi trembled, and stammered out: "I can not enough thank your honor."

The squire said: "You have nothing to thank me for, Rudi. The meadow is yours by the laws of God and man."

Rudi clasped his hands together, wept aloud, and said: "O, my mother's blessing is upon me! She died on Friday, your honor! and before she died, she said to me: 'All will go well with thee, Rudi. Think of me, Rudi!' O, sir, I am so grieved for my dear mother!"

The squire and the pastor were much affected, and the squire said: "God's blessing will indeed be upon you, good and pious man."

"O, sir! it is owing to my mother's blessing! The blessing of the most religious, patient woman," said Rudi, weeping.

"How troubled I am, pastor, that this man should have been so long kept out of his right," said the squire.

"It is all over now, sir!" said Rudi, "and suffering and want are blessings from God, when they are gone through. But I can not sufficiently thank you for all; for the work at the church, which cheered and comforted my mother on her death-bed; and then for the meadow. I know not what I ought to say or do, sir. O! if she had only lived to see it!"

Squire. "You are an excellent man, and she will rejoice in your welfare, even in heaven. Your sorrow and your filial love have affected me so much, that I had almost forgotten to tell you, that the bailiff is bound to pay you arrears, with costs."

Pastor. "Permit me, sir, here to speak a word to Rudi. The bailiff is in very straitened circumstances. He is, indeed, bound to pay you arrears, with costs, Rudi. But I know that you are too kind-hearted to push him to the uttermost, and to bring him to beggary in his old age. I promised, in his affliction, to do all I could to obtain mercy and compassion for him, and I must perform my promise now. Rudi, have pity upon his distress."

CHAPTER XCVI.—GENEROSITY OF A POOR MAN TOWARD HIS ENEMY.

Rudi. "Say not a word about the arrears, reverend sir; they are out of the question: and, if the bailiff is so poor—I don't like to seem to boast—but I will certainly do what is right toward him.

"The meadow will furnish hay for more than three cows; and, if I keep two out of it, I shall have enough and more than I durst hope for; and I will willingly let the bailiff have enough to keep one cow, as long as he lives."

Pastor. "It is acting generously, and like a Christian, Rudi; and God will grant his blessing upon the remainder."

Arner. "This is all well and good, my dear sir. But we must not take the good fellow at his word, now. He is overcome by his joy. I admire you for your offer, Rudi; but consider the thing over quietly for a day or two. It will be time enough to promise, when you are sure you will not repent."

Rudi. "I am but a poor man, your honor; but not so poor as to repent having promised to do what is right."

Pastor. "The squire is right, Rudi. It is enough for the present that you will not exact the arrears. If you find that the bailiff is in want; when you have well considered the thing, you can do what you like."

Rudi. "If the bailiff is in want, I am sure I shall wish to do as I have said, your reverence."

Squire. "Well, Rudi, I want this to be a happy, cheerful day for you. Would you rather stay and rejoice with us here, or go home to your children? I will take care that you have a good supper in either place."

Rudi. "Your honor is very good! but I wish to go home to my children. There is nobody to take care of them. Alas! my wife is in her grave—and my mother also."

Squire. "Then go home to your children, Rudi. In the pastor's cow-house, below, you will find a cow, which I give you to reconcile you to my dear grandfather, who did you wrong; and that you may this day rejoice over his memory, with your children. I have also ordered a quantity of hay to be carried from the bailiff's barn, for it is yours. You will find it at home; and, if your cottage or your cow-house want repairs, take what wood is necessary out of my forest."

CHAPTER XCVII.—HIS GRATITUDE TO THE SQUIRE.

RUDI knew not what to say, he was so completely overcome; and this joyful confusion, which could not utter a word, pleased Arner more than any expression of thanks.

At last Rudi stammered out a few words, but Arner interrupted him, and said, smiling: "I see that you are grateful, Rudi." He then again shook him by the hand, and added: "Go, now, Rudi. Drive home your cow, and depend upon my help; whenever I can be of service to you in any way, it will always be a pleasure to me."

Then Rudi left Arner, and drove home the cow.

CHAPTER XCVIII.—A SCENE TO TOUCH THE HEART.

THE pastor, and all who were present, had tears in their eyes, and remained silent for some moments after the man left the room.

At last Theresa exclaimed: "What an evening this has been! How fair is creation, and with what pleasure and joy does the face of nature inspire us; but human happiness is more delightful than all the beauties of earth!"

"Yes, my love, it surpasses all earthly beauties," said the squire.

The pastor added: "I thank you, from my heart, sir, for the touching scenes you have brought before us. Throughout the course of my life, I never met with purer and nobler greatness of soul than in the deed of this man. But it is most certain that the purest elevation of the human heart, is to be sought for amongst the unfortunate and distressed."

The pastor's wife pressed her children, who were much affected, to her heart, bent over them, and wept in silence.

After a while, the children said to her: "Let us go and see his poor children, and send them our supper."

And the pastor's wife said to Theresa: "Will you like to go with the children?"

"Very willingly," answered Theresa. And the squire and the pastor expressed their wish to accompany them.

Arner had brought a roasted quarter of veal in the carriage with him, for the poor family; and the pastor's wife had added to this some good nourishing broth, and given orders for it to be taken to them: but now she sent also her own and the children's supper, and Claus carried all to the poor man's cottage.

All the villagers, young and old, men, women, and children, were collected at Rudi's door, and round the hay-cart and the fine cow.

Claus was followed almost immediately by the squire and his lady, the pastor's wife, and all the children. They went into the room and found nothing but sickly, half-naked children, the pictures of hunger and want. All were much affected by the distress of the family; and Arner said to his companions: "Yet this very man is now willing to give the bailiff, who has been the cause of all this misery for so many years, a third part of the hay from his meadow!"

"It ought not to be allowed," said Theresa, hastily, in the warmth of her compassion for so much distress. "This man, with all his children, ought not to be allowed to give a farthing of what belongs to him to that wicked wretch."

"But, my love, would you set bounds to the course of that virtue and magnanimity which God has raised, through suffering and want, to such a height?—a height which has so deeply affected your own heart, and forced tears from you?"

"No, not for worlds," answered Theresa. "Let him give all he has, if he will. God will never forsake such a man!"

Arner then said to Rudi: "Give your children something to eat."

But Rudeli pulled his father by the arm, and whispered in his ear: "Father, may I take Gertrude something?"

"Yes," said Rudi; "but wait a little."

Arner had heard the word Gertrude, and asked what the little fellow was saying about her.

Then Rudi told him about the stolen potatoes, and his mother's death-bed; and the goodness of Leonard and Gertrude, and that the very shoes and stockings he had on came from them; adding: "This is a blessed day for me, your honor! but I can not enjoy one mouthful, if these people do not come and share it."

How Arner praised them, and how they all admired the quiet goodness of a poor mason's wife, and the holy death of Catharine; and how Rudeli ran with a beating heart to invite Leonard and Gertrude; and how they declined till Arner sent Claus again for them and their children, and then came abashed and with downcast eyes; how Charles and Emily begged their papa and mamma to give them shoes and stockings, and some of their old clothes, for all the children, and helped them to the nicest food; and how kind the pastor's wife was to them; and how Rudeli and his sisters were not content till Gertrude came, and then ran to her, seized hold of her hand, and jumped into her arms. All this I will not seek to describe by many words.

Arner and Theresa stood for some time gazing on the scene, deeply touched by the sight of so much misery, which was now cheered and entirely relieved. At last, with tears in their eyes, they quietly took leave; and the squire said to the coachman: "Drive gently for a mile or two."

Leonard and Gertrude remained with Rudi till eight o'clock, joyfully sympathizing in his good fortune.

Chapter XCIX.—A pleasing prospect.

For the last few weeks, there has been a general report in the village, that Gertrude wishes to bring about a marriage between Rudi and young Meyer's sister, who is her dearest friend.

And as Rudi's meadow is worth at least two thousand florins, and it is said that the squire has told her brother he should rejoice in the match, people suppose she will not refuse him.

The mason goes on extremely well with the building, and the squire likes him better every day.

Chapter C.—The poulterer's reward.

The poulterer came in for his share of good fortune. Theresa saw him, as they were driving home, and said to Arner: "He should not go unrewarded; for, in reality, it was he, and his night journey, which brought all this about."

Then Arner called out to the poulterer, and said: "Christopher! my wife insists upon having you paid for your devil's business:" and he gave him a couple of crowns.

The poulterer made a low bow, and said: "Please your honor, I should like to do such devil's business every day of my life."

"Yes," said Arner; "provided you could be sure of having the dogs kept well chained up."

"Very true, your honor," said the poulterer; and the carriage drove on.

REMARKS BY THE EDITOR.

THE foregoing pages, although constituting a tale complete in itself, and the whole work as originally published in 1781, are but about one-fourth part of "*Leonard and Gertrude*," as enlarged in subsequent editions.

As introductory to the chapters on the *School in Bonnal*, which are the only portion to be given from the remainder of the work, it will not be improper to give a brief account of all of it.

The first volume of the collected edition of Pestalozzi's works [1818—26,] contains all the portion above printed. The story proceeds with a continuation of Arner's efforts for the improvement of the village, with the help of the pastor, of Gluelphi, a retired military officer who becomes schoolmaster, Meyer, a cotton manufacturer, and Gertrude, whose simple and effective practical methods of managing and instructing her own and Rudi's children, furnish indispensable patterns to the benevolent and well-educated but inexperienced gentry.

The school, though a prominent feature in the story, is only one feature. It includes a combination of measures set on foot by Arner for the moral, social, and physical improvement of the people of the village, both rich and poor. The action of the tale consists of the progress of these measures, and of the opposition to them, resulting from the obstinate adherence of the rich to their long-established habits of oppression and extortion, and from the low vices of falsehood, hypocrisy, &c., which have naturally infected the poor.

One of the chief measures undertaken by Arner for ameliorating the physical condition of the village, is the partition among the landowners of a certain common, into equal shares for rich and poor; a scheme promising material advantage to the latter, and perfectly fair to the former. This is bitterly opposed by the large landowners, however; and the clumsy cunning with which they scheme together to prevent the partition, and the energetic movements of Arner toward the accomplishment of it, form a very curious and graphic picture of the social life of the villagers of the period.

The feudal authority possessed by Arner, however, is too great to admit of any other than underhand and secret methods of opposition to his various reforms; and these would necessarily fail at furthest with the disappearance of the older generation from the scene, and with the gradual substitution in their places of those growing up under the influence of the reformatory measures and better education introduced. But the progress of events renders it proper for Arner to make application to the government for purposes connected with his plans, and some meddlesome relatives of his take the opportunity to make unfavorable representations to a conservative minister, with the design of breaking off his enterprise. This the minister endeavors to do, from apprehensions of some revolutionary contagion which is to be spread among Arner's peasantry, thence into the vicinity, and thence onward. But no serious injuries ensued; and the whole result of Arner's undertaking was, as might be expected, the beginning of a reform among the younger portion of the community, and an increased degree of outward propriety among the elder.

The career of Hummel, the bailiff, is somewhat elaborately illustrated by an episodical history of his previous life. Two sermons by the pastor, though also digressions from the thread of the story, are not without interest, as giving Pestalozzi's views of what the spirit and methods of popular education should be. Hummel himself, after undergoing public punishment, is exhibited at the close of the work, with more truthfulness than is usual in a story, as relapsing, so far as his failing health and diminished riches and influence permit, into his old habits of vile language, swindling, and bullying.

But the story comes to no regular conclusion at the end of the fourth volume;—it drops all the threads of the village life, suddenly and without any gathering together; although the first volume, which was written a year or two before the others, they being added to it by after-thought, is reasonably complete as a work of art.

The following chapters upon the *School in Bonnal*, are from various parts of the three last volumes; and are selected as furnishing, in their connected succession, a good specimen of the style of the remainder of the work, and as presenting an exemplification of Pestalozzi's favorite doctrine of the intimate relation between domestic and school instruction.

VIII. PESTALOZZI.—THE SCHOOL IN BONNAL.*

1. A Good School is Founded.

Since the squire had returned from Cotton Meyer's, he had spent every moment he could spare with the lieutenant, in consultation with him on the organization of the new school. They both came to the conclusion that a child is always well-educated, when he has learned to practice skillfully, orderly, and to the benefit of him and his, what is to be his future occupation.

This principal object of all education seemed to them at once the first requisite of a reasonable school for human beings. And they perceived that the lieutenant, and any person proposing to establish a good school for farmers' and factory children, must either himself know and understand what such children need to know and do, in order to become capable farmers and factory workers; or, if he does not himself understand it, that he must inquire and learn about it, and have those at hand who do know and can show him.

They naturally thought first of Cotton Meyer himself, and immediately after this conversation, and their meal, they went to him.

"This is the man of whom I have said so much to you," said the squire to the lieutenant, and then, to Meyer, "And this is a gentleman who, I hope, will encourage you about your school."

Meyer did not understand; but the squire explained to him, saying that this was to be the schoolmaster of the village.

Meyer could not sufficiently wonder at this, and after a time he said, "If the gentleman is willing to take so much pains, we can not thank him enough; but it will require time to become well acquainted with our condition and ways, in the village."

Lieutenant. "I presume so; but one must begin some time or other; and I shall not regret any pains I take to examine as thoroughly as possible what is needed, and what your children can properly learn, in order to be well-fitted for their farming and manufacturing."

Meyer. "That will be an excellent beginning."

Lieut. "I do not know how else I ought to begin; and I shall take every opportunity of becoming acquainted with all manner of house and field labor, so as to learn correctly what training and what example your children need, in order to the right education for their vocation and circumstances."

Meyer's Mareieli was quite at home with the lieutenant. She showed him all about the house, and in the stables, what the children must do, to learn to do in good order whatever was necessary for themselves and their parents; made them dig in the garden and throw earth hither and thither, to even the ground and improve its appearance, and adjust the edges; and to scatter fodder correctly. The more he saw, the more questions he asked; inquired how they

* From Part III. of "*Lienhard and Gertrud*," as extracted in Christoffel's "*Pestalozzi's Life and Views*," Zurich, 1847.

measured hay, reckoned tithes, and kept account of the cotton manufacture; what was the difference of wages in different kinds of cotton, and a hundred other things. These they explained to him as far as they could. Then he proposed to teach the children how to spin. But Mareieli said, "We take in some hundred *zentners** of yarn in a year, and I have never yet brought them to spin right well. And I can not complain about it, either; for they have to do a good deal in the fields and about the cattle. But if you desire to see a good arrangement for the matter of spinning, you must go to see the mason's wife. With her, there is something to be seen on that point; but not with us."

Lieut. "Is not the mason's wife, of whom you speak, named Gertrude?"

Mareieli. "It seems that you know her already?"

Lieut. "No; but the squire had proposed to go directly from you to her."

Mar. "Well; then you will see that I told you correctly."

2. A Good School is the Foundation of all Good Fortune.

Gertrude's room was so full, when they entered, that they could scarcely pass between the wheels. Gertrude, who had not expected to see any strangers, told the children, as the door opened, to get up and make room. But the squire would not let one of them move, but gave his hand first to the pastor and then to the lieutenant, to lead them behind the children, next the wall, to Gertrude's table.

You could not believe how much the scene delighted these gentlemen. What they had seen with Cotton Meyer seemed as nothing, in comparison.

And very naturally. Order and comfort, about a rich man, do not surprise. We think, hundreds of others do not do so well, because they have not money. But happiness and comfort in a poor hut, showing so unanswerably that every body in the world could be comfortable, if they could maintain good order and were well brought up—this astonishes a well-disposed mind, almost beyond power of expression.

But the gentlemen had a whole room full of such poor children, in the full enjoyment of such blessings, before their eyes. The squire seemed for a time to be seeing the picture of the first-born of his future better-taught people, as if in a dream; and the falcon eyes of the lieutenant glanced hither and thither like lightning, from child to child, from hand to hand, from work to work, from eye to eye. The more he saw, the fuller did his heart grow with the thought: She has done, and completely, what we seek; the school which we look for is in her room.

The room was for a time as still as death. The gentlemen could do nothing but gaze and gaze, and be silent. But Gertrude's heart beat at the stillness and at the marks of respect which the lieutenant showed to her during it, and which bordered on reverence. The children however spun away briskly, and laughed out of their eyes to each other; for they perceived that the gentlemen were there on their account, and to see their work.

The lieutenant's first words to Gertrude were, "Do these children all belong to you, mistress?"

"No," said Gertrude, "they are not all mine;" and she then pointed out, one after another, which were hers, and which were Rudi's.

"Think of it, lieutenant," said the pastor, "these children, who belong to Rudi, could not spin one thread, four weeks ago."

* Hundred weight.

The lieutenant looked at the pastor, and at Gertrude, and answered, "Is it possible!"

Gertrude. "That is not remarkable. A child will learn to spin right well in a couple of weeks. I have known children to learn it in two days."

Squire. "It is not that which I am wondering at in this room, but quite another thing. These children of other people, since the three or four weeks ago when Gertrude received them, have come to look so differently, that in truth I scarcely knew one of them. Living death, and the extremest misery, spoke from their faces; and these are so gone that no trace of them is left."

The lieutenant replied, in French, "But what does she do to the children, then?"

Squire. "God knows!"

Pastor. "If you stay here all day, you hear no tone, nor see any shadow of any thing particular. It seems always, and in every thing she does, as if any other woman could do it; and certainly, the commonest wife would never imagine that Gertrude was doing, or could do, any thing which she herself could not."

Lieut. "You could not say more to raise her in my estimation. That is the culmination of art, where men think there is none at all. The loftiest is so simple that children and boys think they could do much more than that."

As the gentlemen conversed in French, the children began to look at each other and laugh. Heireli and the child who sat opposite to her made mouths to each other, as if to say, "*Parlen, parlen, parlen.*"

Gertrude only nodded, and all was still in a moment. And then the lieutenant, seeing a book lying on every wheel, asked Gertrude what they were doing with them."

Ger. "Oh, they learn out of them."

Lieut. "But, not while they are spinning?"

Ger. "Certainly."

Lieut. "I want to see that."

Squire. "Yes; you must show us that, Gertrude."

Ger. "Children, take up your books and learn."

Children. "Loud, as we did before?"

Ger. "Yes, loud, as you did before; but right."

Then the children opened their books, and each laid the appointed page before him, and studied the lesson which had been set. But the wheels turned as before, although the children kept their eyes wholly on the books.

The lieutenant could not be satisfied with seeing, and desired her to show him every thing relating to her management of the children, and what she taught them.

She would have excused herself, and said it was nothing at all but what the gentlemen knew, and a thousand times better than she.

But the squire intimated to her to proceed. Then she told the children to close their books, and she taught them, by rote, a stanza from the song,

"How beautiful the sunbeams' play,
And how their soft and brilliant ray
Delights and quickens all mankind—
The eye, the brain, and all the mind!"

The third stanza, which they were then learning, reads thus:—

> "The sun is set. And thus goes down,
> Before the Lord of Heaven's frown,
> The loftiness and pride of men,
> And all is dusk and night again."

She repeated one line at a time, distinctly and slowly, and the children said it after her, just as slowly, and very distinctly, and did so over and over, until one said, "I know it now." Then she let that one repeat the stanza alone, and when he knew every syllable, she permitted him to repeat it to the others, and them to repeat after him, until they knew it. Then she began with them all three of the stanzas, of which they had already learned the first two. And then she showed the gentlemen how she taught them arithmetic; and her mode was the simplest and most practical that can be imagined.

But of that I shall speak again in another place.

3. Recruiting Officer's Doings.

The lieutenant was every moment more convinced that this was the right instruction for his school; but he was also convinced that he needed a woman like this, if the giving it was to be not merely possible, but actual.

A Prussian recruiting officer does not contrive so many means of getting into the service a fellow who comes up to the standard, as the lieutenant contrived to decoy into his trap this woman, who came up to his standard in school teaching.

"But, mistress," he began, "could not the arrangements in your room here be introduced into a school?"

She thought a moment, and replied, "I don't know. But it seems as if what is possible with ten children is possible with forty. But it would require much; and I do not believe that it would be easy to find a schoolmaster who would permit such an arrangement in his school."

Lieut. "But if you knew of one who desired to introduce it, would you help him?"

Ger. (*Laughing.*) "Yes, indeed; as much as I could."

Lieut. "And if I am he?"

Ger. "Are what?"

Lieut. "The schoolmaster, who would be glad to organize such a school as you have in your room."

Ger. "You are no schoolmaster.'

Lieut. "Yes I am. Ask the gentlemen."

Ger. "Yes, perhaps, in a city, and in something of which we know neither *gigs* nor *gags*."

Lieut. "No; but, honestly, in a village."

Ger. (*Pointing to the wheels.*) "Of such children?"

Lieut. "Yes, of such children."

Ger. "It is a long way from me to the place where schoolmasters for such children look like you."

Lieut. "Not so far."

Ger. "I think it is."

Lieut. "But you will help me, if I undertake to organize my school in that way?"

Ger. "If it is far away, I will not go with you."

Lieut. "I shall remain here."

Ger. "And keep school?"

Lieut. "Yes."

Ger. "Here in the room?"

Lieut. "No; in the school-room."

Ger. "You would be sorry, if you should be taken at your word."

Lieut. "But you still more, if you should have to help me."

Ger. "No; it would please me."

Lieut. "You have said twice that you would help me."

Ger. "I have—and I say so three times, if you are our schoolmaster."

Here he and the other gentlemen began to laugh; and the squire said "Yes, Gertrude; he is certainly your schoolmaster."

This perplexed her. She blushed, and did not know what to say.

Lieut. "What makes you so silent?"

Ger. "I think it would have been well if I had been as silent for a quarter of an hour back."

Lieut. "Why?"

Ger. "How can I help you, if you are a schoolmaster?"

Lieut. "You are looking for excuses; but I shall not let you go."

Ger. "I will beg you."

Lieut. "It will be of no use; if you had promised to marry me, you must abide by the promise."

Ger. "No, indeed!"

Lieut. "Yes, indeed!"

Ger. "It is out of the question."

Squire. "If there is any thing which you know, Gertrude, do it as well as you can; he will not ask any thing more; but, whatever you do to help him, you will do to help me."

Ger. "I will, very willingly; but you see my room full of children, and how I am tied down. But, with regard to advice and help in matters relating to work, which a gentleman naturally can not understand, I know a woman who understands them much better than I; and she can do whatever I can not."

Squire. "Arrange it as you can; but give him your hand on the bargain."

4. A Proud Schoolmaster.

The new condition of affairs raised the courage of the pastor, who had been almost in the state of a slave under the old squire; and his acquaintance with the son contributed much toward accomplishing his ancient plans. On the next Sunday he explained to the people some chapters of the Bible; and, at the end of the service, called for whatever else was to be done. Then the squire took the lieutenant by the hand, and told him to say himself to the congregation what he desired to do for their children.

The lieutenant arose, bowed to the squire, the pastor, and the congregation, took off his hat, leaned on his stick, and said:—"I have been brought up with a nobleman, and am myself a nobleman; but I am not for that reason ashamed to serve God and my fellow-men in the situation which Providence calls me; and I thank my dear parents, now under the ground, for the good education they gave me, and which enables me now to put your school on such a footing that, if God will, your children shall all their lives be respected for having attended it. But it is not my business to make long speeches and sermons;

but, if it please God, I will begin my school instruction to-morrow, and then every thing will be made plain. Only I will say that each child should bring his work, whether sewing, or spinning cotton, or whatever it be, and the instruments for the same, until the squire shall purchase such for the school."

"And what will he do with spinning-wheels in the school?" said men and women to each other in all their seats, and one, behind him, so loud that he heard it.

The lieutenant turned round, and said aloud, "Nothing, except to make the children learn to read and cipher, of each other."

This the farmers could not get into their heads how the scholars could learn to read and cipher of each other; and many of them said, at the church-door, "It will be with him as it was with the madder-plants, and the beautiful sheep that the old squire had brought from two hundred leagues away, and then let them die miserably at their fodder." But some older and experienced men said, "He does not look at all like the madder-plants; and has not the appearance of a man who talks carelessly."

That evening the lieutenant went into the school-room, and nailed up, immediately opposite to where he was going to sit, a beautiful engraving. This represented an old man, with a long white beard, who, with wrinkled brow, and eyes wide open, lifted up his finger.

The squire and the pastor said, "What is that for?"

Lieut. "He is to say to me, 'Gluelphi, swear not, while you sit there before me!'"

They replied, "Then we will not pull him down, he fills too important a place."

Lieut. "I have been considering about it."

5. School Organization.

Next morning, the lieutenant began with his school. But I should not readily recommend any other schoolmaster to do what he did, and after such a Sunday's proclamation, which was considered proud by every body, then cause his school to be put in order by a farmer's wife. Still, if he be a Gluelphi, he may do it, and it will not injure him; but I mean a real Gluelphi, not a pretended one.

He let Gertrude put the children in order, just as if she had them at home.

She divided them according to age, and the work they had, as they could best be put together; and placed her own and Rudi's children, who were already accustomed to her management, between others. In front, next the table, she put those who did not know their A, B, C; next behind them, those who were to spell; then those who could read a little, and last those who could read fluently. Then, for the first row, she put only three letters on the blackboard, and taught them to them. Whichever knew them best then was to name them aloud, and the others were to repeat them after him. Then she changed the order of the letters, wrote them larger and smaller, and so left them before their eyes, all the morning. In like manner she wrote up several letters, for the scholars who were learning to spell, and those who could read a little had to spell with these letters. But these, as well as those who could read fluently, were to have their books always open by their spinning-wheels, and to repeat in a low tone of voice after one who read aloud. And every moment they were saying to that one "Go on."

For the work, Gertrude had brought a woman with her, named Margaret, who was to come to the school every day; as Gertrude had no time for that purpose.

This Margaret understood her business so well that it would not be easy to find another like her. As soon as any child's hand, or wheel, was still, she stepped up to him, and did not leave him until all was going on in good order again.

Most of the children carried home that evening so much work, that their mothers did not believe they had done it alone. But many of the children answered, "Yes; it makes a difference whether Margaret shows us, or you." And in like manner they praised the lieutenant, their schoolmaster.

In the afternoon he conducted the school, and Gertrude watched him, as he had her in the morning; and things went so well that she said to him, "If I had known that I could finish all my work in helping you organize the school in a couple of hours, I should not have been so troubled on Thursday."

And he was himself pleased that things went so well.

That evening he gave to each of the children over seven years old, a couple of sheets of paper, stitched together, and a couple of pens; and each child found his name written thereon as beautifully as print. They could not look at them enough; and one after another asked him how they were to be used. He showed them; and wrote for them, for a quarter of an hour, such great letters that they looked as if they were printed. They would have watched him until morning, it seemed so beautiful to them, and they kept asking him if they were to learn to do the same.

He answered, "The better you learn to write, the better I shall be pleased." At dismissal, he told them to take care of their paper, and to stick the points of their pens into rotten apples; for that was the very best way to keep them.

"To this, many of the children answered, "Yes, that would be nice, if we had any rotten apples; but it is not winter now."

At this he laughed, and said, "If you have none, perhaps I can get them for you. The pastor's wife has certainly more than she wants."

But other children said, "No, no; we will get some, we have some yet."

6. School Organization—Continued.

The children all ran home, in order quickly to show their beautiful writing to their parents; and they praised the schoolmaster and Margaret, as much as they could. But many answered, "Yes, yes; new brooms sweep clean;" or some such singular expression, so that the children did not understand what they meant. This troubled the good children, but still they did not cease to be pleased; and if their parents took no pleasure in their beautiful writing, they showed it to whomever they could, to their little brothers in the cradle, and to the cat on the table; and took such care of them as they had never in their lives taken of any thing before. And if the little brother reached out his hand, or the cat its paw, after them, they quickly drew them back, and said, "You must only look at it with your eyes; not touch it." Some of them put theirs away in the Bible. Others said they could not open such a great book, and put them in a chest, among the most precious things they had. Their joy at going to school again was so great that the next morning many of them got up almost before day, and called their mothers to get them quickly something to eat, so that they might get to school in good season. On Friday, when the new writing-benches, which the squire had had made, were ready, their pleasure was very great. During the first lesson, they would all sit together; but the lieutenant divided them into four classes, in order that there should not be too many of them, and that none should escape him, and none could make a single mark that he did not see.

In this study also, most of the children did very well. Some learned so easily, that it seemed to come to them of itself; and others, again, did well, because they had been more in the habit of doing things that required attention. Some, however, who had never had very much in their hands except the spoon with which they ate, found great difficulties. Some learned arithmetic very easily, who found writing very hard, and who held the pen as if their hands had been crippled. And there were some young loafers among them, who had all their lives scarcely done any thing except run about the streets and fields, and who, nevertheless, learned almost every thing far quicker than the rest.

So it is in the world. The most worthless fellows have the best natural endowments, and usually exceed, in intelligence and capacity, those who do not wander about so much, but sit at home at their work. And the arithmeticians among the farmers are usually to be found at the tavern.

The schoolmaster found these poor children generally much more capable, both in body and in mind, than he had expected.

For this there is also a good reason. Need and poverty make men more reflective and shrewd than riches and superfluity, and teach him to make the best use of every thing that will bring him bread.

Gluelphi made so much use of this fact, that, in every thing he did, and in almost every word he used, in the school, he had the distinct purpose of making use of this basis laid down by nature herself, for the education of the poor and of countrymen. He was so strenuous, even, about the sweat of daily labor, that he claimed that whatever can be done for a man, makes him useful, or reliable for skill, only so far as he has acquired his knowledge and skill in the sweat of his years of study; and that, where this is wanting, the art and knowledge of men is like a mass of foam in the sea, which often looks, at a distance, like a rock rising out of the abyss, but which falls as soon as wind and wave attack it. Therefore, he said, in education, thorough and strict training to the vocation must necessarily precede all instruction by words.

He also maintained a close connection between this training to a vocation and training in manners, and asserted that the manners of every condition and trade, and even of the place or country of a man's abode, are so important to him, that the happiness and peace of all his life depends on them. Training to good manners was thus also a chief object of his school organization. He would have his school-room as clean as a church. He would not even let a pane be out of the windows, or a nail be wrongly driven in the floor; and still less would he permit the children to throw any thing on the floor, eat during study, or any thing else of the kind. He preserved strict order, even in the least thing; and arranged so that, even in sitting down and rising up, the children would not hit against each other.

In muddy weather they were made to leave their shoes at the door, and sit in their stockings. And if their coats were muddy, they had to dry them in the sun, or at the stove, as the case might be, and clean them. He himself cut their nails for many of them, and put the hair of almost all the boys in good order;

and whenever any one went from writing to working, he was obliged to wash his hands. They had, likewise, to rinse out their mouths at proper times, and take care of their teeth, and see that their breath was not foul. All these were things they knew nothing about.

When they came into the school and went out, they stepped up to him, one after the other, and said to him, "God be with you." Then he looked at them from head to foot, and looked at them so that they knew by his eye, without his saying a word, if there was any thing wrong about them. But if this look did not serve to set things right, he spoke to them. When he saw that the parents were to blame for any thing, he sent a message to them; and, not uncommonly, a child came home to its mother with the message, "You, the schoolmaster sends his respects, and asks whether you have no needles, or no thread; or if water is expensive with you," and the like.

Margaret was as if she had been made on purpose to help him about these things. If a child's hair was not in good order, she placed it with its spinning-wheel before her, and braided it up while the child studied and worked. Most of them did not know how to fasten their shoes or their stockings. All these things she showed them; adjusted their neckcloths and aprons, if they were wrong, and, if she saw a hole in their clothes, took a needle and thread and mended it. At about the close of the school, she went through the room, praising or blaming the children, as they had worked well, half-well, or ill. Those who had done well, then went first up to the schoolmaster, and said to him, "God be with you," and he then held out his hand to them and replied, "God be with you, you dear child!" Those who had done only half-well, came then to him; and to them he only said, "God be with you," without holding out his hand to them. Lastly, those who had not done well at all had to leave the room before the others, without daring to go to him at all.

If one of them came too late, he found the door shut, like the gate of a fortress that is closed. Whether then he cried or not, made no difference; the master said to him, briefly, "Go home again, now; it will do you good to think a long time about it. Every thing that is done must be done at the right time, or else it is as if it is not done at all."

7. God's Word is the Truth.

Thus, every word he said, was intended, by constantly accustoming the children to what they would in future have to say and do, to lead them into true wisdom in life; for he endeavored, with every word, to plant deep in their minds such a foundation of equanimity and peace, as every man can possess in all circumstances, if the difficulties of his lot are early made to be another nature to him. And this is the central point of the difference between his mode of instructing the children, and that of other schoolmasters.

The efficiency of his labors soon convinced the pastor of Bonnal of the importance of that distinction; and caused him to see that all verbal instruction, so far as it aims at true human wisdom, and that highest end of this wisdom, true religion, must undoubtedly be subordinated to constant exercises in useful domestic labor; and that that mouth-religion which consists in memory-work and controversial opinions may be forgotten, as soon as, by constant exercises in useful practical exertion, a better foundation is laid for good and noble aspirations; that is, for true wisdom and true religion.

But the pastor saw that he himself knew little of any such management of men, and that the lieutenant, and even Margaret, accomplished more in that direction than he did by preaching for hours, or by doing whatever else he could. He was ashamed of himself in the comparison, but he aided their undertaking, learned from both of them whatever he could, and, in every thing which he taught his children, founded upon what the lieutenant and Margaret practiced. But in proportion as these latter accustomed their children to useful labor, so much did he shorten his verbal instructions.

This he would gladly have done long before; but he did not know how to begin it, or how to continue it. He had indeed dreamed of what the lieutenant and Margaret were doing; but he could not deprive his children of such benefits as were derivable from the old system of instruction, for the sake of mere dreams of what he could not execute. But now that he saw a better truth, and the advantage of practice in doing over practice in teaching, he followed after that better truth, and in his age made giant strides in the change of his method of popular instruction.

From this time forward he permitted his children to learn no more dogmas by rote—such, for example, as those apples of discord, the questions which for two hundred years have split good Christians into so many parties, and which certainly, for country people, have not made easier the way to everlasting life; for he was every moment more convinced that man loses little or nothing by losing mere words.

But while he, like Luther, with the help of God, struck down the foolish verbiage of a mere mouth-religion, still he did not serve up instead of it a new one of the same kind, one of his own instead of the strange one; but united his efforts with those of the lieutenant and Margaret, to train his children, without many words, to a peaceful and laborious life in their vocations; by constantly accustoming them to a wise mode of life, to stop up the sources of ignoble, shameful, and disorderly practices, and in this manner to lay the foundations of a quiet and silent habit of worship of God, and of a pure, active, and equally and silent benevolence to men.

To attain this end, he based every word of his brief instructions in religion upon the doings and omissions of the children, their circumstances and duties in life; so that, when he talked with them of God and eternity, he seemed to be speaking of father and mother, of house and home—of things closely connected with this world.

He pointed out to them with his own hand the few wise and pious portions which they were still made to learn by rote from the book. Of the rest of the prolix, quarrelsome gabble, which he desired to empty out of their brains, as the summer melts away the winter snow, he saved nothing at all; and if any one began to talk to him about it, he said that he saw more clearly every day that it was not good for men to have heads filled up with too many whys and wherefores, and that daily experience showed that, just in proportion as men carried about such whys and wherefores in their heads, they lost in their degree of natural understanding, and the daily usefulness of their hands and feet. And he no longer permitted any child to learn a long prayer by heart; saying openly that it was contrary to the express spirit of Christianity, and to the command which the Saviour gave to his disciples, "But thou when thou prayest," &c.

8. To be as Good as a Man can be, he must Appear Bad.

The best thing about him was, that he said plainly, all that he did, "If I had not seen the lieutenant and Margaret doing this in their school-room with the children, I should have remained, as to their instruction, even until death, the old pastor in Bonnal, without any change, just as I have been for thirty years. I was not in a condition to undertake the chief parts of the true instruction of these children; and all that I can do for it, even now, is this: not to lay any hindrance in the way of the lieutenant and Margaret."

He was quite right; for of the ordinary employments of men, and of most things upon which the lieutenant based his proceedings, he knew nothing whatever. He both knew men, and did not know them. He could describe them in such a way that you would have to say, "Yes, they are thus." But he did not know them so that he could mingle with them, and correct or accomplish any thing about them. And the lieutenant often told him directly that he was not capable of accomplishing any real reform amongst men; that he would only destroy them with his goodness. For how kind soever the lieutenant might seem always, no one could easily have stricter principles of education than he.

He openly maintained, that "Love is useless in the training of men, except behind or by the side of fear. For they must learn to root up thorns and thistles; and men could never do that willingly, never of themselves, but only when they are obliged, or have become accustomed to. One who would set any thing right with men, or bring them up to any proposed point, must gain the mastery of their evil qualities, must follow up their falsehood, and must make them sweat with pain, for their crooked ways. The education of men is nothing except the polishing of single members of the great chain by which all humanity is bound together. Faults in the education and guidance of men consist mostly in this, that we take single links out of the chain and undertake to ornament them, as if they were isolated, and were not links belonging to that great chain; and as if the power and usefulness of that single member depended upon its being gilded, or silvered, or set with precious stones; and not upon its being well-knit to its next neighbors without any weakening, and being strongly and pliantly adapted to the daily vibrations of the whole chain, and to all its movements."

Thus spoke the man whose strength consisted in his knowledge of the world, to the clergyman, whose weakness consisted in his ignorance of it.

But it was the labor of the life of the former to acquire a knowledge of men; and he always felt gratitude to his deceased father, for having made this his design from youth up. His father had thought many men good who were not, by reason of insufficient knowledge with them; and the sorrow therefrom resulting cost him his life. A few days before his death, he called Gluelphi, then eleven years old, to his bedside, and said, "Child, trust no one, all your life, until you have experience of him. Men betray and are betrayed; but to know them, is worth gold. Respect them, but trust them not; and let it be your daily task to write down every evening what you have seen and heard."

And therewith the last tears came from his eyes, and soon they were closed. And from that day, Gluelphi had not omitted, any evening, to follow the death-bed advice of his father. He had also preserved all his written records, from youth. They are to him a treasure of knowledge of human nature; and he calls them by no name except the good bequest of his dear deceased father;

and he often moistens them with tears. They make a thousand heavy hours pleasant to him, and have been, in his school also, a guide which has quickly led him to the object he has desired.

He knew the children in a week, better than their parents in seven years; and, according to his principles, set himself to make them sweat for pain if they undertook to keep any thing secret from him, and especially to keep their hearts always open to his eyes.

9. He who Separates the Principles of Arithmetic and of Susceptibility to Truth, puts Asunder what God has Joined.

But how much soever he cared for the hearts of his children, he took as much care for their heads; and required whatever went into them should be as clear and comprehensible as the silent moon in the heavens. He said, "Nothing can be called teaching, which does not proceed in that principle; what is obscure, and deceives, and makes confused, is not, teaching, but perverting the mind."

This perversion of the mind, in his children, he guarded against, by teaching them, above all, to see and hear closely; and by laboriously and industriously teaching them habits of cool observation, and at the same time by strengthening in them the natural capacity which every man possesses. To this end, he practiced them especially in arithmetic; in which he carried them so far, within a year, that they very soon yawned if any one began to talk to them about the wonderful puzzles with which Hartknopf's friends so easily astonished the rest of the people in the village.

So true is it, that the way to lead men away from error is, not to oppose their folly with words, but to destroy the spirit of it within them. To describe the night, and the dark colors of its shadows, does not help you see; it is only by lighting a lamp, that you can show what the night was; it is only by couching a cataract, that you can show what the blindness has become. Correct seeing and correct hearing is the first step toward living wisely; and arithmetic is the means by which nature guards us from error in our searches after truth; the basis of peace and prosperity, which children can secure for their manhood only by thoughtful and careful pursuit of their employments.

For such reasons, the lieutenant thought nothing so important as a right training of his children in arithmetic; and he said, "A man's mind will not proceed well, unless it gains the habitude of apprehending and adhering to the truth, either by means of much experience, or of arithmetical practice, which will in great part supply the place of that habitude."

But his methods of teaching them arithmetic are too extended to be given here.

10. A Sure Means Against Mean and Lying Slanders.

In this matter also he succeeded with the children as he desired; and it could not but happen that one, who accomplished so much for them, should become dear to many people. But it was far from being the case that all were satisfied with him. The chief charge against him was, that he was too proud for a schoolmaster, and would not talk with the people at all. He said one thing and another to defend himself, and tried to make them understand that he was using his time and his lungs for their children; but the farmers said that, notwithstanding all that, he might stop a moment or two when any one wanted to say something to him; and, if pride did not prevent him, he would.

All the children, to be sure, contradicted their parents in this, and said that he certainly was not proud, but they replied, "He may be good to you, and may be proud nevertheless."

But the rainy weather, in the third week of his school-keeping, accomplished for him, what the good children could not do, with all their talking.

It was an established principle in Bonnal, that an old bridge, in front of the school-house, decayed for twenty years, should not be replaced; and so, whenever it rained for two days together, the children had to get wetted almost to their knees, to get to the school. But the first time that Gluelphi found the street so deep in water, he stood out in the street, as soon as the children came, in the middle of the rain, and lifted them, one after another, over the stream.

This looked very funny to a couple of men and their wives, who lived just opposite the school-house, and who were exactly those who had complained most that his pride would scarcely let him say good day and good night to people. They found great pleasure in seeing him get wet through and through, in his red coat, and thought he would never keep at it a quarter of an hour, and expected every moment that he would call out to them to know whether nobody was coming to help him. But when he continued right on with his work, just as if not even a cat lived any where near him, not to say a man, and was dripping wet, clothes and hair, and all over, and still showed no shadow of impatience, but kept carrying over one child after another, they began to say, behind their windows, "He must be a good-natured fool, after all, to keep it up so long, and we seem to have been mistaken about him. If he had been proud, he would certainly have stopped long ago."

At last they crept out of their holes, and went out to him, and said, "We did not see, before, that you were taking so much trouble, or we would have come out to you sooner. Go home and dry yourself; we will carry the children over. We can bear the rain better than you. And, before school is out, we will bring a couple of planks, too, so that there shall be a bridge here, as there used to be."

This they did not say merely, but did it. Before eleven o'clock, there was actually a bridge erected, so that after the school the scholars could go dry-shod over the brook. And, also, the complaints about his pride ceased; for the two neighbors' wives, who had been the loudest in making them, now sang quite another song.

If this seems incredible to you, reader, make an experiment yourself, and stand out in the rain for the sake of other people's children, without being called on to do so, or receiving any thing for it, until you are dripping wet; and then see whether those people do not then willingly speak good of you, and do good to you; and whether they say any thing evil of you, except in regard to something actually and very evil, or something which they absolutely can not see and understand to be otherwise than bad.

11. Foolish Words, and School Punishments.

But it was not long before the people had something else to complain about; and, indeed, something worse than before. The Hartknopf party in the village, that is, discovered that the lieutenant was not a good Christian; and began quietly to make good and simple people in the village believe it. One of the first to find comfort in this story, and to endeavor to propagate it, was the old schoolmaster. He could not endure that all the children should so praise and love the new schoolmaster. As long as he had been schoolmaster, they had hated him; and he had become so used to this, in thirty years, that he believed it must be so; and asserted that the children, not being able to understand what is good for them, naturally hate all discipline, and consequently all schoolmasters. But he made not much progress with this theory; and he fancied people were going to tell him that the children loved their present schoolmaster because he was good to them.

This vexed him; for he could not endure, all his life, to have it flung at him that his own foolishness was the reason that the children did not love him, although it was the honest truth. If he observed the least thing which he disapproved, the first word was, "You are killing me, body and soul; you will bring me into my grave. If you did not deserve hell for any other reason, you deserve it on account of me;" and the like.

Such language, especially to children, does not cause good feelings; and they must have been much more than children to be able to love a fool, who spoke to them in that way every moment. They knew whom they were dealing with, and when he was most enraged, they would say to each other, "When we kill again, and bring him some sausages and meat, we shall not go to hell any more, at least as long as he has any of them left to eat."

With the new schoolmaster the case was quite otherwise. His harshest reproofs to the children, when they did wrong, were, "That is not right," or "You are injuring yourself," or "In that way you will never arrive at any thing good," &c. Little as this was, it was effectual, because it was the truth.

Gluelphi's punishments consisted mostly in exercises intended to help the faults which they were to punish. For instance, if a child was idle, he was made to carry stone for the guard-fence, which the teacher was making some of the older boys construct, at the sand-meadow, or to cut fire-wood, &c. A forgetful one was made school-messenger, and for four or five days had to transact whatever business the teacher had in the village.

Even during his punishments, he was kind to the children, and scarcely ever talked more with them than while punishing them. "Is it not better for you," he would often say to a careless one, "to learn to keep yourself attentive to what you do, than every moment to be forgetting something, and then to have to do every thing over again?" Then the child would often throw himself upon him with tears, and, with his trembling hand in his, would reply, "Yes, dear Herr schoolmaster." And he would then answer, "Good child. Don't cry; but learn better; and tell your father and mother to help you overcome your carelessness, or your idleness."

Disobedience, which was not carelessness, he punished by not speaking publicly to such a child, for three, or four, or five days, but only alone with him; intimating to him, at the close of school, to remain. Impertinence and impropriety, he punished in the same way. Wickedness, however, and lying, he punished with the rod; and any child punished with the rod, was not permitted, during a whole week, to join in the children's plays; and his name and his fault stood entered in the Register of Offenses, until he gave unmistakable evidence of improvement, when they were stricken out again.

So great was the difference between the old and the new organization of the school.

CHRISTOPHER AND ALICE.

In the year 1782, Pestalozzi, with a view of directing the attention of the readers of "*Leonard and Gertrude*" from the story to the moral lessons which it was intended to convey, and to correct some erroneous impressions which the people had got from the picture he had drawn of the depravity of subordinate functionaries in the villages, published his "*Christopher and Alice,*" (*Christoph and Else.*) This work consists of a series of dialogues, in which Christopher, an intelligent farmer, discusses with his family, chapter by chapter, the history of Bonnal. The principal interlocutors are, besides Christopher, his wife Alice, Josiah, his head-servant, and Frederic, his eldest son. Some of his neighbors occasionally drop in, and take part in the discussion, which is replete with the soundest views of life, and of parental duty, and opportunity, conveyed in homely but expressive language. But it lacked the interest of action, and never reached the class of people for whose special benefit is was intended.

We extract the principal portion of one of the dialogues, in which Pestalozzi exalts the training office of the mother and the home above that of the schoolmaster and the school room—a leading principle of his educational labors through life—one of the earliest and latest of his aspirations for the advancement of his father-land, and of humanity.

HOME AND SCHOOL TRAINING. DOMESTIC EDUCATION.

"That is my chapter, father!" said Alice, when Christopher had read the twelfth chapter of our book;* "a pious mother, who herself teaches her children seems to me to be the finest sight on the earth."

"It is a very different one from a school room, at all events," said Josiah.

Alice. "I did not mean to say that schools are not very good."

Christopher. "Nor would I allow myself to think so."

Josiah. "Well, and it is true, after all, that nothing of what the schoolmaster can say will ever reach children's hearts in the same way as what their parents teach them; and, generally speaking, I am sure there is not in school-going all the good that people fancy there is."

Christopher. "I am afraid, Josiah, thou art rather straining thy point. We ought to thank God for all the good that there is in the world; and, as for the schools in our country, we can't thank Him enough for them."

Josiah. "Well spoken, master. It is well that there are schools; and God forbid that I should be ungrateful for any good that it has done to us. But, with all this, I think that he must be a fool who, having plenty at home, runs about begging; and that is the very thing which our village folks do, by forgetting all

---

* This chapter represents Gertrude in the midst of her children, teaching them, at the same time that they are engaged in spinning.—B.

the good lessons which they might teach their children at home, and, instead thereof, sending them every day to gather up the dry crumbs which are to be got in our miserable schools. I am sure that is not quite as it ought to be."

Christopher. "Nor is it, perhaps, quite as thou hast put it."

Josiah. "Nay, master! but only look it in the face, and thou'lt surely see it the same as I do. That which parents can teach their children is always what they stand most in need of in life; and it is a pity that parents should neglect this, by trusting in the words which the schoolmaster makes them get by heart. It is very true, they may be good and wise words, and have an excellent meaning to them; but, after all, they are only words, and coming from the mouth of a stranger, they don't come half as near home as a father's or a mother's words."

Christopher. "I can not see what thou would'st be at, Josiah."

Josiah. "Look, master! The great point in bringing up a child is, that he should be well brought up for his own house; he must learn to know, and handle, and use those things on which his bread and his quiet will depend through life; and it seems to me very plain, that fathers and mothers can teach that much better at home, than any schoolmaster can do it in his school. The schoolmaster, no doubt, tells the children of a great many things which are right and good, but they are never worth as much in his mouth as in the mouth of an upright father, or a pious mother. The schoolmaster, for instance, will tell the child to fear God, and to honor his father and mother, for that such is the word of God; but the child understands little of what he says, and mostly forgets it again before he comes home. But if, at home, his father gives him milk and bread, and his mother denies herself a morsel, that she may give it to him, the child feels and understands that he ought to honor his father and mother, who are so kind to him, and he will not forget his father's words, which tell him that such is the word of God, as easily as the empty word of the schoolmaster. In the same way, if the child is told at school to be merciful, and to love his neighbor as himself, he gets the text by heart, and perhaps thinks of it for a few days, till the nice words slip again from his memory. But at home he sees a poor neighbor's wife calling in upon his mother, lamenting over her misery, her hunger, and nakedness; he sees her pale countenance, her emaciated and trembling figure, the very image of wretchedness; his heart throbs, his tears flow; he lifts up his eyes full of grief and anxiety to his mother, as if he himself was starving; his mother goes to fetch some refreshments for the poor sufferer, in whose looks the child now reads comfort and reviving hope; his anguish ceases, his tears flow no longer, he approaches her with a smiling face; at last his mother returns, and her gift is received with sobs of gratitude, which draw fresh tears from the child's eye. Here then he learns what it is to be merciful, and to love one's neighbor. He learns it, without the aid of words, by the real fact; he sees mercy itself, instead of learning words about mercy."

Christopher. "I must own I begin to think thou art not quite mistaken in saying that too much value is put upon the schoolmaster's teaching."

Josiah. "Of course, master! If thou sendest thy sheep up into the mountain, thou reliest upon their being well kept by the shepherd, who is paid for it, and thou dost not think of running about after them thyself; but if thou hast them at home, in thy own stables, thou lookest after them thyself. Now it is just the same thing with the school; only there is this difference, that it is easy to get for the sheep pasture which is infinitely better than the food they have in the stable; but it is not so easy to find a school in which the children are better taught than they might be at home. *The parents' teaching is the kernel of wisdom, and the schoolmaster's business is only to make a husk over it, and there even is a great chance whether it turn out well.*"

Alice. "Why, Josiah, thou makest one's brains whirl all round, about one's children. I think I see now what thou art at; and I fancy many a poor, ignorant mother, who now sends her children to school, without thinking any thing about it, merely because it is the custom to do so, would be very glad to be taught better."

Josiah. "There is yet another part of the story, master. What helps the common people to get through the world, thou knowest, and to have their daily bread, and a cheerful heart, is nothing else but good sense and natural understanding; and I have never found in all my life a useful man who was what they call a good scholar. The right understanding with the common people is, as it were, free and easy, and shows itself always in the proper place and season; so that a man's words don't fit but at the very moment when they are spoken, and a quarter of an hour before or after they would not fit at all. But the school understanding, brings in all manner of sayings which are fit at all times, in summer and winter, in hot and cold, in Lent and at Easter; and that is the reason why this school understanding does not do any good to common people, who must regulate themselves according to times and seasons; and that is the reason, again, why their natural understandings, which are in them, ought to be drawn out more. And for this, there are no better teachers than the house, and the father's and mother's love, and the daily labor at home, and all the wants and necessities of life. But if the children must needs be sent to school, the schoolmaster should, at least, be an open-hearted, cheerful, affectionate, and kind man, who would be as a father to the children; a man made on purpose to open children's hearts, and their mouths, and to draw forth their understandings, as it were, from the hindermost corner. In most schools, however, it is just the contrary; the schoolmaster seems as if he was made on purpose to shut up children's mouths and hearts, and to bury their good understandings ever so deep under ground. That is the reason why healthy and cheerful children, whose hearts are full of joy and gladness, hardly ever like school. Those that show best at school are the children of whining hypocrites, or of conceited parish-officers; stupid dunces, who have no pleasure with other children; these are the bright ornaments of school rooms, who hold up their heads among the other children, like the wooden king in the ninepins among his eight fellows. But, if there is a boy who has too much good sense to keep his eyes, for hours together, fixed upon a dozen letters which he hates; or a merry girl, who, while the schoolmaster discourses of spiritual life, plays with her little hands all manner of temporal fun, under the desk; the schoolmaster, in his wisdom, settles that these are the goats who care not for their everlasting salvation. . . ."

Thus spoke good Josiah, in the overflowing of his zeal, against the nonsense of village schools, and his master and mistress grew more and more attentive to what he said.

"Well, I trust," said Christopher, at last, "there still may be some other light to view the matter in."

But Alice replied: "There may be twenty more lights to view the matter in, for aught I know. But I care not; I know this one thing, that I will have my children more about me in future; it seems very natural, indeed, that fathers and mothers should themselves teach their children as much as they possibly can. I think there is a great deal in what Josiah says, and one really shudders, when one comes to reflect what sort of people our village schoolmasters generally are. There are many of them, I know, Christopher, whom thou wouldst not trust with a cow, or a calf, over winter; and it is very true, that one ought to look more one's self after one's children, and not fancy all is well, provided one sends them to school."

EVENING HOUR OF A HERMIT.*

BY JOHN HENRY PESTALOZZI.

MAN, as he is, the same whether on a throne or under the forest leaves; man in his essence; what is he? Why do not the wise tell us? Why do not great intellects inform us what is the reality of our race? Does a farmer use oxen, and not study to understand them? Does a shepherd not investigate the nature of his sheep?

And ye who use men, and say that you protect and cherish them; do you care for them as a farmer does for his oxen? Have you such care of them as a shepherd over his sheep? Is your wisdom a knowledge of your race, and are your benefits those of enlightened shepherds of your people?

What man is, what he needs, what elevates him and degrades him, what strengthens him and weakens him, such is the knowledge needed, both by a shepherd of the people and by the inmate of the most lowly hut.

Everywhere, humanity feels this want. Everywhere it struggles to satisfy it, with labor and eagerness. For the want of it, men live restless lives, and at death they cry aloud that they have not fulfilled the purposes of their being. Their end is not the ripening of the perfect fruits of the year, which in full completion are laid away for the repose of the winter.

Why does man investigate truth without order or purpose? Why does he not seek after what his nature needs, that therewith he may secure pleasure and blessings for his life? Why does he not seek Truth, which will afford him inward peace, will develop his faculties, make his days cheerful and his years blessed?

Source of the deepest peace of our existence, pure power of our nature, blessing of our being, thou art no dream. To seek thee, to investigate after thee, is the end and destiny of man; thou art both a necessity to me, and an impulse from the deepest part of my soul, O end and destiny of man!

By what road shall I seek thee, O truth, who liftest my nature toward perfection? Man, driven by his wants, will find the path to this truth, by the way of his own inmost soul.

The powers of conferring blessings upon humanity are not a gift of art or of accident. They exist, with their fundamental principles, in the inmost nature of all men. Their development is the universal need of humanity.

Central point of life, individual destiny of man, thou art the book of nature. In thee lieth the power and the plan of that wise teacher; and every school education not erected upon the principles of human development, leads astray.

The happy infant learns by this road what his mother is to him; and thus grows within him the actual sentiment of love and of gratitude, before he can

---

* Abendstunde eines Einsiedlers.—*Pestalozzi, Werke*, vol. 5, p. 271.

understand the words, Duty or Thanks. And the son who eats his father's bread, and is kept warm from his flocks, finds by the same nature-directed way the blessing upon his studies, and his duties as a child.

All humanity is in its essence the same; and to its content there is but one road. Therefore that truth which rises from our inmost being, is universal human truth; and would serve as a truth for the reconciliation of those who are quarreling by thousands over its husks.

Man, it is thou thyself, the inner consciousness of thy powers, which is the object of the education of nature.

The general elevation of these inward powers of the human mind to a pure human wisdom, is the universal purpose of the education even of the lowest men. The practice, application and use of these powers and this wisdom, under special circumstances and conditions of humanity, is education for a profession or social condition. These must always be kept subordinate to the general object of human training.

Wisdom and power based upon simplicity and innocence, are efficient blessings in all human circumstances, and in every misfortune, as well as an indispensable necessity in every elevation of position.

To him who is not a Man, a man developed in his inmost powers, to him is wanting a basis for an education suited to his immediate destiny and to his special circumstances, such as no external elevation can excuse. Between the father and the prince, the needy man struggling with difficulties for his sustenance and the rich oppressed by cares still more burdensome, the ignorant woman and the renowned philosopher, the indolent slumberer and the genius whose eagle powers influence all the world, there are wide gulfs. But if those, in their loftiness, lack real manhood, dark clouds surround them; while in these, a cultivated manhood, pure, elevated and sufficing human greatness, will of itself shine forth from the lowest hut.

Thus a prince in his greatness may long for a wise and upright code of regulations for his prisons, yet may offer in vain a purse filled with gold for it. Let him bring real manhood into his council of war, his councils of forestry and of exchequer, and let his conduct be truly fatherly within his own house, and let him wisely, earnestly and paternally train up judges and protectors for his prisoners.

Without this, the name of enlightened laws is, in the mouth of heartless men, only another name for selfishness.

So far art thou perhaps, O Prince, from the blessing of truth which you seek.

Meanwhile are laboring in the dust beneath your feet, good fathers with their ill taught children. Prince, learn the wisdom applicable to your prisoners from the tears of their night watchings; and delegate thy rights over life and death to men who seek that wisdom in that source. Prince, educated humanity is the blessing of the world; and only through it is enlightenment efficient, and wisdom, and the inmost blessing of all laws.

Educated powers of humanity, these sources of your mighty deeds and peaceful pleasures are no purposeless impulse, nor deceitful error.

The path of nature, for developing the faculties of humanity, must be open and easy; and the method for educating men to true and satisfying wisdom, simple, and universally applicable.

Nature develops all the human faculties by practice; and their growth depends upon their exercise.

The method of nature for educating humanity is, the explanation and practice of its knowledge, its gifts, and its qualities.

Therefore the simplicity and innocence of that man are educated by nature, who uses a thorough and obedient explanation of his knowledge, and with silent industry uses his powers, and develops them into a true human wisdom. On the other hand, that man is incapable of the pleasure of the blessings of truth, who violates within himself this natural order, and weakens his sensibility for obedience and knowledge.

Men, fathers, force not the faculties of your children into paths too distant, before they have attained strength by exercise, and avoid harshness and over-fatigue.

When this right order of proceedings is anticipated, the faculties of the mind are weakened, and lose their steadiness, and the equipoise of their structure.

This you do when, before making them sensitive to truth and wisdom by the real knowledge of actual objects, you engage them in the thousand-fold confusions of word-learning and opinions; and lay the foundation of their mental character and of the first determination of their powers, instead of truth and actual objects, with sounds and speech—and words.

The artificial mode of the schools, which everywhere crowds in this affair of words, instead of the easy and slower waiting method of nature, endows men with an artificial show of acquirement which ornaments over their lack of inner natural powers, and which satisfies such times as the present century.

The miserable exhausting struggle for the mere shadow of truth, the struggle for the accent and sound and words only, of truth, where no interest can be felt, and no application is practicable; the subjection of all the powers of growing humanity to the opinions of a hard and one-sided schoolmaster; the thousand-fold niceties of word-changing and fashionable style of teaching, which are made the basis of human education—all these are sad defections from the path of nature.

Moreover, a strict and stiff adherence to one order is not nature's way of teaching. If it were, she would train one-sided characters; and her truth would not accommodate itself easily and freely to the feelings of all men.

Such a severe course would not develop the truth within man to be his useful servant, nor to be a good and affectionate mother, whose happiness and wisdom are the happiness and necessity of her children.

The power of nature, although unquestionably leading to truth, leads with no stiffness. The voice of the nightingale sounds out of the darkness; and all the appearances of nature operate, in an enlivening freedom, without the shadow of constraint anywhere, according to a prescribed order.

Man loses all the balance of his powers, the efficacy of his wisdom, if his mind is too one-sidedly and forcibly applied to any subject. Nature's mode of teaching is therefore not a forcible one.

But her teaching is steady and consistent; and her method is strictly economical.

Education of man to truth, thou art the education of his existence and his nature to satisfying wisdom.

Man who seekest truth after this method of nature, you will find it in proportion as you make it your stand point and your path.

In proportion as that truth is requisite to your repose and your enjoyment, as it is your guiding star in your troubles and the support upon which your life rests, in that proportion it will be your blessing.

The circle of knowledge, through which every man in his own place becomes blessed, begins immediately around him; from his being; from his closest relations; extends from this beginning; and at every increase must have reference to truth, that central point of all powers for blessing.

Pure sensibility to truth grows up within a narrow sphere; and pure human wisdom rests upon the solid basis of the knowledge of the nearest relations, and of an educated capacity for dealing with the nearest circumstances.

This wisdom, which reveals itself through the necessities of our condition, strengthens and educates our practical capacity; and the mental training which gives it, is simple and steady, consisting of the action of all the powers upon the phenomena of nature in their actual relations; and thus it is related to truth.

Power and feeling and practical certainty are its expressions.

Elevating path of nature, the truth to which thou leadest is power and action, origin, training, completion, and destination of the whole of humanity.

Thou dost educate with certainty; not to a rapid show of growth; and the son of nature is confined by limits;—his speech is the expression and consequence of full knowledge of facts.

The disconnected confusion of the sciolist is as little the basis which nature points out.

The man who with rapid course flits about every subject of knowledge, and does not fortify his acquirements by silent steady investigation, loses the power of observing cheerfully, and with steady search, and the still and genuine pleasure of sensibility to truth.

Unsteady will be the progress of that man who, in the hurlyburly of his sciolisms, finds, to be sure, material for many words, but sacrifices to them the quietness of real wisdom. Amidst his noisy pride, you will discover, close around him, in the place where the power of a blessed wisdom would beam brightly, only empty solitudes and darkness.

Also the slothful empty wastes of dark ignorance lead away from the path of nature. Lack of knowledge of thy nature, O man, contracts the limits of thy knowledge, more than the necessities of thy being. Misapprehension of the first principles of thy condition, deadly oppressive tyranny, withholding of all the pleasures of truth and blessing; unnatural want of general national enlightenment in relation to the most important actual needs and relations of men, overcloud and darken thee, as the deep shadow of night darkens the earth.

The effect of actual life in opposition to the inner consciousness of right, undermines our power of recognizing truth, and perverts the purity of the lofty and noble simplicity of our fundamental ideas and susceptibilities.

Therefore, all human wisdom is based upon the strength, of a good heart, and one obedient to truth; and all human blessings, upon its simplicity and innocence.

Education of humanity in this purity of simplicity and innocence, thou art the guardian of humanity, who dost protect and guide rightly the undestroyed principles of the heart, in the course of their mental development.

Man must be trained to inward peace. Content with one's condition, and with the pleasures attainable in it, patience, reverence and faith in the love of the Father under all restrictions, that is the right training to wisdom.

Without inward peace, man wanders about in wild ways. Thirst and longing after impossible forms, deprive him of every pleasure which present blessings offer, and of all the powers of a wise, patient, and obedient spirit. If the feelings are not regulated by inward peace, their power destroys the inward strength of the man, and plagues him with dark tortures, in days during which the cheerful wise man would laugh.

The discontented man worries himself within his happy home, because his dancing at the festival, his violin at the concert, his address in the public hall, were not distinguished.

Peace, and quiet pleasure, are the first purposes of human education, and its darling children. Man, thy knowledge and ambition must be subordinate to these high purposes, or thy curiosity and ambition will become gnawing agonies and curses.

Man, thou livest not for thyself alone, on earth. Nature educates thee for relations with those without thee.

In proportion as these relations are near to thee, O man, are they important for the training of thy being for its ends.

The complete mastery over a near relation, is a source of wisdom and powe over more distant ones.

Fatherhood trains princes, brotherhood, citizens, Both produce order i family and in the state.

The domestic relations of man are the first and most important re nature.

Man labors in his calling, and endures the burden of a citizen's thereby he may enjoy in quiet, the pure blessings of his domestic ha

Therefore the education of man for his professional and social pos be subordinated to the ultimate purpose, the pleasures of his pure happiness.

Therefore art thou, home, the origin of all the purely natural education o humanity.

Home, thou school of morals and of the state.

First, man, thou art a child; afterward an apprentice in thy calling.

Childish virtue is the blessing of thy days of learning; and the first training of thy faculties to the enjoyment of all the blessings of thy life.

Whoever departs from this natural order, and forces an unnatural education for state, vocation, authority, or servitude, turns humanity aside from the enjoyment of the most natural blessings, to voyage upon a rocky sea.

See ye not, O men, feel ye not, sons of earth, how your upper classes have lost their inner powers by their education? Seest thou not, humanity, how their divergence from the wise order of nature, brings empty and barren curses upon them and from them downward amongst their people? Feelest thou not, O Earth, how the human race wanders away from the happiness of its domestic relations, and everywhere crowds to wild glittering shows, to make game of wisdom and to tickle its ambition?

Erring humanity wanders afar off.

God is the nearest resource for humanity.

Even thy family, O man, and the wisest of thy pleasures, will not last thee forever.

To suffer pain and death and the grave, without God, thy nature, educated to mildness, goodness, and feeling, has no power.

In God, as the father of thy house, the source of thy blessings, in God as thy father:—in this belief findest thou peace and power and wisdom which no pain nor the grave, can shake.

Faith in God is a tendency of human feeling, in its highest condition; it is the confiding childlike trust of humanity, in the fatherhood of God.

Faith in God is the fountain of peace in life; peace in life is the fountain of inward order; inward order is the fountain of the unerring application of our powers; and this again is the source of the growth of those powers, and of their training in wisdom; wisdom is the spring of all human blessings.

Thus, faith in God is the source of all wisdom and all blessings, and is nature's road to the pure education of man.

Faith in God, thou art buried deep in the being of man. As the sense of good and evil, as the ineradicable sense of right and wrong, so immovably fast art thou lodged in our inmost nature, as a foundation for human development.

Faith in God, thou art the portion of the people in every misery, in every clime. Thou art the power of men in every exaltation, and their strength in every adversity.

Faith in God, thou art not a sequel and result of educated wisdom; thou art e endowment of simplicity; the hearkening ear of innocence to the voice ure, whose father is God.

keness and obedience are not the result and invariable consequence of e education; they must be the primitive and spontaneous first princi- an training.

der of wise men in the depth of creation, and their searches into the the creator, are not an education to this faith. In the abysses of e searcher can lose himself, and in its waters he can wander ignorantly, y from the fountains of the bottomless ocean.

God, father; God, an existence within the dwellings of men; God, within my own inmost being; God, the giver of his own gifts and of the pleasures of my life;—he is the training of man to this faith; this is the power of nature, who bases all faith upon pleasure and experience.

Otherwise, arouse thyself, O man—I call upon the people—arouse, O man, to the lesson of preponderating goodness. Let this encourage or soothe thee; that either happiness will on the whole preponderate. When the flames of misery burn over thy head and destroy thee, will this dictum of wise men support thee?

But when thy Father strengthens thee inwardly, makes thy days cheerful, lifts thy being above all sorrows, and develops within thyself an overbalance of blessed enjoyments; then thou enjoyest the education of nature to faith in God.

The bread which my child eats from my hand develops its child's feelings; not its wonder at my night watches and my care over its after years. Much judgment upon my deeds would be folly, and might lead its heart astray, and away from me.

Simplicity and innocence, pure human feelings of thankfulness and love, are the source of faith.

On the pure childlike nature of men, is based the hope of everlasting life; and a pure human faith in God is not possible for it without this hope.

The tread of a tyrant upon his brethren, upon the children of his God, makes the inmost soul of humanity to shudder. The widows and orphans of the ranks of his victims wail, tremble, hunger, believe, and die.

If God is the father of men, then the day of their death is not the day of the fulfillment of their existence.

If there is any perception of truth in thee, O man, speak. Does it not conflict with thine inmost convictions, to believe that God is the father of men, and also that the lives of these wretches are completed so?

God is not the father of men, or else death is not the completion of our life.

Man, thy inward sense is a sure guide to truth and to thy duty; and dost thou doubt, when this sense summons thee to immortality?

Believe in thyself, O man; believe in the inward intelligence of thine own soul; thus shalt thou believe in God and immortality.

God is the father of humanity; God's children are immortal.

Within thine inmost being, O man, lies that which with faith and reverence recognizes truth, innocence and simplicity.

But simplicity and innocence are not possessed by all men.

To many, this inward consciousness of humanity is a mere dream; and faith in God and immortality, based upon this inner consciousness, a contempt and a reproach.

God, who within my being dost with strength and power teach me truth, wisdom, holiness, faith and immortality; God, who hearest all the children of God;—God, whom all the good, feeling, pure and loving among men understand all alike;—God, shall I not listen to the lessons within my inmost nature, which are true and which must be true? Shall I not believe what I am and what I do?

Faith in God causes a separation of men into the children of God and the children of the world. Faith in the fatherhood of God is faith in immortality.

God, father of man; Man, child of God; this is the aim of faith.

This faith in God is a tendency of man in his relations to his blessings.

Parental love and filial love, these blessings of thy house, O man, are results of faith.

Thy rightful enjoyments, husband and father, the pleasant submission of thy wife and the deep and soul-elevating gratitude of thy children, are the results of thy faith in God.

Faith in my own father, who is a child of God, is a training for my faith in God.

My faith in God is a reinforcement of my faith in God, and of every duty of my house.

So, O elevating nature, thou dost bind together, in thy discipline, my duties and my pleasures; and at thy hand man is guided from pleasures enjoyed to new duties.

All humanity, prince or subject, master or servant, is disciplined for the especial duties of its station by the enjoyment of its most intimate natural relations.

The prince who is the child of his God, is the child of his father.

The prince who is child of his father, is father of his people.

The subject who is child of his God, is child of his father.

The subject who is child of his father, is child of his prince.

Station of prince, representation of God, father of the nation. Station of subject, child of the prince, are each, the child of God. How soft and strong and subtle is this interweaving of the natural relations of humanity.

O humanity in thy loftiness!

But vain is the sense of thy worth, to a degraded people.

I scarcely venture to name thy rank, householder. What art thou, and what canst thou be? An ox for sale? The master of thy house. The representative of the prince, within thy hut, O man in thy degradation! O Lord and Father of all!

In whatever low state, the servant is in his essence like his master; and is by nature entitled to the satisfaction of his necessities.

For the raising of the people to the enjoyment of the proper blessings of their existence, are the high the fathers of the low.

And all the people depend, for the enjoyment of their domestic happiness, upon their pure childlike confidence in the paternal feeling of their lords; and upon the fulfillment of the paternal duties of their lords, for the education and elevation of their children to the enjoyment of the blessings of humanity.

Is this expectation of men a dream? Is their childlike expectation a mere vision in their sleep and weariness of their degradation?

Faith in God, thou art the strength of their hope.

Princes who believe in God, and understand the brotherhood of men, find in this belief a stimulus to every duty of their station. They are men trained by divine power for the blessing of their people.

Princes who disbelieve the fatherhood of God and the brotherhood of men, find in this unbelief the sources of a terrible annihilation of their recognition of their duties. They are men of terror; and their power works destruction. In the recognition of the supreme paternal authority of God, princes assume to themselves the obedience of their people as a religious duty.

And the prince who does not found his own rights and duties upon obedience to God, founds his throne upon the mutable sands of popular belief in his own power.

Faith in God is in this view the bond of union between prince and subjects; the bond of the intimate connection amongst the relations of men for happiness.

Unbelief, disbelief in the brotherhood and fraternal duties of man, disrecognition and contempt of the paternal rights of God, obstinate hardiness in the misuse of power, are the dissolution of all the pure bonds of the happy relations of humanity.

The clergy are the announcers of the fatherhood of God and of the brotherhood of men; and their station is the central point of union between the natural relations of men, and the blessings which come from faith in God.

Faith in God is the source of all the pure paternal and filial feelings of men; the source of all uprightness.

Faith in God without paternal or filial feeling, is a mere glittering nonentity, without power for blessing.

The haughty administration of laws, the passing of sentences according to the ancient blasphemies which have grown up in the studies of the law and the courts, is a mummery in imitation of justice, and no blessing to the people.

Security and innocence, those sources of pure virtue among the people, those consequences of wise and fatherly justice, are consequences of faith.

Hardy and outrageous attacks upon innocence, right and truth, those evidences of the absence of a paternal feeling in the administration of the laws of a country, are the consequences of unbelief.

Violence and impudent bold usurpation contrary to right and innocence, in the spirit of a nation, are sources of national powerlessness; and thus unbelief is a source of such powerlessness.

And on the other hand, fatherly and childlike feelings in the national spirit, are the sources of all pure national blessings.

In like manner, the belief in God among the people, is a source of all pure national virtue, all popular blessings, and all national power.

Sin is the source and consequence of unbelief. It is the action of men contrary to the inner teachings of our nature as to right and wrong. Sin, the source of the perversion of our first fundamental ideas, and of our pure natural feelings. Sin, the destruction, O man, of thy faith in thyself, and in thine inward nature, destruction of thy faith in God, of thy childlike feelings toward him.

Open sin; defiance of God by man.

Abhorrence of sin; pure feeling of the childlike relation of man to God, expression and result of the faith of humanity in the revelation of God within its own nature.

Abhorrence of open sin: feelings of a child toward a man who insults his father and mother.

National abhorrence of a people against public sinners; pledge and seal of national faith, and of the childlike feelings of the people toward their supreme head.

National abhorrence by a people of the open defiance by their prince of God, is a sign of national virtue, and of the weakening of the faith and obedience of the people toward their supreme head.

Unbelief; source of the destruction of all the inner bonds of society.

Unbelief in rulers; source of disobedience in subjects.

Paternal feeling and paternal treatment by rulers establishes and assures the obedience of subjects.

Unbelief destroys the source of obedience.

Under a ruler who is not a father, the tendency of the people can not be toward the understanding of a popular character, pure in thought and happy in childlike obedience.

The consequences of unbelief:—Daily increasing burdens, daily decreasing paternal goodness, arbitrary exertion of power for no good purpose, fantastic and unnatural abuses of governmental authority, oppressive intermediate officers, decrease of power in the people to oppose them, are among the inevitable consequences of a government without faith; which despises the rights of God and of humanity.

The perception by the people of the perversion of paternal authority is the dissolution of the pure bonds of nature between the prince and his people.

Thou, good and motherly nature, dost knit the bands of social relations through the blessings of mutual happiness.

And it is the popular perception, the national feeling of the blessing of this happiness, which blesses and sanctifies these relations through the gratitude, love and faith of the people toward their ruler. Here therefore is the sacred source of all patriotism and civic virtue.

I am touching strings unused, and not accordant with fashionable tones. Despise the sound, dance-music, trilling calumnies, and drown my voice; leaving pure humanity and truth unnoticed.

All the powers of humanity only accomplish blessings through faith in God;

and the paternal character of princes, the only sources of blessings for the people, are the consequence of this faith in God.

Man, how low thou standest! If thy prince is a child of God, his authority is paternal.

Harsh and insolent exercise of authority is not paternal; is not a sign of faith in God. It is the destruction of the highest attributes of both prince and country; of the pure childlike feeling of the people toward the prince.

I can not apply to such conduct, although so common among penetrating minds in the service of princes, the name of high treason.

But what less is it, when they interpret the paternal authority of the prince to include the right of both good and evil, of both right and wrong?

What less is it, when in the prince's name they destroy the happiness of households, rob them of their goods, and cover innocence with infamy and shame?

Bond of union between humanity and its blessings, belief of prince and people in the supreme Lord of humanity, faith in God, thou alone protectest mankind from such perils.

All unbelief is arrogant; but faith in God, the childlike feeling of humanity toward God, gives a quiet sublimity to every exertion of its powers.

A brilliant and flashing creation of humanity, is that hardy laughing courage at danger and destruction, which is a human power; but it is unfavorable to a childlike feeling toward God.

Diligent economical use of every gift, aspiration after the strengthening of the faculties, is the path of nature to the development and strengthening of all the powers; and in every degradation and every weakness this is an inclination of the pure childlikeness of humanity to God.

A proneness to degrading shadows, impulse to make sport with the faculties and powers, and to hide its weaknesses, is a mark of the lowest and weakest humanity, turned aside from the natural order of development.

Outward and inward human nobleness, cultivated in the natural method, is understanding and paternal feelings toward a lower order of endowment.

Man, in thy elevation, use thy powers for this purpose.

Paternal exercise of high endowments toward the undeveloped and weak flock of common humanity.

Pure blessing of humanity, thou art the power and the result of faith.

O my cell, pleasure be within thee! Thou also art a consequence of this faith.

Hail, myself and my hut!

In order that humanity may believe in God, I abide in this hut.

The faith of the people in the true ministers of God is the source of the peacefulness of my life.

The priests of God are the representatives of the pure paternal relation of humanity.

Thy power consecrated, is the enlightenment of God.

God's enlightenment is love, wisdom, and fatherhood.

O thou who wanderest near my hut, would that I were even a shadow of the power of my God.

O Sun, thou picture of his power, thy day is completed. Thou goest down behind my mountain, O day of my completion. O hope of the coming morning, O power of my faith.

I base all freedom upon justice; but I see no certain justice in this world, except that inspired by simplicity, piety and love, and in humanity as enlightened by this inspiration.

All family administration of justice, which is the greatest, purest and most generally enjoyed in all the world, has as a whole no source except love; and yet, in the simplicity of all the nations, it accomplishes the general blessing of the world.

As all justice rests upon love, so does freedom upon justice. Pure childlikeness is the real source of freedom, which rests upon justice; and pure fatherhood is the source of all such government as is elevated enough to do justice, and to love freedom.

And the source of justice and of all worldly blessings, the sources of the love and brotherhood of men, these rest upon the great idea of religion: that we are the children of God, and that the belief in this truth is the sure foundation of all human happiness. In this great idea of religion lies the spirit of all true political wisdom which seeks the real happiness of the people; for all the moral faculties, all enlightenment and human wisdom, rest upon the same basis of the faith of humanity in God.

Forgetfulness of God, neglect of the filial relation of humanity to God, is the source of the destruction of all the power of morality, enlightenment and wisdom, for the blessing of humanity. Therefore is this loss of filial feeling toward God the greatest of human misfortunes, since it renders all God's paternal instruction impossible; and the restoration of this lost filial feeling is the salvation of the lost children of God on earth.

The man of God who through the sorrows and death of humanity re-establishes this universally lost filial feeling toward God, is the saviour of the world, the sacrificed priest of God, the mediator between God and God-forgetting humanity. His teachings are pure justice, an instructive philosophy for all people; the revelation of God the Father to the lost race of his children.

VII. PESTALOZZI,—TEACHING AS THE FATHER OF A FAMILY.

[FROM BIBER'S LIFE OF PESTALOZZI.]

The spirit in which Pestalozzi presided over his house can not be better described than by his own words, in the discourses which he addressed to the whole family every Christmas Eve and New-Year's Day. One of these, delivered on Christmas Eve, 1810, will be read with interest, as it is not only a faithful expression of the tone which he maintained in his establishment, but affords, at the same time, a pleasing picture of that peculiarity of continental custom, by which Christmas Eve and New-Year's Day are consecrated as the two great family festivals.

Children, sons and daughters of this house, and ye matured men, my friends and brethren!

What is there in this day that calls for rejoicing! For nearly twice ten centuries, this hour has ever been an hour of gladness! Is its joy, peradventure, worn out with age, and do we possess no more than the dregs and forms of its sacred solemnity? If so, I would rather not partake in it; I would not rejoice, but mourn, in this hour of ancient joy. And I ask: That ancient joy, what was it? And I look around me, to see what it is now. I have heard of the ancients, and I have partly seen it in my own days, that Christmas Eve was a night on the earth above all earthly nights. Its shades were brighter than the noon-day of highest earthly joy. The anniversaries of national emancipation from the thraldom of tyranny were not to be compared to that heavenly night, the night of heavenly rejoicing. Through the holy silence of its service resounded the words: "Glory to God in the highest, and on earth peace, and unto men purity of heart." It was as if the angels were again gathering together over the heads of men in that hour, praising God that a Saviour was born unto the world. Oh! in those days, Christmas Eve was indeed a holy night, whose joys no words can describe, its bliss no tongue declare. The earth was changed into a heaven every such night. God in the highest was glorified, on earth there was peace, and gladness among the children of men. It was a joy flowing from the innermost sanctuary of the heart, not a joy of human affection. The joys of human affection are tied to place and outward circumstances; they are individual joys. But the joy of our ancient Christmas Eve was a universal joy, it was the common joy of humankind; for it was not a human, but a divine rejoicing.

Friends and brethren, and ye, my children; Oh that I could lead you back to Christendom of old, and show you the solemnity of this hour in the days of simplicity and faith, when half the world was ready to suffer death for the faith in Christ Jesus!

My friends and brethren! Oh that I could show you the joys of Christmas

Eve in the mirror of those days! The Christian stood at this hour in the midst of his brethren, his heart filled with the Holy Ghost, and his hand with earthly gifts. Thus stood the mother among her children, the master among his workmen, the landlord among his tenants. Thus assembled the congregation before its pastor; thus the rich entered the cottage of the poor. This was the hour in which enemies offered each other the hand of reconciliation, in which the heavily laden sinner knelt down, praying in tears for the pardon of his transgressions, and rejoicing in his heart that a Saviour was born to take away sin.

This hour of heavenly joy was an hour of sanctification; the earth was a heaven-like earth, and, though the dwelling-place of mortal man, breathed the breath of immortality. Death and sorrow seemed to have departed from the earth. The holy joys of that night lightened the burdens of the poor, and eased the pangs of the wretched. Prisoners, who had long been shut out from the light of day, were liberated on that night, and returned, as if led by an angel of God, to their desolate homes, to their wives and children, who were kneeling, weeping, and praying for their deliverance; for the heart of the judge had softened itself in the joy, that to him too a Saviour was born, and it had grown milder toward his fellow-men, his enemy, and his captive. . Even the criminal under sentence of death, whom no human power could rescue from his fate, was more kindly treated; words of peace, words of life everlasting, instilled comfort into his trembling nerves. He felt not merely his guilt and misery; he felt the pardon of iniquity, and when his hour drew near, he went to meet his end with manly composure. Many thousands, entangled in debt by the necessity or the weakness of life, and persecuted by the arms of the law with merciless rigor, obtained in this sacred interval remission of their debts from the more generous feelings of their creditors, who, in the joy of having a Redeemer born to them, became themselves the redeemers of unfortunate debtors.

Oh, what a night was Christmas Eve to ancient Christendom! Oh that I could describe its blessings, and your hearts would be moved to seek God's Holy Spirit, and your hands would tremblingly give and receive human gifts sanctified by the solemnity of this hour; for you would remember, that in this hour was born unto you Christ the Saviour, and you would rejoice in him with a holy joy.

Oh that Christ Jesus would now appear to us in spirit! that we might all be like unto our children, to whom the invisible love of God is made manifest in the Christ-child* under the form of an innocent babe, like unto them in appearance, but descending from heaven with pleasant gifts. Oh that the joy of this hour, wherewith we rejoice over the birth of our Saviour, could enable us to see in spirit the divine love of Christ Jesus, giving himself up to death to be a ransom for us. Let us rejoice in the hour in which he was made flesh, in the hour in which he brought into the world the great gift of his death to be deposited on the altar of divine love. From this hour was he the Lord's High Priest, the victim for our sins.

My friends, my brethren and sisters! let us pray: "Bring back, Oh Lord, bring back unto the world those happy days, when mankind were truly rejoicing

* Christmas Eve abroad is the time when children receive gifts of every kind from their parents, godfathers, &c.; but instead of "Christmas boxes," they are "Christmas trees,"—young fir-stems, lighted up with little wax-tapers, on the twigs of which all the glittering gifts are hung. The preparation of the "Christmas tree" is a family mystery, and if the child ask from whence all the goodly things come, the answer is, "The Christ-child brought them."—B.

in their Saviour Jesus Christ, and in the hour of his birth. Bring back unto us those times, when at this hour the hearts of men were filled with the Holy Ghost, and their hands with gifts of brotherly love. Oh heavenly Father, thou wilt bring them back if we seek for them. And, as one of old asked Jesus Christ: 'Lord, what must I do to be saved?' even so let us ask: 'Lord, what must we do, that Christmas Eve may bring unto us those blessings which it brought to the Christian world in its better days? what must we do that the joy of Christmas may be an universal joy to our house, as it was in the days of old to all mankind?'"

It is by answering this question, my friends and brethren, that I will endeavor to edify you in the solemn moments of this festival, so sacred to the Christian's heart.

My friends, my brethren! the joy of Christmas was to our fathers a universal joy, the common joy of humankind, because it was the joy of holy and heavenly love. In like manner in our house, the joy of Christmas will become a universal joy only if it become among us a joy of holy and heavenly love. The fellowship of love is the only true source of fellowship in rejoicing; its divine power alone can break the bonds by which joy is restrained in the human breast. In the absence of that love, our joy is only the joy of individuals in single objects, in whose excitement selfishness is enthroned. The troop of the joyful is separated from the multitude of the mournful; and the latter are left to their fate without one feeling of sympathy, while the former, full of envy and anxiety, are jealously guarding the sources of their joy, lest any of those that are rejoicing with them should divert its streams into their own channels. Such is the joy which, fettered by the bonds of human selfishness, is unable to rise into a holy and divine feeling.

My friends and brethren! wherever the fellowship of love is wanting, the fellowship of joy is precluded. If, then, we desire to make Christmas Eve a festival to our hearts, as it was to the hearts of our fathers, the fellowship of love must first be established and secured among us. But this is wanting wherever there is not the mind of Jesus Christ and the power of his Spirit.

My friends and brethren! unless that mind and that power be in the midst of us, our house will prove to be built on sand. In vain shall we seek for the fellowship of joy, if we have not that of love.

My friends and brethren! if there be no other but human and temporal ties to bind us, we are inwardly divided already, and our external union will and must be broken up, as a spider's web by the strong wings of a wasp, or by a gush of wind.

My friends and brethren! it is no small thing for men to be united for a holy purpose. They must sanctify themselves in their union, that their purpose may remain to them a holy purpose, and that the work of their hands also may be holy. But it is far more common for men to corrupt than to sanctify themselves by their union.

My friends and brethren! let us not overlook the dangers of every union between man and man. Wherever men unite in their human capacities, their union will not lead to their purification or sanctification. It is only where a divine life forms the tie of union, that man by his union with other men can become purified and sanctified; but the union in the tie of a divine life is only possible by the fellowship of the mind of Christ and the communion of his Holy Spirit. Whoever has not the mind of Christ, nor his Spirit, will not be ennobled by any union with man. Let us not be blind, therefore, my brethren, to the dangers of our union. They are great, very great. It is the work of thy mercy, Oh Lord, that they have not ensnared us already. For how variously has in our union the human nature of the one attached itself to the human nature of the other! how manifold has been among us the fellowship of weakness! Have we not endeavored each of us to make the weakness of others a cloak wherewith to cover his own. Oh, how little has the success of our undertaking effected toward raising us to a higher state, and strengthening in us the power of divine grace! How often have we rejoiced with a merely human joy, unsanctified by the divine Spirit, in that outward success which became the more illusory as we took a merely human view of it! Oh Lord, how little have we been strengthened, and how much have we been enfeebled, by our prosperity. My friends and brethren! let us not conceal this matter from ourselves; the history of our union is nothing else than the history of the merciful dealings of divine grace, with the weakness of men united together for a holy purpose. We have pursued this purpose after the fashion of men, but the Lord has blessed our labors with the blessing of heaven. Of that blessing we have proved ourselves unworthy, for in the midst of his loving kindness toward us, our weaknesses not only remained the same, but they were often increased.

My friends and brethren! the days of our prosperity have not, as they ought to have done, prepared and strengthened us for the days of adversity; and yet adversity must necessarily come upon us, lest we should be subdued by our human weaknesses, which are in open conflict with the divine purpose of our union. My friends and brethren! are we to give way to those weaknesses of our human nature, and see our house stride on toward dissolution; or shall we, by elevating ourselves above them, save our work from destruction?

My friends and brethren! is the coming Christmas to be to us a day of deep mourning, or a joyful day of triumph, to celebrate our conquests over ourselves and our infirmities? The decisive moment is come. We must no longer rely upon outward prosperity for the success of our undertaking; for there is no prosperity that can now become really conducive to its progress; nothing but righteousness can any longer advance the object of our union. You are left, my friends, almost without a leader. My strength is gone. I am no longer an example for you of what you ought to be day by day, as members of our family. Your task is an important one. You are to educate yourselves as well as the children intrusted to our care. You are to resist the world and its vain works, and yet you are to satisfy men who have grown grey-headed in its vanities. You are to pave a new road through impervious tracts, and to walk on it as if it had been paved long ago. You are to act the parts of youths in your development, and that of men in your position to the world.

My friends! our meeting together was on a less high, it was on a human ground; nor has our temporal connection raised us to such an elevation; and yet it is indispensable for the attainment of our end, that we should rise to that point.

Oh my friends, my brethren! in what a sublime light does this purpose present itself to my view. Oh that it were possible for me to present it to you in the like manner as I did the Christmas joy of our forefathers. The purpose of our union is not founded upon our human nature, but upon the divine spark implanted within it; it is on this account that it embraces the whole of humankind; it is a universal purpose, because it addresses itself to that divine seed which God has universally deposited in the hearts of men. Our means likewise are not derived from our human nature; they emanate from a divine life within us. So far only as we are alive to that purpose in its divine character, so far as it is unfolded in us by divine means, so far only has it in us a real foundation; and it is so far only, that the attainment of it can become to us a source of universal peace and tranquillity.

My friends and brethren! if that be wanting among us, our union for the purpose of education is no more than a vain dream; from which when we wake, we shall find our eyes filled with tears.

My friends and brethren! if we be united by no better tie than that which binds men together in the vanity of their common pursuits, our union will share the fate of all vain human associations. The fetters of this vain world will then keep our union in an unholy bondage, and we shall sink, as man always does in union with man, except he be raised above the degrading influence of merely human relationship by sanctification in a divine bond. Mean selfishness will then preside among us, as it presides every where in human society, and it will cause our union to perish in itself, like a house thrown on a heap by an earthquake, in the same manner as it has ruined before thousands of human associations. Fix your view upon this prospect, my friends; do not turn your eyes from this picture. How should we feel if all this should be fulfilled in us? Oh! do not turn away your eyes from this picture of truth. If ever we should be overcome by our own weakness, and obliged to separate; if any of us should forsake the common cause and look to their private interests, some in the apparent calmness and satisfaction of selfishness, and some in the selfish sorrow of weakness; if we should part from each other; if those that are strong among us should abandon the weak ones to their fate; if any of us should become intoxicated with the narcotic of vain glory, or should endeavor for the sake of contemptible gain to obtain for themselves the credit due to all. * * * * * My friends and brethren! is it possible for you to place this picture of dissolution, degradation and ruin before your eyes, and not to feel a sacred determination kindled in your bosom, to do all in your power to avert the day of such a calamity?

It is impossible, my friends, my brethren, that you can be indifferent to that prospect: you will, I know you will, be elevated and united. Oh! let us deliver ourselves and our cause from danger, by elevation and unity of spirit. Can we do otherwise? Could we have cherished for years the idea of raising the condition of the people by a better education, and now allow it to sink into oblivion? Is it possible for us to forget those sacred hours in which our hearts were filled with pious enthusiasm at the recollection of our great purpose; those hours in which, separated from the world, and firmly united among ourselves, we acknowledged each other as devoted instruments of that purpose, and gave each other the solemn promise, which also we have openly declared before men, that we would consecrate ourselves to the holy cause for which we are called, and assist each other in its pursuit, until every one of us should have obtained strength and ability to pursue it by himself, independently of any farther assistance? Who that has for a moment felt in his bosom the spirit of our union, could consent to abandon the least among us that is truly attached to our cause, instead of lending him a helping hand, and leading him to become a mature instrument for the common purpose? Is it possible to see our blooming youth, whom none can equal in cheerfulness, in native wit, in intelligence and practical acquirements, in physical power and agility, whose whole education is so evidently superior to that commonly imparted, and not to mourn at the thought that our union should ever be dissolved? Is it possible to view the improvements produced in the method of instruction, by rendering it conformable to the nature of the human mind, and to be indifferent to the idea that the experiment, out of which these improvements arose, should be interrupted? No, it is impossible. I know you, and though I may have to complain of much frailty among you, yet I am sure, that many of you would rather die, than suffer the blessed fruits of our union to be arrested in their growth by your failings.

No, no! my brethren! let the voice of union be raised among us with a shout in the solemn hour of this festival: the voice of that union which has raised us to the privilege of becoming the servants of our brethren. Let us be faithful to that union, let us not depart from the path prescribed to us by the love of mankind. Let our object be now and forever, to consecrate ourselves to our holy calling, and to remain faithful to each other in coöperating for the attainment of our great purpose; to remain faithful to the beloved children who grow up in the midst of us, in the flower of youth; to remain faithful to truth and love in all the means that we adopt; and in the whole sphere of our exertions to preserve purity of heart.

My friends and brethren! let this day, consecrated to the remembrance of a Saviour's birth, be the day of a holy renovation of our union! let it be the day of a holy renovation of ourselves for the purposes of our calling! let the joy that Jesus Christ came in the flesh, be one with the joy that we are united in his service; let our joy be the joy of faith and love in Him! Let the sacred, the divine character of our calling, raise us far above ourselves, and above the dangers of human weakness, which exist in our union as in the union of all our brethren. Let us be sincere with ourselves, let us not deceive ourselves by the vain jingle of words, let us not contaminate the holy night of our Lord by the delusion of selfishness! Whoever seeks in our union to serve himself only, let him depart from us! Whoever makes our union a scene for the freer indulgence of his weakness, let him depart from us! Whoever feels that in our union he grows more frail and faulty than he would have allowed himself to become elsewhere, let him depart from us!

We are brought together by chance; it could not be otherwise; but let not chance keep us together like fishes caught in a net, who must all perish together. No, no! the hour is come to separate the wheat from the chaff. The hour is come, when our union must cease to afford food for the wicked. It is enough! It is enough! The goodness of God has given to each of us a time of grace and long suffering. For those who have abused that time, it is now at an end, it must be at an end! Whoever does not serve the holy purpose of our union, whoever disturbs it by his presence, let him depart from us!

My brethren! The ties of chance must this day be broken! No other tie can henceforth be suffered to exist among us than that of love and righteousness. Let us part rather than perish! We must either part and follow every one his own appointed way, or else we must stand together this day, before God and men, with one heart and one soul! resolved to follow our common calling. Such is our duty this day!

My friends, my brethren! let us be faithful to that calling; let us cheerfully run our race together! I am the weakest among you, but I am ready to bring any sacrifice that may be required of me for the attainment of our holy purpose.

My friends and brethren! be you also ready to bring those sacrifices which will be required of you! They will not be small. It is no small matter to put one's hand to the work of educating mankind; to stand forward among men, and to say: "Come to us and see the great thing which we propose to do for improving the education of the human race, for benefiting the world, and securing the welfare of our species."

My friends and brethren! This is the view which has been taken of the object of our union, and we ourselves have represented it nearly in the same light. Feeling the corrupt state into which education has fallen, and suffering under its mistakes, the world has awarded confidence to the language of my enthusiasm, and has crowned us with laurel, when we had hardly begun to search after the means by which a beautiful dream might be realized. I was myself under a great mistake. I thought the way to my end much shorter than it actually is; while the incense with which we were perfumed, as well as the unexpected success of some unripe experiments, confirmed us in that mistake, and had a prejudicial influence on our union and our institution. The seeds of corruption began to unfold themselves among us. We contradicted one another with our unripe opinions in dogmatical arrogance, and ills began to spring up in our house, which, when the fashion of praising us had grown old, afforded the world an opportunity of abusing us, likewise as a matter of fashion. Our time of trial is come, but it is better for us than the hour of vain praise. Let us not deceive ourselves. The voice of censure is becoming severe against us, and times of trouble are at hand. My poor house! thy lovers are become thy accusers, and know thou that the accusations of lovers are severe, and that their blame will become a testimony against thee in the mouth of thy enemies. My poor house! thou art grown up as a beautiful flower of the field; the gardeners envy thy beauty, because it shakes the faith of the world in their hot-houses, and verily they will take vengeance upon thee!

My friends, my brethren! despise not this time of tribulation! Our gold will be purified, and the heat of the refiner's fire will bring the dross to the surface! The world will for awhile see nothing but dross, and will lose for a time all faith in the gold, which is underneath the drossy bubbles.

My friends, my brethren! let not this offend you, but rejoice rather that your dross shall be separated from the gold of our holy cause. If the dross be permitted to swim on the surface, and all that is good and valuable among us be hidden from the eyes of the world, which can not see beyond the surface, rejoice ye! The hour of purifying will pass over; the vain dross of our labors will be thrown away, and be lost like chaff in the fire, but that which is purified will remain. Think on this, pass it not over lightly! Ask yourselves: "What then will remain! much, very much, of what we consider as gold, is now boiling up with the dross. But be ye not offended. The gold of our cause is not to be found in our outward labors, in our outward success; it is within you; there you must seek it, there you shall find, there you must value it. Our cause can have no value to us, except that which we possess in ourselves; and that value is great, it can not be little; nor must we allow ourselves to lose it in the unstable estimation formed of our external undertaking, like a diamond in a heap of sand. No! the intrinsic value of our cause is great. It requires an uncommon elevation of heart, singleness of sight, absolute submission to the guidance of Providence, indefatigable exertion, undaunted courage, constant self-denial, the humility of love, and the strength of heroes.

My friends, my brethren! let us not deceive ourselves, our aim is one which heroes only can hope to reach. Whence shall we get that heroic strength of which we stand in need?

My brethren! remember that the strength of the Lord is made perfect in weakness. The Saviour came into the world, lying in a manger, a helpless infant; and the glory of the only begotten of the Father was declared unto poor shepherds that kept watch over their flocks.

May the holy reminiscences of this day inspire us with a high and holy courage for our work. My brethren! if we are able to celebrate this festival in the spirit of our noble-hearted ancestors, in the spirit of genuine Christians, then are we capable likewise of accomplishing our work. The Lord Jesus has said: "If ye have faith as a grain of mustard seed, ye shall say unto this mountain: 'Remove hence to yonder place!' and it shall remove." My friends, if ye have faith as a grain of mustard seed, though obstacles should lie in your way like mountains, whose feet are rooted in the depth of the earth, and whose tops reach unto heaven, ye shall say to them: "Remove hence to yonder place!" and they shall remove. My friends! if we celebrate this holy festival in true faith, we shall in the same faith accomplish our task. Cast back your looks upon the times of old, and see how this festival was celebrated by true faith. His heart filled with the Holy Spirit, and his hand with gifts of human kindness, the Christian stood at this hour in the midst of his brethren. The solemn hour of heavenly joy was an hour of sanctification to our species. The earth was at this hour a heavenly earth. The dwelling-place of mortal man was filled with the breath of immortality.

If we celebrate this hour in the spirit of ancient Christendom, in the spirit of better days that are gone by, our hearts will be filled with the Holy Spirit, as well as our hands with earthly gifts. Thus shall every one of us stand in the midst of his brethren, in the cheerful circle of our children. With the hand of kindness will we seek their hands, and their eye shall find in ours the beam of love. Then will the joys of this day be to us heavenly joys, then shall we be sanctified in the rejoicing of this hour. Then, my friends, my brethren, will our house be a heavenly house, and the dwelling-place of our weakness be filled with the breath of immortality.

My friends, my brethren! the fellowship of our joy will then be a fellowship of love, and our house will no longer be built on sand. Selfishness and sensual appetite will then no longer rule over our pleasures, nor embitter our sufferings. Our union will no longer be disturbed, for heartless indifference will be banished from among us, and whoever sins against love, will stand confounded before the image of offended and weeping love. Then shall our union rest, not upon a human but upon a divine basis, and then it will and must become a source of blessing to all its members. The pangs of the suffering, the sorrows of the afflicted, and the burden of the oppressed, will then disappear. I may then adopt with truth the language of internal tranquillity, and say: "I cast my burden upon thee, Oh Lord; thou wilt sustain me." My friends, my brethren! our cause is secured, if the fellowship of love dwell among us. Oh heavenly Father, grant Thou us the grace of fellowship in Thy Spirit!

All human fellowship disturbs the high fellowship of love, which is only to be found in a divine fellowship, and of this none can partake but those who have the mind of Christ Jesus, and follow after him in the strength of his Spirit.

My friends, my brethren! let this holy night be consecrated by earnest prayer to God for the mind of Christ Jesus, and for the strength of his Spirit, that our house may be established, and the work of our calling accomplished in the fellowship of love.

And you, my beloved children, who celebrate this Christmas in the simplicity of your hearts, what shall I say to you? We wish to be partakers of your simplicity, of your child-like joy. We know, that except we be converted and become as little children, except we be elevated to the simplicity of a child-like mind, we shall not enter into the kingdom of heaven, we shall not attain the fellowship of love, by which alone our house can be established on a sure foundation. Beloved children! it is for your sakes that we are united in one family; our house is your house, and for your sakes only is it our house. Live in our family in the simplicity of love, and trust in our faithfulness and our paternal affection toward you. Be ye children, be ye innocent children in the full sense of the word. Let this festival establish you in the holy strength of a child-like mind. Behold Christ Jesus, the Saviour of the world; behold him with the graces of holy childhood at the bosom of his mother; behold him in the manger with the sweet look of holy innocence. Remember him, how he grew, and waxed strong in spirit, filled with wisdom, and how the grace of God was upon him; how he was subject unto his parents; how in fear and love toward them he increased in wisdom and stature, and in favor with God and man; how, being yet a child, he sat in the temple in the midst of the wise men, and astonished all that heard him by his understanding and answers; how grace and love never departed from him all his days; how he drew the souls of men toward him by the excellency of his life; how he took unto him little children, and declared their sweetness and simplicity to be the source of life everlasting in and with God; how his grace and love was made manifest in his sufferings and death, as the power of God to the salvation of mankind; how it forsook him not even in the last hour, that in the midst of its torments his lips instilled consolation into the soul of his mother. Oh, my children, may this solemn hour inspire you with that spirit of grace and love that was in Him, and may you be preserved in it all the days of your lives! We too, my children, stand in need of your grace and love, to nourish and to strengthen these paternal feelings, which we pray God that he may grant unto us, and without which we can not render you any service of love and righteousness

Children, let the graces of childhood elevate our souls, and purify us of all contamination of anger and wrath, and hastiness in your education. May your love animate our hearts and refresh our spirits, that we may not grow weary in the duties of our office.

Children, I must conclude: I will again speak to you in a little while. For the present let it suffice. Children, young men, men, friends and brethren, let our Christmas be unto us a day of holiness! May God in heaven sanctify it unto us! Glory be to God in the highest, and on earth peace, and meekness of heart among the children of men! Amen!

PESTALOZZI.—NEW YEAR'S ADDRESS, 1809.

* * * I bow down my face, fall down, and ask myself, Am I worthy of the benefactions of my Father? Am I worthy of that salvation of my work, and of all the value which God has given, during the past year, to me, and to my house? O God! dare I even ask it? Is man ever worthy of God's benefits? and dare I, for a moment, imagine myself worthy of the wonderful manner in which the paternal goodness of God has carried our existence, with all its weaknesses, through the dangers of the past year? The year was an important one for us. We saw what our work requires more clearly than ever before; we saw its power, and felt our own weakness, more clearly than ever. The force of circumstances had nearly swallowed up our existence. The means we used, to extricate ourselves from perils beyond our strength, increased the evil. Let an everlasting veil fall over the human part of our labors. Let the first festive hours of this day be devoted to the gratitude which we owe to the Saviour of our work, the Father of our life, the everlasting source of all that is holy or good within our association. I will thank him. I will look within myself, and acknowledge how little I was worthy of his goodness; how little I was worthy that he should thus rescue the labor of my life. O thou good God, how much did it require, even to undertake that work! Father in Heaven, what an expanse of duty did even the dream of my work lay before me! I myself dare scarcely think of the accomplishment of all those duties. Fear and shame must seize hold upon me, when I reflect what is officially required of me by the religious and human duties, and the extent, of my house. What have I done, in taking such extensive burdens on my shoulders? Near the grave, feeling more than ever the need of rest, too weak for ordinary duties, uneasy at almost every occurrence, unforeseeing its almost every danger, inconsiderate in almost every conclusion, unskillful, helpless, and unpractical in almost every thing which I begin and ought to finish. I see myself placed in relations to you, which demand the utmost calmness, the greatest foresight, the deepest deliberation, and the utmost skill and practical dexterity, that any one human task ever required. I have had nothing to oppose to all these defects of mine, except my love, and my presentiment of the possibility of good results; which have never left me. But this presentiment, and this love, were not re-enforced for my work, either by corresponding inner powers nor corresponding outward means. Thus stood my enterprise for years. Yet it was not my enterprise: I did not seek what I found; I did not know the ocean in which I was to swim, when I threw myself into the stream which has borne me into it. What I do, is not my work; I did not begin what I now see completed here; nor am I completing what I began. I stand here, surrounded by benefits from my fate, which fate yet controls; by benefits from God, which he yet controls; by friends, whom God himself has given to me, and whom he yet controls. My work exists, my friends, through you, who are around me; my work exists through you. I have ever the least share in it. My powers of sharing it, how small soever, are continually becoming smaller. What has

come to pass, has come to pass through you; and what is to come to pass, must happen through you. God's providence will never leave me to lose you, and to be obliged to seek out new supports for my work. I could thank you—but what words could render thanks for what you are to me, and to my work? Sorrow takes hold upon me. How little am I to you, in comparison with what you are to me! I look within myself, and acknowledge how much I have been wanting to my work; how my weaknesses have almost hindered my work more than they have advanced it. . . .

. . . Deeply beloved children; you too should, in this festive hour, raise your hearts to your Father in heaven, and promise him to be his children; with thanks and devotion, to be his children. Children, your good fortune is great. At a time when the great majority of children go on in neglect and abandonment, with only want for their teacher, and their passions for their guides; in days when so many, so innumerably many, better and more fortunate children, suffering under a combination of harshness, violence, and bad guidance, diverted from the paths of nature, not educated, but trained only into a one-sided, empty show of knowledge, and an equally one-sided pretense and fashion of practical efficiency, and thus offered up to the world; in such a time, you are not given over to abandonment and neglect: want is in no respect your bad counselor; nor are the dubious impulses of passion used in your training. Amongst us, neither vanity nor fear, neither honor nor shame, neither reward nor punishment, as they are elsewhere almost universally used, purposely and as part of the method, are used to show you the path in which you are to go. The divine nature, which is in you, is counted holy in you. You are, among us, what the divine nature within you and without you summon you to be. We oppose no vile force against your gifts or your tendencies; we constrain them not—we only develop them. We do not instil into you what is ours, what exists in us as corrupted by ourselves; we develop in you what remains uncorrupted within yourselves. Among us, you are not under the misfortune of seeing your whole being, your whole humanity, subordinated, and thus sacrificed to the training of some single power, some single view of your nature. It is far from us to make you such men as we are. It is far from us to make you such men as the majority of the men of the time are. Under our hands, you will become such men as your natures require; as the holy, the divine, within your natures, require. Father in heaven, grant to us that the purpose of our labors may be visibly and undeniably in thee, and through thee. Men around us assert that we propose, as the ultimate end of our labors, not thine understanding, thy wisdom; but thy humanity. No, no! It is far from me to resign myself to the cunning and art of my race, confined to the limits within which those faculties do their work. It is far from me to seek, as the end of my labor, a confined development of the lower endowments of men, and of their material senses. O God, no! What I seek is, to elevate human nature to its highest, its noblest; and this I seek to do by love Only in the holy power of love do I recognize the basis of the development of my race to whatever of the divine and eternal lies within its nature. All the capacities for intellect, and art, and knowledge, which are within my nature, I hold to be only means for the divine elevation of the heart to love. It is only in the elevation of man that I recognize the possibility of the development of the race itself to manhood. Love is the only, the eternal foundation of the training of our race to humanity. The error was great, the deception immeasurable, of believing that I sought the complete development of human nature by a one-sided cultivation of the intellect; by the exclusive study of arithmetic and mathematics. No. I seek it through the universality of love. No, no. I seek not training to mathematics, I seek training to humanity; and this comes only through love. Let your lives, your whole lives, my children, show that the whole purpose of my instruction was only love, and elevation to humanity through love. They will show it. The error of believing that I sought any other end, of believing that my method was intended only to obtain for the poor better means of earning bread, will disappear. Deeply beloved children, you will cause it to disappear. This error has arisen, not from me, not from my labors, not from my instructions to you; but only from hasty glances at my books, the special means of developing single faculties.

Your existence is a contradiction of this opinion, which gladdens my heart. Since your examination, I have seen you only for a moment yesterday, I have spoken with you but little; but my heart is full of affection for you. How little were those miserable mechanical accomplishments, which we dealt with, filling your minds! Freedom, courage, elevating strife after the lofty, the noble; these were upon your brows, in your eyes, in your glances, in your whole being. The bliss of love beamed from many eyes. Peace was upon your lips. You were far more yourselves, and for the sake of God, than you were created by us. The talents which you possess appear in their own form, as you possess them, and not at all as we have given them to you. It is true that, among us, the bonds of the folly, the self-seeking, and the misery of our day, are loosed. With us, a man may be poor. With us, any one may be destitute of all those means toward artistic training which are attainable by wealth and by favor, and may yet claim all the elevation of mind and of heart for which human nature is created. Among us, the saying is not heard, that he who is born to eat hay may eat hay. We know no class of men born only to live like beasts. We believe that the lofty endowments of human nature are found in all ranks and conditions of men. We believe that as every man, who does righteously, is acceptable before God his creator, so that every man, to whom God himself has given lofty powers of mind and of heart, is entitled to assistance, before the eyes of men, and in the midst of them, in the development of the powers which God has given him. Therefore is it that we simplify the means of that development; and therefore that we found upon the holy power of love. Children, that this love may increase, and be assured within you, is all that we propose for our object. Instruction, as such, and of itself, does not produce love, any more than it produces hate. Therefore it is that it is not the essence of education. Love is its essence.

PESTALOZZI.—ADDRESS ON HIS SEVENTY-THIRD BIRTHDAY.

Upon closer investigation of all these practical means of elevating the poor, we shall not be able to conceal from ourselves the fact that they all alike lack the firm certainty arising from the inmost pure spirit of all true and profoundly thorough human education, namely, the divinely-given instinct of father and mother; the divinely-given impulse of childlike instincts; the everlasting purity of brotherly and sisterly affection, which never passes beyond the narrow circle of the domestic relations. They all lack the certainty and continuity which comes from the connection of material stimuli to faith and love with similarly powerful stimuli to intellectual and physical activity, which appeal to the whole of human nature in freedom and by conviction. They all lack the lofty, holy influence of home. Their external scale of magnitude, on one hand, deprives them all of the genial intimateness of domestic life, which can only exist within a narrow circle of little close relations; and, on the other hand, their organization always rather makes forcible impressions by public or at least by external force, than exerts the blessed influence of domestic piety; and who can conceal from himself how unfatherly and unmotherly are the human beings often sent forth by such institutions, owing to their circumstances, and especially to all sorts of influences and interests from directors, managers, stewards, &c.? Who can estimate the difficulties which must arise from this source, in such institutions, in the way of the inner, holy essence of true human education? Such institutions, however, owing to the present condition of non-education, and of the corresponding moral, mental, and domestic debasement from overrefinement, are at present an urgent necessity. May God grant that the heart of those of the present day may be interested in the object, and take pity even according to the prevailing contracted views on the want and degradation of the poor, in all that concerns both soul and body—but that, at the same time, it will not be forgotten that good institutions for the relief of sufferers by fire and water are not good institutions for the education of the poor. Provident regulations for the prevention of losses by fire and water may, after a fashion, be classed under the head of institutions for educating the poor; but institutions for relieving actual losses by them can not.

The only sure foundation upon which we must build, for institutions for popular education, national culture, and elevating the poor, is the parental heart; which, by means of the innocence, truth, power, and purity of its love, kindles in the children the belief in love; by means of which all the bodily and mental powers of the children are united to obedience in love, and to diligence in obedience. It is only in the holiness of home that the equal development of all the human faculties can be directed, managed, and assured; and it is from this point that educational efforts must be conducted, if education, as a national affair, is to have real reference to the wants of the people, and is to cause, by its influence, the coinciding of external human knowledge, power, and motives with the internal, everlasting, divine essence of our nature.

If the saying is true, "It is easy to add to what is already discovered," it is infinitely more true that it is easy to add to the inward eternal goodness of human nature, whatever external goodness human skill can communicate to our race; but to reverse this process, to endeavor to develop that eternal inward goodness of human nature, out of our mere miserable human art, deprived of its divine foundation; this is the cause of the deepest error of the wretched debasement of the present time. The homes of the people—I do not say of the mob, for the mob have no homes—the homes of the people are the centers where unites all that is divine in those powers of human nature which admit of education. . . .

The greatest evil of our time, and the greatest and almost insurmountable obstacle to the operation of any thorough means is this, that the fathers and mothers of our times have almost universally lost the consciousness that they can do any thing—every thing—for the education of their children. This great falling away from their faith, of fathers and mothers, is the universal source of the superficial character of our means of education.

In order to improve the education of the people as a national interest, and universally, it is, above all, necessary that parents should be awakened again to consciousness that they can do something—much—every thing—for the education of their children. Fathers and mothers must, above all, learn to feel vividly how great an advantage—as intrusted by God and their own conscience with the duty of educating their own children—they enjoy, over any others to be employed as assistants therein. And, for like reasons, it is indispensable that there should be a general public recognition of the fact that a child who has lost father and mother is still a poor, unfortunate orphan, even though his guardian can employ the first among all the masters of education in the world to teach him. . . .

. . . Truth is every where and nowhere; and only he lives in the truth who sees it every where, as a phenomenon bound up with a thousand others, and nowhere, as an exacting, isolated idol before him. But the visionary weakness of man easily leads him to carve a graven image out of every great idea which he takes to his bosom, and to recognize and admit all truth, all the rights of men, only with a one-sided reference to this idol, and to whatever may serve its selfish requirements. Even great men, and deep thinkers, are not secure from the danger of seeing isolated opinions become almost a sort of monomania; not indeed as absolutely as those, the terror of mankind, which are heard from hopeless bedlamites; yet it is undeniable that favorite conceptions pushed too far, and views which become daily familiar, are liable, even in deep thinkers, to acquire such a sort of hardness that it easily becomes impossible to treat them as they are, moral and intellectual, without prejudice, and freely, but the thinker becomes a servant to his idea. The world is full of men thus prejudiced for some particular views. Are there not hundreds in every profession—military, civil, judicial, or any other, distinguished each in his department—who are holden by their opinions relative to their favorite pursuit, in a manner at least very similar to those possessed by a monomania? I must proceed still further. I must ask myself whether there are not, amongst us, many traces of this hardening into views of some great idea? I must ask, distinctly, have not incompatible ideas become equally fixed, in this way, in our heads? This I believe so truly to be the case, that I am completely convinced that we can in no way arrive at a universal internal union of the hour, and at an actual harmony of views relative to what we call our method, except by efforts to put upon an equality within us all views relative to that method—whether mathematical, theological-philosophical, natural-philosophical, humanist, philanthropist, or whatever—and by not permitting ourselves to be governed by any idea which is in progress of becoming fixed, as I have described. If we can lift ourselves to this point, the stand to which our efforts have come, by means of the determination of some of us to conform ourselves in certain views, would, by means of the increased power of each of us within his department, become really valuable for the whole of our enterprise; and I am certain that, in that case, none of us would intrude himself beyond the circle in which he can work most profitably for the promotion of our designs. In that case, I myself should not be entirely without that circle. On the contrary, I am sure that the sentence of death, of moral and intellectual failure, would no longer be passed upon me with so much zeal and pleasure as has been the case for years immediately around me. Many would then be convinced that I am alive. The misunderstandings which are and must be every moment crowding about me, as things are, are innumerable. But if they are for ever and ever to be taken as true against me, because they last long and are accompanied with the influence of men very active hereabouts, what must I think of such a fate? What I do think is this: that courts which condemn the accused on such evidence will be abhorred by the whole unprejudiced world. And for the future I have no fears on this account. I am not ungrateful, and never shall be known as such. . . . Friends, brothers! coldnesses have crept in among us, which are the result of the whole extent of the history of our association and of that outwardly chaotic condition, which has overpowered the goodness and nobility which lay and still lies at the bottom of our association, and have brought it to pass that, here and there among us, one looks at another through spectacles whose glasses are no longer clear, and can be clear no more. Brothers! the evils of our house are not of to-day, nor of yesterday. They came from afar. From the beginning of our union, we have admitted among us habits and ways of living which must necessarily, by their very nature, produce disagreements; and it is absolutely necessary that, in order to judge of these, we should look carefully back to the days of the beginning of our association. It was in truth then that the origin of the evils, under which we have lain so long, sprouted and took root. What is passed is no longer here; but, even though we forget it, its influence is no less upon the present. Friends, brothers! the hours when we united ourselves in the beginning, were hours of perfect dreaming; and of great error in that dreaming. In those days the world seemed to seek what we sought, and to love what we loved. The delusion of the time fell in with our efforts; the interests of the public authorities seemed at that time to have become the same with our own; even the selfishness of thousands, now in opposition to us, seemed then to coincide with our views. What we did was thought excellent before it was understood; even before we ourselves understood it. Honors and praises carried us almost beyond ourselves. The pecuniary prosperity of our undertaking seemed to us to be secured, almost without effort and without care. But the vision of this paradise in the air soon passed by. The thorns and thistles of the world soon began to grow up around us, as they do round the lives and doings of all men. But the dreams of those days profited us nothing. They weakened our powers, when they so variously and so urgently needed strengthening. Truly, the climate of those days was too pleasant for us. We prepared ourselves for living in the warm South, when the hard, cold days of the North were awaiting us. Why should we conceal from ourselves the truth? The vigor and purity of our ardor for our object grew weak in those days, and became, in some cases, only a pretense while good fortune lasted, not knowing the power of that zeal which in misfortune still burns, and is not extinguished even in days of the greatest trouble. I myself see in those days the origin of the evils which oppress us now; and consider incorrect all opinions respecting our later condition, which do not have reference to these earlier sources of them. It is always necessary, in judging of any particular situation or occurrence among us, to have reference to the character of the bond which united us to each other; whose peculiar quality was this, that no one of us was, by virtue of that bond, any other than what the peculiarities of his own personal, individual nature made him. Consider the importance of this point; that among us nature did every thing, art nothing. In reference to the persons of the adult members of our house, we lived without government, and without obedience. No more free development of our individuality can be imagined; nor any condition more dangerous and oppressive to my home and my place. Friends! in your judgments upon my condition and my conduct, consider this, and reflect, further, upon the great concourse of persons who became members of the establishment, without knowing what we sought, without desiring what we had, without the abilities which we needed; and who thus were, in reference to myself, presuming, and unrestrained in their conduct, just in proportion as I was under constraint with reference to them. Friends! consider the establishment in the extent of all its relations: all the necessities into which I fell, all the burdens which came upon me; and compare them with my destitution of all those means and powers which were required to meet, even in a distant degree, the external and internal requirements of our association. Friends! our innocence at the beginning of our association was praiseworthy, and the aims of that innocence were praiseworthy. But did innocence ever overcome the power of the many? And is it not a mere natural necessity that it should yield to that power? Or did it ever perfect an enterprise which ventured to throw itself, with all its outward weaknesses, into the power of the world and the current of it, without a strong steersman, as our enterprise did? Truly, we, in the dreams of our first innocence, sought for such a life as ancient piety dreamed of in a cloister; and at the same time we lived in the utmost imaginable freedom. The youngest of our inmates soon almost universally practiced a freedom of speech which the world permits to no novices; and of the elder ones, none thought of any privileges of a father-prior. And I represented the abbot of the monastery; when, in some respects, I was much more fit for the donkey of the monastery, or at least the sheep, than the abbot. Friends! I speak plainly on this point. All this is well understood; and does not at all derogate from the real good which has been planted, has taken root, and still exists among us, and which is so perfectly well known by its results on so many of our pupils, and by the conduct and the success of so many adult men who have been trained among us. But it is now time, and also a duty, to turn our attention, with truth, freedom, and earnestness, to a subject important in itself, and which on various accounts has attracted the attention of the world. We must endure the responsibilities of our places; and it would be well if a deeper consciousness of this obligation prevailed among us. From this responsibility we can not escape. All that is noble and pure—even that which is noblest and purest in the world—if it increases and grows great rapidly, must then decrease and deteriorate; and we grew much too fast, in our efforts after our good object, to know and practice sufficiently the rules which would have maintained and strengthened the growth of what was good amongst us. The greater number of those who called themselves ours, came to us rather by chance than by election or our choice; and however the temporary appearance of many things amongst us might have been understood by a practiced eye to indicate only their ephemeral nature, most of them thought my imprudence and weakness perennial. This could of course not do otherwise than to originate almost incurable evils amongst us. Even the best enterprise, if it increases too rapidly, becomes degraded by the evil qualities of the mass which accretes to it; then seizes, with the vigorous radical power of evil, upon the usually weak roots of what is good; and then becomes, even while intermingled with the overpowered goodness yet remaining, a recruiting-station for evil, which gathers in every incautious passer-by; and experience shows that men once enlisted on the side of evil soon become sworn conspirators for it, and, although feeble in the ordinary operations of life, show great power and much bad cunning in promoting their evil objects, whether idleness, disorder, impudence, or whatever they may be—or at least in obstructing the dominion of their opposites. When things come to this pass, whether in a small or large association of men, the necessity of some governing authority, competent to control such a state of affairs, becomes fully recognized; and, at however late a period, aid from such authority is sought for. But the very cause that makes such control sought for, disenables those who apply to such authority from judging of it. Judgments formed in such cases are, therefore, commonly wrong; and the necessitous state into which such applicants have fallen, is almost always a bad counselor. This was the case with us. We sought and sought, but did not find. And at no time was there more error relative to myself. Every one thought me unfit to govern; but I was still permitted to remain, as if I were fit, and the relations of all remained such as if I were so. This condition of affairs could lead to no relief. I should surely have succumbed under it, had not the protecting providence of God so graciously watched over me, that often the apparently unavoidable results of my faults passed by, as if they had not happened. This is so true, that I myself do not know, and can not explain it to myself, how I have been able to pass through the turbulent and trackless chaos into which I have been cast, without entire ruin; and to attain to that point of power and efficiency upon which I see and feel myself to be standing.

HOW GERTRUDE TEACHES HER CHILDREN.

THIS work was written in 1801, and is in the form of letters to Pestalozzi's friend Gesner, of Zurich, son of the author of "*The Death of Abel;*" and was, indeed, drawn up at his request. Its purpose is to present in a condensed form the history of the development of Pestalozzi's views on the principles and practice of instruction, up to the period of the composition of the work.

The name is not appropriate to the actual contents of the book; for instead of containing such details of rudimentary instructions as mothers might give, it is mainly a careful and condensed compend of an extended course, adapted to the minds of teachers of some experience. The title was given with reference to the previous work, "*Leonard and Gertrude*," in which Gertrude is represented as a pattern teacher for young children; and it signifies merely that the present work sets forth at greater length the principles and practice of the former one. It has an allusive propriety only.

The work commences with reference to Pestalozzi's early confusion of ideas respecting education, and states briefly his early labors for improving the condition of the poor. But he says his early hopes, as expressed in Iselin's "*Ephemerides*" (1782,) were no less comprehensive than his later ones. His progress had been in working out the details of the application of his principles to practical instruction. In the course of the unsuccessful experiment at Neuhof, he proceeds, he had acquired an acquaintance with the real needs of the Swiss people, altogether deeper than that of his cotemporaries. In the despondent years then following, he endeavored to do something toward supplying those needs, by composing and publishing his "*Inquiries into the Course of Nature in the Development of Mankind.*" But Pestalozzi was not made for a master of theories, whether in social or mental philosophy, or elsewhere. His work neither satisfied him nor commanded the attention of the public.

Pestalozzi then traces his career as a practical educator, beginning with his sudden resolution to become a schoolmaster, and his bold assumption, single-handed and without money, books, apparatus, or any thing except a ruinous old building, of the charge of the school of homeless poor children at Stanz, and pausing to give brief accounts, partly autobiographical, of his three assistants, Krüsi, Buss, and Tobler.*

Besides the exposition of his practical views, of which the following pages present an abstract in his own words, the work contains a consider-

* These autobiographies will be found in the "*American Journal of Education*," Vol. V., p. 155.

able portion of polemic matter, directed against cotemporary evils and errors in received modes of education. A principal origin of the superficial and unsubstantial character of these modes he finds to have been the introduction of printing, which, according to him, has caused an excessive devotion to mere language, without regard to thought, and has resulted in making book-men, instead of thinkers.

The latter portion of the work contains a somewhat obscure and unsatisfactory statement of the position of religious education in his system, and of the mode of giving it; which, however, is by no means to be taken as an adequate presentation of Pestalozzi's views on this point.

The positive part of the book may be considered as an extended answer to the question, "What is to be done to give the child all the theoretical and practical knowledge which he will need in order to perform properly the duties of his life, and thus to attain to inward contentment?"

This answer professes to discuss both the theory and the practice referred to in the question; but the former is predominant, although there is an honest effort to give the latter its proper place.

The following pages will sufficiently present the chief features of the most important portion of the work, that which sets forth the system of instruction within the three primary divisions of Number, Form, and Speech. For a more full account and analysis of this book, see "*American Journal of Education*," Vol. IV., Number 10, (Sept. 1857,) p. 72, *et seq.*

PESTALOZZI'S ACCOUNT OF HIS OWN EDUCATIONAL EXPERIENCE.

POPULAR education once lay before me like an immense marsh, in the mire of which I waded about, until I had discovered the sources from which its waters spring, as well as the causes by which their free course is obstructed, and made myself acquainted with those points from which a hope of draining its pools might be conceived.

You shall now follow me yourself for a while through these labyrinthine windings, from which I extricated myself by accident rather than by my own art or reflection.

Ever since my youthful days, the course of my feelings, rolled on like a mighty stream, was directed to this one point; namely, to stop the sources of that misery in which I saw the people around me immersed.

It is now more than thirty years since I first put my hand to this same work, which I am still pursuing. Iselin's "*Ephemerides*" bear witness that my present dreams and wishes are not more comprehensive than those which I was even then seeking to realize.

I lived for years together in a circle of more than fifty pauper children; in poverty did I share my bread with them, and lived myself like a pauper, to try if I could teach paupers to live as men.

The plan which I had formed for their education embraced agriculture, manufacture, and commerce. But, young as I was, I knew not what attention, and what powers, the realization of my dreams would require. I allowed myself to be guided by a deep and decided feeling of what seemed to me essential to the execution of my project; and it is true that, with all the experience of after life, I have found but little reason to modify the views I then entertained. Nevertheless my confidence in their truth, founded upon the apparent infallibility of my feeling, became my ruin. For it is equally true, on the other hand, that in no one of the three departments above-mentioned did I possess any practical ability for the management of details, nor was my mind of a cast to keep up a persevering attention to little things; and, in an insulated position, with limited means, I was unable to procure such assistance as might have made up for my own deficiencies. In a short time I was surrounded with embarrassments, and saw the great object of my wishes defeated.

In the struggle, however, in which this attempt involved me, I had learned a vast deal of truth; and I was never more fully convinced of the importance of my views and plans than at the moment when they seemed to be for ever set at rest by a total failure. My heart too was still aiming at the same object; and, being now myself plunged into wretchedness, I had a better opportunity, than any man in prosperity ever can have, of making myself intimately acquainted with the wretchedness of the people, and with its sources. I suffered even as the people suffered; and they appeared to me such as they were, and as they would not have shewn themselves to any one else. For a length of years I sat amongst them like the owl among the birds. I was cast away by men, and their sneers followed after me. "Wretch that thou art!" they exclaimed; "thou art less able than the meanest laborer to help thyself, and yet thou fanciest thyself able to help the people!" Yet amidst the scorn which I read on all lips, the mighty stream of my feeling was still directed to the same point; to stop the sources of the misery in which I saw the people around me sinking; and in one respect, at least, my power was daily increased. My misfortune was a school, in which Providence had placed me to learn truth for my great object; and I learned of it more and more. That which deceived no other, has ever deceived me; but what deceived every one else, now deceived me no longer.

I knew the people in a manner in which no one around me knew them. The glitter of prosperity arising from the newly-introduced manufactures, the freshened aspect of their houses, the abundance of their harvests, all this could not deceive me; nor even the Socratic discoursing of some of their teachers, nor the reading associations among bailiffs' sons and hair-dressers. I saw their misery, but I lost myself in the vast prospect of its scattered and insulated sources; and while my knowledge of their real condition became every day more extensive, my practical capability of remedying the evils under which they labored, increased in a far less proportion. Even "*Leonard and Gertrude*," the work which sympathy with their sufferings extorted from me, was, after all, but the production of my internal inability to offer them any real help. I stood among my contemporaries like a monument which bespeaks life, but is in itself dead. Many cast a glance upon it; but they could appreciate me and my plans no better than I myself was able to form a correct estimate of the various powers, and the details of knowledge, necessary to carry them into effect.

I grew careless; and, being swallowed up in a vortex of anxiety for outward action, I neglected to work out to a sufficient depth, within my own mind, the foundations of what I intended to bring about.

Had I done this, to what internal elevation might I have risen for the accomplishment of my purposes! and how rapidly should I then have reached my aim! I attained it not, because I was unworthy of it; because I sought it merely in the outward; because I allowed my love of truth and of justice to become a passion which tossed me about, like a torn-up reed, on the waves of life, nor would permit me to take root again in firm ground, and to imbibe that nourishment and strength of which I stood so much in need for the furtherance of my object. It was far too vain a hope, that some one else would rescue that loose reed from the waves, and secure it in the ground in which I myself neglected to plant it.

Oh, my dear friend! Who is the man that has but one feeling in common with my soul, and knows not how low I must now have sunk? And thou, my beloved Gesner, before thou readest on, wilt consecrate a tear to my course. . . . . . .

Deep dissatisfaction was gnawing my heart; eternal truth and eternal rectitude were converted by my passion into airy castles. With a hardened mind I clung stubbornly to words and sounds which had lost within me the basis of truth. Thus I degraded myself every day more with the worship of commonplaces, and the trumpeting of those quackeries, wherewith these modern times pretend to better the condition of mankind.

I was not, however, insensible to this internal abasement, nor did I fail to struggle against it. For three years I toiled, more than I can express, over my "*Inquiries into the Course of Nature in the Development of Mankind,*" chiefly with a view to get settled in my own mind as to the progress of my favorite ideas, and to bring my innate feelings into harmony with my notions of civil right and moral obligation. But this work, likewise, is no more than a testimony of my internal incapacity; a mere play of my reflective faculties. The subject is not comprehensively viewed, nor is there a due exercise of power to combat myself, or a sufficient tendency to that practical ability which was requisite for my purposes. It only served to increase that deficiency within myself, arising from a disproportion between my power and my knowledge, which it was indispensable that I should fill up, though I grew every day more unable to do so.

Nor did I reap more than I sowed. My book produced upon those around me the same effect as did every thing else I did; hardly any one understood me; and in my immediate neighborhood there were not two men to be found, who did not hint that they considered the whole book as a heap of nonsense. And even lately, a man of importance, who has much kindness for me, said with Swiss familiarity: "Don't you now feel yourself, Mr. Pestalozzi, that when you wrote that book you did not know what you wanted to be at?" Thus, however, to be misunderstood and wronged was my lot: but instead of profiting by it, as I ought to have done, I warred against my misfortune with internal scorn and a general contempt of mankind; and by thus injuring the foundation, which my cause ought to have had within myself, I did it infinitely more harm than all those could do, by whom I was misunderstood and despised. Yet I had not lost sight of my aim; but my adherence to it was no more than the obstinacy of a perverted imagination and a murmuring heart; it was on a profaned soil that I sought to cherish the sacred plant of human happiness.

I, who had just then, in my "*Inquiries,*" declared the claims of civil right as mere claims of our animal nature, and therefore essential impediments to moral purity, the only thing that is of real value to human nature, now descended so low, that amidst the violent convulsions of the revolution I expected the mere sound of social systems, and of political theories, to produce a good effect upon the men of my age, who, with few exceptions, lived upon mere puff and swell, seeking power, and hankering after well-set tables.

My head was gray; yet I was still a child. With a heart in which all the foundations of life were shaken, I still pursued, in those stormy times, my favorite object; but my way was one of prejudice, of passion, and of error. To bring to light the inveterate causes of social evils, to spread impassioned views of the social constitution and the unalterable basis of man's rights, nay, to turn to account the spirit of violence which had risen up amongst us, for the cure of some of the ills under which the people suffered; such were the means by which I hoped and sought to effect my purpose. But the purer doctrines of my former days had been but sound and word to the men among whom I lived; how much less, then, was it to be expected, that they should apprehend my meaning in the view which I now took. Even this inferior sort of truth they contaminated by their filth: they remained the same as ever; and they acted toward me in a manner which I ought to have anticipated, but which I did not anticipate, because the dream of my wishes kept me suspended in mid-air, and my soul was a stranger to that selfishness by which I might have recognized them in their true colors. I was deceived not only in every fox, but also in every fool; and to every one that came before me, and spoke well, I gave full credit for the sincerity of his intentions. With all this I knew more than any one else about the people, and about the sources of their savage and degraded condition; but I wished nothing further than that those sources might be stopped, and the evils which sprang from them arrested; and the new men, (*novi homines*) of Helvetia, whose wishes went further, and who had no knowledge of the condition of the people, found, of course, that I was not made for them. These men, in their new position, like shipwrecked women, took every straw for a mast, on which the republic might be driven to a safe shore; but me, me alone, they took for a straw not fit for a fly to cling to.

They knew it not, they intended it not; but they did me good, more good than any men have ever done me. They restored me to myself; for, in the amazement caused by the sudden change of their ship's repair into a shipwreck, I had not another word left, but that which I pronounced in the first days of confusion: "I will turn schoolmaster." For this I found confidence. I did turn schoolmaster. Ever since I have been engaged in a mighty struggle, and compelled, as it were, in spite of myself, to fill up those internal deficiencies by which my purposes were formerly defeated.

To lay before you, my friend, the whole of my existence, and my operations, since that period, is my present task. Through Legrand I had made some interest with the first Directoire for the subject of popular education, and I was preparing to open an extensive establishment for that purpose in Argovie, when Stanz was burnt down, and Legrand requested me to make the scene of misery the first scene of my operations. I went; I would have gone into the remotest clefts of the mountains, to come nearer to my aim; and now I really did come nearer. . . . But imagine my position. . . . Alone, destitute of all means of instruction, and of all other assistance, I united in my person the offices of superintendent, paymaster, steward, and sometimes chambermaid, in a half-ruined house. I was surrounded with ignorance, disease, and with every kind of novelty. The number of children rose, by degrees, to eighty: all of different ages; some full of pretensions; others inured to open beggary; and all, with a few solitary exceptions, entirely ignorant. What a task! to educate, to develop these children, what a task!

I ventured upon it. I stood in the midst of these children, pronouncing various sounds, and asking them to imitate them; whoever saw it, was struck with the effect. It is true it was a meteor which vanishes in the air as soon as it appears. No one understood its nature. I did not understand it myself. It was the result of a simple idea, or rather of a fact of human nature, which was revealed to my feelings, but of which I was far from having a clear consciousness.

PESTALOZZI.—METHODS OF ELEMENTARY INSTRUCTION.

1. The Elementary Means of Instruction Depend upon Number, Form, and Speech.

Ideas of the elements of instruction were for a long time working in my mind, vividly though indistinctly, until at last, like a "*Deus ex machina*," the conception that *the means of the elucidation of all our intuitional knowledge proceed from number, form, and speech*, seemed suddenly to give me new light on the point which I was investigating.

After long consideration of the subject—or rather, uncertain dreams about it—I at last set myself to conceive how an educated man proceeds, and must proceed, when endeavoring to abstract, and gradually make clear, any subject now floating confusedly and dimly before his eyes.

In such a case, he will—and must—observe the three following points:—

1. How many subjects, or how various ones, are before him.
2. How they look; what is their form and outline.
3. What they are called; how he can recall each to mind by means of a sound, a word.

The doing this evidently presupposes, in such a man, the following developed powers:—

1. The power of considering unlike objects in relation to their forms, and of recalling to mind their material.
2. That of abstracting these objects as to their number, and of distinctly conceiving them either as one or as many.
3. That of repeating by language, and fixing, so as not to be forgotten, the conception of an object as to number and form.

Thus I conclude that number, form, and speech are commonly the elementary means of instruction, since they include the whole sum of the external qualities of an object, so far as relates to its extent and number, and become known to my intellect through speech. Instruction, as an art, must thus, by an invariable law, proceed from this threefold basis, and endeavor

1. To teach the children to consider any object brought before their consciousness, as a unity; that is, as separate from whatever it seems to be bound up with.
2. To teach them an acquaintance with the form of each such object; its size and relations.
3. To make them as early as possible acquainted with the whole circle of words and names of all the objects known to them.

The instruction of children being to proceed from these three elementary points, it is evident, again, that the first efforts of the art must be directed to develop, establish, and strengthen, with the utmost psychological skill, the fundamental knowledge of numbering, measuring, and speaking, upon whose correct attainment depends the right knowledge of all visible objects; and afterward to bring the means of developing and training these three departments of mental attainment to the highest degree of simplicity, of perfection, and of agreement together.

The only difficulty which occurred to me upon the recognition of these three elementary points was this: Why are not all those conditions of things, which we recognize through the three senses, not elementary in the same sense, as number, form, and speech? But I soon observed that all possible objects have number, form, and name; but that the other attributes, recognized through the five senses, are not possessed in common with all others as those are, but only sometimes one and sometimes another of them. Between the three attributes of number, form, and name, and others, I also found this substantial and distinct difference—that I was unable to make any of the others elementary points of human knowledge; while, on the contrary, I saw just as clearly that all other such attributes of things as are recognized by the five senses, permit themselves to be put into immediate relations with those three; and in consequence, that in the instruction of children, knowledge of all the other qualities of subjects must be deduced immediately from the preliminary knowledge of form, number and name. I saw that by my acquaintance with the unity, form, and name of an object, my knowledge of it becomes *definite* knowledge; that by gradually aiming to know all its other qualities, I acquire a *clear* knowledge; and by understanding the relations of all facts relative to it, I acquire an *intelligent* knowledge.

I now proceeded further, and found that all our knowledge proceeds from three elementary faculties, namely:—

1. The active faculty, which renders us capable of language.

2. The indefinite power of mere perception by the senses, which gives us our consciousness of all forms.

3. The definite power of perception not by the senses alone, from which must be gained the consciousness of unity, and through it the power of counting and computing.

I thus concluded that the art of educating our race must be based upon the first and simplest results of these three fundamental elements—sound, form, and number; and that instruction in any one department could and would never lead to a result beneficial to our nature, considered in its whole compass, unless these three simple results of our fundamental faculties should be recognized as the universal starting-points for all instruction, fixed as such by nature herself; and unless these results were accordingly developed into forms proceeding universally and harmoniously from them, and calculated efficiently and surely to carry instruction forward to its completion, through the steps of a progression unbroken, and dealing alike and equally with all three. This I concluded the only means of proceeding in all three of these departments, from indistinct intuitions to definite ones, from intuitions to clear perceptions, and from clear perceptions to intelligent ideas.

Thus, moreover, I find art actually and most intimately united with nature, or rather with the ideal by means of which nature makes the objects of the creation known to us; and so was solved my problem, *viz.*, to discover a common origin of all the means of the art of instruction, and, at the same time, that form of it in which the development of the race is defined by the constitution itself of our nature:—and the difficulty removed, in the way of applying the mechanical laws, which I recognized as at the foundation of human instruction, to that system of instruction which the experience of thousands of years has given to the human race for its own development; that is, to writing, arithmetic, reading, &c.

2. The First Elementary Means of Instruction is, Accordingly,

SOUND.

From this arise the following subdivisions of instruction:—

A. In Tones; or, the means of training the organs of speech.

B. In Words; or, the means of becoming acquainted with single objects.

C. In Language; or, the means of becoming able to express ourselves with clearness relatively to such objects as become known to us, and to all which we are capable of seeing in those objects.

To repeat these subdivisions.

A. *Instruction in Tones.* This, again, divides itself into instruction in speaking tones, and singing tones.

a. Speaking tones.

With respect to these, it should not be left to chance whether they are heard by the child at an early or late period; and in great number or in small. It is important that he should hear all of them, and as early as possible.

His knowledge of them should be complete, before he has attained the ability to form them; and in like manner his power of imitating them all and with facility should be completely developed, before the forms of the letters are laid before him, and before his first exercises in reading.

The spelling-book must therefore contain all the sounds of which language consists; and should in every family be daily repeated by the child who is studying them, in the presence of the child in the cradle; so that the knowledge of those sounds may thus by frequent repetition become deeply impressed upon the latter, and indeed be made quite indelible, even before it is able to repeat one of them.

No one who has not seen it can imagine how the pronunciation of such simple sounds as ba, ba, ba, da, da, da, ma, ma, ma, la, la, la, &c., excites the attention of young children, and stimulates them; or of the gain to the general powers of acquisition of the child which comes from the early acquaintance with these sounds.

In accordance with this principle of the importance of the knowledge of sound and tones, before the child can imitate them, and in the conviction that it is equally important what representations and objects come before the eyes of young children, and what sounds come to his ears, I have composed a "*Book for Mothers;*" in which I explain, by illuminated wood-cuts, not only the fundamental points of number and form, but also the most important other attributes with which the five senses make us acquainted; and in which, by an acquaintance with many names, thus assured, and rendered vivid by much actual inspection, future reading is prepared for and made easy. In the same way also, by practice in sounds, preparatory to spelling, I prepare and facilitate this study also; for by this book, I make these sounds at home and, I may say, quarter them upon the child's mind, before the child can pronounce a syllable of them.

I intend to accompany these cuts, for the youngest children, with a book of methods, in which every word which must be said to the child upon each subject elucidated, shall be stated so clearly that even the most inexperienced mother can sufficiently attain my purpose; for the reason that not a word will need to be added to those which I shall set forth.

Thus prepared from the "*Book for Mothers*," and acquainted by actual practice from the spelling-book with the entire extent of sounds, the child must, as soon as his organs become trained to articulation, become accustomed to repeat over the various columns of sounds in the spelling-book, with as much ease as he does such other purposeless sounds as people give him to imitate.

This book differs from all previous ones in this: that its method is universal; and that the pupil himself proceeds in a visible manner, beginning with the vowels, and constructing syllables by the gradual addition of consonants behind and before, in a manner which is comprehensive, and which perceptibly facilitates speech and reading.

My method is: to take each vowel with all the consonants one after another, from b to z, and thus to form at first the simple easy syllables, ab, ad, af, &c.; and then to put before each of these simple syllables such consonants as are actually so placed in common language; as, for instance, before ab, in succession, b, g, sch, st, &c.; making bab, gab, schab, &c. By going through all the vowels in this manner, with this simple prefixing of consonants, I formed first easy syllables, and then, by prefixing more consonants, more difficult ones. This exercise necessitated manifold repetitions of the simple sounds, and a general and orderly classification of all the syllables which are alike in their elements; resulting in an indelible impression of their sounds, which is a very great assistance in learning to read.

The advantages of the book are explained in it, as follows:—

1. It keeps the child at spelling single syllables, until sufficient skill is acquired in the exercises.

2. By the universal employment of similarities of sound, it renders the repetition of similar forms not disagreeable to the child, and thus facilitates the design of impressing them indelibly on the mind.

3. It very rapidly enables the children to pronounce at once every new word formed by the addition of new consonants to syllables already known, without being obliged to spell them over beforehand; and also to spell these combinations by heart, which is afterward a great assistance in orthography.

In the short introduction prefixed to the book, explaining the use of it, mothers are required themselves to repeat daily to their children, before they can read, these series of sounds, and to pronounce them in different successions, so as to attract attention, and to give an acquaintance with each separate sound. This recitation must be prosecuted with redoubled zeal, and begun again from the beginning, as soon as the children begin to speak, to enable them themselves to repeat them, and thus to learn quickly to read.

In order to make the knowledge of the written characters, which must precede spelling, easier to the children, I have annexed them to the spelling-book, printed in a large character, in order to make their distinctions more easily discernible by the eye.

These letters are to be pasted separately on stiff paper, and put before the children. The vowels are in red, to distinguish them, and must be learned thoroughly, as well as their pronunciation, before going further. After this they are by little and little to be taught the consonants, but always along with a vowel; because they can not be pronounced without a vowel.

As soon as the children, partly by their exercise, partly by the spelling which I am about to describe, begin to have a sufficient knowledge of the letters, they may be set at the threefold series of letters, also appended to the book; where, in a smaller type, is given, over the German printed letter, the German written, and the Roman printed letters. The child, reading each syllable in the form of letter already familiar to him, and then repeating it in the other two, will learn to read in all three alphabets, without any loss of time.

The same principle is still to be adhered to in these exercises: that every syllable is nothing but a sound constructed by the addition of a consonant to a vowel; the vowel being thus always the foundation of the syllable. The vowel should be laid down first—or slid out on the spelling-board hung up on the wall, which should have a groove at the upper and lower side, in which the letters should stand and move easily backward and forward—and the consonants added, in the order given in the book. Each syllable should at the same time be pronounced by the teacher and repeated by the children, until indelibly impressed on their minds. Then the teacher may ask for each letter, in its order or out of it; and make them spell the syllables when covered up out of sight.

It is very necessary, especially in the first part of the book, to proceed slowly, and never to proceed to any thing new until what precedes it has been learned beyond the power of forgetting; for upon this depends the foundation of the whole course of instruction in reading, upon which what follows is to be built by small and gradual additions.

When in this way the children have arrived at a certain degree of facility in spelling, it may be interchanged with exercises of another kind. Thus, for example, a word may be spelled by beginning with one letter and adding the others, one after another, until it is complete, pronouncing it as each letter is added; as, p, pi, pin. Then the reverse process may be followed, by taking away one letter after another, and thus going backward in the same manner; repeating it until the children can spell the word by heart, correctly. The same thing can also be done by beginning at the end of the word, instead of the beginning.

Lastly, the word may be divided into syllables, the syllables numbered, and repeated and spelled promiscuously by their numbers.

Great advantages may be gained in schools, by teaching the children, from the beginning, to repeat the words all together at the same moment; so that the sound produced by all shall be heard as a simple sound, whether the words were repeated to them, or pointed out by the number of the letters or syllables. This keeping time together renders the instructor's part quite mechanical, and operates with incredible power upon the senses of the children.

When these exercises in spelling have been gone through with on the tablet, the book itself is then to be put into the child's hand, as a first reading-book; and he is to be kept at work upon it until he has acquired the most complete facility in reading it.

So much for instruction in the sounds of speech. I have to add a word, on the sounds of singing. But as singing proper can not be reckoned a means of proceeding from indistinct intuitions to clear ideas, that is, as one of the means of instruction which I am at present discussing, but is rather a capacity, to be developed from other points of view, and for other purposes, I put off its consideration to the time when I shall consider the system of education; saying at present only this: that singing, according to the general principle, begins with what is simplest, completes this, and proceeds only gradually from it, when completed, to the beginning of what is new.

B. The second department of the domain of sound, or of the special elementary means of instruction derived from sound, is—

Instruction in words, or rather in names.

I have already remarked that the child must receive its first instruction in this department, also, from the "*Book for Mothers.*" This is so arranged, that the most important subjects of the world, and especially those that, as generic names, include whole classes of subjects within themselves, are discussed; and the mother is enabled to make the child well-acquainted with the most important of all these names. By this course of proceeding, the child is prepared, even from its earliest years, for instruction in names; that for the second special means of instruction depending on the power of uttering sounds.

The instruction in names is given by means of series of names of the more important subjects, from all the realms of nature, history, geography, and human vocations and relations. These columns of words are put into the child's hand immediately after the end of his studies in the spelling-book, as a mere exercise in learning to read; and experience has shown me that it is possible for the children to have completely committed to memory the columns, within no more time than is required to learn to read them readily. The advantage of so complete a knowledge of such various and comprehensive views of names at this stage, is immeasurable, in relation to the facilitation of subsequent instruction.

C. The third special means of instruction proceeding from the faculty of sounds is—

Instruction in language itself.

And here is the point at which begins to be developed the proper method by which the art of instruction, by taking advantage of the development of the capacities of the human mind, can give an acquaintance with language which shall keep up with the course of nature in general development. But I should say, rather, here begins to develop itself the method by which, according to the will of the Creator, man can secure himself from the hands of mere natural blindness and natural capability for instruction, to be put into the hands of the higher powers which have been developing in him for thousands of years; the method by which the human race, independently—man—can secure for the development of his powers that more definite and comprehensive tendency and that more rapid progress, for which nature has given him power and means but no guidance, and in which she can never guide him while he is man only; the form in which man can do all this without interfering with the loftiness and simplicity of the physical development of nature, the harmony that exists in our merely sensuous development; without taking away any part of ourselves, or a single hair of that uniform protection which mother nature exercises over even the mere physical development.

All these attainments must be reached by means of a finished art of teaching language, and the highest grade of psychology; thus securing the utmost perfection in the mechanism of the natural progression from confused intuitions to intelligent ideas. This is, in truth, far beyond my powers; and I feel myself to be, on this subject, as the voice of one crying in the wilderness.

But the Egyptian, who first fastened a shovel with a crooked handle to the horn of an ox, and thus taught him to perform the labor of a man at digging, thus prepared the way for the invention of the plow, although he did not bring it to perfection.

My services are only the first bending of the shovel-handle, and the fastening of it to a new horn. But why do I speak by similitudes? I ought to and will state what I mean, plainly, and without circumlocution.

I desire to remove the imperfections from school instruction; both from the obsolete system of stammering servile old schoolmasters, and from the later system which has by no means taken its place—in the common schools; and to knit it to the immovable power of nature herself, and to the light which God kindles and ever maintains in the hearts of fathers and mothers; to the desires of parents that their children may be respectable before God and man.

In order to define the form of our instruction in language, or rather the various forms in which its object can be gained, that is, through which we are to become able to express ourselves distinctly on subjects with which we are acquainted, and as to every thing which we see about them, we must inquire:—

1. What is man's ultimate object in language?

2. What are the means, or rather what is the progression, through which nature herself, by the gradual development of the faculty of language, brings us to this end?

The answer to the first question is, evidently: To bring our race from obscure intuitions to intelligent ideas; and to the second: The means by which she gradually brings us to this end have, unquestionably, this order of succession, viz.:—

a. We recognize an object generally, and designate it as a unity—an object.

b. We become generally acquainted with its characteristics, and learn to designate them.

c. We acquire, through language, the power of defining more in detail these traits, by verbs and adverbs, and making clear to ourselves their modifications by modifications in words themselves, and in their juxtaposition.

1. On the effort to learn the names of objects, I have already spoken.

2. Efforts to comprehend and to teach the names of the qualities of objects as desirable, are divided into—

a. Efforts to teach the child to express himself with distinctness in relation to number and form: (Number and form, as qualities possessed by all things, are the two most comprehensive universal abstractions of physical nature; and are the two central points to which are referred all other means of rendering our ideas intelligent.)

b. Efforts to teach the child to express himself with distinctness upon all other qualities of things, besides number and form; as well those qualities which are perceived through the five senses, as those which are perceived, not by means of a simple intuition of them, but by means of our faculties of imagination and judgment.

Children must early become accustomed to consider with ease form and number, the first physical universal qualities which the experience of thousands of years has taught us to abstract from the nature of all things; and to consider them, not merely as qualities inherent in each particular thing, but as physical universal qualities. He must not only learn early to distinguish a round and a triangular thing as such, but must as early as possible have impressed upon his mind the idea of circularity, and triangularity, as a pure abstraction; so that he may be able to apply the proper term, expressing this universal abstract idea, to whatever occurs to him in nature which is round, triangular, simple, fourfold, &c. Here also comes up clearly the reason why speech is to be and must be treated as a means of expressing form and number, in a special manner, differing from its treatment as a means of expressing all the other qualities which we observe in natural objects by the five senses.

I therefore began, even in the "*Book for Mothers*," to lead the children toward the clear knowledge of those universal qualities. This book furnishes both a comprehensive view of the most usual forms and the simplest means of making the first relations of numbers intelligible to the child.

More advanced steps toward this purpose must, however, together with the corresponding exercises in language, be put off to a later period, and must be connected with the special exercises in number and form, which two, as the elementary points of our knowledge, must be taken up after a full course of exercises in language.

The cuts in the elementary manual for this instruction, the "*Book for Mothers*, or for the earliest childhood," are so selected as to bring forward all the universal physical qualities of which we become aware through the five senses; and as to enable mothers readily to give their children the command of the most definite expressions relative to them, without any pains of their own.

As relates, next, to those qualities of things which become known to us, not immediately through the five senses, but through the separating powers of our faculty of comparison, imagination, and faculty of abstraction, in regard to them also, I adhere to my principle, not to endeavor to bring any human opinion to a premature ripeness, but to make use of the necessary knowledge of the appropriate abstract terms by the children, as a mere exercise of memory; and also to some extent as a light nourishment for the play of their imaginations and of their powers of forethought.

In reference to such objects as we recognize immediately by the five senses, and in reference to which it is necessary to teach the child as quickly as possible to express himself with precision, I take from a dictionary substances whose most prominent qualities are such as we can distinguish by the five senses, and put down with them the adjectives which describe those qualities; as—

(*Aal.*) Eel. Slippery, worm-shaped, tough-skinned.

(*Aas.*) Carcass. Dead, offensive.

(*Abend.*) Evening. Quiet, cheerful, cool, rainy.

(*Achse.*) Axle. Strong, weak, greasy.

(*Acker.*) Field. Sandy, clayey, sowed, manured, fertile, profitable, unprofitable.

Then I reverse this proceeding, and in the same way select from the dictionary adjectives expressing distinguishing qualities of objects recognized by the five senses, and set down after them the substantive names of objects possessing them; as—

Round. Ball, hat, moon, sun

Light. Feather, down, air.

Heavy. Gold, lead, oak-wood.

Hot. Oven, summer-day, fire.

High. Tower, mountain, giants, trees.

Deep. Oceans, seas, cellars, graves.

Soft. Flesh, wax, butter.

Elastic, Steel-springs, whalebone.

I did not endeavor, by completing these explanatory suffixes, to diminish the field of the child's independent intellectual activity; but only gave a few terms, calculated to appeal distinctly to his senses, and then inquired, in continuation: What else can you mention of the same sort?

In far the greatest number of cases the children found that their experience furnished them additional terms, frequently such as had not occurred to the teacher; and thus their circle of knowledge was widened and elucidated in a manner either impossible by the catechetical method, or possible only with a hundred times greater expenditure of art and exertion.

In all proceedings by catechisation, the child is constrained, in part by the limits of the defined idea respecting which he is catechised, in part by the form in which it is done, in part by the limits of the teacher's knowledge, and lastly, and more important, by the limits of a painful care lest they should get out of the regular artistic track. What unfortunate limitations for the child! but in my course they are avoided.

Having finished this portion of study, I proceed, by means of the dictionary, to communicate to the child, now variously acquainted with the objects of the world, a further increase of the gradually growing clearness of his knowledge of objects so far as known to him.

For this purpose, I divide language, that great witness of the past respecting all that now exists, into four chief heads, viz.:—

1. Geography.
2. History.
3. Nature.
4. Natural History.

But in order to avoid all unnecessary repetition of the same words, and to make the form of instruction as brief as possible, I divide these chief heads into some forty subheads, and bring the names of objects before the children only under these latter subdivisions.

I then turn attention to that great object of my intuitions, myself; or rather, to that whole series of terms in language which relate to myself; by bringing all that language, that great witness of the past, says upon man under the following chief heads.

First head. What does language say of man, considered as a merely physical being; as a member of the animal world?

Second head. What does she say of him as striving toward physical independence by means of the social state?

Third head. What does she say of him as a reasoning being, striving for inner independence; or self-improvement?

I then divide these three chief heads, as before, into some forty subheads, and bring them before the children only under the latter.

The first exhibition of these series of names, both relating to men and to the other subjects of the world, must be strictly alphabetical, without any intermixture of any opinion, and not as any consequence of any opinion; but a gradually increased clearness in the knowledge of them must be attained merely by the juxtaposition of similar intuitions, and similar intuitional ideas.

When this has been done, when the witness of the past as to all that now exists has thus been made useful in the whole simplicity of her alphabetical arrangement, I propose this question:—

How does the method arrange these subjects further, for fuller definition? To answer this, a new labor begins. The same columns of words with which the child has become acquainted in seven or eight columns, in an alphabetical order, almost beyond the possibility of forgetting them, are laid before him again, in the same columns, but in a classified manner, by which the method arranges them very differently, and enables the child himself to arrange them on the new principle.

The plan is this: The different heads, under which the words are to be newly arranged, are put in a row, and distinguished by a series of numbers, abbreviations, or some other arbitrary marks.

The child must, during his first studies in reading, become thoroughly master of this series of heads; and he may then find, in the columns of words, against each word, the mark of that head under which it belongs; and thus he can, at first sight of the figure, tell under what head it belongs, and thus himself alter the alphabetical nomenclature into a scientific one.

I do not know that this plan needs to be illustrated by an example; but, though it seems to me almost superfluous, I will still give one, on account of the newness of the plan. Thus, for instance, one of the subdivisions of Europe is Germany. Let the child first become acquainted, beyond the power of forgetting them, with the subdivision of Germany into ten circles. Now let the names of the cities of Germany be laid before him in alphabetical order, to be read; there being, at the name of each city, the number of the circle in which it lies. As soon as he can read these names of cities fluently, let him be shown how the numbers annexed to them refer to the heads above, and the child will after a few lessons be able to locate all the cities of Germany according to the heads thus set above them. Let there be put before him, for instance, the following names of German places, with figures:—

Aachen, 8	Allendorf, 5	Altona, 10
Aalen, 3	Allersperg, 2	Altorf, 1
Abendberg, 4	Alschausen, 3	Altranstädt, 9
Aberthan, 11	Alsleben, 10	Altwasser, 13
Acken, 10	Altbunzlau, 11	Alkerdissen, 8
Adersbach, 11	Altena, 8	Amberg, 2
Agler, 1	Altenau, 10	Ambras, 1
Ahrbergen, 10	Altenberg, 9	Amöneburg, 6
Aigremont, 8	Altenburg, 9	Andernach, 6.
Ala, 1	Altensalza, 10	
Allenbach, 5	Altkirchen, 8	

He may then read these as follows:—

Aachen is in the Westphalian circle.

Abendberg is in the Franconian circle.

Aacken is in the Lower Saxon circle; &c.

The child will thus evidently be enabled, at the first glance at the number or mark which distinguishes the head under which any word belongs, to determine it; and thus, as was said, to change the alphabetical nomenclature into a scientific one.

And having gone so far, I find myself, in this direction, at the limit of my course, as peculiar to me; and the powers of the children so developed, that they can, in any department of the method to which their disposition inclines them, and to which they are inclined to attend, make an independent use for themselves of the means of assistance which already exist in all these departments, but which are of such a character that, hitherto, only a few fortunate persons have been able to use them. To this point, and no further, have I sought to attain. What I desired, and desire, was, not to teach the world any art or science—for I know none—but to make more easy for the people at large the mastery of the points of commencement of all arts and sciences; to open to the powers of the poor and weak in the country, neglected and given up to desolation, the approaches to learning, which are the approaches to humanity; and, if possible, to burn down the barrier which keeps the more lowly of the citizens of Europe far behind the barbarians of the north and south in respect to independent intellectual power, which is the basis of all efficient acquirement. It keeps them so, because, notwithstanding our windy boastings on universal enlightenment, it deprives ten men to one of the right of all men in society, the right of being instructed; or at least of the possibility of making use of this right.

May that barrier, after my death, burn up with a bright flame! But yet I know that I myself am only one feeble coal, lying among wet straw. But I see a wind, and that not far off, which shall kindle the coal into a blaze; the wet straw around me will gradually dry, grow warm, kindle, and at last burn. Yes, however wet it is round me now, it will burn, it will burn!

But I have occupied so much time with the second of the special means of instruction in language, that I find I have not yet said any thing of the third of those means, by which is to be attained the last purpose of instruction, the rendering our ideas intelligent. It is this:—

c. The endeavor to enable the child correctly to define, by language, the connections of objects with each other, and their intermodifications by number, time, and relation; or, rather, to make still better understood the existence, the qualities, and the powers of all those objects of which knowledge has been gained by the study of names, and made clear to a certain extent by juxtaposition of their names and their qualities.

From this point of view we may discern the foundations on which a real grammar is to be constructed, and, at the same time, the further progression by which, through this means, we are to arrive at the last purpose of instruction, the rendering intelligent of ideas.

Here, also, I prepare the children for the first steps by very simple but still psychological instruction in speaking; and, without a word of any form or rule, I cause the mother first to repeat to the child, as mere exercises in speaking, sentences, which are to be repeated after her, almost as much on account of the training of the organs of speech, as of the sentences themselves. The two objects, practice in speaking and the learning of words as language, must be kept apart from each other; and the former must also be attended to by itself, by proper exercises. In the exercises for both purposes at once, then, the mother repeats to the child the following sentences:—

The father is kind.
The butterfly has variously-colored wings.
Cattle eat grass.
The pine is straight-stemmed.*

When the child has pronounced these so often that it is easy for him, the mother inquires, "Who is good? What has various-colored wings?" And again, "What is the father? What has the butterfly?" And so on, as follows:—

Who is? What are?
Carnivorous beasts eat flesh.
Deer are light-footed.
Roots are spread out.

Who has? What has?
The lion hath strength.
Man has reason.
The hound has a keen scent.
The elephant has a trunk, &c., &c.

Thus I proceed, through the whole extent of the declensions and conjugations, to unite the first and second steps of these exercises; going also, in particular, into the use of the verbs, after a mode of which I give the following examples:—

Simple Connection.

Regard—the teacher's words.
Breathe—through the lungs.
Bend—a tree.
Tie—a sheaf, the stockings, &c.

After this comes the second species of exercise, in verbs in composition; as,

Regard. I regard (*achte*) the teacher's words, my duty, my estate. I regard one person more than another; I judge (*erachte*) whether a thing is so, or otherwise; I take an important matter into consideration (*obacht*;) I watch over (*beobachte*) a man whom I do not trust, an affair which I am desirous of arranging, and my duty; a good man honors (*hochachtet*) virtue, and despises (*verachtet*) vice.

So far as a man regards any thing, he is attentive (*achtsam*) to it; so far as he does not regard it, he is inattentive (*unachtsam*.)

I regard myself more than every thing else; and care more for (*achten auf*) myself than every thing else.

Then I proceed to enlarge the sphere of these exercises by additions gradually more extensive, and thus progressively more variously developed and more definite; as, for instance:—

I shall.
I shall gain.
I shall gain my health by no other means.
I shall gain my health, after all that I have suffered, by no other means.
I shall gain my health, after all that I have suffered in my illness, by no other means.
I shall gain my health, after all that I have suffered in my sickness, by no other means than by temperance, &c., &c.

All these sentences are then each to be carried through the whole tense-conjugation; as,

I shall gain.
Thou wilt gain, &c.
I shall gain my health.
Thou wilt gain thy health, &c.

The same may then be carried through the different tenses.

Care is taken to select, for these sentences, so firmly to be fixed in the child's

* In the German, all these sentences are constructed precisely like the first; and are as simple.—*Trans.*

mind, such as shall be particularly instructive, elevating, and suitable to his condition.

With them I join examples of description of material objects, in order to exercise and strengthen in the children the powers which these exercises develop in them. For instance:—

A bell is a bowl or vessel, open below, wide, thick, round, usually hanging free, growing smaller from below up, egg-shaped at the top, and having in the middle of it a perpendicular bar, hanging loose, which, upon a violent motion of the bell, strikes it from below on both sides, and thus occasions the sound which we hear from it.
Go. To move forward step by step.
Stand. To rest on the legs with the body upright.
Lie. To rest upon any thing with the body horizontal, &c., &c.

I would gladly leave these exercises in language, at my death, as a legacy to my pupils, making them, by means of brief observations annexed to the more important verbs, a vehicle for conveying to their minds the same impressions which have been made upon my own, by the experiences of my life on the subjects of their significance. Thus I would make these exercises in words a means of imparting truth, correct views, and pure feelings on all the doings and failings of men. For example:—

Breathe, (*athmen.*) Thy life depends upon a breath. Man! when thou snortest like a tyrant, and inspirest the pure air of the earth like poison into thy lungs, what doest thou but to hasten to become breathless, and so free humanity, weary of thy snorting, from thy presence.

But I must leave this part of the subject.

I have dwelt at length upon language as a means of the gradual clearing up of our ideas. But it is the most important means for that purpose. My method of instruction is distinguished especially in this, that it makes more use of language, as a means of lifting the child from obscure intuitions to intelligent ideas, than has heretofore been the case; and also in this, that it excludes from the first elementary instruction all combinations of words which presuppose an actual knowledge of language. Any one who admits how nature leads to intelligent comprehension of all things by a clear comprehension of single things, will admit also that single words must be clearly understood by the child before he can intelligently comprehend them in connection; and any one who admits this, rejects at once all the received elementary books of instruction; for they all presuppose an acquaintance with language in the child before they communicate it to him. It is a remarkable fact that even the best schoolbook of the last century forgot that the child must learn to talk before he can be talked with. This omission is remarkable, but it is true; and since I observed it, I have wondered no longer that we can develop children into other men than were trained by those who had so far forgotten both the piety and the wisdom of antiquity. Language is an art—an immeasurable art; or, rather, the compendium of all the arts which our race has acquired. It is in a peculiar sense the reflection of all the impressions which the whole extent of nature has made upon our race. As such I use it, and seek, by means of its spoken sounds, to produce in the children the same impressions which have occasioned the production of the sounds by mankind. The gift of speech is a great one. It gives the child, in a moment, what it has taken nature thousands of years to give mankind. It is said of the poor beast, What would he be if he knew his strength? And I say of man, What would he be if he knew his strength—through language?

It is a great defect in the very heart of human education, that we have been so forgetful of what was proper, as not only to do nothing toward teaching the lower classes to speak, but as to have permitted the speechless to learn by rote isolated abstract terms.

In truth, the Indians could not do more in order to keep their lower classes eternally in stupidity, and in the lowest ranks of humanity.

Let these facts be denied by any one who dares. I appeal to all clergymen, all authorities, all men who live among the people, who, in the midst of their so great carelessness, are subjected to such a distorted and mistaken model of fatherly care. Let any one who has lived among such a people stand forward, and testify whether he has not experienced how difficult it is to get any idea into the heads of the poor creatures. But all are agreed on the point. "Yes, yes," say the clergy; "When they come to us they do not understand one word of our instructions." "Yes, yes," say the judges; "However right they are, it is impossible for them to make any one understand the justice of their cause." The lady says, pitifully and proudly, they are scarcely a step in advance of beasts; they can not be trained to any service. Fools, who can not count five, look upon them as more foolish than themselves, the fools; and villains of all sorts cry out, each with the gesture natural to him, "Well for us that it is so! If it were otherwise, we could no longer buy so cheaply, nor sell so dearly."

Nearly the same is the speech of all the boxes of the great European Christian comic theater, regarding the pit: and they can not speak otherwise of it; for they have been for a century making the pit more mindless than any Asiatic or heathen one would be. I repeat my position once more:—The Christian people of our portion of the world is sunken to this depth, because, for more than a century, in its lower schools, a power over the human mind has been accorded to empty words, which not only in itself destroyed the power of attention to the impressions of nature, but destroyed the very susceptibility itself of men to them. I say, once more, that while this has been done, and has made of our European Christian people the most wordy, rattle-box people on the face of the earth, *they have not been taught to speak.* This being the case, it is no wonder that the Christianity of this century and this part of the world has its present prospects; it is, on the contrary, a wonder that, considering all the bungling methods which have been proved upon it in our wordy and rattle-box schools, it has retained so much of its native force as can still be recognized every where in the hearts of the people. But, God be praised! the folly of all these apish methods will always find an end, an antagonist in human nature itself; and will cease to injure our race, when it has reached the highest point of its apishness which can be endured. Folly and error, in whatever garb, contain the seeds of their own transitoriness and destruction; truth alone, in every form, contains within itself the seeds of eternal life.

The second elementary means, from which all human knowledge, and consequently the existence of all means of instruction, proceeds and must proceed, is

FORM.

Instruction in form must precede the conscious intuition of things having form; whose representation, for purposes of instruction, must be deduced in part from the nature of the means of intuition, and in part from the purpose of instruction itself.

The whole sum of our knowledge comes,

1. Through the impressions derived from all things around us, when brought into relation with our five senses. This mode of intuition is without rule, confused, and its progress is very confused and tedious.

2. Through whatever is brought before our senses by the intervention of methodic guidance, so far as this depends upon our parents and teachers. This mode of intuition naturally corresponds to the intelligence and activity of our parents and teachers, in respect to comprehensiveness and connection; and is of a more or less correct psychological character; and, according to the same rule, it pursues a course more or less rapid, and leading with more or less speed and certainty toward the purpose of instruction, the attainment of intelligent ideas.

3. Through our own determination to attain to knowledge, and to obtain intuitions by our independent striving after the various means of them. Knowledge thus attained possesses a positive and proper value; and, by giving to the results of our intuitions a free existence within ourselves, brings us nearer to the attainment of a moral influence upon our own education.

4. Through the results of effort and labor in our callings, and all activity which has not mere intuition as its object. This department of knowledge connects our intuitions with our situations and relations; brings the results of those intuitions into agreement with our duty and with virtue; and, both by the constraining force of its progress and by our purposelessness as to its results, a most important influence upon the correctness, completeness, and harmony of our views, as related to the attainment of our purpose, intelligent ideas.

5. Through a means analogous to our intuitional knowledge; inasmuch as it instructs us in the properties of things not pertaining properly to our intuitions, but in which we perceive a similarity to things which we know by our intuitions. This mode of intuition enables us to make our progress in knowledge, which, as a result of actual intuition, is only the work of the five senses, the work of our minds and of all their powers; so that thus we enjoy as many kinds of intuition as we have powers of mind. But the term intuition, in this latter sense, has a more extended meaning than in the common usage of language; and includes the whole range of feelings which are by nature inseparable from my mind.

It is important to be acquainted with the distinction between these two kinds of intuitions; in order to be able to comprehend the rules which apply to each of them.

With this purpose, I return to the course of my discussion.

From the consciousness of intuition of things having form, comes the art of geometry. This however depends upon a power of intuition which it is important to distinguish from the primary means of knowledge, as well as from the mere simple intuition of things. From this power of intuition are developed all the departments of geometry and those deduced from them. But this very faculty of intuition leads us, by the comparison of different objects, beyond the rules of surveying, to a freer imitation of the relations between those objects—to drawing; and, lastly, we make use of the art of drawing in writing.

GEOMETRY.

This presupposes an intuitional A B C; that is, the power of simplifying and defining the rules of geometry by the accurate distinction of all the dissimilarities which come before the intuition.

I will draw attention again to the empirical succession which led me to my views on this subject, and will give for this purpose an extract from my Report.

In this I say, "Having granted the principle that intuition is the basis of all knowledge, it follows irresistibly that correct intuition is the proper basis of the most correct opinions.

"But with reference to the method of education, thorough correctness of intuition is evidently a result of measuring the subject to be judged of, or else of a faculty of perceiving relations, so far developed as to make such measuring superfluous. Thus a readiness at measuring correctly has, in education, an immediate relation to the necessity of intuition. Drawing is a linear definition of forms, whose shape and contents are correctly and fully defined by means of a developed power of measuring.

"The principle that practice and readiness in measuring should precede practice in drawing, or at least must keep pace with it, is as obvious as it is unused. But the process of our methods of education is, to begin with incorrect seeing; to build awry, then to pull down, and so on ten times over, until after a long time the sense of relations becomes developed, and then at last we come to what we should have begun with—to measuring. Such is the proceeding of our methods, and yet we are so many thousands of years older than the Egyptians and Etruscans, whose drawings all depend upon a trained power of measuring, or in fact were at bottom nothing than measurings.

"And now the question comes up, By what means is the child to be trained to this basis of all art, the right meaning of objects which come before his eyes? Evidently by a succession including the whole of all possible intuitions; and by an analysis of the square, according to simple, certain, and definite rules.

"Young artists, in the absence of such elementary exercises, find the means, by long practice in their art, of acquiring greater or less facility in so placing any object before their eyes and imitating it as it is in nature. And it can not be denied that many of them, by painful and long-continued efforts, have, from the most confused intuitions, attained to a sense of relations so far advanced that the measuring of objects is superfluous to them. But then each individual had a different system; none of them had any nomenclature, for none of them had any distinct conscious comprehension of the system; and, accordingly, they could not properly communicate it to their scholars. The latter were thus in the same condition in which their teachers had been, and were obliged to attain the same result—correct sense of relations—with the extremest exertion and by long practice, and with their own means, or rather with no means at all. Thus art remained in the possession of a few fortunate individuals, who had time and leisure to travel by such an incommodious road to the requisite attainment. Art could not be considered as concerning all men, nor could instruction in it be demanded as a universal right, although it is such. At least, this can not be denied by any one who admits that it is the right of living men, in an enlightened state, to be able to learn reading and writing; for the tendencies to draw, and the capacity for measuring, develop naturally and freely in the child; while the painstaking efforts which must be made in order to bring him to spell and read, must be applied either with great skill or with harshness and violence, if they are not to injure him more than reading is worth to him. And drawing, if it is to promote the aim of instruction, the attainment of intelligent ideas, is necessarily connected with the measuring of forms. The child before whom an object is placed to be drawn before he can represent to himself its proportions in their whole form, and express himself upon it, can never make the art, as it should be, an actual means of proceeding from obscure intuitions to intelligent ideas; nor procure from it the actual substantial advantage, throughout his whole education and in harmony with the great purpose of it, which it ought to and can afford him."

In order to establish the art of drawing upon this basis, it must be subordinated to that of geometry; and the subdivisions into angles and curves which proceed from the rudimental form of the square, as well as the divisions of curves by straight lines, must be arranged into regularly classified geometrical forms. This has been done; and I believe that I have arranged a series of geometrical forms, whose use will as much facilitate the child's acquisition of geometry, and his acquaintance with the proportions of all forms, as does the alphabet of sounds his studies in language.

This intuitional alphabet* is a symmetrical subdivision of an equilateral square into fixed geometrical forms, and evidently requires a knowledge of the origin of the square; that is, of horizontal and perpendicular lines.

The subdivision of the square by right lines produces means of determining and measuring angles, circles, and all curves.

This is brought before the child in the following manner:—

The qualities of the right line are first explained to him by itself alone, and drawn in various arbitrary directions; until a variety of exercises has given him a clear apprehension of it, without reference to any ulterior application. He is next made acquainted with right lines, as horizontal, perpendicular, and oblique, and to distinguish them as inclining or extending toward the right or left; then with various parallel lines and their names, as horizontal, perpendicular, and inclined parallels; then with the names of the different varieties of angles formed by the intersection of these lines, so that he can distinguish them as right, acute, and obtuse angles. He is then made acquainted with the primitive of all geometrical forms, the equilateral triangle, which is formed by the junction of two angles, and with its divisions into halves, fourths, sixths, &c.; and then with the circle and its variations, and to recognize and name them and their forms.

All these definitions are to be done merely by the power of the eye; and the names of the geometrical forms are, in this part of the studies, merely square; horizontal and perpendicular quadrilateral, or rectangle; circle, semicircle, quarter-circle; first-oval, half-oval, and quarter-oval; second, third, &c., oval; and thus he must be introduced to the use of these forms as means of geometrical study; and must learn the nature of the relations by which they are generated.

* I should here observe that the alphabet of intuition is the indispensable and only true means of instruction in judging correctly of the forms of all things. Yet it has hitherto been entirely neglected, until it is entirely unknown. For instruction in number and speech, on the contrary, there are a hundred such means. But this want of means of instruction in form is not merely a simple defect in the system of education to human knowledge—it is also a breach in the necessary foundations of all knowledge. It is a defect of knowledge upon a point to which knowledge of number and speech must be subordinated. My alphabet of intuition will supply this serious defect in instruction, and assure the basis upon which all other means of instruction must be founded. I beg such Germans as may be inclined to form an opinion on the subject, to consider this position as the basis of my method; upon whose correctness or incorrectness depends the value or worthlessness of all my researches.

The first means of reaching these results is—

1. The endeavor to teach the child to recognize and name the relations of these geometrical forms.

2. To enable him to know and make use of them independently.

Preparation for this purpose has already been made in the "*Book for Mothers;*" and various objects set before him—triangular, round, oval, wide, long, and narrow. After this, various detached portions of the alphabet of intuition are set before him, as a quadrilateral in quarters, eighths, sixths, &c., and circles, and half and quarter-circles, ovals, and half and quarter-ovals; thus furnishing him in advance with an obscure consciousness of the clear conception which he must acquire under the instruction of the method, and the subsequent application of these forms. He is also prepared for this conception and application in the "*Book for Mothers,*" in which are given, on one hand, the rudiments of a definite nomenclature for these forms, and, on the other, the commencement of arithmetic, which presupposes geometry.

The study of the alphabet of intuition will lead toward the same end; for in that alphabet speech and number, the means before used for attaining an obscure consciousness, are made more clearly applicable to the definite aim of geometry, and thus the pupil will gain a more assured power of expressing himself definitely as to the number and proportion of all forms.

3. The third means of attaining this purpose is the copying of forms themselves; by means of which the children, using at the same time the two other means above-mentioned, will generally gain not only intelligent ideas as to each form, but the power of laying off each form with certainty. In order to gain the first of those steps, the relations of the forms known to them in the first course as horizontal and perpendicular quadrilaterals, are now to be brought out by teaching them that "Horizontal quadrilateral, two are twice as long as wide; perpendicular quadrilateral, two are twice as high as wide," &c.; going through all the parts of the figure also. In this exercise, also, on account of the various directions of the inclined lines of some quadrilaterals, it must be shown that, of the horizontal ones, some are once and a half times as high as wide, &c., until the description is easy. In like manner are to be studied the various directions of inclined lines, and of acute and obtuse angles, as well as the various subdivisions of the circle, and the ovals and their parts, arising from the subdivisions of the square.

By the recognition of these definite forms, the geometrical faculty develops from an uncertain natural faculty of intuition to an artistic power according to definite rules; from which comes that power of judging correctly of the relations of all forms, which I call the power of intuition. This is a new power; which must precede the former usual and recognized views of the artistic cultivation of our powers, as their common and actual basis.

By means of it, every child arrives, in the simplest manner, at the power of rightly judging of every object in nature according to its inner relations, and its relations to other objects; and of expressing himself with distinctness relatively to it. By this method of proceeding he becomes able, when he sees any figure, to define it accurately, not only as to the proportion between hight and breadth, but as to the relations of every variation of its form from the equilateral triangle, in curves and crooked outlines; and to apply to all these the names by which these variations should be designated in the alphabet of intuition. The means of attaining this power are within geometry itself, and are to be developed still further by drawing, especially by linear drawing; and carried to such a point, that his power of definitely measuring objects, with such a degree of skill and accuracy, that after completing his course of elementary exercises he will no longer need, even in the case of the most complicated objects, to proceed by actual geometrical rules, but can without assistance correctly determine the relations of all their parts amongst each other, and express himself distinctly respecting them.

Even children of inferior capacity attain to indescribably great results by the development of this power. This assertion is no dream. I have taught children on these principles; and my theory on this subject is nothing except a result of my experience upon it. Let any one come and see the children. They are still at the beginning of the course, but their beginning has carried them so far that it must be a very extraordinary kind of man who can stand by and not quickly be convinced; and still their progress is by no means extraordinary.

DRAWING

Is the ability to represent to one's self, in similar lines, the outlines of any object and what is contained within them, by means of merely looking at the object, and thus to imitate it correctly.

This art is facilitated out of all measure by the new method, since it is, throughout, an easy application of forms which have not only been brought before the intuition of the child, but by practice in imitating which he has acquired actual geometrical ability.

The mode pursued is as follows:—As soon as the child can correctly and readily draw the straight horizontal lines with which the alphabet of intuition begins, there are sought for him, out of the chaos of intuitions, figures whose outline requires nothing but the application of the horizontal lines which are already easy to him, or at most only a not noticeable departure from them.

Then we proceed to the perpendicular line, and then to the right-angled triangle, &c.; and, in proportion as the child is more assured in the simple application of these forms, we gradually pass from them to the application of them. The results of the application of this rule, entirely coincident with the essence of physico-mechanical laws, are no less in drawing than are those of the use of the alphabet of intuition upon the geometrical powers of the child. In this course they become thoroughly acquainted with the first elements of drawing before going further; and accordingly, even in the first stages of their progress, there is developed in them a perception of what the consequences of the thorough mastery of the whole subject will be, and with this an endeavor after perfection, and a perseverance in the attainment of their object, such as the foolishness and disorderliness of the usual methods would never produce. The basis of this progress is not merely in the cultivation of the hand; it is founded upon the innermost powers of human nature; and practical books of geometrical forms coming in succession afterward, enable the children, pursuing this course on correct psychological principles, and under the proper conditions of physico-mechanical laws, gradually to attain the desired point, namely, that the further use of geometrical lines to be employed by the eye shall gradually become entirely superfluous, and that, of the means of attaining their art, nothing shall remain but the art itself.

WRITING.

Nature herself subordinates this art to drawing, and to all the means by which the latter is taught to the child and carried to perfection; and, accordingly, is actually and especially subordinate to geometry.

Writing ought, even still less than drawing, to be begun and pursued without previous training in linear geometry; not only because it is itself a kind of linear drawing, and does not allow arbitrary variations from the fixed lines of its forms, but more particularly because, if facility is acquired in it before drawing, it must necessarily injure the hand for the latter, by confirming it in particular forms before it has been sufficiently trained to a universal capacity for all forms, such as drawing requires. It is another reason why drawing should precede writing, that it beyond measure facilitates the proper formation of the letters by the child, thus saving him a great loss of time spent in weaning himself from wrong forms which he has been acquiring for years together. This, again, is of advantage to him during his whole course, in that, even in the first beginnings of study, he becomes conscious of the power to be acquired by the mastery of it; so that, even in the first part of his studies in writing, he becomes resolved not to leave any thing incomplete or imperfect, in his rudimentary acquirements.

Writing, like drawing, must be first commenced on the slate, with a pencil; children being competent to make a perfect letter on the slate, at an age when it would be infinitely difficult to teach them how to guide the pen.

This use of the slate-pencil before the pen is to be recommended, both in writing and drawing, for the additional reason that it admits of the easy rectification of errors; while, by the remaining on the paper of a faulty letter, a worse one is always made next.

And I shall cite, as a material advantage of this method, that the child will wash from the slate even perfectly good work; an advantage incredible to all who do not know the importance of educating children without presumption, and so as to prevent them from vanity in attaching value to the work of their hands.

I divide the study of writing into two epochs:—

1. That in which the child is to become familiar with the forms of letters and their connection, independently of the use of the pen; and

2. That in which his hand is to be trained to the use of the pen, the proper instrument for writing.

During the first of these epochs I place the letters before the child, in strictly correct forms; and have caused a copy-book to be engraved, by means of which the child, if he has the advantages consequent upon pursuing my whole method, can acquire facility in writing almost by himself without assistance.

The characteristics of this writing-book are:—

1. It dwells sufficiently long upon the rudimentary and fundamental forms of the letters.

2 It proceeds gradually, only from the simple forms of the letters to the complex.

3. It practices the child in the combination of several letters, beginning from the moment when he can correctly write a simple one; and goes on, step by step, in the writing of such words as contain those letters only which he is already able to make perfectly.

4. Lastly, it has the advantage of being cut up into single lines; so that the line to be written upon can always be made to stand immediately under the copy.

In the second epoch, in which the child is to be introduced to the use of the pen, the proper instrument for writing, he is practiced in the forms of the letters and in their combinations, even to a higher degree of perfection; and the teacher's work is then only to apply this perfected skill in drawing these forms to writing proper, by the use of the pen.

But the child must here also come at the new step in his progress with those he has already made. His first copy for the pen is precisely like his copy for the pencil; and he must commence his practice with the pen by writing the letters as large as he drew them, and only gradually becoming accustomed to imitating the smaller usual forms of writing.

The psychology of all departments of education requires a clear distinction to be preserved between their means; and a keen discrimination as to which of them the child can and should be made to practice at any age. As in all departments, I apply this principle in writing also; and by a steady adherence to this principle, and with the help of the book of slate-pencil copies founded on it, which has been prepared for children of four and five years of age, I confidently assert that by this method even an unskillful schoolmaster, or a very inexperienced mother, can instruct children, up to a certain point, in both plain and ornamental writing, without having themselves been previously able to do it. It is, in this particular, as every where, the main design of my method to make home instruction again possible to our neglected people; and to enable every mother, whose heart beats for her child, to follow my elementary exercises in a progressive order, quite to their end; and to practice them throughout with her children. To do this, she need be but a little way forward of the child itself.

My heart is lifted up by the blessed wishes that spring from this idea. But when I first expressed distantly something of these hopes, I was answered, from all sides, "The mothers among the people at large will not approve of it;" and not only men from the common people, but men who teach the common people—who teach them Christianity!—said to me, scoffingly, "You may search all our villages up and down, but you will find no mother who will do what you require from her." I answered them, "Then I will, by the use of these means of mine, enable heathen mothers from the furthest north to do it; and, if it is really true that Christian mothers in peaceful Europe—that Christian mothers in my fatherland—can not be carried forward as far as I will carry heathen mothers from the wild north;—then I will call upon these gentlemen, who are to-day thus insulting the people of the fatherland, whom they and their fathers have hitherto taught, instructed, and directed; and, if they dare wash their hands of the blame, and say, "We are guiltless of this inexpressible shame of the people in peaceful Europe, we are guiltless of this unspeakable disgrace of the best natured, most teachable, and patient of all the European nations, the Swiss"—if they dare say, "We and our fathers have done what it was our duty to do, in order to remove from our father-land the nameless unhappiness of this inhuman condition of our country and our father-land, to prevent this decay of the first foundations of morality and religion in our country and our father-land"—to these men, who dared to tell me, "You may search the land up and down, but its mothers will not do nor desire what you wish," I will reply, "Cry out to these unnatural mothers of our father-land, as did Christ to Jerusalem, 'Mothers, mothers, how often have we wished to gather you under the wings of wisdom, humanity, and Christianity, as a hen gathers her chickens under her wings, and ye would not!'" If they dare do this, then I will be silent, and believe their assertion and their experience, instead of believing in the mothers of the country, and in the hearts which God has put into their breasts. But if they dare not, I will not believe in them, but in the mothers, and in the hearts which God has put in their breasts; and will moreover meet the miserable statement with which they have rejected from themselves the people of the land, like the production of an evil creation, and proclaim it an insult to the people, to nature, and to truth; and will go my way, like a wanderer who in a distant forest hears a wind whose blowing he does not feel. I must go my way, for the sake of what I desire to speak. I have all my life seen all manner of such word-men, hardened in systems and ideals, with no knowledge or respect for the people; and the appearance of those who to-day are, as I have shown, insulting the people, is more similar to theirs than any other that I know. Such men believe themselves to be upon an eminence, and the people at a depth far below them; but they are mistaken on both points, and like wretched apes, by the arrogance of their miserable nature, hindered and made incapable of right judgment on the real value of actual animal power, or that of real human endowments; thus these wretched word-men are, even by the loftiest attainments of their unnatural course, become incapable of observing that they are walking on stilts, and that they must get down from their wretched wooden legs, in order to be planted as firmly as common people are, upon God's earth. I am forced to pity them. I have heard many of these wretched word-men say, with such a mixture of nun-like innocence and rabbinical wisdom, "What can be better for the people than the Heidelberg catechism and the psalter?" that I have been forced, out of consideration for humanity, to give up my respect for even the foundation of this error. And even if I would excuse the error, it would still be an error, and will be. Men are ever like themselves; and book-learned men, and their pupils, have likewise been so. I will therefore open my mouth no longer against the verbiage of their human sayings, and the tinkling bells of their ceremoniousness, and the delightful foolish frame of mind which must naturally thence arise; but will only say, with that greatest of men, who ever beneficially advocated the cause of truth, the people, and love, against the errors of the book-learned, "Lord, forgive them, for they know not what they do."

But to return: The study of writing seems to appear, in the third place, as an introduction to learning speech. It is, indeed, essentially, nothing but a peculiar and special application of the latter.

As, therefore, writing, considered as a study of form, comes according to my method into connection with geometry and drawing, and thus enjoys all the advantages derivable from the early development of those studies, so, as a special department of the study of speech, it comes into connection with all that has been done, from the cradle upward, by the method for the development of that faculty, and enjoys the same advantages which were secured and established for it, from the previous training of it by the "*Book for Mothers*," and the spelling and reading-book.

A child taught by this method knows the spelling-book and the first reading-book almost by rote; he knows, to a great extent, the basis of orthography and speech; and when he has acquired facility in the forms of writing, by means of the pencil-book and the first exercises, so far as concern single letters and their connection, he will need no special copies to proceed in his studies in writing, for he will then, by means of his knowledge of speech and orthography, have the substance of all the copies in his head, and can write down, from the acquaintance he has acquired with the spelling and reading-books, whole series of words; by which his knowledge of language is continually increased, and his memory and imagination trained.

The advantages of exercises in writing thus arranged, and connected with those in language, are as follows:—

1. They continually increase the grammatical facility which the child has already acquired, and make its basis in his mind more firm. This can not fail to be the case; for the arrangement of the reading-book, in which nouns, adverbs, verbs, conjunctions, &c., stand in separate columns, enables him to write them down as they stand; by which means he acquires the power of determining at once in which series any word belongs that comes before him. In this manner even the rules applicable to these classes of words will shape themselves in his mind.

2. By these exercises in language, according to the method, is also cultivated the general power of arriving at intelligent ideas; for the child may, as a writing-exercise, write out his dictionary, according to the headings and distinctions of the series of subdivisions which he has already learned, into groups of words, and thus arrange for himself orderly, generalized views of the various classes of things.

3. The means of gradually attaining to intelligent ideas by writing-exercises are re-enforced in two ways: first, because the pupil gains practice both by the writing and reading-lessons, through the elucidatory juxtapositions of the important nouns, verbs, adverbs, &c.; and, second, he gains independent power in discovering and adding the ideas derived from his own experience to the various series of terms whose chief conceptions he has made his own while engaged in studying reading.

Thus, in the writing-exercises, for example, he sets down not only the names of what he has learned in the reading-book to call "high" and "pointed," but he practices himself, and the very task stimulates him to do so, in remembering and adding such objects as he recollects, within his own experience, of that form.

I will give an example, to illustrate the investigating spirit of children as to such additions.

I gave out to them the word "Three-cornered;" of which, along with a country schoolmaster, they furnished the following instances:—

Three-cornered: Triangle; plumb-level; half a neck-cloth; carpenter's square; a kind of file; bayonet; prism; beech-nut; engraver's scraper; wound left by leech; blade of a sword-cane; buckwheat kernel; leg of a pair of dividers; the under surface of the nose; leaf of "Good Henry;" spinach leaf; seed-pod of tulip; figure 4; seed-pod of shepherd's pouch.

They found still others on tables, and in round windows, which they were unable to give names for.

The like is the case with reference to the addition of adjectives to the nouns.

For instance, the children annexed to the nouns eel, egg, evening, not only all the adjectives which they had learned as annexed to them in the reading-book, but those also which their own experience enabled them to add as appropriate. Thus, by this mode of collecting the qualities of all things, they arrive, by the simplest of processes, at the means of becoming acquainted and familiar with the nature, essence, and qualities of all things, from various directions, and in a mode harmonizing with their own experience. The same is true of verbs; as, for instance, if the children are to elucidate the verb "to observe," by adding nouns and adverbs to it, they would elucidate or accompany them, not only with the words which they had found accompanying them in the reading-book, but would add others, as in the previous case.

The consequences of these exercises are far-reaching. The descriptions which the children have learned by rote, as of the bell, going, standing, lying, the eye, the ear, &c., become definite and universal guides to them, by means of which they become able to express themselves, both orally and in writing, as to every thing with whose form and contents they become acquainted. It will of course be observed, that this result can be reached, not by isolated, exclusive practice in writing, but by connecting it with the whole series of means by which the method gradually elevates its pupils to the attainment of intelligent ideas.

It is also, as standing in connection with the whole course of instruction, that I say of the study of writing, that it should be completed, not merely as an art, but as a business acquirement; and that the child should be carried to such a degree of facility in it, that he shall be able to express himself as distinctly respecting it, and use it as easily and as universally, as speaking.

The third elementary means of our knowledge is

NUMBER.

While sound and form lead us toward the intelligence of ideas, and the intellectual independence which are attained through them, by the use of various means of instruction subordinate to themselves, arithmetic is the only department of instruction which makes use of no such subordinate means, but seems, throughout the whole extent of its influence, to be only a simple result of the primitive faculty, by which we represent clearly to ourselves, in all cases of intuition, the relations of greater and less, and, in cases where measurement is impossible, to form a perfectly clear idea of the relation.

Sound and form often, and in various ways, contain within themselves a germ of error and delusion; but number, never: it alone leads to infallible results; and, if geometry makes the same claim, it can be only by means of the application of arithmetic, and in conjunction with it; that is, it is infallible, as long as it arithmeticizes.

Since, therefore, this department of instruction, which leads with most certainty toward the purpose of all instruction—intelligent ideas—must be honored as the most important of all the departments, it is therefore evident that it must also be pursued universally, and with the utmost care and wisdom; and that it is of the utmost importance for the attainment of the ultimate object of education; and also that it should be put in a form which shall admit all the advantages which a profound psychology and a most comprehensive knowledge of the invariable laws of the physical mechanism of instruction can secure. I have, therefore, made the utmost efforts to bring arithmetic before the intuition of the child, as the clearest result of these laws; and not only to reduce the element of it in the mind to that simplicity which they wear in the actual phenomena of nature, but also to preserve this same simplicity without any variation, strictly and without exception, in every step of onward progress; in the conviction that even the furthest attainments in this study can only be the means of true enlightenment—that is, means of attaining to intelligent ideas and correct views—so far as it is developed in the human mind in the same order of progress in which it proceeds from nature herself, from the very beginning.

ARITHMETIC.

This arises wholly from the simple collocation and separation of several unities. Its primitive formula is evidently as has been stated. One and one make two, and one from two leaves one. Every figure, whatever its value, is in itself only a mode of abbreviating this rudimentary form of all computation. It is, however, important that the recollection of the primitive form of the relations of numbers should not be weakened in the mind by the abbreviated means of arithmetic; but that they should, by means of the forms in which the study is pursued, be carefully and deeply impressed upon it; and that all progress in this department toward the end proposed should be founded upon that deeply-seated consciousness of the material relations, which lies at the basis of all arithmetic. If this does not happen, the very first means of attaining intelligent ideas would be degraded to a mere plan of memory and imagination, and thus made powerless for its real object.

This must, of course, be the case; for if, for instance, we learn by rote that three and four are seven, and then proceed to use this seven as if we *really* knew that three and four made it, we should deceive ourselves; for the inner truth of the seven would not be in us, since we should not be conscious of the material basis which alone can give the empty words any truth for us. The fact is the same in all the departments of human knowledge. Drawing, in like manner, if not based upon the geometry from which it is deduced, loses that internal truthfulness, by means of which only it can lead us toward intelligent ideas.

I begin, in the "*Book for Mothers*," to endeavor to make upon the child that firm impression of the relations of numbers, as such actual interchanges of more and less, as may be observed in objects discernible by the eye. The first tables of that work contain a series of objects intended to bring distinctly before the eyes of the children the ideas of one, two, three, &c., up to ten. Then I let the children select from the pictures the objects which represent one; then the twos, threes, &c. Then I make the same relations familiar to them by their fingers, or with peas, small stones, or such other objects as may be at hand; and I daily renew the consciousness of the numbers hundreds and hundreds of times, by the division of words into syllables and letters on the spelling-board, and asking, How many syllables has that word? What is the first? The second? &c. In this manner the primitive form of all arithmetic becomes deeply impressed upon the children's minds, by which means they become familiar with the means of abbreviating it, by figures, with the full consciousness of their inner truth, before proceeding to the use of the figures without keeping this background of intuition before their eyes. Aside from the advantage of thus making arithmetic a basis for intelligent ideas, it is incredible how easy the study thus becomes, even to children, through this assured preparation of the intuition; and experience shows that the beginning even is difficult only because this psychological rule is not used to the proper extent. I must, therefore, go somewhat more into detail upon such of my rules as are here applicable.

Besides the steps already mentioned, and after them, I make use of the spelling-tablets also as a means of teaching arithmetic. I call each tablet one, and begin with the child at a time when it can learn its letters, to instruct it in the knowledge of the relations of numbers. I lay down one tablet, and ask the child, "Are there many tablets?" He answers, "No; only one." Then I put one more, and say, "One and one. How many is it?" The child answers, "One and one are two." And so I go on, adding only one at a time, then two, three, &c., at a time.

When the child has thoroughly mastered the combinations of one and one, as far as ten, and states them with entire facility, I put the spelling-tablets before him in the same manner, but vary the question, and say, "If you have two tablets, how many times one tablet have you?" The child sees, reckons, and answers correctly, "If I have two tablets, I have twice one tablet."

When he has thus, by the limited and often-repeated computation of their parts, gained a clear understanding of the number of ones in each of the first numbers, the question is varied again, and he is asked, with the tablets in sight as before, "How many times one are two? how many times one are three?" &c.; and again, "How many times is one in two; in three?" &c. When the child has thus become acquainted with the simplest rudimentary forms of addition, multiplication, and division, and intuition has enabled him to master the essence of the processes, the next step is to make him thoroughly acquainted, in like manner, by intuition, with the rudimentary forms of subtraction. This is done as follows:—From the whole ten tablets together I take away one, and ask, "If you take away one from ten, how many remains?" The child reckons, finds nine, and answers, "If I take one away from ten, there remain nine." Then I take away another, and ask, "One less than nine is how many?" The child reckons again, finds nine, and answers, "One less than nine is eight." And so it proceeds to the end.

This mode of explaining arithmetic can be practiced by means of the following series of figures:—

1 11 11 11 &c.
1 111 111 111 &c.
1 1111 1111 1111 &c.

When the additions in one of these columns are finished, they may be used for subtraction; e. g.:—

If one and two are three, and two and three make five, and two and five make seven, &c., up to twenty-one; then two tablets may be removed, and the question asked, "Two less than twenty-one is how many?" and so on, until none are left.

The knowledge of the greater or less number of objects, which is awakened in the child by the laying before him of actual movable bodies, is strengthened again by the use of arithmetical tables, by means of which the same successions of relations are set before him in lines and points. These tables are used as guides, in reference to computing with real objects, as the spelling-book is in connection with writing words on the blackboard; and when the child has proceeded as far, in reckoning with real objects, as these tables, which are entirely based on intuition, his apprehension of the actual relations of numbers will have become so strengthened, that the abbreviated modes of proceeding by the usual figures, even without the intuition of objects, will be incredibly easy to him, while his mind will have been preserved from error, defects, and fanciful instructions. Thus it may be said, with strict correctness, that such a study of arithmetic is exclusively an exercise of the reason, and not at all of the memory, nor any mechanical routine practice; but the result of the clearest and most definite intuitions, and leading to nothing except to intelligent ideas.

But as increase and decrease takes place, not only by increase and decrease of the number of single objects, but by the division of single objects into several parts, there thus arises a second form of arithmetic, or, rather, a method is offered by which each single object may itself be made the basis of an infinite partition of itself, and an infinite division into single parts existing within it.

And as, in the previous form of arithmetic, the number one was taken as the starting-point for the increase and decrease in the number of single objects, and as the basis of the intuitional knowledge of all their changes, in like manner a figure must be found in the second form of arithmetic which shall occupy the same place. It must be infinitely divisible, and all its parts alike; a figure by which the parts in fractional arithmetic, each first as part of a whole, and again as independent, undivided unities, may be brought before the intuition in such a way that every relation of a fraction to its integer may be presented to the child's eye as definitely and accurately as, by our method, in the simple form of arithmetic, the number one was seen by him to be distinctly contained three times in three.

No figure will serve this purpose except the equilateral square.

By means of this figure we can place before the eye of the child the relation of the parts to unity; that is, the progressive series of fractions, beginning with the universal starting-point of all increase and decrease, the number one, with as much distinctness as we formerly set before him in a sensible form the increase and decrease of whole unities. I have also prepared an intuitional table of fractions, in eleven columns, each consisting of ten squares. The squares in the first column are whole, those in the second are divided into two equal parts, those in the third into three, &c., as far as ten. This simply-divided table is followed by a second, in which these simple intuitional divisions are continued in a further progression. The squares, which in the first table are divided into two equal parts, are now divided into two, four, six, eight, ten, twelve, fourteen, sixteen, eighteen, and twenty parts; those in the next column into three, six, nine, twelve, &c.

As this intuitional alphabet consists of geometrical forms, which are derived from the tenfold subdivision of an equilateral square, it is evident that we have established a common source for the alphabet of intuition, and this arithmetical alphabet; or, rather, that we have established such a harmony between the elementary means of instruction in form and number, that our geometrical forms are made the primary basis of the relations of numbers, and the fundamental relations of numbers, on the other hand, the primary basis of the geometrical forms.

In this manner we arrive at the conclusion that we can not teach children arithmetic, under our method, except by the use of the same alphabet which we used previously as an alphabet of intuition in the more restricted sense; that is, as a basis for measuring, writing, and drawing.

The child's apprehension of the actual material relations of all fractions will become so clear by the use of this table, that the study of fractions in the usual figures, as in the case of the arithmetic of integers, will become incredibly easy. Experience shows that by this method the children arrive four or five years earlier at a proper facility by this method than could possibly be the case without its use. These exercises also, as well as the previous ones, preserve the child's mind from confusion, omissions, and fanciful instructions; and in this respect also it may be said, with distinctness, that this mode of studying arithmetic is exclusively a training of the reason; in no sense a mere exercise of memory, nor any routine mechanical process. It is the result of the clearest and most definite intuitions; and leads, by an easy path, through correct understanding, to truth.

[The following "Course of Instruction" pursued in the Normal and Model Schools of the British Home and Colonial Infant and Juvenile School Society, on Gray's Inn Road, London, presents some interesting applications, as well as modifications, of Pestalozzi's methods of elementary instruction as set forth in the foregoing extracts from "*How Gertrude Teaches Her Children.*"]

COURSE of INSTRUCTION for the TEACHERS in training at the HOME and COLONIAL INFANT and JUVENILE SCHOOL SOCIETY.

I. SCRIPTURE.—The authenticity of the Bible and the evidences of Christianity; a general view of the different books of the Bible; a daily Scripture text with remarks, chiefly of a practical nature; instruction in the most important doctrines of the Bible to promote real religion, the lessons especially bearing upon the duties and trials of teachers.

II. WRITING AND SPELLING.

III. LANGUAGE.—Grammar; etymology; composition.

IV. NUMBER.—Mental arithmetic; ciphering.

V. FORM.—Lines and angles; superficies; solids.

VI. NATURAL HISTORY.—Mammals; birds; plants.

VII. ELEMENTARY DRAWING.—For the cultivation of taste and invention; as an imitative art.

VIII. VOCAL MUSIC.—Singing; the notation of music.

IX. GEOGRAPHY.—A general view of the world; England and its colonies; Palestine.

X. OBJECTS.—The parts, qualities, and uses of common objects; the essential properties of matter.

XI.—EDUCATIONAL LESSONS.—Principles of education as founded on the nature of children; on the government of children, and moral training; on subjects for lessons; on graduated instruction; on methods of teaching; on writing and giving lessons.

XII. PHYSICAL EXERCISES.

First or Lowest Class.—Six Weeks.

The students in this class are chiefly occupied in receiving instruction for their own improvement, with a view to their future training.

H. M. *Morning.*

8 15. The business of the day is commenced with a text from Scripture, and remarks. This is followed by an educational motto, setting forth some principle or practice of education, on which a few remarks are also made.
8 30. A lesson on Scripture.
9 15 Practice in singing pieces from "Hymns and Poetry."
9 30. A lesson on objects, or the properties of matter.
10 30. Recreation.
10 45. Observing a lesson given to the children in one of the practicing schools by the superintendent of those schools.
11 30. A lesson on language.
12 30. Dismissal.

Afternoon.

2 0. A lesson previously given in the preparatory or practising schools, examined as to its object, and the method of giving it.
3 0. A lesson on number.
4 0. A lesson in singing and the notation of music, or in drawing, for the cultivation of taste and invention.
5 0. Walking exercise on Monday, Wednesday, and Friday.
5 30. Dismissal on Tuesday and Thursday.

Evening.

6 30. Scripture instruction, or analyzing lessons in "Model Lessons."
7 30. Entering heads of lessons in note-books.
9 15. Dismissal.

Saturday.

8 15 A Scripture text and educational motto, as on the previous days.
8 30. Scripture instruction.
9 30. Gymnastics, under a drill-sergeant.
10 30. Scripture instruction.
11 30. Entering heads of lessons in note-books.

Note.—The afternoon of Saturday is a holiday for all the teachers in the Institution.

Second Class.—Twelve Weeks.

As the students now begin what may properly be called their *training*, more time is appropriated to the principles and practice of early education.

H. M. *Morning.*

8 15. A Scripture text and educational motto as to the lowest class.
8 30. A lesson to the upper section of the class in geography, or on the principles and practice of early education, and to the lower section on Scripture.
9 15. A lesson on number or drawing as an imitative art.
10 0. In charge of classes of children in the schools, or a continuation of the lesson on drawing.
10 45. A lesson on the principles and practice of early education.
11 30. Attending and remarking on gallery lessons given by students of the class
12 30. Dismissal.

H. M. *Afternoon.*

2 0. In charge of classes of children in the schools.
2 30. Observing a lesson given to the children by the mistress of the infant school.
3 0. Drawing up sketches of lessons, or analyzing lessons in "Model Lessons," or other exercises of the same kind.
4 0. Notation of music, or practising drawing.
5 0. Walking exercise on Monday, Wednesday, and Friday.

Evening.

6 30. A lesson on Scripture, or natural history.
7 30. Entering notes in daily journals.*
9 15. Dismissal.

Saturday.

8 15. A Scripture text and educational motto, as in the other days of the week.
8 30. A lesson to the upper section of the class on geography, and to the lower section on Scripture.
9 30. Gymnastics.
10 30. A lesson on Scripture.
11 30. Entering notes in daily journals.

Third Class.—Six Weeks.

The previous instruction and practice of the students is now brought to bear upon the government of large numbers of children, and the time is chiefly employed as assistants in the schools, or in taking the entire management of one of the small practicing schools. When they are not so employed, their time is occupied as follows, viz.:

H. M. *Morning.*

8 15. A Scripture text and educational motto.
8 30. A lesson on the principles and practice of early education, or on geography.
9 15. In the schools employed as general assistants.
12 30. Dismissal.

Afternoon.

2 0. In the schools as before.
5 0. Dismissal.

Evening.

6 30. A lesson on natural history or Scripture.
7 30. Entering notes in daily journals.
9 15. Dismissal.

Saturday.

8 15. A Scripture text and educational motto.
8 30. A lesson on geography.
9 30. Gymnastics.
10 30. A Scripture lesson.
11 30. Entering notes in daily journals.

Time allotted to each subject of study.

The following table exhibits the time weekly allotted in the different classes to each subject of study, and also the average weekly time.

—	First or Lowest Class.		Second Class. First Period.		Second Class. Second Period.		Third Class.		Av'rage Weekly	
	H.	M.	H.	M.	H.	M.	H.	M.	H.	M.
I. General Improvement:—Scripture	8	30	7	0	7	0	3	45	6	34
Writing and spelling, reports of lessons, &c.	10	30	12	30	12	30	10	30	11	30
Language	6	15	2	15	0	0	0	0	2	7
Number and form	5	0	0	0	2	15	0	0	1	49
Natural history	0	0	3	0	3	0	3	0	2	15
Geography, including the Holy Land	0	0	1	0	1	15	2	30	1	11
Objects	6	15	0	0	0	0	0	0	1	34
Vocal music	4	15	3	0	3	0	0	0	2	34
Drawing	3	0	5	0	5	0	0	0	3	15
Gymnastics and walking exercise	1	0	1	0	1	0	1	0	1	0
II. Lessons on the principles and practice of early education	11	15	12	30	12	45	3	0	9	45
III. Practice in the Schools:—Taking charge of classes, and afterwards of galleries of children	0	0	4	0	4	0	0	0	2	0
Giving an opinion on the lessons of other teachers, Giving lessons publicly	0	0	4	30	4	30	0	0	2	15
Attending as assistants in the schools	0	0	0	0	0	0	32	15	0	0
Having the sole charge of schools under inspection	0	0	0	0	0	0	0	0	10	15
Recapitulation:—General improvement	44	45	35	0	34	45	20	45	34	0
Principles and practice of education	11	15	12	30	12	45	3	0	9	45
School practice	0	0	8	30	8	30	32	15	12	15
Total number of hours weekly	56	0	56	0	56	0	56	0	56	0

* Much time and attention are given to these journals, both by the students and those who instruct them, as well as by the ladies of the Committee, to whom they are sent for examination.

It is deemed unnecessary to give any syllabus of the courses of ordinary instruction, but the following syllabus of lessons on the principles and practice of early education, is annexed, as it shows what is in some degree peculiar to this institution.

First Course.

It is a distinctive feature at this course that the ideas are chiefly gained from examples presented to the students. The lessons are mainly explanatory of the examples.

I. Lesson on the daily routine of employment in the Institution. The instructions by the committee for students. General rules and regulations.

II. Examination and analysis of lessons from "Model Lessons," viz.:—

Lessons on objects, Part I. p. 51–93.
" color, Part I. p. 149–157.
" animals, Part I. p. 160–165.
" number, Part I. p. 103–140.
Scripture Lessons, Part III. p. 1–28.

III. Drawing out sketches of lessons on various subjects, after the example of those analyzed.

I.—*On Objects.*

1. On a shell or leaf, according to the model of a lesson on a feather.
2. Copper or iron . . . . " " lead.
3. Tea or sealing wax . . . " " loaf sugar.
4. Vinegar or ink . . . . " " milk
5. Recapitulation.
6. Parchment . . . . . " " paper.
7. Cloth . . . . . . " " leather.
8. Pipeclay . . . . . . " " chalk.
9. Wood or rice . . . . " " coal.
10. Recapitulation.
11. A candle or hammer . . " " lead.
12. A turnip or acorn . . . " " a rose-leaf.
13. An egg . . . . . . " " honeycomb.
14. A bird or bee . . . . " " a butterfly.
15. Recapitulation.

II.—*On Animals.*

1. Sheep . model—hare. 2. Goat . model—cow.

III.—*On Color.*

1. The color blue . model—red. 2. Color yellow . model—green.

IV. Lessons in which "Practical Remarks" form the text-book.

V. On the art of questioning children, and on the different methods of giving lessons.

The students afterwards draw out lessons in full, according to models given.

VI. On the best method of drawing out children's observation upon the objects around them, and upon the circumstances in which they are placed, and on fixing the knowledge so gained in the mind.

VII. The characteristics of young children that must be kept in view and acted upon, in order to secure their attention, to interest them in their lessons, and to gain ascendency over them.

1. Love of activity.
2. Love of imitation.
3. Curiosity, or love of knowledge.
4. Susceptibility to kindness and sympathy.
5. Deficiency in the power of attention.
6. The love of frequent change.
7. The force of early association.
8. Disposition to repeat the means by which they have once attained their ends.

VIII. On the senses, and the use to be made of them in early education.

IX. The gallery lessons given to the children of the preparatory or practicing schools, as to the subjects, the manner of treating them, and their bearing upon the education of the children.

First Preparatory School.—1. Form—1st step.
2. Color—1st and 2nd step.
3. Size—1st step.
4. Actions—1st step.
5. Human body—1st step.
6. Objects—1st step.
7. Number—1st step.
8. Religious instruction—1st step.
9. Sounds—1st step.

Second Preparatory School.—1. Form—2nd step.
2. Color—3rd and 4th step.
3. Size—2nd step.
4. Actions—2nd step.
5. Place—1st step.
6. Objects—2nd step.
7. Animals—2nd step.
8. Number—2nd and 3rd step.
9. Moral instruction—2nd step.
10. Religious instruction—2nd step.
11. Sounds—2nd step.

X. A general view of the different subjects of instruction in the preparatory schools, with a view to lead the students to draw from them principles and plans of teaching.

Second Course.

I. Instructions on familiar or conversational lessons, and on the subjects chosen for these lessons, in the preparatory schools.

II. Analysis of lessons in "Model Lessons."

1. Form, Part II. p. 150–226.
2. The human body, Part I. p. 24–50.
3. A flower, Part II. p. 65–76.
4. Scripture lessons, Part II. p. 1–21.
5. Bible examination, Part II. p. 125–132.

III. Drawing up sketches of lessons in writing, according to a given model. first, singly, and then in a series or course.

Objects.

1. On sugar, after the model of the lesson on bread.
2. Spices and liquids " " corns.
3. Leather and silk " " cotton.

Animals.

1. On a tiger . . . Model—A pheasant
2. The elephant and the cat . " A pig.
3. Different kinds of teeth . " Different kinds of .... of animals.
4. Comparison of parts of a quadruped and bird. . . " Hand and foot.

Scripture Illustrations.

1. The sun and the dew. Model—The rainbow.
2. Sheep—lion " The vine.
3. Fishermen of Galilee " The shepherds of Judæa.

Scripture Narratives.

1. On the Prodigal Son, and on } Model—Joseph's forgiveness
2. The Brazen Serpent . . } of his brethren.

3. David's Veneration for his King " Solomon's respect for his mother.

4. The Nobleman's Son. " Mark x. 46 to 52.

In Series or Course.

1. A variety of sketches, after the model of the lesson on water.
2. A series of sketches on a given subject " on prayer, &c., as in "Model Lessons," Part III. p. 24, &c.
3. A graduated series of sketches on the " on a same subject. straw, a cat, &c.
4. On the subjects appointed for lessons weekly at the different galleries.

IV. Writing out lessons in full on specified subjects—As

1. To develop the idea of Inodorous.
2. " " Pliable.
3. " " Tasteless.
4. " " Soluble and fusible.
5. " " Semitransparent.
6. " " Elastic.
7. " " Aromatic.
8. " " Natural and artificial.
9. " " Lesson on an elephant.
10. " " Comparison of the cow and pig.
11. " " A piece of poetry.
12. " " The rainbow.
13. " " The addition or subtraction of 8.
14. " " Explanation of the terms—sum, remainder, product, quotient.
15. " " Substance of lesson X. in Reiner's "Lessons on Form."
16. " " On the illustration of the general truth, "God is angry with the wicked every day."

Note.—The number of sketches and lessons which the students are enabled to draw out during their training of course depends upon their ability and upon the previous education they have received. Some of these lessons are examined publicly, that their excellencies or errors may be pointed out for the improvement of the class, the name of the writer being withheld.

V.—*Gallery Lessons.*—With reference to the Gallery Lessons, instructions are given on the following points:—

1. The sketch.
2. The subject-matter.
3. The summary.
4. The application of a moral subject.
5. On maintaining order and interest.
6. The exercise of the minds of the children, and the knowledge gained.
7. The manner of the teacher.
8. Voice—pronunciation.
9. Importance of attention to the whole gallery of children.
10. On the use to be made of incidental circumstances.
11. On the questions to the children.
12. Mechanical plans.

VI.—On the subjects taught in the schools, their suitability to the children, and the mode of treating them:—

1. Color.
2. Form.
3. Size.
4. Weight.
5. Physical actions and operations.

6. Number.
7. Place, as preparatory to geography.
8. Sounds, as preparatory to singing and the notation of music.
9. Objects, including models of common utensils.
10. Teaching by pictures of common objects, and drawing objects before children.
11. The human body.
12. Animals.
13. Moral instruction.
14. Religious instruction.
15. Teaching pieces of poetry.
16. Drawing and writing.
17. Reading and spelling.
18. Language, including composition, grammar, and the explanation of words.
19. Number, form and language, as the elements of intellectual instruction.
20. Summary of the principles learnt in considering the subjects of lessons for infants.
21. Drawing out sketches of the different methods of giving lessons, and the uses to be made of them, showing which are bad and which are good, and those suitable to different subjects.

VII.—Miscellaneous:—

1. A course of educational mottoes.
2. On intuitive knowledge and early development.
3. On principles and plans of education.
4. Anecdotes of occurrences in the school, brought forward with a view to form right principles of moral training and intellectual development.
5. On the play-ground, especially in reference to its influence in the intellectual and moral training of children.

Third Course.

I.—The practice of the school-room, and the principles on which it should be regulated:—

The school-room and its apparatus, including library, collection of objects &c.
The opening and general arrangements of a school.
Attendance, and the best method of raising and filling a school.
Admission payment, and first treatment of children.
General order and qnietness.
The physical state of the children, health, cleanliness, neatness.
The exercises of the school-room and play-ground.
The division of time, and the subjects of lessons in a school.
Modes of leading elder scholars to work, independently of the master's direct teaching.
The government of a school with respect to its spirit and plans.
The influence of numbers in teaching and moral training.
Rewards, punishments, emulation.
Assistance, including paid assistants and monitors; the monitorial system.
The defects and advantages of the individual, and simultaneous methods of instruction, and the use of the ellipses.
Examinations by the teacher, for parents and for subscribers.
Holidays.

II.—Points respecting teachers:—

The intellectual and moral qualifications of a teacher, and the circumstances which affect him in his labors.
The conduct of teachers to parents, committees, inspectors, and the public.
The means by which teachers may carry on their own improvement.

III.—On the mental and moral constitution of children with reference to the principles on which education should be based:—

Mental.

The various operations of the mind, intellectual and moral, and the wisdom and goodness of God which they display.

The dependence of one intellectual faculty upon another, and the necessity for the orderly and progressive development of the whole.

The intellectual diversities of children, and the method of treating each variety of character.

Moral.

The importance of moral training on a religious basis, showing how the Bible should be our guide.

Diversities in the moral character of children, and the method of treating each, viz.,

Attachments of children.
Anger, and the treatment of passionate children.
Quarrelsome children.
Children disposed to injure and destroy.
Cunning children.
Covetous children.
Fear, and its use and abuse, as a means of discipline with children.
Firmness, and its tendency to become obstinacy.
The love of distinction and applause.
The cultivation of benevolence.
The sense of right and wrong.
Respect.
Obedience.

IV.—General truths respecting the operations of the minds and moral feelings, and the uses to be made of them in the education of children.

The Graduated Course of Instruction pursued in the Model Schools.

I. Religious Instruction.—*1st step: Moral Impressions.*—The children of this gallery are very young, direct religious instruction can scarcely be attempted at first, but their moral sense is to be cultivated, and moral habits formed. For instance, little acts of obedience are to be required from them—their conduct towards each other regulated, and little conversational lessons are to be given upon the kindness of their parents and teachers, with a view to develop the feeling of love, and to instruct them in their duties.

2nd step: First Ideas of God.—The object, as the children advance, is to produce the first impressions of their Heavenly Father—to lead them to feel somewhat of his power from its manifestation in those works of his with which they are familiar; and somewhat of his benevolence, by comparing it with the love shown them by their parents and friends.

3rd step: A Scripture Print.—The story to be gathered from the picture, by directing the attention of the children to it, and by questioning them. A portion of the Scripture should be given, that the children may connect the narrative with the Bible, and receive it as Divine instruction. The children should also be encouraged to make their remarks, by which the teacher may ascertain how far their ideas are correct. The object of the lesson should be to make a religious and moral impression.

4th step: Scripture Narratives.—The incidents or characters should be chose with a view to inculcate some important truth or influential precept. Elliptical teaching should be introduced to help the children to receive the story as a whole, and to sum up the lesson. In giving these lessons, the story itself should be either read from the Bible, or partly read and partly narrated, and pictures only used occasionally, to illustrate and throw interest into the subject. Teachers ought well to consider the different positions that pictures should occupy in the different stages of instruction.

5th step: Scripture Illustrations of Doctrines and Precepts.—Narratives, chosen with a view to inculcate some of the most simple and fundamental doctrines of Christianity. For instance, sin, its nature, introduction into the world, its consequences, and the remedy provided for it in the sacrifice of the Saviour. As the children advance, some lessons to be given to illustrate the natural history of the Bible.

NOTE.—In the first or early lessons on Scripture narratives, the truth or precept should be drawn from the story by the children. In the later lessons, the precept or religious truth or duty may be stated as the subject of the lesson, and the children required to discover what Scripture narratives illustrate the truth or precept they are considering.

6th step.—A course from the Bible, or a course on the Natural History of the Bible. On Monday, Scripture geography.

II. OBJECTS.—*1st step.*—Distinguishing or naming three or four common objects, and telling their uses; or distinguishing and naming the parts of common objects, and stating their uses.

2nd step.—*One Object* chosen that exhibits in a remarkable degree some particular quality, that the idea of that quality may be developed. *Another*, having distinct parts, which the children are to discover, and of which they are told the names.

3rd step: One Object.—The children to find out the qualities that can be discovered by the senses alone; also to distinguish and name the parts.

4th step: Miscellaneous Objects, Metals, Earths, Liquids, &c. One Object.—The children to extend their observations to qualities, beyond those which are immediately discoverable by the senses. *A little simple information* to be given at this stage on the natural history or manufacture of the object, after the children's observation has been called out.

5th step: Several objects.—The children to compare them, and point out their points of resemblance and difference.

III. TOYS.—Model toys of kitchen utensils, common carpenters' tools, &c., naming them, and telling or showing their uses.

IV. PICTURES.—*1st step.*—Groups of objects or single figures,—naming and talking about them.

2nd step.—Part of the lesson to be on the recollection of a picture used in a former lesson—part on a picture of common objects.

V. HUMAN BODY.—*1st step.*—Distinguishing the principal parts of the human body, the teacher naming them; or the children exercising any part of the body as directed. This lesson should be accompanied with considerable action, to animate the children.

2nd step.—Distinguishing the secondary parts of the body. This lesson to be extended to the parts of the principal parts of the human body, the teacher continuing to name them: a good deal of action still to be used.

3rd step.—Distinguishing the parts of the principal parts of the human body—the children naming them, and telling their uses.

VI. FORM.—*1st step.*—Distinguishing the patterns of shapes for the purpose of developing the idea of form—the children to distinguish them—no names being used.

2nd step.—The children continuing to select the patterns of shapes, according to the one shown; when perfect in this, they may select all those that have the same number and kind of edges, and the same number of corners.

3rd step.—The children to determine the number of sides and corners in planes, whether the sides are straight or curved; also to learn the names of the planes.

4th step.—A solid is shown, and the children select all those that resemble it in some points; the names of the solids are not to be given. The letters of the alphabet to be examined, and the number and direction of their lines to be determined.

5th step.—To determine the length of different measures, learn their names, and practice the introductory lessons on Form in "Model Lessons," part II.

6th step.—The course of lessons on Form in "Model Lessons," part II.

VII. ANIMALS.—*1st step: A Domestic Animal.*—A picture or a stuffed specimen may be shown. The children to be encouraged in talking about it, to say what they observe or know, without reference to any arrangement, the aim of the instruction being to elicit observation, to cultivate the power of expression, and especially to encourage humane and benevolent feelings towards the inferior creation. At this stage it is well sometimes to allow the children themselves to propose the animal that they are to talk about.

2nd step: A Domestic Animal.—Children to name its parts, color, size, and appearance. An attempt should be made in this stage, at a little arrangement of the subject, but it should not be too rigidly required. One principal object should be to encourage humane and benevolent feelings towards the lower animals.

3rd step: A Domestic Animal.—Children to describe the uses of domestic animals, their different actions, and with what limb they perform any action, the sounds they make, our duties with respect to them, &c. These alternate weekly with

4th step: Animals and Human Body.—The children to describe where the different parts of the human body are situated, and to compare those parts with the parts of animals, pointing out in what they are alike, in what they differ, and how fitted to the habits and wants of man, or of the different animals. See course in "Model Lessons," part I.

5th step: Wild Animals.—Children to tell their parts, color, size, and appearance; to point out how particularly distinguished, and to learn something of their habits and residence; being led to perceive how the animal is fitted by the Almighty for its habits and locality.

VIII. Plants.—*1st step.*—Naming the parts of plants, and telling their uses to man as food, &c.

2nd step.—See course in "Model Lessons," part II.

IX. Number.—*1st step: First Idea of Number.*—The idea of the numbers from 1 to 5 or 6, to be developed by the use of the ball frame and miscellaneous objects, as exemplified in Reiner's introductory lesson, "Lessons on Number," reprinted, by permission of the author, for the use of the teachers of the institution, in "Papers on Arithemetic;" to which may be added many additional exercises, such as those in the 1st and 2nd sections of "Arithmetic for young Children," &c.

2nd step: First Idea of Number.—The idea of the numbers from 6 to 10 to be developed by the use of the ball frame, as before; also the first and second exercises in "Model Lessons," part i., to be used as directed in that work.

3rd step: Addition and Subtraction.—The remaining exercise under section I., also the whole of the exercises on subtraction in the same work.

4th step.—The more difficult exercises in "Model Lessons," part i., &c., accompanied by selected exercises from "Arithmetic for Children."

5th step: The Four Simple Rules.—Exercises on the four simple rules, in number from 10 to 100, from "Papers on Arithmetic," and "Lessons on Number;" also simple explanations of the rules, leading the children to think of the operation they have been performing; also, by numerous exercises, to lead them to perceive some of the general properties of number.

X. Color.—*1st step.*—Selecting colors according to a pattern shown, and arranging colors, no names being used.

2nd step.—Learning the names of the different colors, and selecting them when called for by name.

3rd step.—Distinguishing and naming colors and shades of colors, and producing examples from surrounding objects; with exercises on beads of different colors.

4th step.—Distinguishing and naming shades of color, and producing examples from memory.

5th step.—The lessons in this step to be given on a specific color; the children are also to learn from seeing them mixed, how the secondary colors are produced from the primary.

XI. Drawing.—From the age of the juveniles, and also from drawing not coming under the head of "Gallery Lessons," the following course of exercises cannot be so well arranged into stages for the various schools. It is also thought desirable that one of the courses of lessons should be presented in a continuous form, that the extent and variety of exercise which they are intended to give to the mind may be observed. The courses form two series of exercises, commenced in the infant-school, and completed in the juvenile-school.

First Series—To Exercise the Eye alone.

Measuring relatively.—Let the children determine the relative length of lines drawn in the same direction on the slate, *i. e.*, which is longest, which is shortest, &c. Whenever there is a difference of opinion, prove who is correct, by measuring.

Determine the relative length of lines drawn in different directions on the slate.

Determine the relative distances between dots made on the slate.

Determine the relative difference of the distances between different parallel lines.

Determine the relative size of angles.

Determine the relative degree of inclination of lines from the perpendicular—first, by comparing them with a perpendicular line, drawn on another part of the slate—and afterwards without this assistance.

The same exercise with horizontal lines.

Determine the relative size of circles, and then of portions of circles.

Children called out to divide straight lines, drawn in different directions, into 2, 3, 4, &c., equal or given parts, the others to state their opinions as to the correctness with which the operation has been done.

The above exercise repeated with curved lines in different directions.

Note.—Several of the above exercises may be applied to the lengths, &c., of the objects and pictures in the room.

Measuring by current Standards.—The teacher to give the children the idea of an inch, nail, quarter of a yard, foot, half a yard, and yard, which, at first, should be drawn in a conspicuous place, for the whole class to see.

To decide the length of lines.—First practice the children upon the inch, then upon the nail, and so on up to the yard; continually referring to the standard measures.

Note.—These exercises should be continued until the eye can decide with tolerable accuracy.

Determining the length of lines combined in various rectilinear geometrical figures.

Determining the circumference or girth of various objects.

Determining distances of greater extent, such as the floor and walls of the room, the play-ground, &c., &c.

Measuring by any given Standard.—Measuring sizes, heights, lengths, &c., by any given standard.

How often a given standard will occupy any given space, with respect to superficies.

Second Series—To Exercise both the Eye and Hand.

Before commencing these exercises, it would be advisable to give the children instruction (in a class around the large slate) with regard to the manner of holding the pencil, the position of the hand in drawing lines in various directions. This will be found to diminish the labor of attending to each individual separately. Instruction as to the position of the body may be left till the children are placed at the desks.

Note.—The standard measures, used previously, should be painted on the walls, or placed conspicuously before the class in some manner, both horizontally and perpendicularly, in order to accustom the children to them.

The children to practice drawing straight lines in different directions, gradually increasing them in length. First perpendicular, second horizontal, third right oblique, fourth left oblique.

To draw lines of given lengths and directions.

To divide the lines they draw into given parts.

To draw curved lines in different directions, gradually increasing in size.

To try how many angles they can make with 2, 3, 4, &c., lines.

To try what they can make of 2, 3, 4, &c., curved lines. Then proceeding to copies; first copying those formed of straight lines, then those of curved lines.

To draw from copies.

NOTE.—In the course of forming figures out of straight and curved lines, the children should be taught to make the letters of the alphabet.

XII. GEOGRAPHY.—*1st step.*—The course consists of the following series of lessons: 1. The cardinal points. 2. The semi-cardinal points. 3. The necessity of having fixed points. 4. The relative position of objects. 5. The boundaries of the school-room. 6. The boundaries of the play-ground. 7. The relative distances of the parts and objects of the school-room. 8. The relative distances of the parts and furniture of the school-room marked on a map, drawn on the large slate or black board with chalk, before the children. 9. The scale of a map. 10. The relative positions and distances of different places on a map of the neighborhood. 11. The map of England. 12. The map of the Holy Land.

PATERNAL INSTRUCTIONS.

DURING that happiest period of Pestalozzi's career, his labors at Burgdorf, he sketched out many rough drafts of lessons, to be filled up by his assistants, in their class room exercises, as a sort of encyclopedia of social science. Many of these fragments came into the possession of Krüsi, who, after the death of Pestalozzi, edited and published them under the title of "*Paternal Instructions*, a Bequest of Father Pestalozzi to His Pupils." We give a few extracts from Biber's volume.

Almsgiving.

"The best alms is that which enables the receiver to cease begging."

Changing.

"Change, my child, change all that thou doest and performest, until thou hast perfected it, and thou be fully satisfied with it. Change not thyself, however, like a weathercock, with every wind; but change thyself so that thou mayest become better and nobler, and that all that thou doest may be ever more excellent and perfect. No such change will ever cause thee to repent."

Baking.

"Baking is, like all cooking, a fruit of civilization. The savage knows of no preparation of his food; he eats every thing raw, like the brutes, and, accordingly, he eats it, like them, with brutal greediness. A wise diet of meat and drink is only possible when the food is prepared by art, and it is then only that man can guard himself against the voracity of the animal. Baking, therefore, and every other sort of cooking, is a far more important business than it appears to be at first sight. It procures to us the most wholesome of all nutriments—that bread which, as a common necessary of life, we daily ask of God, in the most sublime of all prayers."

Bathing.

"By bathing we cleanse ourselves from bodily impurities; the impurities of the soul, however, are not removed either by common or by consecrated water, but only by a renovation of mind in faith and love."

Quaking.

"The most violent quaking, which causes houses and cities to fall in ruins, and which shakes even the foundations of the mountains, is that terrible convulsion of nature which we call an earthquake; but infinitely more terrible is the secret quaking of a guilt-laden soul, at the prospect of the inevitable discovery and punishment of its crimes."

Beginning.

"The beginning of every thing precedes its existence and its continuation. The first day of creation was the beginning of the world. From the beginning God hath set forth his almighty power, his wisdom, and goodness, in all that he has made. From the beginning, the hand of his providence has ordained the destinies of mankind; it has ordained thy destiny also, my child. Rejoice, therefore, and put thy trust in him, who is, and was, and shall be, the everlasting God."

Bowing and Bending.

"Man, the only creature that carries his head so erect, should he never bow it? Verily, he does! For God has deeply impressed upon his heart the feeling of his weakness, and a reverential awe for all that is great and lofty. His head is involuntarily bowed down under the oppressive consciousness of his guilt. His eye sinks in gratitude before the saver of his life, his wife, his child. Verily, verily, it was no art that bent the knee of the first man who prostrated himself in the dust at the sight of the rising sun. It was God within him, who thus laid him low; and he rose more humanized in his feelings, than if he had proudly faced its bright beam. But the work of God is defiled in the bowings and bendings of hypocrisy, by which human nature is as much degraded as it is elevated and ennobled by pious adoration, lowly modesty, and kneeling gratitude."

Blossoming.

"Youth, thou season of blossoms, how fair thou art! But, remember that thy charms are destined quickly to pass away. Thou canst not ripen, unless they vanish. Therefore, value thou the lasting fruits of life above the fleeting beauty of its blossoms."

Thanking.

'Good men and good things, my child, cause joy to the man of pure heart, even though he derive no benefit from them; but when he is benefited by them, his joy is increased. He then seeks the author of all goodness and of all joy; and, when he has found him, his voice is drowned in the overflowing of his feelings. Tears glisten in his eyes. These, my child, are the thanks of the heart, which elevate and ennoble the soul. Whoever thanks not God, deserves not to be called man; and whoever thanks not his fellow-men, is unworthy of all the good which God bestows upon him through the hand of man."

Thinking.

"Thinking leads men to knowledge. He may see and hear, and read and learn whatever he please, and as much as he please; he will never know any of it, except that which he has thought over, that which, by thinking, he has made the property of his mind. Is it then saying too much, if I say that man, by thinking only, becomes truly man. Take away thought from man's life, and what remains?"

Threatening.

"It is a misfortune if one man threaten another. Either he is corrupt who does it, or he who requires it."

Failing.

"All men fail, and manifold are their failings. Nothing is perfect under the sun. But, unless a man despise himself, he will not think lightly of any of his failings."

Refining.

"Man wishes to have things not only good, but shining; therefore is there so much refining in the world. Silver, gold, and steel are polished; the finest silk, the softest wool, the clearest cotton, the mellowest tints, the most exquisite fragrancies, the most delicate sounds, the most delicious spices, and the most luxurious pillows are preferred. But where human nature has attained the greatest refinement of sense, a man of nerve is hardly to be found. The highest degree of this refinement is generally the point from which the decline of individuals and nations takes its beginning.

"The builder, who wishes to erect a durable structure, must do it with strong timber; he must not, by sawing and planing, make his bearers and planks so thin as to render them unfit for the purpose for which they are intended. And in the same way, parents and teachers ought never to refine the children, nor governments the nations, to such a point as to make them lose the strength of their limbs, the freshness of their cheeks, and the muscle of their arms."

Darkening.

"The setting of the sun darkens the earth; and the failing of hope the soul of man. Why, then, is it that every hope of man is not daily renewed, like that of the rising sun. It is well that he should not forever set his hope upon outward things; but seek his repose and his happiness within himself, in those things which do not rise and set daily, like the sun of this earth."

Hoping.

"Hoping and waiting make many a fool. And are we, then, not to hope at all? How unhappy would man be without that beam of hope which, in suffering and sorrow, sheds light through the darkness of his soul. But his hope must be intelligent. He must not hope where there is no hope. *He must look at the past with a steady eye, in order to know what he may hope of the future.*"

www.ingramcontent.com/pod-product-compliance
Lightning Source LLC
LaVergne TN
LVHW020930110826
845150LV00004B/821

* 9 7 8 1 4 2 5 5 5 3 5 1 7 *